DEFINED BY A HOLLOW

Ralahine Utopian Studies

Series editors:
Raffaella Baccolini (University of Bologna, at Forlì)
Joachim Fischer (University of Limerick)
Tom Moylan (University of Limerick)

Managing editor:
Michael J. Griffin (University of Limerick)

Volume 6

PETER LANG
Oxford · Bern · Berlin · Bruxelles · Frankfurt am Main · New York · Wien

Darko Suvin

DEFINED BY A HOLLOW

ESSAYS ON UTOPIA, SCIENCE FICTION AND POLITICAL EPISTEMOLOGY

PETER LANG

Oxford · Bern · Berlin · Bruxelles · Frankfurt am Main · New York · Wien

Bibliographic information published by Die Deutsche Nationalbibliothek
Die Deutsche Nationalbibliothek lists this publication in the Deutsche
Nationalbibliografie; detailed bibliographic data is available on the
Internet at http://dnb.d-nb.de.

A catalogue record for this book is available from the British Library.

Library of Congress Cataloging-in-Publication Data:

Suvin, Darko, 1930-
  Defined by a hollow : essays on utopia, science fiction and political
epistemology / Darko Suvin.
     p. cm. – (Ralahine utopian studies ; v. 6)
  Includes bibliographical references and index.
  ISBN 978-3-03911-403-0 (alk. paper)
  1. Utopias in literature. 2. Science fiction–History and criticism.
3. Dystopias in literature. I. Title.
  PN56.U8S86 2010
  809'.93372–dc22

                                        2010005219

Cover image: *Intérieur* by Miljenko Stančić (1971), oil, 81cm x 65cm,
in the possession of Darko Suvin, reproduced by kind permission of
Melita Stančić and Ivan P. Stančić, Zagreb.

ISSN 1661-5875
ISBN 978-3-03911-403-0

© Peter Lang AG, International Academic Publishers, Bern 2010
Hochfeldstrasse 32, CH-3012 Bern, Switzerland
info@peterlang.com, www.peterlang.com, www.peterlang.net

Printed in Germany

Contents

Ralahine Readers

Utopia has been articulated and theorized for centuries. There is a matrix of commentary, critique, and celebration of utopian thought, writing, and practice that ranges from ancient Greece, into the European middle ages, throughout Asian and indigenous cultures, in Enlightenment thought and Marxist and anarchist theory, and in the socio-political theories and movements (especially racial, gender, ethnic, sexual, and national liberation; and ecology) of the last two centuries. While thoughtful writing on Utopia has long been a part of what Ernst Bloch called our critical cultural heritage, a distinct body of multi- and inter-disciplinary work across the humanities, social sciences, and sciences emerged from the 1960s onward under the name of "utopian studies." In the interest of bringing the best of this scholarship to a wider, and new, public, the editors of Ralahine Utopian Studies are committed to publishing the work of key thinkers who have devoted a lifetime to studying and expressing the nature and history, problems and potential, accomplishments and anticipations of the utopian imagination. Each Ralahine Reader presents a selection of the work of one such thinker, bringing their best work, from early days to most recent, together in one easily accessible volume.

Dedication

This book, spanning texts from 1973 to 2008, is among other things a salvaging of insights and memories, projecting past upon the future.

It will bear no private dedicatees.

But it should recall the great ancestors and masters of thinking whose shadows hover over it, giving inspiration, provoking doubt, testing it and being tested:

> The prose and verse writers I have assiduously frequented *en masse* all my life and learned from more than from anywhere else: their name is legion.
>
> Karl Marx, whom I encountered in 1945.
>
> Vladimir I. Lenin and Miroslav Krleža, whom I encountered in 1946.
>
> Raymond Williams and Bertolt Brecht, whom I encountered in the mid-1950s.
>
> Ernst Bloch, whom I encountered in the late 1950s.
>
> Walter Benjamin, whom I encountered in the early 1960s.
>
> Fredric Jameson, whom I encountered in the late 1960s.

Three among them I had the privilege of personally speaking with, in Zagreb, Cambridge (UK), and North America.

Without them, much of the book would have been poorer or largely non-existent.

But there would have been no book at all, because my life would have been snuffed out by the Nazis and, later, because the air I breathed would have been quite different. So I dedicate this work:

*To the memory of all the Partizan fighters against fascism in Yugoslavia
during the People's Liberation Struggle 1941–1945, led by Josip Broz
Tito, general secretary of the Communist Party of Yugoslavia, twofold
liberator of my ex-country (which exists no longer).
That was then.
But thus it was once, and thus, changing what needs to be changed, we
could again be.*

Lucca (Italy), September 2009

Seven Citations from Rimbaud and Brecht

– Ce qu'on ne sait pas, c'est peut-être terrible.
– On est exilé dans sa patrie!!!
– Quels bons bras, quelle belle heure, me rendront cette région d'où viennent mes sommeils et mes moindres mouvements?
– (Démocratie) Aux pays poivrés et détrempés! – au service des plus monstrueuses exploitations industrielles ou militaires.[...] Conscrits du bon vouloir, nous aurons la philosophie féroce; ignorants pour la science, roués pour le confort; la crevaison pour le monde qui va.

(– What we don't know is perhaps terrible.
– One is exiled in one's own country!!!
– Which good arms, what good hour, will give me back that region from which stem my dreams and my every movement?
– (Democracy) To the spicy and soaked countries! – in the service of the most monstrous industrial or military exploitations. [...] Recruits of good will, we shall hold a ferocious philosophy; ignorant for science, merciless for comfort; bursting asunder the world as it is.)

— ARTHUR RIMBAUD, 1870–74

– Zwischen der wahren Philosophie und der wahren Politik ist kein unterschied.
– Sage ich etwas, negiere ich etwas anderes, enthalte es also.
– Die große Wahrheit unseres Zeitalters (mit deren Erkenntnis noch nicht gedient ist, ohne deren Erkenntnis aber keine andere Wahrheit von belang gefunden werden kann) ist es, dass unser Erdteil in die Barbarei versinkt, weil die Eigentumsverhältnisse an den Produktionsmitteln mit Gewalt festgehalten werden [... W]ir können die Wahrheit über barbarische Zustande nicht erforschen, ohne an die zu denken, welche darunter leiden, [... und] ihnen die Wahrheit so zu reichen, dass sie eine Waffe in ihren Händen sein kann [...]

(– There's no difference between true philosophy and true politics.

– If I say something, I deny something else, thus I contain it.

– The great truth about our age (whose understanding doesn't suffice, but without whose understanding no other significant truth can be found) is that our continent is plunged into barbarism because the property over means of production is violently maintained. [...] We cannot research the truth about barbaric conditions unless we think of those who suffer under them, and hand them the truth so that it may become a weapon in their hands.)

— BERTOLT BRECHT, 1928–35

Acknowledgements

I have always gladly disseminated drafts and publications to a wide range of acquaintances and attempted to listen to reactions. Certainly, I ought to thank many more whom I have forgotten. I am sorry.

Thanks are due to David Willingham, editor of *Paradoxa* magazine, and Sylvia Kelso, editor of its special issue on Ursula K. Le Guin, for accepting a large part of Chapter 18 as a preprint in that issue. Many editors and other friends who helped are acknowledged and thanked in the first note to each chapter.

The following authorizations to reprint are noted with acknowledgement and thanks to the editors and publishers of the original venues:

Chapter 2: "'Utopian' and 'Scientific': Two Attributes for Socialism from Engels," first published in *the minnesota review* no. 6 (1976): 59–70.

Chapter 5: "Locus, Horizon, and Orientation," first published in Jamie O. Daniel and Tom Moylan, eds, *Not Yet: Reconsidering Ernst Bloch*, London: Verso, 1997, 122–37.

Chapter 6: "On Gibson and Cyberpunk SF," an earlier version first published in *Foundation* no. 46 (1989): 40–51.

Chapter 8: "Where Are We? How Did We Get Here? Is There Any Way Out?" a part of which was first published as "Novum Is as Novum Does" in Karen Sayer and John Moore, eds, *Science Fiction, Critical Frontiers*, London: Macmillan, 2000, reprinted with permission of Palgrave Macmillan.

Chapter 9: "Utopianism from Orientation to Agency," first published in *Utopian Studies* 9.2 (1998): 162–90.

Chapter 10: "On Cognition as Art and Politics," first published as a major part of Darko Suvin, *For Lack of Knowledge*, Working Papers Series in Cultural Studies, Ethnicity, and Race Relations, ed. Epifanio San Juan Jr, Pullman: Washington State University, 2001.

Chapter 11: "What Remains of Zamyatin's *We* after the Change of Leviathans," first published in *Envisioning the Future*, ed. Marleen Barr, Middletown: Wesleyan University Press, 2003.

Chapter 12: "What May the Twentieth Century Amount To," first published in *Critical Quarterly* 44.2 (2002): 84–104.

Chapter 13: "A Little Tractate on Dystopia 2001," first published as "Theses on Dystopia 2001," in Raffaella Baccolini and Tom Moylan, eds, *Dark Horizons*, New York and London: Routledge, 2003, 187–201.

Chapter 15: "Living Labour and the Labour of Living," first published in *Critical Quarterly* 46.1 (2004): 1–35.

Chapter 16: "Inside the Whale, or *etsi communismus non daretur*," first published in *Critical Quarterly* 49.1 (2007): 119–37.

PHILLIP E. WEGNER

Preface: Emerging from the Flood in Which We Are Sinking: Or, Reading with Darko Suvin (Again)

> Eine brechtsche Maxime: Nicht an das Gute Alte anknüpfen, sondern an das schlechte Neue.
> [A Brechtian Maxim: take your cue not from the good old things, but from the bad new ones.]
>
> — WALTER BENJAMIN

> They are coming out of the trenches of rock toward the brick shadows. They are always coming.
>
> — CHINA MIÉVILLE

> I believe we can survive in utopia …
>
> — EJIGAYEHU "GIGI" SHIBABAW

> Just wait, 2048 is still to be.
>
> — DARKO SUVIN

For a work so deeply concerned with defining particular genres and practices — of utopia, dystopia, anti-utopia, science fiction, fantasy, and so forth — Darko Suvin's *Defined by a Hollow* is itself difficult to classify, challenging as it does the disciplinary boundaries and protocols of traditional academic studies. It is, to be sure, what its title declares itself to be, an invaluable collection of more than three decades of writings from one of the twentieth century's most significant Marxist students of Utopia (alongside his predecessor Ernst Bloch and his contemporary Fredric Jameson, figures invoked again and again in these pages). But it is much else besides: an engaged intellectual's memoir of the last decades of the turbulent and tragic twentieth century, what he names in Chapter 12, "a time of betrayals" (see page 362); an experiment in cultural criticism; a temperature taking of the present; a philosophical notebook in the spirit of Marx's *Grundrisse*, Lenin's *Philosophical Notebooks*, Gramsci's *Quaderni*, and Benjamin's *Passagenwerk* (all of which are recalled in these pages as well); a declaration of fundamental principles; a trenchant call to action; and a letter to those Bertolt Brecht names *Die Nachgeborenen*, those who come after: *Gedenkt unsrer/ Mit Nachsicht* [Think upon us/with leniency]. Perhaps then we should draw upon one of Suvin's dominant figures throughout this book, and say that it is a *toolkit*, a collection of resources that we might use in our continuing struggles both to imagine and to act in a way to bring into being a considerably better world than that of the violent global neo-liberalism we currently inhabit. My hope in this Preface is thus to offer something of a user's manual for this toolbox, helping to orient the reader, much like the figure of the utopian guide from More's Hythlodaeus to Bellamy's Dr Leete, by providing some context for the wonders they will encounter herein.

In his Introduction to this volume, Suvin notes "a certain break in time, and perhaps even more in tone" between the traditional academic studies of the book's first six chapters and the more experimental nature of those that follow the interlude of Chapter 7, "The Doldrums: Eight Nasty Poems 1989–99". While Suvin maintains that this shift is in a large part the consequence of a significant change of political climate (something I will return to momentarily), I would also suggest that the more experimental style of the later chapters is itself a sign of the lasting achievement of the earlier essays. For Suvin's own efforts – as a scholar, teacher, anthologist, and a founding editor of the journal *Science-Fiction Studies* – played a significant role in establishing utopia and science fiction as legitimate fields of academic inquiry.

For readers perhaps less familiar with Suvin's intellectual trajectory, a bit of biographical information would be pertinent here. Suvin was born on 19 July 1930 in Zagreb, Croatia, which in 1918 had become part of the Kingdom of Yugoslavia (its name until 3 October 1929 being the Kingdom of Serbs, Croats and Slovenes), and which during his adolescence would become, under the leadership of Josip Broz Tito, first the People's and then later the Socialist Federal Republic of Yugoslavia. He earned his doctorate from Zagreb University, the oldest and among the most prestigious of the universities in southeastern Europe, where he also began his teaching career. It was in these earliest studies that Suvin combined his interests in Marxism and science fiction in ways that would enable him to contribute in original and imaginative ways to the scholarship in both fields. After running afoul of some of the political currents at the university, Suvin immigrated to North America, and ultimately settled at McGill University in Montreal in the banner year of 1968, where he would serve as Professor of English and Comparative Literature until his retirement in 1999. He then relocated to Italy where he resides today. Suvin's first published scholarly essays on science fiction, utopia, and dystopia appeared in the mid-1950s, and in English at the end of the 1960s, including his groundbreaking "On the Poetics of the Science Fiction Genre" printed in the important 1972 issue of *College English* edited by Richard Ohmann.[1] Many of Suvin's early essays on science fiction and utopia were brought together in his landmark book, *Metamorphoses of Science Fiction: On the Poetics and History of a Literary Genre* (1979). In the same year, he was named the tenth recipient of the Science Fiction Research Association's Pilgrim Award to honor his lifetime contributions to science fiction and fantasy scholarship.

In the years that he was producing these field-defining essays, Suvin along with R.D. Mullen founded *Science-Fiction Studies* in 1973. This was a moment when academic literary studies were becoming increasingly receptive – in response, in part to the student militancy of the New Left, and in part to the innovations of a burgeoning critical theory (movements that also both deeply influenced Suvin's thought) – to scholarly work in the area of what was then referred to as "paraliterature," popular and genre fiction, including science fiction, fantasy, mystery, horror, romance, and comics. Suvin refused the marginalization of science fiction implied by this characterization, not only locating the genre within a long literary tradition

---

1   For further discussion of this essay, see Moylan, *Scraps* 42–45. And for an extensive bibliography of Suvin's writings from the 1950s through the late 1990s, see Parrinder 272–90.

of transgressive popular fictions that stretched back to the work of Lucian
of Samosata, Thomas More, and François Rabelais, but also consistently
maintaining that the finest contemporary science fiction is among the best
of all literature produced in the present. "The stakes," Suvin would later
argue in an essay on paraliterature, "thus, are the highest imaginable [...]:
the education of *Homo sapiens* for earthly salvation" (*Positions* 20). Here
we see the fusion of artistic, philosophical, and political commitment
characteristic of all of Suvin's writing, and deeply evident throughout this
collection.

Of course, as Suvin famously argues in "Defining the Literary Genre of
Utopia" (reprinted from *Metamorphoses* as the first chapter here), science
fiction and utopia are inseparable: "utopia is not a genre but *the sociopolitical
subgenre of science fiction*" (see page 42). This is not to advance the idealist
claim that science fiction represents some ahistorical eternal practice –
indeed, Suvin has recently written about the potential end of the genre –
nor does it mean, as George Slusser has recently suggested ("The Origins"
40), that Suvin finds in More's *Utopia* the beginnings of science fiction.[2]
(This, he makes clear, occurs with H.G. Wells: "He endowed later SF with a
basically materialist look back at human life and a rebelliousness against its
entropic closure. For such reasons, all subsequent significant science fiction
can be said to have sprung from Wells's *Time Machine*" [*Metamorphoses*
221]). Rather, as he puts it in Chapter 13, "utopian fiction is, today and retrospectively, both an independent aunt and dependent daughter of SF" (see
page 383). With this, Suvin demonstrates the deeply dialectical nature of
his thought – and he invokes in Chapter 15 the dialectic as "an inalienable
part of valid cognition today" (see page 428) – advancing the claim that
only after the establishment of the full range of possible science fictional
imaginaries is utopia recognized, as an older genre, as one of its the most
important roots of modern SF, and simultaneously repositioned within the
newly established generic system as "social-science-fiction or SF restricted

2   For Suvin's discussions of the end of SF, see "The Final Chapter of SF?" and "The
      Final Chapter? Part Two."

to the field of socio-political relationships or to socio-political constructs understood as crucial for the destiny of people" (*Positions* 38).

On this basis, Suvin illustrates the important features shared by utopia and science fictions. First, both are a form of what Suvin describes as the "literature of cognitive estrangement" (*Metamorphoses* 12). The force of this influential definition is two-fold. On the one hand, Suvin's emphasis on the element of "cognition" – the outlook that "sees the norms of any age, including emphatically its own, as unique, changeable, and therefore subject to a *cognitive* view [...] not only a reflecting *of* but also *on* reality" (*Metamorphoses* 7 and 10) – suggests the connection of utopian and science fictions to nineteenth century literary realism, and hence their common distance from other traditional and modern estranging forms such as myth, folk (fairy) tales, and fantasy. Even more significant is Suvin's application of the concept of "estrangement" to these practices. Suvin takes the notion of "*ostranenie*" first from the literary critics of the early twentieth-century Russian Formalist School, most prominently Viktor Shklovsky, and second, from the further elaborations on the concept offered by the great German Marxist playwright and thinker, Brecht. The latter writer, as the essays in this volume make abundantly clear, has been a deep and abiding influence upon Suvin; and Suvin in turn has been one of the last half century's most preeminent scholarly champions of Brecht's work. By stressing these estranging labors – the ability to view the present moment through a critical, distancing eye – Suvin undercuts the assumption that utopia or science fiction are forms of futurology, narrow prognostications of technical or social developments to come.[3]

This then leads Suvin to argue for a second essential trait of science fiction and its subgenre of utopia. In Chapter 3, "SF and the Novum" (also taken from *Metamorphoses*), he maintains that utopias in particular and science fiction more generally are "distinguished by the narrative dominance or hegemony of a fictional 'novum' (novelty, innovation) validated by cognitive logic" (see page 67). The concept of the novum – which Suvin defines

---

3   Also see the discussions of Suvin's concept cognitive estrangement in Moylan, *Scraps* 41–45, and Jameson, *Archaeologies* 410.

here as other than the merely new and rather "a totalizing phenomenon or relationship deviating from the author's and implied reader's norm of reality" – is borrowed from Suvin's most important predecessor in the study of utopia, Ernst Bloch (see page 68).[4] Tom Moylan argues of this crucial insight, "By not only tracking what was at hand in the tendencies of the historical moment as portrayed in the alternative world but also pointing, through the textual novum, toward the potential for radically new directions in the latencies of the moment, Suvin's claim for SF brought it to a level of sociopolitical value that many sensed but never fully theorized" (*Scraps* 45).

In Chapter 5, "Locus, Horizon, and Orientation," Suvin introduces the further axiom that "any utopian novel is in principle an ongoing feedback dialogue with the reader." This leads him to postulate the important concept of utopian "possible worlds," induced in the reader's imagination by "the interaction between the fictional elements presented in a text and the presuppositions of the implied reader" (see page 126). To dispense with the lingering commonplace that utopian fictions necessarily represent closed static worlds – something in fact challenged from the very origins of the genre by works in what Suvin calls, again following Bloch's lead, its "warm current" (Rabelais, William Morris, Le Guin, etc.) – Suvin introduces the twinned concepts of "locus" and "horizon," and on this basis generates a fourfold schema of possible worlds: "open-ended or dynamic utopia," "closed or static utopia," "heterotopia," and "abstract or non-narrative utopia(nism)" (see pages 124–29). An even fuller system of these possible worlds, expanded now to include dystopias, is then developed in Chapter 13.

On a personal note, "Locus, Horizon, and Orientation" was a special influence for one of my own earliest forays into the field, an essay published in *Utopian Studies* on Yevgeny Zamyatin's *We*. This essay then became part of my doctoral dissertation – for which Suvin served as an immensely generous, invaluable, and even utopian outside reader. In the revised book chapter, I further explore the concept of possible worlds in drawing a link between Zamyatin's project in *We* and that in a work it clearly influenced,

4   See Bloch, *The Principle of Hope* 198–205.

Ursula K. Le Guin's great "ambiguous utopia," *The Dispossessed*. (Suvin discusses the contemporary significance of Zamyatin and Le Guin's masterpieces in the face of "the change of Leviathans" – from the state to the Post-Fordist free market – in Chapters 11 and 18 respectively.)[5]

All of this points toward an underappreciated dimension of Suvin's original theorization of science fiction. His works helps us grasp the genre itself as a crucial dimension of the great efflorescence of cultural, political, and social experimentation known as *modernism*. Emerging in the late nineteenth century, the genre of science fiction appears in the midst of the first wave of modernisms; and as an original narrative technology (*techné*), science fiction is as deeply modernist as film, the two developments converging early on in Georges Méliès's *Le Voyage dans la lune* (1902), a film derived in part from Wells's *The First Men in the Moon* (1901). Moreover, drawing upon Fredric Jameson's periodizing narrative of film presented in *Signatures of the Visible*, I argue that there are two distinct modernist periods within the genre itself, the first culminating in the late 1920s, and the second arising in the late 1950s and extending into the mid-1970s – the moments, respectively, of Zamyatin and Le Guin, and both central foci of much of Suvin's work on SF.[6] The latter modernist period also witnesses a great outpouring of utopian SF, the most important text of which is Le Guin's *The Dispossessed*, a work that Suvin describes in this book's final chapter as "the qualitative culmination of the great SF age or wave of 1961–75" (see page 512).

One of the most significant indicators of the waning of the energies of this second moment of SF modernism is the rise of cyberpunk, exploding on both the science fiction and more general reading publics with the publication of William Gibson's *Neuromancer* in 1984 – a year that also saw the appearance of such other classics of postmodernism as Don DeLillo's *White Noise*, James Cameron's *The Terminator*, Martin Amis's *Money*, the Macintosh Superbowl commercial (these last two both

---

5   Readers should also consult Suvin's earlier discussion of Zamyatin in *Metamorphoses* 254–59; and of Le Guin in *Positions* 134–50.

6   See Wegner, "Ken MacLeod's Permanent Revolution" and "Jameson's Modernisms."

explicitly arguing for the obsolescence of George Orwell's statist dystopian vision), the English translation of Jean-François Lyotard's *The Postmodern Condition*, and Jameson's essay, "Postmodernism, Or, The Cultural Logic of Late Capitalism." Suvin first analyzed cyberpunk with a high degree of critical acumen and skepticism in his essay from the late 1980s reprinted here as Chapter 6. While sympathetic to certain formal innovations of cyberpunk, especially in its widening of the genre to include "the new vocabulary of lyricized information interfaces," Suvin argues that the practice has retreated from the utopianism of a previous generation of SF writers by too readily conceding to the central Thatcher/Reagan-era doctrine dubbed TINA ("There is no alternative") (see pages 11, 148). In such a view, Suvin argues, the global neo-liberal free market order is presented as "inevitable and unchangeable," and the primary concern becomes how one might survive within it (see page 146). This essay then already looks forward to the darker vision that we see in the later contributions in this book.

This postmodern moment also witnessed a new prominence for a more nostalgic and conservative fantasy. Elsewhere, Suvin extends this analysis, and argues that if science fiction "appeals to social groups with confidence that something at present can be done about a collective, historical future – if only as dire warnings," fantasy on the contrary, appeals "to uncertain social classes or fractions who have been cast adrift and lost that confidence" ("Considering the Sense" 238; "The Final Chapter?" 4). The story of how we arrived at this situation is also of great interest in the later chapters of this book.

At the same time, the late 1980s and early 1990s saw a shift within the academic field of science fiction studies. Accompanying its increasing institutional respectability was a certain waning of the radical political energies of its earlier formative stage. One indicator of this change was a displacement in *Science-Fiction Studies* of the Marxism of its early years by post-structuralist and postmodern theories and a new emphasis on formalism, a development that contributed to Suvin's break with the journal he helped found. (This is alluded to in a number of the later essays reprinted here, most pointedly in Chapter 8.) This development helps us further understand the shift in focus, tone, and style of some of these more recent essays. If at an earlier moment, simply to do academic work on science fiction was an experimental and even transgressive gesture, later, new cognitive strategies became necessary to challenge what was fast becoming a discipline in its own right, a form of what Jacques Rancière calls an institutional "distribution of the sensible," "the system of self-evident facts of sense perception that simultaneously discloses the existence of something in common [*le commun*, what makes or produces a community] and the delimitations that define the respective parts and positions within it" (*Politics* 12). In this regard, the following description of Rancière's project is applicable to the one Suvin undertakes here as well: "The essence of *politics* consists in interrupting the distribution of the sensible by supplementing it with those who have no part in the perceptual coordinates of the community, thereby modifying the very aesthetico-political field of possibility" (Rancière, *Politics* 3).

However, while these generic and institutional changes played a role in the more general reconsideration of intellectual strategies that we witness in the essays composing the second part of this book, the Event – in Alain Badiou's sense of being utterly unexpected and unplanned for – that looms most largely over them takes place on 11 November 1989: more precisely, at 10:30 p.m. C.E.T., with the opening of the border crossing between East and West Germany at Bornholmer Strasse in Berlin. Although significant challenges had occurred throughout Eastern Europe earlier that year, and equally dramatic ones would quickly follow, it was the unexpected "fall of the Berlin Wall" that signaled for the world the real beginning of the end of both the Soviet Union and its sphere of influence and a nearly half-century of East and West Cold War.[7] One of the most dramatic early consequences of this geopolitical Event would be the dissolution of the federative enterprise of Yugoslavia – under which Suvin had been formed intellectually and politically and to which he had regularly returned since his departure in the late 1960s – and the ultimate disintegration of its former territories into violence, civil war, and chaos. It is these latter developments in particular that will dramatically shape the concerns of Suvin's work throughout the 1990s and beyond.

---

7   For a brief discussion of the context and events of the "1989 revolutions," see Eley, *Forging Democracy* 429–56.

Suvin is in no way nostalgic for bureaucratized state communism, whose effects he had experienced directly in the mild Titoist version and from which he had in the mid-1960s concluded he could be an alienated intellectual just as well outside its borders. Rather, for Suvin the events of the early 1990s alluded to above signaled the final collapse of the modernist utopian promise of the Bolshevik revolution and the apparent evaporation of any organized leftwing challenge to the predatory violence of global capitalism (the rightwing challenges to this reputed "end of history" would become clear soon enough). For similar reasons, Badiou also marks the long wave of modernism he names "The Century" as extending from 1917 to 1989. It was this full unleashing on a global scale of an unchecked neo-liberal capitalism that led Suvin to shift his intellectual focus to a careful study of the economic realities of "Post-Fordism" – including what he pointedly describes in Chapter 9 and elsewhere as the "Disneyfication" of our political and cultural lives – and the lessons that the traditions of dystopia have for our understanding of the present.

Moreover, Suvin was quick to recognize that this Event made possible new forms of state violence, evident first in the United States' war of "liberation" in Kuwait, and then in the carnage in Suvin's one-time homeland of Yugoslavia and Croatia. The deep personal pain of this latter event in particular is registered in the moving poems collected in Chapter 7 – "They are bombing Beograd & Novi Sad/ No more festivals in springtime/ Blood silting up all rivers" (see page 158) – and echoes in all that follow. Here too it might be useful to note the significant role poetry plays in this volume. Collected together in Chapters 4, 7, 14, and 17, and also resurfacing in a number of the other chapters, these lyrical documents disrupt the conventional argumentative structure, offering a deeply affective self-reflective counterpoint to the essay's more analytic turns, while underscoring the emotional shifts and swerves that are a crucial part of the essays' context. This takes the form of a migration that Suvin also alludes to in his Introduction from an earlier guarded optimism ("After Eric, after us, *der Nachgeborenen*: not 1848, not 1948–/ Just wait, 2048 is still to be." [see page 95] "The Great Creativity will not find this behavior/ Entirely useless. & that this is enough/ For one life, on one leg" [see page 104]); to a sense of immanent catastrophe ("Punished by gazing hungrily at Finland

Station/ In the whorehouse that once was Leningrad" [see page 164]); to a recommitment in a situation of dystopia to the struggle for Utopia ("If you, O masters, will not let us/ Be saved, entirely we must/ Remove you" [see page 416] "This is the hidden hour of our ignoble oblivion./ You can live toward a good death or a bad death" [see page 506]).

The diverse experimental texts from the 1990s and the first decade of the new millennium that Suvin presents us with here are thus invaluable both in their strident refusal of the triumphalism of the period's victors (and this enemy has not ceased to be victorious), and in the rare glimpse they offer into the moment's dark underbelly from the perspective of what we might characterize as the utopian horizon of the now vanished Second World. In preserving this horizon – a labor also undertaken in Wolfgang Becker's film *Good Bye Lenin!* (2003), and which in this case as well is something very different than nostalgia – Suvin fulfills the task of Benjamin's historical materialist, who "acts in accord with the following truth: nothing that has ever happened should be regarded as lost to history" (*Selected Writings*, Volume 4 390).

And yet, as one reads these essays, Suvin's deeply dialectical sensibility comes to the fore again, and another sense of this historical moment emerges: not only as one of endings and conclusions, of catastrophe and dystopian realities, all of which are very much the case, but also of new possibilities. Suvin first asks "where are we to look for liberating currents in this needy paltry, poor age (*dürftige Zeit*) of ours?" and then begins the arduous work of forging an answer (see page 300). I argue in *Life Between Two Deaths: U.S. Culture, 1989–2001* that the unexpected end of the Cold War unhinged a good many things, in the First and Third worlds as much as the Second: as Suvin too notes, 1989 "also marked the end of US hegemony over the world, the paradoxical *Pax Americana et Atomica* of the Cold War" (see page 179). This made the 1990s one of those fleeting moments – akin to Benjamin's "nineteenth century," the modernist 1920s, and the 1960s – in which history felt as if it might move in any number of radically different directions. Unquestionably, there were dark forces marshalling their efforts to define the future in a very specific way, and they seemed to have triumphed on 11 September 2001 with the inauguration of the global war on terror and a new frontal assault on personal liberties. It is for this reason, I argue, that the 1990s comes to an end on that terrible "Tuesday in September," already figured in so many of the other cultural documents of the period.[8] However, in the context of its historical situation, the neo-conservative project represented only one position in what in fact became a highly contested struggle for hegemony—and acknowledging these struggles has immense value for us today.

Three developments in particular help establish a context for an understanding of this second dimension of Suvin's project. First and most significantly, the late 1990s witness the explosive emergence of a counter-globalization "movement of movements," whose moments of crystallization bear the names, among others, of Chiapas, Seattle, Genoa, Quebec City, and Porto Allegre.[9] An early collection of discussions from the World Social Forum held at the last site bears the title *Another World is Possible*, bearing witness to the deep and thoroughgoing Utopian aspirations of the movement(s): its aim was not only to reinvent Left politics in the aftermath of Cold War, but to transform the world itself. Giving full expression to these ambitions, Arundhati Roy declares, "Another world is not only possible, she's on her way. Maybe many of us won't be here to greet her, but on a quiet day, if I listen very carefully, I can hear her breathing" (*War Talk* 75). Second, the 1990s sees the flourishing of a new generation of engaged political and utopian science fiction visionaries – whose tasks include wresting fantasy from its more conservative practitioners – a group that encompasses, among others, Ian Banks, Octavia Butler, Nalo Hopkinson, Gwyneth Jones, Ken MacLeod, China Miéville, Alan Moore, Philip Pullman, Kim Stanley Robinson, and Joss Whedon.

Finally, the 1990s gives rise to a series of original and influential "universalizing" theoretical projects. Michael Hardt and Antonio Negri's efforts in *Empire* (2000) and *Multitude* (2004) are perhaps the most celebrated, but this is also the case in the intellectual work of a truly global group of

8   The phrase "Tuesday in September" comes from a never filmed prologue to *Terminator 2: Judgment Day* (1991), a film I discuss in some detail in *Life Between Two Deaths*, Chapter 3.

9   Also now see the discussion of these sites and movements, in Negri, *Goodbye Mr. Socialism*.

scholars, including, but by no means limited to, Giorgio Agamben, Badiou, Judith Butler, Jacques Derrida, David Harvey, Jameson, Kojin Karatani, Gayatri Spivak, Roberto Unger, and Slavoj Žižek. All of these projects mark an authentic "negation of the negation," a post-postmodernism or movement beyond the paralyses of the postmodern, in the theoretical domain at least, and a resurgence of the radical transformative energies of a new modernism.[10] It is to just such a reconsideration and resurgence that these later essays by Suvin contribute as well.

Such a labor is linked to another major concern of all of these ambitious and wide-ranging essays, one made explicit in the title of Chapter 9: "Utopianism from Orientation to *Agency*: What Are We *Intellectuals* Under Post-Fordism To Do?" Throughout this collection, Suvin works to teach us a fundamental materialist lesson: to think about Utopia is in fact always already to think about intellectuals and intellectual labor. Suvin reminds us that intellectual labor has been a prominent concern throughout his career by republishing as the second chapter of this volume his important 1977 essay on the contemporary value of Friedrich Engels's *Socialism: Utopian and Scientific* (1880). However, these issues become even more pressing in the new situation in which he is composing the book's later essays.

Suvin is deeply aware of the precarious place of intellectuals in our global information economy, something that is also of central concern in recent work of one of Suvin's great contemporaries (they were in fact born within six months of one another) and fellow student of Brecht: Jean-Luc Godard in his *Notre musique* (2004). Godard's film unfolds in three parts, modeled on the canticles of Dante's *Divina Commedia*. The first section, "Hell," takes the form of an unblinking montage of images of war's violence, drawn from documentary and fictional film history; the third, "Heaven," conversely, presents a fenced-in waterfront paradise, a pocket utopia, access to which is carefully controlled by the US military (shades of Baghdad's Green Zone). The longest segment and the one nestled between these two extremes, "Purgatory," focuses on intellectuals – journalists, Native

---

10 For a related discussion of the importance of Utopian strong thought in this moment, see Moylan, "Realizing Better Futures."

American activists, students, the recently deceased Palestine poet Mahmoud Darwish, and even a filmmaker, Godard himself – whose paths cross and re-cross in the wreckage and reconstruction of contemporary post-war Sarajevo. In this way, the film brilliantly figures the contemporary condition of radical intellectuals: like the spaces of Sarajevo, the film suggests, intellectuals occupy an intermediate place, bearing the scars of the violence suffered by the majority of the world's peoples while also having access to the privileges of a few. The question of the intellectual's responsibilities, and what they might do to address this situation, remains with the film's conclusion an open one.

In a formula strikingly resonate with the vision of Godard's film, Suvin also describes the intellectual's position as an in-between one: "we can say that fortunately all intellectuals are partly exiles from the Disneyland and/or starvation dystopia, but we are an 'inner emigration' for whom resistance was always possible and is now growing mandatory" (see pages 257–58). Suvin acknowledges the deep challenges faced by radical intellectuals, especially those who work in the university, in the face of contemporary global neo-liberalism. As he already noted in 1998, "Our immediate interests are oppositional because capitalism without a human face is obviously engaged in large scale 'structural declassing' of intellectual work, of our 'cultural capital.' There is nothing more humiliating, short of physical injury, than the experience of being pushed to the periphery of social values – measured by the only yardstick capitalism knows, our financing – which all of us have undergone in the last quarter century. Our graduate students are by now predominantly denied Keynesian employment, condemned to part-time piecework without security" (see page 254). This is a situation that has only become increasingly dire in the last decade, as Marc Bousquet, Christopher Newfield, and others have amply documented. However, Suvin also suggests that our position offers us an immensely important opportunity to challenge this situation, and to work to reinvent utopia for a new world: "The choice is [...] between oligarchic or direct-democracy collectivities and subject-positions. And it is *the intelligentsia* that will formulate (is already formulating) the tools for thinking either. Intellectuals are the name givers of categories and alternatives" (see page 187).

To do so, however, requires a radical reconsideration of both the form and the content of our labors as intellectuals. To this end, Suvin marshals an immense range of resources, past and present, in order to offer a Brechtian refunctioning of the domains of classical philosophy, science, art, politics, and religion, emphasizing in each case what he calls their "salvational" dimensions. What Suvin also demonstrates throughout these essays is the essential place of Utopian thought and literature in these efforts – "only mobilizing Paradise or Utopia can Hell or Fascism be defeated" (see page 259).

All of these labors, and indeed many of the argumentative strands of the book as a whole, come together in the crescendo suite formed by Chapters 15–18, all originally published in the first decade of the new millennium and in the global "moment of danger" (*Augenblick der Gefahr*) inaugurated on 11 September 2001. Chapter 15 functions as a dialectical counterpart to the "Tractate on Dystopia" of Chapter 13, and offers a detailed rereading of the political epistemology of Marx – "indispensable to any looking forward that attempts to avoid catastrophe for humanity" (page 419) – in terms of the interlocking domains of "cognition, liberty, and pleasure." To this end, Suvin invokes a variety of earlier traditions of thought, including those of Lucretius ("The *parenklisis* or swerve (*clinamen* in Lucrece's Latin) [...] breaks the chains of Fate" [see pages 422–23]) Epicure ("Epicure's breakthrough was to conjoin being wise, honourable, and friendly" [see page 424]), Hegel, and Fourier ("an 'absolute swerve' [*écart absolu*) based on the pleasure principle" [see page 433]). The main body of the chapter concludes with a detailed engagement with Marx's *Grundrisse*, of which Suvin argues, "Marx's main innovation was to alter *the people's body* into *labour's living body*, which makes out of the cosmic presupposition of ever-living fire a concrete, everyday matter of *living labour's formative fire*" (see page 444).

In Chapter 16, Suvin unabashedly affirms the utopian dimensions of communism as a "fully worldly, fleshly and material" belief system, which "if it openly assumes the strengths of salvationalism, nobody can, as Benjamin remarked, win against it" (see pages 476 and 488–89). This is followed by a brief group of poems, entitled "Farewell Fantasies," in which Suvin again thematizes the aim of sifting through the cultural and intellectual legacies of the past and then reworking them to best serve our present purposes (this work is especially evident in the longest poem of the group, "Pillaging the Gnostics"). Finally, Suvin brings both this movement and the book as a whole to a close with a new tribute to the continued vitality of *The Dispossessed* as "that actually rather rare thing, a real *science fiction* novel: a work of fiction seriously exploring science for systematic cognition – both a human way of knowing and as human social activity" (see page 524). Even this essay is not without critical interrogations – Suvin especially challenges the novel's "failure of interest" in the question of political revolt, and the fact that "the properly economico-political critique [...] is missing in the Urras story" (see pages 545 and 547). Crucially, however, Suvin concludes, "With warts and all, *TD* establishes a horizon of thisworldly justice centered on people and their knowledge" (see page 548).

Finally, Suvin not only discusses the necessity of another way of being and doing in the world, he enacts one in the very form of these essays. "No toolkit is viable unless fusing the lessons of political & artistic practice," he writes in Chapter 12, a fundamental lesson reinforced throughout these pages (see page 12). The frequent shift of tone, from the analytic to the personal to the messianic, the use of poetry, the formal strategies of the wedges and the braids – "Indeed, perhaps the compositional principle of all fictional utopias (including dystopias) is necessarily the braiding of showing and telling, lecture and action" (see page 325) – all work, like the toolkits of the earlier generations of modernists from which Suvin draws so much, to develop another way of engaging in our intellectual labors. This makes Suvin's text a challenging one; but it also exponentially increases its rewards.

Moreover, drawing upon a rich array of voices and traditions, listening carefully to what they have to teach us, and then placing them in startlingly new juxtapositions and contexts, Suvin creates a truly dialogic and collective text. As with the modernist tradition of the notebook form that I invoked in the opening of this Preface, these essays express "the passion for totality" that Negri sees as a fundamental aspect of Marx's *Grundrisse*, while also remaining open to the possibility of the unexpected, the truly new, the redemptive novum (*Marx Beyond Marx* 13). In these ways, Suvin's work becomes a bridge, resonant of Benjamin's lightning arc, linking the legacies of a past utopian radicalism with what still remains the world "always coming," much like the figure of the train of history glimpsed at the conclusion of Miéville's recent monumental utopian fiction, *Iron Council* (2005). Suvin's work demonstrates an unwavering fidelity to the project of putting this train back upon its track so that it might begin again its tiger leap forward.

For all of these challenges and pleasures, and many others besides, it has been a great privilege to have had the opportunity to read these works once again—or more precisely, to have read with Suvin one more time — and I invite you now to do the same.

Works Cited

Badiou, Alain. *The Century*. Trans. Alberto Toscano. Malden: Polity, 2007.
——. *Ethics: An Essay on the Understanding of Radical Evil*. Trans. Peter Hallward. New York: Verso, 2001.
Benjamin, Walter. *Gesammelte Schriften*, Vol. I. Frankfurt am Main: Suhrkamp Verlag, 1985.
——. *Selected Writings, Volume 3, 1935–1938*. Cambridge, MA: Harvard University Press, 2002.
——. *Selected Writings, Volume 4, 1938–1940*. Cambridge, MA: Harvard University Press, 2003.
Bousquet, Marc. *How the University Works: Higher Education and the Low-Wage Nation*. New York: New York University Press, 2008.
Brecht, Bertolt. *Selected Poems*. Trans. H.R. Hays. New York: Grove, 1959.
Eley, Geoff. *Forging Democracy: The History of the Left in Europe, 1850–2000*. Oxford: Oxford University Press, 2002.

Fisher, William F., and Thomas Ponniah, eds. *Another World is Possible: Popular Alternatives to Globalization at the World Social Forum*. New York: Zed Books, 2003.

Jameson, Fredric. *Archaeologies of the Future: The Desire Called Utopia and Other Science Fictions*, New York: Verso, 2005.

———. *Signatures of the Visible*. New York: Verso, 1990.

Miéville, China. *Iron Council*. New York: Del Rey, 2005.

Moylan, Tom. "Realizing Better Futures, Strong Thought for Hard Times." *Utopia Method Vision: The Use Value of Social Dreaming*. Ed. Tom Moylan and Raffaella Baccolini. Oxford: Peter Lang, 2007. 191–221.

———. *Scraps of the Untainted Sky: Science Fiction, Utopia, Dystopia*. Boulder: Westview, 2001.

Negri, Antonio. *Goodbye Mr. Socialism*. Trans. Peter Thomas. New York: Seven Stories, 2008.

———. *Marx Beyond Marx: Lessons on the* Grundrisse. New York: Autonomedia, 1991.

Newfield, Christopher. *Unmaking the Public University: The Forty-Year Assault on the Middle Class*. Cambridge, MA: Harvard University Press, 2008.

Notre musique. Dir. Jean Luc Godard. Avventura Films, 2004.

Parrinder, Patrick, ed. *Learning from Other Worlds: Estrangement, Cognition, and the Politics of Science Fiction and Utopia*, Durham: Duke University Press, 2001.

Rancière, Jacques. *The Politics of Aesthetics: The Distribution of the Sensible*. Trans. Gabriel Rockhill. London: Continuum, 2004.

Roy, Arundhati. *War Talk*. Cambridge, MA: South End, 2003.

Slusser, George. "The Origins of Science Fiction." *A Companion to Science Fiction*. Ed. David Seed. Blackwell, 2005. 27–42.

Suvin, Darko. "Considering the Sense of 'Fantasy' or 'Fantastic Fiction': An Effusion." *Extrapolation* 41.3 (2000): 209–47.

———. "The Final Chapter of SF?: On Reading Brian Stableford." *SFRA Review* 266 (2003): 5–9.

———. "The Final Chapter? On Reading Brian Stableford – Part Two." *SFRA Review* 267 (2004): 2–6.

——. *Metamorphoses of Science Fiction: On the Poetics and History of a Literary Genre*. New Haven: Yale University Press, 1979.

——. *Positions and Presuppositions in Science Fiction*. Kent: Kent State University Press, 1988.

Wegner, Phillip E. *Imaginary Communities: Utopia, the Nation, and the Spatial Histories of Modernity*. Berkeley: University of California Press, 2002.

——. "Jameson's Modernisms; or, the Desire Called Utopia." *Diacritics* 37.4 (Winter), 2007: 2–20.

——. "Ken MacLeod's Permanent Revolution: Utopian Possible Worlds, History, and the *Augenblick* in the 'Fall Revolution'." *Red Planets: Marxism and Science Fiction*. Ed. Mark Bould and China Miéville. London: Pluto, 2009. 137–58.

——. *Life Between Two Deaths: U.S. Culture, 1989–2001*. Durham: Duke University Press, 2009.

——. "On Zamyatin's *We*: A Critical Map of Utopia's 'Possible Worlds'." *Utopian Studies* 4.2 (1993): 94–116.

Introduction 2008:
On Hollows, or an Alarmed Door

Le choix que je suis
[the choice that is me]
     — JEAN-PAUL SARTRE, *L'Etre et le néant*, 1943

0. A Note to Myself: In the Ice Age
(A Counter-project to Xiung Xi-ling)

All that we feel is the freezing storm
But who is there to grieve for the warmth?
As you're leaving, bequeath this wish:
Everybody should afford happiness!

1. On the Situation

It's lonely in the saddle since the horse died.
     — Graffito in Paddington NSW (Australia), ca. 1997

Must I make my peace
with Clausewitz; or with Hobbes's law?
[...] Suddenly they are upon us, the long
columns, the immense details
of betrayal: as always predicted
yet wholly unforeseen.
     — GEOFFREY HILL, *The Triumph of Love*, 1988

This book is a unified collection of some essays and batches of poems, grouped chronologically and written inside what are to my mind two historical Leviathans where I lived: the end of Fordism and post-World War Two Welfare State (1973–91) and Post-Fordism, where company is wolf to company, State to State, human to human, and the resulting psychophysical horrors are unmitigated (mid-1990s to the present).

It might be objected that Fordism, or the last aftershocks of the Leninist period and of the ensuing Welfare State, ended economically about 1973. But my understanding was certainly very laggard: I only began to realize it after 1989, while full illumination dawned on me with the NATO bombs on Belgrade in the 1990s. Thence a certain break in time, and perhaps even more in tone, between Chapters 1–6 and Chapters 8–18 of this book, marked by the batch of poems called "The Doldrums: 1989–99." The central shift of horizons, though not of orientation (see Chapter 5), is that up to 1991 I was still confident that the antifascist impetus and achievements of my youth could be carried on – with whatever modifications towards a New Left and whatever huge difficulties in finding a way between capitalism and Stalinism (see Chapter 11 on Zamyatin's *We*). After the mid-1990s I was not: my team was in full defeat and rout, and all that could be done was to try and understand how come, why, and how to envisage possible rearguard skirmishes. As the Reaganite slogan went, which I met in Canada too, "That was then; this is now." New subject-matter demanded to be met – laboriously, since for all my interest I had never analytically dealt with it. This I found I could only do bit by bit, in essays which, though incorporating much research, diverged from the scholarly norm I had followed for almost half a century. Concomitantly, their bulk shifted from the academically acceptable six to nine thousand words to thirteen to seventeen thousand; this did not ease their publication, which shifted to non-academic, though largely as marginal, venues (with one exception, whose editor is thanked in Chapter 15).

A look at the contents of the book shows that the first six essays could be inscribed in a somewhat heretic or innovative wing of some academic pursuits, themselves marginal to orthodoxy, such as studies of science fiction and utopian studies. The poems of the time (Chapter 4), while facing the personal price to be paid by an émigré, still held to the larger framework of

Blochian hope, which indeed culminated in the utopian "soft primitivism" of *Visions off Yamada* and other similar poems of a more intimate nature (see Suvin, "Parentheses"). The poems of Chapter 7, during and after the break-up and civil wars in Yugoslavia, culminate to my mind in the cosmic desolation of "Imagine a Fish," a hyperbole for the dystopian period I grappled with after the mid-1990s. Parallel to this, the stocktaking of Chapters 8–12 issues in an overt discussion of dystopia (Chapter 13). Nonetheless, the horizon of a history that has no end is not forgotten, it lives in the poems of Chapter 14 as the value stance from which all is judged and at times even surfaces. The final three essays are lengthy reflections about a ground to stand on, *ubi consistam*: in the Marxian depths of labour, in the Benjaminian horizon of salvation, in the best of imaginative fiction. All of them communicate with our empirical Possible World Zero, indicating places of Hope the Principle. Through the darkness of dystopia, which must be observed because we are living it (Chapters 13 and 17), they reaffirm eutopia, the radically better place to be striven for in every here and now.

2. On the Approach

> The writing of this book [...] has been a series of experiments in methods of thinking about anthropological material, and it remains to report upon how I was led to carry out these experiments [...] and to stress what I regard as my most important results.
>
> — GREGORY BATESON, Epilogue to *Naven*, 1936

What happened around and to me propelled me towards two quasi-disciplinary perspectives, epistemological and political. I adopt the definition of *epistemology* as the theory of cognition (where psychology should meet philosophy) dealing with the possibilities and limits of human knowledge, the analysis of conceptual and other cognitive systems – in my case especially metaphors and figurations in general – and in particular the critique of language and other sign-systems as concrete consciousness, pioneered by my late friend Raymond Williams. As to politics, I am comfortable with the Hellenic approach to it as "affairs of the community," but in today's global dynamics I would rather treat them as ongoing *history*, if updated by Marx's insights into the class structure of people's life together. I have however been unable, perhaps also unwilling, to follow any disciplinary mainstream. Instead, I found whatever illumination I could in dissidents (visible in my Works Cited lists), in poets, whether writing verse, prose or plays, and in a few *maîtres à penser* from whom I took whatever I could and left aside what I could not: Marx, Brecht, Benjamin, Jameson ... (Also Ernst Bloch: having reread him just now, I found my thought so imbued with his that no reference could do it justice, or perhaps that I recognize in him what oft I thought but he best expressed – no doubt both are true. He was the first to note the huge difference between true and fake novum, the strategic importance of Epicure's deviation, and so many other points that recur in this volume. He too was, as a theologian called him, "a hope in search of reason/s – *spes quaerens intellectum*.")

The results here are to be excused by Aristotle's maxim that each field allows its own mode of (im)precision, so that the field of rapidly evolving and hugely conflictual views about present-day Destiny surely must be allowed a lot of imprecision, perhaps kindly thought of as experimental approximations. As Merleau-Ponty put it:

> It would be false rigor to expect fully worked out principles in order to speak philo-sophically about politics. Challenged by events, we meet what is for us unacceptable, and the interpretation of this experience becomes thesis and philosophy. It is therefore permissible to narrate it frankly, with its repetitions, its ellipses, its disparities, and with a possibility of rechecking it. (9)

Max Weber says somewhere that history teaches us the true meaning of what we have willed. And history, when it is not simply a "God word," is constituted by each of us but then also by all of us, and furthermore by forces institutionalized and solidified by some (classes) among us which operate in ways both evident and very opaque. What is evident is their results: bombings, murders, hunger, unhappiness, the exponentially rising moral and material pollution under the triumph of late capitalism. What is opaque are their hidden springs, the causal system (however complex and multiplex) which I have just ventured to name. I am under no illusion that the simple act of naming explains all, but without it – without a proper mental map of pertinent categories and their relationships – no explanation will work. History permeates and constitutes us, it is the atheist equivalent of gods and metamorphosis of Destiny, it is a teacher of life and a delusive siren, past and present in feedback eating at future, a promise and a threat. It is *unumgänglich*: not to be circumvented. But if its results at some point become unbearable, one stops and says "Here I stand, I cannot do otherwise." There the effort to comprehend, as at least a first step towards doing something, inscribes itself.

If then I follow Gramsci in recognizing that our horizons are inescapably a matter of thisworldly collectives, I would see *historicism* as the understanding of our relationships within the societal network of power and knowledge but only if I may add to this two crucial – both epistemic and political – matters. First, syntagmatically, for any particular event strategic primacy belongs to the category of *situation* (see Jameson, *Modernist* x–xi), a delimited and always historical and dynamic totality in view of given interests (I developed this at length in "Two Cheers"). Second, paradigmatically, both an overall social network and a particular situation are strongly determined by the conflicting *class interests* indwelling in each, even if we today know classes themselves are overdetermined. Epistemology and history could fully meet in pragmatics, but I have not seen linguists make enough of that. For, as I discuss in Chapter 5, pragmatics is constitutive of and probably overarching to both semantics and syntactics: an object, person, or event becomes a sign only in a *signifying situation*, constituted by the relation between signs and their users. A user can take something to be a sign only as it is spatio-temporally concrete and as it relates to the user's disposition towards potential action; both the concrete localization and the user's disposition are always socio-historical. Furthermore, they postulate a reality organized not only around signs but also around subjects – psychophysical personalities and collective representations (classes, nations ...).

It is of central cognitive value here to go on and say with Lenin: "Form is essential. Essence is formed" (144); or, in updated vocabulary with Jameson, "absolute historicism [...] is also an absolute formalism" (*Modernist* xiii). Any situation is a form, a mini-monad, a Brechtian self-governing episode. To my mind, it is only with these two additions that the question haunting us on the Left today can be properly envisaged: Is history intelligible? I could answer that the very term and concept of "history" epistemologically implies or presupposes that it is intelligible, that people's collective praxis makes sense (in all meanings), as opposed to Macbeth's "tale told by an idiot, full of sound and fury, signifying nothing." But that answer would be something of a vicious circle or at least Pascalian wager, for history is of course never *fully* intelligible, fixed once and for always as a butterfly-object pinned down to wriggle under the entomologist-subject's gaze. Obviously, it develops, and indeed fairly radically changes epochal models. But most important, *by and for whom* is history intelligible, *cui bono*? That is, the moment we see a situation as functioning for or against given interests sustained in time and across human classes, the wager on intelligibility is at least in theory won: Yes, history could be, up to a point and for given interests in given situations, intelligible. Whether we do understand it and how well depends on our strengths and limitations. And as already Protagora knew, "Many are the things that hinder knowledge: the obscurity of the matter and the brevity of human life."

In that sense, history is a macro-example of both situation and horizon: a prospect of vision, an intimation of not yet experienced but glimpsed possibilities. They are all under the sign of *risk*. The odds against a species with a conscience/consciousness arising are astronomical, as huge as against life itself. We are this improbable animal that lives "nonetheless," the risky creature that cannot dispense with rational planning, culture, material and visionary instruments. History, and the possibility of liberation through it, may be our (so far) supreme visionary invention.

This book wishes and aspires to be a building block of that wager and vision. It is perhaps, as a friend who knew me well put it, a meeting of Joachimite epistemology and political economy. He thought of this mainly as dubious, perhaps akin to the meeting of an umbrella and a sewing machine on an operating table. Yet not only has our world become quite surreal(ist), I would claim that this meeting is not (as in Lautréamont's phrase) fortuitous, but exactly the heart-piece of what can and must be learned from Marx – lest darkness fall. Salvation can only come by way of a critique of political economy: we are living this every day.

3. On Textual History and Method

> In these great times which I knew when they were this small; which will become small
> again, provided they have time left for it; and which […] we had better call fat times
> and, truly, hard times as well; in these times in which things are happening that could
> not be imagined and in which what can no longer be imagined must happen […]; in
> these times you should not expect any words of my own from me – none but these
> words which barely manage to prevent silence from being misinterpreted.
>
> — KARL KRAUS, *In These Great Times*

At this point I have to glance, however briefly, at the substance of the book. I shall unavoidably use insights and terms developed within it. The benevolent reader is invited to read this as it was written, that is: after finishing the book.

To avoid endless prolix explanations of deep-down principles, I have had recourse to the axiomatic method. I have at the outset presupposed, and wherever possible overtly posed, certain axioms as theses. Maybe I should call this a semi-axiomatic method, for I have tried to indicate their inductive roots as precipitates of mass experiences that include mine, but then I think every axiomatic approach is in that way impure (except maybe in mathematics). Beside brevity, this approach works for clarity and elaboration of an open system (explained in Chapter 10), in favour of critical demystification and theoretical richness, and it seems to me the best way to encounter the growing complexity and obfuscation of life under brainwashing turbo-capitalism. No doubt, I have often oversimplified, but usually with an up-front purpose and I hope always harmlessly.

However, this book does not run a straight course. It searches, it probes. Its essay-chapters are part indignant self-understanding, part proposals for thinking further (*Denkvorschläge*). Beside a claim to strategic value, their title often indicates tentativeness. They cannot but often vary recurrent themes, striving to be a widening spiral through the thickets rather than consecutive steps in a neat path. For there was no path (though there were many fellow-explorers before me, without whom it would have been difficult to move). A bit like Old Antonio, the utopian guide, says to the Subcomandante's narrator, the path had to be made out of the experiences of many refracted through an "I" (*Zapatista* 118). As events more and more massively struck, I found that always, as one of my early poetic enthusiasms, Jules Laforgue, put it in "Complainte du Sage de Paris":

> Mais comme Brennus avec son épée, et d'avance,
> Suis-je pas dans un des plateaux de la balance?
> [But from the outset, like Brennus with his sword,
> Am I not in one of the trays of the balance?]

Therefore I attempted to find different joints at which to cut reality, hoping to at least adumbrate a comprehensible, bloody macro-body. At least in thoughts I would not be merely a manipulated, most unwilling object but also a subject, empowered cognitively if not, for want of a collective, also empowered politically. This was my best approximation to Aristotle's and Rancière's democracy: a State in which each citizen in turn obeys and is obeyed.

A brief pragmatic overview of how this book was written might be useful. Chapters 5, 6, and 8 were responses to invitations, as detailed in the last note to each, but such that allowed me to develop what I was anyway aiming to do. Chapter 9 was written for a somewhat anomalous scholarly session: it was at the pleasingly unorthodox Society of Utopian Studies and specially organized so it could be longer than usual. It is in some ways a transition towards essays written using some compositional experimenta-tion ("wedges" in Chapter 10, "braiding" in Chapter 11, and then settling into the theses or tractate format in Chapters 12, 13, and 15), which was facilitated by their not being destined for any express venue. As I say in the note to Chapter 11, the experiments were attempts to escape what I felt as the ghetto of Idealist literary studies and esthetics, which take history into account only if it is the history of other books and writings. While methodological problems how to do this are still with us, and I cannot pretend these essays are more than attempts, this seemed much prefer-able to not trying anything. I should say that in 1997–99 I was teaching half-time and spending three to four months per year in Berlin, while as of 2001 I moved as a pensioner to Lucca, Italy, where all chapters begin-ning with Chapter 13 were written. It does not make much difference to an intellectual where he writes (Chapter 6 was written largely, and Chapter 12 partly, during longer stays in Japan and Germany), but as of Chapter 13 my dialogues with colleagues became mainly electronic and my reading of new books was mainly done once per year at the British Library in London (and as of 2004 also once per year at libraries of the University of Uppsala, where part of Chapter 16 and the whole of Chapter 18 were written). An exceptionally direct dialogue was maintained, both by not quite regular attendance and by participation in its written projects, with the German Institut für kritische Theorie led first in Berlin and then near Stuttgart by W.F. and Frigga Haug (attempts to do something similar in London and Paris did not work out except in welcome brief patches). More can be glimpsed from the Acknowledgements.

I have discreetly retouched the essays by adding to them arguments and info bytes I would have put in originally had I only had time to find their sources and think about them, but I forbore to modify the original horizons – even when mine would today be somewhat different. Exceptions are some references to my later works which I hope might help, and notes expressly marked by an underlined later date. This preserves the essays' own historicity at a fast changing time and allows me to keep the reference, at the beginning of each essay, of the year of its writing, "branding" (as Brecht put it) "each work with its date as a calf on the ranch." I cut a bit and would have cut more had I not thought what is left may be useful: before this book jelled, a long debate about the financial limits of publishing led to the exclusion of essays on SF and on theory deemed tangential to this venture, as can in good part be seen through my (alas not rare) self-references in the Works Cited. Substantive matters of the book's arguments and their evolution – say, the links between the book's constituent parts or the additions to my stock of semi-authorities evident from the Works Cited – I leave to the interested reader. I much hope that the chronologically placed batches of poems will help to understand and enrich the essays.

And finally, my experience as teacher and critic has not convinced me a certain amount of repetition is needless. Within the book's web of forward and backward references between essays, where a few repetitions said what I could not say better, I let them stand, and trust this is forgivable.

4. Things Could Be Otherwise

> I began reading science fiction in the 1950s and got from it a message that didn't exist anywhere else then in my world. Explicit sometimes in the detachable ideas, implicit in the gimmicks ... most fully expressed in the strange life-forms and strange, strange, wonderfully strange landscapes was the message: *Things can be really different.*

Thus the marvellous Joanna Russ (xiv–xv). I do not wish to rehearse here the debate on my infamous suggestion that utopian fiction is today a part of SF (see Chapter 1 – this is empirically correct) and that this remix of cards makes it useful to see retrospectively all utopia as sociopolitical SF, though this book flows out of and explores that suggestion. I shall only point out that strong affinities are clearly present, even to Russ's slogan which is in fact Raymond Ruyer's definition of utopia. Some aspects would differ: for example, classical utopias do not stress technoscientific gimmicks, but even this has exceptions such as Francis Bacon and is obsolete by the time eutopia appears within SF in Ursula K. Le Guin (see Chapter 18), Marge Piercy, or Joan Slonczewski (see Suvin, "Starship"), and indeed a quarter of a century earlier for the SF dystopia, the radically worse society from Frederick Pohl to Philip K. Dick. Even the more important difference of the (sub)generic traditions, in classical utopias addressed to high intellectuals and in narrative form an "anatomy," in classical SF addressed to the masses and in narrative form an action romance with inserted lectures, melds in rich ways after the 1960s in United States SF or such European masters as Stanislaw Lem and the Strugatsky brothers (see Moylan, *Demand* and *Scraps*, and Suvin, *Positions*). I would only add that when I started reading SF, at the same time as Russ, it was after reading Jules Verne, H.G. Wells, and the utopians as a boy in the 1940s, and most important, that Russ's slogan was for me not only compatible with what I was imbibing as Marxism and socialism in Tito's Yugoslavia but that it enriched (and no doubt modified) such doctrines in unforeseen and pleasing ways. Taking the best from both currents, as ideal types, they were natural allies. This seems to me much strengthened in Post-Fordism, where classical realism becomes problematical and where, even before capitalism deconstructed our education into trade schools, it had become more complex "to possess a truth in a soul and a body," as Rimbaud demanded. Following on Brecht and Walter Benjamin, I find this persuasively argued by Jameson as "a gap between individual and phenomenological experience and structural intelligibility":

> if, in the newly decentered situation of the imperialist network, you live something strongly and concretely, it is unintelligible, since its ultimate determinants lie out-side your own field of experience. If on the other hand you are able to understand a phenomenon abstractly or scientifically, [...] then this knowledge fails to add up to a concrete experience, remains abstract and sealed away in a compartment of the mind reserved for pure knowledge and intellection. (*Modernist* 240–41)

To the contrary, SF and utopia construct social models; while "the genius of Marx, the secret of his enduring power, lies in his having been the first to construct true social models" (Braudel 39). A few of us in the journal *Science-Fiction Studies*, started by my lamented friend Dale Mullen in 1973, and prominently including Jameson, tried to elucidate such horizons until 1981.

But all such talk grew taboo in the heyday of Post-Modernism (and Jameson even got kicked off its Board). Yet this heyday came finally a cropper with the Second Iraq War. Even as the great wave of utopian SF seems to have subsided after Kim Stanley Robinson's *Mars* trilogy, some revival of interest in utopian concepts is evident today, most notably in Jameson's *Archaeologies of the Future*, that deals with both utopia/nism and SF. As he does there, we have to liberate the TINA slogan hijacked by Mrs Thatcher and say that there is no (acceptable) alternative to eutopia, a radically better organization of people's lives together. For the alternative is the electronico-genetic police state based on caste, whose Argus eyes we see today hanging above every street-corner.

Alas, we may not have SF to kick around if and when the revival begins to reach towards fiction, unless it finds its way through Fantasy. I consider this rather unlikely, but history is always slyer than the historiographers (see Suvin, "Considering," "Final," and "On U.K. Le Guin's").

5. A Prospect

Mais le remède? Je n'aime pas les médécins qui parlent j'aime ceux qui guerissent.
[But the remedy? I don't like the physicians who talk, I like those who heal.]
— LOUIS DE SAINT-JUST, *De la nature*

Ich bin nicht mehr sicher, dass der Kommunismus [...] das Schicksal der Menschheit ist, aber er bleibt ein Menschheitstraum, an dessen Erfüllung eine Generation nach der anderen arbeiten wird bis zum Untergang unserer Welt.
[I am no longer certain that communism [...] is the destiny of humankind, but it remains a dream of humanity that one generation after another will work toward fulfilling until the end of our world.]
— HEINER MÜLLER, "Das Liebesleben der Hyänen"

There is no conclusion to this book, an ongoing project, nor to its Introduction: we have lost the belief of an immanent *telos* to history, and this is probably to the good. But at the end I would like to face the secret problem of all utopians or utopologists: communism.

When Lenin resuscitated the word as name for his party amid the most murderous First World War, he did so as a gesture of mental hygiene, to wash off the dirt accumulated on the once useful name of a social democracy that had with more or less enthusiasm participated in that war. Many glories were associated with his reborn term during the struggle against war, exploitation, and especially against fascism. Yet also horrors: the ossifications of a hierarchic Party in power, the blood and cruelty of High Stalinism, and finally the betrayal of a rising new class of exploiters. As of somewhere in the 1950s, communism ceased to be *salonfähig* (admissible to polite society) for the "western" Left, that much preferred the unclear term of socialism, which anyway led to fewer reprisals. I know because I participated in that. But after the 1990s there is no more CPSU, or its dwarfish satellites, to differentiate oneself from, and the socialist politicians (they never had theoreticians to speak of) are indistinguishable from the anti-socialist ones. And our plight is as bad as in the First World War.

For we have to note how around us and through us a fully radical alternative has arisen: "What if it were the failures [...] of socialists and communists which left in their wake a universal disillusionment in which only consumption and narrow fanaticism (market and confessional) seem possible, at least for the present?" (Jameson, *Modernist* 291). Against the propaganda of enemies that insisted communism was terror (abetted by Trotsky's pugnacious choice to espouse that term) we have today to inquire what is terrorism. I have written about this at length and concluded the only tenable definition is this: a strategy which consists in pursuing political power by striking dread into the civilian population through exemplary killings among them. Thus, there is State and group terrorism, or should we say capitalist and patriarchal? The States dispose of supersonic bombers and ABC weapons, the groups have to improvise with cheaper ones, the cheapest (costing zero) being human life. As Benjamin saw already in Weimar and Nazi times, the final, most radical novelty of the commodity economy is Death (I touch upon this in almost all chapters from chapter 8 on, especially 9 and 10). Capitalism daily results in thousands of deaths by hunger, war, associated preventable diseases, and so endlessly on. The only way to prevent it from ruining the planet and all our lives is "the desire called utopia," an opposed and normative value-system based on use-values: but that is in its final horizons a redefined communism. The most recent definition I know, by Resnick and Wolff, runs: "A communist class structure exists if and when the people who collectively produce a surplus are likewise and identically the people who collectively receive and distribute it" (9). Not to enter into fine details (what should one call the egalitarianism without a surplus, for example, in tribal societies?), it is striking how analogous this is to Aristotle's quality of a citizen in a democracy, only *more economico*: "the citizen must know and share in both ruling and being ruled" (*Politics* 1277a 31–32 in *Selections* 470; see also 1275a). In other words: there is no full and lasting democracy without communism, and vice versa. The failure to observe this has led to our plight today.

Towards the end of the book I therefore propose we rethink the term for our, no doubt utopian, horizons and consider whether there is a better one for our poetry and prose than communism (I further meet this head on in my newest essay, "Death into Life"). I do not see any. And terms are akin to *terminus*, limit: they delimit reality, shaping it as this, rather than that. This does not mean I know how to get to this supreme political good.

But this book finally strives to establish that it is our necessary horizon and orientation from our present most unhappy locus.

The alternative is what Lucretius called "accepting (or cleaving unto) old religions and cruel lords": "rursus in antiquas referuntur religiones/ et dominos acris adsciscunt."

In the new British Library at Camden, I noted with surprise and some delight the inscription leading to staircases: "alarmed door." I would like this book to have such a function for you, Reader.

Works Cited

Aristotle. *Selections*. Ed. and trans. Terence Irwin and Gail Fine. Indianapolis: Hackett, 1995.

Braudel, Fernand. "History and the Social Sciences." *Economy and Society in Early Modern Europe*. Ed. Peter Burke. London: Routledge, 1972. 11–42.

Jameson, Fredric. *Archaeologies of the Future: The Desire Called Utopia and Other Science Fictions*. London: Verso, 2005.

——. *The Modernist Papers*. London: Verso, 2007.

Lenin, Vladimir I. *Collected Works. Vol. 38: Philosophical Notebooks*. Trans. Clemence Dutt. London: Lawrence and Wishart. 1980.

Marcos, Subcomandante. *Zapatista Stories*. Trans. Dinah Livingstone. London: Katabasis, 2001.

Merleau-Ponty, Maurice. *Les aventures de la dialectique*. Paris: Gallimard, 2000.

Moylan, Tom. *Demand the Impossible: Science Fiction and the Utopian Imagination*. New York: Methuen, 1986.

——. *Scraps of the Untainted Sky: Science Fiction, Utopia, Dystopia*. Boulder: Westview, 2000.

Resnick, Stephen A., and Richard D. Wolff. *Class Theory and History: Capitalism and Communism in the U.S.S.R.* New York: Routledge, 2002.

Suvin, Darko. "Considering the Sense of 'Fantasy' or 'Fantastic Fiction.'" *Extrapolation* 41.3 (2000): 209–47.

——. "Death into Life: For a Poetics of Anti-Capitalist Alternative." (circulating)

——. "The Final Chapter of SF? On Reading Brian Stableford." *SFRA Review* 266 (2003): 5–9.

——. "The Final Chapter of SF? On Reading Brian Stableford – Part Two." *SFRA Review* 267 (2004): 2–6.

——. "Of Starship Troopers and Refuseniks: War and Militarism in US Science Fiction, Part 2." *Extrapolation* 48.1 (2007): 9–34.

——. "On U.K. Le Guin's 'Second Earthsea Trilogy' and Its Cognitions." *Extrapolation* 47.3 (2006): 488–504.

——. "Parentheses: An (Auto)biography Sparked by Verse." *Abiko Annual* 24 (2004): 132–258.

——. *Positions and Presuppositions in Science Fiction*. Kent: Kent State University Press, 1988.

——. "Two Cheers for Essentialism and Totality." *Rethinking Marxism* 10.1 (1998): 66–82.

Defining the Literary Genre of Utopia: Some Historical Semantics, Some Genology, a Proposal, and a Plea (1973)

> For if the matter be attentively considered, a sound argument may be drawn from Poesy, to show that there is agreeable to the spirit of man a more ample greatness, a more perfect order, and a more beautiful variety than it can anywhere (since the Fall) find in nature. [...] it [Poesy] raises the mind and carries it aloft, accommodating the shows of things to be desires of the mind, not (like reason and history) buckling and bowing down the mind to the nature of things.
> — FRANCIS BACON, *De Augmentis Scientiarum*

0. Introduction

"Utopia," the neologism of Thomas More, has had a singularly rich semantic career in our time.[1] Having at its root the simultaneous indication of a space and a state (itself ambiguously hovering between, for example, French *état* and *condition*) that are nonexistent (*ou*) as well as good (*eu*), it has become a territory athwart the roads of all travelers pursuing the implications of the question formulated by Plato as "What is the best form of organiza-

---

1   I use "Utopia" with capital U only for Thomas More's State and title, and "utopia" with lower-case u for all other references. I would dearly wish to see this basic semantic hygiene followed more widely. I also use, again in this whole book, SF for science fiction, and State with capital S when I mean the political power structure rather than condition.

tion for a community and how can a person best arrange his life?" (*Laws* 3, 702b, 85). And have not the urgencies of the situation in which the human community finds itself made of us all such travelers?

Utopia operates by example and demonstration, deictically. At the basis of all utopian debates, in its open or hidden dialogues, is a gesture of pointing, a wide-eyed glance from here to there, a "traveling shot" moving from the author's everyday lookout to the wondrous panorama of a far-off land:

> But you should have been with me in Utopia and personally seen their manner and customs as I did. [...] (More, *Utopia* Book 1)

> [...]it was winter when I went to bed last night, and now, by witness of the river-side trees, it was summer, a beautiful bright morning seemingly of early June. (Morris, *News from Nowhere* chapter 2)

> We should both discover that the little towns below had changed – but how, we should not have marked them well enough to know. It would be indefinable, a change in the quality of their grouping, a change in the quality of their remote, small shapes. [...] a mighty difference had come to the world of men. (Wells, *A Modern Utopia*, Chapter 1)

Morris's abruptly beautiful trees can be taken (as they were meant to be) for an emblem of this space and state: utopia is a vivid witness to desperately needed alternative possibilities of "the world of men," of human life. No wonder the debate has waxed hot whether any particular alternative is viable and whether it has already been found, especially in the various socialist attempts at a radically different social system. In the heat of the debate, detractors of this particular set of alternative conclusions – often shell-shocked refugees from it – have tried to deny the possibility and/or humanity of the utopian concept as such. Other imprudent apologists – often intellectuals with a solid position within the defended system – have taken the symmetrically inverse but equally counter-utopian tack of proclaiming that *Civitas Dei* has already been realized on Earth by their particular sect or nation, in "God's own country" of North America or the laicized Marxist (or pseudo-Marxist) experiments from Lenin to Castro and Mao. Historians have transferred these debates into the past:

were Periclean Athens, Emperor Akbar's India, Emperor Friedrich's Sicily, Münzer's Mühlhausen, the Inca state, or Jeffersonian USA utopian?

Such fascinating and tempting questions cannot fail to influence us in an underground fashion – defining our semantics – in any approach to a definition of utopia. But I propose to confine myself here to a considera-tion of utopia as a literary genre. No doubt this is not the first point about utopias – that would pertain to collective psychology: why and how do they arise? – nor is it the last one – that would pertain to the politics of the human species and perhaps even to its cosmology: how is *Homo sapiens* to survive and humanize its segment of the universe?

Such a politico-eschatological question has understandably arisen out of twentieth-century heretic reinterpretations of the two most systematic bodies of thought about humans in our civilization: the Judeo-Christian one (in spite of its usual pat transfers of the answer into the blue yonder of otherworldly post-mortems) and the Marxist one (in spite of Marx's and Engels's scorn of subjective theorizing about ideal futures in their pred-ecessors, the "utopian socialists"). Ernst Bloch's monumental philosophical opus, culminating in *The Principle of Hope*, has reinterpreted utopia (as have some theologians such as Martin Buber and Paul Tillich) as being any overstepping of the boundaries given to humans, hence a quality inherent in all creative thought and action. In a narrower and more academic version, a similar reinterpretation of "utopia" as any orientation that transcends reality and breaks the bounds of existing order, as opposed to "ideology" which expresses the existing order, was introduced by Karl Mannheim.[2]

However, all these horizons, interesting and even inspiring as they are, are beyond my scope here. I propose that an acknowledgment that utopias are verbal artifacts before they are anything else, and that the source of this concept is a literary genre and its parameters, might be, if not the first and the last, nonetheless a central point in today's debate on utopias. If this is so, one cannot properly explore the signification of utopia by considering

2   See Tillich (a representative essay from which is reprinted in Manuel ed.), Buber, Bloch, and Mannheim; also the rich anthology on the concept of utopia: Neusüss ed.

its body (texts) simply as a transparency transmitting a Platonic idea: the *signifiant* must be understood as well as the *signifié*. Thus, especially at this time of failing eschatologies, it might even be in the interests of utopia (however widely redefined) if we acted as physiologists asking about a species' functions and structure before we went on to behave as moralists prescribing codes of existence to it: perhaps such codes ought to take into account the makeup of the organism? And since discussions of utopias are an excellent demonstration of the saying that people who do not master history are condemned to relive it, the physiological stance will have to be combined with an anamnestic one, recalling the historical semantics (in sections 1 and 2) of utopia while trying to tease out its elements (in section 3) and genological context (in sections 4 and 5).

1. Historical Semantics: Antediluvian

The first point and fundamental element of a literary definition of utopia is that any utopia is a verbal construction. This might seem self-evident, but it is in fact just beginning to be more widely recognized in the vanguard of "utopology." The *Oxford English Dictionary*, for example, defines utopia in the following ways:

1. An imaginary island, depicted by More as enjoying a perfect social, legal and political system.
   b. *transf.* Any imaginary, indefinitely remote region, country, or locality.
2. A place, state, or condition ideally perfect in respect of politics, laws, customs, and conditions.
   b. An impossibly ideal scheme, esp. for social improvement.

Obviously, the *OED* – whose latest examples come in this case from the turn of the century – has not yet caught up to the necessity and practice of defining utopia as a literary genre.[3] If we nonetheless look for clues in the above four definitions, we shall see that the first one pertains to More's "depiction" of a locus which is, for the *OED*, defined by two aspects: (1) "imaginary" removal from the author's (and presumably the reader's) empirical environment; (2) sociopolitical perfection. The first aspect is then isolated in the semantic practice leading to definition 1.b, and the second in the practice leading to 2, which is further treated derisively by hardheaded pragmatists or ideologists of the status quo in 2.b. From all this a definition of utopia as a literary form should retain the crucial element of an alternative location radically different in respect of sociopolitical conditions from the author's historical environment. However, this element must be valorized in the context of a literary-theoretical approach.

Only in *OED* 1 is there even a discreet mumble about the utopia being an artistic artifact, hidden in the ambiguous "depicted" (about which more later). All the other definitions refer to its qualities of perfection, remoteness or impossibility. This ontological equating of utopia to England, Germany, or any other empirical country was an accepted nineteenth- and early twentieth-century way of defining it. I shall adduce only a few definitions from some better-known and more helpful works pertaining to such a way of thinking, which might well – regardless of their actual year – be called antediluvian:

1. Utopias [...] are ideal pictures of other worlds, the existence or possibility of which cannot be scientifically demonstrated, and in which we only believe (Voigt, 1906).
2. More depicted a perfect, and perhaps unrealizable, society, located in some nowhere, purged of the shortcomings, the wastes, and the confusion of our own time and living in perfect adjustment, full of happiness and contentment (Hertzler, 1923).

---

3   See the stimulating discussion, with more lexicographic material, in Schulte-Herbrüggen; also further French, German, and Spanish material in Rita Falke, "Utopie – logische Konstruktion und chimère," in Villgradter and Krey eds.

3. [...] an ideal commonwealth whose inhabitants exist under seemingly perfect conditions (*Encyclopedia Britannica*, accepted by
Berneri 1950).[4]

All of the above definitions or delimitations consider utopia simply as
a Platonic idea and proceed to examine its believability and realizability.
Hertzler (see 2) is the most effusive and prolix among them: she defines
utopias in general by means of a definition of More's work, prefaced with
the statement that this isolates the distinctive characteristic applicable to
all "imaginary ideal societies." The vagueness ("perhaps," "some nowhere")
and non-sequiturs (More depicted a society purged of "the confusion
of our own time") make Hertzler a very good example – though greater
offenders could be found in the antediluvian age – of the uselessness to
our endeavors of most surveys of "Utopian Thought" as being idealistic
and ideological.

All the above definitions, moreover, do not (except by vague suggestions inherent in "commonwealth" or "society") distinguish between various religious "ideal pictures of other worlds" and utopias. This echoes the
(once?) widely held unexamined premise that utopias are really lay variants
of paradise. Now if this is true, it is so only in the sense which would make
a counter-project out of a variant. Whereas it remains very important to
pursue the historical underground continuation of absolutistic religious
and mythological structures (especially those drawn from the Islands of
the Blessed and Terrestrial Paradises) in Plato, More or a number of other
utopian writers, it should seem clear that there is little point in discussing
utopias as a separate entity if their basic humanistic, this-worldly, historically alternative aspect is not stressed and adopted as one of their *differ-
entiae genericae*. "A wishful construct has been explicated, a rational one,

---

4   These definitions can be found in the following books (whenever in my quotes the
     subject and predicate are missing, "utopia is" is implied): Voigt, p. 1; Hertzler, pp. 1–2;
     Berneri, p. 320. A number of very useful approaches to utopia are not referred to
     here, as they were not found cognate to a primarily literary-theoretical viewing; a still
     greater number were found of little use except for a history of "utopologic thought."
     All the translations in this book, unless otherwise indicated, are mine.

that does not possess chiliastic certainties of hope any more, but postulates the possibility of being constructed by its own forces, without transcendental support or intervention," observes Bloch (*Prinzip* 607) even about More's Utopia.

What is literally even more important, such a construct is located in this world. Utopia is an Other World immanent in the world of human endeavor, dominion, and hypothetic possibility – and not transcendental in a religious sense. It is a nonexistent country on the map of this globe, a "this-worldly other world." No doubt, there is the pragmatic, Macaulayan sense of utopia being anything intangible and impossibly far-off, as opposed to immovable property in one's own property-owning environment ("An acre in Middlesex is better than a principality in Utopia"); this sense would also sneer at all Heavenly and Earthly Paradises.[5] But from any point of view except that of a property-owner and pragmatist, religion is, as Raymond Ruyer notes, counter-utopian. It is directed either towards Heaven (transcendence) or towards Middlesex (bounded empirical environment): in either case, it is incompatible with a non-transcendental overstepping of empirical boundaries.[6] The *telos* of religion is, finally, eternity or timelessness, not history. On the contrary, just as the satire is an impossible possible – what is empirically possible is felt as axiologically impossible; it should not be possible – utopia is a possible impossible. Subversion and rhetoric embrace in a paradoxical socio-political revaluation of the Petrarchan "icy fire" *impossibilia* – a "positive *adynaton*" in Barthes's term (122).

Thus, *chemin faisant*, we have found that the (still not too precise) element of historical alternative enters any definition which would leave utopia intact as a literary genre and object of exploration. We have still to pursue the metaphors adopted as a first try at untying the embarrassing knot of utopia's being a concept and belief and yet, at the same time, obviously a (literary) artifact – a "picture" (see 2 and 4) or a "description" (see 4 and 5):

5   Quoted in the *OED*; see Macaulay, "Lord Bacon," 2: 229.
6   Ruyer 31; see also Schwonke 1–3, in whose book this is a basic theme, and Gerber 6–7.

4. a. Nom donné par Thomas Morus au pays imaginaire qu'il décrit
dans son ouvrage: *De Optimo reipublicae statu, deque nova insula
Utopia* (1516), et dans lequel il place un peuple parfaitement sage,
puissant et heureux, grâce aux institutions idéales dont il jouit.
b. Se dit par extension de tous les tableaux représentant, sous la
forme d'une description concrète et détaillée (et souvent même
comme un roman), l'organisation idéale d'une société humaine.
(Lalande, edn of 1968, but the text goes back at least to 1928)
[a. Name given by Thomas More to the imaginary country which
he describes in his work *De Optimo reipublicae statu, deque nova
insula Utopia* (1516), and into which he collocates a people that is
perfectly wise, powerful, and happy, thanks to the ideal institutions
with which it is provided.
b. Said by extension of all pictures representing, by means of a
detailed and concrete description (often even as a novel), the ideal
organization of a human society.]

5. La description d'un monde imaginaire, en dehors [...] de l'espace
et du temps historiques et géographiques. C'est la description d'un
monde constitué sur des principes différents de ceux qui sont à
l'oeuvre dans le monde réel. (Ruyer, 1950)[7]
[The description of an imaginary world, outside[...] of historical and
geographic space and time. This is a description of a world based
on principles that differ from those underlying the real world.]

"Description" is derived etymologically from "writing," but in an
archaic and ambiguous sense which, as it were, echoes the derivation of
writing from drawing. Above it is clearly employed within the semantics
pertaining to painting: "il décrit [...] il place" (in 4a placing pertains to the
way a landscape painter would arrange his figures); and "tableaux représentant, sous la forme d'une description" is a classic witness for my thesis (see

---

7   These definitions can be found in Lalande 1179 – and see the whole discussion on
1178–81 – and Ruyer 3. The definition of Dupont (14) is transitional between the
first group of definitions and this one.

4b). Even 5, which is more abstract than the previous definitions, continues its discussion in the immediately following line by contrasting such descriptions to those of a non-utopian novelist, who "collocates imaginary characters and adventures into our world" (Ruyer 3). Utopia, as well as "our world," is a scene for *dramatis personae* and actions; the metaphor of author as puppeteer (stage manager), never far beneath the metaphor of author as painter (scenographer), has here come nearer to the surface.

Such a dramatic metaphor, linked as it is to the "all the world's a stage" topos, is potentially much more fruitful – since drama fuses painting and literature, temporal and spatial arts – and very appropriate for this dialogic form. Unfortunately, it has not, to my knowledge, been taken seriously in defining utopias. Thus such attempts at acknowledging the artificial character of utopia have remained half-hearted. They have failed because they did not acknowledge that it is a literary artifact. This is crucial because the problems of "depicting" a radically different (see 5) because perfect (see 4) imaginary world are in a literary artifact quite distinct from the problems of a "tableau," which exists in an arrested moment of time and in a synoptic space. A picture may perhaps approximate the status of a mirror of external reality (though even the mirror reverses). In literature, a concrete and detailed "description" or, better, verbal construction is not, in any precise sense, a "re-presentation" of a pre-existing idea which would be the content of that representation or description (where would such an idea preexist? with the *Zeitgeist*?). Literary texts cannot be divided into body and soul, only into interlocking levels of a multifunctional body, which is a human construct out of verbal denotations and connotations. Only within such a context can the definition of its thematic field – practically identical from 2 to 5 – become a valid part of a literary definition. The imaginary community (the term seems preferable to the ambiguous "world") in which human relations are organized more perfectly than in the author's community can be accepted as a first approximation to identifying the thematic nucleus of the utopian genre.

One further point should account for my substitution of "more perfectly" in place of the "perfect" in 2 to 4. Though historically most of the older utopias tried to imagine a certain perfection, after Bacon's *New Atlantis* and Fénelon's *Télémaque* (not to forget Plato's *Laws*) a suspicion ought to have arisen that this is not inherent in the genre. That suspicion should have grown into a certainty after Saint-Simon and Morris. By the time Wells wrote his celebrated first page of *A Modern Utopia* distinguishing between static and kinetic utopias, the laggard academic and literary critics of the genre found their work done for them. Since then we have had no further excuse for insisting on absolute perfection, but only on a state radically better or based on a more perfect principle than that prevailing in the author's community, as a hallmark of the utopian genre.[8] As for the "author's community," this phrase can be left conveniently plastic to embrace whatever the author and his ideal readers would have felt to be their community – from city to nation to planet.

2. Historical Semantics: Postdiluvian

In the last twenty years, at least in literary criticism and theory, the premise has become acceptable that Utopia is first of all a literary genre or fiction. The Cold War "end of ideology" climate might have contributed to this (it can be felt, for example, in the disclaimers in the book by Negley and Patrick discussed below), but more importantly, it has been part of a deeper epistemological shift in literary scholarship – a belated recognition that,

---

8   See the analogous argument in Walsh 25. The position of utopia midway between the corruptible world of class history and ideal perfection is quite analogous – as will be discussed in section 4 of this chapter – to the position of Earthly Paradise in religious thought; see for example the definition of Athanasius of Alexandria: "The Terrestrial Paradise we expound as not subject to corruption in the way in which our plants and our fruits get corrupted by putrefaction and worms. Nor is it, on the other hand, wholly incorruptible, so that it would not in future centuries decay by growing old. But if it is compared with our fruits and our gardens, it is superior to all corruption; while if it is compared to the glory of the coming Good, which eye hath not seen nor ear heard nor the heart of man comprehended, it is and is reputed to be vastly inferior" (Athanasius, quoted in Coli 39). The insistence on utopia as wholly "ideal" can still be found in Schulte-Herbrüggen – see note 9.

as Northrop Frye wrote, the literary critic "should be able to construct and dwell in a conceptual universe of his own" (*Anatomy* 12). I shall again adduce only a few definitions as characteristic examples for works of this period, after the deluge of two world wars and two cycles of worldwide revolutions:

6. There are three characteristics which distinguish the utopia from other forms of literature or speculation:
   a. It is fictional;
   b. It describes a particular state or community;
   c. Its theme is the political structure of that fictional state or community.
   Utopias are expressions of political philosophy and theory, to be sure, but they are descriptions of fictional states in which the philosophy and theory are already implemented in the institutions and procedures of the social structure (Negley and Patrick, 1952).

7. The literary ideal image of an imaginary social system (*Staatsordnung*). (Schulte-Herbrüggen, 1960)

8. The utopian novel is the literary manifestation of a playful synopsis of man, society, and history in a variable, image-like (*bildhaft*) thought model possessing spatio-temporal autonomy, which model permits the exploration of possibilities detached from social reality yet relating to it. (Krysmanski, 1963)

9. La description littéraire individualisée d'une société imaginaire, organisée sur des bases qui impliquent une critique sous-jacente de la société réelle. (Cioranescu, 1972)
   [The individualized literary description of an imaginary society, organized on bases which imply an underlying critique of the real society.][9]

---

9   These definitions can be found in the books by Negley and Patrick, 3–4; Schulte-Herbrüggen, 7; Krysmanski, 19; and Cioranescu, 22.

Negley and Patrick (see 6) seem to have been the first to expressly enunciate a differentiation between the utopia of political scientists and *Geisteswissenschaftler* ("expressions of political philosophy and theory") and that of the literary critics and theorists ("fictional states", theme and ideas "implemented"). Their pioneering status is evident in certain uneasy compromises with the older conception which they are abandoning.[10] But as well as their use of the by-now dead metaphor of describing (which in a proper context it would perhaps be pedantic to fault), their failure to elaborate what exactly fictional implementation entails and the de facto concentration in their book on sociopolitical ideas and structure unrelated to the literary structure leave their definition somewhat isolated and without consequences. Yet their useful and influential book at least indicated the horizons of studying what they called in their preface, in a mixture of conceptual styles, both "utopian thought in Western civilization" (old style) and also, somewhat shamefacedly, "the literary genre of the utopists" (new style).

On the other hand, Schulte-Herbrüggen (see 7) starts boldly and happily by identifying utopia as literary, but then leaves it dangling in intense vagueness by calling it not only "imaginary" but also the "ideal image." Later in this work, he has many just and stimulating things to say about its delimitation from other genres. In particular, he has been a pioneer in drawing some structural consequences from defining utopia as possessing a literary mode of existence. However, a number of his parameters, including his definition, seem to fit More (his particular paradigm), or indeed a utopian program, better than they would an ideal-typical utopia.

Krysmanski's (see 8) sociological exploration of German "utopian novels" of the twentieth century (which ought rather to be called science fiction, SF, as I shall argue in section 5) set itself the laudable aim of discovering and fully defining "the specific nature of the utopian novel": his

---

10   No doubt, there were earlier implicit or incidental suggestions that fictional utopia was primarily a literary genre, e.g. in Dupont – in spite of his definition and title – and in Frye, *Anatomy*. But the voices of these, and possibly of other, precursors fell on deaf ears.

definition is the conclusion of a chapter with that title. Unfortunately, for an analysis of a "literary manifestation" (*Erscheinungsform*) it is far too little conversant with fundaments of literary theory and criticism. One's sympathy and tolerance lie with his Aristotelian basic approach, striving for a definition which must be precise and comprehensive, in which case technical jargon is almost impossible to avoid. Nonetheless, it is not only the Teutonic and Mannheimian "sociology of knowledge" nature of the jargon which makes one pause, it is primarily the arbitrariness and vagueness of the elements of the definition, which seem to prove that modern definitions can be every bit as prolix-cum-insufficient as the antediluvian ones. It may be useful to draw our attention to the elements of playfulness, of simultaneous viewing or synopsis (*Zusammenschau*) of humans, society, and history, or of an exploration of possibilities. But why "manifestation of a synopsis" (the German is still worse: "Erscheinungsform der Zusammenschau")? Why "variable," "image-like," and "spatio-temporal autonomy" – is not every *Denkmodell* such? And the final clause evidently pertains to SF in general, being too wide for utopia, which is bound up with the (here missing) "more perfect community" concept.

I shall return later to Cioranescu's book on "utopia and literature," a work full of stimulating and provocative statements. At this point, it might suffice to point out with relief how neat and with unease how over-generalized his definition is (see 9). Are not Paradise, an Island of the Blessed, or satirical SF covered by it as well? And, not to boggle at minor matters, just what is "the real society"?

3. A Proposed Definition: Utopia as Verbal Construction

The historico-semantical discussion of the preceding two sections has come up with the following elements for defining utopia: a radically different and historically alternative sociopolitical condition; an alternative locus; an imaginary community in which relations are organized more perfectly than in the author's community; the fictional or, more clearly, "verbal construction" character of any such condition, location, or community; the particular or fleshed out character of any such construct as opposed to general and abstract utopian projects and programs. I shall now commit the utopian imprudence of proposing after the above critique a construct or definition of my own:

Utopia is the verbal construction of a particular quasi-human community where sociopolitical institutions, norms, and individual relationships are organized according to a more perfect principle than in the author's community, this construction being based on estrangement arising out of an alternative historical hypothesis.[11]

I have indicated earlier in general outline the importance to be allotted to the element of verbal construction. This can be fully demonstrated only in particular analyses of utopian works. But its relevance can be seen even in a general answer to the question: what type of verbal construction? Utopia belongs to a narrative form and tradition which Frye has persuasively called anatomy (or Menippean satire), rather than to the novel. The anatomy deals less with illusionistic "people as such than with mental

---

11   *Footnote 2008:* This definition is deficient in at least two important respects. The first is technical, an imperfect differentiation existing at the time between utopia and its particular case of eutopia: utopia is radically different, only eutopia is radically more perfect. The second is political, a naïve "early Marx" humanism which omits a collective (class) stance or bearing from the vantage of which perfection (or more neutrally, radical difference) is judged. My proposed definition, updated in Chapter 13 of this book (not by chance written in 2001), now reads: "UTOPIA will be defined as: the construction of a particular community where sociopolitical institutions, norms, and relationships between people are organized according to a *radically different principle* than in the author's community; this construction is based on estrangement arising out of an alternative historical hypothesis; it is created by discontented social classes interested in otherness and change, and its difference is judged from their point of view or within their value-system. All utopias involve people who radically suffer of the existing system and desire to radically change it." For "radically different," EUTOPIA (which is really all this chapter speaks about) substitutes "radically more perfect," and the perfection is judged within that value-system.

attitudes" and at its most concentrated "presents us with a vision of the world in terms of a single intellectual pattern" (*Anatomy* 309 and 310). Our critical judgments should take this into account; in particular, there is no point in expecting from a characterization and plotting which are more allegorical than naturalistic the qualities and criteria induced from the psychological novel, from Prévost to Proust or Samuel Richardson to Henry James.[12] To take one example, the conclusions of Richard Gerber's interesting book on twentieth-century utopias (or rather SF) are vitiated by his assumption and definition of utopia as a novel.[13] To take another, Robert C. Elliott has aptly complained about one of the dominant interpretations of More's *Utopia*:

> We are given no sense [...] that these questions exist, not as abstract political, religious, or philosophical propositions, but as constitutive elements in a work of art. What is wanted instead of the Catholic interpretation of communism is an interpretation of *Utopia* that will show us how the question of communism is incorporated into the total structure of the work. (Elliott 28–29)

Further, some basic structural characteristics of utopia seem to flow logically from its status as a discourse about a particular, historically alternative, and better community. Since such a discourse will necessarily present an opposition which is a formal analogy to the author's delimited environment and its way of life, any utopia must be 1) a rounded, isolated locus (valley, island, planet – later, temporal epoch). Since it has to show more perfectly organized relationships, the categories under which the author and his age subsume these relationships (government, economics, religion, warfare, etc.) must be in some way or other 2) articulated in a panoramic sweep whose sum is the inner organization of the isolated locus; as Barthes remarks

---

12   The famous quarrel between James and Wells – available in *Henry James and H.G. Wells* by Edel and Ray (eds) (1958) – which resulted in a draw rather than in the vindication of the psychological novel the Jamesians saw it, is a clear example of the collision between the "anatomic" or allegorical and the "novelistic" or individualistic orientations.

13   Gerber, final two chapters, and in particular 121–22. See the critique by Elliott 104 and his whole chapter "Aesthetics of Utopia."

about Charles Fourier (and some other writers), the syntax or composition
of elements is identified with creation in such works.[14] Since not only the
elements but also their articulation and coordination have to be based on
more perfect principles than the categorization in the author's civilization
(for example, the federalist pyramid from bottom up of More's Utopia as
opposed to the centralist pyramid from top down of More's England and
Europe), 3) a formal hierarchic system becomes the supreme order and thus
the supreme value in utopia: there are authoritarian and libertarian, class
and classless utopias, but no unorganized ones. (Morris's reticence about
organization and hierarchy in *News From Nowhere* places that work halfway between utopia and Earthly Paradise; see my *Metamorphoses of Science
Fiction* (*MOSF*), chapter 8). Usually the installation of the new order must
be explained – a contract theory, as Frye observes, is implied in each utopia
(King Utopus, the socialist revolution, gas from a comet, etc., being the
arbiters or contract-makers). The utopian contract is necessarily opposed
to the contract-myth dominant in the author's society as the more reverent
"contract behind the contract" (Frye, "Varieties" 38), a human potential
which existing society has alienated and failed to realize. Lastly, utopia is
bound to have 4) an implicit or explicit dramatic strategy in its panoramic
review conflicting with the "normal" expectations of the reader. Though
formally closed, significant utopia is thematically open: its pointing reflects
back upon the reader's "topia." I have already hinted at that in section 1,
and one critic has even conveniently found a three-act dramatic structure
in More's *Utopia*.[15] Whether this is exact or not, there is no doubt that an
analysis of ideational protagonists and settings in "dramatistic" terms is
here appropriate (see Burke).

    For example, utopia is invariably a frame-within-a-frame, because it is a
specific wondrous stage, set within the world stage; techniques of analyzing
the play-within-the-play could be profitably employed when dealing with

14   Barthes 9; this whole discussion is indebted to Barthes's book, though I do not wholly
    share his horizons.
15   Surtz, "Utopia as a Work of Literary Art," in idem and Hexter eds, 4: cxxv–clii,
    especially in the chapter "Dramatic Technique, Characterization, and Setting."

it. The varieties of the outer frame – usually some variant of the imaginary voyage[16] – have been readily noticeable and as such the object of critical attention; less so the correlation of say, the humanistic symposium of More or the socialist dream-which-might-be-a-vision of Morris with the experience in the inner frame. Even on the stylistic and not only compositional level, such a strategy should be fruitful: "l'écriture," remarks Barthes of Fourier, "doit mobiliser en même temps une image et son contraire" [the writing must mobilize at the same time an image and its opposite, 115].

Finally, "verbal construction" as a definitional element by-passes, I hope, the old theologizing quarrel whether a utopia can be realized, whether in fact (according to one school) only that which is realizable or on the contrary (according to another but equally dogmatic school) only that which is unrealizable can be called utopia. Neither prophecy nor escapism, utopia is, as many critics have remarked, an "as if," an imaginative experiment or "a methodical organ for the New."[17] Literary utopia – and every description of utopia is literary – is a heuristic device for perfectibility, an epistemological and not an ontological entity. "L'utopie est un jeu, mais un jeu sérieux. L'utopiste a le sens des possibilités autres de la nature, mais il ne s'éloigne pas de la notion de la nature [Utopia is a game, but a serious game. The utopian author envisages the other possibilities of nature, but he does not let go of the notion of nature]" argued Ruyer in his first two chapters, which remain among the best written on the "utopian mode."[18] He referred to utopian subject matter as "les possibles latéraux" [the lateral possibilities] and compared the utopian approach or view to the hypothetico-

---

16 Historically this is especially significant in Antiquity and the Renaissance, when most utopias and imaginary voyages were combined, but it does not have to persist as an explicit combination. See the excellent survey of Gove, much in need of newer follow-ups.

17 For first quote see Vaihinger. The verbal mode appropriate to this is the subjunctive: see Elliott 115; Delany; Holquist, particularly illuminating in his discussion of utopias as a literature of the subjunctive in "hypothetical or heuristic time," 112; and Dubois, "Une architecture." Second quote Bloch, *Prinzip* 180.

18 Ruyer 4 and 9. Unfortunately, the analysis of actual utopian characteristics and works in the rest of Ruyer's book is much less felicitous.

deductive method in experimental sciences and mathematics (for example, non-Euclidean geometries). If utopia is, then, philosophically, a method rather than a state, it cannot be realized or not realized – it can only be applied. That application is, however, as important as it has been claimed that the realization of utopia is: without it human beings are truly alienated or one-dimensional. But to apply a literary text means first of all (wherever it may later lead) to read as a dramatic dialogue with the reader.[19] Besides requiring the willingness of the reader to enter into dialogue, the application of utopia depends on the closeness and precision of her reading.

4. Comment: Utopia as Historical Estrangement

I have thus far worked upon certain premises, among them that scholarly inquiry is possible only when oriented towards, and by, an at least approximately delimited and defined field and that valid definitions in literary studies – as in anything – are historical and not transcendental, or "contextualist" and not "essentialist." Proceeding further, it is necessary to add that the basic diachronic way to define the context of a work of art is to insert it into the tradition and system of its genre (meaning by that a socio-esthetic entity with a specific inner life, yet in a constant osmosis with other literary genres, science, philosophy, everyday socioeconomic life, and so on). Understanding particular utopias really presupposes a definition and delimitation of their literary genre (or, as we shall see, subgenre), its inner processes, logic, and *telos*. What is, then, the distinctive set of traits of the literary genre "utopia," its *differentia generica*?

19   Some of my conclusions are very similar to those of Harry Berger, Jr, in his more synoptic, seminal introductory discussion of the "other world." Regretfully I must add that I believe his particular argument about *Utopia* – that More differs radically from Hythloday – to be wholly unconvincing.

I have argued in the first two chapters of my *MOSF* for a division of prose literature into naturalistic and estranged genres. The literary mainstream of the individualistic age endeavors faithfully to reproduce empirical textures, surfaces, and relationships vouched for by human senses and common sense. Utopia, on the contrary, endeavors to illuminate people's relationships to other people and to their surroundings by the basic device of a radically different location for the postulated novel human relations of its fable; and I have proposed to call literary genres which have such a different formal framework "estranged." One should insist on the crucial concept of a radically different location, of an alternative formal framework functioning by explicit or implicit reference to the author's empirical environment. Without this reference, non-utopian readers, having no yardstick for comparison, could not understand the alternative novelty. Conversely, without such a return and feedback into the reader's normality there would be no function for utopias or other estranged genres: "the real function of estrangement is – and must be – the provision of a shocking and distancing mirror above the all too familiar reality."[20] No-place is defined by both not being and yet being like Place, by being the opposite and more perfect version of Place. It is a "positive negation,"[21] a "merveilleux réel" (Barthes 101), it stands on its head an already topsy-turvy or alienated world, which therefore becomes disalienated or truly normal when measured not by ephemeral historical norms of a particular civilization but by "species-specific" human norms.

Utopia is thus always predicated on a certain theory of human nature. It takes up and refunctions the ancient *topos* of *mundus inversus*: utopia is a formal inversion of significant and salient aspects of the author's world which has as its purpose or *telos* the recognition that the author (and reader) truly lives in an axiologically inverted world. It follows, as has

---

20 Bloch, *"Entfremdung, Verfremdung"* 10. For "estrangement," see the discussion and references to Shklovsky and Brecht in the first chapter of my *MOSF* as well as Bloch, *Das Prinzip*.

21 "Positive negation" is the term used in Mikhail Bakhtin's fundamental *Rabelais* 403: but his whole book is a rich and persuasive account of folk humor as the source for inverting and negating a dominant, upper-class feeling of reality.

been increasingly recognized in modern investigations (and as has been mentioned in passing in section 1), that the explicit utopian construction is the logical obverse of any satire.[22] Utopia explicates what satire implicates, and vice versa. Furthermore, there are strong indications that the two are in fact phylogenetically connected in the folk-inversions and "saturas" of the Saturnalias, whose theme was sexual, political, and ideological reversal – in fact total existential "reversal of values, of social roles, of social norms" (Elliott 11). The best argument in favor of that can be found in the ontogenesis of individual works, in – to stick to utopias and cognate estranged genres – the most prominent titles of the tradition which I examined in *MOSF* as running from Lucian's *True Histories* and More's *Utopia* through Fourier, Bellamy, Morris, Wells, and Zamyatin to modern SF. A guess could even be hazarded that the significance and scope of writings in this tradition can be gauged by the degree of integration between its constructive-utopian and satiric aspects: the deadly earnest blueprint and the totally closed horizons of "new maps of hell" both lack esthetic wisdom.

However, besides satire (which can be, like utopia, both a mode and a genre) the estranged literary genres comprise several which are differentiated from utopia by not situating what Aristophanes calls their *topos apragmon* in the field of an alternative *historical* hypothesis. The most relevant ones are, in ascending order, myth, fantasy, folktale, Cockayne, and Terrestrial Paradise.

I have tried to disentangle the semantics of myth in *MOSF*, and I can only repeat that, although it is also shaped as a specific form of estrangement, myth is diametrically opposed to a historical approach.[23] Conceiving human relationships to be fixed and supernaturally determined, myth claims to explain phenomena by identifying their eternal essence; conceiving human relationships to be changeable and materially determined, history

22   See Frye, *Anatomy* 309–12; Lalande 1180; Negley and Patrick 5–6; and especially Elliott chapter 1, "Saturnalia, Satire, and Utopia."
23   See also Ruyer 4–6. For all my admiration of Professor Frye's insights, here I obviously disagree with the horizon and main terminology of his work – and in particular with his classifying Dante Alighieri's *Paradiso* and *Purgatorio* as utopian, in Manuel, ed. 34.

attempts to explain phenomena by identifying their problematic context. From a historical point of view, myth itself is a historical phenomenon and problem, an illusion when not a fraud. Literature is, in fact, never truly a myth (though mythological tales are literature) but only, in certain cases, formally analogous to mythical structure or mythomorphic. Thus, for example, the myth of the Golden Age can have many formal analogies and elements in common with utopia, but utopia is its opposite:

> [...] man's effort to work out imaginatively what happens – or what might happen – when the primal longings embodied in the myth confront the principle of reality. In this effort man no longer merely dreams of a divine state in some remote time; he assumes the role of creator himself.
> A characteristic of the Golden Age [...] is that it exists outside history, usually before history begins: *in illo tempore*. (Elliott 8–9)

Folktale and Fantasy stories, being morphological and ideological descendants of fragmented mythology (in the case of Fantasy privatized to boot), can be regarded in a similar way. Neither of them pretends to be historically oriented or in historical time. Both take place in a context of supernatural laws oriented towards the protagonist, whereas for humanistic historiosophy – including utopia – nature is neutral and man's destiny is man.

Somewhat closer to utopia is Cockayne (*Cuccagna, Schlaraffenland*), a widespread folk legend of a land of peace, plenty, and repose, probably refurbished by the student-poets of goliardic and "prandial" libertinism.[24] The land where roasted fowls fly into your mouth, rivers flow with cream or wine, and sausages with a fork stuck into them run around crying "eat me, eat me!" is obviously an inverted image of the hunger, toil, and violence in the authors' everyday lives. Cockayne is already an inverted parallel world that relates, if not yet to a historical hypothetical possibility organized into institutions, then at least to everyday human needs and not to transcendental doctrines:

---

24   See Bakhtin's chapter "Banquet Imagery," especially 296–98, and Morton 15–27. For some further references to Cockayne see Ackermann, Bonner, Boas 167–68, Patch 51 and 170–71, Gatz 116–21, Graus, the Manuels, and the following note 25.

La fiction parallèle, la préoccupation pour le destin de l'homme et la solution stricte-
ment matérialiste sont les trois traits fondamentaux qu'ont en commun l'utopie et
la pays de Cocagne [...]
Le matérialisme ainsi entendu ignore les restrictions mentales et transcende la matière
pour la transformer en divinité tutélaire et en providence. (Cioranescu)[25]
[The parallel fiction, the preoccupation with human destiny and the strictly materialist solution are the three fundamental traits which Utopia and Cockayne have
in common [...].
Taken thus, materialism ignores mental restrictions and transcends matter in order
to transform it into patron deity and providence.]

Clearly, as Cioranescu notes, this does not jibe with the fundamental
utopian context of a neutral nature: but utopia wishes to achieve by cognitive means and in a context of hypothetically inflected history what the
legend of Cockayne achieved in a pure wish-dream outside the terrible
field of history. While still a folktale, Cockayne can be readily transferred
to the vicinity of utopia by allying its dream to a cognitive context, as in
Rabelais.

The Earthly Paradise may be even nearer to utopia. Outside official
Christianity, it is as a rule not transhistoric, but can be reached by an ordinary voyage. It is divided from other lands by a barrier, which makes it usually an island in the sea – an Island of the Blessed, as the Greek tradition
from time immemorial has it and as many other writings, anonymous or
famous, also know it, to wit, the Celtic blessed island or Dante's Paradiso
Terrestre in the western sea.[26] Often, especially in versions unaffected by
religious rewriting, the inhabitants are not disembodied, but are simply

25   Cioranescu 57 and 59, but see his whole passage 55–62, which presents the best
      analysis of Cockayne I know of. For connections with satire see also Elliott 16–17.
26   A general survey on ideas about the Golden Age, Eden, and Paradise is to be found
      in Manuel and Manuel, who, however, fail to make the crucial distinction between
      heavenly and earthly paradise. On Greek tales see Bonner, Lovejoy and Boas, the com-
      ment in Bloch *Prinzip*, ch. 36, Gatz, Finley, Pöhlmann, and Winston. For medieval
      tales and beliefs about localized "other worlds" see Boas, Coli, "Il Mito del Paradiso
      Terrestre" in Graf, Patch, as well as Curtius, Graus, and Westropp; Coli 130 and Patch
      135 comment on the accessibility and material reality of Eden for medieval minds.
      See also Giamatti for Renaissance echoes.

more perfect people. The implied critique of the author's environment is explicated in a whole group of "other world" tales (see Patch 128, and Coli 130). The magical or folktale element is clearly present in the perfect climate, the freedom from cares and strife, and often in the arrested time on such blessed islands (so that a return from them entails instant aging or turning to dust). And yet, the proximity of utopia to Terrestrial Paradise in its unbowdlerized versions is impressively indicated by a tale such as that of the Guarani Land-Without-Evil. That land, also called the House of Our Ancestress,

> [...] is difficult to reach, but it is located in this world. Although [...] it entails paradisiacal dimensions [...] (for instance, immortality) – the Land-Without-Evil does not belong to the Beyond [...]. One arrives there [...] [not only] in soul or spirit, but in flesh and bones [...]. [It] is thus a world at once real and transfigured, where life continues according to the same familiar model, but [...] without misery or sickness, without sins or injustice, and without age. (Eliade)[27]

Is such a country outside history, as Eliade thinks? It is certainly outside empirical or known history, but it is at the same time an alternative, hypothetically possible, and supremely desirable history on Earth. All the above qualifications could be applied to utopia, not only in my proposed definition but according to most of the quoted definitions too. It lacks only More's great discovery of focusing on sociopolitical institutions and norms as a key to eliminating misery, sickness, and injustice. The usual utopian answer, communal or communist ownership, is here preserved (the Guaranis did not need to attain it) by means of what Bloch calls a "medical utopia" (search for immortality, eternal health, and youth). If not utopia, this is a fraternal genre: an early and primitive branch of SF.

---

27   Mircea Eliade, "Paradise and Utopia." in Manuel ed., 273–75. For paradises located on Earth see also Boas 154–74, Graf 15 and 24, and Coli 91; and for the arrival in flesh at Earthly Paradise the Hellenic testimonies in Lovejoy and Boas 25–30 and 290–303, where further bibliography can also be found.

5. Comment: Utopia as a More Perfect Organized Community

Finally, the relationships of utopia to other genres of what I have in *MOSF* called "cognitive estrangement" – SF, pastoral, and nonfictional works – should also be discussed.

This will account for the necessity of all my definitional elements between "verbal construction" and the final clause. Just like Cockayne, the pastoral is akin at least to libertarian utopia in its rejection of money economy, cleavage between town and country, and State apparatus. But just like Cockayne, it is primarily a *unomia*, a land without formalized institutions, without organized superstructures of community life (Cioranescu 60–61). If Cockayne is the land for sensualists, Earthly Paradise for heroes, and pastoral for swains (shepherds as philosophers, poets, and lovers), utopia is the land for naturalistic human figures just slightly larger (more virtuous) than everyday nature.

The definitional element of a particular community is necessary (as observed in section 3), in order to differentiate utopia from general beliefs, programs, and unlocalized projects. However, as soon as the blueprints and beliefs become localized and approach a narrative (as in much of the writing of utopian socialists), there is little delimitation provided by any definition of utopia I can think of. The usual escape clause is that utopia is *belles lettres* or fiction, while Saint-Simon or Fourier are *lettres* or nonfiction. But that distinction, though sufficiently normative in the eighteenth-century to allow Jonathan Swift to base the formal framework of *Gulliver's Travels* on playing with it, is historically a fugitive one. What was the Guarani legend of Land-Without-Evil or Columbus's letter on finding the Terrestrial Paradise beyond the Orinoco for the authors, fiction or nonfiction? And for us? What is, for that matter, the Bible – theology or "literature" in the sense of fiction? The term "literature" has always wavered between a populist or sociological inclusive extreme (everything published in printed form) and an elitist or esthetical exclusive extreme (only those "*belles*" works worthy of entering into a normative history of "literature"). In brief, the eighteenth-nineteenth century escape clause does not seem to me to work any longer, since it deals in subjective values and intangible intentions. Suppose it were found that the *Supplement to Bougainville's Voyage* had been written by Bougainville instead of Diderot – would it cease to be utopian? And if Fourier had published his vision of anti-lions and a sea of lemonade with Jules Verne's editor, would it thereby become SF? We are beginning to move in the Borgesian world, where the same text has opposite meanings according to the intention of the author. This is good satiric fun, but any literary theory which can be built upon such premises would have to reject most that we now dignify with such a name.

The same dilemma applies to ethnological reports: if literature is not defined by being right or wrong but by illuminating human relationships in certain ways and by certain means, I see no way of delimiting Lévi-Strauss's sequence on myths from fictional literature or *belles lettres*. Reports on the perfect Inca empire, it has been argued, had inspired More. This is probably inexact, but such a report, especially if related at second hand, would have been generically indistinguishable from the *Utopia* (although, among other things, surely less witty). If I have argued all along in this chapter for utopia as literature, it is precisely because of such a breakdown in the philosophy of literature. The resulting inchoate mass should at least be judged by taking into account the whole text and not arbitrary essences abstracted from it: as imaginative, though not imaginary (Frye, "Varieties" 32).

The definitional element of quasi-human refers to such communities as those of Swift's Houyhnhnms, Olaf Stapledon's Eighteenth Men (*Homo sapiens* being the First Men), or the numerous aliens and cybernetic intelligences of modern SF.[28] It connotes that utopias are in a strange and not yet clarified way an allegorical genre akin to the parable and analogy. In the parable or analogy, the premises do not have to be realistic as long as the upshot is clear. Thus, utopia is always aimed at human relations, but its characters do not have to be human or even outwardly anthropomorphic.

---

28 See e.g. Boguslaw's discussion of men as "operating units," passim, which effects a witty juxtaposition of utopias and "system design."

Their relationships and communities, though, will make sense only insofar as the reader can judge them to be similar or dissimilar to human ones.

The element of community differentiates utopias on the one hand from "robinsonades," stories of castaways outside any community (see Brüggeman, especially 187–89). On the other hand, this terminology tries to steer a middle course in the debate which seems to have raged in *Mitteleuropa* between State worshippers and Kantian or anarchist individualists among critics, an echo of which is heard in Krysmanski's Solomonic solution of a "synopsis" of humans, society, and history. The "anarchists" (for example, Berneri) stressed the moral behavior of individuals, the "archists" the normative power of institutions. Too narrow an interest in governmental apparatus leads to the deadly boredom of eighteenth-century *Staatsromane* in the narrow sense – say, certain works extolling constitutional monarchies in the South Seas. Too wide a sense of utopia, which with Bloch would embrace medical, biological, technological, erotic, and even philosophical wish-dreams, leads to incorporating Don Juan and Faust, the *Theses on Feuerbach* and *The Magic Flute*, into utopia: a somewhat overweening imperialism. The middle course suggested in what is, I hope, my prudent use of "community where sociopolitical institutions, norms, and individual relationships are organized according to a more perfect principle" (see section 3), focuses on the sociopolitical concern with justice and happiness, on the "radical eudemonism" (Barthes 86) of utopia's "detailed, serious discussion of political and sociological matters" (Elliott 110). And if utopia is not a myth valid for all eternity but a historical genre, the acknowledgement of its context in the adjunct "than in the author's community" seems mandatory – most utopias would not be such for most of us today without that adjunct, since one man's perfection is another man's (or class's) horror.

Yet, finally, it cannot be denied that sociopolitical perfection, though I believe it historically crucial in our epoch, is logically only a part of Bloch's spectrum, which extends from alchemy through immortality to omniscience and the Supreme Good. All cognition can become the subject matter of an estranged verbal construction dealing with a particular quasi-human community treated as an alternative history. This "cognitive estrangement" is, I have argued at length, the basis of the literary genre of SF. Strictly and precisely speaking, utopia is not a genre but the sociopolitical sub-genre of science fiction. Paradoxically, it can be seen as such only now that SF has expanded into its modern phase, "looking backward" from its subsumption of utopia. Further, that expansion was in some not always direct ways a continuation of classical and nineteenth-century utopian literature. Thus, conversely, SF is at the same time wider than and at least collaterally descended from utopia; it is, if not a daughter, yet a niece of utopia – a niece usually ashamed of the family inheritance but unable to escape her genetic destiny. For all its adventure, romance, popularization, and wondrousness, SF can finally be written only between the utopian and the dystopian horizons. All imaginable intelligent life, including ours, can be organized only more or less perfectly. In that sense, utopia (eutopia and dystopia) is first of all a literary genre; but finally, as Bloch notes, it is a horizon within which humanity is irrevocably collocated. My main point is that without a full, that is, literal and literary, analysis we are bound to oversimplify and misconstrue those horizons. For any sane understanding of utopia, the simple basic fact to start from remains that it is not hypostasis of the Holy Ghost, the *Zeitgeist* or whatnot, but a literary genre induced from a set of man-made books within a man-made history.

Works Cited

Further titles, including those on extra-European utopias, may be found in *MOSF*.

Ackermann, Elfriede Marie. "'Das Schlaraffenland' in German Literature and Folksong: Social Aspects of an Earthly Paradise, with an Inquiry into its History in European Literature." Chicago: University of Chicago dissertation, 1944.
Bacon, Francis. "De Augmentis Scientiarum," *The Works of Francis Bacon*. Vol. 4, Book 5. Ed. James Spedding, Robert L. Ellis, and Douglas

D. Heath. 14 vols. Stuttgart-Bad Cannstatt: F. Frommann Verlag G. Holzboog.

Bakhtin, Mikhail M. *Rabelais and His World*. Trans. Hélène Iswolsky. Cambridge, MA: MIT Press, 1968.

Barthes, Roland. *Sade, Fourier, Loyola*. New York: Farrar, Straus, and Giroux, 1976.

Berger, Harry Jr. "The Renaissance Imagination: Second World and Green World." *The Centennial Review* 9 (1965): 36–78.

Berneri, Marie-Louise. *Journey Through Utopia*. New York: Schocken, 1971.

Bloch, Ernst. *Das Prinzip Hoffnung*. 2 vols. Frankfurt: Suhrkamp, 1959.

——. *Verfremdungen*. Vol. 1. Frankfurt: Suhrkamp, 1962.

——. "*Entfremdung, Verfremdung:* Alienation, Estrangement," *Brecht*. Ed. Erika Munk. Trans. Anne Halley and Darko Suvin. New York: Bantam, 1972. 3–11.

Boas, George. *Essays on Primitivism and Related Ideas in the Middle Ages*. New York: Octagon, 1966.

Boguslaw, Robert. *The New Utopians: A Study of System Design and Social Change*. Englewood Cliffs: Prentice Hall, 1965.

Bonner, Campbell. "Dionysiac Magic and the Greek Land of Cockaigne." *Transactions and Proceedings of the American Philological Association*. 41 (1910): 175–85.

Brüggemann, Fritz. *Utopie und Robinsonade*. Weimar: Duncker, 1914.

Buber, Martin. *Paths in Utopia*. Boston: Beacon, 1949.

Burke, Kenneth. *The Philosophy of Literary Form. Studies in Symbolic Action*. New York: Vintage, 1957.

Cioranescu, Alexandre. *L'Avenir du passé: Utopie et littérature*. Paris: Gallimard, 1972.

Coli, Edoardo. *Il Paradiso Terrestre dantesco*. Florence: Carnesecchi, 1896.

Curtius, Ernst R. *European Literature and the Latin Middle Ages*. Trans. Willard R. Trask. New York: Harper and Row, 1963.

Delany, Samuel R. "About Five Thousand One Hundred and Seventy-Five Words" *SF: The Other Side of Realism*. Ed. Thomas D. Clareson. Bowling Green: Bowling Green University Press, 1971. 130–46.

Dubois, Claude-Gilbert. "Une architecture fixionelle." *Revue des sciences humaines.* 155–56 (1974): 449–72.

——. *Problèmes de l'utopie.* Paris: Lettres modernes, 1968.

Dupont, Victor. *L'Utopie et le Roman Utopique dans la Littérature Anglaise.* Toulouse: Didier, 1941.

Edel, Leon, and Gordon N. Ray (eds). *Henry James and H.G. Wells.* Urbana: University of Illinois Press, 1958.

Elliott, Robert C. *The Shape of Utopia: Studies in a Literary Genre.* Chicago: University of Chicago Press, 1970.

Finley, Moses I. "Utopianism Ancient and Modern." *The Critical Spirit: Essays in Honor of Herbert Marcuse.* Ed. Kurt H. Wolff and Barrington Moore, Jr. Boston: Beacon 1967. 3–20.

Frye, Northrop. *Anatomy of Criticism: Four Essays.* New York: Atheneum, 1966.

——. "Varieties of Literary Utopias." *Utopias and Utopian Thought.* Ed. Frank E. Manuel. Boston: Beacon, 1967. 25–49.

Gatz, Bodo. *Weltalter, Goldene Zeit und sinnverwandte Vorstellungen.* Spudasmata XVI. Hildesheim: Olms, 1967.

Gerber, Richard. *Utopian Fantasy.* New York: McGraw-Hill, 1973.

Giamatti, A. Bartlett. *The Earthly Paradise and the Renaissance Epic.* Princeton: Princeton University Press, 1966.

Gove, P[hilip] B[abcock]. *The Imaginary Voyage in Prose Fiction.* New York: Columbia University Press, 1975.

Graf, Arturo. *Miti, leggende e superstizioni del Medio Evo.* Vol. 1. Bologna: Forni, 1965.

Graus, F[rantisek]. "Social Utopias in the Middle Ages." *Past and Present* 38 (1967): 3–19.

Hertzler, Joyce O. *The History of Utopian Thought.* New York: Cooper Square, 1965.

Holquist, Michael. "How to Play Utopia: Some Brief Notes on the Distinctiveness of Utopian Fiction." *Game, Play, Literature.* Ed. Jacques Ehrmann. Boston: Beacon, 1971. 106–23.

Krysmanski, Hans-Jürgen. *Die utopische Methode.* Köln: Westdeutscher Verlag, 1963.

Lalande, André. "Utopie". *Vocabulaire technique et critique de la philosophie*. Paris: Presses universitaires de France, 1968.

Lovejoy, Arthur O., and George Boas. *Primitivism and Related Ideas in Antiquity*. New York: Octagon Books, 1965.

Macaulay, Thomas Babington. *Critical, Historical and Miscellaneous Essays and Poems*. Albany: James B. Lyon and Co., 1887.

Mannheim, Karl. *Ideology and Utopia: An Introduction to the Sociology of Knowledge*. New York: Harcourt Brace, 1936.

Manuel, Frank E. (ed.). *Utopias and Utopian Thought*. Boston: Beacon, 1967.

——, and Fritzie P. Manuel. "Sketch for a Natural History of Paradise." *Daedalus* 101 (1972): 83–128.

Morris, William. *News from Nowhere; Or, An Epoch of Rest*. Boston: Roberts Brothers, 1890.

Morton, Arthur L. *The English Utopia*. London: Lawrence & Wishart, 1969.

Negley, Glenn, and J. Max Patrick. *The Quest for Utopia*. College Park, MD: McGrath, 1971.

Neusüss, Arnhelm ed. *Utopie. Begriff und Phänomen des Utopischen*. Berlin: Luchterhand, 1968.

[OED] The Compact Edition of the Oxford English Dictionary. Oxford: Oxford University Press, 1991.

Patch, Howard R. *The Other World, According to Descriptions in Medieval Literature*. New York, 1970.

Pöhlmann, Robert von. *Geschichte der sozialen Frage und des Sozialismus in der antiken Welt*. 2 vols. München: C.H. Beck, 1925.

Ruyer, Raymond. *L'Utopie et les utopies*. Paris: Presses Universitaires de France, 1950.

Schulte-Herbrüggen, Hubertus. *Utopie und Anti-Utopie*. Bochum: Pöppinghaus, 1960.

Schwonke, Martin. *Vom Staatsroman zur Science Fiction. Eine Untersuchung über Geschichte und Funktion der naturwissenschaftlich-technischen Utopie*. Stuttgart: Ferdinand Enke, 1957.

Surtz, Edward, S.J., and Jack H. Hexter (eds). *The Complete Works of St. Thomas More*. New Haven: Yale University Press, 1965.

Suvin, Darko. *Metamorphoses of Science Fiction.* New Haven: Yale University Press, 1979.

Tillich, Paul. *Politische Bedeutung der Utopie im Leben der Völker.* Berlin: Weiss, 1951.

Vaihinger, Hans. *Die Philosophie des Als Ob.* Leipzig: Felix Meiner, 1920.

———. *The Philosophy of "As If."* Trans. C.K. Ogden. New York: Harcourt Brace, 1924.

Villgradter, Rudolf, and Friedrich Krey (eds). *Der utopische Roman.* Darmstadt: Wissenschaftliche Buchgesellschaft, 1973.

Voigt, Andreas. *Die sozialen Utopien: Fünf Vorträge.* Leipzig: Göschen, 1906.

Walsh, Chad. *From Utopia to Nightmare.* Westport: Greenwood, 1972.

Wells, Herbert G. *A Modern Utopia.* Leipzig: Tauchnitz, 1905.

Westropp, Thomas Johnson. "Brazil and the Legendary Islands of the North Atlantic." *Royal Irish Academy Proceedings* 30 (1912): 223–60.

Winston, David. "Iambulus' *Islands of the Sun* and Hellenistic Literary Utopias." *Science-Fiction Studies* 3 (1976): 217–27.

CHAPTER 2

"Utopian" and "Scientific": Two Attributes for Socialism from Engels (1976)[1]

Donner un sens plus pur aux mots de la tribu.

— STÉPHANE MALLARMÉ

If socialism is to emerge from the blind alley into which it has strayed, among other things the catchword "utopian" must be cracked open and examined for its true content.

— MARTIN BUBER, *Paths in Utopia*

---

1   Engels's essay is analyzed from *Die Entwicklung des Sozialismus von der Utopie zur Wissenschaft*, Verlag Marxistische Blätter (Frankfurt, 1971), which follows the text of vol. 22 in the East Berlin (Dietz Verlag) 1959 edition of Karl Marx-Friedrich Engels, *Werke*. All quotes from it (and from other German works) in this essay have been translated by me, after checking with the standard translation by Edward Aveling. The page numbers in parenthesis refer first to the above cited German edition, and after the semi-colon and SW to the (apparently) only available English-language edition which also contains Engels's Introduction to the English edition of 1892: Karl Marx and Frederick Engels, *Collected Works in One Volume*, London: Lawrence and Wishart, 1968 (published simultaneously by Progress, Moscow, and International Publ., New York, apparently in the same pagination). Thus, "44; SW 399–400" means: p. 44 of the above cited German (Frankfurt) edition; English (not necessarily in the identical translation) on pp. 399–400 of the above cited London edition. One significant deviation from the Aveling translation is discussed in note 9; cf. also note 5.

In this chapter an analysis is attempted[2] of some key usages of the term science/scientific[3] in its opposition to utopia/utopian,[4] and of their immediate context, in Friedrich Engels's fundamental formulation of *Socialism: Utopian and Scientific* (1882, though based on materials dating back to the 1840s – further *SUS*). This analysis is conducted to check whether the usage found there is still valid in a very much changed existential and linguistic practice. My hypothesis is that the most important connotations of the two terms have changed so much that Engels's main meanings are indeed no longer immediately usable. If this is correct, many brilliant historical passages in *SUS* would remain largely valid, but its up-to-now most meaningful passages – including the title – would not, so that its usefulness in ideological and political propaganda would be over, and the

2   Thus, this essay is not intended to be a survey of: historical semantics of the terms and concepts "science" or "utopia" (see for the latter note 3), even within the socialist thought of the last 150 years, since that would be almost equivalent to sketching its epistemologies or models for understanding the world; or of Engels's role in Marxist thought (though it is not only piety towards our teachers but elementary probability which demands that we refuse the total opposition of a bad, "positivistic" Engels and a good, "structuralist" Marx – were they incapable of recognizing such a mutual incompatibility by themselves?).

3   The difference between noun and adjective, which for both terms arises in the translations from German to English, French, etc. and not out of the deeper structure, will be disregarded here.

4   I have attempted to analyze the historical semantics of utopia as a literary genre in "Defining the Literary Genre of Utopia," (now chapter 1 in this book), where the most relevant secondary literature can be found. Of the huge secondary literature on science and/or Marxism, I am listing here only the titles most immediately stimulating for this essay even when I partly disagreed with them, any quotes from which will be adduced in parenthesis, with the author's name and page only, within the body of the essay. They are by Bloch – first and foremost; Bottomore and Rubel; Buber; Fromm ed.; Gramsci; and Lenin. It should also be mentioned that Herbert Marcuse, for all his oscillations between the Engelsian devaluation and the Blochian revaluation of utopia, has perhaps been the most meritorious stimulator of its re-evaluation in English-speaking countries; and that the most inspiring fictional example of fusing utopian and revolutionary horizons in the last half century can be found in Brecht's essays, poems, and plays such as *The Caucasian Chalk Circle* and *Coriolanus* (see now essays on both within my book *To Brecht*).

basic opposition embodied in the title would have become misleading and even counter-productive.

Many fascinating possibilities of inquiry are here reluctantly waived in order to concentrate on three main areas: 1) the basic oppositions clustering around the axis of "utopia" vs. "science" in *SUS*; 2) the nineteenth-century natural science as the epistemological model for historiosophy, and therefore for political action; 3) some consequences of 1 and 2. Also, *SUS* is organized like a Beethoven symphony, and its main themes have to be teased out gradually, as they develop. This chapter will try to follow roughly such a development, by dealing with the three parts of *SUS* in three sections.

1. Two Oppositional Models – Exclusive or Polemical and Subsumptive or Cognitive

In the very first paragraph of *SUS*, early – i.e., pre-Marxist – socialist theory is defined as a union of vertical, synchronic growth from roots of "material economic facts" (class antagonisms and anarchy in production) and horizontal, diachronic continuation of earlier theoretical principles (from the French Enlightenment). In the second paragraph, very revealingly, the French Revolution is said to have stood the world on its head, in two senses: first, in the bad or idealist sense of a claim that the human head and the principles found by its thought ought to be the basis of all human actions and socializations (see note 4; 44, 64; SW 399–400, 414); but second, in the good or subversive sense (quoted from Hegel) of reality being in deed or in fact (*in der Tat*) stood on its head in the name of reason – however deficient that particular form of bourgeois reason eventually turned out to be. Here we have to do with a complex double dichotomy: first and basic, between the anarchic class society and the two disparate ways of denying it; second, and central for the purposes of *SUS*, between the improper and the proper way of denying it – one which we could call mere ideational inversion, and which Engels very soon identifies as utopian and idealistic; and a different one which Engels properly calls subversion (*Umsturz*, note on 44; SW on 399) and will later identify as scientific and materialistic. In Parts 1 and 2 of *SUS* (49, 64–65; SW 403, 414) two opposed clusters emerge to embody this second dichotomy, which can, using Engels's own terms, be tabulated as:

IDEALISTIC AND UTOPIAN	MATERIALISTIC AND SCIENTIFIC
head – thinking – principles – reason	reality – facts and deeds – real things and economic processes
from outside the society	[from within the society]*
absolute truth	historical view

Now, no doubt, utopian fantasies are superior to reactionary philistinism which makes its peace with class society and its anarchic reality (490; SW 403), and are to be treated with respect and even admiration insofar as they were prefigurations of later, Marxist scientific truths; but, for the purpose of discussing the development and prospects of socialism as a movement and theory – which is the purpose of *SUS* – the "utopians" are to be resolutely and even sarcastically rejected because they "built a near-perfect system" pretending to a final "absolute truth" instead of practicing a "historical view" and examining "the economic process" (64–65, 67; SW 414, 416).

On the face of it, for anybody knowing the painstaking economic calculations of Robert Owen, the fundamental role allotted to industry and production in Henri de Saint-Simon, or even the maniacal distribution of daily occupations in Charles Fourier, the accusation of not having at least tried to cope with economic processes must sound strange. As for

---

*   Engels does not actually use the term, but it's clearly demanded by his logic and present in an – as it were – zero-form in 49; SW 403. It should be noted that Aveling often (unnecessarily) substitutes "mind" or "brain" for "head" (*Kopf*).

history, Engels himself acknowledges that Fourier's sweeping overview was a work of genius (it clearly underlies the *Communist Manifesto*), and that Saint-Simon's views on politics vs. production as well as on European cooperation evinced great historical foresight (Owen was, admittedly, an insular Briton). Conversely, Marx also surely thought with his head, applied reason, had principles, had a view from the margins of society, and so on. The true difference might be that, in him, building a system pretending to an asymptotic approximation toward a near-perfect truth coexisted with the acute consciousness that it is always historical and therefore modifiable. We begin to realize that the context of *SUS* is almost wholly unknown to us today, that it must in fact be recreated if we are to understand that essay's formulations. This recreation cannot be explicitly attempted here; but it might be suggested implicitly by considering the presence in *SUS* of two basic models.

I would submit it is impossible to take Engels seriously if we stick to the absolute "EITHER/OR," A vs. −A, black-or-white, *exclusive* model briefly identified above. On the contrary he makes sense if we take him as using a dialectical "NOT ONLY/BUT ALSO," AB vs. A, blending-of-colours, *subsumptive* model. What matters in the subsumptive model is not the fact that the "utopian socialists" built a system from their head: Marx did so too. But he, as different from them, NOT ONLY used reason, his head, principles, etc., BUT ALSO took into account reality, facts, and historico-economical processes – all of which culminated in his discovery of the theory of surplus value which revealed the innermost secret of capitalist production (*SUS*, end of part 2). This seems to me a perfectly tenable position. The trouble with *SUS* is that it oscillates between the two models. While its concrete historical analyses are as a rule subsumptive, its generalizations are as a rule exclusive. Since generalizations are the most easily remembered part of a political essay, the dominant rhetorics of *SUS* tend to heap scorn on the "only" half of the not only/but also model, and to induce the average reader into taking it too for a Manichean, either/or model, in which anything the brother-enemy does is automatically bad: *SUS* on the whole implies that either you build a system OR you examine

the historical economic process. I do not see how Marx can be differentiated from the major "utopian socialists" using such a model.[5]

What I do see is how effective it is as polemics; and the fact is that
SUS goes back to a long history – beginning with the writings of Marx and
Engels in the 1840s and in particular the various drafts of *The Communist
Manifesto* – which is basically one of a direct political polemic against the
degraded sub-fourierism, sub-owenism, and sub-saintsimonism of most
"socialists" at the time (66; SW 415), the near and partly dear brother-
enemies – who are, just because of that, more infuriating than reactionaries
far away. In the first half of *SUS*, for all his valiant tries at fairness, remem-
bering his own youthful "utopian socialism," Engels falls time and again
into such theological politics: *corruptio optimi pessima*, and erring brothers
should be combated in the same way as – only harder than – full-fledged
enemies. In times of acute revolutionary crisis, such as 1848 and 1917, this
method may become momentarily unavoidable; in general, however, it is
a slippery and often self-defeating path for a stable Left to follow (witness
the rise of Nazism and today). Thus the underlying cognitive model of "A
vs. AB," and the Marxian novelty of adding a crucial factor B (the theory of
surplus value, etc.) to the A of the "utopian socialists" (cooperative classless
society, etc.), is obscured by turning it into a "scientific" historical materialism as against their "utopian" unhistorical idealism. This is the first reason
Engels's basic opposition in *SUS* is no longer useful.

From the identified stance, Engels then analyzes the faults of the three
"utopian socialists" as consisting mainly in: 1) not being the representatives
of the proletarian class interests but of a spurious absolute truth, reason, and
justice – discussed in Part 1 of *SUS* (46, 57; SW 401, 409–10); 2) lacking
the knowledge of dialectics – discussed in Part 2. Both parts culminate in
announcing the solution: making socialism into a "science" (58, 68; SW
410, 416), a task made historically possible by the development of modern

5   Tangentially, Saint-Simon was certainly one of the historical "founders" or stimula-
     tors of socialism, but he was himself in his doctrine as certainly no socialist. It might
     be time to stop calling him (even utopian) one; which would mean finding a better
     term for all the para-Marxian socialists.

industry and proletariat, and realized by Marx who applied dialectics to the actual historical economic process in capitalism. But what exactly does Engels here mean by the term "science"? What is this (we must assume) dialectical activity or body which is in the interest of the proletarians?

2. Some Versions of "Science"

In order to attempt an answer, we must briefly examine the semantic context of "science" in Engels's time and space. In German, *Wissenschaft* originally meant "knowledge, intelligence, notion, understanding" (the Grimms gloss it as *notitia, cognitio, notio*), and secondarily "erudition" and "skill."[6] But such meanings – though they can here and there still be found, with suggestions of being old hat, in Kant, Schiller and Goethe – soon crossed over into "objective knowledge; a branch of knowledge and studies." This in turn led into, and was during the eighteenth-century Enlightenment largely absorbed by, a third main cluster of meanings in which science means "science as a formal discipline." That final semantic cluster can be subdivided – by a violent simplification of ten closely printed columns in the Grimms – first, into the meaning of "a single formal discipline," such as metaphysics or philology; in that sense it seems to be first tentatively applied to history by the great ideological pioneer of German Romanticism, Herder: "Rather early on, I often had the thought whether – since all that exists has its philosophy and science [*Wissenschaft*] – that which is of greatest importance to us, the history of mankind as a whole, should not also have its own philosophy and science."

Then it was applied to philosophy as the "science of sciences" by another prominent Romantic, Friedrich Schlegel: "All philosophy is but

6   All my lexical examples and quotes are from the brothers Grimm, cols. 781ff. It has been impossible to discuss the quite parallel English and French developments, but I have profited from the entries in *OED* and Lalande.

the science of all the sciences permanently flowing into each other and separating again." ["die Wissenschaft aller sich ewig mischenden und wieder trennenden Wissenschaften."] Engels's comments on history as a science (discussed later in this chapter) and on the redundance of a specialized philosophy once "each special science" has illuminated its own position in the total context of natural sciences (65–66; SW 414–15) are clearly a development viz. inversion of the Romantic ideologists, and unthinkable without them.

   A second subdivision of this third (and here the only relevant) semantic cluster of "science as a formal discipline" tries to narrow down its broad meaning by supplying it with adjectives, of which the most important in the nineteenth century is "natural science(s)." But for our present purpose the crucial subdivision is the Grimms' *Wissenschaft als Gesamtbegriff* – "science as a general or collective notion." Its use begins in the eighteenth century with Leibniz and the first philosophical formulation in Christian Wolff (itself reposing on medieval scholastics and ultimately Aristotle): "[...] the capacity of inferring whatever is asserted from sure principles and through legitimate conclusions is called science." It triumphs in the Romantics, such as A.W. Schlegel, and in the following formulation by Kant, the second part of which must be thought as underlying all the nineteenth-century discussions:

> Only that science can be called a proper one, the certainty of which is apodictic [...].
> Any whole body of cognition that is systematic can for that very reason be called
> science, and, if the knitting together of cognition in this system is a correlation of
> principles and consequences, then it can even be called rational science.

Engels seems, thus, to be trying to play off the first part of Kant's definition (by equating "apodictic," which in the tradition leading up to Kant means "clearly and firmly demonstrated," with "based on real historico-economic processes") against the too formal, "system-building" second part of the formulation which had alone become classical. As against a merely rational science, Engels is calling for a proper (*eigentliche*) one. Here too, he is following the Romantic demystifying turn which – e.g., in Strauss's

Life of Jesus – opposed science to such undoubtedly "systematic ensembles of cognition" as theology, earlier the knowledge or science *par excellence*.

As the Grimm dictionary remarks, such examples with their culmination in Kant's definition testify to an inner transmutation of the notion: "science" becomes a value notion and judgment, and eventually an almost incantatory substitute for further argumentation. Parallel to that, the adjective *wissenschaftlich* (scientific) takes on the meaning of "corresponding to the demands of science" rather than merely "associated with science or the sciences," and becomes a strong value-judgment (e.g., in Goethe and A.W. Schlegel). The same shift can be observed in English, where the new adjectival meanings seem first to have appeared apropos of Humphry Davy's writing and the tradition of the Royal Society. At a second remove, the noun *Wissenschaftlichkeit* (scientificalness – the quality of being scientific) appears as a neologism, in German for the first time apparently in Lavater's discussions of physiognomy (1775), and then in Fichte, F. Schlegel, and even Schopenhauer, in English (probably influenced by German) in 1866. Thus, to quote the Grimms, "Science [*Wissenschaft*] has become the measure for the truth and value content of a cognitive correlation" (col. 797); and from Schiller on examples are found of something being called "not scientific" in the seriously defamatory or (the other side of the coin) "scientific" in the ironic sense – both of which twists are used to great effect in Engels's polemic. The Grimms conclude with quotes from F. Schlegel, Goethe, and possibly the most significant German nineteenth-century historian Mommsen, which show how, from the very beginning of that century, *Wissenschaft* had with exceptional rapidity risen to mean one of the two supreme goods of the German nation and indeed of mankind (the other being the much older *Kunst* or art). There is no doubt that Engels too takes it in this sense, thus accepting the semantic developments of bourgeois practice, philosophy, and culture from the eighteenth century through Kant and the Romantics to the "positive" science of the nineteenth century, and only proposing to redefine the "apodictic" in Kant's definition in the sense of that "historical materialism" which finally crystallizes in *SUS*.

In the body of *SUS* (as distinct from the title and prefaces), curiously and significantly enough the first mentions of science occur in connection with Saint-Simon – both in the sense of "science as a social institution," i.e., the official scientists (50; SW 404 – see also 63; SW 413), and in the more usual sense of "science as a formal cognition" (for Saint-Simon's genius is among other things manifested in his declaring that "politics is the science of production" [51; SW 405]).[7] Immediately thereafter in *SUS*, Fourier is said to be at his most sublime in a historiosophy which is explicitly compared to natural sciences (52–53; SW 406). This parallel is picked up again and developed further in the usual symphonic fashion during the discussion of dialectics in Part 2. "Real natural science" has been developing since the second half of the fifteenth century, gathering "details" for a later dialectical understanding (60; SW 411). Modern materialism concludes from this development that "Nature also has its history in time" (65; SW 414). Conversely, the parallel to "the positive science of nature," a positive science of history (66; SW 415), was in a less fortunate situation until the 1840s when it (and socialism, which is in a way a theory of history) could begin using the lessons of proletarian class struggle, of German dialectics, and of "modern natural science" (67; SW 416). It is at this point, as already mentioned, that Part 2 of *SUS* culminates with the name of Marx and his theory of surplus value as the examples of the union of proletarian interests, dialectics, and "scientificalness." Saint-Simon is here tacitly extrapolated into the formula, "history is the science of economics" (which Marx, of course, never used).

Thus, the positive science of nature is for Engels identical with existing natural science – chemistry, astronomy, physics, physiology, and the like (22, 25; SW 386, 387) – as interpreted by a consistent dialectician (presumably regardless of any class interests); it is always materialist insofar as it is science (23; SW 386). The positive science of history (as discussed in the last part of *SUS* and the later written preface) is historical materialism (24; SW 386–87); it is fully as materialist as the science of nature but requires dialectics and the acknowledgement of the economic development of society

7   Strangely enough, the cited twentieth century edition of Grimm does not list that obviously important meaning, nor do *OED* and Lalande (though *OED* hesitates on the brink of it): too mundane for the theoretical grid of the lexicographers?

and of the resulting class struggles as "final causes and [the] decisive motive power of all significant historical events." A tabulation might again help:

POSITIVE SCIENCE OF NATURE	POSITIVE SCIENCE OF HISTORY
Developed from fifteenth century	Developed after Hegel and the 1840s
Its interpretation demands dialectics	Its constitution demands dialectics
Must acknowledge existence of matter and its laws	Must acknowledge existence of economy-based class conflict and its laws
? ? ? ?	Must be representative of proletarian class interests, not "absolute truth" etc.

If this tabulation is correct, the constitutive parallel of Engels's contains nonetheless a glaring blind spot (marked by the question-marks above), which invalidates much of his reasoning. For either science too is finally an ideology, a "superstructure" (*Überbau*) on the "real [...] economic structure of society" just as the "religious, philosophical, and other ways of imagination (*Vorstellungsweise*) of a given historical period" are (66–67; SW 415), and then a new science must be sought after, as radically different from the "value-free" post-Galileian or Baconian one as theirs was from the medieval one; or, if science is allowed to be an approximation of absolute truth, then the quite parallel historiosophy must be given rein to be such too, and all the fulminations against the "utopians'" search after absolute truth, justice etc. are unwarranted. In the first case (to which I personally incline), science and scientificalness could no longer serve as an immaculate epistemological model for historical materialism, as science would be itself ideologically corrupted by class society. In the second case, utopianism would not, and the utopians would not, be wrong in principle – though they might very well be wrong in their concrete doctrines (a fact not too difficult to establish from a brief perusal), which it would therefore be necessary to combat ideologically and politically. In both cases the opposition of "utopian" and "scientific" does not hold. And in either case, the hypostasis of nineteenth-century science into the only absolute epistemological model for Marxist or socialist historiosophy is illogical. (Let us note that this is in *SUS* never explicitly argued – it is a hidden premise.)

Indeed, it is the practical lessons of what bourgeois "value-free" science lends itself to – concentration camps, atom bombs, napalm, ecocide, and so on – which at the latest since 1945 precludes a socialist from accepting it as anything more than an extremely powerful, in its ascending historical phase extremely liberating, always potentially useful, but finally also quite sinister ideology. Modern investigations into the history, theory, and sociology of science, from Brecht's *Life of Galileo* to specialized studies such as Thomas Kuhn's, have confirmed this.

Thus, it seems that the history of the term "science" is entering into the phase of a new, fourth semantic cluster, where its absolute or mythological pretensions are being challenged and demystified; on a higher rung of the dialectical spiral, "science" is being reconducted to something like the medieval notion of knowledge (*scientia*) which is not synonymous with wisdom (*sapientia*) but can oscillate between that and its opposite. This is the second reason Engels's basic opposition in *SUS* is no longer useful.

3. The Reality Principle and the Hope Principle

The contradiction inherent in defining historical materialism as a "science" has an obvious bearing on the unsolved tensions within it between necessitarianism and voluntarism, or between economic predetermination and ideologico-political free-will. The third and final part of *SUS* begins somewhat promisingly by requiring that means of social change "are not to be invented out of one's head, but discovered by means of one's head in the existing material facts of production" (69; SW 417). But this opposition is not fully clarified (does not an inventor deal as much with existing material facts or laws as a discoverer does?),[8] so that it is possible to find in the next paragraph perhaps the extreme deterministic formulation of the essay: the modern conflict between productive forces and mode of production "exists in the facts, objectively, outside of us, INDEPENDENT OF THE WILL OR COURSE (*Laufen*) even of the men that have brought it about" – and thus *a fortiori* independent of the will of any men; and "modern socialism is NOTHING BUT THE REFLECTION IN THOUGHT (*Gedankenreflex*) of this factual conflict" (70; SW 418; caps DS).[9] This prevailing determinism leads on the one hand to a crassly mechanical materialism, such as when the capitalist accumulation of riches on the one pole and of misery, degradation, and so on, on the other pole of society is set parallel to the accumulation of hydrogen and oxygen on the positive and negative poles during water dialysis (79; SW 424).

Complementarily but somewhat incompatibly, determinism leads to a historical optimism politically as unrealistic as that of the utopians from Saint-Simon to Bellamy – e.g., "no people would stand for a production conducted by trusts, for such a naked exploitation of the community" (82; SW 427). Perhaps the most just way of dealing with this is to repeat Gramsci's diagnosis (Gramsci Part 2, e.g. 69–70, 100–07) that deterministic confidence had a role to play in the Marxist as much as in religious

---

8   Just as elsewhere Aveling "hardens" some formulations of Engels's (e.g., "*Geschichtsbetrachtung*," 52–53, is rendered as "historical science," SW 406), so here he smoothes over his exclusive opposition; his translation is: "These means are not to be invented by deduction from fundamental principles, but are to be discovered in the stubborn facts of the existing system of production." Since this is not what Engels wrote, and the authorized translation of Aveling's has no consistent drift which would indicate some second thoughts of Engels's, I have not gone into the (by itself very intriguing) philological comparisons of the German with this English and with Lafargue's French translation.

9   This "clear glass," "mirroring" or "nothing but" theory of thinking, this slighting of mediations, dialectical method and the NOT ONLY/BUT ALSO model, leads directly to Lenin's theory of reflection in *Materialism and Empiriocriticism*, the disastrous Zhdanovian consequences of which are known. It is to the Lenin of the *Philosophical Notebooks* and in particular *The State and Revolution* we should return.

revolutionary movements, but that this role is over after the first serious defeats (i.e., the rise of fascism after World War I – an epoch from which one can date the obsolescence of *SUS* too). Once the propagandistic role of deterministic optimism is exhausted, however, the cognitive role of the *SUS* "scientific" definitions, while undoubtedly a very valuable contribution in a historical perspective, is revealed as insufficient. It is a great cognitive step to have stressed that "an unclear future ideal" or "will" (of socializing the productive forces) must also become possible through concrete economic conditions; but that possibility is not defined precisely enough simply by speaking of "historical necessity" (87; SW 432). The sublime ideal of men becoming masters of nature by mastering history (that is, the laws of their own social activity – 489–90; SW 432) with which Part 3 of *SUS* closes, remains itself an "unclear future ideal" unless historical necessity is defined as only one – strong but merely potential – force, which can be actualized or repressed by other forces in and among people. In such a dialectics, determinisms work – or do not work – through voluntary actions; in other words, "scientific" preconditions must in their turn be fused with "utopian" élan and projects. And this is the third reason why Engels's basic opposition in *SUS* is no longer useful.

Thus, the so-called utopian socialists are rightly to be criticized for not taking both the inertia and the potential real forces of material history into account; theirs is "a picture of society designed as though there were no other factors at work than conscious human will" (Buber 8). On the other hand, the scientistic so-called historical materialists are as rightly to be criticized for stressing economic determinism. Surely the dialectically mature use of these somewhat one-sided oppositions, the only use liable to be a good guide to action, is a synthesis of the bold, vertical utopian will to revolution and the careful, horizontal knowledge of preconditions for revolution; of the single unwavering absolute and the myriad supple contingencies; of the Hope principle (Bloch) and the Reality principle (Freud). And this leads us straight back – and forward! – to Marx's own usage and epistemology.

This chapter cannot deal with the much more interesting ways in which Marx thought of his socialism as a guide to action. It will have to suffice, in order to suggest his precise distance from Engels, to mention that for

Marx "materialist" is an adjective derived from matter rather than from materialism; and to discuss a single very suggestive passage of his from *The Poverty of Philosophy* (which of course underlies Engels's essay):

> [...] utopians [...], in order to remedy the distress of the oppressed classes, impro-
> vise systems and pursue a regenerative science. But as history continues, and as the
> struggle of the proletariat takes shape more clearly, they have only to observe what
> is happening before their eyes, and to make themselves its vehicle of expression. As
> long as they are looking for a science and only create systems, as long as they are at
> the beginning of the struggle, they see in poverty only poverty, without noticing its
> revolutionary and subversive aspects, which will overthrow the old society. But from
> this moment, the science produced by the historical movement, and which consciously
> associates itself with this movement [that is, the "socialists and communists who are
> the theoreticians of the proletariat" as Marx says a few lines earlier], has ceased to be
> doctrinaire and has become revolutionary. (Bottomore and Rubel 81)

Many expressions in this passage of Marx's are used as in *SUS*: the utopians (here Proudhon) "improve systems," "look [...] in their own minds," etc. But strangely enough, some crucial expressions are used in a diametri-cally opposed way: it is a science the utopians are pursuing! Clearly, such an improvised system is a "bad" science and not an absolute value, it is a Kantian "systematic whole body of cognitions" on the order of metaphys-ics, only privatized; and furthermore, it is simply a "positive" or tauto-logical science (poverty = poverty) instead of a dialectical one (poverty = NOT ONLY poverty BUT ALSO subversion). Gratifyingly enough, it is the NOT ONLY/ BUT ALSO model we find dominating this pas-sage of Marx's: the observation of "what is happening before their eyes" (though still polemically accompanied by an "only") is to result in theoreti-cal "expression"; but it is, quite clearly, "ONLY creat[ing] systems" that is NOT enough or is wrong. Finally, the utopianism is defined as a doctrinaire science, as opposed to the cognitive socialism and communism associated with the historical movement of the working class which is defined as a revolutionary science. The development from Proudhon, Owen, etc., to Marxism is thus NOT a development from "utopia" to "science," but from a "doctrinaire" to a "revolutionary" science! Science is here, obvi-ously, thought of by Marx neither as an official social institution nor as an absolute epistemological model, but as a usable and misusable ensemble of cognition – which is, as in Kant, a pioneering prefiguration of that fourth semantic cluster I was postulating earlier. The *differentia specifica* between Proudhon (or other utopians) and Marx is, thus, that notion and activity in which theory and practice, inversion and subversion, determinism and free-will, utopia and knowledge meet, the basis, center, and purpose of Marxian socialism: it is revolution.

Finally, all the paradoxes discussed in this chapter are in a way paradoxes arising out of the concept of a non-deterministic future history. In it, the two-valued, A or −A, logic necessarily fails. Of a fixed isolated moment in the present and the past, we can affirm something either is or is not true (or better, correct); but of the future, all we can say is that the existence plus the non-existence of a given A is (or is not) true or correct.[10] In the case of "future contingents," only dialectical logic, shunning EITHER/OR models, helps.[11] For past or present history, in our hindsight, an attitude is either "realistic" or "utopian"; within a positive science of the nineteenth-century type, something is or is not true and thus possible. But in a future history, which is only postulated and contingent, science and utopia, necessity and possibility, the vertical and the horizontal, embrace (as in the medieval godhead of the Schoolmen). The future is a thisworldly Other World, which replaces the transcendental and unhistorical Other World of the Schoolmen – but replacing means also taking its place. If you wish, socialism is a science because it is an unquenchable future-oriented

---

10 *Additional note 2008*: See now for a lengthy discussion of the One Truth vs. historical correctness as well as of science, my "On the Horizons of Epistemology and Science", forthcoming in *Critical Quarterly* 52.1.

11 Future contingents are events that have not yet happened and are not predetermined. Aristotle's famous example in *On Interpretation*, Chapter 9, 18a–19b, is that it is not necessary either a) that a sea-battle should take place tomorrow, or b) that a sea-battle should not take place tomorrow; c) "yet it is necessary that it either should or should not take place tomorrow" – in Gale ed. 182. For further comments on Aristotle see that volume, and Smart ed., with a bibliography on pp. 428–29.

utopia; and it can be a utopia because it is a science not in any "positive" but in the Marxian, revolutionary sense.[12]

Works Cited

Bloch, Ernst. *Das Prinzip Hoffnung*. Frankfurt: Suhrkamp, 1959.

Bottomore, T.B., and Maximilien Rubel. "Marx's Sociology and Social Philosophy." *Karl Marx: Selected Writings in Sociology and Social Philosophy*. Ed. Tom B. Bottomore and Maximilien Rubel. Harmondsworth: Penguin, 1963.

Buber, Martin. *Paths in Utopia*. Boston: Beacon, 1949.

Engels, Friedrich. "Die Entwicklung des Sozialismus von der Utopie zur Wissenschaft." *Werke*. Karl Marx and Friedrich Engels. Vol. 22. [East] Berlin: Dietz Verlag, 1959.

Fromm, Erich (ed.). *Socialist Humanism*. New York: Doubleday, 1965. (Especially the essay by Maximilien Rubel, "Reflections on Utopia and Revolution".)

Gale, Richard (ed.). *The Philosophy of Time: a Collection of Essays*. Garden City NY: Doubleday, 1967.

Gramsci, Antonio. *The Modern Prince and Other Writings*. New York: International Publishers, 1972.

Grimm, Jacob and Wilhelm. *Deutsches Wörterbuch*, Vol. 14, Part 2. Leipzig: S. Hirzel, 1913.

Lalande, André. "Utopie". *Vocabulaire technique et critique de la philosophie*. Paris: Presses universitaires de France, 1968.

Lenin, Vladimir I. *The State and Revolution*. Peking: Foreign Languages Press, 1973.

---

12   My thanks go to Fredric Jameson for whose issue of *the minnesota review* on utopia this essay was first written.

Marx, Karl, and Frederick Engels. *Collected Works in One Volume*. London: Lawrence & Wishart, 1968.

[OED] *The Compact Edition of the Oxford English Dictionary*. Oxford: Oxford University Press, 1991.

Smart, J.J.C. (ed.). *Problems of Space and Time*. London and New York: Macmillan, 1964.

Suvin, Darko. *To Brecht and Beyond: Soundings in Modern Dramaturgy*. Brighton: Harvester, 1984.

Science Fiction and the Novum (1977)

0. Introduction

It is often thought that the concept of a literary genre (here science fiction, SF) can be found directly in the works investigated, that the scholar in such a genre has no need to turn to literary theory since he/she will find the concepts in the texts themselves. True, the concept of SF is in a way inherent in the literary objects – the scholar does not invent it out of whole cloth – but its specific nature and the limits of its use can be grasped only by employing theoretical methods. The concept of SF cannot be extracted intuitively or empirically from the work called thus. Positivistic critics often attempt to do so; unfortunately, the concept at which they arrive is then primitive, subjective, and unstable. In order to determine it more pertinently and delimit it more precisely, it is necessary to educe and formulate the *differentia specifica* of the SF narration. My axiomatic premise in this chapter is that *SF is distinguished by the narrative dominance or hegemony of a fictional "novum" (novelty, innovation) validated by cognitive logic.*

1. The Novum and Cognition

1.1

What is the common denominator, the presence of which is logically necessary, and which has to be hegemonic in a narration in order that we may call it an SF narration? In other words, how can the proper domain of SF be determined, what is the theoretical axis of such a determining? The answering is clouded by the present wave of irrationalism, engendered by the deep structures of the irrational capitalist way of life which has reduced the dominant forms of rationality itself (quantification, reification, exchange value, and so on) to something narrow, dogmatic, and sterile inasmuch as they are the forms of reasoning of the dominant or of the dominated classes. Nonetheless, I do not see any tenable intrinsic determination of SF which would not hinge on the category of the novum, to borrow (and slightly adapt) a term from the best possible source, Ernst Bloch (in particular: *Das Prinzip Hoffnung* and *Experimentum Mundi*). A novum or cognitive innovation is *a totalizing phenomenon or relationship deviating from the author's and implied reader's norm of reality*. Now, no doubt, each and every poetic metaphor is a novum, while modern prose fiction has made new insights into people its rallying cry. However, though valid SF has deep affinities with poetry and innovative realistic fiction, its novelty is "totalizing" in the sense that it entails a change of the whole universe of the tale, or at least of crucially important aspects thereof (and that it is therefore a means by which the whole tale can be analytically grasped). As a consequence, the essential tension of SF is one between the readers, representing a certain number of types of people of our times, and the encompassing and at least equipollent Unknown or Other introduced by the novum. This tension in turn estranges the empirical norm of the implied reader (more about this later).

Clearly the novum is a mediating category whose explicative potency springs from its rare bridging of literary and extraliterary, fictional and empirical, formal and ideological domains, in brief from its unalienable historicity. Conversely, this makes it impossible to give a static definition of it, since it is always codetermined by the unique, not to be anticipated situationality and processuality that it is supposed to designate and illuminate. But it is possible to distinguish various dimensions of the novum. Quantitatively, the postulated innovation can be of quite different degrees of magnitude, running from the minimum of one discrete new "invention" (gadget, technique, phenomenon, relationship) to the maximum of a setting (spatiotemporal locus), agent (main character or characters), and/or relations basically new and unknown in the author's environment.

Tangentially I might say that this environment is always identifiable from the text's historical semantics, always bound to a particular time, place, and sociolinguistic norm, so that what would have been utopian or technological SF in a given epoch is not necessarily such in another – except when read as a product of earlier history; in other words, the novum can help us understand just how is SF a historical genre.

I.2

The novum is postulated on and validated by the post-Baconian scientific method. This does not mean that the novelty is primarily a matter of scientific facts or even hypotheses; and insofar as the opponents of the old popularizing Verne-to-Gernsback orthodoxy protest against such a narrow conception of SF they are quite right. But they go too far in denying that what differentiates SF from the "ahistorical" literary genres (mythical tales, fairy tales, and so on, as well as horror and/or heroic Fantasy in the narrow sense) is the presence of scientific cognition as the sign or correlative of a method (way, approach, atmosphere, sensibility) identical to that of a modern philosophy of science.[1] Science in this wider sense of methodically systematic cognition cannot be disjoined from the SF innovation, in spite of fashionable currents in SF criticism of the last fifteen years – though it should conversely be clear that a proper analysis of SF cannot focus on its ostensible scientific content or scientific data. Indeed, a very useful distinction between "naturalistic" fiction, Fantasy, and SF, drawn by Robert M.

---

[1] Beyond the discussion in *MOSF* chapter 1, see also my essays "'Utopian' and 'Scientific,'" *the minnesota review* (1976), now chapter 3 of this book, and "Science and Marxism, Scientism and Marquit," ibidem no. 10 (1978). *Addition 2008*: On Fantasy (which I have realized is a congerie of ahistorical rather than necessarily supernatural genres, and which I write with capital F to avoid confusion) see now my essay "Considering," and on science much more in my "On the Horizons of Epistemology and Science" (forthcoming in *Critical Quarterly*).

Philmus, is that naturalistic fiction does not require scientific explanation, Fantasy does not allow it, and SF both requires and allows it.[2]

Thus, if the novum is the necessary condition of SF (differentiating it from naturalistic fiction),[3] the validation of the novelty by scientifically methodical cognition into which the reader is inexorably led is the *sufficient* condition for SF. Though such cognition obviously cannot, in a work of verbal fiction, be empirically tested either in laboratory or by observation in nature, it can be methodically developed against the background of a body of already existing cognitions, or at the very least as a "mental experiment" following accepted scientific, that is, cognitive, logic. Of the two, the second alternative – the intrinsic, culturally acquired cognitive logic – seems theoretically the crucial one to me. Though I would be hard put to cite an SF tale in which the novelty is not in fact continuous with or at least analogous to existing scientific cognitions, I would be disposed to accept theoretically a faint possibility of a fictional novum that would at least seem to be based on quite new, imaginary cognitions, beyond all real possibilities known or dreamt of in the author's empirical reality. (My doubts here are not so much theoretical as psychological, for I do not see

2   The distinction is to be found in Philmus 5–6. My defining of SF is indebted to some earlier discussions. In particular, I find myself in some respects near to Kingsley Amis's definition in *New Maps* – with the significant difference of trying to go beyond his evasive basing of the SF innovation "in science or technology, or pseudo-science or pseudo-technology" (18).

3   Works avowedly written within a nonrealistic mode, principally allegory (but also whimsy, satire, and lying tall tale or Münchhauseniade), constitute a category for which the question of whether they possess a novum cannot even be posed, because they do not use the new worlds, agents, or relationships as coherent albeit provisional ends, but as immediately transitive and narratively nonautonomous means for direct and sustained reference to the author's empirical world and some system of belief in it. The question whether an allegory is SF, and vice versa, is, strictly speaking, meaningless, but for classifying purposes has to be answered in the negative. This means that – except for exceptions and grey areas – most of the works of Kafka or Borges cannot be claimed for SF: though I would argue that *In the Penal Colony* and "The Library of Babel" would be among the exceptions. But admittedly, much more work remains to be done toward the theory of modern allegory in order to render more precise the terms underlined in this note (see also section 2.2 of this chapter).

how anybody could imagine something not even dreamt of by anyone else before: but then I do not believe in individualistic originality.) But besides the "real" possibilities there exist also the much stricter – though also much wider – limits of "ideal" possibility, meaning any conceptual or thinkable possibility the premises and/or consequences of which are not internally contradictory (see the stimulating discussion by Foht). Only in "hard" or near-future SF does the tale's thesis have to conform to a "real possibility" – to that which is possible in the author's reality and/or according to the scientific paradigm of his culture. On the contrary, the thesis of any SF tale has to conform to an "ideal possibility," as defined above. Any tale based on a metaphysical wish-dream – for example omnipotence – is "ideally impossible" as a coherent narration – can an omnipotent being create a stone it will not be able to lift? – and so forth, according to the cognitive logic that human beings have acquired in their culture from the beginnings to the present day. It is intrinsically or by definition impossible for SF to acknowledge any metaphysical agency, in the literal sense of an agency going beyond *physis* (nature). Whenever it does so. it is not SF, but a metaphysical or (to translate the Greek into Latin) a supernatural fantasy-tale.

1.3

Science is then the encompassing horizon of SF, its "initiating and dynamizing motivation" (Trzynadlowski 272; see also Lem, Nudelman "Conversation," and Russ 8–15). I re-emphasize that this does not mean that SF is "scientific fiction" in the literal, crass, or popularizing sense of gadgetry-cum-utopia/dystopia. Indeed, a number of important clarifications ought immediately to be attached: I shall mention three. A first clarification is that "horizon" is not identical to "ideology." Our view of reality or conceptual horizon is, willy-nilly, determined by the fact that our existence is based on the application of science(s), and I do not believe we can imaginatively go beyond such a horizon; a machineless Arcadia is today simply a microcosm with zero-degree industrialization and a lore standing in for zero-degree science. On the other hand, within a scientific paradigm and horizon, ideologies can be and are either fully supportive of this one and only imaginable state of affairs, or fully opposed to it, or anything in between. Thus, anti-scientific SF is just as much within the scientific horizon (namely a misguided reaction to repressive – capitalist or bureaucratic – abuse of science) as, say, literary utopia and dystopia both are within the perfectibilist horizon. The so-called speculative fiction (for example, J.G. Ballard's) clearly began as and has mostly remained an ideological inversion of "hard" SF. Though the credibility of SF does not depend on the particular scientific rationale in any tale, the significance of the entire fictive situation of a tale ultimately depends on the fact that "the reality that it displaces, and thereby interprets" (Philmus 20) is interpretable only within the scientific or cognitive horizon.

A second clarification is that *sciences humaines* or historical-cultural sciences like anthropology-ethnology, sociology, or linguistics (that is, the mainly nonmathematical sciences) are equally based on such scientific methods as: the necessity and possibility of explicit, coherent, and immanent or non-supernatural explanation of realities; Occam's razor; methodical doubt; hypothesis-construction; falsifiable physical or imaginary (thought) experiments; dialectical causality and statistical probability; progressively more embracing cognitive paradigms; and similarly on. These "soft sciences" can therefore most probably better serve as a basis for SF than the "hard" natural sciences; and they have in fact been the basis of all better works in SF – partly through the characteristic subterfuge of cybernetics, the science in which hard nature and soft humanities fuse. A third clarification, finally, is that science has since Marx and Einstein been an open-ended corpus of knowledge, so that all imaginable new corpuses which do not contravene the philosophical basis of the scientific method in the author's times (for example, the simulsequentialist physics in Ursula Le Guin's *The Dispossessed*) can play the role of scientific validation in SF.

1.4

It may be objected to this that a look into bookstores will show that a good proportion of what is sold as SF is constituted by tales of more or less supernatural or occult Fantasy. However, this is the result of an ideological and commercial habit of lumping together SF (fiction whose novum is cognitively validated) and fantastic narrative. A misshapen subgenre born of such mingling is that of "science-fantasy," extending from Poe through Merritt to Bradbury, about which I can only repeat the strictures of the late James Blish, who noted how in it "plausibility is specifically invoked for most of the story, but may be cast aside in patches at the author's whim and according to no visible system or principle," in "a blind and grateful abandonment of the life of the mind."[4] In supernatural Fantasy proper, the supposed novelty rejects cognitive logic and claims for itself a higher "occult" logic – whether Christian, a-Christian and indeed atheistic (as is the case of Lovecraft), or, most usually, an opportunistic blend of both, openly shown in the more self-confident nineteenth century by something like Marie Corelli's "Electric Christianity" (the enormous popularity of which is echoed right down to C.S. Lewis). The consistent supernatural Fantasy tale – one which does not employ only a single irruption of the supernatural into everyday normality, as in Gogol's *Nose* or Balzac's *Peau de Chagrin*, but develops the phenomenology of the supernatural at the expense of the tension with everyday norm – is usually (in England from Bulwer-Lytton on) a proto-Fascist revulsion against modern civilization, materialist rationalism, and such. It is organized around an ideology unchecked by any cognition, so that its narrative logic is simply overt ideology plus Freudian erotic patterns. If SF exists at all, this is not it.

One of the troubles with distinctions in genre theory is, of course, that literary history is full of "limit-cases." Let us briefly examine one of considerable importance, Robert L. Stevenson's *The Strange Case of Dr Jekyll and Mr Hyde.* Despite my respect for Stevenson's literary craftsmanship, I would contend that he is cheating in terms of his basic narrative logic. On the one hand, his moral allegory of good and evil takes bodily form with the help of a chemical concoction. On the other, the

4   Atheling 98 and 104. A further warning of his that the hybrid of SF and detective tale leads – as I would say, because of the incompatibility between the detective tale's contract of informative closure with the reader and the manifold surprises inherent in the SF novum system – to a trivial lower common denominator of the resulting tale has so far been developed only by Nudelman, "Approach."

transmogrification Jekyll-Hyde becomes not only unrepeatable because the concoction had unknown impurities, but Hyde also begins "returning" without any chemical stimulus, by force of desire and habit. This unclear oscillation between science and fantasy, where science is used for a partial justification or added alibi for those readers who would no longer be disposed to swallow a straightforward fantasy or moral allegory, is to my mind the reason for the elaborate, clever, but finally not satisfying exercise in detection from various points of view – which in naturalistic fashion masks but does not explain the fuzziness at the narrative nucleus. This marginal SF is therefore, to my mind, an early example of "science fantasy." Its force does not stem from any cognitive logic, but rather from Jekyll's anguish over his loss of control and from the impact of the hidden but clearly underlying moral allegory. The latter is particularly relevant to Victorian bourgeois repressions of the non-utilitarian or unofficial aspects of life and it also holds forth an unsubstantiated promise that the oscillation between SF and Fantasy does not matter since we are dealing with full-blown allegory anyway (see note 3).

2. Narrative Consequences of the Novum

2.1

The presence of the novum as the determining factor of an SF narration is crucially testable in its explanatory power for the basic narrative strategies in this genre. First of all, the dominance or hegemony of the cognitive novelty means that an SF narration is not only a tale that includes this or that SF element or aspect: utopian strivings or dystopian terrors of some kind, as in the greater part of world literature; moral allegories or transcendental visions of other worlds, better or worse from our own, as in much literature down to Milton, Swedenborg, and countless imitators; use of new technological gadgets, as in many James Bond tales; and so on. An

SF narration is a fiction in which the SF element or aspect, the novum, is *hegemonic*, that is, so central and significant that it determines the whole narrative logic – or at least the overriding narrative logic – regardless of any impurities that might be present.[5]

2.2

Furthermore, the novum intensifies and radicalizes that movement across the boundary of a semantic field, as defined by the author's cultural norm, which always constitutes the fictional event (Lotman 229 ff.). In "natural-istic" fiction this boundary is iconic and isomorphic: the transgression of the cultural norm stands for a transgression of the cultural norm; Madame Bovary's adultery stands for adultery. In SF, or at least in its determining events, it is not iconic but allomorphic: a transgression of the cultural norm is signified by the transgression of a more than merely cultural, of an ontological, norm, by an ontic change in the character/agent's reality either because of her/his displacement in space and/or time or because the reality itself changes around him. I do not know a better characterization than to say that the novelty makes for the SF narration's specific *ontolytic*

5   A major objection against so-called thematic studies of SF elements and aspects, from Bailey's work – in 1947 no doubt pioneering – to present-day atomistic and positivistic SF critics, is that these studies ignore the determining feature of what they are studying: the narrative logic of a fictional tale. Correlatively, they tend to become boring catalogs of raisins picked out of the narrative cake, and completely desiccated in the process. This does not mean that critical discussions of, say, artificial satellites, biological mutations, or new sexual mores in SF (or other fiction) cannot be, for some strictly limited purposes, found useful; and for such purposes we should probably know where the mutations, satellites, or sex patterns first appeared and how they spread. But we should not be lured by this very peripheral necessity into annexing any and every tale with a new gadget or psychic procedure into SF as, for example, Bailey did with Wilkie Collins's *Moonstone* and Thomas Hardy's *Two on a Tower*. SF scholarship that does this is sawing off the branch on which it is sitting: for if these and such works are SF just like, say, Wells's *Invisible Man*, then in fact there is no such thing as SF.

effect and properties. Or perhaps – since, as differentiated from Fantasy tale or mythological tale, SF does not posit another superordinated and "more real" reality but an alternative on the same ontological level as the author's empirical reality – one should say that the necessary correlate of the novum is an alternate reality, one that possesses *a different historical time* corresponding to different human relationships and sociocultural norms actualized by the narration. This new reality overtly or tacitly presupposes the existence of the author's empirical reality, since it can be gauged and understood only as the empirical reality modified in such-and-such ways. Though I have argued that SF is not – by definition cannot be – an orthodox allegory with any one-to-one correspondence of its elements to elements in the author's reality, its specific modality of existence is a feedback oscillation that moves now from the author's and implied reader's norm of reality to the narratively actualized novum in order to understand the plot-events, and now back from those novelties to the author's reality, in order to see it afresh from the new perspective gained. This oscillation, called estrangement by Shklovsky and Brecht, is no doubt a consequence of every poetic, dramatic, scientific, in brief semantic novum. However, its second pole is in SF a narrative reality sufficiently autonomous and intransitive to be explored at length as to its own properties and the human relationships it implies. (For though mutants or Martians, ants or intelligent nautiloids can be used as signifiers, they can only signify human relationships, given that we cannot – at least so far – imagine other ones.).

2.3

The oscillation between the author's "zero world" and the new reality induces the narrative necessity of a means of reality displacement. As far as I can see, there are two such devices: a *voyage* to a new locus, and *a catalyzer* transforming the author's environment to a new locus; examples for the two could be Wells's *Time Machine* and *Invisible Man*. The first case seems better suited to a sudden and the second to a gradual introduction of a new reality; no doubt, all kinds of contaminations and twists on these two means are thinkable. When the *in medias res* technique is used in any particular SF tale, the means of displacement can be told in a retrospective or they can, apparently, totally disappear (more easily in a spacetime displacement: our hero is simply a native of elsewhere/elsewhen). However, this semblance conceals the presence of displacement in a zero-form, usually as a convention tacitly extrapolated from earlier stories; the history of the genre is the missing link that made possible, for example, tales in another spacetime without any textual reference to that of the author (as in most good SF novels of the last twenty years).

2.4

The concept of novum illuminates also the historical vicissitudes of justifying the reality displacement. In naturalistic tales the voyage can only start in the author's space, and the account of the new reality has to arrive back into that space so that its telling may be naturalistically plausible. However, it would then be logically necessary that the account of such a sensational voyage to a new reality should in its turn become a catalyzer, inducing changes in the author's and reader's environment. Since this in fact, as the reader knows, has not happened, naturalistic SF has had to invent a number of lightning-rods to dissipate such expectations. Verne pretended not to notice its necessity, while Wells in some of his tales pretended we all knew it already – ploys which today make those narrations sound as if they assumed an alternate time-stream in which Nemo or the Invisible Man had in fact (as different from the reader's time-stream) been the scourge of the seas or of southern England. Many earlier writers went through other extraordinary contortions to satisfy naturalistic plausibility, usually a contamination of the "manuscript in a bottle" device (the news of a voyage to the Moon just having arrived by volcanic eruption from it and just being served piping hot to you, dear reader) and the "lost invention" device (a one-shot novelty confined to the experience of a few people and unable to extend beyond them because the invention has been lost), as in *The First Men in the Moon*. But the most plausible variable for manipulation was time, inasmuch as setting the tale in the future immediately dispensed with any need for empirical plausibility. The shift of SF from space into future time is not simply due to an exhaustion of white spots on the *mappa mundi*. Rather, it is due to an interaction of two factors: on the one hand, such a narrative convenience, stunted within strict positivist ideology; on the other, the strong tendency toward temporal extrapolation inherent in life based on a capitalist economy, with its salaries, profits, and progressive ideals always expected in a future clock-time.

Thus space was a fully plausible locus for SF only before the capillary dominance of the capitalist way of life, from very early tales about the happy or unhappy valley or island – known to almost all tribal and ancient societies – to More and Swift. An Earthly Paradise or Cockayne tale, a humanist dialogue and satire, all happen in a literary or imaginative space not subject to positivistic plausibility. But a triumphant bourgeoisie introduces an epoch-making epistemological break into human imagination, by which linear or clock-time becomes the space of human development because it is the space of capitalist industrial production. The spatial dominions of even the largest feudal landowner are finite; capital, the new historical form of property – that shaper of human existences and relationships – has in principle no limits in extrapolated time. Through a powerful system of mediations infusing the whole human existence, time becomes finally the equivalent of money and thus of all things. The positivist ideology followed capitalist practice in eventually perfecting an image of time rigidified "into an exactly delimited, quantifiable continuum filled with quantifiable 'things' [...]: in short, [time] becomes space."[6] Imaginative times and spaces are now resolved into "positive," quantified ones. All existential alternatives, for better or worse, shift into such a spatialized future, which now becomes the vast ocean on whose other shore the alternative island is to be situated. Positivism shunts SF into anticipation, a form more activist than the spatial *exemplum* because achievable in the implied reader's own space. When the

---

6   Lukács 90 – the whole seminal essay "Reification and the Consciousness of the Proletariat," developing insights from Marx's *Capital*, is to be consulted; also Simmel, Sombart, and Mumford. I have tried to apply Lukács's approach to uantification and reification in my essays "On Individualist" and "Beckett's," and in the historical part of *MOSF*, especially in the essay on Verne as the bard of movement in such a quantified space.

industrial revolution becomes divorced from the democratic one – a divorce which is the fundamental political event of the bourgeois epoch – activism becomes exasperated and leads to the demands for another epistemological and practical break, signalled by Blake's Jerusalem in England's green and pleasant land and the cosmic "passionate attraction" of Fourier's phalansteries. Such imaginative energies converge in Marx, the great prefigurator of the imaginative shift still being consummated in our times. Rather than identify it as "postindustrial" (a fairly reified and vague term), I would tend to call the new paradigm – since it is in our century marked by names such as Einstein, Picasso, Eisenstein, and Brecht – one of spatiotemporal covariance, simulsequentialism, or humanist relativism and estrangement: in brief, one of alternate historical realities. I would argue that in such a historical perspective, all significant SF from Zamyatin, Čapek, and Lem to Le Guin, Thomas M. Disch, and Samuel Delany is neither simply spatial, as in Lucian or More, nor simply temporal, as in all the followers of *The Time Machine* and *When the Sleeper Wakes*, but spatiotemporal in a number of very interesting ways, all of which approximate a reinvention and putting to new uses of the precapitalist and preindividualistic analogic times and spaces of the human imagination.

The main difference with such medieval and pre-medieval conceptions could perhaps be expressed in terms of *destiny*. As Lotman remarks, literary functions can be divided into two groups, the active forces and the obstacles (239). Right down to Swift (in SF and in literature in general), the obstacles are inhuman and superhuman forces, at best to be ethically questioned by the tragic poet and hero but not to be materially influenced. Whether they are called gods, God, Destiny, Nature, or even History is relatively less important than the fact that they are transcendental, empirically unchangeable. The great enlightening deed of the bourgeoisie was to reduce the universe to individuals, which also meant identifying the obstacles with people, who are reachable and perhaps removable by other people. I would imagine that a truly modern literature (and SF), corresponding to our epoch, its *praxis* and *episteme*, would correspond to the third dialectical term to follow on such fatalistic collectivism and humanistic individualism. We have learned that the institutional and imaginative products of people – states, corporations, religions, wars, and the like – can very well become a destiny for each of us: tragedy is again possible in the twentieth century (as the October Revolution and Second World War, Dubček and Allende can teach us), though it is the tragedy of blindness – of failed historical possibilities – rather than of lucidity. The obstacles are superindividual but not inhuman; they have the grandeur of the ancient Destiny but they can be overcome by people banding together for the purpose. People together are the historical destiny of each person; the synthesis in this historical triad is a *humanistic collectivism*.

2.5

The alternate reality logically necessitated by and proceeding from the narrative kernel of the novum can only function in the oscillating feedback with the author's reality suggested in 2.2 because it is as a whole – or because some of its focal relationships are – an *analogy* to that empirical reality. However fantastic (in the sense of empirically unverifiable) the characters or worlds described, always *de nobis fabula narratur*. Though SF is not orthodox allegory, it transmits esthetic information in direct proportion to its relevance and esthetic quality. The alternative is for it to operate in semantic emptiness spiced with melodramatic sensationalism as a compensatory satisfaction, in a runaway feedback system with corrupt audience taste instead of with cognition of tendencies in the social practice of human relationships.[7] The clear dominance of that kitsch alternative in the

---

7   "The information gained, concerning a hypothesis, may perhaps be thought of as the ratio of the a posteriori to the a priori probabilities (strictly the logarithm of this ratio)" – Cherry 63. Thus, the information gained from a work of literature is a logarithmic (that is, alas, much diminished) ratio of the existential possibilities imaginable and understandable by an ideal reader after reading, to those imaginable and understandable before the reading. The information is a function of the rearrangement of the reader's understanding of "human relationships". "In general, where we speak of information, we should use the word form," argues Thom in his impressive *Stabilité*, 133.

present historical period should not, however, prevent us from discussing the significant models of SF, its horizons and yardsticks.

In *MOSF* I considered heuristic models of SF under the headings of 1) extrapolation, which starts from a cognitive hypothesis incarnated in the nucleus of the tale and directly extrapolates it into the future, and 2) analogy, in which cognition derives only from the final import or message of the tale, and may perhaps be only indirectly applicable to pressing problems in the author's environment. This analysis was, so far as it goes, useful in challenging the defining of all SF as extrapolation (to which the title of a critical journal devoted to SF still witnesses); but it does not go far enough. I also noted that any futurological function SF might have was strictly secondary, and that stressing it was dangerous since it tended to press upon SF the role of a popularizer of the reigning ideology of the day (technocratic, psionic, utopian, dystopian, hip, or whatever). Thus, although extrapolation was historically a convention of much SF (as analyzed at length in the second section of that book), pure extrapolation is flat as any quantity, and the pretense at it masks in all significant cases the employment of other methods. Theoretical defining of any SF as extrapolation should therefore be decently and deeply buried.[8] It seems clear that SF is material for futurology (if at all) only in the very restricted sense of reflecting on the author's own historical period and the possibilities inherent in it: Bellamy's and Morris's different socialist twenty-first centuries use the anticipation device so effectively because they are about incipient collective human relationships in the 1880s as they (differently) saw them, while *1984* or *2001* are about incipient collective human relationships in 1948 or 1967 as certain aspects of or elements within Orwell's or Kubrick's mind saw them.

Any significant SF text is thus always to be read as an analogy, somewhere between a vague symbol and a precisely aimed parable, while extrapolative SF in any futurological sense was (and is) only a delusion of

---

8   Wells knew this already in 1906, see chapter 10 of *MOSF* for his self-criticism. On the discussion of extrapolative, analogical, and other models for SF see also Philmus, both articles by Jameson – and now (2008) also my note "Goodbye to Extrapolation."

technocratic ideology – no doubt extremely important for the historical understanding of a given period of SF, but theoretically untenable. For extrapolation itself as a scientific procedure (and not pure arithmetic formalization) is predicated upon a strict – or, if you wish, crude – analogy between the points from and to which the extrapolating is carried out: *extrapolation is a one-dimensional, scientific limit-case of analogy*. As Peirce puts it, a scientific "effect" (or "phenomenon") "consists in the fact that when an experimentalist shall come to *act* according to a certain scheme that he has in mind, then will something else happen, and shatter the doubts of skeptics, like the celestial fire upon the altar of Elijah" (Peirce, para. 425, p. 284).

Specifically, the SF "future-story" has been well identified by Raymond Williams as "the finding and materialization of a formula about society. A particular pattern is abstracted, from the sum of social experience, and a society is created from this pattern [...] the 'future' device (usually only a device, for nearly always it is obviously contemporary society that is being written about [...]) removes the ordinary tension between the selected pattern and normal observation" (307). Clearly, neither is the future a quantitatively measurable space nor will the ensemble of human relationships stand still for one or more generations in order for a single element (or a very few elements) to be extrapolated against an unchanging background – which is the common invalidating premise of futurological as well as of openly fictional extrapolation. The future is always constituted both by a multiple crisscrossing of developments and – in human affairs – by intentions, desires, and beliefs rather than only by quantifiable facts. It is Peirce's scheme or Williams's pattern rather than the end-point of a line. Furthermore, anticipating the future of human societies and relationships is a pursuit that shows up the impossibility of using the orthodox – absolute or scientistic – philosophy of natural science as the model for human sciences. It is a pursuit which shows, first, that all science (including natural sciences) is and always has been a historical category, and second, that natural or "objective" and human (cultural) or "subjective" sciences are ultimately to be thought of as a unity: "Natural science will in time include the science of man as the science of man will include natural science. There will be one science" – remarked an acute if deviant observer already in the first part of the nineteenth century (Marx 312). As a corollary, the valid SF form or subgenre of anticipation – tales located in the historical future of the author's society – should be strictly differentiated from the technocratic ideology of extrapolation on the one hand and the literary device of extrapolation on the other. Extrapolating one feature or possibility of the author's environment may be a legitimate literary hyperbole equally in anticipation tales, other SF (for example, that located in space and not in the future) or indeed in a number of other genres such as satire. However, the cognitive value of all SF, including anticipation tales, is to be found in its analogical reference to the author's present rather than in predictions, discrete or global. Science-fictional cognition is based on an esthetic hypothesis akin to the proceedings of satire or pastoral rather than those of futurology or political programs.

The problem in constructing useful models for SF is, then, one of differentiating within analogy. If every SF tale is some kind of analogy – and I think that *The Time Machine* or *The Iron Heel*, Heinlein's *Future History* or Pohl–Kornbluth's *Space Merchants*, even Stapledon's *Last and First Men* or Yefremov's *Andromeda*, are primarily fairly clear analogies to processes incubating in their author's epoch – then just what is in each case the degree and the kind of its anamorphic distortion, its "version" of reality? How is their implied reader supposed to respond to and deal with a narrative reality that is an inverted, reverted, converted, everted, averted, subverted Other to his certainties of Self and Norm – certainties which, as Hegel says, are clouded by their very illusion of evidence and proximity, *bekannt* but not *erkannt* (28). A partially illuminating answer to this group of questions would also clear up why some of these versions pretend – sometimes with conviction, most often by pure convention – to be situated in an extrapolated future.

2.6

A final narrative consequence of the novum is that it shapes the SF "chronotope" (or chronotopes?). A chronotope is "the essential connection of temporal and spatial relationships, as shaped in literary art." In it, "the characteristics of time are unfolded in space, while space is given meaning and measured by time" (Bakhtin 234–35) – and both are blended into a particular plot structure. Now the novelty in SF can be either a new locus, or an agent (character) with new powers transforming the old locus, or a blend of both. The connection between the active forces (the protagonists) and the obstacles to be reduced (the locus) determines the homogeneity of a tale. If the protagonists and the loci necessarily imply and richly reinforce each other – as do Wells's Time Traveller and the sequence of his devolutionary visions of the future, or Le Guin's Shevek, his physics, and the binary planetary sociopolitics and psychology of *The Dispossessed*[9] – then we have a tale of a higher quality than the wish-dreams of, say, a Van Vogt, where all the obstacles are fake since the protagonist is a superman enforcing his will both on enemies and supposed allies.

As for plot structures, if SF is organized around an irreversible and significant change in its world and agents, then a simple addition of adventures, where *plus ça change plus c'est la même chose*, is an abuse of SF for purposes of trivial sensationalism, which degrades the genre to a simpler and less organized plot structure. Nudelman has to my mind brilliantly demonstrated the incompatibility of the plot structures of the cyclical detective tale, the conclusion of which returns the universe "to its equilibrium and order," the linear or additive adventure tale, and the spiral structures of valid SF, the plot of which alters the universe of the tale ("Approach" 240–50). On the contrary, the easiest narrative way of driving a significant change home is to have the hero or heroine grow into it (or better, to have the hero or heroine define it for the reader by growing with it), and much valid SF uses the plot structure of the "education novel," with its initially naive protagonist who by degrees arrives at some understanding of the novum for her/himself and for the readers.

As these two examples and other discussions in this chapter may indicate, it should be possible to engage in analytic evaluations of SF that would be neither purely ideological nor purely formalistic, by starting with the necessities of literary structure brought about by some variant of a novum.

9   *Addition 2008*: see now Chapter 18 of this book on *The Dispossessed*.

3. The Novum and History

3.1

The novum as a creative, and especially as an esthetic, category is not to be fully or even centrally explained by such formal aspects as innovation, surprise, reshaping, or estrangement, important and indispensable though these aspects or factors are.[10] The new is always a historical category since it is always determined by historical forces which both bring it about in social practice (including art) and make for new semantic meanings that crystallize the novum in human consciousnesses (see 1.1 and 2.2). An analysis of SF is necessarily faced with the question of why and how was the newness recognizable as newness at the moment it appeared, what ways of understanding, horizons, and interests were implicit in the novum and required for it. The novelty is sometimes directly but sometimes in very complex ways (for example, not merely as reflection but also as prefiguration or negation) related to such new historical forces and patterns – in the final instance, to possibilities of qualitative discontinuity in the development of human relationships. An esthetic novum is either a translation of historical cognition and ethics into form, or (in our age perhaps more often) a creation of historical cognition and ethics as form.

3.2

Probably the most important consequence of an understanding of SF as a symbolic system centered on a novum, which is to be cognitively validated within the narrative reality of the tale and its interaction with reader expectations, is that the novelty has to be convincingly explained in concrete,

10　For development of estrangement and similar notions after the Formalists and Brecht, see Jauss, as well as critiques of and improvements on Jauss handily assembled in Hohendahl ed.

even if imaginary, terms – that is, in terms of the *specific* time, place, agents, and cosmic and social totality of each tale. This means that, in principle, SF has to be judged, like most naturalistic or "realistic" fiction and quite unlike horror Fantasy, by the density and richness of objects and agents described in the microcosm of the text. Another way of interpreting Philmus's distinction from 1.2 would be to set up a further Hegelian triad, where the thesis would be naturalistic fiction, which has an empirically validated effect of reality, the antithesis would be ahistorical genres, which lack such an effect, and the synthesis would be SF, in which the effect or reality is validated by a cognitive innovation. Obversely, the particular essential novum of any SF tale must in its turn be judged by how much new insight into imaginary but coherent and this-worldly, that is, *historical*, relationships it affords and could afford.

3.3

In view of this doubly historical character of the SF novum – born in history and judged in history – this novum has to be differentiated not only according to its degree of magnitude and of cognitive validation (see 1.1. and 1.2.), but also according to its *degree of relevance*. What is *possible* should be differentiated not only from what is already real but also from what's equally empirically unreal but axiologically *necessary*. Not all possible novelties will be equally relevant, or of equally lasting relevance, from the point of view of, first, human development, and second, a positive human development. Obviously, this categorization implies, first, that there are some lawlike tendencies in people's social and cosmic history, and second, that we can today (if we are intelligent and lucky enough) judge these tendencies as parts of a spectrum that runs from positive to negative. I subscribe to both these propositions and will not argue them here – partly for rhetorical brevity, but mainly because I cannot think of any halfway significant SF narration that does not in some way subscribe to them in its narrative practice (whatever the author's private theories may be).

Thus a novum can be both superficially sweeping and cognitively validated as not impossible, and yet of very limited or brief relevance.

Its relationship to a relevant novelty will be the same as the relationship
of the yearly pseudo-novum of "new and improved" (when not "revolutionary") car models or clothing fashions to a really radical novelty such
as a social revolution and change of scientific paradigm, making, say, for
life-enhancing transport or dressing. The pseudo-novum will not have
the vitality of a tree, an animal species, or a belief but, to quote Bergson,
the explosive, spurting *élan* of a howitzer shell exploding into successively
smaller fragments, or "of an immense fireworks, which continually emits
further fire-sparks from its midst."[11] In brief, a novum is fake unless it in
some way participates in and partakes of what Bloch called the "front-line
of historical process" – which for him (and for me) as a Marxist means a
process intimately concerned with strivings for a disalienation of people
and their social life. Capricious contingencies, consequent upon market
competition and tied to copyright or patent law, have a built-in limit and
taboo defined precisely by the untouchable sanctity of competition (a
palpable ideology in much SF). Of brief and narrow relevance, particular rather than general (*kath'hekaston* rather than *kath'holon*, as Aristotle
puts it in *Poetics*), they make for a superficial change rather than for a true
novelty that deals with or makes for human relationships so qualitatively
different from those dominant in the author's reality that they cannot be
translated back to them merely by a change of costume. All space operas
can be translated back into the Social Darwinism of the Westerns and
similar adventure-tales by substituting colts for ray-guns and Indians for
the slimy monsters of Betelgeuse. Most novels by Asimov can be returned
to their detective-story model by a slightly more complex system of sub-
stitutions, by which, for example, Second Foundation came from Poe's
Purloined Letter.

11   Bergson, 99 and 270; see also Bloch's comment on him in *Das Prinzip* 231 – my whole
      argument in 3.1–3.4. is fundamentally indebted to Bloch. See on originality within
      a capitalist market also Brecht passim – for example, 15:199–200 – and Adorno 257
      ff.

3.4

Since freedom is the possibility of something new and truly different coming
about, "the possibility of making it different," the distinction between a true
and fake novum is, interestingly enough, not only a key to esthetic quality in SF but also to its ethico-political liberating qualities, its communal
relevance.[12] Finally, the only consistent novelty is one that constitutes an
open-ended system "which possesses its novum continually both in itself
and before itself; as befits the unfinished state of the world, nowhere determined by any transcendental supraworldly formula" (Bloch, *Experimentum*
143). This connects with my argument in 1.3 about validation for SF being
based on science as an open-ended corpus of knowledge, which argument
can now be seen to be ultimately and solidly anchored to the bedrock fact
that there is no end to history, and in particular that we and our ideologies are not the end-product history has been laboring for from the time
of the first saber-toothed tigers and Mesopotamian city-states. It follows
that SF will be the more significant and truly relevant the more clearly it
eschews final solutions, be they the static utopia of the Plato–More model,
the more fashionable static dystopia of the Huxley–Orwell model, or any
similar metamorphosis of the *Apocalypse* (let us remember that the end of
time in the *Apocalypse* encompasses not only the ultimate chaos but also
the ultimate divine order).[13]

3.5

An imaginary history each time to be reimagined afresh in its human
significance and values may perhaps borrow some narrative patterns from
mythological tales, but the "novelty" of gods validated by unexplained

12   Bloch, *Experimentum* 139; see also Gramsci, *Il Materialismo storico e la filosofia di
      Benedetto Croce*, quoted from *Selections* 360, to whom I am also much indebted.
13   I have attempted to expand on this in my "Open-Ended"; it is incorporated into a
      parallel to the orthodox Soviet and US SF models in my "Stanislaw Lem." Both are
      now available as Chapter 8 of my *Positions*.

supersciences at the beck and call of the Cambridge School's or von Däniken's supermortals is a pseudo-novelty, old meat rehashed with a new sauce. SF's analogical historicity may or may not be mythomorphic, but – as I have argued in *MOSF* – it cannot be mythopoetic in any sense except the most trivial one of possessing "a vast sweep" or "a sense if wonder": another superannuated slogan of much SF criticism due for a deserved retirement into the same limbo as extrapolation. For myth is re-enactment, eternal return, and the opposite of creative human freedom.

True, even after one subtracts the more or less supernatural tales (science-fantasy, sword-and-sorcery, and the like), 90 percent of SF will have plot structures escaping from history into Westerns, additive sensationalist adventures, or rehashes of mythography. However, as Kant said, a thousand years of any given state of affairs do not make that state necessarily right. Rather, reasons for the wrongness should be sought.

3.6

Thus this analysis has finally arrived at the point where history, in the guise of analogical historicity, is found to be the next and crucial step in the understanding of SF: story is always also history, and SF is always also a certain type of imaginative historical tale (which could be usefully compared and contrasted to the historical novel). All the epistemological, ideological, and narrative implications and correlatives of the novum lead to the conclusion that significant SF is in fact a specifically roundabout way of commenting on the author's collective context – often resulting in a surprisingly concrete and sharp-sighted comment at that. Even where SF suggests – sometimes strongly – a flight from that context, this is an optical illusion and epistemological trick. The escape is, in all such significant SF, one to a better vantage point from which to comprehend the human relations around the author. It is an escape from constrictive old norms into a different and alternative time-stream, a device for historical estrangement, and an at least initial readiness for new norms of reality, for the novum of disalienating human history. I believe that the critic, in order to understand it properly, will have to integrate sociohistorical into formal knowledge, diachrony into synchrony. History has not ended with the "post-industrial" society: as Bloch said, Judgment Day is also Genesis, and Genesis is every day.

Works Cited

Adorno, Theodor W. *Aesthetische Theorie*. Frankfurt: Suhrkamp, 1970.

Amis, Kingsley. *New Maps of Hell*. New York: Harcourt Brace, 1975.

Atheling, William, Jr [pseud. of James Blish]. *More Issues at Hand: Critical Studies in Contemporary Science Fiction*. Chicago: Advent, 1970.

Bailey, J.O. *Pilgrims Through Space and Time: Trends in Scientific and Utopian Fiction*. Westport: Greenwood Press, 1972.

Bakhtin, M[ikhail] M. *Voprosy literatury i èstetiki*. Moscow: Khudozhestvennaja literatura, 1975.

Bergson, Henri. *L'évolution creatrice*. Paris: Alcan, 1907.

Bloch, Ernst. *Experimentum Mundi*. Frankfurt: Suhrkamp, 1976.

——. *Das Prinzip Hoffnung*, 2 Vols. Frankfurt: Suhrkamp, 1959.

Brecht, Bertolt. *Gesammelte Werke*. 20 Vols. Frankfurt: Suhrkamp, 1973.

Cherry, Colin. *On Human Communication*. Cambridge, MA: MIT Press, 1966.

Foht, Ivan. "Slika čovjeka i kosmosa." *Radio Beograd: Treći program* 2 (Spring 1974): 523–60.

Gramsci, Antonio. *Selections from the Prison Notebooks*. Trans. and ed. Quintin Hoare and Geoffrey Nowell Smith. New York: International Publishers, 1971.

Hegel, Georg W.F. *Phänomenologie des Geistes. Sämtliche Werke*. Vol. 2. Leipzig: Meiner, 1949.

Hohendahl, Peter Uwe (ed.). *Sozialgeschichte und Wirkungsästhetik*. Frankfurt: Athenäum, 1974.

Jameson, Fredric. "Generic Discontinuities in SF." *Science-Fiction Studies: Selected Articles in Science Fiction 1973–1975*. Ed. R.D. Mullen and Darko Suvin. Boston: Gregg, 1976. 28–39.

——. "World Reduction in Le Guin: The Emergence of Utopian Narrative." *Science-Fiction Studies: Selected Articles in Science Fiction 1973–1975.* Ed. R.D. Mullen and Darko Suvin. Boston: Gregg, 1976. 251–60.

Jauss, Hans Robert. *Literaturgeschichte als Provokation.* Frankfurt: Suhrkamp, 1970.

Lem, Stanisław. *Fantastyka i futurologia.* 2 vols. Krakow: Wydawnictwo Literackie, 1973.

Lotman, Jurij. *The Structure of the Artistic Text.* Trans. Ronald Vroon. Michigan Slavic Contributions, 7. Ann Arbor: University of Michigan Press, 1977.

Lukács, Georg. *History and Class Consciousness: Studies in Marxist Dialectics.* Trans. Rodney Livingstone. London: Merlin, 1971.

Marx, Karl. "Private Property and Communism." *Writings of the Young Marx on Philosophy and Society.* Ed. and trans. Loyd D. Easton and Kurt H. Guddat. Garden City, NY: Doubleday, 1967.

Mumford, Lewis. *Technics and Civilization.* New York: Harcourt, Brace and Co., 1963.

Nudelman, Rafail. "An Approach to the Structure of Le Guin's SF." Trans. Alan G. Myers, *Science-Fiction Studies: Selected Articles in Science Fiction 1973–1975.* Ed. R.D. Mullen and Darko Suvin. Boston: Gregg, 1976. 240–50.

——. "Conversation in a Railway Compartment." Trans. Daniel Scoones. *Science-Fiction Studies* 5 (1978).

Peirce, Charles S. "What Pragmatism Is." *Collected Papers.* Ed. Charles Hartshorne and Paul Weiss. Cambridge, MA: Harvard University Press, 1934.

Philmus, Robert M. "Science Fiction: From its Beginning to 1870." *Anatomy of Wonder: Science Fiction.* Ed. Neil Barron. New York: Bowker Company, 1976.

Russ, Joanna. "Towards an Aesthetic of Science Fiction." *Science-Fiction Studies: Selected Articles in Science Fiction 1973–1975.* Ed. R.D. Mullen and Darko Suvin. Boston: Gregg, 1976. 8–15.

Simmel, Georg. *Philosophie des Geldes.* München: Duncker & Humblot, 1930.

Sombart, Werner. *Der Moderne Kapitalismus*. 3 vols. München: Duncker & Humblot, 1917.

Suvin, Darko. "Beckett's Purgatory of the Individual." *Tulane Drama Review* 11.4 (1967): 23–36.

——. "Considering the Sense of 'Fantasy' or 'Fantastic Fiction.'" *Extrapolation* 41.3 (2000): 209–47.

——. "Goodbye to Extrapolation." *Science-Fiction Studies* 22.2 (1995): 301.

——. "On Individualist World View in Drama." *Zagadnienia rodzajów literackih* 9.1 (1966).

——. "On the Horizons of Epistemology and Science." (forthcoming in *Critical Quarterly*).

——. "The Open-Ended Parables of Stanislaw Lem and *Solaris*." Afterword. *Solaris*. Stanislaw Lem. New York: Walker, 1976.

——. *Positions and Presuppositions in Science Fiction*. London: Macmillan, and Kent: Kent State University Press, 1988.

——. "Stanislaw Lem und das mitteleuropäische soziale Bewusstsein der Science Fiction." *Stanislaw Lem. Der dialektische Weise aus Krakow*. Ed. Werner Berthel. Frankfurt: Insel Verlag, 1976. 157–71.

Thom, René. *Stabilité structurelle et morphogénèse*. Reading: Benjamin, 1972.

Trzynadlowski, Jan. "Próba poetyki science fiction." *Z teorii i historii literatury*. Ed. K. Budzyk. Warsaw, 1963.

Williams, Raymond. *The Long Revolution*. Harmondsworth: Penguin, 1971.

Poems of Doubt and Hope 1983–1988

Part 1. Twelve Diary Poems of the Mid-1980s

Shipwreck in Pannonia: A Sonnet with a Tail

— To the unquiet shade of M. Krleža —
Auf die Schiffe! (Nietzsche)
Quis mundis plaga? (Seneca)

Obese car wreckers, stressful owners of private weekend-houses,
Obscene shore-polluting yachts or leaky rowing boats,
Petty managers, at best hunters of sexual game, comrades of my
Generation are dying out one by one. Now to be or not

Is perhaps neither good nor bad, the neutral fleet of
Old admiral death weighs anchor towards unfathomed oceans;
Yet the failure to obstinately sail with one's tribe into the dawn
It had set its heart on, sea by unknown sea, preempts even

The excuse of unmapped eternity. These heroes of one decade
Went thru war, suffered greatly, tried to turn suffering
Into charting of ocean floors: fat clogged the generous arteries

& delicate capillaries halfway, they never became truly
What they suffered for, explorers & dredgers in permanent warm
Currents, a permanently creative revolution. Heart arrest,

Brain stroke, defeats without from defects within, the malignant
Cells of fratricide spreading, shipwrecked in Pannonia all of us again,

No excuse, desolation.

Jugendbewegung

To GT

Niké, o Victory from Sarmatia to the Alps!
How many times beheaded, driven
Under ground, lost sight of, given
Up for lost! How many heads ground to pulp,

Bodies cut up into shuddering flesh, icepick
Wedged into Trotsky's brain, flies sup=
Ping in Che, bulldozers scooping up
Bladefuls of skinny bones like kindlewood sticks

Not only in Belsen. Worse still, the dulled
Fattening face, faithless excuses, bold
A-whoring after false gods! –
                              Yet i behold
Thy absent face on the red-haired girl, jacket full

Of leaflets for the whores in Old Zurich Town:
& i hear the mighty wings a-swooping down.

Eightie-Foure is Icummen In: Lhude Sing Goddam!
Or: 1948–1984–2048

Poor Eric, all eaten up with TB & hate
At the hypocrisies of Airstrip Number One, the skull
Of Oceania grinning underneath the Victorian musty
England, my England, your England of the upper-class
Terror from public school to Burma; poor George,
Paying homage to bluff common-sense England in Catalonia,
Looking at us smelly animals who are all unequal, but some
More than others; poor Orwell/Blair, reaching for the granddad
Of all us satirists, rationally absurd Jonathan, to flesh
Out cool Evgeniy, invert the bounder Bertie Wells; fashioning
Out of his pain, rage & dead despair a finally – we must admit –
Bad book, more important than a score of Jameses on ladies
(Or flower-girls) leaving the shopping mall at five; supplying –
Mediocre language stylist, insular politician, memorable
Politician of the English language – our century with its
Small change in slogans, alas still with us in these 80s:
War is Peace. Slavery is Freedom. Bigotry is Strength.
Yet in spite of Eric, at the end of George's 1984
There falls the shadow of the huge Prole woman. Brecht
Would see there the proletarian Mother, Mother of those to come
After Eric, after us, **der Nachgeborenen**: not 1848, not 1948 –

Just wait, 2048 is still to be.
(But i shall not live to taste the tea-scented sea.)

Rebellions

It just got thru to me, i'll die
Much too soon.
The universe is full of indignities, stacked
Against us.
How is it that even in dreams, my mind's eye
Can't see you,
A faint record only remains, like Callas's
Casta Diva?
Make that why.

The Two Fishes: An Amphibian Fable

> Dies septima nos ipsi erimus.
> Augustine of Hippo

Two fish flop in the dry river-bed.
Heroically, they bounced across the rough shallows.
One gasps. Too late he is sorry for
His mistake. Now he wants to slide back
& warn all the other fishes.
The other flops on. Almost dead.

Suddenly, her fins bite soil. They are claws.

Parliament Of Foules

To Vanna Gentili, for *La Recita della follia*

Fierce-clawed eagles tear down entire cities
Of swallows' nests; large-beaked crows peck out
Eyes of hens & ducks; neither swallows nor hens
Know whence the strike, how to guard against it.

The wise owls, stuffed to their fill & so stuffy
With comfort esoteric, compute the elegant curves
Of eagle & crow flight, the nesting mechanics,
The protein content of eyes like oysters.

The unique phoenix, redeemer of our bird kingdom
Has disappeared for this generation, far behind eastern
Seas. Parrot, parrot, you who have sharp ears, beady eyes,
Quick brain, clever tongue, O fool, why don't you
Call him aloud, how can you bear the bore
To simply sit there chattering to yourself?

A Letter to my Friend, Disenchanted After 1968

To know the perfect horizon without knowing the misery
Within one's own mind is a peril you have avoided. Well
& good: i rejoice for you, my sister. Yet
It is equally perilous to know one's misery & forget
The moving horizon of classless harmonies. The first dearth
Engendered rigidity, lack of sympathy, a monotone
Fixation on militant monoliths; you have rightly
Rejected this mirage, no longer working. The second dearth
Engenders formlessness, forgets the aim, our common focus,

Expends the energy in a waste of divergent driblets:
Will your cool intelligence refuse it as resolutely?
The former forever runs to a father for light & shelter,
The latter refuses to be a parent for coming generations.
I beg you, therefore, after the hard monster
                                  avoid also the soft one:
Let the doctrine of our fathers reincarnate in you as a mother,
Let the pursuit of truth be your just light & warm shelter.

Three Commentaries on *The Way and the Power*

1. STRAW DOGS

First the straw dogs are carefully lined up in a basket
Swaddled in precious needlepoint clothes.
He who plays the dead person & those that invoke it
Fast before being allowed to handle them.
Then the dogs are offered in sacrifice.
                                The passers-by
Begin kicking them on their heads & their backs.
Finally they are swept up by the gleaners of dead branches
& thrown on a heap to feed the fire.

Myriads of beings walk under the unblinking heavens
If there's to be any concern, it has to come from us being them.

2. PEASANT DIALECTICS

The Way has the homogeneous wholeness of the formless
When the formless is formulated, delimited terms appear.
The way that merits to be called the Way
Is & is not a fixed way.
The terms that are truly naming Terms
Are & are not fixed terms.
The term of Non-Being stands for the male origin

Its time is before, between & after.
The term of Being stands for the female source
Its presence is the myriad sensual bodies.
Only when Non-Being penetrates Being
Can space become the place of growth.
The sustained interplay of Non-Being & Being
Sees prodigies arising from the see-saw between both.
To recognize Goodness is to establish evil
To recognize Beauty is to admit ugliness.
Since terms needs must be, the Sage has to get hold of them
He who knows what stance to take will not be harmed.

3. A STRONG VISION

There is no norm for normality
What is today normal is tomorrow strange
What is here sinister is there right
But truly, people are blinded for too long.

Some matters that are now small
Are baby figures of masses to be.
Some motions that are now weak
Are baby muscles of giants to come.

To perceive those small matters
Means to have vision.
To stick to those weak motions
Means to be strong.

After the Fall

> Infandum, regina, iubes renovare dolorem.
> — VIRGIL, *Aeneid*

You command me, O princess, here in a strange climate,
White-haired, sick at heart, eyes wet with tears,
To renew bittersweet memories of the old times & places:
Bear Mountain & the city along Mud River, now
Filled with children speaking a foreign tongue
(To my ears no language); in Phoenix Park now
The untended high trunks gnarled entrap the bright new
Moon; the Upper Palace stands dreary in the dusk,
Broken tiles on its long fading roofs thick with red
Leaves, crumbling walls covered with heavy moss.

I first entered the Theatre Academy in Mahzhong Park
Before the Ma Po revolt. I was adept at reading old scores
& spent satisfying years in the capital, debating
Fine points of musical doctrine, that pillar of the state.
At that time, the reign was peaceful, stable, growing
More prosperous. Each Fall, audiences crowded into
The Lower Palace, officials rode busily by, from afar
Embassies arrived to hear us making music, women wore
Their hair long & ogled us as they fanned themselves;
Thru Winter snows & Spring winds, the rounds of pleasure

In great halls went on long into the white nights. Yet
The enemy was menacing us all the time; but the enemy
(Now i see) was within us by some unknown flaw, & erupted
Suddenly into the city streets & squares, filling the air
With the sounds of tribal gutturals & expletives;
The Emperor was forced to give way, the beloved beauty,
Our patroness, sacrificed to appease the army, a life-

Style changed like a hairpin river, a horizon winked out
Like the setting sun; our music suddenly found only deaf ears,
The theatre of the world closed in on our too little theatre.

Since then, O princess, i have wandered over the whole Earth.
Now, in my exile, i am one of the very few to remember it all,
The dreams, the hopes, the warm nights, the airs, the taste
Of that youthful moment. I gaze over the waters of your river
In the Autumn mist, i drink a glass of mulled wine
On a lone boat in the evening rain; i am a dried fish
Long out of water, a stalk of withered reed:
I who once basked in the sun of the capital city
& made confident music in its parks & palaces,
At the center of imperial horizons.
                                    Once a year
I am permitted back to sweep the ancestral graves;
A eunuch comes to make offerings for the dead:
Straw dogs, paper money, cold food.

Song of the Insufficiency of Human Endeavours in Late Capitalism and Early Socialism

> Judgment Day is also Genesis, and Genesis is every day.
> — ERNST BLOCH

> Today is the first day of the rest of your life.
> — ANON.

I have said so little
I have done so little
I have been too polite with shifty movers
Too lukewarm with dolphins & lovers

The swift river flows
It freezes for the Day of Judgment

& yet i had seen the world's body burst in terror
Melt, reshape, & get wound up as galvanized error
Screaming in jets rocking round the clock
Lurching Shiva-like along time's spiral stairs
Reproducing pale babies clutching at the lacking air

You understand
The mirror of your eyes my Judgment

& yet sometimes i was gladly beguiled
By a woman walking in the sun with dreamy smile
Or i looked up from words that a book unwound
With tears in my eyes when Luna was like to a pearl
Wondering at the suppressed tenderness of the world

The swift river flows
The mirror of your eyes my Judgment

I have given too much in to feeling virtuous & blue
I should have been more pious toward the messy New
I should have understood that people & planets are brittle
Bathed by the sardonic Moon, warmed in the Sun's tresses
I should have steeled myself to more tender caresses

You understand
Now & in the day of our past Judgment

One-Legged Life (Intimate Dialogue with a Crane)

– An eagle swoops on a chick, ripping it open.
Crows & hawks fight over a limp goose. Sparrows
Struggle to find a crumb to eat, a nesting place.
You, however, stand on a tree or the water's edge
      Thru sleet & rain (O crane)

With one leg raised, meditating, not moving; aloof,
Loafing, pale, impractical. How, pray, do you justify
Such bathetic, unperipatetic, theoretical, intellectual=
Izing behaviour? – Indeed, our flesh & fowl society
      Is built on pain (quoth the crane),

Cruelly it crushes life; only few, by chance,
Gain time for standing still on the ice or
Atop a high pine, looking for a firm branch
Or ledge to grasp. Who would not like to see
      Sparrows fed, crows

Exterminated, hawks & jackdaws retrained, geese
Educated? Neither do i believe this to be impossible,
The nature of birds & men is malleable; nor
That it's none of my business, work for cranes
      Too vulgar & low:

All birds are kin, & i am my brother's keeper.
A good half of my life, persecuted myself, i flocked
Together with a multitude of feathers, sparrows
Or swallows, attempting to found a Republic of Birds
      Free to fly without fear

Everywhere, even to the Sun where Cyrano found us
Triumphant. Alas, the wily crows were too many, the eagles

Treacherous, for my generation the Great Creativity
Was brought low in a welter of blood & lies.
        How am i then to bear,

What should i do with the rest of this only life?
It is my deep delight to stand on one leg & meditate:
To wake up, go to sleep with a warm, moving vision
Is act erotic. If i then theorize so as to herd
        Into a conceptual net

A squirming bit of how the defeat felt, what
Its experience, its efficient & final cause,
Perhaps even meaning; if i then, a minor Galileo,
Give what lens i managed to grind for others' use;
        I must hope, i must bet

The Great Creativity will not find this behaviour
Entirely useless. & that this is enough
        For one life, on one leg.

Disputing Sōgyō

even the greatest truth
may grow into skyward wall
hiding all fireflies

or i may climb up
atop the great wall-tower
to see the fireflies

or i may grow up
playing on the great tower
amid all these fireflies.

Part 2. Visions Off Yamada (1988)

— FOR YK —

In Yamada on the coast a mirage can be seen every year. It is said that
it is usually the scenery of a foreign country: an unknown capital with
many carriages in the streets & people coming & going. It's quite amaz-
ing. From year to year, the shapes of the houses & other things don't
change in the least.

— YANAGITA KUNIO, *Tōno monogatari*

1. In Praise of a Wonderful Sight

Come see this bridge.
How can we build it?
Cross it this way & that?
Get there, across the bridge?

***

Come see this main gate.
It is made of solid red wood
It is an auspicious wide gate

Push open the doors, look:
What a wonderful age,
There, behind the straight gate!

I wish i could come
See & push open the gate,
Enter the wonderful age.

***

Come see the spacious houses
Of the people, for the people
Built by skilled carpenters

For themselves, by their own hands,
Own designs. They do not have to kill,
Choke off food, air, water, eat

Up brain synapses so as
To live: they vie to interpret
Their enterprise – yours & mine!

     ***

The curving roofs look like wood bark
Karamatsu pines grow above
Springs flow non-acid to the left & the right
Scoop it up & drink, the water never fails.
Come see the great Hall of the Commune
Morning & evening sunshine on that temple
A hundred rosy-cheeked children run into it,
Run out of it, like water down the mountain,

Bubbling, falling, going on.

     ***

Come see my own home
In that wonderful age.

Now, I rent a too crowded apartment.
Then, it's the house of a kind-hearted person.

Here, all my children are arranged words.
There, they are also bodies, blended with yours.

2. Choosing the Stag's Wife

As soon as it's born, the fawn runs about the hills
    We too go around, run about the park.
Try to gaze around attentive, find a doe
    But heavy smog hides all mountain tops.
O happy we! The cruel wind has blown off the smog
    We are off in search of the doe.

Let us celebrate the Siberian wind, sweet rain,
    Let's gather & drink warm rice-wine
Let us worship the twohundredandtenth day,
    October, the stormiest month of the year.
Which direction shall we salute? Salute the North!
    The North Wind wins over the polluted mist.

Now we have made a barn for the doe
    We cut **kikyô** flowers & morning grass
The barn is bright with the beauty of flowers
    Of course, it took so long to furnish it!
Wherever the doe hides, i'll search all the ways
    I'll walk on roads & thru waving grasses:

Like bamboo stems, tall & appetizing, wherever
    She hides, the pretty doe will be found.
Look at the doe & stag, their bodies lusty,
    Their hearts full of tender affection
They need to hurry together, browse together,
    Sleep together, have offspring, in a brief world.

Deep in the mountain passes a stag dances
    Still burning with passion for the doe.
Look at the pines up the slope, the silly ivy
    Clings to the pine; without good luck

The ivy leaves will fall off the pine. In the park
    We are planting another pillar
The stag may rub his antlers, grow young. Out at sea,
    The plover sways with the waves,
Cries, in the end flies smoothly off. Let us dream
    A Spring not far behind.

3. Where the Waves Meet

When i hear a good singer in this gathering
I'm ashamed to dance & sing.
I learned yesterday what i give you today
Please be kind   forgive the mistakes.

The flowered mats with their fine designs
Let's bring them to this gathering
The silver-lacquered rice-wine set
Let's drink from it to this gathering.

The Queen of May pours **sake** herself
The gathering brightens with joy
Drink a cup of this wine from the celadon set
Believe that we can all live well.

The King of October roasts the **yakitori** himself
With the wine goes also sea-bream,
Mountain trout, swordfish cut into steaks,
Tuna from the wave off Kanagawa.

To begin the banqueting, somebody sing!
To say my song is good
Is impossible. Who will come to hear
This well-wishing song? Everyone is welcome!

What carpenter made this stand?
It is solid, a treasure is inside.
What wine do you think this is?
It's **kiku no sake** from the famous fields.

Where does this rice-paper come from?
From Harima? From Kashima?
Never mind, it folds well,
It's good paper, you can read from it.

Which is the spot that holds the fan together?
It's **uchi no miya**, the pivot point
It folds well, snaps closed ready for use.
Friends, let us bow deep & be going.

4.

That's all there is to the story.

(If only life were not a crystal.)

NOTE: This poem has been catalyzed by Yanagita's famous collection of Japanese folklore cited in the epigraph; many lines are pieced together from Yanagita's stories and poems, with small alterations but against a different horizon. "Yakitori" = chicken brochette; "kiku no sake" = special rice wine with chrysanthemum leaves; "That's all there is to the story" (Kore de dondo hare) = the obligatory ending to any Japanese folktale (but in the poem it is not the ending).

Locus, Horizon, and Orientation: The Concept of Possible Worlds as a Key to Utopian Studies (1989)[1]

To the memory of Ernst Bloch

The truth is not in the beginning but in the end, or better in the continuation.

— LENIN, *Philosophical Notebooks*

1. The Pragmatics of Utopian Studies

1.1

Pragmatics has been much neglected in literary and cultural studies. In the semiotic sense in which I am using it, it was defined already by Charles Morris as the domain of relationships between the signs and their interpreters, which clarifies the conditions under which something is taken as a sign. From Peirce, G.H. Mead, and Bühler, through Bakhtin/Vološinov, Morris, Carnap, and the Warsaw School, to (say) Richard M. Martin, Léo Apostel, and John R. Searle, pragmatics has slowly been growing into an independent discipline on a par with syntactics (the domain of relationships between the signs and their formally possible combinations) and with semantics (in this sense, the domain of relations between the signs

---

1   All translations in the text, unless otherwise indicated, are mine.

and the entities they designate). But what is more, there are since the late 1950s strong arguments that it is constitutive of and indeed overarches both semantics and syntactics. The basic – and to any materialist sufficient – pair of arguments for it is, first, that all existents and events are (only or also) signs and, second, that any object or event becomes a sign only in a signifying situation; it has no "natural" meaning outside of it (e.g., in More's *Utopia* gold is a sign of shame). This situation is constituted by the relation between signs and their users; a user can take something to be a sign only as it is spatio-temporally concrete and localized, and as it relates to the user's disposition toward potential action. Both the concrete localization and the user's disposition are always socio-historical. Furthermore, they postulate a reality organized not only around signs but also around subjects, in the double sense of psychophysical personality and of a socialized, collectively representative subject. The entry of potentially acting subjects reintroduces acceptance and choice, temporal genesis and mutation, and a possibility of dialectical negation into the frozen constraints of syntax (in fact, by the most orthodox Structuralist standards, only such dynamics can make the – temporary – stability of any structure meaningful). It also re-grounds semantics: each and every semantic presupposition is also a pragmatic one, effected by a subject – atomic or collective – as a choice in a sociohistorical signifying situation.

Thus, pragmatics could also be taken as the mediation between semiotics and an even more general theory of action or practice. Only pragmatics is able to take into account the situation of the sign producers and its social addressees and the whole spread of their relationships within given cognitive (epistemological and ideological) presuppositions, conventions, economical and institutional frames, etc. The pragmatic presuppositions about the signs' possible uses by their users, as argued above, necessarily inscribe historical reality – as understood by the users – between the lines of any text.

In this semiotic perspective, "text" is understood in the widest sense of an articulated and recordable signifying micro-system, of a coherent unit of signic work. Any spatio-temporal organization which can stand still for such a recording – e.g., any verbal or graphic description of a utopian colony – qualifies for this sense of "text"; and in fact semiotics began with ancient medicine taking the body for its text or ensemble of signs (signifying health or various sicknesses). Yet there are problems if this imperialistic sense of text is absolutized: against the deconstructionists, I believe that bodies and objects (and subjects) are not only texts, for I don't see how a text can experience loss, delight, or indeed death. In other words, organic and inorganic molecules may be no more or less material than signs, but they are material in different ways from signs. Thus, even if the sciences are, no doubt, texts (though not purely verbal ones), the book of science is also – for all its partial autonomy – an interpretation of the book of nature, which is the presupposition of all scientific propositions. Furthermore, what exactly are the pertinent categories which constitute any object of investigation (in the widest sense, including a whole discipline) in the first place? This delimitation, which constitutes not only the cognizable domain but also the possible ways of envisaging and cognizing it, cannot be established from the object alone but only from its interaction with the social subject whose pragmatic point of view or approach is defining the pertinence, and by that token constructing the object's cognitive identity (though not necessarily the extra-signic pre-existence of the object's elements etc.).

1.2

Now in the light of such an approach (for which see further Suvin, "Can People?"), what is the first pragmatic fact about utopian scholarship? Let me take as emblematic the situation in North America, which also has undoubtedly the largest number of scholars and investigations in the "utopian" field (Italy and West Germany probably coming a close second), who meet regularly at national or international conferences, often publish in the same organs, etc. The central fact about their activities, it seems to me, is that they encompass what is at a first glance two rather different foci and scholarly corpuses, namely utopian fictional texts and utopian movements and communities. While it is undeniable that there are certain overlaps between these two corpuses, mediated by imaginary projects and attitudes related to a fictional imagination but intended to be the basis or seed for empirical construction of a micro- or macro-society, the corpuses are usually subjects of different disciplines and rather different methodologies and discourses. In one case, literary and textual approaches are mandatory, in the other a spectrum of approaches about which I am too ignorant to pontificate – sociological, geographical, etc. Again, it should not be denied that psychology can be applied to authors of both corpuses, that philosophy is applicable to the first principles of anything, that everything happens within given social and political histories, etc. Thus, it is not only semioticians who can and do claim that their discipline can explain – at least an important aspect of – anything and everything: philosophers, historians, etc., have just as good a claim to mediate (indeed, it is my stance that unless semiotics is informed by philosophy and social history – as in a number of Italian scholars – it remains at best a sterile and at worst a dubious syntax – as in most Parisian versions). Nonetheless, for all the existing and welcome mediations, I hope not to encounter too much resistance if I note that, for all the partial overlap in corpuses and for all the possibilities of fertile cross-pollination between approaches to them, there are still two distinct "wings" to "Utopian Studies", which I shall in a simplified manner call *the literary (or fictional)* and *the sociological (or factual)*.

This could be well documented by a glance at the agendas of various conferences on utopia/s, but I shall here substantiate it only with help of the *Directory of Utopian Scholars*, edited by the meritorious pioneer of our field, Dr Arthur O. Lewis, and used in its May 1986 edition. It contains 349 names of scholars (of which 62 from outside North America) with a brief self-characterization of "Utopian Interests" and "Related Interests." Striving for a loyal interpretation of these interests, I find that they substantiate my above impression, for they are best divided into three large groups. The two opposed poles are a dominant interest in empirical utopian communities and movements vs. a dominant interest in fictional utopias. By my imperfect count (since the interests are not always clearly spelled out) the "empirical" pole accounts for ca. 45 percent and the "fictional" pole for ca. 33 percent of the entries. In between them is a dominant interest in utopian philosophy and thought which accounts for ca. 20 percent (while 1–2 percent of the entries do not permit identification). Now I will readily concede not only that my interpretation of the scholars' interests may well not be final, but furthermore that for other purposes other groupings could be just as legitimate. Nonetheless, I find that the "empirical" group is professionally mainly in social science departments or indeed in political or social agencies outside of universities, with a few geographers, architects or art historians as well as a few teachers of religion and of literature or natural sciences who are breaking out of the discipline boundaries. Their "related interests" are usually history, political theory, planning, religion, ecology, and/or futurology, more rarely literature or science and technology, even more rarely philosophy or feminism. On the contrary, in the opposite "fictional" group, the most frequent "related" interests are science fiction, women's studies, literary theory and various segments of literary history or political philosophy, more rarely Fantasy literature, religion, or science. Finally, the "in between" or "utopian philosophy" group relates most strongly in its interests to intellectual history (including political thought) but there is also a smattering of most diverse interests from computers through esthetics and space to peace and mysticism.[2]

Thus, in spite of a number of scholars with significant overlaps between two of the above three groups (ca. 15 percent), in spite of the intermediate philosophy group, and finally in spite of the fact that utopian scholars as a whole are indeed a group with unusually and refreshingly interdisciplinary interests, I think that this little survey confirms a question that might occur to anybody who has assisted at one of the national or international conferences of Utopian Studies or who has read some of the volumes arising from their work: Just what is the common denominator, in corpus or methodology, between the interest in New Harmony or the Shakers and the interest in Morris's or Wells's fictional texts? Now we all know that Bellamy's books started a political movement with partly utopian hues; that the Marxists call most writers of societal blueprints from Morus to Wells and further "utopian socialists", with respect accorded to people before 1848 and increasing impatience with regard to people after that; etc.

2   In a 1988 letter to me, Lyman Tower Sargent observed that "the balance of scholarship that you record would change if the membership of the National Historic Communal Societies Association and the International Communal Societies Association were taken into account." In 1992 he thought the two wings may be approximately equal in size. I trust that my basic argument would not be affected.

I am not at all arguing that there were or are no good reasons for scholarly interested to be so bifurcated as that of the "utopian scholars." But even if we conceded their corpus presented some continuities (which would still leave many discontinuities and problems), just what is the methodological common denominator in approaches to and discourses about Oneida "free love" and Morus's use of dialogue and satire? Personally, I must confess that I often think of being in the presence of a two-headed monster. And if utopian scholarship centrally or predominantly uses two (or more) different discourses or methodologies, is not this at least a radical pragmatic problem and perhaps even an intellectual scandal? In sum, is Utopian Studies one discipline or (at least) two?

It could be objected that there is in practice a common denominator which has been used to rationalize this budding discipline, namely the concept of "utopian thought" practiced by pioneering scholars as different as Mannheim and the Manuels (and for which Bloch too is sometimes claimed). This is empirically correct but, to my mind, philosophically and methodologically quite inconclusive. I cannot discuss this anywhere near as fully as it deserves, but it seems fairly clear that – psychologically, philosophically or politically – free-floating "thought" pre-existing to wholly different methodologies and largely different corpuses is a woolly concept that raises as many questions as it solves. If Utopian Thought created the universe of Utopian Studies, one must ask about this creator the same questions as about a monotheistic God: and who or what created god (or the idea of utopia)? If one stops at the notion of the Creator or of the Platonic Idea, this is an act of belief, necessary but insufficient for scholarship. Rather than an explanation, this philosophically Idealist concept itself needs to be explained: it is not a solution but a problem. Indeed, there is to my mind something despotic about watertight conceptual systems that are not dissolved in and humanized by other aspects of contradictory societal practice; and historical practice – just as that of texts – is never fully reducible to an Idea. (It must be added that the best people in "intellectual history," from Mannheim to W. Warren Wagar, have in practice often transcended their doctrine, and that Bloch is to my mind not to be categorized as such anyway.) In sum: the touchstone and minimal requirement for a real unity of our field would be, I believe, the existence of *some common and centrally significant tools of inquiry*, ensuring the possibility of some common *lines of inquiry*. Can they be found? The rest of this chapter is a much too brief, admittedly schematic attempt to answer this question in a cautiously positive vein.

2. Paradoxes and Ambiguities in the Denial of Utopia

2.0

In this section I shall make an only apparent detour into a consideration of central ideological objections to utopia which dominate present-day bourgeois and techno-bureaucratic attitudes in the "real world" and are not rarely introjected by scholars dealing with utopia. The detour is apparent because, as argued above, pragmatics subsumes – but also needs to be based upon – not only syntactics but also semantics (in this case, of utopian studies).

2.1

Without pretending to an even approximate survey of the state of the art in the burgeoning utopian studies (*Utopieforschung*), I shall postulate there are two related paradoxes within them. I call the first *the paradox of incoherent denial of utopia* – of both utopian fiction and empirical projects for utopian communities. Utopia is denied *in toto* and *a limine* as static, dogmatic, and closed. And yet this critique is incoherent because a lot of evidence exists – marshalled into arguments by Wells, Zamyatin, Bloch, and others since them (for example, Hansot) – that utopian fiction and projects have historically not always been closed, that indeed theoretically they may be either open or closed, and that no easy (much less automatic) correspondence exists between utopia on the one hand and either openness or closure on the other.

I shall in this second section focus on verbal, predominantly on fictional, texts (and only later see whether the argument can be extended to an approach to all fields of utopian investigation). Here it seems, first, arguable that most of the significant utopian texts historically *were not* closed but subject to varying degrees of openness or opening. Second, I see no good (methodo)logical reason why utopian texts *have to be* closed.

2.2

This sub-section could be called "true, but." *True*: historically utopias arose at least once (with Morus) as a secularization of the static millennium and projection of a final Paradise onto Earth, as a political version of Earthly Paradise. *But*: even in Morus there is change (the Utopians open up to Greek knowledge and Christian religion). Not to speak of non-fictional – i.e., doctrinal or what the French call "doxic" – texts such as Gioacchino da Fiore's or Condorcet's, in Bacon and Mercier the notion of a more or less ongoing evolution appears. *True*: there are notoriously dogmatic elements in these three texts too, and such elements grow almost seamless in such "cold stream" centralizers as Campanella, who delineated his utopian locus as an astrological prison, or Cabet, who expressly calls his locus "an Eden, [...] a new Earthly Paradise" (Cabet 3). *But*: there was always a critique of such closure from within utopianism, from its "warm stream": Pantagruel's unending voyage balances Hythloday's arrival, Morris responds to Bellamy, the use of the conditional tense and approach in Wells's *A Modern Utopia* throws into relief the weakness of most other utopian fictions of his. Often this dialectics between the cold and warm currents within the utopian ocean of possibilities that opposes the status quo is to be found within a single text – in Morus's ancestral dialog, in the succeeding hypotheses of Wells's equally paradigmatic Time Traveller, or in the succeeding series of stations of Mayakovsky's *Mystery Bouffe* and Platonov's *Chevengur* (for more on Russian utopias see *MOSF* chapter 10 and Striedter 57–59). This is also quite clear in the latest utopian fiction wave, the best US utopian SF of the 1960s–1970s: *The Dispossessed* by Ursula K. Le Guin, the (highly unjustly neglected) *Daily Life in Nghsi-Altai* tetralogy by Robert Nichols, *Woman on the Edge of Time* by Marge Piercy, etc. (see Suvin, *Positions* 83–85).

2.3

However, even if we were to find that almost the whole past tradition of utopian fiction was in fact static, dogmatic, and closed, this would not answer the logical and methodological question of whether utopia as a genre and orientation is since Wells (or since tomorrow) *necessarily* such. As Bloch rightly noted: "utopian thinking cannot be limited to the Thomas More kind any more than electricity can be reduced to the Greek substance *elektron* – amber – in which it was first noticed" (*Prinzip* 14). This has then a counterpart in the re-reading of history necessitated by the industrialized *epistémé* which entails that "we cannot breathe in a closed world. We have invented the productivity of the spirit [...]" (Lukács 33–34). Following such methodological and historical leads, I argued in *MOSF* that utopia was "an 'as if', an imaginative experiment," and that literary utopias in particular were "a heuristic device for perfectibility, an epistemological and not an ontological entity;" and I concluded that "if utopia is, philosophically, a method rather than a state it cannot be realized or not realized – it can only be applied" (now in the first chapter of this book). This argument of mine was based on a quite respectable philosophical tradition, perhaps first noted in Socrates' dictum that he was tracing "a theoretical *model* of a good city" (Plato, *Politeia* 472e, 1099; emphasis added) and continuing down to Bloch's discussions of fashioning models for an unfinished and open world-process (see the latest formulation in his *Abschied* 131 and passim). The dogmatic and eschatological *forma mentis* found in all laicized religious psychologies – e.g. in those partisans and enemies of socialism which believed that a perfect, utopian state could be realized (say, Stalin and Berdyaev) – is therefore fundamentally wrong. As Italo Calvino wrote in "Per Fourier" (252): "l'utopia come città che non potrà essere fondata da noi ma fondare se stessa dentro di noi, costruirsi pezzo per pezzo nella nostra capacità d'immaginarla, di pensarla fino a fondo" ("utopia [is] as a city which cannot be founded by us but can found itself within us, can build itself bit by bit in our capacity to imagine it, to think it through"). I would today reaffirm my quoted claim that utopia is a *method* rather than a *state*, but I would add that it is a method camouflaging as a state: the state of affairs is a signifier revealing the presence of a semiotic process of signification which induces in the reader's imagination the signified of a Possible World, *as a rule not identical with the signifier*.

In effect, "any true understanding is dialogic in nature [...]. Meaning is the effect of interaction between speaker and listener [...]" (Vološinov/ Bakhtin 102–03; see Suvin, "Performance"). It follows from such considerations – as I also claimed in my earlier chapter – that "to apply a literary text means first of all (wherever it may later lead) to read it as a dramatic dialogue with the reader"; and that, therefore, "utopia is bound to have an implicit or explicit dramatic strategy in its panoramic review conflicting with the 'normal' expectations of the reader. Though formally closed, significant utopia is thematically open: its pointings reflect back on the reader's 'topia'"; and I cited Barthes à propos of Fourier to the effect that the utopian *écriture* must mobilize at the same time an image and its contrary. Converging with this, in a rich essay on Russian utopias, Striedter has pointed out that the utopian state represented in a novel should not be confused with the function of that novel: "The explicit or implicit reference to the external context, the dialogue with this polyphonic reality, counteracts the isolation and the abstract idealism of the utopian 'polis' itself" (38; see now also the argument of Ruppert's book). In other words, even in the case of perfect stasis and closure in the signifier, the signifying process inscribed in or between the text's lines, and finally proceeding to contextual reference, will make for a larger or smaller opening of the signified. Or, in a probably much more adequate terminology: whether the vehicle be open or closed, the tenor will finally be a – more or less – open meaning. As Ricoeur (who with good reason renames meaning into "reference") put it,

> The sense of the work is its internal organization, whereas the reference is the mode of being unfolded in front of the text (93).[3]
> The sense is the ideal object which the proposition intends, and hence is purely immanent in discourse. The reference is the truth value of the proposition, its claim to reach reality. (140)

Any utopian novel is in principle an ongoing feedback dialogue with the reader: it leaves to him/her "the task of transforming the closing of the 'completed' utopia (and utopian novel) into the 'dynamics' of his own mind in his own world" (Striedter 55). But conversely, if the reader is Stalin or Berdyaev, even the dynamic Marxian permanent revolution will for him freeze into an ossified stasis: "the application of utopia depends on the closeness and precision of his reading" (*MOSF* 53). And if this bent reader's readings come to rule, they will destroy the method (the Way) in order to preserve the state (the supposedly final Goal).

Possibly the most sophisticated argument for this thesis can be found in a remarkable review sparked by a remarkable book, Fredric Jameson's "Of Islands and Trenches" à propos of Louis Marin's *Utopiques*. Jameson sees in Marin's stance a proposal to grasp utopian discourse as a process (in Humboldt's terms, the creative power of *energeia* rather than the created piece of work or *ergon*, in Spinoza's terms *natura naturans* rather than *natura naturata*). This proposal is also the repudiation of the

> conventional view of utopia as sheer representation, as the 'realized' vision of this or that ideal society or social ideal [...]. [I]t is possible to understand the utopian text as a determinate type of *praxis*, rather than as a specific mode of representation, [...] a concrete set of mental operations to be performed on [...] those collective representations of contemporary society which inform our ideologies just as they order our experience of daily life.
> In this vein, the utopian "real" is not "something outside the work, of which the latter stands as an image or makes a representation [...]." What is "real" or perhaps operative in a utopian text is rather a set of elements participating in an allegorical

---

3   For a longer discussion that begins with Frege's *Sinn* vs. *Bedeutung* and goes on to consider the trickiness of reference (in fiction always "second-order reference"), see Suvin, "Proposal."

referentiality, "interiorized in [the text's] very fabric in order to provide the stuff and the raw material on which the textual operation must work". (Jameson 81)[4]

2.4

Thus, I claim that utopia is not necessarily static and dogmatic, that indeed it is at least as probable to suppose it may intrinsically not be such as to suppose the opposite. If so, what are the reasons for the paradox of incoherent denial of utopia? My hypothesis is there are two:

First, *the errors of utopophiles*, who stressed either the openness of texts considered as final objects of analysis and/or the ideas to be found in the texts, neglecting the real location of utopian fiction and horizons in a feedback traffic with readers. As against this error, my thesis is that *utopias exist as a gamut of Possible Worlds in the imagination of readers, not as a pseudo-object on the page*. It becomes evident here that (even without going into the complex formalizations of an Eco), we cannot do without some elementary but indispensable semiotic distinctions, such as the one between syntactics, semantics, and pragmatics, or between signifier and signified, or vehicle and tenor. As a Bakhtinian dialog with contextual readers, utopian Possible Worlds are in principle not closed.

Second, *the errors of utopophobes*, who ab/used the (practical as well as – or more than – theoretical) errors of utopophiles to concentrate on the vehicle – the utopian text on the page, in order to impugn both the

---

4   My argument here is not to be confused with Abensour's interesting distinction between systematic and heuristic utopias, developed by Raymond Williams (202–03; see also Moylan 5–6, 49, and passim), i.e., with focusing on institutions vs. focusing on direct relationships between people; this is an old debate between anarchist and "archist" utopians (see my chapter 1) or, in Fourier's terms, between the focus on Need and on Desire (see Barthes 90, also 114–15). No doubt, Abensour's argument and mine arise within the same horizon and from cognate preoccupations, but they seem to me aslant to each other. I would be more sympathetic to a distinction between a praxis gelled into fixed concepts and one developing so quickly it largely has to be rendered by polysemic but also cognitive metaphoric systems, as I argue in my essay "On Metaphoricity" and apply to *Life of Galileo* in "Heavenly."

semantic meanings and the syntactic closure-cum-value-hierarchy which is formally unavoidable in it. Omitting the pragmatic tenor, they identified, without much ado, both these levels of the vehicle with political repression. The best one can say of this procedure is that it oscillates between ignorance and bad faith.

2.5

This situation permits the second paradox, that of a very unhealthy ambiguity between objectors to utopian orientation as such (or in general) and objectors to closed utopias (in particular). To somewhat simplify, the first group objects to utopian orientation because that orientation radically doubts and transcends the bourgeois construction of human nature and the capitalist economico-political power-system. The second group objects to utopias because they *did* not – or, in metaphysical hypostasis, because they in principle *can* not – find the otherwise necessary way out of backward-looking ideologies and out of a globally destructive system. A strange alliance has thus come about, it seems, between bourgeois conservatives and anti-Stalinist leftists understandably (but also inconsistently) shell-shocked from the three totalizing political experiences of Fascism, Stalinism, and massified consensus capitalism spreading from the US. Perhaps the best names for this alliance are on the one hand Karl Popper, Thomas Molnar, and C.-G. Dubois, and on the other hand Theodor W. Adorno and Michel Foucault. I wish I could enter into this at more length, but this rather easily provable point must be left for documentation in another place (see Brenner). There is little doubt that it has powerfully contributed to the pragmatics of what Neusüss has called "the denunciation of utopia" (33–80), which has since grown into a stifling one-dimensional orthodoxy.

3. Locus, Horizon, Orientation, and Possible World

3.1

To help in disambiguating the pragmatic puzzles presented so far, I propose in the spirit of semiotics to introduce the paired concepts of *utopian locus vs. utopian horizon*. Since most of the present discussions around utopia are a mediated reaction to Marxist projects or to developments claiming to be Marxian, it might be appropriate to go back to the origins:

> Der Kommunismus ist für uns nicht ein Zustand, der hergestellt werden soll, ein Ideal, wonach die Wirklichkeit sich zu richten haben [wird]. Wir nennen Kommunismus die wirkliche Bewegung, welche den jetzigen Zustand aufhebt. (Marx and Engels 35)
> [Communism does not mean for us a state of affairs that ought to be brought about, an ideal which reality will have to follow. We call communism the real movement which abolishes the present state of affairs.]

This is a constant attitude in the classical Marxist tradition. On the one hand, it is pretty clear what communism should NOT be – a way of people's living together with war, exploitation, and State apparatus, i.e., neither today's US nor today's USSR; so that from Marx's key notion of alienation a utopian horizon can be inferred by contraries (see Ollman) and so that Lenin can write perhaps the greatest utopian work of this century, *The State and Revolution*. Yet on the other hand in this vein, the same Lenin answered Bukharin's query about future socialism by a vigorous affirmation that "what socialism will be [...], we do not know [...]" (122; see a somewhat different translation in Striedter 36).

As Bloch noted, ever since Plato used the term *topos ouranios* (heavenly space or place, the locus of Plato's Ideas), a clear signal had been given that utopian location (*Ortung*) is only seemingly spatial, if spatial is to be taken in the positivistic sense of photographable places (Bloch, *Abschied* 43, 45–46). To find this signal indicative and illuminating is quite independent from ideological agreement with Plato's notion that such a non-positivistic space is a transcendent or heavenly place for ideas: "it ain't necessarily so" (a watered-down Platonism is, as noted above, my main objection to the notion of "utopian thought" by the Manuels and company). What is to be retained from Plato's intuition is that in the utopian tradition *the actual place focused upon is not to be taken literally*, that it is less significant than the orientation toward a better place somewhere in front of the oriented. In the most significant cases, furthermore, even the place to be reached is not fixed and completed: it moves on. It is thus situated in an imaginary space which is a measure of and measured as value (quality) rather than distance (quantity): "it is a true not-yet-existing, a novum which no human eye hath seen nor ear heard" (Bloch, *Abschied* 46). The necessary elements for meaningful (and certainly for utopian) movement are, then: first, an agent that moves, and second, an imaginary space in which it moves. In this chapter I have unfortunately, for reasons of spacetime, to bracket out the extremely important agential aspects, on which I have written at length elsewhere ("Can People?"); they would contain the properly political problematic of who is the bearer of utopia/nism (I approach this in chapter 10 of this book). However, I hope that sufficient initial illumination may come from the pertinent aspects of space. They are:

a. the place of the agent who is moving, her/his *locus*;
b. the *horizon* toward which that agent is moving; and
c. the *orientation*, a vector that conjoins locus and horizon.

A horizon is the furthest reach of that agent's visual and cognitive imagination at a given moment; yet it is characteristic of horizon that it moves with the location of the moving agent, as was exhaustively argued by Giordano Bruno (cited in Mahnke 54). Obversely, it is characteristic of orientation that it can through all the changes of locus remain a constant vector of desire and cognition. As Musil was to formulate it in a self-reflection on writing ironic utopias, in *The Man Without Characteristics* – a text that is itself emblematic for its intended signification of permanent movement through various loci in a fixed direction which is also a movable, expanding horizon: "Eine Utopie ist aber kein Ziel, sondern eine Richtung" [A utopia, however, is not a goal but an orientation] (1594; see also Plattel 97).[5]

3.2

The use of notions such as locus, horizon, and orientation is predicated on an analogy with conceptions of the empirical world. The Possible Worlds (further PWs) of utopian fiction, which exist in the imagination of given social types and implied addressees of utopian texts, take their structures – wherever these are not expressly modified – from "natural worlds" (i.e., dominant conceptions thereof). A highly important aspect is that for a PW "the term of 'world' is not a manner of speaking: it means that the 'mental' or cultural life borrows its structures from natural life" (Merleau-Ponty 225), that "our *hic et nunc*" has "a preferential status" (Eco, *Role* 223). In the same vein, Marin concluded (significantly, by advancing from an avowed parabolic text) that

> the natural world, as an organized and perceptually structured spatiotemporal ensemble, constitutes the original text [...] of all possible discourse, its "origin" and its constitutive environment [...]. All possible discourse is enunciated only against the ground of the perceived world's significant space, by which it is surrounded [...]. ("Théorie" 167 and 175)

The fact that we can meaningfully effect this metaphoric analogy, that we can transport these three notions into a discussion not of practice but of verbal (or of all signic) constructs constitutes, therefore, itself a highly significant meta-meaning. My contention (developed at length in my essay "Performance") is that the interaction between the fictional elements presented in a text and the presuppositions of the implied reader induces in

---

5   For a first sketch on the semiotics of horizon in West European literatures from Bacon to the nineteenth century see Koschorke; on orientation as "the Ur-form of theoretical work" and its etymological root in astronomy see Negt and Kluge 1002, and my "Haltung" for the synonyms of "bearing" or "stance," which connect it with the agential discussion.

the readers a specific PW. This PW is constructed by and in the reader's constrained imagination, it is a tenor (signified) to be clearly distinguished from the isolated text or the text surface which is a vehicle (signifier). As argued in Section 1, an element (work, agent, shape, color, change, or indeed a whole corpus, etc.) that can help to induce and constrain a PW for the reader becomes a sign only in a signifying situation. In the particular case of reading fiction, the specific, imaginary PW of a fictional text is constituted by complex and intimate feedback with the readers on the basis of its not being identical with, and yet being imaginatively supported by, their empirical world (or empirical PW). This interaction ensures (among other things) that, whatever the spatiotemporal and agential signifiers, it is always *de nobis* or, more precisely and significantly, *de possibilibus pro nobis* that the fable narrates. It is the tension between the finite, often closed texts and the multivalent (im)possibilities facing the reader that creates the fictional utopia's basic openness.

3.3

Let me pursue some consequences of the three terms proposed in 3.1, so that they may be judged by their fruits. Since without a utopian orientation our field of inquiry does not exist, so that its discussion has to be left to the discussion of utopian agents, what are the mutual relationships – or indeed the combinatorics – of locus and horizon? Can they give rise to a typology which would be a useful grid for utopian studies as a whole?

My approach has been (for all my abiding demurral against his panutopianism) stimulated and largely shaped by Bloch, the most important philosopher of utopia. The concept of horizon comes from phenomenology, from which (Husserl, Merleau-Ponty, Ricoeur) I believe we also have much to learn. But Bloch refunctioned it into a sociopolitically concrete tool within a "warm stream" Marxism. As I argued in *MOSF* upon his tracks, imaginary space shifts into time with the industrial and bourgeois revolutions. Therefore, I shall here briefly discuss Bloch's late hypothesis on elastic temporal structure in history, on the analogy of Riemannian space.

Riemann assumed that the metrical field is causally dependent upon matter and that it changes with matter: the field is not a pre-existent static and homogeneous fixity but a process of changeable material feedback. With all due caution toward analogies from natural sciences (e.g., the awful example of Heisenberg's Indeterminacy): historical matter is at least as unequally distributed as matter in relativistic physics. No doubt, history would have to add to this at least the latent tendencies possibly present – and in the form of dominant alternatives, most probably present – in its matter (see Bloch, *Tübinger* 129ff., in particular 133 and 136). Adapting Bloch's final *Theses on the Concept of Progress*, I would say that the goal of utopia is in principle not a defined, localized or fixed humaneness but a not-yet-manifest type of human relationships, a hominization in Engels's or Teilhard's sense. This is "a depth dimension (*Tiefenbeziehung*) of the Onwards" (ibid. 147); from which it follows that there can be no final, "classical" or canonic locus of utopianism.

In my proposed terms, this can be systematized as *the dominance of Horizon over Locus*. Locus does not coincide with but interacts with Horizon: this makes for a dynamic, open utopia (e.g. Platonov's *Chevengur*, Le Guin's *The Dispossessed*). I shall characterize it in the words of a brilliant graduate student of mine: "The tension in *The Dispossessed* is not between a voyager from here and now (the familiar) and the utopian locus (the strange), but between the utopian hero and the utopian locus" (Somay 34). I would add that this is so because the hero or protagonist embodies here the orientation toward a moving (in this case, an anarcho-communist) utopian horizon.

The second possibility would be that *Locus coincides with or swallows Horizon*: this makes for a dogmatic, static, closed utopia (e.g., Campanella's *Civitas Solis*, Cabet's *Voyage en Icarie*):

> A doctrinaire, or dogmatic, utopian text [...] asserts the utopian focus as "ultimate" and drastically limits the possibilities of the utopian horizon; an open-ended text, on the other hand, portrays a utopian locus as a mere phase in the infinite unfolding of the utopian horizon, thereby abolishing the limits imposed on it by classical utopian fiction. (Somay 26)

The third possibility would be to have *Locus alone*, i.e., without a uto-pian Horizon (by now to my mind a pseudo-utopian locus): this makes for heterotopia. The best theoretical example is of course Foucault, and the best fictional one his disciple Samuel Delany's *Triton*, also a direct polemic with "ambiguous utopia" of *The Dispossessed*, and explicitly couched in terms of heterotopia.

> [Both these SF novels do away] with the doctrinaire identification of the utopian locus with the utopian horizon. Delany, however, goes one step further: he also does away with the utopian horizon itself. In Le Guin, too, the utopian horizon is not actual, solid; yet the utopian horizon, appearing as an urge towards certain actions, furnishes her narrative agents with a purpose; whereas in Delany, the horizon and the urge are [...] absent, and that absence leaves his characters purposeless and con-fused. (Somay 33)

The final logico-combinatorial possibility is to have in a text *Horizon alone*, without a utopian Locus. This is where non-localized "utopian thought" belongs, such as all the abstract blueprints, utopian programs, etc. I have difficulty in seeing how a horizon without concrete locus – without Bakhtin's chronotope – can be a fictional narration in any strict technical sense (though it can of course be called both fictional in an ironic and narrative in a loosely metaphoric sense, both of which I would find irksome).

To resume the above locus/horizon combinatorics:

1. H > L: *open-ended or dynamic utopia*;
2. L = H or L > H: *closed or static utopia*;
3. L (H = 0): *heterotopia*;
4. H (L = 0): *abstract or non-narrative utopia/nism*.

Thus, there seems to be no obstacle to applying these terms (as well as a further set of agential terms) as analytic tools to the whole range of utopian studies – fictions, projects, and colonies.

3.4

The interaction of locus and horizon in the case of the dynamic utopia constitutes it as not too dissimilar from – possibly as a special case of – Eco's definition of a semiotic encyclopedia:

> Essa appare [non come un oggetto finito ma] piuttosto come un progetto aperto: non una utopia come *terminus ad quem*, e cioè uno stato di perfezione da raggiungere, ma una utopia come idea regolativa, come progetto *ante quem*, la cui forza è data proprio dal fatto che esso *non può e non deve* essere realizzato in modo definitivo. (Eco, "Quattro" 108)
> [It appears not as a finished object but rather as an open project: not a utopia as *terminus ad quem*, i.e. a state of perfection to be reached, but a utopia as a regulating idea, as a project *ante quem*, whose force stems precisely from the fact that it *cannot* and *should not* be realized in any definitive form.]

Let me add here (as an epistemological complement) that Eco himself is somewhat more agnostic or pessimistic – or "post-modern" or "weak thought" – than I would be, since he identifies such an open utopia with a rhizomatic encyclopedia only, which I would in its "disorganized organization" rather liken to my possibility no. 3. I am very skeptical toward "shapeless shapes" (ibid. 107), unless they are simply initial stages of our still partly inchoate understanding – or construction – of a new kind of organization and shape. While fully agreeing with Eco (and Deleuze) that it is an ideological illusion knowledge could be organized in a definitive and permanent fashion, I would not share their distrust toward global (or indeed total) organization of knowledge (ibid. 121) on the same presuppositions as those of utopia no. 1 above: on condition that this globality is conscious of itself as a synchronic cross-cut for well-defined interests and with a limited pertinence. Nonetheless, there is no reason that would necessarily prevent such an organization (e.g., a dynamic utopia) from defining strategically central cognitions necessary and available for action aimed at radical or global change at a given spacetime point (see Suvin, "Two Cheers").

4. Towards a Conclusion: Physician, Heal Thyself

I conclude with some questions and open proposals of a partly self-critical nature, in light of further reflection (including further reading of Bloch) within our evolving ideologico-political situation. In chapter 1 of this book (written at the beginning of the 1970s), I stressed the specificity of utopian fictions as *verbal constructs* (and of course this is readily extrapolated to other textual constructs in a wider acceptation of "text," i.e., to paintings). I believe that such a stress was at that initial point mandatory. Indeed, it still seems to me the indispensable beginning, or A, of all wisdom when discussing utopian texts (and remember that any description, verbal or pictorial, of a project or colony is also a text). Still, I would today advance from this position by saying that after A there follow B, C, etc., and that I was perhaps too narrowly focused when I claimed Blochian methodology for texts only. The dichotomy of the field of utopian studies into texts vs. practices, supposedly unified by "utopian thought" but in fact separated by a tacit gap, is *à la longue* untenable. It is also one of the utopophiles' errors, or at least areas of lack, that gives great comfort to the utopophobes, as mentioned in Section 2. For, logically, either utopian texts and utopian practices are two fields, in which case there should be two disciplines and two professional organizations to study them. Or, on the contrary, we should attempt to establish at least some traffic across the existing gap. I have argued why the only present footbridge of "utopian thought," always flimsy, seems by now rather worm-eaten and not too *tragfähig*, unable to support much burden. The concept of Possible Worlds, on the contrary, as adapted and humanized from a sociohistorical and pragmatic semiotics of mainly Italian provenience (a critical view of its sources can be found in Suvin, "Performance", and a development in "Can People?") – and in particular its spatial categories of orientation, locus, and horizon – has some chances to become a real bridge. But of course, this is only a hypothesis. It remains to be proven by further, if possible cooperative, exploration.

Allow me, nonetheless, to provisionally close this open-ended utopian modest proposal by reiterating, with Bloch, that we should hold a steadfast

orientation toward the open ocean of possibility that surrounds the actual
and that is so immeasurably larger than the actuality. True, terrors lurk in
that ocean: but those terrors are primarily and centrally not (as the utopophobes want to persuade us) the terrors of the not-yet-existing, but on
the contrary simple extrapolations of the existing actuality of war, hunger,
degradation, and exploitation of people and planets. On the other hand,

> there exists a process and we people are at the advanced front-line of this world-
> process; it is given unto our hands to nurture the possibilities already pending [...].
> The seventh day of creation is still before us, the seventh day of which Augustin
> said: "dies septima ipsi erimus, we ourselves shall be the seventh day" [...]. (Bloch,
> *Abschied* 63, and see also 59)

But in order to understand how to approach such open adventist possibilities given into our perhaps feeble hands, I believe we have first to learn the
lesson of the dynamic utopias, where locus constantly tends toward and
yet never fuses with horizon. The best formulation I can find of this is in
the stupendous close of Brecht's *Badener Lehrstück vom Einverständnis*
(1929 – *Baden Learning Play on Consent, Gesammelte Werke* 2):

THE LEARNED CHORUS
When bettering the world, you might have perfected the truth,
Now go on perfecting the perfected truth.
Give it up!

CHORUS LEADER
March!

THE LEARNED CHORUS
When perfecting the truth, you might have changed humanity,
Now go on changing the changed humanity.
Give it up!

CHORUS LEADER
March!

THE LEARNED CHORUS
Changing the world, change yourself!
Give yourself up!

CHORUS LEADER
March!

And as Brecht added in his radio theory: "If you deem all of this utopian, I beg you to reflect on the reasons which render it utopian" (*Gesammelte Werke* 18: 30).[6]

Works Cited

Barthes, Roland. *Sade, Fourier, Loyola*. Paris: Seuil, 1971.
Bloch, Ernst. *Abschied von der Utopie*. Frankfurt: Suhrkamp, 1980.
——. *Das Prinzip Hoffnung*. Frankfurt: Suhrkamp, 1959.
——. *Tübinger Einleitung in die Philosophie*. Frankfurt: Suhrkamp, 1970.
Brecht, Bertolt. *Gesammelte Werke*. 20 vols. Frankfurt: Suhrkamp, 1973.
Brenner, Peter J. "Aspekte und Probleme der neueren Utopiediskussion in der Philosophie." *Utopieforschung. Interdisziplinäre Studien zur neuzeitlichen Utopie*. Vol. 1. Ed. Wilhelm Vosskamp. Stuttgart: Metzler, 1982. 111–63.
Cabet, Etienne. *Voyage en Icarie*. Paris: Ressources, 1979.
Calvino, Italo. *Una pietra sopra*. Torino: Einaudi, 1980.

6   My thanks go to Giuseppa Saccaro Del Buffa, without whose help and patience this chapter would not have been written, also to Daniela Guardamagna and Igina Tattoni, who helped in Rome. It was first given in an abbreviated form at the world conference of Utopian Studies organized by Professor Del Buffa in Frascati 1986 and first published, in a slightly different form, in volume 1 of *Utopia e modernità* edited by her and Arthur O. Lewis (Rome: Gangemi, 1989).

Eco, Umberto. "Quattro forme di enciclopedia ..." *Quaderni d'italianistica* 2.2 (1981): 105–22.

——. *The Role of the Reader*. Bloomington: Indiana University Press, 1979.

Hansot, Elisabeth. *Perfection and Progress*. Cambridge, MA: MIT Press, 1974.

Jameson, Fredric. "Of Islands and Trenches." *The Ideologies of Theory*. Vol. 2. Minneapolis: University of Minnesota Press, 1988. 75–101.

Koschorke, Albrecht. "Der Horizont als Symbol der Überschreitung und Grenze: Zum Wandel eines literarischen Motivs zwischen Aufklärung und Realismus." *Proceedings of the 12th Congress of the ICLA*. Vol. 2. Ed. Roger Bauer et al. München: Iudicium, 1990. 250–55.

Lenin, Vladimir I. *Sochineniia*, Vol. 27. Moscow: Gos.izd. politicheskoi lit., 1950.

Lukács, Georg. *The Theory of the Novel*. London: Merlin, 1971.

Mahnke, Dietrich. *Unendliche Sphäre und Allmittelpunkt*. Stuttgart: Frommann, 1966.

Marin, Louis. "Pour une théorie du texte parabolique." *Le Récit évangélique*. Ed. Claude Chabrol et al. Paris: Aubier Montaigne, 1974.

——. *Utopiques, jeux d'espaces*. Paris: Minuit, 1973.

Marx, Karl, and Friedrich Engels. *Die Deutsche Ideologie. Werke (MEW)* Vol. 3. Berlin: Dietz, 1956.

Merleau-Ponty, Maurice. *Phénoménologie de la perception*. Paris: NRF, 1945.

Moylan, Tom. *Demand the Impossible: Science Fiction and the Utopian Imagination*. New York and London: Methuen, 1986.

Musil, Robert. *Der Mann ohne Eigenschaften*. Hamburg: Rowohlt, 1972.

Negt, Oskar, and Alexander Kluge. *Geschichte und Eigensinn*. Frankfurt: Zweitausendeins, 1981.

Neusüss, Arnhelm (ed.). *Utopie*. Neuwied: Luchterhand, 1968.

Ollman, Bertell. *Alienation*. Cambridge and New York: Cambridge University Press, 1976.

Plato. *The Republic. Complete Works*. Ed. J.M. Cooper. Indianapolis: Hackett, 1997.

Plattel, Martin G. *Utopian and Critical Thinking*. Pittsburgh: Duquesne University Press, 1972.

Ricoeur, Paul. *Hermeneutics and the Human Sciences*. Ed. J.B. Thompson. Cambridge: Cambridge University Press, 1981.

Ruppert, Peter. *Reader in a Strange Land*. Athens: University of Georgia Press, 1986.

Sargent, Lyman Tower. Letter to D. Suvin. 6 December 1988.

Somay, Bülent. "Towards an Open-Ended Utopia." *Science-Fiction Studies* 11.1 (1984): 25–38.

Suvin, Darko. "Can People Be (Re)Presented in Fiction?" *Marxism and the Interpretation of Culture*. Ed. Cary Nelson and Lawrence Grossberg. Urbana: University of Illinois Press, 1987. 663–96.

——. "Haltung (Bearing) and Emotions: Brecht's Refunctioning of Conservative Metaphors for Agency." *Zweifel – Fragen – Vorschläge: Bertolt Brecht anlässlich des Einhundertsten*. Ed. T. Jung. Frankfurt: Peter Lang, 1999, 43–58.

——. "Heavenly Food Denied: *Life of Galileo*." *The Cambridge Companion to Brecht*. Ed. Peter Thomson and Glendyr Sacks. Cambridge: Cambridge University Press, 1994. 139–52.

——. *Metamorphoses of Science Fiction*. New Haven: Yale University Press, 1979 [cited as MOSF].

——. "On Metaphoricity and Narrativity in Fiction." *SubStance* 48 (1986): 51–67.

——. "A Modest Proposal for the Semi-Demi Deconstruction of (Shakespeare as) Cultural Construction." *Semeia: Itinerari per Marcello Pagnini*. Ed. Loretta Innocenti et al. Bologna: Il Mulino, 1994. 67–76.

——. "The Performance Text as Audience-Stage Dialog Inducing a Possible World." *Versus* no. 42 (1985): 3–20.

——. *Positions and Presuppositions in Science Fiction*. London: Macmillan, 1988.

——. "Two Cheers for Essentialism and Totality." *Rethinking Marxism* 10.1 (1998): 66–82.

Striedter, Jurij. "Journeys Through Utopia." *Poetics Today* 3.1 (1982): 35–60.

Vološinov, Valentin N. [= M.M. Bakhtin]. *Marxism and the Philosophy of Language*. Trans. Ladislav Matejka and Irwin R. Titunik. New York: Seminar Press, 1973.

Williams, Raymond. *Problems in Materialism and Culture: Selected Essays*. London: Verso, 1980.

CHAPTER 6

On William Gibson and Cyberpunk SF (1989–1991)[1]

To the memory of Raymond Williams

0. Preliminary Reflections

More so than for other literary genres, a commentator of current SF has to cope with its very spotty accessibility. It is well known that new books in what the market very loosely calls SF come and go quickly, and are apt to be taken off the bookstore shelves in weeks if not days. Even in the case of those recognized names whose titles get reprinted, the reprinting is as a rule patchy, both selective and short-lived, governed by long-ago contracts and bureaucratic middlemen in publishing and distribution whose reasoning may be accessible to some ESP godhead but not to earthly logic. In Summer and Fall 1988, for example, in North America from the numerous SF titles by Samuel Delany there were two in print. How is a critic or historian to cope with that?

---

[1]   After the first mention, the often cited works by Gibson will be as a rule abbreviated as follows: *Burning Chrome* as *BC*, *Count Zero* as *CZ*, *Neuromancer* as *N*, and the collective anthology *Mirrorshades* as *M*.

    Addition 2008: I have since realized, in the wake of Tom Moylan's analyses, that the second significant name in "cyberpunk", beside Gibson, is Pat Cadigan. Also, today what Moylan has rightly called the "implosion" of the horizons and in particular of the utopian aspect of Gibson's first trilogy can be counterbalanced by his interesting later works. This essay is what I was able to grasp by the late 1980s.

One way, favoured by fans, used to be building up a huge personal library. Even in the days before 1970, when a strict definition of the genre would have found considerably fewer than 200 new titles in English yearly, this was a somewhat crazy undertaking, often accompanied by enforced specialization on some subset of SF. To speak from direct experience, until the second half of the 1970s I tried to stay atop the field by reading if not 200 new books per year then an appreciable fraction thereof which would permit me to follow all significant authors and trends. I discontinued this endeavour in despair when the SF field mushroomed – catalyzed by the big money of a few Hollywood adulterations à la *Star Wars* and the horror mass media successors (in literal and metaphorical senses) to the often tolerable and sometimes actually thoughtful *Star Trek* series – and when the esthetic-cum-cognitive quality simultaneously dropped off sharply in direct response to the New Right dominance in the US media: a case of quality turning into quantity indeed.

All this is to say that in the 1980s no single person can follow the field, unless perhaps this is the economic mainstay of her or his life. Coming to the matter at hand, "cyberpunk" SF (the name seems less brainless than either "Golden Age" or "New Wave" and I shall henceforth use it without quotation marks) – a state of ingent confusion seems to prevail as to what ought to or may be included into and excluded from it. If narratives by Greg Bear, Pat Cadigan, Marc Laidlaw, Rudy Rucker, Lucius Shepard, Lewis Shiner, and John Shirley – people included in the important *Mirrorshades: The Cyberpunk Anthology* – as well as by a number of further names which I have at various points seen associated with it, are to be called cyberpunk SF, then I am not competent to talk about this phenomenon as an extensive whole: I have not read many of their writings – or at least I cannot remember having read them, which may be in itself some kind of a significant comment. I have in my ongoing readings plus a 1988 attempt to catch up succeeded in locating – beside William Gibson and Bruce Sterling – only most books by Rucker, and some by Bear, Shepard, and Shirley. Yet it would be easy to show that, e.g., Bear's *Blood Music* is – under an initial and misleading overlay of hard science (biotechnology) and thriller – a naive fairytale relying on popular wish-dreams that our loved ones not be dead and that our past mistakes may all be rectified, all of this infused with rather dubious philosophical and political stances. On the other extreme, Shepard's much more considerable, if possibly somewhat overlush, *Life During Wartime* focuses on a soldier in the field, his participation in a drug-saturated war, and his eventual ethical revulsion from such a dehumanization. Thus – in spite of its politically illiterate attribution of global power struggles and protracted wars to an *Illuminatus*-type conspiracy, based yet on two Panamanian families in control of a rare drug source – it is the weightiest contribution I know of (beside Gibson) by a new writer to SF in the 1980s. However, its narrative texture and composition is nearer to the 1960s, like an impressive cross between Mailer's *The Naked and the Dead* (or indeed Pynchon's *Gravity Rainbow*) and one of the better John Brunner novels (say *Stand on Zanzibar*): something like a drug-perfected ESP story used for anti-war purposes. Obviously, we are here fast approaching the limits of "cyberpunk SF" as a meaningful synchronic category. Conversely, Norman Spinrad's *Little Heroes*, by almost any definitional element I can think of: its cheerless future world, tough, gritty, and disillusioned protagonists, streetwise future slang, erasing of "hard" vs. "soft" boundaries or melding of personal experience and politics with biochips and the entertainment industry, etc., could be taken – in its characteristics and in its significance – for a central cyberpunk novel. Yet it equally seems rather uneconomical to put Spinrad into the same category as Gibson and co. This problem may be overcome by saying that Spinrad was himself (say in *Bug Jack Barron*) a major precursor of cyberpunk and that he has in feedback turn been reinvigorated by Gibson and co. I would in fact assume both of these semi-reasons are correct. Nonetheless, they also indicate that the usefulness of cyberpunk as a self-contained diachronic category has here become doubtful.

An encompassing survey of cyberpunk SF looks therefore not only materially impossible but also methodologically dubious. My solution in this pragmatic dilemma is to opt for representative intension rather than extension. As I hinted above, I have read all the books authored exclusively by Gibson and Sterling, who seem to be – by accessibility as well as by critical attention paid them – the most popular, and who are taken to be the most representative, writers of this trend. They will therefore in this first approach figure as the positive and negative pole of cyberpunk, as well as a gauge of whether there is in fact an esthetic cohesion to it (as different from coterie mutual admiration). Nonetheless, should anybody wish to stress the "preliminary reflection" nature of this chapter, implied by the "On" in its title, I shall happily assent. Still, it seems to me legitimate to begin by discussing cyberpunk SF from what are, within the range of my knowledge, undoubtedly its best works, i.e., the less than half a dozen of Gibson's short stories published from 1981 to 1983 in *Omni* and Terry Carr's *Universe 11*, and the novel to which they led and in which they culminate, *Neuromancer* of 1984. I shall assume that these works constitute the furthest horizon of cyberpunk and try to briefly characterize it. Then I shall compare it to Gibson's *Count Zero* and to some aspects of Sterling's writing, and proceed to a tentative conclusion.

1. Pro: Utopia

The critics said it almost unanimously: Gibson "brings an entirely new electronic punk sensibility to SF" (*Asimov's SF Magazine*), a "technopunk sensibility" (New York's prestigious *Village Voice*). I would say it consists in a truly novel SF formulation of the structure of feeling dominant among some fractions of the youth culture in the affluent North of our globe (more about this in the conclusion). All of Gibson's protagonists are somewhere between fifteen and thirty years of age, all of them are totally immersed in – or indeed, it would be more accurate to say, their sensibility is constituted by – the international pop culture. They have been socialized into the new space of the 1980s, which

> [...] involves the suppression of distance [...] and the relentless saturation of any
> remaining voids and empty places [...]. [The body] is now exposed to a perceptual
> barrage of immediacy from which all sheltering layers and intervening mediations
> have been removed. (Jameson, "Mapping" 351)

As the propagandist of the movement, Sterling, has testified, for cyberpunks technology is inside, not outside, the personal body and mind itself:

> Eighties tech sticks to the skin, responds to the touch: the personal computer, the Sony Walkman, the portable telephone, the soft contact lens [...] prosthetic limbs, implanted circuitry, cosmetic surgery, genetic alteration. (Sterling, *M* xiii)

And even further, cyberpunk is centered on the mind-invasion motifs of "brain-computer interfaces, artificial intelligence, neurochemistry – techniques radically redefining the nature of humanity, the nature of self" (Sterling, *M* xiii). The pop culture, that largest sub-culture of our times, stemmed from the punk music and life-style of the 1970s as it was internationalized by global media and jet travel; it is international in the sense of a global market of junk (the *gomi* of Gibson's story "The Winter Market"). This is well approximated in Julie Deane's office, the first interior the reader encounters in *N*:

> Neo-Aztec bookcases gathered dust against one wall of the room [...]. A pair of bulbous Disney-styled table lamps perched awkwardly on a low Kandinsky-look coffee table in scarlet- lacquered steel. A Dali clock hung on the wall between the bookcases, its distorted face sagging to the bare concrete floor. Its hands were holograms that altered to match the convolutions of the face as they rotated, but it never told the correct time [...]. (12)

Delany has observed that "The bricolage of Gibson's style, now colloquial, now highly formal, now hardboiled, makes him as a writer a *gomi no sensei* – a master of junk. Applied to Gibson, it is a laudatory title" (Delany, "Some Real Mothers" 8). I would argue that this too is a development of the astounding "kipple" chapters in P.K. Dick's much underrated *Martian Time-Slip*. But here the punk tradition meshes with the high-tech of the 1980s, in particular with the burgeoning of modern computerized communications; in Gibson, their world is discreetly and very reasonably extrapolated into new drugs or hologram games, and mainly into biotechnics which come to provide their new software. These characteristics of Gibson's stories are well-known. What may be less noticed is that the "hard science" elements function as narrative mediations and common-denominator connectives between the two poles of Gibson's agential system. These poles I take to be the overwhelming Powers-That-Be and the Little Man caught in their killing meshes. In a world whose inhabitants increasingly function as literally software (this is, e.g., the theme of "The Winter Market" and its "neuroelectronics"), the distinction between hard and soft sciences is difficult to maintain.

Case in *N* thinks his destiny is "spelled out in a constellation of cheap crome," in the knife-edge little *shuriken* stars (11–12). But underneath the symbolic glitz, the role of Destiny is in Gibson's narratives perspicaciously allotted to the power-systems dominant in our 1980s world, the ruthlessly competing "multinational corporations that control entire economies" (*Burning Chrome* 103), well symbolized by the Japanese name but also tradition of *zaibatsu*. Although Gibson's views of Japan are inevitably those of a hurried if interested outsider who has come to know the pop culture around the Tôkyô subway stations of Shibuya, Shinjuku, and Harajuku, I would maintain there is a deeper justification, a geopolitical or perhaps geo-economical and psychological logic, in choosing such "nipponizing" vocabulary. This logic is centered on how strangely and yet peculiarly appropriate Japanese feudal-style capitalism is as an analog or indeed ideal template for the new feudalism of the 1970s–1980s corporate monopolies: where the history of capitalism, born out of popular merchant-adventurer revolt against the old sessile feudalism, has come full circle – Worm Ouroboros carrying us back to Leviathan. (The focus on neo-feudalism, by the way, also explains Gibson's undoubted affinities with the Bester of *Tiger, Tiger*.) Not only Night City in *N*, but the whole "biz" world is "like a deranged experiment in Social Darwinism, designed by a bored researcher who kept one thumb permanently on the fast-forward button" (7). Gibson's major SF precursors are Dick and Delany (and then Spinrad and John Varley). However, in between Dick's nation-state armies or polices and Delany's Foucauldian micro-politics of bohemian groups, Gibson has – to my mind more realistically – opted for global economic power-wielders as the arbiters of peoples' lifestyles and lives. This can be exemplified in his *femme fatale* Sandii, who is symbolically a "Eurasian, half gaijin, long-hipped and fluid," and who moves the way "the crowds surg[e] around Shinjuku station, wired electric night [...] rhythm of a new age, dreamy and far from any nation's soil" (*BC* 104–07).

Dick's (and John le Carré's) focus on the increasing role of intelligence agencies has in Gibson been transferred to industrial espionage, conducted either through cyberspace or by organizing corporate defection: these two activities account for practically all of his plots. Thus, the second and narratively central pole or focus of Gibson's are the "computer cowboys" riding this cyberspace range as the hired hands, wildcard operators, hustlers, mercs or outlaws in the "intricate dance of desire and commerce" (*N* 11). They are the hero(in)es of his writings: Case in *N*, or Bobby and Angela of *CZ*. A secondary role is that of a "street samurai" (*N* 30), a mercenary of the monopoly wars: Molly in *N*, Turner in *CZ*, Sandii in *New Rose Hotel*. Usually, his narrative agents come in pairs. Gibson's theme, or at least his central agential relationship, is often a love story: *Romeo and Juliet in the world of zaibatsu* (Case and Molly in *N*, Turner and Allison, Bobby and Angela, Jaylene and Ramirez in *CZ*, Johnny and Molly in "Johnny Mnemonic," Lise and Casey in "The Winter Market," Jack and Rikki in *BC*). Such an updated Juliet, the female co-heroine, whom the narrative spotlights almost but not quite equally, is refreshingly independent and strong: Delany acutely points out the parallel between Molly and Russ's Jael, though he seems to me to overstate the case of direct filiation between Gibson and Russ or Le Guin (Delany, "Some *Real* Mothers" 8). Sometimes this Juliet turns out to be a le-Carréan traitor, a Kim Philby of the *zaibatsu* wars, as in "New Rose Hotel," sometimes she simply at the end walks away, as in *N* and *BC*, or shifts into inaccessible cyberspace, as in "The Winter Market"; but in this cruel world the love story usually ends badly. Gibson's basic affect is to be the bearer of bad news, as was Dick. A happy ending is in his work a signal for a lowering of narrative intensity, as in "Johnny Mnemonic" (so that this is rightly taken back through Molly's incidental memories in *N*). Or it is even a sign of outright low-quality faking, as in Angela's silly transition from voodoo to TV goddess at the end of *Count Zero*.

In a world laced with pills and drugs, cyberspace is itself a kind of super-drug vying in intensity with sexual love. Cyberspace, that central metaphor, is defined by Gibson as "consensual hallucination," "[a] graphic representation of data abstracted from the banks of every computer in the human system [...] in the nonspace of the mind" (*N* 51), a "monochrome nonspace where the only stars are dense concentrations of information, and high above it all burn corporate galaxies and the cold spiral arms of military systems" (*BC* 170). Sometimes not only his console cowboys but he too seems to consider cyberspace as the new sensorium of an undifferentiated human species, as "mankind's extended electronic nervous system" (*BC* 170) in which anything is possible. An abstract logic and cultural ecstasy is hidden beneath this hardboiled technical vocabulary, a yearning to get out of the dinginess and filth of everyday life that can, in Gibson's most woolly-minded moments, easily branch off into heterodox religion (as in the voodoo that vitiates much of *Count Zero*). More prudently and plausibly, cyberspace can be seen as a landscape simulation (extrapolated from "primitive arcade games [...] [and] graphics programs," *N* 51) of the mathematizable data fed into all the corporate computers, into which his hustler heroes plug by means of cranial jacks (extrapolated from present-day military experimentation). Its matrix is "bright lattices of logic" (*N* 5), contrasting with their closed horizons, the sordid temperfoam of a coffin hotel. Case in *N* sees the black-market quarter of Ninsei "as a field of data, the way the matrix had once reminded him of proteins linking to distinguish cell specialties [...] the dance of biz, information interacting, data made flesh [...]" (16). It has clear affinities with erotics. Case's first orgasm with Molly is one of Gibson's fine lyrical passages lurking just below the cynical, street-wise surface, and therefore chopping up the rhythms of a prose poem into brief clauses: it is described as "flaring blue in timeless space, a vastness like the matrix, where the faces were shredded and blown away down hurricane corridors, and her inner thighs were strong and wet against his hips [...]" (33). Even more strikingly, toward the end of *Neuromancer* sexual love is seen as a kind of life-affirming ocean of super-information; since the passage is situated in cyberspace, where Case is meeting his first love, Linda Lee, as a ROM construct, the two-way traffic between eroticism and cyberspace grows intricate:

"No," he said, and then it no longer mattered, what he knew [i.e., that she was an illusion], tasting the salt of her mouth where tears had dried. There was a strength that ran in her, something he'd known in Night City and held there, been held by it, held for a while away from time and death, from the relentless Street that hunted them all [...]. It belonged, he knew – he remembered – as she pulled him down, to the meat, the flesh the cowboys mocked. It was a vast thing, beyond knowing, a sea of information coded in spiral and pheromone, infinite intricacy that only the body, in its strong blind way, could ever read. (239)

Cyberspace is a utopia out of video-arcades or *pachinko* parlors (see Gibson's interview, *Mississippi Review* 226), a mathematized love-philtre of computer hacker lore; and – like Harlan Ellison or Spinrad – Gibson is on the side of his petty juvenile criminals trying to penetrate the corporate "blue ice." (Ice means, we are told, "intrusion countermeasures electronics," but it obviously also connotes the extremely rarefied, lonely, Antarctic edge of exhilaratingly dangerous exploration among those informational super-glaciers.) The cowboy-samurai love affairs usually end badly, but at least they (and only they – not the rulers obscenely devoted to money or power) are capable of it.

2. Con: Ideology

The rapt utopia of bright logic and teeth-gritting erotic tenderness contrasts strangely, sometimes in interesting and sometimes in kitschy ways, with the melodramatic plots full of double-crossings out of le Carré or Spinrad. The ending of *N* was already ambiguous, and somewhat vague: one Case was left in cyberspace with Linda Lee, another in "real" space alone, while the artificial intelligences (whose unshackling – the reader comes to realize – had constituted the hidden plot of *N*) pursued their unclear extraterrestrial contacts somewhere in the background. We are not too far here from Arthur Clarke's homespun quasi-mysticism, somewhat updated into the era of Fritjof Capra and of the pleasures or indeed (literally) ecstasies of the computer, that emblematic informational super-machine of "the great suprapersonal system of late capitalis[m] [...]" (Jameson, "Pleasure" 73).

Among the different senses of ideology let me use here Althusser's sense of a twisted representation of the subject's relationship to his or her real conditions of existence. In fiction on the capitalist market a quite basic and all-permeating ideology is the need for permanent excitement and mounting reader stimulation (see Suvin "Commodities"). As Gibson's work expands but also weakens in *Count Zero*, it becomes clear that this more and more obtruding ideology and its narrative concomitant, melodrama, are *within the utopia itself.* Of the four or five principal narrative agents in *Count Zero*, three veer off, more or less strongly, into mystical realms: Marly and Turner rely on their intuition or "edge" – "that superhuman synchromesh flow that stimulants only approximated" (14) – while Angela's biotechnical enhancement manifests itself even more sensationally as voodoo and then (as already mentioned, inconsequentially) ends up as a simstim ("feelies") entertainment-industry career. Yet, in spite of his plot oscillation between defeatism and kitschy happy-endings, which is an indicator of a real dilemma this very intelligent writer finds himself in as to the direction of history and even as to the possibility of meaningful action within it, Gibson's powers of observation, the flip face of his verbal inventiveness, are on the whole very refreshing. His work does not accept the values of the black, closed world he evokes with such skill: he hates the status quo. But his balancing act accepts the status quo a bit too readily as inevitable and unchangeable.

Paradoxically, this is for me too "realistic" in the pedestrian sense, too direct a reflection of the short-term situation all of us who radically doubt the dominant values of the new capitalist feudalism find ourselves in. I believe a deeper, or longer-range, view would be to hold fast to a belief in really possible, even if statistically at the moment not very probable, radical changes. Neither the tough-guy lyricism of erotics nor the excitement of cyberspace, acceptable and even fine as they undoubtedly can be, seem to me finally satisfactory as utopias. Both, it will be noticed, are deeply socialized but still privatized utopias – or in fact utopian surrogates. Cyberspace is "[...] an information map of the economically grounded world of data and documentation: not history, certainly, but history's material fallout"

(Delany, *Mississippi Review* 33). Perhaps unwittingly, Delany has here put the finger on a basic ambiguity in this characteristic imaginary or narrative space: *cyberspace is simultaneously an acknowledgement of the overriding role of History and a flight from it.* The only way to cope with blue ice is to serve it or to destroy (a part of) it; the single person Chrome can be "burned" but the *zaibatsu* system as a whole cannot. History is an all-encompassing cruel Destiny, more than a little transcendental in its very intimate insertion into the flesh of the little protagonists. The dilemma of how personal actions and conduct relate to social change is simultaneously inescapable and insoluble within Gibson's model. I have suggested earlier that a solution logically latching on to cyberspace, and allowing a surrogate reconnecting [*re-ligio*] between disparate people and their destinies outside of and against history, is then religion. As Delany goes on to acutely observe, religion is therefore a permanent temptation of the cyberpunkers: "The hard edges of Gibson's dehumanized technologies hide a residing mysticism" (*Mississippi Review* 33).

In sum, a viable thisworldly, collective and public, utopianism simply is not within the horizon of the cyberpunk structure of feeling. When Sterling interprets the cyberpunk emblem of mirrorshades, mirrored sunglasses reflecting the light, as "prevent[ing] the forces of normalcy from realizing that one is crazed and possibly dangerous" (*M* xi), he seems to me wrong. It is true that the mirrorshade wearer's gaze is obscured for the observer, who cannot tell whether she or he is being looked at or not. Nonetheless, it is not too difficult to gauge a person's behaviour even when the eyes are hidden. Rather, in my opinion mirrorshades are a two-way transaction between the wearer and his social environment: they conjoin a minor degree of effective withdrawal with a large degree of psychological illusion of withdrawal in the wearer. In political terms, such an illusory dead end becomes obvious when Sterling continues the cited sentence by listing those dangerous mirrorshade visionaries: "the biker, the rocker, the policeman, and similar outlaws" (sic! – these macho associations of mirrorshades justify my "his" for the wearer). As Delany points out, "[mirrorshades] both mask the gaze and distort the gaze"; he then rightly proceeds to read them as an emblem or "a nice allegory of what is happening in this particular kind of SF" (Delany, "Some *Real* Mothers" 8).

Thus an evaluation of cyberpunk depends, I think, on the works examined. Even where I disagree with Gibson's horizons, he has certainly identified some real or even central problems of our spacetime. He latches onto some great precursors on the margins of SF and "high lit," such as Pynchon (in honour of whose Oedipa Maas Gibson's recurring villainous *zaibatsu* of Maas Biolabs has been named), or William Burroughs, who pioneered the insight that the hallucinatory operators are real. It is mainly in his hands that cyberpunk has been "that current SF work which is not middle-class, not comfortable with history, not tragic, not supportive, not maternal, not happy-go-lucky [...]. But it's only as a negative [...] that cyberpunk can signify." (Delany, *Mississippi Review* 30) Gibson's first two books have refreshed the language and sensibility of SF. In fact, it is correct but not quite sufficient to praise Gibson for broadening the range of SF (or indeed of modern literature) with the new vocabulary of lyricized information interfaces. The new vocabulary is, as always, a sign for new human relationships. To say, as does the first sentence of *N*, "The sky above the port was the color of television, tuned to a dead channel," means to foreground electronic interfaces into a new nature, a second nature that has grown to be a first nature.

Sterling, on the contrary, does not play in the same league. His general form is that of a rather loose and verbose picaresque string of adventures. The yawning gap which I feel exists between Gibson and Sterling can be illustrated by comparing the erotic relationship between the junkie protagonist of *Involution Ocean* and the alien, physiologically incompatible woman Dalusa to the couples discussed earlier in Gibson. Sterling's love affair lacks the tension between Eros and Thanatos characteristic of Gibson. While the situation as set up is potentially interesting, it never gets beyond rather thin sadomasochism, where the pain inflicted (primarily on the woman) is another sexual thrill. The tension is here abolished in favor of the only remaining horizon of death. Furthermore, after two readings I cannot see either a causal or an analogical function for the love-story within the "involution ocean" quest of Captain Desperandum – itself a not very interesting foal sired by Captain Ahab's quest out of *Dune*.

Perhaps it may not be fair to judge anybody by a first novel. And in fact Sterling's second one, *The Artificial Kid*, is to my mind his most interesting work. There is much inventiveness in the protagonist's "combat-artist" youth subculture – with "technomedicine" including superdrugs – that arises in response to the long-lifers' grip on society, i.e., on economics and politics. This subculture is both an analogy and a writing large of contemporary punk plus violent sports plus (most interestingly) their use for mass entertainment under the rulers' patronage. These fun touches, however, are accompanied by naive or outright dubious disquisitions on politics, such as Manies's "Chemical Analog" theory of society (where individuals function as molecules – not a great advance on Asimov's psychohistory). True, at least there is in this novel an essay at a range of meditations on social organization, which includes also Chairman Moses' attempt at redesigning society, St Anne's eco-theology, and perhaps most important Arti's own experiential trajectory. In spots, the novel therefore approaches allegorical validity. Unfortunately, not only are these aspects rather shallow, they are also thrown about in a slapdash manner and usually given as long speeches breaking up the tension. The plot itself meanders about and ends up in the last third echoing some fairly old SF conventions (e.g., some early Aldiss) as well as dodging the initial youth-culture issues by means of a happy ending based on friendship between young and old oiled by prosperity.

Sterling's next novel, *Schismatrix*, is a somewhat updated space opera flitting from colony to colony, in a rather forced derivation from something like the Italian Renaissance city-states and their different systems with internal intrigues of little relevance. It is an advance on his earlier novels in ambition but not in execution. It recirculates with a new sauce, pretending to some metaphysical depth of "Prigoginic levels of complexities," the hoariest clichés of 1940s–1950s SF, say from Heinlein to Farmer. As usual, some interesting themes (loneliness, flesh vs. disembodied mind) are hurriedly tossed off and quite buried under a torrent of micro-ideas neither fully digested nor integrated into the narrative. Thus the basic plot tension between the Mechanics and the more biologically inclined Shapers, transferred from five stories of his between 1982 and 1985 and evolving against a horizon of ultimate futility, does not seem to me meaningfully worked out either as concept or in the plot (see Tom Maddox, *Mississippi Review* 237–44). Again, there are amusing fragments and witty passages in the novel, but the principle of how they are strung together escapes me. Finally, for all the inventive and hip, "postmodernist" conceptual proliferation, neither the political canvas of Sterling's *Schismatrix*, nor the supposedly biological one *of Involution Ocean*, nor the attempt to combine the two in *The Artificial Kid*, have anything like the lyrical force, intrinsic fascination, or indeed referential relevance of Gibson's cyberspace.

***

I must confess, at the end of this section and in the nature of a post-scriptum to it, that the neat polarization between a worthy Gibson and an unworthy Sterling is somewhat shaken by their latest novels. Upon my first two readings, Gibson's *Mona Lisa Overdrive* confirms and solidifies his trajectory from critical to escapist use of cyberspace, masked by plot recomplication. The ending, where the Romeo-and-Juliet pair (continued from *Count Zero*) willingly withdraw from empirical to cyberpunk space, is tired old stuff, identical, for example, to the end of Fritz Lang's expressionist movie *Der müde Tod* (*The Tired Death*, translated also as *Destiny*, 1921), where the space into which the lovers enter after all the empirical defeats is more accurately – if less science-fictionally – identified as the domain of a friendly Death. As is well known, Death is the final horizon of melodrama.

On the other hand, Sterling's *Islands in the Net* is technically his smoothest work. Yet it is achieved, first of all, at the cost of a withdrawal from the earlier, more exuberant multiplicity of viewpoints to old-fashioned single-protagonist focus on Laura Webster. Further, it is politically woolly-minded, or if you prefer, its extrapolated twenty-first century has too many loose ends. Though centered on power-struggles which grow quite violent, this is a much more cheerful vision than Gibson's. True, in this "post-millennium" world the detente and international cooperation through the UN means in fact the domination of multinational companies. However, not only is this a world without the nuclear threat in bombs or power plants, without traffic jams, and without network television, its corporations also come in a spread running from responsible "economic democrats" (like Laura's Rizome) to data pirates and straightforward fascists (like the tiny nation-states of Grenada, Singapore, and Mali where most of the derring-do occurs, and which are at the end dispossessed). Due to the exertions and sufferings of our candid and sturdy heroine, the good guys of Rizome, who value creativity and a feeling of belonging (which Sterling persists in spelling *gemeineschaft*), i.e., who sympathize with the "scientist and engineers, and architects, too, [...] who do the world's true work" (*Islands* 94–95), are at the end left in control of the field. Their framework and symbol is the omnipresent audiovisual and information Net, "Computers [...] fusing together [...] [t]elevision – telephone – telex. Tape recorder – VCR – laser disk" (*Islands* 15). The Net is a poor parent of Gibson's Cyberspace both because it is flatly extrapolative, and because its value and its values are never doubted; both of these mean that it is quite alien to Cyberspace's utopian core. Outside the Net are the disadvantaged: people like the dyslexic Carlotta, and most of the Third World population. It is interesting to look at the provenience of some names given to his narrative agents: Valeri Chkalov and Sergei Ilyushin were (in the readers' historical world) famous Russian aviation people of the 1930s–1940s, Lacoste is a famous present-day brand of clothing etc., Yaobang is the first name of a recent secretary of the Chinese Communist party, etc. Such second-hand tags from daily papers or historical handbooks indicate well the superficiality of Sterling's international politics. The fake alternative of Atom Bomb vs. The Net, on which the novel is based, is finally simply the alternative between old-style military capitalism (against which much indignation is directed) and new-style informational invasion: neither of which could in a reasonable extrapolation exist without the other. It speaks well for Sterling's ideological instincts, but badly about his narrative framework, that he was on page 292 (out of 348) forced to bring out of nowhere an anarchic rebel, extrapolated from T.E. Lawrence, to save Laura and let her properly inform the world, in a triumph of media freedom against international UN bureaucracy ... The hoariest clichés of US liberalism, those which gave it a deservedly bad name, celebrate their rebirth here.

3. Parting Doubts

A general conclusion therefore might be that Gibson best demonstrates how "Today, one need not 'be a Marxist' to realize that aesthetics, politics, economics, technology, and social relations are interdependent cultural phenomena" (Sobchak 8): though I would add one need to have at least – and that is no small least – absorbed some central propositions of Marxism. This interdependence means also that literary utopianism cannot grow any more into an independent literary genre, but only (as I have had occasion to argue) into a dominant component of SF.

Furthermore, Gibson's work also presents (at any rate, for the moment) the coalescing of a new structure of feeling. A structure of experience and of feeling is, as the late and regretted Raymond Williams formulated it, "a particular quality of social experience and relationship [...] which gives the sense of a generation or of a period"; however, that remains only "social experiences in solution" or "a [semantic] formation at the very edge of semantic availability" until it precipitates and becomes "more evidently and more immediately available" (131–34). In Gibson, a structure of feeling has indeed become formulated and therefore more immediately available for our collective discussion.

There can be few higher praises than this for a work of verbal or any other art. But for cyberpunk SF as a whole, at least two questions in mutual feedback remain to be tentatively answered or indeed simply posed. First, whose structure of feeling might this be? Second, what ideological horizons or consequences does it imply?

It is, of course, quite insufficient and improper to call this structure of feeling simply one of the 1980s. No doubt, it is such – but of everybody living in the 1980s? in the whole world? Based on both external and internal evidence, I would speculate that cyberpunk SF is representative for the structure of feeling of an important but certainly not all-inclusive international social group. As I hinted at the beginning, this is some fractions of the youth culture in the more affluent North of our globe. More particularly, cyberpunk is correlative to the technicians and artists associated with the new communication media, and to the young who aspire to such a status.

It is, of course, quite irrelevant whether a formulator of such an ideology (e.g., Gibson) is personally a computer hacker or video-arcade addict. It is only necessary that the formulator's ideology be an ideal representation of the experience from which cyberpunk arose, persuasively characterized by Sterling as follows:

> [...] high-tech recording, satellite video, and computer graphics [have turned] the artists at pop's cutting edge [...] quite often [into] cutting-edge technicians in the bargain. They are special effects wizards, mixmasters, tape-effects techs, graphics hackers, emerging through new media to dazzle society with head-trip extravaganzas like FX cinema and the global Live Aid benefit. (*M* xii)

Now this group is widespread, international, and significant beyond its numbers as a cutting edge. However, it is certainly a small, single-digit percentage even of the youth or fifteen-to-thirty age group, even in the North (never mind the whole world).

As to my second parting question, let me here too start from the language at the end of Sterling's quite representative passage just cited. It is, to put it mildly, puzzling. Is cyberpunk then proudly proclaiming itself to be another extravaganza to dazzle society in head-trips and (let me add) to be integrated into the profit-making and highly ideologized culture industry? Is it to be, as Delany observed, reactionary macho cynicism, "at its best conservative and at its worst rebarbative – if not downright tedious," so that it could well be "co-opted to support the most stationary of status quos" (Delany, "Some *Real* Mothers" 9–10; see also Csicsery-Ronay, *Mississippi Review* 266–71)? Or is it something more – perhaps even a cognitive poetry of the horizons of that social group, important for all of us? To put the crucial question: In its forte, the integration of agents and action into technosleaze, is cyberpunk the diagnostician of or the parasite on a disease? Such items as Sterling's and Shiner's collaborative short story "Mozart in Mirrorshades" (*M* 223–39), which have nothing to envy Robert Adams's genocidal "mercenaries' SF" (if I may so baptize it) – and might be even more repulsive for the slick sheen they add to it – certainly testify that it can be the parasite.

Is cyberpunk then, despite all trendy mimicry of rebelliousness, complicitous with the owners and managers of the culture industry, finally with the death-dealing *zaibatsu* so well described by Gibson, and merely trying to get some crumbs off their table by flaunting its own newness as a marketable commodity; or is it truly (at least in intention and in part) a coalescing oppositional world-view whose final horizon would be a historical world of liberated erotics and cognitive cyberspace, without the zaibatsu or escapist head-trips? Only time will tell. But the evolution (or if you wish, the involution ocean) of cyberpunk after 1984 does not, at the moment, bode too well. The dilemma has, with some exaggeration, been put provocatively thus:

> So cyberpunks, like near-addicts of amphetamins and hallucinogens, write as if they [we]re both victims of a life-negating system and the heroic adventurers of thrill. They can't help themselves, but their hip grace gets them through an amoral world, facing a future which, for all intents and purposes, has gone beyond human influence, and where the only way to live is in speed, speed to avoid being caught in the web [...]. (Csicsery-Ronay, *Mississippi Review* 276)

The attitude thus described is, of course, properly an adolescent one. "Adolescent" does not necessarily mean invalid; indeed, it means very probably at least partly valid; but it also, finally, means untenable à la longue. We can only hope pessimists such as Csicsery-Ronay and I will be confounded by Gibson and some new stars, or at least shuriken.

Or perhaps (unkind thought, subject to verification by further SF writings): perhaps we should simply stop talking about "cyberpunk SF," that witty coinage of Gardner Dozois's? Perhaps it might be more useful to say that there is the writer William Gibson, and then there are a couple of expert PR-men (most prominently Sterling himself) who know full well the commercial value of an instantly recognizable label, and are sticking one onto disparate products?[2]

---

2   My thanks go to Prof. Takayuki Tatsumi and to the organizers of the "SF Seminar" meeting at Ochanomizu in Tokyo, June 1988, who asked me to prepare a first draft of this essay as a lecture. Dr Tatsumi also kindly gave me some materials and information on "cyberpunk SF." Special warm thanks to my friend Ms Kazuko Yamada whose translation of the lecture and then of an intermediary version of this essay into Japanese, following on the heels of a 1987 interview where she first challenged me about cyberpunk, has in fact made her into a collaborator in this text. The article was written in Köln, June 1989, and slightly revised in April 1991.

Works Cited

Bear, Greg. *Blood Music*. New York: Ace, 1986.

[Delany, Samuel R.] "Some *Real* Mothers: An Interview with Takayuki Tatsumi." *Science Fiction Eye* 1.3 (1988): 5–11.

——. "Is Cyberpunk a Good Thing or a Bad Thing?" *Mississippi Review* 16.2–3 (1988): 28–35.

Gibson, William. *Burning Chrome*. New York: Ace, 1986.

——. *Count Zero*. New York: Ace, 1987.

——. *Neuromancer*. New York: Ace, 1984.

Jameson, Fredric. "Cognitive Mapping." *Marxism and the Interpretation of Culture*. Ed. Cary Nelson and Lawrence Grossberg. Urbana: University of Illinois Press, 1988. 347–57.

——. "Pleasure: A Political Issue," *The Ideologies of Theory*. Vol. 2. Minneapolis: University of Minnesota Press, 1988. 61–74.

Mississippi Review 47/48 (1988). [Special Issue on Cyberpunk, ed. Larry McCaffery.]

Shepard, Lucius. *Life During Wartime*. New York: Bantam, 1987.

Sobchack, Vivian. *Screening Space*. New York: Ungar, 1987.

Spinrad, Norman. *Little Heroes*. New York: Bantam, 1987.

Sterling, Bruce. *The Artificial Kid*. New York: Ace, 1987.

——. "Introduction." *Mirrorshades*. Ed. Bruce Sterling. New York: Ace, 1988. ix–xvi.

——. *Involution Ocean*. New York: Ace, 1988.

——. *Islands in the Net*. New York: Arbor House, 1988.

——. "Preface." Gibson, *Burning Chrome*. ix–xii.

——. *Schismatrix*. New York: Ace, 1986.

Suvin, Darko. "Two Holy Commodities: The Practices of Fictional Discourse and Erotic Discourse." *Sociocriticism* 2 (1985): 31–47.

Williams, Raymond. *Marxism and Literature*. New York: Oxford University Press, 1981.

The Doldrums: Eight Nasty Poems of 1989–1999

The Return of the Ancestors (End of March)

> Mrijeti ti ćeš kada počneš sâm
> U ideale svoje sumnjati.
> [Thou wilt die when thyself beginnest
> Doubting your own ideals]
> — SILVIJE S. KRANJČEVIĆ

Our dead return. We must meet them
With short fir branches, light the lanterns.
The fire is lighted: Grampa, Granma
Ride a cow, ride a bull
Please come by this light, take a drink with us.

Our dead ask: What have you done of our work,
How continued our lives? Why are the dams collapsing,
Who lives in the big house ruling the hill? What
Interests extort blood in peacetime, brothers killing
Brothers? Do you have too many sons to feed?

Our dead do not bless us. Their stare is of stone.
The branches grow brown. The lanterns gutter.
The fire is damped. Granma, Grampa
Ride a bull, ride a cow
Please go back by this light, have pity on us.

O sons, O grandchildren, look how fat you are,
Look how hard your women must work, where's
Your powerful sisterhood & brotherhood? Pay
Your ingent debts, to us, to yourselves, flow
Over the banks: unclog your veins, have pity
On us, on yourselves.

Le Ceneri di Tito (Berlin Day, End of C20)

is there peace in this world?
the torture of humans continues
evening light   island just floating
shaking like a baby carriage
even archeologists perish in the end ...

— HAYASHI FUMIKO, 1930

German winter   elder ladies with mink coats
Peroxide hair   too much makeup
Lines slashing from both mouth corners down & out
I burrow into sleep quietly on morning islands
At the bottom of the ocean   schools of fish
Soft murmur of weary voices
They are bombing Beograd & Novi Sad
No more theatre festivals in springtime
Blood silting up all rivers.

Whispering of fish   jealousy of fish
If sharks were men
Big gangsters eat little gangsters
Peasants are burned out of their villages
City people bombed out of their homes
Thousands of Munch faces screaming
Humans   from their womb humanity forcibly ripped
By progressive technology & humanism

Demanding oceans of blood

Western brainwashed in uniform shoot at Balkan brainwashed
The center doesn't tolerate too much periphery
Top dollar American mercenaries bomb scared Serbian draftees
Bristly bearded gangsters from Beograd
                cleaning Albanians out of medieval monasteries
They are madly in love with the Serbian destiny to suffer
Smooth shaven gangsters from Washington
                upgrading armament technology
They are madly in love with the profits of arms industries
Booms in Balkan skies   booms on the stock-markets
Communicating slaughterhouse vessels

Oceans of blood   oceans of profit
Who is king of the world jungle must be made quite clear
Sharks are not so clever   except in fable

Now you can touch what we lost with Tito's brotherhood & unity
Now you see how a people's revolution is eradicated
One million & three quarters dead in the partizan war
A ton of TNT to wipe out every dead partizan
These dead are dangerous   they must be killed again by bombs & lies
The grounds salted with durable uranium

Counter-revolution by the center against the periphery
Blood on stone   blood & stones
Thou shalt not get out from under world banks   fish mouth silently
This is Moses & the prophets

Glossary: Le Ceneri di Tito = The Ashes of Tito

Ein garstig Lied

In my dream i find again
The purity of the militant:
An abiding carnal ache.

Köln, am Dom (Nichtsdestotrotz)

For Michael Hulse

Und das Versäumte geht um, gross wie die Schemen der Zukunft.
— PAUL CELAN, *Nachts*

Minding time, the software
Won't quite work, letters fail
In stranger land. The Nô recorder wails,
Neigh the Houyhnhnhms of night.

We still hold what should,
Only
No sweet maidens sing
What holds. Notwithstanding

We have almost lived, between Here & Not-Yet-There
On the rapids of Sometimes, in a
Dream-fast canoe,
At the rosy teats of time.

Let me understand: first
Things last,
No finger-post is finally lost. Yet O you
Swaying castrato-high spires,

Blinding light
　　diesscling down
　　　　solidified
　　　　　　space

Of not working cathedrals
Subwayed out beneath Einerlei rock;
& O you vanishing beds
Of the electric trains we didn't track.

Glossary: Title = Cologne, by the Cathedral; subtitle: Nevertheless,
Notwithstanding; motto from Celan: And what was omitted, spooks
around/ Huge like the blueprints of the future; Einerlei: Never-mind (echo
to Lorelei, the Rhine nearby)

Montréal 1994

For Tamura Ryûichi

The wolves of freezing
　　　　O god of Puritans
howl down the canyons of Montréal
　　　　or is it just the nineties
i am
　　into regretting
uphill from regretting
are reasons　　　entwined like roots of the wisdom molar
milling away　　　splitting down the middle
waiting for bridge & forceps

a february blizzard took the last as always
warmth from anywhere in the alluvial plain
built over by banks & electricity
too many cold confused people   i am there too
water pipes freeze forty feet below the ground
superintendent please keep the warm water running at all times
somewhere in the house
if anybody will
be in the house

in my medium-sized condo
inside the study   & the bedroom
i light the type R-30 movable lamps
they radiate much heat from their 100 watts
i draw them to the height of my front
          above my writing hands
just aslant above my eyes
& work at the regretting
like a competent midwife
        proscribed by the medical faculty
she's seen it all for centuries

it's toward the end of this cold century
babies are always bloody & howl
        with fright pain & maybe regret
a baby forgets it's working at regretting
at collecting   with much luck replacing
      seashells of nostalgia by the seashore
(the roots entwining
        like twin pines in pain)
in training for unemployment
       the brief joys of the slave.

Imagine a Fish

Imagine a fish living out of water

The water is
The air is
The fish is

He has some water in his bladder
He flops along gravelly roads

Up to her eyes coated with dust
How does she see desiccated the world
Imagine

Sometimes it flops up a stump
And attempts to sing
The birds are in the water

(Imagine)

Old Age, Letting Go

Homage to Tanikawa Shuntarô

I.

I wish a wandering asteroid wd whoosh down
When nobody expected it any more
Ringed like Saturn with promises
The size of red Jupiter
& blow this infested planet to smithereens.

This is what my life has added up to
Almost
Like a blind mangy kitten.

      ***

Get rid of yr affections
Let go vanity hope even wounds.

You have vanquished O pale Galilean
Sweat blood & snot running down the cross of gold
From which we hang in vain
Punished by gazing hungrily at Finland Station
In the whorehouse that once was Leningrad.

      ***

Reader try as i may i have lost
Yr image. My compassion runs dry
I won't get to be a Bodhisattva.
I go on for accidental reasons. Scarcely
Believable of the man who attacked
The written page as a wolf, with iron jaws
& slavering appetite.

Slaves must perforce be stoic,
Patients patient.

      2.

A poet lies on his double bed,
Writing. Fiftythousand neurons die in his head
Each day. The ceiling in his study leaks,
Five years already, nobody can find out why.

What is he writing, to whom, what for?

Mad hatters & dormice
slit each other's throats
in a Bosnian shelled city.

In my memory you smile at me
wet from monsoon rains
which warmly sweep the macadam.

Do you really know how the world
ends? My bed sails the broad ocean.
People you loved tell me

You talk to nobody.

When father died, we got a snapshot of his grave
The copyrights of his manuals are also left to me
My desire to claim either has vanished.
I walk to the top of the hill & pretend not to hear
The little demons guffawing behind the bushes.

                    3.
You that may read these fragments, you in
A new cool harmony we are condemned to
Disbelieve in, you that i lived with & for
Until this senility, if i had any feelings left
Parting with you wd break my heart. Let go,
Let go, unimaginable others, defined by a hollow.

On or about January one, Nineteenninetytwo,
The short Twentieth Century – just seventyfive years –
Winked out, the future became a thing of the past.
We embark upon extra-vehicular spacewalks empty-handed,
Isolated by non-conducting gloves, technological prestige
& helmets with virtual faceplates. O Harmonians
How long, justify how long you let us wait.

***

It's tiresome to wake up. For threehundred readers
It is tiresome to write. No doubt, you'll fit
This high-pitched note into a chord, Harmonians,
Martian "ulla, ulla" on Hampstead Heath. But now
Only old music remains for me, & some bodies
(Not mine). The kalpa is muzak-meretricious
Or silent.

Earnestly she reads on Wallerstein & Hobsbawm, in warm
Scarves swathed. I am haunted by songs of auld lang syne:
"Avanti popolo ..." "O bella ciao ..."
"Omladino zemlje ove ...". Azure, the azure!

                    ***

Learning
How to non-write
Not unwrite.
The dead are not safe.
Learning, still.

Glossary: "Omladino zemlje ove ..." = "O youth of this country", Partizan
round-dance song

Alas Indeed! Disputing Cao Ji

Alas indeed! – the many rolling tumbleweeds
In this only life-world how discarded
A quarter of century uprooted into dying
Day & night without rest or respite
Eastward, westward, passing seven paths

Northward, southward, crossing nine roads.
The years look down from high-rise loggias
They wisely wave goodbye goodbye.

Young we met a rising whirlwind
Propelling us up inside the clouds
We thought, this is the end-reach of skies!
Older we were cast down to the abyss
The terrible storm carried us off
The south-pointing needle now shows the north
We set sail for Cathay & the land was California
All too soon Leningrad is not even Petrograd.
Drift on, drift on, what may we lean on?
Finally perish but finally be.

Floating up beyond the warm Adriatic
Flying on over the North Atlantic
Flowing, tumbling, no abiding dwelling.
Should the future care for our bitter straits?
I wish we might be grass amid the forest
Where raging fires follow Fall & burn.
The pains would be frightening, slash & pierce,
But our ash would return to roots, connected
In the mashing cycle that now wheels downward
In the awesome cycle that will wheel upward.

CHAPTER 8

Where Are We? How Did We Get Here? Is There Any Way Out? Or, News from the Novum (1997–1998)[1]

For Fredric Jameson: who keeps the faith
and to the shade of William Morris

Hic est itaque finis, ad quem tendo, talem scilicet naturam acquirere, et, ut multi mecum eam acquirant, conari; hoc est, de mea felicitate etiam est operam dare, ut alii multi idem atque ego intelligant, ut eorum intellectus et cupiditas prorsus cum meo intellectu et cupiditate conveniant; utque hoc fiat, necesse est tantum de Natura intelligere, quantum sufficit, ad talem naturam acquirendam; deinde formare talem societatem, qualis est desideranda, ut quamplurimi quam facillime et secure eo perveniant. [This is therefore the end to which I tend, namely to obtain such a [perfected] state and to strive as best I can so that many people may obtain it together with me; for it is part of my happiness to work at having many others understand what I understand, so that their intellect and desire may accord with my intellect and desire; and in order that this may be, it is necessary to understand nature insofar as is sufficient to reach that [perfected] state, and after that to build such a society which is to be desired so that the greatest possible number of people may reach it in the securest and easiest way.]
— BARUCH SPINOZA, *De Intellectus Emendatione (Of Bettering the Intelligence)*

It would be very pretentious of me to think that I am subversive. But I would say that, etymologically speaking, yes, I try to subvert. To come up underneath conformity, underneath an existing way of thinking, in

---

1   Translations from titles adduced in foreign languages are mine. All unreferenced verse is mine.

order to shift it a little [...]. To unstick matters, to make them a bit more
mobile, to let in doubt. I always try to discomfit what is supposedly natural, what goes without saying.

— ROLAND BARTHES, *The Grain of the Voice*

What liberates us is the knowledge of who we were, what we became,
where we were, whereunto we have been thrown, whereto we speed,
wherefrom we are redeemed, what birth is and what rebirth.

— VALENTINUS THE GNOSTIC

1. Bombed Back to Gilgamesh: The Politico-Economic (Thence Epistemic) Deluge and Three Axioms

The concept of progress should be anchored in the idea of catastrophe. The fact of
"it going on" is the catastrophe: not what is in each case in front of us but what is
in each case given.

— WALTER BENJAMIN

1.0

All cultural artefacts, discursive propositions or indeed non-discursive
sense-makings are constituted in the reader by continuous, multiplex allud-
ing to her more or less collective imaginary encyclopedia, with its fluctuating
entries and presuppositional cross-references. Where SF differs from most
(though not all) other modes and genres is by using strategically placed
non-existents – for instance spacetimes and psychozoa – to allude if not
to point-like existents familiar to the reader/s (that point-to-point allusion
would be old-fashioned allegory) but then, in most cases, to *relationships*
between familiar existents. Now to allude is to refer.

So my *first axiom* is that *SF makes sense by referring to the readers' here-
and-now through not referring to familiar empirical existents*. This is the fundamental device, charm, and perhaps paradox of SF, and all discussions of

it. The salient textual existents are empirically non-existent; the syntagmatic development of the text uses the simulacrum of a paradigm (Angenot), its textual Possible World, in order to reconstitute the paradigm implied in the reader's encyclopedia. It is a detour, a slowed-down understanding or deferred cognitive gratification which, as the Russian Formalists well realized, de-automatizes our reading by forcing us to think what the textual deployment – unfolding and show – may *mean*. Again, it shares this with the story of Agamemnon, Prince Genji, Rastignac or Mother Courage, but only by redoubling the work of reading. Analogously to Freud's dreamwork, SF builds a second tier of displacement and condensation by means of the principal agents' journey through spacetimes unfamiliar to the implied readers. This journey is also the readers' voyage toward making sense, simultaneously, of the story being read and of one's own position under the stars and banks. This means SF is (or at least, is best interpreted as being) a hidden parable about some aspect/s of the times in which it is written and offered for reading.

1.1

Thus might begin a paper, essay or speech I would have made ten or twenty years ago to a gathering of SF critics and readers. But if there is a fundamental presupposition to all I have said up to now, i.e., in the last forty years, about SF, it is that the flow of here-and-nows is what we usually call history, that whatever encyclopedia is being referred to is specific to a sociohistorical class, that whatever very significant constants can be found in SF from Wells or Percy and Mary Shelley or Thomas More on, they are in practice only apprehended in concrete socially determined points of reading. Can the critic, however interested in long duration, be outside history, a simulacrum of the monotheistic God judging if not his then other Creations? Maybe so in slower and more confident times. But not today. If our value-horizon, however battered, does not have to change – I hope mine has not changed overmuch during my lifetime, I do not like convert-renegades – s/he who does not learn in and from history is dead. Our speaking voice is necessarily modified in its registers in a different atmosphere, now thoroughly intermixed with fumes of pollution. The voices sound tinny and squeak, unless they sound hoarse from ranting against the tinniness: their pitch has to be adjusted. Also their yaw, in the noosphere where bellowing instead of argumentation has become the carefully patented and profitable trademark of Post-Modernism, from born-again Christians and Moslems through the various mutually murderous nationalisms and ethnicisms to the terrorism of atopia, and where I do not know who I am speaking to (though I still know what I am speaking for).

For a new overwhelming global experience has intervened between the early 1970s and today, which demands to be given voice and contours to: we have lived a politico-economical and epistemic earthquake. Or maybe it should be called the Deluge. The trickle-down began so slowly that I for one had not realized any need to face the small rain when finishing my book *Metamorphoses of SF* by writing the essay on the novum for Teresa de Lauretis's panel at a Milwaukee conference in 1977 (Chapter 3 in this book). But it can today be for our profession approached by saying with Gayatri Chakravorty Spivak: "literary people are still caught within a position where they must say: Life is brute fact and outside art; the aesthetic is free and transcends life [...]. If 'literary studies' is to have any meaning [...], [this] ideology might have to be questioned" (95). In other, my words: The assumption of esthetic transcendence means Formalism in criticism: the artistic artifact has its own immanent laws of shaping, and elucidating them is our professional business. I still believe this is partly true (as autonomy), but a partial truth may turn into the worst lie. This has been happening to people deriding Noah for building the Ark, who then drowned. While Noah always needs shipwrighting criticism, if professionalism means refusing to be citizens, then it is a pernicious ideology serving the crumbling status quo.

Faced with this, one of my two Faustian souls has always envied the ancient Daoist sages or Mitteleuropean rabbis who could devote their life to sitting at the temple's gate and meditating. Alas, as Brecht and Weill noted in a Chorus of *The Threepenny Opera*, "die Verhältnisse, die sind nicht so": the conditions around us are not such. We are rather living the deepest ancient Chinese malediction, "may you live in interesting times" – the times of permanent conflict of each against each for which Hobbes used the slanderous comparison to wolves. So it is our curse and glory, at any rate necessity, to engage in combat: agon is the only (bitter) remedy in agonizing times.

1.2

One consequence of our politico-epistemic earthquake-cum-deluge is that we need not only new maps of hell but also new conventions of cartography, mapping zigzags through simultaneous and alternative times. For one example: description gets very complicated when the analysis has simultaneously to question its presuppositions, and when the only way to do that is to interweave it with prescription supplying values and opening the presuppositions up to the reader's judgment. Why bother describing just *this* matter from just *that* aspect? "Pure" description (a beast as frequent as the unicorn) is insidiously on the side of the Powers-That-Be, while prescription is overtly and clearly on the side it chooses. I have been quite rightly accused of committing this heinous sin in *Metamorphoses*. I hope it makes that book similar to what every fiction writer does: a narration with a barely concealed system of tropes subtending both description and evaluation (I have been accused of that too, in an ill-placed preface to its Italian translation).

For a second example: with quicker obsolescence and market diversification, a greater number of unfamiliar existents, events, and relationships has to be accommodated into our shifting cognitive paradigm; so while there's no induction at all without an initial (deductive) guesstimate what to induce from and against which, however approximate, horizons, the relative weight of induction will rise. And third, the criteria of choice between hypotheses are, even in strictest natural science with predictive power, finally reducible to a preference for one model over another: the criterion of simplicity underlying all science assumes that nature itself follows a given *model* of unity or coherence (Hesse 101–29). Every theoretical explanation is thus also a "metaphoric redescription of the domain of the explanandum," so that "rationality consists just in the continuous adaptation of our language to our continually expanding world, and metaphor is one of the chief means by which this is accomplished" (Hesse 157 and 176–77; see Suvin *Positions*, final essay). Indeed, reasoning by analogy, that scorned prerogative of poets and mystics, will be seen to ultimately (though not at all centrally) underlie all the Kuhnian paradigms of however positive a science: most famously, Einstein's God who does not play at crap-shooting. Finally: the scientist faith, still rampant in our schools of engineering and newspapers, that objects can be seen "objectively," i.e., regardless of the type of subject and other conditions of seeing it, is being replaced by a struggle to understand how valid cognition can arise from openly acknowledged "subject-positions" (competing in the plural, though I have argued elsewhere – as have the best Feminists – that some of them are more equal than others).

So my *second axiom* might run like this: *Conceptual argumentation is absolutely necessary but only if shot through by poetry may it be sufficient.* Formalism is absolutely necessary as the A and B of scholarship, but the alphabet has many more letters: perhaps indeed the atomic binaries of A and −A should be replaced by something akin to the Chinese characters as units of understanding? (If we only understood what Chinese characters were!)

In an age of broad social hopes incarnated in strong sociopolitical movements of working people, including intellectuals – parties, trade unions, liberation movements, co-ops such as the Kibbutzim, and other NGO groupings – the role of scholars in humanities has always seemed to me to be one of a critical support for them. This means support for these movements' horizons and general strategy plus critique of their tactics – in particular, of their frequent blindness to the power and specificity of semiotics and storytelling. Thus, when Lenin's and Trotsky's, or Tito's, or Gramsci's and Togliatti's, or Cabral's, or Ho's, or Castro's communist party was spearheading crucial political battles, cultural scholars not only could but had to be Formalists. (I am here speaking from a Left-wing perspective, but I think my stance might be applicable to Rightwing constellations too, so that we could learn something from the relation of Pound or indeed Jim Blish to Mussolini or of Martin Heidegger to Hitler.) But today, Formalism – or Structuralism, or any heirs to them – can only be a preliminary to a more comprehensive civic analysis, to politics in the Aristotelian sense:

there is no movement to take the onus away from any of us. The comforting economic and psychic roofs (Bellamy's and Bai Ju-yi's collective umbrella or blanket covering an entire city or province) holding us warm against the blasts of a then disputable Destiny have been torn down. *The barrier between so-called "culture" and citizenship, which today means economically based politics, has been wiped out in practice by the Right wing*: it is time all of us recognized this in our laggard theory or we shall be naked unto our enemies, forced to accept them as overwhelming Destiny (i.e.: to shift from SF to horror Fantasy or apocalypse).

Of course, Formalism was deeply enmeshed with epistemology, i.e., with how do we identify anything at all – for example as being such-and-such politics that go with such-and-such homologous economics. I shall hint at this toward the end of the essay. In the meantime, I shall claim that epistemology cannot function without asking the political question "what for?" or *cui bono*. So if we grasp that the barrier between our "cultural" discussions and politics-cum-economics is simply sterile categorization, our politically and epistemologically corrected theory would then be only following, fifteen if not thirty years late, two generational waves of SF: William Gibson or Octavia Butler or Marge Piercy or Stan Robinson, who showed us how Dick's Palmer Eldritch or Debord's and Burroughs's addictive image-virus is reproducing within all of us, manipulating our takes on reality: "The scanning program we accept as 'reality' has been imposed by the controlling power on this planet, a power primarily oriented towards total control," said William – not Edgar R. – Burroughs (*Nova* 51, and see for political-economic grounding Haug). The time for isolated formal poetics is over when the *Geist* has been colonized (see for a golden oldie the argument of Arnheim); I must respectfully posit as known my theoretical arguments from the first part of *Metamorphoses* and most importantly from the concluding chapter on chronotope and parable of *Positions*, and move to wider waters.

And so, to round off my axiomatics into a trinity, I would like to offer you what you may call the *"Suvin axiom for cultural studies"*: *Every man her own Gramsci*: each of us makes sense only as a prefigurative component of the allegorical collective intellectual this unique unifier of cultural theory and political practice, argument and passion, demanded.

2. You and Me in the Deluge

> [...] today we need [to run the risk of] simple-mindedness in order to be able to
> say anything at all.
>
> — ERNEST BECKER, *The Denial of Death*

2.1

And therefore: What can you expect me to give you in this potlatch /sym-
posion, what can I be expected to offer you in this end of the age of the
so-called White race, this dark moment of a planet under the far-off stars
almost cabalistically invoked as the new, evil millennium?

> In the dark times, will there be poetry written?
> There will be poetry written about the dark times. (Brecht)

Faced with almost (but never quite) total and ever-growing desolation,
as a young man asked at the beginning of our wasteland century, what is
to be done, *chto delat'*? Well, at least bear witness:

> Reading books won't save you from death.
> Writing books won't save you from poverty.
> But if you leave off and never speak out:
> How will the young know to tell their stories?
>
> So the verse-smith forges you these words,
> Words commodity-worshippers won't believe.
> Sugar is addictive; birds are charmed into the snake's maw;
> Yet wholesome food, wisely chosen, furthers life ...
>
> ("Metacommentaries," 1981)

Or consider the following fragment of a love poem:

Having seen this, what do you and I do, love? Much must be done
By us as citizens banding together, much again as lovers,
But as writers one thing, our stock in trade and secret weapon –
To slice up the world by *nomination*. Master Kung Fu,
Our forebear, changed "killed" to "murdered", thus branding for all
     the ages
The unjust deeds of a king; "to right the names", he called
Such revisionist calligraphy. Plebeian scribes,
Minions of creative truth, we unveil and tattle out the taboo names
Of dragons and men, profanely unfold them in the public eye
Like holy fools, indiscreet lovers, irrepressible drunks:
General Motors, Hitachi, Nestle, Siemens, Boeing,
Con Edison, Canon, General Electric, all are involved
With the generals' Beast of Abomination that poisons our loves ...

And so Darko will offer you a view from the belly of the Beast, 666, Leviathan, the great super-global worm Ouroboros biting his own tail and strangling us in his Laokoon coils, the politico-economical whale out of which we Jonahs attempt to spout our prophecies about the fall of Nineveh or Babylon the great scarlet whore, to assemble a toolkit or set of lenses for neo-Galilean starry messages. So, first of all, always first of all, a name-giving and description: What is this rough Beast slouching toward Bethlehem or Armageddon? In the more adequate Buddhist terms, what Law decayed in this evil-yet-propitious age and world-system? Or finally, what Atlantis collapsed in the Deluge and why? I shall treat of What in terms of politics and of Why in terms of economics, ineluctably intertwined. We have all been trained to dislike such terms: but we have to disintoxicate ourselves, or perish.

I give you two warnings at the outset: First, I certainly have no more than a first approximation to an answer; but if all of us do not start to debate it right now, there are very good chances we shall in the twenty-first century – amid scores of dirty wars, a changed climate, and serious food and energy starvations – have to look back at Hitler and Stalin as we are now looking back on Nixon, Johnson, and Khrushchev: the good old times, when there was hope. Second, my focus on what is not only logically prior to all texts but also informing and strongly co-determining them means I shall not discuss any in detail, only plead for a grid and horizon of future discussions.

In a book-length study, place would have to be found for macro-events of the post-1973 era. On the one hand, there is the invasion of the minimax-strategy SF-snatchers by the corporate conglomerization of Hollywood, TV, and the mega-middlemen of the book trade – publishing houses, distributors, bookstore chains. US SF in Fordism was rendered possible and shaped by the double market in competing genre pulps and paperbacks, which lay a strong stress on the story's horizon's (ideology) – i.e., on what was being produced, and not simply on financial profit. The Post-Fordist "tight money" for culture resulted from the end of Cold War competition with what was perceived as the Left. This delivered the field to a totalizing "bottom line" orientation where the Powers-That-Be are not simply trying to make a profit, but as much profit as possible, this year, now. This Post-Fordist mode is dominated by circulation (sales, marketing, advertising), tied into the movie and TV arms of the same "vertically integrated" corporation, and it leads to increased government as well as middlemen censorship, an oligopoly disempowering thoughtful editors and forcing upon us both Fantasy and sequels-cum-series as well as the low standards of bestsellerdom and SF movies or comics.[2] On the other hand, opposing the suppression of thoughtfulness, there are the bright spots of most SF by and about women and of other brave new names. None of this can be dealt with here. I have also restricted a look backward at my *Metamorphoses* book to a single matter, doubts about the novum.

2   See Sedgewick, Stableford, Broderick 90, Greenland 44, and Pfeil 83. Yet "[the worst publisher] is still a nun in the whorehouse alongside the major players in the music industry and the art market or, to take a comparable industry elsewhere in the economy, some of the ethical drug companies" (Solotaroff 80).

2.2 *The Politics and Economics of the Deluge*

In touching democratic unison, the New Disorder commonsense has concluded that it was the evil empire of Leninism which collapsed under the
onslaught of the valiant white-clad forces of Princess Leia – as allegory for
legitimate property – and Luke and Han Solo – as allegory for the ideolog-
ical-cum-technical supremacy of US individualism. In fact, the Star Wars
company outspent its rivals: but that does not make a good media story
... No doubt, 1989 saw the end of a Leninism that had degenerated into a
bureaucratic State despotism and resulted in a Soviet power-grab around
its borders and world rivalry with the West. Yet not only! It also marked
the end of US hegemony over the world, the paradoxical *Pax Americana et
Atomica* of the Cold War. What collapsed in 1989 had a twofold beginning
in 1917: not only Lenin's revolution but also Woodrow Wilson's entry into
the age of World Wars (started twice by German industries and ruling classes
in the misguided belief that *they* will be the successor empire to Britain).
This had led already in 1919 to US troops fighting the young Red Army.
The enemy brothers – perspicaciously allegorized already in an early 1920s
poem by Mayakovsky – had in common key presuppositions:

> that humanity could rationally and consciously construct the good society [...], that
> the State was a key instrument of this construction [...], [that] nations were all to be
> "equal" [..., and finally, the eschatological] view that history was moving inevitably
> and ever more rapidly in the direction of their universalizing ideals which, in the end
> [...] would exclude no one. (Wallerstein 5; see also Derrida, *Spectres*)

Though diametrically opposed, Leninism became what Liberalism had
always been, a Statist ideology of constructing an interclass wealthy future
that would embrace the whole population on the basis of continual expansion of production. I am persuaded by Wallerstein's lengthy analyses that
the triple-headed hell-gates' dog of Keynesianism, Fordism, and Wilsonism
has also been collapsing after its pseudo-Leninist Siamese twin was excised
from him, only in slower motion, a domino-principle not dreamed of by
General Westmoreland!

As to economics: the real capitalists have always known, but reproached
the Marxists for tattling out, that the "bottom line" of all politics is glorified

pork-barrelling: insuring such economic profits for the capitalists that the rest of the nation could also be bought off. In the boom-and-bust cycle, the ascending part that began in the 1930s found in Fordism and Keynesianism the remedies to the dangerous 1920s bust. These strategies effected a limited but real redistribution of wealth: Fordism through higher wages rendered possible by mass production of goods but neutralized by total production alienation (Taylorism, conveyor belt) and consumer brainwashing (see Hirsch and Lipietz, though the earliest and in many ways still most stimulating analyses are in Gramsci's "Americanism and Fordism" and in Brecht's *St Joan of the Stockyards*), Keynesianism through higher taxation neutralized by bourgeois control of the State. They functioned, and could only function, in feedback with the rise of production and consumption 1938–73, itself inextricably enmeshed with imperial extraction of surplus-value, armament production, and the warfare State. The ideology adequate to this greatest economic expansion in history, to a continuous change of form but augmentation of substance in market circulation, was State-inflected Liberalism. The dominance of Liberalism did not mean it was not fiercely contested from the conservative or Fascist Right and the Socialist Left: it meant that any contestation had to address itself precisely to New Deal Liberalism. It had to show that their "new deal" would give a greater share in affluence and other perks to given groups (for example the German or Japanese or Russian peoples) than the Liberal one: but no contestation ever questioned the need for a car industry, conveyor belts, and a contained labour force. And yet "the private car, together with the dismantling of public transport, carves up towns no less effectively than saturation bombing, and creates distances that can no longer be crossed without a car" (Haug 54; see Noble 6 and passim).

In class terms, both Soviet pseudo-Leninism and RoosevTeltian Liberalism were compromises with and co-optations of the pressures and revolts by plebeian or labouring classes. In economic terms they meant the institution of a modest but real "security floor" to the working classes of selected "Northern" countries (what was in Mao's China called "the iron rice-bowl") as well as a great expansion of middle classes, including all those hearing or reading this, with a fairly comfortable financial status and an appreciable margin of manoeuvre for ideologico-political independence.

Now such compromises are revoked by the capitalists as unnecessary. In a fierce class war from above, through a series of hidden or overt putsches by the Right wing (hidden in the "North," from Britain to the USSR, overt in the "South" – China being the pivot between the two), what Marx called "the extraction of absolute surplus value" is sharply increased: the security floor is abolished (in the US, one half or more of all working people have no full or permanent employment), a large class of chronically poor is created, while the middle class is squeezed back into full dependency by abolishing financial security, and split into a minority of "organic" mercenaries – the engineers of material and human resources, including the new bishops and cardinals of the media clerisy (see Debray) – and a majority of increasingly marginalized and pauperized humanists and teachers, disproportionately constituted by women and non-"Whites." Some new elites, say Japanese or Brazilian, may still join the affluent, everybody else – the South and the middle and lower classes of the North – will be kicked back, by threat of starvation and bullets, into the pre-Keynesian state: we may be doubling back to a Dickensian "two nations" society, with more computers, more (or at least more talk about) sex, and more cynicism for the upper classes. In world politics, just as after 1873 there came about a hegemony shift from the UK to the rival successors, US and Germany, so the post-1973 dispensation, after the end of national liberation wars, shifts to a tripartite tension between the mega-spheres of decaying North America, Western Europe and Japan (in the future perhaps East Asia?) – a classical precursor-constellation of the last two World Wars.

In this Wallersteinian scheme, 1917 meant the irruption of the periphery or South into the world-system's core, a bid of the objects to become subject-players themselves. Wilson and Lenin were taken after 1917 to announce – and both the Soviet and US post-1945 ideologies certainly trumpeted – that everybody could live as well as the affluent North, glamorized and rendered present to the whole world by Hollywood and then TV. But the shock of 1973, when we entered upon the "bust" part of the cycle that began with the 1930s–1940s boom (the oil crisis, debt crisis, global domination of the World Bank, etc.), revealed what should have been evident to anybody with a smattering of geography and demographics: that the planet just did not have sufficient resources for that. It is a finite system that cannot expand indefinitely to bear six or ten or twenty billion people up to the immensely wasteful "Northern" standards: raping nature will not beget a child upon her (see Kapp). The South as a whole cannot be co-opted, only repressed: Wallerstein has argued that the demise of Leninism is simply the harbinger of the demise of all "developmentalist ideologies" (97).

Furthermore, Keynesianism has brought about huge masses of exploitable people, but exploiting such numbers is in the age of automation etc. not profitable any longer. Not needed as producers, these masses may still be useful as consumers as long as the welfare safety-net gives them some means: but these means are being retracted by the capitalists in favour of direct enrichment of the rich. Since the by now unnecessary people are still voters and potential rebels, the liquidation of unnecessary stocks of human lives goes on cautiously, but it can be accelerated in civil or national wars which go merrily on, profiting the armament and drug industries. Thence on the one hand the revocation by the Northern ruling classes of both the Keynesian compromise with the lower classes and the Wilsonian promise to the peripheric "South"; and on the other hand the increased world concentration of capital now dominated by cartels of "multinationals," the shuffling off of lower-profit branches like textile, metallurgy, and even electronics to the lower paid periphery while the richer core concentrates on biotechnology and microprocessors as well as on the "acute politicized competition [...] for the tighter world market" (Wallerstein 124).

2.3

There is no doubt we are today seeing the rolling back of Keynesianism. Some data: the US capitalist class comprises 5 per mille of the population, but even if we take the top 1 percent of the US population, the 834,000 households constituting it had at end of the 1980s a net "worth" of ca. $5,700 billion, which was "worth" more than the bottom 90 percent of the US population, 84 million households with ca. $4,800 billion net worth (Phillips; see also for this whole paragraph Chomsky). In the relatively moderate Canada, according to a report by Morrissette and Bérubé of

Statistics Canada, in the last twenty years the chasm between upper and lower classes has grown rapidly, with middle incomes disappearing into part-time work or overtime of a multitude of badly paid jobs. This means that ca. 40 percent of the workforce is by now unemployed or on insecure part-time or "self-employed" work (Wood 285–86), while CEO pay packages rose by one third in the last three years only (Zacharias). According to the very tame ILO, worldwide unemployment affects in one form or another one billion people or nearly one third of the global workforce (*Second*). In the European Union, two thirds of workers under the age of twenty-five work on a temporary or "self-employed" basis (Andrews).

Obversely, in the US, the top tax on CEO wages fell from 94 percent in 1945 to 28 percent in 1991, so that the average pay in that class grew to be 85 times the income of the average industrial worker (Miyoshi 738). The not too startling conclusion for anybody who has studied the reasons for a State apparatus is that the welfare-state transfer of wealth from one class to another goes on in spades but *for the rich*. The latest report to have percolated into public domain tells of the US Congress and FCC handing $70,000,000.000 – yes, seventy billion dollars – to the TV conglomerates in free space on public airwaves ("Bandwidth"). No wonder the number of US millionaires from 1980 to 1988 rose from 574,000 to ca. 1,300,000, while the official 1991 statistics count one seventh of the population as poor, which given their obfuscations probably means one fifth or ca. 50 million (Phillips 9–10 and Miyoshi 739). And so whole generations, as well as the planetary environment for centuries into the future, are being warped by an arrogant 0.5 percent on the top and a faceless world money market.

Coddling the poor is a barefaced lie: another report by Mimoto of Statistics Canada (who got into trouble for his pains) shows that only 1 percent of debt growth is due to unemployment insurance, 8 percent to increased spending on police, military, and prisons, and 44 percent to interest payments (Sprung). The new contract enforced on the "downsized" is: "Workers undertake to find new occupations where they can be exploited in the cleverest and most efficient way possible" (Lipietz 77). Rocketing indigence and aimlessness provide the ideal breeding ground not only for petty and organized criminality – business by other means – but also for its legitimization in discrimination and ethnic hatred (for example in India or Yugoslavia). Internationally, the gap between the rich "North" and the poor "South" of the world system has doubled from 1960 to 1992, with the poor "transferring more than $21 billion a year into the coffers of the rich" (*The Economist*, see Chomsky 62). This dire poverty gap between classes and nations can be suggested by the fact that the most trustworthy international source estimated in the mid-1980s some 40 million people die from hunger each year and (I do not know which is worse) the UN reported that in 1996 "[n]early 800 million people do not get enough food, and about 500 million are chronically malnourished" (Drèze-Sen *Hunger* 35; *Human* 20). This means that only a small minority in the North will have enough food, energy, and medical attention or adequate education and transport, so that all societies are being turned into two-tier edifices, with good services for the rich and shoddy ones or none for the dispensable poor. Human groups divide into resentful islands who do not hear the bell tolling; the "absolute general law of capitalist accumulation: accumulation of wealth is at the same time accumulation of misery, agony of toil, slavery, ignorance, brutality" (Marx, *Selected* 483), has been confirmed in spades. No wonder SF is getting contaminated by sorcery and horror: we live in a world of capitalist fetishism run wild, against which the Cthulhu entities are naive amateurs.

The only question is then:

> What if we cannot dismiss the rantings of the [R]ight and it really is true [...] that workers' rights, social citizenship, democratic power and even a decent quality of life for the mass of the population are indeed incompatible with profit, and that capitalism in its most developed forms can no longer deliver both profit or "growth" and improving conditions of labor and life, never mind social justice? (Wood 287)

In brief, can the Keynesian class compromise be dismantled without burying under its fallout capitalism as a whole? If one doubts this, as I do, then two further questions come up. First, will this happen explosively, for example in a quite possible Third World War, or by a slow "crumbling away" which would generate massive breakdowns of civil and civilized relations, on the model of the present "cold civil war" smouldering in the US, which are (as Disch's forgotten masterpiece *334* rightly saw) only comparable to daily life in the late Roman Empire? And second, what kind of successor formation will then be coming about? The age of individualism and free market is over, the present is already highly collectivized, and demographics as well as insecurity will make the future even more so: the only alternative is between the models of the oligarchic (i.e. centrally Fascist) war-camp and open plebeian-democratic commune.

I have always held that SF was a "neo-medieval" genre in its collectivist procedures of shared generic presuppositions and indeed worlds (see the brilliant Russ 3–14). While I earlier thought of this, optimistically, as proto-socialist, a richer explanation is – alas – Eco's "new Middle Ages," where "a period of economic crisis and weak authority" is blended with "incredible intellectual vitality" (491), "an immense operation of bricolage, balanced above nostalgia, hope, and despair" (504). I cannot pursue here his witty, detailed, and very early parallels between the collapse of the international Great Peace of Roman *virtus* and that of market individualism (both limited to a part of Europe and some adjacent areas), resulting in what I have called the creeping "cold civil war" returning the Third World with poetic justice to the metropolitan cores; Eco accurately noted that the major insecurity and unlivableness of our new "Middle Ages" is based on excess of population. However, some of the parallels, such as the proliferation of cutthroats, sects, and mystics where divine grace is often another drug, were being signalled by much SF from Dick on. Other voices have focused on the collapse of State authority resulting in "a lasting, semistabilized disorder, which feeds on itself " and "grey zones" where the only authority is that of the drug barons (Alain Minc and N. Stone, BBC 1994, cited in Morley 352–53). In particular, you will recognize here the scenarios of much among the best SF of the last thirty years, say from William Gibson, Pat Cadigan, Norman Spinrad, and Marge Piercy through Octavia E. Butler and Carolyn J. Cherryh to Gwyneth Jones and Stan Robinson. You will also recognize what Broderick rightly called "hymn[s] to corporate fascism": his example is Larry Niven and Jerry Pournelle (79) but let me at least add two whole new sub-genres. First, the misnamed "libertarian" (a better name would be US-Fascist) SF which comprises, for example, John Norman's *Gor* novels and the militia-oriented works published outside commercial SF circuits by people like Phil Bolger and "Jill von Konen" (see the important essay by Orth), and which should be taken seriously because they are very seductive. Second, the "mercenary" SF extolling killing (for example by Robert Adams, who once expressed to me a heartfelt desire to kill my unworthy Commie self). Within depictions of "thick" Possible Worlds (usually called fiction), SF is to my knowledge the only genre engaged in this public debate, and to its further great credit it must be said that all good SF sees the answer to the crucial second question as depending on social actions by all of us.

3. On SF and SF Criticism: Responses at the Cusp

> There are [...] ways of thinking with the seeds of life in them, and there are others, perhaps deep in our minds, with the seeds of a general death. Our measure of success in recognising these kinds, and in naming them making possible their common recognition, may be literally the measure of our future.
>
> — RAYMOND WILLIAMS

3.0

Tom Shippey once noted, in a phrase that echoes deservedly from Patrick Parrinder through Adrian Mellor to Broderick, that SF has at some points been a "machine for thinking," and he accurately added, for people outside recognized official support (108) – i.e., for thinking in unorthodox ways, often cuckoo but probably not more often wrong than the hegemonic, academically blessed and megabuck-anointed, machines. Surely the narrative ploy and metaphor of superluminal speed is less crazy than the bitter earnest and yet metaphor of supply-side economics? But for thinking to illuminate there is a precondition: that it choose a mature or urgently relevant stance, rather than an irresponsible one: "A denial of authorial responsibility, a willed unconsciousness, is elitist, and it does impoverish much of our fiction in every genre" (Le Guin 5). One could talk about such a bearing with a preferential option for the humiliated and exploited in many ways, but let me talk first about binarism and the thematic foci, and come back at the end to the place SF plants its klieg-light in.

3.1

Binaries are an Aristotelian, undialectical simplification, granted. Still, there are two fatal reasons we must go for them: first, "I gotta use words when I talk to you" (T.S. Eliot): collapse or upwards curve, bright or black; second, all major decisions finally do come down to binary choices. The choice is, I argued above, between oligarchic or direct-democracy collectivities and subject-positions. And it is the intelligentsia that will formulate (is already formulating) the tools for thinking either. Intellectuals are the name-givers of categories and alternatives. At the beginning of my *Positions* I argued that mass literature has in the twentieth century been largely co-opted so that it is, even to its name, complicitous in the creation of "the masses," an alienated consumer-blob out there analogous to the dispossessed producers, only in relation to which can there be cultural and financial elites (see also de Certeau 119ff. and Williams, *Long* 379, or indeed in all of his works). And looking backwards, many 1968ers can be seen as claiming the mantle of court poets for the New Despotism (see Debray, Klein, and Angenot-Suvin). Clearly the appeal of Frank Herbert, and possibly of Gene Wolfe, derives from this *frisson*, though I suspect that at his best Wolfe may be more complex. Still "popular literature" (Gramsci) is the only directly important one, supplying images to comics, movies, and TV, and thence to the everyday imagination. The Formalists were right that great literature has always arisen from a reworking of that populist side.

What then can we not yet quite proletarianized intellectuals do in the next, say, quarter century, yoked under this maleficent constellation, disaster? As my poem said, in good part we can decide whether to *transmit the memory* and what is more the lessons of 1917 to 1968 or 1989 to the coming generations or not. "[The] historical amnesia characteristic of American culture [is] the tyranny of the New," for example in Post-Modernism (Hall 133). Memory could help rearguard actions to defend the worthiest yet weakest among us:

> The four whales who hold up the corners of heaven:
> Women, workers, the learners, the loving.
>   (*The Long March*, 1984)

And we have to wager it would even facilitate the cusp decisions of 2015 or whenever in favour of radical democracy and survival. The central decision is one – the hippies were right! – between war and love: the arms race and narcotics peddling that has ruined both the USSR and US (look at Germany and Japan!) vs. a use-value production that conserves the planet and heals people (see Lipietz's "Postscript"). We are nearing a Prigoginian bifurcation region, at which, you will remember, "an individual, an idea, or a new behavior can upset the global state," or in other words, where small causes lead to great results: "Even in those regions, amplification obviously does not occur with just any individual, idea, or behavior, but only with those that are 'dangerous'" (Prigogine and Stengers 206). At the cusp begin our distributively Gramscian responsibilities.

3.2

Yet, alas, there is no reason for me to alter a constant quality judgment, only to ask how come that 98 percent of a machine for thinking is at best ephemeral schlock and at worst cocaine for the intellectuals, William Burroughs's "junk" as "the mold of monopoly and possession [...] the ultimate merchandise" (*Naked* xxxviii–ix) or Brecht's "branch of the bourgeois drug trade." I can approach this through one of SF's many articulate writer-critics, who has however the advantage of being simultaneously one of its few grand masters and an unrecognized prophet in his land, Tom Disch. In a 1975 London lecture called "The Embarrassments of SF," Disch concluded that SF writers and readers have "characteristically preferred" adolescent imaginary worlds with little articulation of "sex and love, [...] the nature of the class system and the exercise of power within it" (144). Two converging, more acerbic ways of putting it are: "technotwit satisfactions [... of] great dollops of masculinist [...] adventure and [...] technogadgetry for sexually terrified twelve- and thirteen-year-old boys of all ages"

(Pfeil 85), and an empathy-machine for the adolescent male reader with "some libidinal equation between military power fantasies, war games, and the sublimated sexual dynamic" (Spinrad 185). Sex, duly uncoupled from Disch's other three foci, has been let in after Farmer and Heinlein in the *aggiornamento* of capitalist mores that was going on even as Disch spoke; yet I still remember the impact two books of 1969, *Bug Jack Barron* and *The Left Hand of Darkness*, had on me by at least beginning to relate sex to love, class, and/or power (see Suvin "Science" – nobody, so far as I can remember, not even Ursula Le Guin, has added a consideration of economic strictures to SF thematics). After many telling and highly disenchanted arguments, for example about lower-class resentment rampant in SF, Disch's unique vantage point of oscillation between the very centre and the margins of the genre led him to the equable conclusion that SF as we know it "dealt with the largest themes and most powerful emotional materials – but in ways that are often irresponsible and trivializing" (155).

***

But at this point, gentle hearer, two of my souls (I have many) – the epistemological one of dark subterranean perceptions and the Formalist one of surveying Possible Worlds – are having a new attack of doubting.

3.3 Epistemology

Not that any of the above is wrong, it's just insufficient. Do I want to get into a scolding of all SF (or all US-style SF) à la Stanislaw Lem? For there's the great SF writer of *Solaris, The Invincible, His Master's Voice, The Mask* and rewriter in the SF-vein of fables and non-fictional discourses (essays, speeches, diaries) – and then there is the European elitist, lover of the Hansa patrician Thomas Mann and of Count Jan Potocki. And I remember many other anathemas, for example Samuel Delany's ludicrous essay on *The Dispossessed* in which he goes systematically through all the major points (heterosexual love, anarchist utopianism, discursive clarity, etc.)

that make Le Guin fortunately be Le Guin and not Delany, and therefore
judges as failed that ultimate Kanchenjunga of the 1960s Himalayas. Thus,
while critique began with our great ancestor Lucifer as a cosmic principle
of bringing light into the darkness of the rulers, perhaps critics should not
be activist prosecutors? Could there not be a defensive critique which sees
(say) Delany's own writings not simply as only partly successful if richly
suggestive dazzle, info overload mystifyingly foregrounded as cognition –
but more generously as very good approximations to an impossible ideal?
If we note with Broderick that some of Delany's lines are "increasingly
embarrassing" (126, on *The Einstein Intersection*) or that the "evelmi" in
Stars in My Pocket come across as Donald Duck's nephews, a sleight-of hand
to present "too lovable a blend of large lolloping dogs, sweet-natured children, natural wonders, and all-round nice, wise folks," and that at least one
sentence, "The door deliquesced," is "decorative special effects" though in
some ways absurd (144–45) – should we then not proceed with Broderick
to drown it in the billows of our admiration for Delany's immensely eru-
dite and energetic blends of Black discourse à la Wright and Ellison, gay
discourse, and bohemian discourse à la the Beats?

     This would be the proceeding, to use Scholastic language, of a trium-
phant rather than a militant Church, a Franciscan *poverello* rather than a
Dominican inquisitor. You may see here a huge paradox: how can I daydream of being a triumphant Churchman at the moment of Antichrist's
triumph? And if I were a real Churchman I might answer that the Antichrist
is the necessary prelude to the Messiah's Millennium; but since I am not
one, and my creed of shintoist cybermarxism is not a religion (see Suvin
"Travels"), and yet I need to go gentle into the good night, I shall present
you with the only possible triumph today: a zero-triumph. I speak of the
failed but absolutely necessary triumph of social justice and Homo sapiens
survival that yet remains to judge us, summing up prosecution and defense
– a long-duration horizon. What is a century to such a stance but a brief
moment under the witness stars? And it behooves me to champion such
a critique at what might be, given Time's wingèd chariot, my last major
pronouncement on SF. (But do not bet on not having me to kick around,
as Nixon might have said!) From this stance, looking backward from 2015
or 2050 to the 1996 Decline of the Law (to imagine Bellamy modifying

Gautama the Enlightened), militancy is not denied: that would be desertion under fire. But its enforced strategic retreat is to be blended with and shot through with Hope the Principle, which does not forsake us even in the worst times. Against a stiflingly looming dead future, we have to mobilize all our living pasts, of how the best people coped with the descent *ad inferos*. And traditionally we did so by an active male hero encountering an ancestor figure to guide him with its superior insight: Dante the exile taken in hand by Virgil the mage. We have forgotten most of this today, for already Milton attenuated these figures with a human face into the Holy Light as his internalized ethereal Muse dazzling into the blindness. And worst of all we have forgotten that supernal wisdom is female, Beatrice.

But let me here mobilize only our most adjacent analog and ancestor, the nearest dark time and night of the soul from which even the dawn, though firmly believed in as coming, was invisible: the 1930s, that time when two enemy brothers fed each other from Germany to Muscovy. At that time, most favoured by their position at the heart of all European and world contradictions, Brecht and Benjamin and Bloch diagnosed the ineradicable Principle of Hope even under the Gestapo, the imperial bureaucracy of Hwang Ti or Djugashvili, and the US Federal Communications Commission and FBI. And if you think this Iron Heel has little to do with SF, I will not speak to you of names unknown, swallowed by cruel Father Time, whom Leonardo da Vinci, in at the birth of capitalism, defined as "swift predator of all created things" – such as Savinien Cyrano or Karin Boye or Katherine Burdekin or Yan Larry – but only of those who, equally oppositional in their preferential option for the downtrodden, have evaded Lethe through the odd misreading as useful political PR for the rich: Orwell formulated the position of artists like Henry Miller to be inside the whale, Zamyatin moved from internal exile in the State he had fought for as a socialist to external exile in Paris, only to be refused by pro-Stalin and anti-Soviet circles alike and die writing a piece on the Eastern nomad Attila ending the evil Empire of the West ... Let us, not unreasonably, substitute Disch for Orwell, Delany for Miller, and Johanna and Günther Braun or Gottfried Meinhold or Angela and Karlheinz Steinmüller (whose State, the GDR, evaporated from under them) for Zamyatin, and what this has to do with SF will become apparent.

The difference is largely that excising and curing the cancers of the body politic without including the psychophysical cancers of the body personal has little liberating power under the heel of the new, much more pervasive and invasive Oligarchy. What lessons can we learn from the exasperated defenders of the personal body (say Orwell to Disch) and the ambiguous defenders of the collective body, of Bakhtin's utopian people (say Zamyatin to Le Guin)? The first lesson is, as the Odonians would say, not to believe false categories: body personal is intimately moulded by body politic and vice versa. And whoever falls for the false categories lives falsely: to withdraw to the individual body, in a dream of Rousseauist enjoyable Arcadia, is impossible in today's admass pollution where the labouring body is downgraded in favour of the consumerist body, colonized by fashion, by the billion-dollar cosmetics, sports, exercise, etc. industries (see Featherstone); and teeth-gritting loves are channelled into Harlequin romances or the adolescent technodream of teledildonics.

> O hopes desires
> a little tenderness
>   bodies
> melt in a twinkling
>   ("Last Light," 1988)

At any rate, faced with the two holy commodities – the discourse of fiction and esthetics and the discourse of the body and erotics – I have here to focus on the first one, even if both are not only indispensable for our lives but also for understanding each other, and their product – politics. Alice Sheldon once complained about our world "where the raising of children yields no profit (except to television salesmen)" (45): this has been superseded by the politically shaped technology of Post-Fordism. For it is politics that enables molecular genetics businesses to patent DNA units and companies to copyright trademarks, so that one day we might have to pay royalties for having children (see Chomsky 112–13) as well as for using nouns and verbs such as xerox.

3.4

So, to particularize my querulous query under the gaze of my Formalist soul: can you expect me to give you, can I be expected to offer you a State of the Art report on either SF criticism or (preferably, for wider interest) of SF itself, our focus and *Schmerzenskind*? If so, the expectations will be disappointed: I have no time to read all that is necessary, write it, and regurgitate it to you in fifty minutes ... And if I had, surely you could not be expected to sit through it. So let me instead offer you an unashamed impression only about SF criticism, which has by now advanced and diversified beyond all the dreams and nightmares we pioneers had in the 1960s. We have by now theoreticians for all constituencies and streams: ruling out my own generation from Bruce Franklin, Stanislaw Lem, Joanna Russ, and Fredric Jameson on, if you want the PoMo menu, we can serve you Csicsery-Ronay and the terminal Bukatman, with some Fekete vituperation for sour cream. You prefer the Feminist version of PoMo, here is Donna Haraway as a patron saint of merry cyborgs and primates watched by women researchers, and Sarah LeFanu or Constance Penley as operative spearheads – not to speak of punning feminist humanists such as Marleen Barr. You want a kind of reach-me-down Neo-Historicist, we can come up with Gary Westfahl, who has applied the insight that power is everything into a constant "in your face, buster" style insuring that nobody'll tangle with *him*! You want academics, well of course there's the whole pretentiously theoretical *S-F Studies* crowd carping from the edges of the Empire or the more commonsensical US academic mainstream of *Extrapolation*, blessedly untainted by the fading pinkish colours of their rival and believing with Pangloss that everything that is is right; and on the other NATO lakeshore the eminently British empiricist mixture of writers and academics, sometimes in eminent personal union à la Brian Aldiss and Ian Watson, the professional gentlemen finally talking at each other in *Foundation*, fortunately not quite US-style professionals watching with eagle eye the idiot multitude's beer money ... Beyond parody, I have learned much from all of them, even some from Westfahl – just as they learned much from SF. In fact I would assert that you can gauge the limit-qualities of each critic by noting which SF texts they induce from: Haraway from the best case

of Butler, Penley from the K/S fanzines, Fekete and Broderick from the
later Delany, Aldiss from Shelley (alas the finally upper-class recuperated
Mary without Percy), Parrinder not only from Wells but also from Bernal,
Haldane, and co.

While this is great fun and I could go on all evening and leave at least
those of you who like academic wit rolling in the aisles, it might be more
profitable to focus – not on the State of New SF, but at least on some
cool date-palm oases in what I used to perceive as the rapidly encroaching
desertification of the genre, strip-mined by Hollywood, TV, and fast-buck
publishers pressuring luckless writers into Procrustean trilogies and as much
Fantasy with as many vampires as possible in congress each with more and
more housewives (notoriously the largest reading public after the teens
stopped reading). But Formalism not being on the menu tonight, I cannot
serve you exemplary analyses. I can only say that, having read mo' better SF
in the last few years, I think this hypothetical model is too simple. Binary
oppositions of the desert-oasis kind have a hard time surviving today. We
are at a confluence of an ideology and a market acceleration: the maxim
"if Socialism is dead, everything is permitted"[3] (which would have made
Dostoevsky smile acidly) has grown into a horrendous hegemony pun-
ishing recalcitrants by lack of income, career, and fame; and beyond that,
the diversification of micro-events within the really existing capitalism is
increasing faster than our abilities to hypothesize them into yes and no.
So I shall end with a reconsideration of a general epistemic category as
cognitive tool, which may also be a self-criticism: for I am talking about
(not Jerusalem but) the novum.

3   "In the words of the Master Assassin, Hassan-i-Sabbah (used as the epigraph to
     David Cronenberg's adaptation of *Naked Lunch* [1991]) '*Nothing is true. Everything
     is permitted*'" (cited in Bukatman 91).

4. "Droppin' Science":
The Dream of Reason Begets Monsters, and the Novum

When economic necessity is replaced by the necessity for boundless economic development, the satisfaction of primary human needs is replaced by an uninterrupted fabrication of pseudo-needs which are reduced to the single pseudo-need of maintaining the reign of the autonomous economy.

— GUY DEBORD, *Society of the Spectacle*

Quid novi rabidus struis? [What novelty do you furious plot?]
— SENECA, *Thyestes*

"What's new?" is an interesting and broadening eternal question, but one which, if pursued exclusively, results only in an endless parade of trivia and fashion, the silt of tomorrow. I would like, instead, to be concerned with the question "What is best?," a question which cuts deeply rather than broadly, a question whose answers tend to move the silt downstream.

— R.M. PIRSIG, *Zen and the Art of Motorcycle Maintenance*

Lenin did not want to speak in an old or in a new way. He spoke in a pertinent way.

— BERTOLT BRECHT, "The Debate on Expressionism"

4.1

I have always maintained SF is not "about" science but only correlative to a mature scientific method. Yet let us take a closer look at this method, and principally at who uses it how in whose interest and with what results. It is used by *intellectuals*, as a rule in the service of capitalist collectivities (States or corporations); in the guise of "technology," it has become a directly intervening and decisive force of production; the fruits thereof are contradictory: potentially liberating, today at best mixed, and at worst catastrophic: a good chance at destroying vertebrate life on this planet through profiteering and militarism (see Mumford).

In this century, as capital has been completing its moulting from individual into corporate, Fordism was characterized by "hard" technology (crucially all those associated with mass car transport), semi-automation, State planning, and the rise of mass media and advertising; and Post-Fordism by "soft" technology (crucially computer technology and biotechnology, where gene-splicing techniques invented in 1973 provide a possibly more weighty watershed than the oil-shock), automation, mega-corporations and world market regulation, and the integration of the media with the computer under total domination of marketing. An exemplary case may be the technology of mobility: under Fordism these were telephone via wire cable, cars and roads winning over the older railroad, and postal services; under Post-Fordism, mass use of air transport, fibre-optic cable, and satellite communications leading to fax and e-mail. In both cases, as mentioned in 2.2, more "software" or "human engineering" people were needed than before. One of the century's earmarks is therefore the enormous multiplication and enormous institutionalization or collectivization of the earlier independent artisan and small entrepreneur. This ensured not only higher production but also its supervision and the general ideological updating, i.e., it was "not all justified by the social necessities of production [but] by the political necessities of the dominant [class]" (Gramsci 13). (Writers of books, as opposed to people in "media entertainment," are perhaps the last word-smiths or craftsmen still for the moment not fully dependent – whence for example the praise of the artisan in the clairvoyant Dick.)

These "new middle classes" comprised roughly everybody who works sitting down but does not employ other people: it is in fact a congerie of social classes including teachers, office workers, salespeople, the so-called "free" professions, etc. Often classified as part of a "service" sector, they could be properly called "the salaried classes." Their core is constituted by "intellectuals," largely university graduates (but see more precisely the classical Wright Mills book, Noble, and the Ehrenreichs), people who work mainly with images and/or concepts and, among other functions, "produce, distribute and preserve distinct forms of consciousness" (Mills 142): Hobsbawm calculates that two thirds of the GNP in the societies of the capitalist North are now derived from their labour (so that Bourdieu's metaphor of human "cultural capital" accompanied a literal state of affairs), though their proportion within the population is much inferior. Politically, they (we) may be very roughly divided into servants of the capitalist and/or bureaucratic state, of large corporations, self-proclaimed "apolitical" or "esthetic" free-floaters, and radicals taking the plebeian side; the alliance of the first and fourth group with some non-"intellectual" classes determined both the original Leninism and New Deal. What the Japanese call "salarymen" (though as often as not they are women, in US already since 1940) are "the assistants of authority" (Mills 74), but no authority can abide without their assistance. The socialist tradition from Marx through Lenin to Bukharin, Gramsci, and Brecht has therefore always oscillated between praising the intelligentsia – for example the students – as the conscious interpreter of social contradictions and chastising it with scorpions as the producer of fake consciousness; the Marxists rightly (if as a rule rather schematically) saw in this a homology to the intellectuals' ambiguous status of salaried dependents (see for one example Lenin's polemic with Bernstein, 208–09). Is there perhaps a crucial distinction between the creative intelligentsia proper (to which all of the above names belonged), as opposed to reproductive or distributive intellectuals, for example teachers and engineers (Debray 95 and passim)?

In the Fordist dispensation, liberal ideology claimed that the world is composed of inner-directed atomic individuals within atomic national States, all of which can and will achieve infinite progress in riches by means of technology in a competitive market. The new collectivism, while mouthing Liberal slogans stripped of the State worship, needs other-directed intellectuals. Post-Fordism has had quite some success in making intellectual "services" more marketable, a simulacrum of profit-making. This was always the case in sciences and engineering: industrial production since ca. the 1880s is the story of how "the capitalist, having expropriated the worker's property, gradually expropriated his technical knowledge as well" (Lasch xi, and see Noble). In the age of World Wars this sucks in law, medicine, and "soft-science" consulting in the swarms of "professional expertise" mercenaries. Now, in the polarized and non-Keynesian situation, those who buck the market better get themselves to a nunnery. The class aggressions by big corporations against the immediate producers, corporeal and intellectual (the Belly against the Hands and the Brain, to reuse the fable of Menenius

Agrippa), means that Jack London's dystopian division of workers under the Iron Heel into a minority of indispensable Mercenaries and a mass of downtrodden proletarians (updated, say, by Piercy in *He, She and It*) has a good chance of being realized. The PoMo variant, where the proles buy in the local supermarket the hand-me-down Guccis they have seen on the idiot box model-parades while the mercenaries live in Aspen or Provence and commute through cyberspace, does not invalidate this early Modernist diagnosis ("labour aristocracy" in Lenin's language), rather it incorporates all the talk about status.

We are not quite there yet: in the meantime, most intellectuals share the split orientation of all middle classes, pulled between wage-labour and the desire to control their work: "its individuals live or attempt to live an elite life, evading through 'culture,' while their knowledge serves capitalism [...] They live a double life [...], inside the 'system' but with alibis, [...] in a *jouissance* half real and half illusionary." (Lefebvre 32–33). What Debray calls the reproductive or distributive intellectuals (95 and passim) – the engineers of material and human resources, the admen and "design" professionals, the new bishops and cardinals of the media clerisy, most lawyers and engineers, as well as the teeming swarms of supervisors (we teachers are increasingly adjunct policemen keeping the kids off the streets), etc. – are the Post-Fordist mercenaries, whom PoMo cynicism has dispensed from alibis.

But beyond the cynicism of the fast buck, the horizon of these crucial swing classes, who profited most from "really existing science," has been scientism (including orthodox Marxism). If scientism in the West meant, as Le Guin says, "technological edge mistaken for moral [and political] superiority" (4), then the so-called Post-Modernism is its symmetrical obverse, carried by the mobile fraction of the elite humanist intelligentsia that was rendered homeless by the hurricane that tore down both the Rooseveltian New Deal and "really existing socialism" (see Wolfe 587) and adopted with a vengeance the obfuscating PR techniques of "commodity scientism," plucking a perverse exultation out of despair, "[getting a bang] from the big bang" (Hall 131).

Commodity scientism – a notion exemplified by Michael L. Smith in his essay on the marketing of the NASA Moon venture but applicable as well, for example, to the nuclear bombs and industry – means a systematic fusion of a select technology and image-creation in the service of a politico-ideological project, so that

> [...] the products of a market-aimed technology are mistaken for the scientific process, and those products, like science, become invested with the inexorable, magical qualities of an unseen social force. For the consumer, the rise of commodity scientism has meant the eclipse of technological literacy by an endless procession of miracle-promising experts and products. For advertisers and governments, it has meant the capacity to recontextualize technology, to assign to its products social attributes that are largely independent of the products' technical design or function [i.e., of their use-value]. (179)

In this key operation of consumer capitalism, "progress" is identified with science, science with technology, and technology with new products supposedly enriching life but in fact enriching the financiers while brainwashing the taxpayers (Smith 182). SF writers of the Asimov-to-Bova "integrated" wing have made it a (lucrative) point of honor to spearhead the touting of commodity scientism. Yet SF writers have also, like all intellectuals, split "into those who perceived their interests to be aligned with the military-industrial complex and those who did not" (Smith 233). For one example of the "critical" wing, Vonnegut noted how the Earth in the pretty NASA pictures "looks so clean. You can't see all the hungry, angry earthlings down there – and the smoke and the sewage and trash and sophisticated weaponry" (cited in Smith 207).

4.2

With this I come to my introduction of the novum as the distinguishing hallmark of SF. *The novum* is obviously predicated on the importance, and potentially the beneficence, of novelty and change, linked to science and progress. Perhaps because both socialists and liberals were comfortable with this, I have the impression no other part of my theoretical toolbox has been received with so little demur. I'll now proceed to doubt it.

It's not only that the critical consensus makes me, an inveterate Ibsenian enemy of the solid majority, suspicious: what have I done wrong if I am praised in those quarters? It is also that living under Post-Fordism brings new insights: we are in a whirl of change that has co-opted science, but where has it got us? First, is our overheated society better than the "colder" one of (say) Tang China? There's more of us but do we have more space or more trees, per person? We have less back-breaking toil, but more mind-destroying aimlessness resulting in person-killing by drug and gun; we have WCs but also cancer and AIDS ... (If you read Delany you will see that public toilets is where you get AIDS.) So it suddenly comes into sharper focus that change within one lifetime grew to be normal and mandatory only with industrial capitalism and bourgeois revolutions, and that applied scientific mass production, characteristically, first came about in the Napoleonic Wars. Two hundred years later, we live in an ever faster circulation of what Benjamin called *das Immerwiedergleiche*, the recurring whirligig of fads that do not better human relationships but allow oppression and exploitation to continue with a new lease on life: "The perpetual rush to novelty that characterizes the modern marketplace, with its escalating promise of technological transcendence, is matched by the persistence of pre-formed patterns of life [...]: a remarkably dynamic society that goes nowhere" (Noble xvii, see Suvin "Two"; also Jameson *Late*, on Adorno and the parallels between technological and esthetic novum, especially 162–64 and 189–93). Indeed, in its systematic dependence on foreign and civil wars, i.e., weapons production, as well as on strip-mining human ecology for centuries into the future, this society is based on "a productive system efficient in details but supremely wasteful and irrational in its general tendency" (Lasch xiii, and see Wood 265 and passim).

As to science, I do not want at all to lose its central cognitive impetus and orientation toward the systematic and testable understanding of material processes. I am in favour of its deep reformation *in capite et membris* rather than of its (anyway impossible) evacuation – of Haraway rather than Heidegger. But its reduction to absolute, subjectless, objectivist analysis meant opposing science to art as reason to emotion and male to female. Score one against fiction using it. Science meant incorporating novelty after novelty into a more and more simple explanation of the world that culminated in the fortunately unsuccessful quest for the Unified Field theory in physics. In brief, everything is explainable by generalizations, which can ultimately all be stated in terms of universal laws in Newton's "absolute" spacetime. Score two against fiction, a "thick" description of concrete spacetimes, using it. Science as institution became a cultural pressure system simultaneously legitimating and disciplining the world's cadres or elite, in unholy tandem with the converging pressure-systems disciplining and exploiting the less skilled workforce usually called sexism and racism (this has been exhaustively rehearsed from Weber through the better Frankfurters such as Horkheimer and Marcuse to Mumford, and see Wallerstein 107–22). In the scientists' professional lives – not to speak of the engineers – it enforced narrow specialization that wiped out civic responsibility for knowledge and its insertion into production in favour of almost total identification with the capitalist hegemony (see Kevles and Noble, so far as I remember applied to SF only by the perspicacious Berger), and it got commodified into a series of Minimum Publishable Units. Symmetrically, we have watched the "elite" enthusiasm for bureau-cratized and profit-oriented rationalism causing the understandable (if wrong) mass reaction into mistrust and horror, engendering all possible irrationalisms. Score three, and knockout, against fiction using science-as-we-know-it (as well as irrationalism-as-we-know-it). And I take it I do not have to speak about so-called "hard SF" except to say it is interesting in proportion to its failing to carry out its program (for example in David Brin).

So the only sane way to see science, the world's leading cognitive struc-ture but also (as I argued in 1.2) macro-metaphor and, most important, a historically constituted collective practice fulfilling clear and strongly enforced interests of social groups in power, is not as the Messiah but as Goethe's two-souled Faust. Science as we know it in the last 200 years is a battlefield of "*the productive forces of labour and the alienating and destructive forces of commodity and capital*" – of cognition and exploitation (Mandel 216; and see Feenberg 195 and passim). The productive capacity of labour to wax cognitive may be seen in this – to my mind beautiful and astounding – dialogue:

MARK DERY: What does the hip-hop catchphrase "droppin' science" mean?
TRICIA ROSE: It means sharing knowledge, knowledge that is generally inaccessible to people, together with a fearlessness about stating what you believe to be the truth. There's also the implication that the information you're imparting is going to revolutionize things because this is the truth that has been deliberately and systematically denied. Science, here, stands in for incontrovertible evidence. Science is understood as that space where the future takes place.

(Dery ed. 214–15)

Obversely, the stance of mastery over nature is inextricably intertwined with that over people; let us ponder Lincoln's conclusion, "As I would not be a slave, so I would not be a master" (which was also Brecht's, see the poem "Kicked Out for a Good Reason"). In Marx's words, "modern industry [...] makes science a productive force distinct from labour and presses it into service of capital" (*Capital* 397). Revealingly, the language spoken by and in turn, as Wittgenstein would say, speaking commodified science is permeated by that selfsame warfare which in fact funded and stimulated its exponential growth: "the war on cancer and poverty, the battle against HIV, the struggle against old age and death itself" (Babich, "Hermeneutics" 26). In sum, science and technology's promise of easing life is in capitalism tightly coupled with and as a rule subsumed into its being "a mode of organizing [...] social relationships, a manifestation of prevalent thought and behavior patterns, an instrument for control and domination" (Marcuse 414). As to machines, they have become "means for producing surplus value"; "the central machine from which the motion comes [in the factory is] not only an automaton but an autocrat" (Marx, *Capital* 492 and 549): "technologies clearly have their purposes built into them" (Lummis 83). As to overt ideology, technocratic futurology (the nightmarish Laplace ideal of knowing the paths of each atom and therefore foreseeing every event from now to Doomsday, repeated by Asimov's Hari Seldon), based on the invalid premise of extrapolation (from market research), added "a new knowledge commodity: the opportunity to 'explore' alternative futures within the confines of the existing system," and thus combine corporate profit with the worst aspect of deterministic pseudo-Marxism (Ross 176–77, and see his whole section on 173–92 which includes "futures trading"). This kind of science cannot indicate the way to Hercules at the crossroads: we must indicate the way to it.

I was trying to get at that with my early distinction between true and fake novums: but is this enough? What follows from the strict commodifying parallels of ever shorter cycles: reduction of production and circulation time (including planned use-value obsolescence), reduction of attention-span of the sound-bite generation, reduction of stocks in magazines, quicker turnover of books and of fashions in attention-grabbing ideas, constraint to accelerated though exclusively profit-oriented technological innovation and R-and-D mentality – one intermittent SF theoretician, reputed to be a CIA expert, defined SF as the fiction of R-and-D! – and the fictional or esthetic stress on unceasing circulation of innovations (see Haug 39–44 and Mandel 182 and passim)? What happens when "[t]he key innovation is not to be found in chemistry, electronics, automatic machinery [...], but rather in the transformation of science itself into capital" (Braverman 166)? What if, in such "hotter" capitalism, Einstein's competing time-measurements translate into a choice among spacetimes of capital investments (Kwangtung China vs. Canton Ohio), and "the avant-garde strategy of innovation at any price becomes the paradigm of dominant economic practice" (Goux 218)? "Now everything is new; but by the same token, the very category of the new then loses its meaning [...]" (Jameson, *Postmodernism* 311). What if the great majority of scientific findings are today, axiologically speaking, fake novums? Predetermined by the mega-fake novum of science transubstantiated into capital, our contemporary version of Destiny, in an age when science and technology is "the racing heart of corporate capitalism" (Noble xxv), they produce changes and innovations that make for increased market circulation and profit rather than for a more pleasurable, light, easeful life – brandy tinted brown by caramel rather than aging slowly in oak casks. This is masked behind obfuscating PR; and what if much art is in the same race, incorporating PR into text-immanent sensationalism, curlicues, and kitsch (see in Benjamin's essays the tension between Baudelaire and Brecht)? What happens to "making it new," the battle-cry of great anti-bourgeois Modernism from Baudelaire and Rimbaud on, when the horrors of world-wide wars become the leading, oft-employed, and never-failing labs for technoscientific and hierarchical "modernization" of society under increasing repressive control and conditioning?

A pithy way of putting this is Brecht's note from 1948 about "calls for novelty" from Germany which seemed extremely suspect: "For what these voices really call for is a new repression, a new exploitation, a new barbarism. The real novelty is NO REPRESSION, NO EXPLOITATION, NO BARBARISM ANY MORE" (BBA 154/29–31).

In sum: innovation in art has often precious little to do with new relationships between people, however estranged – including the self-proclaimed orthodox SF task of reflecting upon the social relations shaping technology (see Huntington 179 and passim). "Whoever says 'new,' however, [...] also fatally raises the spectre of Revolution itself, in the sense in which its concept once embodied the ultimate vision of the Novum [...]" (Jameson, *Postmodernism* 311). This was certainly my (anachronistic) perspective in 1977. But in this quintessentially counterrevolutionary age, innovation has deliquesced into a stream of sensationalist effects largely put into service of outdating and replacing existing commodities for faster circulation and profit. Harvey has even suggested that spectacles, with their practically instant turnover time, i.e., "the production of events" rather than of goods, provide the ideal Post-Fordist model (156–57); just as oil, steel or electricity companies can only look with envy at the model monopolization in book publishing (in the US already ten years ago 2 percent of the publishers controlled 75 percent of the books published; three distributors handled 95 percent of all SF and Fantasy – Harvey 160 and Chalker 28). But profitable consumption (the one measured by GNP) is not carried out only by means of spectacles: finally, the novum has in the new hegemony become wedded to war as the most cruel fakery and opposite of any revolution radically bettering human relationships. Competing with Leninist revolution and finally overcoming it, destructive innovations have become THE genuinely formative experience of the post-1914 age.

The function of possibly the nearest cultural analog of SF, pop music, has been characterized as: "The young see in it the expression of their revolts, the mouthpiece of their dreams and lacks, while it is in fact a channelling of imagination, a pedagogy of general enclosure of societal relations into the commodity" (Attali 219). This may be overly monolithic. But for the emblematic example of the US SF films of the 1980s Sobchack has per-suasively shown that their new depthlessness, ahistoricism, and changed emotional tone "no longer figure the alienation generated by a 'whole new economic system,' but rather our *incorporation* of that new system and our *absorption* by it" (252). And clearly, most of the unspeakable SF series, the "endless succession of 1500-page Tolkienesque or military trilogies and worse" (Broderick 52), as well as the final works by Heinlein and Asimov subordinate use-value (cognition and estrangement) to the brand-name "event." As Aldiss noted, "The awful victories of *The Lord of the Rings*, *Star Wars*, and *Star Trek* have brought – well, not actually respectability, but Instant Whip formulas to sf. The product is blander. It has to be immedi-ately acceptable to many palates, most of them prepubertal" (108–09). I would only dissent when he blames this simply on "mass taste": it is a taste manipulated and brainwashed through decades of censorship, aggressive PR, and addictive fixes in all available media and forms.

Overall, the meteoric breakthrough of US SF after the 1930s is part of the High Fordist sea-change of commercialized culture from repeating the familiar commonsense for generations on end to wrapping a more deeply buried commonsense into surface, co-optable novelties (for example, illic-itly extrapolating 1776 or the Cold War into galaxies). The exasperatedly unsatisfied needs and desires of most people have to be reorganized more quickly and sensationally. This is certainly not the whole story of SF, but it is its institutional framework, which broke down to a significant extent only in the "one-eighth revolutions" (Brecht) of the antifascist years and the 1960s. The simulation of quality, equally in everyday life and in formal culture (an excellent example are almost all SF movies and TV serials) may be the rational basis of Dick's and Baudrillard's differing simulacra.

In brief, while expecting a revolution leading to a qualitatively better mode of people living together, it was reasonable or maybe mandatory to bank on the novum. But when getting ever deeper into the belly of the whale, the novum of wandering through its entrails has to be met by much suspicion. So, perhaps a labour-saving and nature-saving society would also need novums, but just how many? Might we not rather wish, as William Morris did, for the true novum of "an epoch of rest"? Philosophically speak-ing, should we not take another look at the despised Aristotelian "final cause"? Religiously speaking, why do the great Asian creeds such as Daoism and Buddhism suddenly look more enlightening than the "hotter" and more frantic monotheistic ones which cleared the ground for capitalism? Politically speaking, what if science is the whore of capitalism helping it to infect the planet, or (if you so desire) a more and more powerful engine in the irrational perpetually automobilized system of cars and highways with capitalism in the driving seat heading for a crash with all of us unwilling passengers – how does one then relate to the novums in car power and design? How does one focus on anti-gravity, or at least rolling roads, or at the very least electrical cars (which could have existed before Ford if the patents had not been bought up and suppressed by the automotive industry)? And what about similar crashes in computer networks, arrived or arriving? Should the life of people without computers, cellular phones, www, and so on, be described as not worth living: as the Nazis called the inferior races' *lebensunwertes Leben*?

I have no full solution to this dilemma (I have myself opted to have a computer and no car), except to say that my quite conscious founding decision in *Metamorphoses*, dating from a silent debate with Brecht in the 1950s, to use the nomination of "cognition" instead of "science" has been fully justified, and should be articulated further. The way out does not seem to me to lie in the direction of Arthur Clarke's equation of science and magic, which is seriously misleading precisely insofar as it stresses the mythical and elitist side of scientism, complicitous with "commodity scientism" (see Smith in 4.1 and Williams *Problems*), and in fact much debased in comparison to (for example) shamanism. I am afraid many feminists fall into the same, if symmetrically obverse, kind of trap if and when they stress magic against science rather than the empowering role-models to be found in either. With Gautama the Buddha and Diderot, I am in favour of enlightenment. And, as Adorno noted, the New is irresistible in modern art (36–37). But at a minimum the incantatory use of the novum category as explanation rather than formulation of a problem has to be firmly rejected. Novum is as novum does: it does not supply justification, it demands justification. This may be formulated as: *we need radically liberating novums only*. By "radically liberating" I mean, as Marx did, a quality opposed to simple marketing difference: a novelty that is in critical opposition to degrading relationships between people – and, I strongly suspect, in fertile relation to memories of a humanized past (Bloch's *Antiquum*). Where is the progress progressing to?

4.3

And yet, let me mark toward the end some unease with, or better contradictions within, the frequent apocalyptic tone of the last twenty years, from which my positions are not so far that they could not profit from some delimitation. To schematize with help of the unavoidable binaries: there is a big difference between the lamentation of a tired emperor in flight, or of a money-changer ejected from the temple, and that of Yeremiyahu (whom the Gentiles call Jeremiah); between the apocalypse as seen by a Parisian intellectual cynic and by the political exile John at Patmos in a kind of Dischian "Camp Concentration"; between profitably elegant snivelling and pessimism of the intellect uncompromisingly seeking lucidity (which, as Sorel and Gramsci taught us, is quite compatible with optimism of the will). The latter refuses the discursive and revelatory monopoly of the rulers. To the former, but I would say only to the former, Derrida's 1980 pastiche ironizing a newly fashionable "apocalyptic tone" applies:

> Verily I tell you, it is not only the end of this here but also and first of that there, the end of history, the end of the class struggle, the end of philosophy, the death of God, the end of religions, [...] the end of the subject, the end of man, the end of Oedipus, the end of the earth, *Apocalypse Now*, I tell you, in the deluge, the fire, the blood, the fundamental earthquake, the napalm that falls from heavens by helicopters [...].
> ("On a Newly" 145, tr. modified; see also Jay)

True, any apocalyptic proposition will say that the end is near or here: but the end of what, and what comes after the end? Is the proper position of a (provisional) survivor of the Deluge the one I mentioned above, "if there's no dry land left [no absolutes], everything is permitted," or is it rather, "how many arks of what kind do we need, and in which direction may the dove look for shores?" Do we have to regret the fallen stone monuments of princes, should we not rather say good riddance and take

as our example dolphins frolicking in the agitated waves, the dying generations in one another's arms? The very act of penning and disseminating an
apocalypse (admitting for the moment but not conceding that that's what I
am doing) means that its hyperboles include the tiny but momentous gate
of salvation, Benjamin's "weak messianic power" that is given unto each
and all of us. Apocalypse is problem and not solution, to invert Stokely
Carmichael: a real, most pressing problem that has to be worked through.
The plagues traditionally accompanying the apocalypse will not be dealt
with by old antibiotics: progress, expanding GNP, onwards and upwards
(excelsior), reason identified with the bottom line. We are in between
two major bifurcations: one ended the "short twentieth century" 1917–89
(Hobsbawm); the other, economists whom I think well of speculate, may
be expected somewhere around 2015 give or take a decade, when the raw
materials of the automobile age run out. Our focus, our fears and hopes,
should be on the future and not on the past bifurcation. The old, including the old New, is dead, the new has not yet managed to see the light of
the day and we are not sure whether it will in our lifetimes (surely not in
mine): and in the meanwhile, a too long while, the old masquerades as the
newest; as Gramsci and Brecht concluded, "in the half-light monsters rise
up" (Lipietz 59).

　　Only too often, the apocalyptic panic is one at the loss of privilege;
and yet the original sense is still that of a disclosure, uncovering (*kalupt-
ein*, to cover), or what Swift properly called, "The Revelation or rather the
Apocalypse of all State-arcana" (*Tale of the Tub*, see *OED* s.v. "apocalypse").
If we today find it useless to call it a revelation of The Truth, we might say:
the constitution of operative truths. These guides to actions are not to be
found through a consensus of the brainwashed but only through a cooperation of Ibsenian Enemies of the People. But they have in common with
the old Truth an orientation toward the whole, toward "the *universalia* of
history, within which people take up their [...] proper place" (Böhme 383).
This kind of apocalypse, as Hartmut Böhme notes, is not the Elysian Fields
of the sated upper class but raw and plebeian, sprung from distress, favour-
ing poetic images not subject to the conceptual discipline of the hegemonic discourse, dealing with hate and loss, passionate sacrifice and cruelty,
tender love and acceptable death. There is a commanding "transcendental

signifier" (and signified), but by Jamesonian contraries, as an awful warning in the subjunctive: "if we don't find ..." (as in Brecht-Weill's Alabama Song) a way out from the genosuicidal mastery that rules us, then "I tell you, I tell you, I tell you we must die." No apocalypse (especially one at the end of huge empires amid huge global wars) can be without blood: in Schiller's phrase "Die Weltgeschichte ist das Weltgericht" (World history is the Judgment Day). Yet secularizing it against the vampiric fundamentalisms of bank and religion, we should today not call for streams of blood but meditate how to minimize them.

4.4

And finally, from this follows for us as students of SF and utopianism: the way out is not the placeless atopia of the playful signifier and absent signified, this unbearably simplifying binary at some point much touted by its best writer, Delany. The static utopia was cognitively dead in the nineteenth century, though its putrefying cadaver poisoned most of the twentieth. Our problem is its successor: atopia is today as dead as utopia was in the nineteenth century and as pernicious as static utopia was in the twentieth (see on atopia's theoretical incarnations Meaghan Morris, especially 25, and Suvin "Polity"). To quote the theoretician of atopia: "Instead of informing as it claims, instead of giving form and structure, information neutralizes even further the 'social field'; more and more it creates an inert mass impermeable to the classical institutions of the social, and to the very contents of information" (Baudrillard 25). He also, quite rightly, identifies meaningless discourse with terrorism (the real, psychic one). The powerful talent of Delany is always tempted by the narcissism of gazing at his own textuality and writing about an incomplete subject-production, while the Ballardian "inner spaces" are a refuge from traumatic post-imperial history but also a Jungian black hole (see Bukatman 7 and passim). Beyond utopia and atopia, we need a space of dynamic alternatives – let me appropriate for it (as in essay 5) the term of heterotopia. Beyond our pernicious polarities of personal vs. public, male vs. female or inner vs. outer (and so on *ad nauseam*), we have to forsake the fake "reason" that "is in fact [...] a standardization of the world imposed fully as much by the economic system as by 'Western science'" (Jameson, *Late* 15), that is at best contaminated by capitalist exploitation and at worst of a piece with it. As was, again, noted by the less apocalyptic among the Frankfurt School, scientistic rationalization tends "to destroy precisely that substance of reason in whose name it invokes progress" (Horkheimer 14). But then we need a new reasonableness: a rationality that incorporates much refurbished science but also permanent self-estrangement and self-criticism under the eyes of plebeian apocalypse, most importantly by practices not reducible to clear-cut concepts yet articulated in topological propositions – for example, those usually called emotions and approached in pioneering ways by some Feminist theoreticians (see Suvin, "Cognitive"). Already Nietzsche had surmised that we have to "look at science in the light of art, but at art in the light of life" (19; see also Babich, *Nietzsche's*).

As can be seen in the best works of today's SF: Butler or Cadigan or Piercy or Stan Robinson.[4]

4   My thanks go to my friend Ziva Ben-Porat, who invited me to give a first sketch of this at a Tel Aviv University symposium on SF in 1995; for clarifying my thoughts about Wallerstein, Hobsbawm, and similar, to the study circle with Andrea Levy, Eugenio Bolongaro, and Qussai Samak; to Babette Babich, Marleen Barr, Wolf Haug, R.D. Mullen, and Erik Simon; and to McGill University for a sabbatical leave in 1995. The final shape was stimulated by the kind invitation of John Moore to give a keynote speech at the Luton University 1996 conference on Alternative Futures. The chapter is inscribed to a friend and maître à penser, Fred Jameson: without his work and our discussions, even those where I disagreed, I doubt this text would be here.

Works Cited

Adorno, Theodor W. *Ästhetische Theorie*. Frankfurt: Suhrkamp, 1981.

Aldiss, Brian W. *The Pale Shadow of Science*. Seattle: Serconia, 1985.

Andrews, Edmund L. "Jobless Snared in Europe's Safety Net." *Gazette* [Montreal] 15 November 1997: 1–8.

Angenot, Marc. "The Absent Paradigm." *Science-Fiction Studies* 17 (1979): 9–19.

——, and Darko Suvin. "A Response to Professor Fekete's 'Five Theses.'" *Science-Fiction Studies* 15 (1988): 324–33.

Arnheim, Rudolf. *Toward a Psychology of Art*. Berkeley: University of California Press, 1966.

Attali, Jacques. *Bruits*. Paris: PUF, 1977.

Babich, Babette. "The Hermeneutics of a Hoax." *Common Knowledge* 6.2 (1997): 23–33.

——. *Nietzsche's Philosophy of Science*. Albany: State University of New York Press, 1994.

"Bandwidth Bonanza." *Time* (Canadian edn). 1 September 1997: 35.

Barthes, Roland. *The Grain of the Voice*. Trans. Linda Coverdale. Berkeley: University of California Press, 1991.

Baudrillard, Jean. *In the Shadow of the Silent Majority*. Trans. Paul Foss et al. New York: Semiotext(e), 1983.

BBA = Bertolt Brecht Archive, Berlin (by folder, lines).

Benjamin, Walter. *Gesammelte Schriften*, 7 vols. Frankfurt: Suhrkamp, 1980–87.

Berger, Albert I. *The Magic That Works*. San Bernardino: Borgo, 1993.

Böhme, Hartmut. "Vergangenheit und Gegenwart der Apokalypse." *Natur und Subjekt*. Frankfurt: Suhrkamp, 1988. 380–91.

Braverman, Harry. *Labor and Monopoly Capital*. New York: Monthly Review, 1974.

Broderick, Damien. *Reading by Starlight*. London and New York: Routledge, 1995.

Bukatman, Scott. *Terminal Identity*. Durham: Duke University Press, 1993.

Burroughs, William S. *Naked Lunch*. New York: Grove, 1959.

———. *Nova Express*. New York: Grove, 1964.

Chalker, Jack L. "Reflections on the Industry." *Fantasy Review* 99 (1987): 28.

Chomsky, Noam. *Year 501*. Montréal and New York: Black Rose Books, 1993.

Debord, Guy. *Society of the Spectacle*. Detroit: Black and Red, 1983.

Debray, Régis. *Le Pouvoir intellectuel en France*. Paris: Ramsay, 1979.

de Certeau, Michel. *Heterologies*. Trans. Brian Massumi. Minneapolis: University of Minnesota Press, 1986.

Derrida, Jacques. "On a Newly Arisen Apocalyptic Tone in Philosophy." *Raising the Tone of Philosophy*. Ed. Peter Fenves. Trans. John Leavey, Jr. Baltimore: Johns Hopkins University Press, 1993. 117–71.

———. *Spectres de Marx*. Paris: Galilée, 1993.

Dery, Mark (ed.). *Flame Wars*. Durham: Duke University Press, 1994.

Disch, Thomas M. "The Embarrassments of SF." *Explorations of the Marvellous*. Ed. Peter Nicholls. London: Fontana, 1978. 139–55.

Drèze, Jean, and Amartya Sen. *Hunger and Public Action*. Oxford: Clarendon Press, 1989.

Eco, Umberto. "Towards a New Middle Ages." *On Signs*. Ed. Marshall Blonsky. Baltimore: Johns Hopkins University Press, 1985. 488–504.

Ehrenreich, Barbara, and John Ehrenreich. "The Professional-Managerial Class," *Between Labor and Capital*. Ed. Pat Walker. Boston: South End, 1979.

Featherstone, Mike. "The Body in Consumer Culture." *Theory, Culture and Society* 1 (1982): 18–33.

Feenberg, Andrew. *The Critical Theory of Technology*. Oxford: Oxford University Press, 1991.

Goux, Jean-Joseph. "General Economics and Postmodern Capitalism." *Yale French Studies* 78 (1989): 206–24.

Gramsci, Antonio. *Selections from the Prison Notebooks.* Ed. and trans. Quintin Hoare and Geoffrey Nowell Smith. New York: International, 1975.

Greenland, Colin. "Redesigning the World." *Red Letters* 14 (1982): 39–45.

Hall, Stuart. "On Postmodernism and Articulation," *Stuart Hall: Critical Dialogues in Cultural Studies.* Ed. David Morley and Kuan-hsing Chen. London and New York: Routledge, 1996. 131–50.

Harvey, David. *The Condition of Postmodernity.* Oxford: Blackwell, 1990.

Haug, Wolfgang Fritz. *Critique of Commodity Aesthetics.* Trans. Robert Bock. Minneapolis: University of Minnesota Press, 1985.

Hesse, Mary B. *Models and Analogies in Science.* Notre Dame: University of Notre Dame Press, 1966.

Hirsch, Joachim. "Auf dem Wege zum Postfordismus?" *Argument* 151 (1985): 325–42.

Hobsbawm, Eric. *The Age of Extremes.* New York: Pantheon, 1994.

Horkheimer, Max. *Zur Kritik der instrumentellen Vernunft.* Frankfurt: Suhrkamp, 1967.

Human Development Report 1996. Ed. UN Development Programme. New York and London: Oxford University Press, 1996.

Huntington, John. *Rationalizing Genius.* New Brunswick: Rutgers University Press, 1989.

ILO. *Second World Employment Report.* Geneva: ILO, 1996.

Jameson, Fredric. *Late Marxism.* London: Verso, 1992.

——. *Postmodernism, or, The Cultural Logic of Late Capitalism.* Durham: Duke University Press, 1992.

Jay, Martin. "Apocalypse and the Inability to Mourn." *Force Fields: Between Intellectual History and Cultural Criticism.* London: Verso, 1992.

Kapp, Karl W. *The Social Costs of Private Enterprise.* Cambridge, MA: Harvard University Press, 1950.

Kevles, Daniel J. *The Physicists.* New York: Knopf, 1978.

Klein, Gérard. "Discontent in American Science Fiction." *Science-Fiction Studies. Second Series.* Ed. R.D. Mullen and Darko Suvin. Boston: Gregg, 1978. 243–53.

Lasch, Christopher. "Foreword". Noble. xi–xiii.

Le Guin, Ursula K. "Introduction". *A Fisherman of the Inland Sea*. New York: Harper, 1994. 1–11.

Lefebvre, Henri. *La Survie du capitalisme*. Paris: Anthropos, 1973.

Lenin, Vladimir I. *Polnoe sobranie sochinenii*. Vol. 4. Moscow: Gos.izd. politicheskoi lit., 1959.

Lipietz, Alain. *Towards a New Economic Order*. Trans. Malcolm Slater. New York: Oxford University Press, 1992.

Lummis, C. Douglas. *Radical Democracy*. Ithaca: Cornell University Press, 1996.

Mandel, Ernest. *Late Capitalism*. Trans. Joris de Bres. London: Verso, 1978.

Marcuse, Herbert. "Some Social Implications of Modern Technology." *Studies in Philosophy and Social Science* 9 (1941).

Marx, Karl. *Capital*. Vol. 1. Trans. Ben Fowkes. Harmondsworth: Penguin, 1976.

——. *Selected Writings*. Oxford: Oxford University Press, 1977.

Mills, C. Wright. *White Collar*. New York: Oxford University Press, 1953.

Miyoshi, Masao. "A Borderless World?" *Critical Inquiry* 19.4 (1993): 726–51.

Morley, David. "EurAm, Modernity, Reason and Alterity." *Stuart Hall: Critical Dialogues in Cultural Studies*. Ed. David Morley and Kuan-hsing Chen. London and New York: Routledge, 1996. 326–60.

Morris, Meaghan. "Banality in Cultural Studies," *Logics of Television*. Ed. Patricia Mellencamp. Bloomington: Indiana University Press, 1990. 14–43.

Mumford, Lewis. *Technics and Civilization*. New York: Harcourt, 1963.

Nietzsche, Friedrich. *Birth of Tragedy*. Trans. Walter Kaufmann. New York: Vintage, 1967.

Noble, David F. *America by Design*. New York: Knopf, 1977.

[OED] *The Compact Edition of the Oxford English Dictionary*. Oxford: Oxford University Press, 1991.

Orth, Michael. "Reefs on the Right." *Extrapolation* 31.4 (1990): 293–316.

Pfeil, Fred. "These Disintegrations I'm Looking Forward to." *Another Tale to Tell*. London: Verso, 1990. 83–94.

Phillips, Kevin. *The Politics of Rich and Poor*. New York: Random House, 1990.

Prigogine, Ilya, and Isabelle Stengers. *Order Out of Chaos*. New York: Bantam, 1984.

Ross, Andrew. *Strange Weather*. London and New York: Verso, 1991.

Russ, Joanna. *To Write Like a Woman*. Bloomington: Indiana University Press, 1995.

Sedgewick, Cristina. "The Fork in the Road." *Science-Fiction Studies* 53 (1991): 11–52.

Sheldon, Alice. "A Woman Writing Science Fiction and Fantasy," *Women of Vision*. Ed. Denise Du Pont. New York: St Martin's Press, 1988. 43–58.

Shippey, Tom A. "The Cold War in Science Fiction, 1940–1960," *Science Fiction: A Critical Guide*. Ed. Patrick Parrinder. London: Longman, 1979. 90–109.

Smith, Michael L. "Selling the Moon," *The Culture of Consumption*. Eds. Richard W. Fox and T.J. Jackson Lears. New York: Pantheon Books, 1983. 175–209 and 233–36.

Sobchack, Vivian. *Screening Space*. New York: Ungar, 1987.

Solotaroff, Ted. "The Paperbacking of Publishing." *Writer's Digest* March 1992: 80 and 78–79.

Spinrad, Norman. "Science Fiction versus Sci-fi." *Isaac Asimov's Science Fiction Magazine* December 1986: 178–91.

Spivak, Gayatri Chakravorty. *In Other Worlds*. New York: Routledge, 1988.

Sprung, Guy. "Chapter One" *Gazette* [Montreal] 8 April 1995: H-1.

Stableford, Brian. "The Way to Write Science Fiction." *Interzone* 28 (1989): 49–50.

Suvin, Darko. "On Cognitive Emotions and Topological Imagination." *Versus* 68–69 (1994): 165–201.

——. *Metamorphoses of Science Fiction*. New Haven: Yale University Press, 1979.

——. "Polity or Disaster." *Discours social/ Social Discourse* 6.1–2 (1994): 181–210.

——. *Positions and Presuppositions in Science Fiction*. London: Macmillan, 1988.

——. "The Science Fiction Novel in 1969." *Nebula Award Stories Five*. Ed. James Blish. New York: Doubleday, 1970, 193–205.

——. "Travels of a Shintoist Cybermarxist" [interviews with Chao-yang Liao and Tami Hager]. *Foundation* 67 (1996): 5–28.

——. "Two Holy Commodities." *Sociocriticism* 2 (1985): 31–47.

Wallerstein, Immanuel. *Geopolitics and Geoculture*. Cambridge: Cambridge University Press, 1992.

Williams, Raymond. *The Long Revolution*. Harmondsworth: Penguin, 1965.

——. "Advertising: The Magic System," *Problems in Materialism and Culture*. London: Verso, 1980. 170–95.

Wolfe, Alan. "Suicide and the Japanese Postmodern." *South Atlantic Quarterly* 87.3 (1988): 571–89.

Wood, Ellen M. *Democracy against Capitalism*. Cambridge: Cambridge University Press, 1995.

Zacharias, Yvonne. "The Pay Gap." *Gazette* [Montreal] 12 October 1996: B-1–2.

Utopianism from Orientation to Agency: What Are We Intellectuals under Post-Fordism to Do? (1997–1998)[1]

To the memory of Bob Elliott, Herbert Marcuse, and Louis Marin
and to Predrag Matvejević, the utopian of "ex"

Monsieur est Persan? Comment peut-on être Persan?
[You are a Marxist/ utopian/ activist? How can one be a Marxist/ utopian/ activist? – PoMo translation]
— MONTESQUIEU, *Lettres Persanes*

"Bring your knowledge of disaster"
(telegram summoning Charles Beard to Tôkyô after the great earthquake)

1   Since I did my survey on at least the definitional aspect of utopia a quarter of century ago (Chapter 1 in this book), a huge amount of secondary literature has come about dealing both directly and indirectly (methodologically) with utopia – not only in English but also (to mention the richest European traditions) German, Italian, and French. It is well-known to most of us, but I wish today to exercise a creative forgetfulness in regard to it. For, my project is to focus not so much on a "horizontally" self-enclosed tradition (which is in part operative as generic memory and in good part constructed by us critics) as it is, primarily and perhaps right now even exclusively, to concentrate on the "vertical" interplay of utopian horizons, existents, and events with the "thick" experience of endangered living together in Post-Fordism. Nonetheless it ought to be apparent that my thinking is centrally stimulated and modified not only by the "indirect" masters such as Barthes, Hall, Jameson, or Williams, but also by the "direct" critics from (say) Bauman to Zamyatin (I find it interesting that most of the first category have also committed some direct writing on utopia/nism).

0. "The Dark Now" (free after Bloch)

We literally do not want to be what we are.

— KIERKEGAARD

0.1

What is to be done by an intellectual wedded to utopianism in what Hölderlin, suffering from the breakdown of the great French Revolution, called the *dürftige Zeit* (forgetting the misinterpretation by Heidegger, this can be rendered as penurious, indigent, shabby, needy, mean, paltry, poor times)? How do we find the proper "point of attack" to begin articulating the lay of this wasted land and the ways that might be found out of it? I shall start with a little known lecture by Foucault (discussed in Macherey, "Natural" 181–84), who poses the question: "What then is this present to which I *belong*? [...] and (what is more) [what is the thinker's] role in this process where he [*sic*] finds himself both an element and an actor." I interpret this to mean that, as opposed to the individualist Me, there is no subjectivity which does not centrally include belonging to what Sartre would call a situation, out of which her projects are elaborated. Foucault goes on to comment that such questioning no longer asks (or I would say, does not only ask) about "his belonging to a doctrine or to a tradition," but about "his *belonging to a certain 'us'* [...]" This "us," I would further update Foucault, participates in a given cultural as well as politico-economical ensemble of synchronic relationships, "present" in all senses of that term. In the vein of Spinoza, all of us are *pars naturae* rather than simply a dis-embodied gaze standing over and above it, and we are constantly interpellated by various necessities of our constitutive situation. The thinker's only alternative is whether to respond by going on to think to some purpose, of finding his freedom (as Engels almost said) in facing the interpellating necessity, or to respond as Dostoevsky's childishly resentful Underground Man by saying "just because of that, I won't respond." In other words, as the good old reactionary Chesterton once remarked, you may be free to draw a camel without humps, but then you will find out that you have not been free to draw a camel ...

If we decide that a thinker or intellectual is, by definition, the one who responds, who is responsive and responsible, then I shall supplement my point of attack by attempting to build upon a great ancestor who is a much less dubious role-model than Foucault, since he was not desperately reacting against the Communist Party, leftwing phenomenology, and Marxism but maintaining a fruitful critical dialog with them – Walter Benjamin. In the highly endangered *Jetztzeit* of the 1930s he concluded that an intellectual work should be judged not only by what is its attitude toward the relations of production but before all, by what is its position within them. It is in and because of this position, Benjamin held, that an intellectual producer is impelled by his professional or class interest to exercise solidarity with the producing workers (*Gesammelte Schriften* II.2: 683–701). I shall go on to discuss how we must today (building on Marx) add the relations of *consumption* as closing the circle of commodity fetishism and re-enchanting it, but also return to Benjamin's realistic central thrust. How does this hold for the writing, criticizing or indeed actualizing of utopias? Is it pragmatically appropriate or pertinent to the demands of the situation, is it oriented toward its nodal points, is it what Brecht called an intervening or meshing thinking (*eingreifendes Denken* – see also Macherey, "Materialist" 145–46)?

0.2

But this general orientation is not enough. One of the major lessons of the "short twentieth Century" has been, I feel, the dethroning of the nuclear, individualist or billiard-ball interior Self (I attempted an orientation in this field in "Polity"). This means raising the Subject into a problem and concomitantly the Body into a (sometimes fetishized) litmus paper for and final line of defence against the alienation of labour, reification of people's mutual relationships, and hegemonically created massification. The Marxian and Nietzschean recognition that agential praxis is the end-all of understanding also spells the death-knell of the neat scientistic division between looking subject and looked-at object.

What then is this particular Darko Suvin able to contribute as a valid stance under the stars in the not quite Blochian *Dunkles Jetzt*? What is he/ am I supposed to say of note to a gathering of people seriously (and usually joyously) concerned with utopian ideas/ fictions/ colonies? Am I supposed to either further buttress or abandon my (in)famous sundering of the latter two, or my even more professionally transgressive refusal to sunder utopia and SF, both dating back to *MOSF*? I assume I have been punished enough for the latter by the almost unanimous refusal of the SF people to get aboard a discussion of utopianism (with a few precious exceptions such as Tom Moylan) unless written by women after Charlotte Perkins Gilman, and of the utopological people to even take into serious consideration what I wrote about More, Lucian, Swift, Blake, Percy Shelley, never mind the Frenchmen and Italians – in fact anything in the 120 pages between the theory and Wells, since it is in a book that has SF in its title; so that I can simply shrug my shoulders and say "transgressing the slots by which one lives in academe doesn't pay, *sed salvavi animam meam*." Or am I to turn to what are, to my mind, essential entries on the agenda of utopology today? – such as:

- the already mentioned *Body*;
- the already mentioned *Subject*, the multiply fragmented and malleable yet holistic Subject so overwhelming on today's collectivized horizons;
- futures that are not simply exponential take-offs from the past, so that breaks in experience mask continuity in augmentation of profits, but whose point is to think the incorporation and revival for the memory of losses and victims: frame-altering, bifurcating *endangered futures*;

– or finally (which is maybe the same in other words: but then all these entries are aspects of one another) *the Dead*, in Benjamin's sense that even they are not safe if the enemy goes on winning, if the break masquerading as extrapolation swallows our past.[2]

But I have written about the Subject, the Body and its emotions, and death as presupposition of life in a number of other places (e.g., "The Subject," "On Cognitive," "Polity," "The Use-Value of Dying" chapter in *Lessons*, "Emotion," last not least in my poetry), and connecting it with the utopian hub from which they spring and/or to which they tend demands another book which I may not have time to write. So that I choose rather to incorporate Subject and Collective Bodies in an investigation which I think of as the continuation of the hint I gave in "Locus, Horizon, and Orientation" (now Chapter 5 in this book) namely that a fuller discussion demands providing a focus on the oriented agents able or failing to dynamize any – but most clearly the utopian – locus against certain horizons. This is a discussion which is in our present, no doubt tainted, terms political in both the most pragmatic daily sense and yet only if that is infused with the classical sense within which we humans were rightly defined as *politika zoa*, living beings of the city-state, communal animals. This might also be the most useful way to define my place not only towards but also within the Post-Fordist Deluge, and to ostend it to you as an articulation, a "polemical sketch of the salient activities and claims" (Ross 13), proposed for a debate we cannot live without.

---

2   A theme I wish I had spacetime to develop here is on intellectuals as the memory bump of society. I find obscene the phrase by Agnes Heller, born out of anti-utopian panic: "The history of the dead is dead history" (*A Philosophy of History in Fragments*, Oxford: Blackwell, 1993, 40). On the contrary, all sense of history is consubstantial with the actuality or fear of death (of the past, but also of the future), the longing in "If I forget thee, O Jerusalem …!".

1. Living in Fantasyland
   (Dystopia, also Fake Utopia and Anti-Utopia)

> As long as there is still one beggar left, there will still be myth.
> — BENJAMIN, *Gesammelte Schriften*

1.1

I shall enter into the thick of the matter by means of two apparently unrelated but I think revealing bits or bytes from the flood of information that so efficiently hides the constellations of extremist reality transformations from us today. One is the estimate of what I take to be the most trustworthy international source that as of the mid-1980s some 40 million people die from hunger each year, which is equal to 300 jumbo jet crashes per day every day with total loss of lives – and the number is steadily rising; or (I do not know which is worse) the UN report that in 1996 "[n]early 800 million people do not get enough food, and about 500 million are chronically malnourished" (Drèze-Sen *Hunger* 35 and *Human* 20; see also the too optimistic World Bank *Poverty*). The second is press reports according to which the ex-Mouseketeer Ms Billie Jean Matay unsuccessfully sued Disneyland not only for a hold-up of her family in the parking lot but also for the emotional trauma her grandchildren, aged five, seven, and eleven, suffered when they were taken backstage and saw Mickey Mouse and the Lion King removing the heads of their costumes (*Gazette* C15 and "Next"; I resist the temptation to linger at the Disney corporation's emblematic progress from mouse to lion in order to follow the broad picture).

Now, I very much doubt the starving hundreds of millions or the couple of billion people eking out a living, at the periphery of the world system or dossing down in the center of the affluent cities of the North, would have time for the Matay family's Disneyland trauma. They are absorbed by surviving the fallout from the civil and overt wars waged by the big corporations, and which with poetic justice migrate from their "hot" foci also into the "Third World inside the metropolis," the creeping war in all our slums so far best described in hip-hop and in the post-Dischian and post-Dickian dystopian SF of Piercy, Butler (Octavia, not Judith), Gibson, Spinrad or Cadigan. Nonetheless I submit to you there is a deep subterranean bond between, on the one hand, the starving bellies and bacterial epidemics among the masses of the South, and on the other hand, the starving minds and brainwashing epidemics moulding all of us in the North: a bond between misery and drugging, best incarnated by the AIDS pandemic, where the collapse of the bodies' immune system is an almost too pat allegory of PoMo capitalism. For, the ideological Disneyfication (and I shall return to the fact that the Disney corporation is by now one of the biggest "vertical" monopolists in movies, media, and book publishing) is a drug of the brainwashing variety. What is perhaps worst – and we intellectuals should know why – is that this drug functions by channelling the imagination rather than by chemical stimulation or inhibition: it uses the brain's imaginative powers to create empathetic images which are a fake Novum or what Louis Marin called a degenerate utopia. As the old theologians knew, the corruption of the best creates the worst, pre-empting any radical Novum or utopia – the indispensable precondition for altering the lot of Ms Matay's grandchildren as well as the millions upon millions of kids as seen (for example) in *Salaam Bombay*.

1.2

As all opiates and fake utopianisms, Disneyfication is predicated upon alienated labour so that people crave compensatory satisfaction in "leisure time" consumption (Kracauer, Ewen). And in a further turn of the screw specific of our "society of the spectacle" (Debord), in Disneyfication as a privileged allegory and simultaneously metonymy of our *Lebenswelt* each citizen viewer is not only cut off from creative, satisfying work rather than "useless toil" under the profit system (as has been superbly formulated by William Morris); furthermore, she is cut off from the producing of (or in) the media and positioned within a mass of atomized fellow-viewers, where a dynamic "desire to consume [...] [is] the only permissible participation in the social process" (Bukatman 36–37). Even more clearly than in the

Keynesian papering over, today's permanent structural unemployment, financial speculation run mad, and ungovernable movements of capital are coupled with the image and spectacle society as an ever deeper loss of autonomy by people (see Jameson, "Five" 182).

Showmanship for the masses is, of course, as American as the six-shooter and apple pie. It started rocketing in importance at the same time as in Europe – in the mid-nineteenth century – but untrammelled by non-capitalist values, it developed more vigorously in the US, issuing in Barnum's great discovery of "making consumers feel both good (full) and bad (empty) about what they are buying. even as they are induced to believe that what they are buying determines who they are" (Roach 47). The full-ness comes through magnetic induction (a feature of US showmanship as mesmerism, which Poe extrapolated presciently into arresting death) or feedback between a huckstered image that is accepted as the consumer's ideal self-image and tautologically found in the product as image. The emptiness preventing surfeit comes from never fully possessing that prod-uct, both because it is offered to a mass and because it will continually be updated as variations within what Benjamin called the always-again-same (*das Immerwiedergleiche*). It focuses on the consumer, explicitly delimited in US PR from Barnays on as "the contrary of the citizen, in a way the antidote to a collective expression of collective needs […] to the care for a common good" (Gorz 66, and see his whole section 64ff.).

The inner springs of this ploy are that a manipulative class hegemony has to offer a consumer specific compensatory gratifications for his/her passivity. These substitutive gratifications are rechannelled *utopian desires* (Jameson, *Political* 287) for the obverse of what determines the consumer in everyday life (say: safety, beauty, abundance, joy ...). The abiding politi-cal, bodily disempowerment is by means of showmanship channelled into a restless rage for addictive consuming as a new anchor for collective una-nimity where, paradoxically, the fake utopia is felt as personal. It has eaten into Ms Matay's brain so deeply that she sobbed uncontrollably in court at the loss of "the happy feeling" she had known in Disneyland and on the Mickey Mouse Club TV show in the 1950s. The slogans of this alienation are "comfort, affluence, consumerdom, unlimited scientifico-technical progress, omnipotence and good conscience, […] values assumed by violence and exploitation appearing disguised as law and order" (Marin 298).[3] Here we see, as Marin taught us precisely on the example of Disneyland, utopia eaten up by the very ideology which it was its original Morean and Morrisian function to fictionally unveil – in order, I would add, to rob ideology of its absolutizing and indisputable power, by interrupting its omnipresence, which then creates a chance of delivering it to the critique of practical reason. The viscous flow of what Marin calls ideology we might today more usefully call thinking saturated and shaped by capitalist pragmatics, a total immersion into the linear flow of consumption time. It is fuelled by an unacknowledged horror at the consumers' life emptied of meaning: "to be caulked off against Nothingness, *every* sense organ must be '*occupied*' (a well-aimed description)" (Anders, *Antiquiertheit* I: 139), and this occupation leads to addictive hunger. To the contrary, recommending reading (and, metaphorically, looking at plays and at life) by leafing and footnotes, as a "complex seeing," Brecht noted: "almost more important than thinking within the flow is thinking above the flow (*das Überdenflussdenken*)" (*Gesammelte Werke* 24: 59).

I shall not follow up here the whole subtle, sometimes perhaps oversubtle, rhetoric of Marin's book about neutralization etc.; it may be of interest if I report that in a discussion we had before his untimely death, he admitted that his basic approach was still too dependent on Engels's by now untenable split between utopia and science (see Chapter 3 above). For our present pressing purposes, I shall focus only on a few generalizable foci of Marin's astute dissection of Disneyland, whose features can be discerned best, I shall argue, if we see it in terms of dystopia masquerading as utopia. This argument comprises two points. First, Marin quite rightly seized on what I would call reproductive empathy, the fact that

---

3   Cf. also some shrewd observations on the representativity of Disneyland by Baudrillard, Eco, and by the PoMo architect Venturi who however feels much more at home in it. It would be useful to get into an as extended analysis of Walt Disney World in Orlando, which I here, alas, cannot do.

[...] the Disneyland visitor is on the stage, an actor of the play being performed, caught by his role like the rat by the trap, and alienated into the ideological character he plays without knowing it [...]. "Performing" Disney's utopia, the visitor "real-izes" the ideology of the ruling class as the mythic legend of origins for the society in which he lives. (298–99)

Marin thus reactualized the founding insight Benjamin reached looking at movies and advertising, that "the commercial glance into the heart of things [...] demolishes the space for the free play of viewing" by abolishing any criti-cal distance (*Gesammelte Schriften* IV.1: 131–32). Second, Disneyland – here read as a pioneering, topologically accessible, and even mappable, *pars pro toto* of the capitalist and especially US admass brainwash – is a "degenerated utopia" in two reinforcing ways, which I shall label transfer ideologizing and substitution commodifying. The analogy to Freud's account of dream-work as removal and condensation (*Verdichtung, Verschiebung*) is striking, but the consumer-visitor's work is imposed on her/his brain from the outside evacuating his/her creativity. It is analogous to a permanent hallucinatory REM-stage without the rest indispensable to prevent the work from turn-ing into Morris's "useless toil" with alienating upshot.

Transfer ideologizing, the first achievement of Disneyland is to perform a "Mickey Mouse" version of ideology: the continually reinforced empa-thizing immersion, the "thick," topologically and figurally concrete, and seamless false consciousness, injects the hegemonic bourgeois version of US history into people's neurons by twisting into a different semantics – thus "naturalizing" and neutralizing – three imaginative fields: *historical time* as the space of alternative choices; *the foreign/ers*; and the *natural world*. Marin does not focus much on historical time, except to suggest that it is turned into ideology, into the myth of technological progress (316 and 320–21), for example a clichetized Wild West in Frontierland (in Disney comics the past appears, if at all, as a space of farcical eccentrics). He does not fully conceptualize either – Marin proceeds rather by a kind of rhe-torical mimicry of Disneyland alienation – how the foreign and nature are denied, how that same Social Darwinism turns them into the primitive, the savage, and the monstrous (321), but I think this can be followed by means of a number of his *chemin faisant* analyses. This holds in particular for the discussion immediately following the spatial and performative "central access" to Disneyland and dealing with the phantasmatic Fantasyland, which is the PR "sign of Disneyland, the trade-mark of the utopia itself [...] the privileged utopian locus of Disneyland" (305–06; I am adapting these pages in the following account).

The very aptly named Fantasyland is constituted by personalized and impersonating images (themselves second-degree empathetic citations of Disney's comics, cartoons, etc.). Reality becomes the double or twin of the image in Marin's earlier and better version of Baudrillard's flashy simulacra. (The great ancestor here was Philip Dick's SF from the 1960s on.) This doubling is itself double: first, the image is turned into a material reality by figures of stone, plastic, plaster or rubber, but most empathetically and emphatically by human representers disguised into such fantasy characters. The representer (*le figurant*) has imaginatively become an embodied, flesh-and-blood represented (*le figuré*) and signified – the unmasking of which as fake when faced with the no doubt sweaty faces of Disney corporation's tired employees then quite rightly shocked the Matays. But second and symmetrically inverse, reality is transformed into image: insofar as the visitor is caught up in Disneyland, there is no other reality but that of the figure or representation into which (as Brecht would say) you creep in an act of psychic vampirism. This is also the proceeding of magic, which elevates its images to the ontological status of another, underlying reality (and it is logical that the Disney World NBA basketball team is the Orlando Magics). Any alternative non-narcissistic imaginary, imagination as consciousness of a possible non-drugged radical otherness or indeed simply as fertile possibility of shuttling in and out of myth (Mannoni), is being neutralized here:

> [...] while you believe you're enjoying yourself, you're absorbing the ideology needed for the reproduction of the relations of production. Historical reality is being concealed from you, it is camouflaged underneath a stylized and fascinating verisimilitude [...]. You're given a prefabricated dream: [...] a homegrown unconscious (*un inconscient maison*), perfectly ideologized. (Mikel Dufrenne, cited in Guattari 96–97)

As Marin established, Disneyland first neutralizes external reality by means of the car and the dollars that got the spectator into it. But it then

substitutes a transmogrified reality produced by the hallucinatory channelling of desire in Fantasyland, which is itself a terror: "the violence exercised
upon the imaginary by the phantasm of that Disneyland district [...]."
When "another" reality appears, it is "as the reality of the banalized, routine
images of Walt Disney movies, poor signs of an imagination homogenized
by the mass media." This fake Other is a trap for desire, its caricatural collective image. Disneyland's careful and most efficacious organization of
desires installs the imprinted *repetition of the familiar* as the supreme good
and demonizes the radically different Other. I find it lamentable that Ms
Matay could not hold Disneyland accountable for transgressing this basic
ideological contract with the brainwashed, for not policing its parking
lot better, not sufficiently occulting that drugging is necessary precisely
for life in PoMo capitalism as gangsterism, as the inescapable obverse of
Disneyland's business coin. This allows the too immediate, destabilizing
shock of the sordid life-world violence and insecurity – a reality which
the unanimous media make visible only for the relatively small or at best
medium gangsters, from the hold-up for the next fix to Saddam Hussein,
while the arms merchants, the starvers of hundreds of millions, and the
druggers of billions of people remain invisible.

The second achievement of Disneyland is, however, a new twist on
age-old ideology-mongering and constitution of graven images. The Golden
Calf is capillarized in the psychic bloodstream as *commodity*. This pervasive
upshot is introduced by "Main Street USA": "commodities are significations and significations are commodities" (Marin 317). It is confirmed at the
centre as "*life is a permanent exchange and perpetual consuming*" (319, Marin's
emphasis). By giving an infantilized connotation of "security blanket" to
images, which Debord famously defined as the final form of commodity
reification (ch. 1), Disneyland produces constantly repeated demand to
match the constantly recycled offer: it commodifies desire, and in particular
the desire for signification or meaningfulness (see Attali 259 and passim,
Eliot, and Schickel). Walt Disney himself stated to *Parade* in 1972 his object
was to sell happiness (cited in Dorfman 29). Disneyfication, then, centrally
means the pursuit of happiness, twisted from its Jeffersonian origins to a
permanent readiness for re-enchanted commodification: "the pursuit of
happiness becomes a lifetime of shopping" (Lummis 48). The dynamic

and sanitized empathizing into the pursuit of commodity is allegorically focused on and by anthropomorphic animals who stand for various affects that make up this pursuit. The affects and stances are strictly confined to the petty-bourgeois "positive" range: so that, roughly, Mickey introduces good cheer, the Lion King courage and persistence, etc. "Just try to get [things such as hunger, lack of shelter, cold or disease] past the turnstiles at Disneyland sometime!" (Dorfman 60) – shades of the Matay family!

This Disney infantilization marks and displaces a double rejection. First, of an active intervention into the real world which would make the pursuit of happiness collectively attainable: it is a debilitating daydream which appeals to the same mechanism as empathizing performances and publicity (see Berger et al. 146–49). Second and obversely, it rejects any reality constriction of one's desire, however shallow: you can never lust for too many commodities (but sex is forbidden in Disneyfication – his females are usually subaltern coquettes, cheery virgins, or villainous witches). While Disneyland is wedded to consumer dynamics, to an ever expanding market (Dorfman 202), it remains deeply inimical to knowledge, which crucially includes an understanding of limits for any endeavour – and in particular of the final personal limit of death. Disneyfication blends out death (see Benjamin, *Gesammelte Schriften* V: 121). Snow White – as so many other cartoon heroes and villains, for example Coyote – must always be magically resuscitated: "*Life is dreamt without death; [...] knowledge is dreamt as consumption and not production*" (Dorfman 170–71, my emphasis; and see 199–204). It is thus a degenerate form of ideology in comparison to religion and other beliefs whose strategic object is to give meaning to death (see Suvin *Lessons*, ch. 5). While Disneyfication is thus a displacement in Freud's sense, it is also more: and it might be more precisely identified as a shaping of *affectual investment into commodifying*. This is a metonymy of what Jameson has penetratingly discussed as the PoMo "consumption of the very process of consumption" (*Postmodernism* 276), say in TV; or of what some German critics have called "the transformation of commodities into fantasy values," where leisure-time has to compensate for the discipline and lack of human values during work-time: "The individual must be linked to [the immense collection of] commodities not only through physical contact and the consumption of goods, but also through imaginary consumption," and this consumption of goods is also the incorporation into an ideology (Negt and Kluge 172; they take their cue from Haug's *Critique*). However, it is not a discursive ideology, which is rather present in prohibitions and Newspeak terminology, but a channelling of affectual forces of their own brain and body as a whole, in a permanent roller-coaster ride. Appadurai calls such an approach to consumption as the driving force of metropolitan capitalist societies "ersatz nostalgia [...] without memory," that produces "the discipline of learning to link fantasy and nostalgia to the desire for new bundles of commodities" and involves labour to produce "the conditions of consciousness in which buying can occur" (82–83).

1.3

How are we to understand the lesson of Disneyfication and its efficient and consistent anti-utopian use of utopia? The best theorizations of consumerism as mind-warping has, until the 1960s, been European. Though there are some ancestral remarks of Marx already in the *Grundrisse* about historically created needs of the worker-consumer, and especially about consumption creating the user for production (e.g., 90–94), I shall in brief mention primarily the developments by Benjamin, Anders, Marcuse, and Debord.

The first and probably still the shrewdest critic of the "pleasure industry," its rise in the world expositions and fairs, its induction of the dreamworld of mass culture and affinities to fascism, as well as its connection with the employee class that produces information/entertainment/persuasion, was Benjamin. He understood well, not least through personal experience, the two prongs of such theorization. First, how "With the new production processes, which produce imitations, appearances (*Schein*) are crystallized in the commodities" (*Gesammelte Schriften* I.2: 668). Second, that their effect stems from the superimposition (*Überblendung*, also filmic fade-over) of proletarianized economic existence by bourgeois wishdream images (*Gesammelte Schriften* III: 220). Applied to what he knew of Disney, mainly the Mickey Mouse shorts, he first noted its ambiguous power of a blend of utopian escape from the resigned dismalness with an anarchist proliferation of metamorphic images (*Gesammelte Schriften* II.1: 218–19), and praised the original disrespectful Mickey (for example in *Steamboat Willie*, drawn with Ub Iwerks) as a "figure of the collective dream" in his much too optimistic first version of "The Work of Art" (*Gesammelte Schriften* 1: 462). However, in the later 1930s he began to meditate about "the usability of Disney's methods for fascism" (*Gesammelte Schriften* I.3: 1045, and see VI: 144–45, VII.1: 377; see the excellent overview in Buck-Morss, especially 83–99, 253–84, 303–17, and 322–27).[4]

Benjamin's favourite theme of a "refunctioning of allegory in the commodity economy" led him to pose the problem of how commodity can be personified and evoke affects. Beyond indicating (as Marx too did) the importance of the prostitute as obvious human commodity, Benjamin did not elaborate, but, latching onto a formulation by Brecht, he identified what we can recognize as Disneyfication by contraries to cognitive poetry. Centrally, in this Modernist poetry, as presented in the ancestral Baudelaire, "sensuous refinement [...] remains free of cuteness [*Gemütlichkeit*, coziness, snugness]" (*Gesammelte Schriften* I.2: 671 and 675). Heiner Müller, a dissident Brechtian, made the same contrast when horrified by *Fantasia*'s "reduc[tion of] the symbolic force of images to one meaning," and at that one of banal allegorizing, as against the early Soviet cinema's "torrent of metaphors" assimilating a rapidly changing reality in the specific tools of art before it was possible to conceptualize it (277). Obversely, the "mature" Disney Studio production after the mid-1930s, as of the *Donald Duck* comics (1934 on) and the first climax in the *Snow White* movie (1936) – when Disney got scared by an incipient workers' revolt, including the 1,500 studio employees, and retreated into a fierce conservatism, strike-busting, and collaboration with the FBI – became totally drenched in often unbearable cuteness.

---

4   On the sentimentalization of Mickey, see Jameson, *Brecht* 8; also Auden's perceptive characterization of Mickey in "Letter to Lord Byron" (93). Zipes analyzes both Disney's turn and the significance of the dwarves in *Snow White* as "the composite humours of a single individual" (114–15).

Benjamin learned much in exchanges with Kracauer and Brecht, and was in turn influential both upon Adorno in his and Horkheimer's horror at Donald Duck as "Cultural Industry" in *Dialectic of Enlightenment*, which however is much more monophonic, and upon the stringent accusations of Anders about conformist drugging or brainwashing by illusions, covertly or overtly religious, as the vehicle of people's cognitive immiseration and dispossession (see *Antiquiertheit* I: 176, II: 145, 169, 380–82, and passim, and on cosiness [*Verbiederung*] I: 125–31). Quite parallel to Benjamin and Brecht is Hanns Eisler's sharp critique in *Composing for the Films* of Hollywood's sentimentality mixed with cheer, with the function of buttressing with clichés illusionism and sensationalist plot-tension leading to the obligatory happy ending. These new developments of the postwar US-type conformism were brought to a point in the spirited book by Marcuse, *One-Dimensional Man* (and society), who found that oppositional horizons are obliterated by incorporating fake "cultural values" into the established order and displaying them on a massive scale. What he called "institutional desublimation" led to the atrophy of mental faculties for grasping contradictions and alternatives, to a "Happy Consciousness" in the service of a technologized Death Instinct (79 and passim, see Anders I: 280). We may wish today to use a less Freudian language, but to my mind it describes Disneyfication precisely.

Debord brought such considerations into a tight focus on the preeminence of spectacular images:

> Spectacle says simply "what appears is good, what is good appears" [...]. It is the sun that never sets on the empire of modern passivity. (13)

> Spectacle is the ceaseless discourse that the present order holds about itself, its laudatory monologue. (17)

> From car to TV, all the *goods selected* by the spectacular system are also weapons of constant reinforcement of the conditions of isolation for the "lonely crowds". (20)

Interestingly, this "specialization of apparent living [...] without depths" (42) unites both meanings of "apparent," the fake and the visible or evident. It is thus a powerful inversion of "utopia," whose two meanings meld the good (*eu*) and the apparently negative (*ou* – non-existent, not visible, not-here-and-now). In utopia, what is good cannot be here-and-now seen, and what appears here-and-now is not good. Obversely, for Debord spectacle is a technological, "material reconstruction of religious illusion" (16) as analyzed by the young Marx, an alienation of humanity by thisworldly means that does not need an immaterial Transcendence. In spectacle, "commodity has become the world, which also means that the world has become commodity" (47).

Thus, we ought to realize with Negt and Kluge – and with global capitalist corporations – that nowadays "intellectual activity [is] the most important raw material," basic for "the realization of [a whole] new range of products." The human brain is increasingly recognized as the core of human labour, and yet this labour is alienated by capitalist valorization of the working people's minds in the interests of profit: "Objective alienation is joined by an alienation from the awareness of this alienation" (183–84). Disneyfication is an important part as well as, to my mind, an emblem or metonymy of the demands and values of commodification being transposed directly into people's imagination. Disney learned how to use allegories of commodity from early cartoons, which were strongly veined with them. The clearest example from among intrawar cartoons is the figure of Popeye, scrawny little sailor version of the Little Tailor from fairy tale or of Chaplin's Tramp without Chaplin's disrespect for established society. Popeye always wins against powerful enemies (the melodramatic villain Pegleg) when he consumes a tinful of spinach – a highly interesting case of the usual fairytale function of magical helper becoming both the *telos* and a metonymy of a commodity to be sold. His mate is another commodity, Olive Oyl, as helpless fluff-head and potential rape victim.

As Featherstone noted, in consumerist practice, and even more so in consumerist ideology, the experience of manual labour, of bodily activity, is backgrounded at the same time as developments in economy favour administrative and supervisory jobs, including huge PR agencies for more consumption, while the greater part of manual jobs is in the more affluent North shuffled off to immigrant workers. The "consumerist body" is a passive one, in a way abstracted and ideologized in tandem with being infantilized and brutalized. Descartes was the first to proclaim that people are minds who "have" and "possess" a body. In other words, the body is had as a thing, or possessed as a saleable commodity; while the bourgeoisie proclaims each body is a subject, it also remains a manipulable object over which potentially violent power can be exercised. Until the compromise with working classes in dominant countries effected by Keynesian and Fordist capitalism, the "mind" function was restricted to the upper classes. Now it became impossible to disallow its democratization to everybody, *on condition* that it be warped conceptually and emotionally. As has been demonstrated on the example of Disneyland, managed consumerism implies invasive persuasion on or over the border of psychophysical violence.

This is no wonder in an enterprise permanently wedded to underpaid assembly-line labour, for which the artist-workers nicknamed Disney studios Goofenwald and Mousewitz, as well as to the cultural imperialism abroad so well documented by Dorfman (alone and with Mattelart). The Disney comics promote an authoritarian patriarchal system, which effects a retraction of the liberal fairy tale (see Zipes 112–13). The producer and the product fit seamlessly: if the product shows (say in the comics) "wealth without wages, deodorant without sweat," then "consumption [is] rid of the original sin of production, just as the son is rid of the original sin of sex represented by the father, and just as history is rid of the original sin of class-conflict" (Dorfman and Mattelart 65) – one should add the *absence of mothers*. Disney's and then his corporation's iron control over the visitors to his theme parks is truly total(itarian): they are steered from the word go to one-way presentations, enclosed in vehicles, hectored by guidebooks and voiceovers telling you how to feel, given no space or time for reflection or spontaneous exploration, "drained of interpretive autonomy" (Fjellman 13, see also Giroux, Bryman 103 and passim). The Disneyland visitor is ceaselessly within the flow, constantly bombarded by subtle and unsubtle solicitations to buy/consume, surfeited by kitschy sensory overloads, not allowed freedom to catch her/his breath even for a moment. Disney's type of "happy feeling" pleasure was the icebreaker for theme parks stuffed down the throats of infants and infantilized visitors "as a substitute for the democratic public realm" (Sorkin xv) where dialogue and even opposition might happen: no poor, no dirt, no work, not even unregulated Nature are permitted to be shown here, all must be predictably, manageably cosy. The fact these illusions are produced by unsanitized people *working* opened an epistemological abyss for the Matay kids! The park employees are in the Disney Newspeak not workers: they are hosts, the customers are guests, and lining-up happens in pre-entertainment areas (Bryman 108–09)... A sophisticated analysis of Disney's movies (Blackmore 349) identifies an agential constellation of what I would call a Transcendental Mandator (analogous to Uncle Walt himself – the Blue Fairy, the Sorcerer) who mandates an intermediary sub-creator (Geppetto, Mickey as Apprentice) to animate the silly quasi-human agent (Pinocchio, the Broom). The character most clearly partaking of transcendental powers is the original Mickey Mouse, a disinterested "ethical" character in cahoots with good luck; later, the more bilious and irate Donald Duck characteristically prevails (see Dorfman and Mattelart 91).This rage against self-determination led to the inglorious despotism of his model community Celebration, a shoddy failure (amply documented in Giroux, and Ross's *Celebration*).[5]

1.4

So my *first thesis* submitted to your discussion is (as seems only proper for a Gramscian, see *Selection* 164) double-pronged, epistemological, and political. *1a*: while I have little doubt that collective realities exist (see more in 1.4 below), *it is dubious that empirical entities can be neatly disjoined from imaginary ones*; in other words, it is dubious – though still perhaps not only useful but unavoidable for pedagogical purposes – that empirical or existent societies can be neatly disjoined from imaginary or non-existent ones. I shall argue in a moment that there is no identification of any token or sample existent without an imaginary type which permits the identifier

---

5   *Note January 2008*: There is a direct line from this pseudo-magic illusionism and showmanship deeply complicitous with violence to the ethos of the Bush Jr presidency. For example, the 2003 pressroom of the US armed forces in Qatar for General Franks's briefings to the world's press, erected into an ultramodern TV studio at the cost of one million dollars, was realised by an ex-Disney and MGM designer with the help of the TV "magician" David Blaine (see Salmon).

to recognize it as such, say the sample Mickey Mouse as type of "Disney's comforting being" (*Geborgenheit*). *1b*: *we live today in dystopia as well as in anti-utopia* – perhaps because the dystopia is an anti-utopia, a deliberate project for subalternity. This was dimly adumbrated in the flash of horror (*Geworfenheit*) the fatherless Matay family had at the backstage divestment.

Is it only professional idiocy to conclude that we desperately need (at least to begin with) some semantic hygiene as to what we are speaking about? Is it only intellectualist expert doodling? Not, I firmly believe, if we are doing this as a link in an ongoing praxis culminating in action. If Rosa Luxemburg, in the midst of World War 1, before the admass efficiency, was possibly too optimistic in believing that "to speak the truth is already a revolution," we must inherit her optimism of knowledge and will, and say that to articulate a category hygiene is the *precondition* for any salvational revolution. I do not therefore see any break in the continuity of my discussion if I immediately segue from politico-economic data and ideological emotions into epistemological discussions of the proper vocabulary and articulation we need in order to see sufficiently steadily the ground upon which we unstably stand, and to see it sufficiently whole – though I shall come back to the complex and indispensable mediations and in particular to ourselves as (potential) intellectuals.

Allow me therefore a very brief and compressed epistemic reminder: All conscious thinking involves imagining what would happen if something were other than the way it is (Ellis 1997). Even for the infant consciousness, identifying an object involves imagining how it could be manipulated: there is no "perceptual consciousness" without imagination and subjunctivity, that is, without an implied counterfactuality (cf. for example Piaget 1928 and 1969). Seeing, as opposed to staring, occurs only when we attend to (look for) the object on which we are to focus, that is, when we ask "Is my imaginative/ry type instantiated by the token in my visual field right now?" Furthermore, a main difference between conscious and non-conscious dealing with perceptions, and *a fortiori* a set of them, is that in the former the imaginative act of arousal and attention precedes the perceptual one (Bruner 1986); Marx even held that this is the species-specific difference between humans and spiders or bees. It originates in desire or interest

which is translated into the formulation of questions (Luria 1973), concepts, and abstractions. Only at this point, when the whole brain knows
what it is "looking for" in this sense, does optic stimulation result in an
attentive seeing of the object. This means that a conscious registering of a
perceptual object leads to much more extensive processing of the data than
the non-conscious registering of it could possibly lead to, concludes Ellis.
Even inchoate "desire" becomes desire in the conscious sense only when
it begins to include the missing elements (as the need-"desire" for cellular
sustenance grows to include images of oneself eating and then representations of edible objects). It is this full use of the brain, the imaginative play
with counterfactuals and Possible Worlds, which is being precluded by
capturing inchoate imaginative desire and channelling it away from full
understanding, into infantilism, in Disneyland. And I propose we can make
sense of this by seeing it with Marin as a fake utopia, which we according
to our interests decipher as a dystopia and therefore also as anti-utopia.

Map-making and naming are after all the founding gestures, the seed or
root (*etymon*) of any utopian venture – narrativized in fiction, empirically
localized in colonies. Baudrillard's consciously outrageous claim that the
map precedes the territory is quite one-sided, though up to a point salutary as a goad to thinking: for no territory can be constituted as territory
(instead of a lot of terrains) unless a drawn and/or verbal map delimits it as
such. While obversely (as is neatly proved by contraries in an ironic story
by Borges) the map is not the territory, it is both a model of the territory
and the territory seen through a grid of epistemic conventions, seen as an
overview instead of as a bodily experience or indeed a buzzing confusion
of random phenomena.

1.5

Thus, what is anti-utopia? And what dystopia? They are incompletely
stabilized neologisms, but to use them as efficient cognitive tools we
should try to stabilize them for collective manipulation. Some years ago
I made such a disambiguating proposal to my student Ron Zajac and it is

briefly sketched in his MA (2).[6] Mr Zajac and I decided to call "dystopia"
a community where sociopolitical institutions, norms, and relationships
between its individuals are organized in a significantly less perfect way than
in the author's community. Accepting the objection (by Wittgenstein or
Brecht) that nothing is seen without being "seen as X" because it is "seen
from the stance Y," I would today add to my original, somewhat formalist
or objectivist definition of utopia and dystopia in *MOSF* as significantly
more (or less) perfect than the norms of the original readers something
like "significantly less perfect, as seen by a representative of a discontented
social class or fraction, whose value-system defines 'perfection.'"

As a secondary recomplication, there is a special case of a sociopolitically different locus which finally also turns out to be a dystopia, but
which is explicitly designed to refute a fictional and/or otherwise imagined
utopia; and I hope we were following the bent of the English language
when we proposed to call it "anti-utopia," evacuating the uneconomical
use of this term as a synonym of dystopia. "Anti-utopia" thus designates
a pretended utopia, a community whose hegemonic principles pretend it
is more perfectly organized than any thinkable alternative, while our representative "camera eye" and value-monger finds out it is significantly less
perfect than an alternative.

Finally, it becomes logically inescapable to invent a name for those
dystopias which are not also anti-utopias, but in order not to abet the
Babylonian confusion of languages around us, I shall simply call it the
"simple" dystopia.

Since we have here a somewhat complex state of affairs, I believe it
might be clarified by a minimal amount of formalization in terms of Possible
Worlds. Let me call PW_0 the dominant ideas or "encyclopedia" about the
describer's and the evaluator's empirical world, and PW_u the imaginative

6   I note with pleasure that our delimitation tallies with Lyman Tower Sargent's (188),
     though his definition insists on objectively "non existent societies" and I have men-
     tioned that I reject commonsense objectivism (see Suvin, "Cognitive"). I should in
     fairness say that I was aware of precursory discussions in North America, usefully
     summarized in Moylan, *Scraps* 124–30 (from whose two books I have taken much),
     and later in Germany, e.g., by Seeber and Groeben.

Other (utopian/dystopian) world. In that case, the intertext of "simple" dystopia (that is, of that cluster of dystopias which is not also antiutopia, say Pohl and Kornbluth's *Space Merchants* or other "new maps of hell") is PW_o, and what is "inter" or shared here are some strategically central tendencies of the author's empirical world. The intertext or referential (Eco would say inferential) foil of anti-utopia, however, is PW_u: a non-empirical PW intended to be significantly better than PW_o but failing to be such. In other words, dystopia (PW_d) traffics between text and the reader's encyclopedia about reality, while anti-utopia is almost exclusively ideological polemics:

$$\text{DYSTOPIA} \begin{cases} \text{ANTI-UTOPIA} \\ \text{"SIMPLE" DYSTOPIA} \end{cases}$$

"SIMPLE" DYSTOPIA: $\quad PW_d \longleftrightarrow PW_o$

ANTI-UTOPIA: $\quad\quad\ PW_{au} \longleftrightarrow PW_u$

The purpose of PW_d is an awful warning against things going on as they do in the original empirical world PW_{o1}, sometimes wedded to a hope that it may be changed – "if others will but see it as I do" (Morris) – into a less dangerous and happier PW_{o2}. The purpose of PW_{au} is an awful warning against a new PW_u, as a rule wedded to a hope that we can get rid of that novel delusion and return to the original PW_{o1}. Seeing Disneyland – standing in for Post-Fordism – as a fake utopia consubstantial with (deciphered as) anti-utopia is a move analogous to those utopographer opponents of Bellamy who have his hero Julian West waking up to the fact he was being hoodwinked by a future evil empire. Seeing Disneyland then simultaneously as a dystopia prevents us from regressive nostalgia for the good old days of (say) the 1960s or of the antifascist coalition, the lessons of which we must nonetheless sublate if we are to have a chance of getting at any happier PW_{o2}.

This little mental exercise does not claim to work out a full system of utopian sub-genres or facets. Still, I wish to add a further important warning. I did begin by saying these distinctions are tricky. I have been arguing that there is strictly speaking no objective "empirical world" out there without its simultaneously and co-constitutively "being seen as" such, and indeed as such-and-such. (This does not at all mean "there's nothing out there" interacting with anybody's gaze or action, as the PoMo vulgate, though not its best people, claimed: try jumping off a skyscraper without a parachute ...) But I would defend my operative distinction between empirical and utopian world by saying that there was – and is! – *a strong, ideologically dominant illusion of such an empirical world*, seen at one glance by God or asymptotically by Science or Mankind, in that modern scientism which impinges deeply on and largely determines our experiential world (cf. Suvin, "On the Horizons"). The distinction depends on the bourgeois or capitalist utopianism, which can be seen in fiction as of Jules Verne, denying that it is utopian and instead being "naturalized" as normal and/ or scientific. This pragmatic micro-utopianism presents the ideology of progress and Social Darwinism as natural (see *MOSF* ch. 7 and both titles by Barthes) and not needing explicit, ideologically foregrounded figuration. Up to, say, the 1950s–1970s, the Powers-That-Be rightly refused – because *they* did not need it – the stroke of genius with which More endowed his King Utopus: cutting off the ideal topology of Utopia from the experiential continent. Then, it was mainly oppositionists (socialist or anarchists on the Left, reactionaries on the Right, with some technocrats à la Skinner – and indeed much Wells – in between) who carried on with both topologically and conceptually or axiologically explicit, let me call them *ruptural* utopias. I shall argue Disneyland, though topologically separate, is not ruptural but continuous to, intensificatory, and celebratory of capitalist experience. No Disneyland is imaginable before Fordism.

It should be added that the dominant ideological horizon of anti-utopia is in any historical monad determined by opposition to the dominant idea/s of utopia, to the dominant imaginary PW_u. In the Modernist "short twentieth century" (Hobsbawm dates it ca. 1917–73, thus underlining its crucial but probably not exclusive parallels with Leninism), this dominant idea was either some kind of socialist – usually perverted or pseudo-socialist – imaginative topology, or technocratic etatism with few if any socialist traits. Thus, as a rule, only the "simple dystopian" horizon applied to high capitalism while the anti-utopian one applied to rotting pseudo-socialism. It seems to me significant for the social class/es of intellectuals which articulated such anti-utopias that at any rate the best examples thereof (for example the Holy Trinity of Zamyatin-Huxley-Orwell) subsumed both capitalist and Stalinist etatism into its foil PW_u, and yet did not envisage this resulting in a radically better PW_{o2}.

However, the unprecedented Post-Fordist mobilization and colonization of people's desires and of all the remaining non-capitalized spaces (making Huxley's Palau in *Island* today possibly more important than *Brave New World*) now requires masked, infantile fantasies. In that light, Asada's playful proposition that our period should not be called mature or late but "infantile capitalism" (631) is quite correct if taken as a kind of infantilized, *gâteuse* senescence which cannot mature further (but may of course grow pragmatically stronger or weaker): the dusk creature on three rather than four legs in the Sphinx's riddle. The capitalist logic of accumulation is purely infantile "since it can tolerate no contradictions or limitations" but only annexation in an additive growth. This reveals a psychic void, a "pursuit of narcissistic identity [inseparable] from the fetishization of commodities," a reified self that "must perforce obsessively proclaim, through the possession of things, a phantom identity [of >feeling good<]." (Davis, "Death's," and see his *Deracination*). Thus it becomes clear why desire, images, "culture" can no longer be disjoined from economics: rather, it is their interpenetration which constitutes the new mode of production's corrupt strength, that is, source of major profits (and a counter-force can only be found in a sane interpenetration). This has been brilliantly argued by Stuart Hall (for example 243), while Jameson has even remarked that "everything in our social life – from economic value and state power to practices and to the very structure of the psyche itself – can be said to have become 'cultural' in some original and as yet untheorized sense" (*Postmodernism* 48) and developed this at length throughout that book.

"Culture" began supplying authoritative frameworks and foci for agency and meaning after "belief became polluted, like the air or the water" (de Certeau 147), so that orthodox religions (including scientism and liberalism) rightly devolved to just another, if more privileged sect – yet a need for religious or analogous values was more in demand than ever amid physical and psychic indigence. Culture co-opted by capitalism is today no longer a fully distinct sphere of activities but a colonization of the "service" or consumption-focussed society in the twin guise of information and esthetics: information-intensive production in working time (the best example is biotechnology, whose output is information inscribed in living matter, so that the engineering involved is the processing or "reading" of this information), and "esthetic" consumption in leisure time (see Haug *Critique*, and Kamper et al. 55–58 and 64ff.). The new orthodoxy of belief proceeds thus "camouflaged as facts, data and events" (de Certeau 151) which are in fact shamelessly manipulated and indeed openly manufactured by those in power, and increasingly consubstantial with "culture industry" images. An exemplary (bad) case of the latter are the edulcorated fables and fairy-tales of Disneyland.

Disneyland's first move is homologous to King Utopus's cutting off Utopia from the everyday continent: a spatial delimitation (splendidly analyzed by Marin's account of the Disneyland layout). Yet this is not a true, qualitative rupture. It is only a mimicry, insect not twig, which by reason of its pervasive and invading ideological continuity with the everyday hegemony functions as harbinger and accelerator of mega-corporate capitalism. At this point – more or less contemporaneous with the exhaustion of Leninist and Social-Democratic socialism, of the Welfare State – a new monster has appeared that must be understood as topologically opposed to PW_o but axiologically intensifying it – rather than oppositional as in the More to Morris canon. Thus it not only mimics a ruptural genre (the classical utopia, PW_u) but it also appropriates a Wellsian dynamic, invasive subversion of empirical reality (PW_o; see chapters 9 and 10 in *MOSF*). Furthermore, if we take the Disney enterprise as an allegorical *exemplum*, its pervasiveness is not only intended to be intensionally total (in all fields of life) but also extensionally total (global) as none before (see Jameson's *Political*, but his whole work bears on this point): Disneylands brainwash impartially and without discrimination (non olet) consumers of all social classes and in the whole world, including Europe and Japan. All of us live in a dynamically aggressive fake utopia whose "degeneracy" we nonetheless absolutely have to – upon pain of brain rot and then bodily collapse – decipher as anti-utopia.

This state of affairs was most stimulatingly seen in Philip Dick's ubiq-
uitously invading stigmata of Palmer Eldritch, whose prescient articulation
merits a longer consideration (see Suvin, "Philip K. Dick's") – thus to my
impenitent mind confirming that it is sterile to cut off "pure utopian lit."
texts from SF. I would today go further and argue that confining utopia
to fiction only or small colonies only, or worse yet to pure ideas, is equally
sterile, channelling it away from praxis.[7] More than ever, we need as clear
as possible distinctions and delimitations of concepts; but only if their
articulation "cuts reality at its joints," that is, performs as good an approximation as possible to the increasingly complex bastardry and impurity of
experience. For one example, the Disneyland experience feels all which is
not being turned into exchange-value for and by corporations, all use-values
not subject to the bottom line of "profit this year" and "as much profit as
possible and the devil take the hindmost," as alien and savage: pollution
finds the Amazon basin dirty. Let me mention only two further glimpses
of invaded mega-fields which happen to be preying on my mind these
years: molecular genetics and copyright. Alice Sheldon once complained
about our world "where the raising of children yields no profit (except
to television salesmen)" (45): this has been superseded by the politically
shaped technology of Post-Fordism. For it is politics, no doubt in tandem
with atomizing possessive individualism, that enables molecular genetics
businesses to patent DNA units and companies to copyright trademarks,
so that one day we might have to pay royalties for having children as well
as for using nouns and verbs such as xerox.[8] It is inside this world-whale all
of us Jonahs, Sindbads, and Nemos today live, cultivating our kale.

---

7   Is it necessary to say that I find much to interest and delight me in utopological writ-
     ing, and that I have, of course, no objection to pragmatic delimitation of any field
     according to the delimiters' interest, but only wish then to reserve the right to judge
     that interest? Yet in fact nowadays we meet a "pure utopia" as often as an okapi, since
     to isolate political organization from all other factors has proved self-defeating.
8   See Chomsky 112–13. This hyperbole is likely to be literally true if we specify "healthy"
     or even "normal life expectancy" children. This whole matter of so called TRIPS
     (Trade Related Intellectual Property Rights) is an extremely important, threaten-
     ing, and neglected spearhead of corporate aggression into the most intimate areas

2. We Intellectuals in Post-Fordism

> You may back off from the world's woes, you're free to do so and it lies in your nature,
> but perhaps this backing away is precisely the only woe that you might avoid.
> — KAFKA, "Reflections on Sin, Woe, Hope, and the Way"

> "It's the economy, stupid!"
> — ANON., first Clinton campaign

2.0

"Let us go then, you and I / When the evening is spread out against the sky / Like a patient etherized upon a table / [...] like a tedious argument / Of insidious intent / To lead you to an overwhelming question ..." (T.S. Eliot) – the question being first, "Why do we live so badly?", and second, "What orientation may get us out of it?" To restate at different level the initial question I adapted from Foucault: pragmatically, in the present to which all of us belong, "What is this present?" and "Who are we?". My working hypotheses for a first delimitation, without the ifs and buts no doubt necessary for further understanding, are: The what is Post-Fordism; the we is intellectuals.

I take the "economy, stupid!" slogan from Clinton's co-opting and obfuscatory Tweedledum campaign; but "thank thee for teaching me the word" (Shakespeare). Its salutary orientation toward action may be supplemented with the *second thesis* I submit to you: as I concluded in Chapter 8, *the barrier between "culture" and citizenship, which today means economically based macro- and micro-politics, has been wiped out in practice by our dystopian capitalist rulers*, and it is time we recognized this in our laggard theory. There is no longer any believable utopian social movement which

of everybody's life world, which is through extension of patent law logic (for genetically engineered food, seeds, micro organisms, pharmaceuticals, and chemicals) to copyright laws, including trademarks, also sucking in language.

we could entrust with the task of economic politics, in which we then participate as citizens but not as professionals. The comforting economic and psychic roofs or blankets holding us warm against the blasts of a then disputable Destiny have been torn down. If there are to be any movements and roofs, they will have to be painfully remade by ourselves. Therefore, Formalism – an enclave of playful creativity amid the material necessities that create consciousness, or Kantian esthetics within a Hegelo-Marxist politico-economical horizon – can today only be useful as the preliminary to a more comprehensive civic analysis, to politics in the Aristotelian and a critique of political economy in the Marxian sense. It is imperative that we realize epistemology does not function without asking the political question "what for?" or *cui bono*. It is not simply that there is no useful politics without clear perception: much more intimately, interests and values decisively shape all perception. So if we grasp that the barrier between such "cultural" discussions and politics-cum-economics is simply sterile categorization and blindness, our politically and epistemologically corrected theory would then be only following, fifteen if not thirty years late, two generational waves of SF and utopianism, from Russ and Piercy to Stan Robinson. The time for isolated formal poetics is over when the *Geist* has been colonized and our debates can no longer presume movements for the liberation of labour – an "existing community of praxis" – as the ground for their figures (see Ahmad 70, 2, and passim); I must respectfully posit as known my theoretical arguments from the first part of *MOSF* and most importantly from chapters 5 and 8 in this book, and pass on.

2.1 Post-Fordism

In a long position paper for the Luton University conference on SF, only a bit more than half of which had been printed ("News") but which is now Chapter 8 in this book, I attempted an overview of Post-Fordism to which I refer for more detailed supporting. I summarize and partly develop it here. The argument is that we should be, economically speaking, at the descending part of the boom-and-bust cycle; this can only be compensated, for a time, by "military Keynesianism." Its ascending part, that began in the 1930s, found in Fordism and Keynesianism the remedies to the dangerous 1920s bust. These strategies effected a limited but real redistribution of wealth: Fordism through higher wages rendered possible by mass production of goods but neutralized by total production alienation and consumerist PR, Keynesianism through higher taxation neutralized by bourgeois control of the State. They functioned in feedback with the rise of production and consumption 1938–73, itself inextricably enmeshed with imperial extraction of surplus-value, armament production, and the warfare State. In class terms, Soviet pseudo-Leninism and Rooseveltian Liberalism – as well as some important aspects of Fascism – were compromises with and co-optations of the pressures and revolts by plebeian or labouring classes. In economic terms they meant the institution of a modest but real "security floor" to the lowermost classes of selected "Northern" countries as well as a great expansion of fairly comfortable and thus fairly independent middle classes. Wallerstein somewhat optimistically numbers these "[sharers] in the surplus value" – us – as 10–15 percent of the world population, of course disproportionately concentrated in the richer North (*Historical* 123).

However, the shock of 1973, when we entered upon the "bust" part of the cycle that began with the 1930s–1940s boom (the oil crisis, debt crisis, global domination of the World Bank and then of the corporate credit system, etc.), revealed that our planet Earth, a finite system, cannot expand indefinitely to bear six or ten or twenty billion people up to the immensely wasteful "Northern" standards (see for example Lummis 60–74). This real emergency was seized upon and twisted by the ruling capitalists into revoking both the Keynesian compromise with the metropolitan lower classes and the Wilsonian promise to the peripheral "South." In a fierce class war from above, through a series of hidden or overt putsches by the right wing all protective barriers and mitigating bumpers are dismantled, so that what Marx called "the extraction of absolute surplus value" may be sharply increased, the security floor is abolished, the permanent Fordist class of chronically poor is now enlarged up to or beyond one third even in the rich North, while the "middle" group of classes is squeezed back into full dependency by abolishing financial security (there is a wealth of uncoordinated data on this, see for example Lash and Urry 160–68). This leads to increased world concentration of capital now dominated by cartels of "multinationals."⁹ Closest to home, control of the major US media had passed from fifty corporations in 1983 to twenty in 1992, so that four movie studios (including Disney's Buena Vista Films), five giant book publishers, and seven cable TV companies – all interlocked with major banks – produced more than half of the revenue in their field (Bagdikian ix–xii and 20–26). The dazzling surface array of diversity hides bland uniformity: there are 11,000 magazines but two magazine publishers dominate the field ... The people running these twenty media monopolies and their bankers "constitute a new Private Ministry of Information and Culture" (Bagdikian xxviii). Rocketing indigence and aimlessness provide the ideal breeding ground not only for petty and organized criminality – business by other means – but also for its legitimization in discrimination and ethnic hatred (for example in India or ex-Yugoslavia). The warfare state had a little hiccup after the end of Cold War but it has recovered nicely (the best estimate seems to show that two thirds of US citizens' taxes go to pay for military technology and wars, see Ross 4). The welfare-state transfer of wealth from one class to another goes on in spades but *for the rich*. The latest report to have percolated into public domain tells of the US Congress and FCC handing $70,000,000.000 (yes, seventy billion dollars) to the TV conglomerates in free space on public airwaves ("Bandwidth"). No wonder the number of US-dollar millionaires has from 1980 to 1988 risen from 574,000 to ca. 1,300,000 (Phillips 9–10) and of billionaires 1982–96 from 13 to 149. The "global billionaires' club" of 450 members had by 1997 a total wealth much larger than that of a group of low income countries comprising 56 percent of the world population (*Forbes Magazine*, cited in Chossudovsky, "Global"): these 450 individuals are richer than 3 billion poor people. Production, the great trump ace of capitalism, has in the core

---

9   *Note January 1998*: The newest such case, the IMF "bailout" of South Korea, means in practice a cut in half in wages expressed in US dollars, huge unemployment of employees and bankruptcies of small businesses, the open door to takeover of Korean banks by foreign finance, strong reduction in government spending on social programs, infrastructure, and credits to business, fracturing of the large domestic conglomerates: in brief, a whole thriving "high tech and manufacturing economy up for grabs" (Chossudovsky, "IMF").

countries been downgraded first for consumption and then for financial speculation. Increasingly, the consumer-goods market dominated by giant corporations supplanted independent small suppliers of products and services (e.g., midwifery) in the lower classes, and indeed even its sociability in participant sports or local social drinking: consumption was unified and totalized (the Ehrenreichs 15–16). Democracy fares poorly in such situations, where elections (if not fraudulent) are bought by the rich, "people [are intentionally kept] structurally illiterate [...] about the forces that are shaping their lives" (Sellars 89), and, ever since the 1930s, censorship has occupied the commanding heights of movies and then TV in the world's two (whilom) great hopes, the USA and USSR.

Not to forget the Walt Disney corporation, in 2004 it was the second largest among US multimedia conglomerates, with an income of $27 billion (*Fortune*, 12 April 2004); its CEO Michael Eisner's salary was $750,000 plus huge bonuses and stock options, at the time a Haitian worker is paid six cents for one "101 Dalmatians" children's garment ("Globaldygook") and a Korean or Chinese girl even less for Christmas toys ("On the Job") – such as possibly worn by or bought for the happy Matay grandchildren. Whole generations, as well as the planetary environment for centuries into the future, are being mortgaged to an arrogant fraction of 1 percent on the top and a faceless world money market. The gap between the rich "North" and the poor "South" of the world system has doubled from 1960 to 1992, with the poor "transferring more than $21 billion a year into the coffers of the rich" (*The Economist*; see Chomsky 62). Lowering "the cost of labour," the ultimate wisdom of capitalism, means impoverishing everybody who lives from her work and enriching top-level managers and the upper mercenaries (ranking politicians, cops, engineers, lawyers, administrators ...). The dire poverty gap is turning all societies into "two nations," with good services for the small minority of the rich and shoddy ones or none for the dispensable poor. Compared to Dickens, the upper classes will have more computers, more (or at least more talk about) sex, and more cynicism, while the Indian, Brazilian, Chinese or our own slums will have TV. Human groups divide into resentful islands who do not hear the bell tolling; Marx's "absolute general law of capitalist accumulation: accumulation of wealth is at the same time accumulation of misery, agony of toil, slavery, ignorance, brutality" (*Selected* 483), has been confirmed in spades.

What then is the balance sheet of the capitalist social formation (see Wallerstein, *Historical* 99–105 and 117–37)? Let me take the two most undoubted material achievements: production and length of life. As to the first, it is clear that human domination over nature has mightily increased: per unit of labour-time, the output of products is considerably greater. In other words, technological productivity under capitalism has finally created the presuppositions for rendering our globe habitable for all. But the habitability has been hijacked: is the required labour-time for production and reproduction per one person, per one lifetime or in the aggregate smaller? Certainly, in comparison to precapitalist formations the working classes "work much harder in order to merely scrape by; they may eat less, but they surely buy more" (ibid. 124). Not only is Paul Lafargue's right to creative laziness nowhere on the horizon, but its reformulation to ecological purposes as the right to slowness (Barthes, "Day" 116) is lost in turbocapitalism. In the last thirty years, at the same time that a fake decolonization redrew political borders outside the metropolitan countries, from Ghana to the Ukraine, "the world proletariat has almost doubled [...] [much of it] working under conditions of gross exploitation and political oppression" (Harvey 423). There is a serious possibility that the classical Marxist thesis of the absolute immiseration of the proletariat as compared to 500 or 200 years ago may after all be correct, if we look at the 85 percent or more of the working people in the world economy rather than only at the industrial workers of the metropolitan countries; and there is no doubt of the huge relative immiseration in comparison to the dominant classes and nations. Obviously, even the latter is politically quite explosive and morally unacceptable: it demoralizes and alienates all classes, if in different ways. Therefore, the rulers need brainwashing.

As to the second, infant mortality has been strongly reduced in peace-time: but have the pollutions of air, water, and food as well as the psychic stresses and unceasing compulsion and insecurity lengthened life for those who survived beyond cared-for infancy? The jury is out on this: but the quality and ease of life has surely fallen sharply within my lifetime, and it is bound to fall exponentially with structural long-term unemployment.

The amount of social waste and cruelty is larger than ever before in the century beginning with the great capitalist world wars (1914). "[C]apitalism cannot deliver world peace" (Wood 265): we will be very lucky if we have no further ABC wars after the Gulf Oil one. Capitalism is positively dependent on ecological devastation, condensing geological change into historical time. True, "really existing socialism" also badly failed at this (not at keeping peace); but ecological vandalism is a measure of capitalism's success, not failure: the more vandalism the more short-term profit (look at Amazonia). So I asked in "News": is our overheated society better than the "colder" one of (say) Tang China or the Iroquois Confederation? There is more of us but do we have more space or more trees, per person? Many of us have less back-breaking toil, but all have more mind-destroying aimlessness resulting in person-killing by drug and gun; we have WCs but also cancer and AIDS ... Most probably, even quantitatively – and with greater certainty qualitatively – the achievements of the bourgeoisie celebrated in *The Communist Manifesto* have been overbalanced by what it has suppressed.

One example of the very ambiguous balance sheet would be universalism and science. I discuss the latter in Chapter 8 (and now at length in "On the Horizons"), and can here only telegraphically note that, while I wish to keep its cognitive orientation toward the systematic and testable understanding of material processes, it is also an institution both legitimating and disciplining the world's cadres, and its subsumption under profit-oriented rationalism has caused a horrified massive reaction into irrationalism. And the destruction of local communities, knowledge, and living species from Columbus on is irreparable. For Homo sapiens and the planet, the price of drug, gun, and profits is too high: the price of capitalism is bankrupting us morally and materially.

2.2 Intellectuals

Post-Fordism is, then, the apparently final moulting of capitalism from individual into corporate. Where Fordism was characterized by "hard" technology (paradigm: personal car), semi-automation, State planning, and the rise of mass media and advertising, Post-Fordism brings "soft" technology (paradigm: personal computer), automation, mega-corporations, and world market regulated so as to override States, as well as the integration of the media with the computer under total domination of marketing. In both cases, more "software" or "human engineering" people were needed to ensure not only production but also supervision and ideological updating of the hegemony: the population increased. I have argued in Chapter 8 that these "new middle classes," constituted of managers and "intellectuals," account for two thirds of the GNP in the societies of the capitalist North now derived from their labour, though their proportion within the population is globally perhaps 10–15 percent. Politically, they (we) may be very roughly divided into servants of the capitalist and/or bureaucratic State, servants of large corporations, self-proclaimed "apolitical" or "esthetic" free-floaters, and radicals taking the plebeian side. It is actually this intermediate class-congeries in the world, the Ehrenreichs' "professional-managerial class" (a nomination that usefully underlines their two wings), that has beyond doubt been materially better off than their earlier historical counterparts: but the price has been very high.

In the Fordist dispensation, liberal ideology claimed that the world is composed of inner-directed atomic individuals within atomic national States. The new collectivism needs other-directed intellectuals, whose consciousness/conscience is fully subsumed under profit. This is where it might be useful to delve further into the Faustian two souls of us intellectuals. It would require complex adaptations of Marxian class theory (see to begin with Gramsci, the Ehrenreichs, Poulantzas, Resnick-Wolff, Guillory, and Robbins ed.) which would take into account a group's relation to both economics and to power and cultural positioning; I can only hope to identify the problem. On the one hand, as Marx famously chided, "the bourgeoisie has stripped of its halo every occupation hitherto honoured and looked up to with reverent awe. It has turned the physician, the lawyer, the priest, the poet, the scientist, into its paid wage-labourers" (*The Communist Manifesto*). On the other hand, the constitution of the intellectuals into professions is impossible without a measure of autonomy: of corporative self-government and, most important, control over one's work. We share to an exasperated degree the tug-of-war between wage-labour and self-determination: even the poorest intellectual participates in privilege through her "educational capital"; even the richest manager may not be able to rid himself of the uncomfortable itch of thinking. The increasingly marginalized and pauperized humanists and teachers are disproportionately constituted by women and non-"Whites," a sure index of subalternity.

Bourdieu has intriguingly described intellectuals as "a dominated fraction of the dominant class" ("Intellectual" 145 and *Other* 319ff.; see Guillory 118ff.). Such semi-Foucauldian brilliancies are too monolithic and undialectical for my taste, but it is true that the funds for this whole congeries of "cadre" classes – "administrators, technicians, scientists, educators […] have been drawn from the global surplus" (Wallerstein, *Historical* 83–84): as Sartre would say, none of us has clean hands. (I myself seem to be paid through loans to Québec by German banks, or ultimately by the exploitation of my ex-compatriots in Eastern Europe.) It is also true that the welfare-and-warfare State epoch saw the culmination of the "cut" from the global surplus we "middle" 10–15 percent were getting; and "the shouts of triumph of this 'middle' sector over the reduction of their gap with the upper one per cent have masked the realities of the growing gap between them and the other [85–90] per cent" (ibid. 104–05). So Bourdieu is getting at our oxymoronic position of a living contradiction: we are essential to the *encadrement* and policing of workers, but we are ourselves workers – a position memorably encapsulated by Brecht's "Song of the [Tame] Eighth Elephant" helping to subdue his recalcitrant natural brethren in *The Good Person of Setzuan*. Excogitating ever new ways to sell our expertise as "services" in producing and enforcing marketing images of happiness, we decisively contribute to the decline of people's self-determination and non-professionalized expertise (see the early acid definition by Sorel 162 and 273, also Fox and Lears 9 and passim). We are essential to the production of new knowledge and ideology, but we are totally kept out of establishing the framework into which, and mostly kept from directing the uses to which, the production and the producers are put. Our professionalization secured for some of us sufficient income to turn high wage into minuscule capital. We cannot function without a good deal of self-government in our classes or artefacts, but we do not control the strategic decisions about universities or dissemination of artefacts. The list of such variants to Dr

Dolittle's two-headed Pushme-Pullyou beast, between self-management and servitude, could be extended indefinitely.

3. The Bifurcations and the Alliances

> The starting-point in critical elaboration is the consciousness of what one really is
> [...] as a product of the historical process to date, which has deposited in you an
> infinity of traces, without leaving an inventory. Therefore, it is imperative at the
> outset to compile an inventory.
>
> — GRAMSCI, *Prison Notebooks*

3.1

The main realization dawning from the preceding subsections is for me, following arguments such as Wallerstein's, that the hope for an eventual bridging of the poverty gap is now over, and it is very improbable the Keynesian class compromise can be dismantled without burying under its fallout capitalism as a whole. Will this happen explosively, for example in a quite possible Third World War, or by a slow "crumbling away" which would generate massive breakdowns of civil and civilized relations, on the model of the present "cold civil war" smouldering in the US, which are (as Disch's forgotten masterpiece *334* rightly saw) only comparable to daily life in the late Roman Empire? And what kind of successor formation will then be coming about? The age of individualism and free market is over, the present is already highly collectivized, and demographics as well as insecurity will make the future even more so: the alternative lies between the models of the oligarchic (that is centrally Fascist) war-camp and an open plebeian-democratic commune.

In this realistically grim perspective, a strong argument could be made that facing a dangerous series of "cascading bifurcations" (Wallerstein, *Historical* 155–56) our liberatory corporate or class interests as intellectuals

are twofold and interlocking. First, they consist in securing a high degree
of self-management, to begin with in the workplace. But second, they also
consist in working for such strategic alliances with other fractions and
classes as would consent us to fight the current toward militarized browbeating. This may be most visible in "Confucian capitalism" from Japan
to Malaya, for example in the concentration-camp fate of the locked-in
young women in industries of Mainland China, but it is well represented
in all our sweatshops and fortress neighbourhoods (see the US example in
Harvey). It can only be counteracted by ceaseless insisting on meaningful
democratic participation in the control not only of production but also of
distribution of our own work, as well as of our neighbourhoods. Here the
boundary between our as it were dissident interests within the intellectual
field of production and the overall liberation of labour as their only guarantee becomes permeable. True, history has shown that alliance-building
is only more painful than base organizing: any Mannheimian dream about
the intelligentsia as utopian arbiter was unrealistic to begin with. But at
least we know it can only be done by bringing into the marriage our honest
interests and uncertainties, by eschewing like the plague the PoMo certainty
and apodictic terrorizing, adapted in a bizarre mimicry of their two rivals,
admass and Stalinism, as the newest variant of the intellectuals' illusion that
they do not suffer from illusions (as Bourdieu somewhere said).

Our immediate interests are oppositional because capitalism without
a human face is obviously engaged in large scale "structural declassing" of
intellectual work, of our "cultural capital" (Bourdieu, and see Guillory
134ff.). There is nothing more humiliating, short of physical injury, than
the experience of being pushed to the periphery of social values – measured
by the only yardstick capitalism knows, our financing – which all of us have
undergone in the last quarter century. Our graduate students are by now
predominantly denied Keynesian employment, condemned to part-time
piecework without security. As Poulantzas observes, capitalism has now
adjoined to the permanent reserve army of industrial labour that of intellectual labour (321–23). The new contract enforced on the "downsized"
generation is: "Workers undertake to find new occupations where they can
be exploited in the cleverest and most efficient way possible" (Lipietz 77). If
the degree of autonomy within the "middle class" is inversely proportional

to a given fraction's domination over workers, so that managers have little autonomy but great powers over workers (including intellectual workers), then university teachers never had any power over productive relations, but now we are bit by bit losing our relatively large autonomy. The difference between intellectuals and managers is analogous to that of monks to territorial priests in the medieval Catholic Church. The best we can today expect from capitalism is the shrinking and proletarianized plastic-tower autonomy of a begging order: the badly supplied but relatively undisturbed monastery of Thomas of Aquinas – certainly not the Abbey of Thélème, beset as it is by an unholy alliance of barbaric businessmen and what Gayatri C. Spivak (in Robbins ed. 167) calls "corporate feminists" (or corporate ethnics). This is not good enough.

3.2

In this bind, we can at any rate say to the supposed realists (Haug, *Versuch* 88–89): Look where you have landed us! There's no more realism without utopia! (Your reality itself works toward a negative utopia.) But what does this practically mean? A number of things.

First, I must be the bearer of painful news: the professionalism of which we were up to a point justly proud has been overwhelmingly corrupted – by outright bribery where it matters, by self-willed marginality in the humanities. The ivory of our towers has been largely ground into powder as aphrodisiac for the corporate bosses and enchantment for the elder Matay sibs. Looking at our class position soberly, we shall have to redefine professionalism as including – rather than complementing – self-managing political citizenship or we shall be political by selling our brains to the highest bidder. This follows necessarily from the above discussions of epistemology and our class position, which are now revealed as two ways of envisaging the same thing. On the one hand, in our classes we shall have to redefine, with Nietzsche, philology not simply as the art of reading rightly (what is there) but the art of reading well (what we may get from it). And outside the class it may mean anything from picketing the University Board or the Faculty of Business Management to lying down on the railway tracks (to use an improbable 1960s parallel). It certainly means striving for activist unionization, at a time when corporations are corrupting academic administrators by making them into well-paid CEOs in exchange for downsizing teachers (see Soley 24–32 and Guillory). Like publishers vs. artistic cognition, universities vs. teaching cognition are now "the swine [...] in charge of the pearls" (Anthony). As Benjamin put it, in the permanent part of an essay which was alas written in a more hopeful situation:

> only by transcending the specialization in the process of production that, in the bourgeois view, constitutes its order can one make this production politically useful; and the barriers imposed by specialization must be breached jointly by the productive forces that they were set up to divide. The author as producer discovers – in discovering his solidarity with the proletariat – simultaneously his solidarity with certain other producers who earlier seemed scarcely to concern him. (*Gesammelte Schriften* II.2: 690–4; trans. E. Jephcott)

Only this can, in his wonderful polysemy, unfetter *die Produktion der Intelligenz*: the production of us intellectuals, but also the productivity of intelligence or reason. And if we at the moment do not find many proletarian organizations to meet us in the middle of the tunnel, we can start by doing utopian cross-pollinations of at least the cultural with the philosophic, economic, political, and other history studies. To wax unabashedly autobiographical, this is one of the reasons why I am a member of the Society for Utopian Studies; or why I consider Attali's remarks on the political economy of music (the age of repetitive evacuation of meaning and big centralized *apparati* determining production and listening as commodified time, best foregrounded in muzak) as one of the most enlightening diagnoses of Post-Fordism; or why one of my books interlarded seven essays and seven sequences of poetry (and the present book does something similar). But I am afraid we will have to relearn the tradition of persecution ranging, say, from Cyrano and Spinoza, through Marx's and Benjamin's exile from universities and many countries, to the Pope's treatment of Liberation Theology: such ecumenical professionalism will entail less reading of papers and much more civic conflictuality.

For, on the citizenship end of the same continuous spectrum it means beginning to fight two even more difficult long revolutions. One is to master what we might call, adapting Said, *critical worldliness*: Brecht called it the art of thinking also in other people's heads. Though we partly become intellectuals in order to get far from the madding crowd, our class and often even personal survival requires us then (now) – without surrendering either our bearings or the clarity of our arguments' articulation! – to get out of the elite ghetto of writing, theatre, etc., into the mass media. The most important politico-cultural position today is obviously the TV station, secondly the radio station, and thirdly the cinema and the video production. This is why they are also, in descending order, the most firmly controlled by millions and laws. Nonetheless, there may be limited chinks in the system, as proved by the stories of the three-kilometre-radius Japanese radio stations in the 1960s and 1970s, or of the movie producing units at the end of "real socialism" in East Central Europe – both successfully used by small self-governing groups. Video production, and in particular computerization and the Internet offer many possibilities, so far used by the Rightwing subversives much more efficiently than by the Left. The second long struggle might be called *global solidarity*: it consists in fighting what would be a Fascist geopolitical involution, turning our privileged Northern continents into an insular *Festung Amerika* and *Festung West-Europa*. The Japanese dissident Muto Ichiyo called it perhaps more precisely "transborder participatory democracy," and Douglas Lummis argues on his tracks that it is a necessity of our time when "imperial power is incarnated in three bodies: pseudo-democracy at home, vast military organizations, and the transnational corporations [...]" (Lummis 138). Its furthest utopian horizon, absolutely necessary if we wish to avoid oblivion or caste society, is the long revolution of achieving "democratic forms of 'social control' of financial markets" (Chossudovsky "IMF").

In sum, the Modernist oases for exiles (the Left Bank, Bloomsbury, lower Manhattan, major US campuses) are gone the way of a Tahiti polluted by nuclear fallout and venereal pandemic: some affluent or starving writers à la Pynchon or Joyce may still be possible, but not as a statistically significant option for us. Adapting Tsvetaeva's great line "All poets are Yids" (*Vse poèty zhidy*), we can say that fortunately all intellectuals are partly exiles from the

Disneyland and/or starvation dystopia, but we are an "inner emigration" for whom resistance was always possible and is now growing mandatory. The only resistance to Disneyland brainwashing is "the invention of the desire called Utopia in the first place, along with new rules for the fantasizing or daydreaming of such a thing – a set of narrative protocols with no precedent in our previous literary institutions [...]" (Jameson, *Seeds* 90). This would be *a collective production of meanings* whose efficacy is measured by "[how many] consumers it is able to turn into producers, in brief, how many readers and lookers-on it can turn to collaborators" (Benjamin *Gesammelte Schriften* II.2: 696, and see Attali): that is, to begin with, critical and not empathetic thinkers (see Suvin "Emotion"). And the only chance to do this is "[to keep] in touch with all kinds of streams of protest and dissent so as to know what's important to say" (Ehrenreich 177–78, and see passim). And a final piece of painful news: this means "doing things we're not used to, like saying things that 'everybody' (meaning everybody in one wing of the profession) 'already knows'" (Bérubé 171, and see the whole section 164–78, esp. 176). The gentle reader will notice I have not quite managed to follow this prescription ...

3.3

Mindful of my Marxian roots, I shall not venture into prophecies about the next generation or two. You can find it better in the dystopian SF I have already alluded to. But I wish to report that I find two of the best "conceptual" people, Raymond Williams from the humanities and Immanuel Wallerstein from the social sciences (*Historical* 162–63), quite independently – such is our bourgeois division of labour that even they, on the same political side in the same language, appear not to have read each other! – coming to a practically identical view of alternatives to capitalist commercialism. They are: Platonic Fascism (authoritarianism), the Guardians being maybe half or less of the affluent 10–20 percent in the North of the globe; Neo-feudalism (paternalism), distinguished from the former by a significant breakdown in globalization and division into local satrapies of different kinds; and finally, federated self-governing communes and workgroups (participatory democracy), a technologized Morrisian Nowhere as the nearest approximation to classless society we may today dream of. And we also have a good yardstick for measuring any change as it occurs: does it increase or reduce the exploitation of labour, of production in the widest sense (that includes art and love, see Suvin, "Brecht"). Again, against the horizon of these blue distances the production of goods and the production of meanings grows indistinguishable.

To conclude: we have no choice but to propose the most daring utopia, which is today, to begin with, not Earthly Paradise but the prevention of Hell on Earth. May the Earth remain our habitable mother, rather than being pushed by greedy classes and imbecilitated masses (as today) the way of ecological catastrophe, and the ensuing great Migration of Peoples, the bitter State and corporation wars, the civil wars of constructed racism and ethnicity! But paradoxically, I am persuaded that finally – which is not at all opposed to other medium-range horizons – only the most radical counterpoise, a flexible system of what Marx called the free association of direct producers, the horizon of a global self-sustaining and self-managing society (which is socialism) has a chance: only mobilizing Paradise or Utopia can Hell or Fascism be defeated. Fuller's slogan "utopia or oblivion" can be interpreted to mean the threatening loss of historical memory for almost all that distinguishes our horizons from a caste society.

Yet, of course, when the status quo collapses, the bifurcations are unforeseeable. Behind the alternative between utopia and disastrous being there lurks utopia vs. non-being. The alternative to a habitable planet is not only the present creeping death of the mind and values but sweeping and totally non-metaphoric death. At any rate, as Brecht wrote in the dark little poem on reading Horace's account of the Great Deluge:

Even the Deluge
Did not last for ever.
At some point
The black waters receded.
And yet, how few people
Lasted that long!

(*Gesammelte Werke* 10: 1014)

So: having arrived within hailing distance of the end of our species and perhaps of vertebrate life on Earth, the wonderful but possibly somewhat elite form of the scholarly essay begins at the end to fail me. I shall therefore try to encapsulate what I had to say here in five slogans (aided by Haug, *Versuch* 89 and 498, and Moylan, *Demand*):

> No way out of dystopia except as orientation to utopia – and viceversa.
> No valid epistemology (perceiving, understanding, culture) without politics – and viceversa.
> No social liberation without self-management (in workplace as well as all other places) – and viceversa.
> No democracy without (the best from) socialism, ecology, and feminism – and triply viceversa.
> "And if you think this is utopian, please think why is it such". (Brecht)

Utopia as static goal has been dead since the nineteenth century, even if its putrefying cadaver poisoned the twentieth. Marx's critique of Cabet's project of emigrating to found a colony as desertion from class struggles (and I find it rather significant that Marx did not focus on criticizing Cabet's earlier – rather poor – utopian novel), could have taught us that "the place of utopia is not elsewhere, but here and now, as other" (Marin 346). As Italo Calvino's "city which cannot be founded by us but can found itself within us, can build itself bit by bit in our capacity to imagine it, to think it through" (252), utopia cannot die. But its latent rebirth depends on us. I give you what I have learned in this truncated half century, through hope and terror and finally compassionate solidarity (the *karuna* of Huxley's Buddhist mynah-birds, the ironic tenderness of Brecht):

> Do not expect from utopia more than from yourselves.

Montreal, September 1997[10]

---

10 My thanks go to Peter Fitting and Lyman Tower Sargent for generously organizing a session devoted to discussing this, and to the latter for help with sources on hunger statistics. Also to Farah Mendlesohn and Tom Moylan for comments on a first draft,

Works Cited

Ahmad, Aijaz. *In Theory*. London: Verso, 1992.

Anders, Günter. *Die Antiquiertheit des Menschen*. 2 vols. München: Beck, 1994–95.

Anthony, Piers. Letter to D. Suvin. 11 November 1997.

Appadurai, Arjun. *Modernity at Large*. Minneapolis: University of Minnesota Press, 2000.

Asada, Akira. "Infantile Capitalism and Japan's Postmodernism: A Fairy Tale." *South Atlantic Quarterly* 87.3 (1988): 629–34.

Attali, Jacques. *Bruits*. Paris: PUF, 1977.

Auden, W[ystan] H. *Collected Poems*. Ed. Edward Mendelson. New York: Vintage, 1991.

Bagdikian, Ben. *The Media Monopoly*, 4th edn. Boston: Beacon, 1992.

"Bandwidth Bonanza." *Time* (Canadian edn) 1 September 1997: 35.

Barthes, Roland. *Critical Essays*. Trans. Richard Howard. New York: Hill and Wang, 1964.

——. "Day by Day with Roland Barthes." *On Signs*. Ed. Marshall Blonsky. Baltimore: Johns Hopkins University Press, 1985. 100–20.

——. *Mythologies*. Trans. A. Lavers. New York: Hill & Wang, 1972.

Benjamin, Walter. *Gesammelte Schriften*. Ed. Rolf Tiedemann and Hermann Schweppenhäuser. 7 vols. Frankfurt: Suhrkamp, 1980–87.

Berger, John, et al. *Ways of Seeing*. Harmondsworth: Penguin, 1972.

Bérubé, Michael. *Public Access*. London: Verso, 1994.

Blackmore, Tim. "Animachinations." *Extrapolation* 39.4 (1998): 338–51.

Bourdieu, Pierre. "The Field of Cultural Production." *Poetics* 12 (1983): 311–56.

to Fredric Jameson for giving me the original version of "Five Theses" and many other drafts of his, to David McInerney for reawakening my interest in Macherey, to Ernie Hakanen for pointing to Giroux, and to Ksenia Krimer for the full Tsvetaeva poem. All translations from non-English titles in the Works Cited are mine.

——. *In Other Words. Essays Towards a Reflexive Sociology.* Trans. Matthew Adamson. Stanford: Stanford University Press, 1990.

Brecht, Bertolt. *Gesammelte Werke in 20 Bänden.* Werkausgabe Edition Suhrkamp. Frankfurt: Suhrkamp, 1967.

Bruner, Jerome S. *Actual Minds, Possible Worlds.* Cambridge, MA: Harvard University Press, 1986.

Bryman, Alan. *Disney and His Worlds.* London and New York: Routledge, 1995.

Buck-Morss, Susan. *The Dialectics of Seeing.* Cambridge, MA: MIT Press, 1995.

Bukatman, Scott. *Terminal Identity.* Durham: Duke University Press, 1993.

Calvino, Italo. "Per Fourier." *Una pietra sopra.* Torino: Einaudi, 1980.

de Certeau, Michel. "The Jabbering of Social Life." *On Signs.* Ed. Marshall Blonsky. Baltimore: Johns Hopkins University Press, 1985. 146–54.

Chomsky, Noam. *Year 501.* Montréal and New York: Black Rose Books, 1993.

Chossudovsky, Michel. "The Global Financial Crisis": 9 November 1997 <http://www.twnside.org.sg/title/mic-cn.htm>.

——. "The IMF Korea Bailout": 1 January 1998 <http://www.kimsoft.com/1997/sk-imfc.htm>.

Davis, Walter A. "Death's Dream Kingdom": <http://www.counterpunch.org/davis/09062003.html>.

——. *Deracination: Historicity, Hiroshima.* Albany: State University of New York Press, 2001.

Debord, Guy. *La Societé du spectacle.* Paris: Lebovici, 1987.

Dorfman, Ariel. *The Empire's Old Clothes.* New York: Pantheon Books, 1983.

——, and Armand Mattelart. *How To Read Donald Duck: Imperialist Ideology in the Disney Comic.* Trans. David Kunzle. New York: International General, 1991.

Drèze, Jean, and Amartya Sen. *Hunger and Public Action.* Oxford: Clarendon Press, 1989.

Eco, Umberto. *Travels in Hyperreality.* Trans. William Weaver. San Diego: Harcourt, 1986.

Ehrenreich, Barbara. "The Professional-Managerial Class Revisited." *Intellectuals.* Ed. Bruce Robbins. Minneapolis: University of Minnesota Press, 1990. 173–85.

Ehrenreich, Barbara, and John Ehrenreich. "The Professional-Managerial Class," *Between Labor and Capital.* Ed. Pat Walker. Boston: South End, 1979. 5–48.

Eliot, Marc. *Walt Disney: Hollywood's Dark Prince.* New York: Carol, 1993.

Ellis, Ralph. "Differences between Conscious and Non-conscious Processing." August 1997 <http://www.focusing\org\com>.

Ewen, Stuart. *Captains of Consciousness.* New York: McGraw Hill, 1976.

Featherstone, Mike. "The Body in Consumer Culture." *Theory, Culture and Society* 1 (1982): 18–33.

Fjellman, Stephen M. *Vinyl Leaves: Walt Disney World and America.* Boulder: Westview, 1992.

Fox, Richard W., and T.J.J. Lears (eds). *The Culture of Consumption.* New York: Pantheon, 1983.

The Gazette (Montreal) 23 August 1997.

Giroux, Henry A. *The Mouse That Roared: Disney and the End of Innocence.* Lanham: Rowman and Littlefield, 1999.

"Globaldygook." *Canadian Perspectives* (Fall 1997): 11.

Goodwin, Barbara, and Keith Taylor. *The Politics of Utopia.* New York: St Martin's Press, 1982.

Gramsci, Antonio. *Selections from the Prison Notebooks.* Ed. and trans. Quintin Hoare and Geoffrey Nowell Smith. New York: International, 1975.

Groeben, Norbert. "Frauen – Science Fiction – Utopie." *Internationales Archiv für Sozialgeschichte der deutschen Literatur* 19.2 (1994): 173–206.

Guattari, Félix. "Le Divan du pauvre." *Communications* 23 (1975): 96–104.

Guillory, John. "Literary Critics as Intellectuals." *Rethinking Class.* Ed. Wai Chee Dimock and Michael T. Gilmore. New York: Columbia University Press, 1994. 107–49.

Hall, Stuart. "The Meaning of New Times." *Stuart Hall: Critical Dialogues in Cultural Studies*. Ed. Dave Morley and Kuan-hsing Chen. London and New York: Routledge, 1996. 223–37.

Harvey, David. *Justice, Nature and the Geography of Difference*. Oxford: Blackwell, 1996.

Haug, Wolfgang Fritz. *Critique of Commodity Aesthetics*. Trans. Robert Bock. Minneapolis: University of Minnesota Press, 1987.

——. *Versuch beim täglichen Verlieren des Bodens unter den Füssen neuen Grund zu gewinnen*. Hamburg: Argument, 1990.

Hobsbawm, Eric. *The Age of Extremes*. New York: Pantheon, 1994.

Human Development Report 1996. Ed. UN Development Programme. New York and London: Oxford University Press, 1996.

Jameson, Fredric. *Brecht and Method*. London: Verso, 1998.

——. "Five Theses on Actually Existing Marxism." *In Defence of History*. Ed. Ellen M. Wood and John B. Foster. New York: Monthly Review, 1997. 175–83.

——. *The Political Unconscious*. Ithaca: Cornell University Press, 1981.

——. *Postmodernism, or, The Cultural Logic of Late Capitalism*. Durham: Duke University Press, 1992.

——. *The Seeds of Time*. New York: Columbia University Press, 1994.

Kamper, Dietmar, et al. "Tendenzen der Kulturgesellschaft." *Ästhetik und Kommunikation* 67/68 (1987): 55–73.

Kracauer, Siegfried. *Die Angestellten*. Frankfurt: Suhrkamp, 1971.

Lash, Scott, and John Urry. *Economies of Signs and Space*. London: Sage, 1996.

Lipietz, Alain. *Towards a New Economic Order*. Trans. Malcolm Slater. New York: Oxford University Press, 1992.

Lummis, C. Douglas. *Radical Democracy*. Ithaca: Cornell University Press, 1996.

Luriia, A.R. *Osnovy neiropsikhologii*. Moscow: Izd. Moskovskogo univ-ta, 1973.

Macherey, Pierre. "In a Materialist Way." *Philosophy in France Today*. Ed. Alan Montefiore. Cambridge: Cambridge University Press, 1983. 136–54.

——. "Towards a Natural History of Norms." *Michel Foucault Philosopher.* Ed. and trans. Timothy J. Armstrong. Hemel Hempstead: Harvester, 1992. 176–91.

Mannoni, Octave. *Clefs pour l'Imaginaire.* Paris: Seuil, 1969.

Marcuse, Herbert. *The One-Dimensional Man.* Boston: Beacon, 1964.

Marin, Louis. *Utopiques: jeux d'espaces.* Paris: Minuit, 1973.

Marx, Karl. *Grundrisse.* Trans. Martin Nicolaus. New York: Vintage, 1973.

——. *Selected Writings.* Ed. David McLellan. Oxford: Oxford University Press, 1977.

Morris, William. "Useful Work versus Useless Toil." *William Morris.* Ed. G.D.H. Cole. London: Nonesuch, 1948. 603–23.

Müller, Heiner. "19 Answers." *The Twentieth-Century Performance Reader.* Ed. Michael Huxley and Noel Witts. London: Routledge, 1996, 276–81.

Moylan, Tom. *Demand the Impossible.* New York: Methuen, 1986.

——. *Scraps of the Untainted Sky.* Boulder: Westview, 2000.

Negt, Oskar, and Alexander Kluge. *Public Sphere and Experience: Toward an Analysis of the Bourgeois and Proletarian Public Sphere.* Trans. Peter Labanyi, Jamie Owen and Assenka Oksiloff. Minneapolis: University of Minnesota Press, 1993.

"Next, Oscar Sues Kermit." *Time* (Canadian edn) 1 September 1997: 58.

"On the Job." *The Gazette* (Montreal) 23 December 2000.

Phillips, Kevin. *The Politics of Rich and Poor.* New York: Random House, 1990.

Piaget, Jean. *Judgement and Reasoning in the Child.* New York: Harcourt Brace, 1928.

——. *Mechanisms of Perception.* Trans. G.N. Seagrim. New York: Basic Books, 1969.

Poulantzas, Nicos. *Les Classes sociales dans le capitalisme aujourd'hui.* Paris: Seuil, 1974.

Poverty and Hunger. Washington: World Bank, 1986.

Roach, Joseph. "Barnumizing the Diaspora." *Theatre Journal* 50.1 (1998): 39–52.

Robbins, Bruce (ed.). *Intellectuals.* Minneapolis: University of Minnesota Press, 1990.

Ross, Andrew. *Strange Weather.* London and New York: Verso, 1991.

Salmon, Christian. "Le magicien de la Maison Blanche." *Le Monde diplomatique.* December 2007: 3

Sargent, Lyman Tower. "Political Dimensions of Utopianism." *Per una definizione dell'utopia. Metodologie e discipline a confronto.* Ed. Nadia Minerva. Ravenna: Longo, 1992. 185–210.

Schickel, Richard. *The Disney Version.* New York: Simon and Schuster, 1968.

Seeber, Hans Ulrich. "Bemerkungen zum Begriff Gegenutopie." *Literarische Utopien von Morus bis zur Gegenwart.* Ed. Klaus L. Berghahn and Hans U. Seeber. Königstein/Ts.: Athenäum, 1983. 163–71.

Sellars, Peter. "Directing a National Consciousness." *Theater* 28.2 (1998): 87–90.

Sheldon, Alice. "A Woman Writing Science Fiction and Fantasy." *Women of Vision.* Ed. Denise Du Pont. New York: St Martin's, 1988. 43–58.

Soley, Lawrence C. *Leasing the Ivory Tower.* Boston: South End, 1995.

Sorel, Georges. *Reflections on Violence.* Trans. T.E. Hulme and Jack Roth. London: Collier Macmillan, 1972.

Sorkin, Michael. "Introduction." *Variations on a Theme Park.* New York: Hill and Wang, 1992.

Suvin, Darko. "Brecht: Bearing, Pedagogy, Productivity." *Gestos* 5.10 (1990): 11–28.

——. "On Cognitive Emotions and Topological Imagination." *Versus* 68–69 (1994): 165–201.

——. "Emotion, Brecht, Empathy vs. Sympathy." *Brecht Yearbook* 33 (2008): 53–67.

——. "On the Horizons of Epistemology and Science." (forthcoming in *Critical Quarterly* 52.1)

——. *Lessons of Japan.* Washington: Maisonneuve, 1996.

——. *Metamorphoses of Science Fiction.* New Haven and London: Yale University Press, 1979 [cited as *MOSF*].

——. "News from the Novum." *Foundation* 69 (1997): 26–43.

——. "Philip K. Dick's Opus." *Positions and Presuppositions in Science Fiction*. London: Macmillan, 1988. 112–33.

——. "Polity or Disaster: From Individualist Self Toward Personal Valences and Collective Subjects." *Discours social/ Social Discourse* 6.1–2 (1994): 181–210.

——. "The Subject as a Limit-Zone of Collective Bodies (Bakhtin, Hobbes, Freud, Foucault, and Counting)." *Discours social/ Social Discourse* 2.1–2 (1989): 187–99.

Venturi, Robert. *Learning from Las Vegas*. Cambridge, MA: MIT Press, 1972.

Wallerstein, Immanuel. *Geopolitics and Geoculture*. Cambridge: Cambridge University Press, 1992.

——. *Historical Capitalism with Capitalist Civilization*. London: Verso, 1996.

Williams, Raymond. *Communications*. London: Penguin, 1976.

Wood, Ellen Meiksins. *Democracy against Capitalism*. Cambridge: Cambridge University Press, 1995.

Zajac, Ronald J. "The Dystopian City in British and U.S. Science Fiction, 1960–1975." Master's thesis, McGill University, 1992.

Zipes, Jack. *Breaking the Magic Spell*. Austin: University of Texas Press, 1979.

CHAPTER 10

On Cognition as Art and Politics:
Reflections for a Toolkit (1997–1999)[1]

My enemies have grown powerful and have distorted the image of my teaching.
— NIETZSCHE, *Thus Spoke Zarathustra*, ca. 1883

Most people lament the lost revolution, Rosa Luxemburg analyzes it.
— BRECHT, *Project for a play on Luxemburg*, 1950s

Preguntando caminamos [we walk while asking]
— EZLN (Zapatista) slogan

Part 1. How May We Know For Salvation

An introduction will establish the work's methodological relationship to dialectical materialism in the form of a confrontation of "salvation" with the customary "apologia."
— BENJAMIN TO HORKHEIMER, 16 April 1938

I wish first to speak of how I ought to speak, and only then to speak.
— AGATHON, in Plato's *Symposium*, fourth century BCE

1   The writing of this chapter in Berlin and Montreal, 1997–99, in part overlapped with that of Chapter 12, and some more or less identical formulations resisted eradication in either.

— He who knows that he knows, knows not yet how to know.
— This is again very good. But it smells of capitulation.

— BRECHT, 1938

Creation – thinking new thoughts as *Ermöglichungen* (making possible) of new lives – hides in the ellipsis.

— R. WYSER, 1999

Wedge 1/ Cognition is Our Unavoidable Horizon: But Who Cognizes How and What for?

A theory is exactly like a box of tools. It must be useful. It must function. And not for itself.

— GILLES DELEUZE, "Intellectuals and Power"

1.1

Nobody lives without cognizing; even the wondrous eye of the octopi does not see without a brain. In that sense, as Gramsci and Brecht's Galileo had it, all of us are philosophers. We always see (perceive, feel, judge, evaluate) our environments as fields of action and value, orienting ourselves according to our interest. Any life-world is saturated with overlapping and competing types, vectors, and tiers of understanding-with-evaluating. But without reflexivity – if you do not know what and how (and why) you are understanding – chances are that you shall see insufficiently and wrongly. Hegel's formulation in the *Lectures on the History of Philosophy*: "The great difference lies in one's knowing what one is; only then is one truly that," may not be sufficient in that it brackets the traffic with practice, but it remains indispensable. Yet even if one trusted intuition more than is reasonable in this age of polluted ground-waters, it would not be possible to adjust one's intuitive seeing without constant corrections from other people and changing experiences of reality, prominently including cognitive delving beneath the surface appearances.

This opens at least three huge questions. First: What is knowing? Hegel's great sentence should obviously be supplemented with other sentences. To begin with, let us consider probably the central knot today – Nietzsche's sentence: "Thou sayest 'I' and art proud of this word. But the greater one [...] is your body and its great understanding [*Vernunft*]: it does not say 'I' but it performs 'I'" (*Also* 28–29). This slides seamlessly into: What is "one" (what are we)? And last not least, as our right now final horizon: How does knowledge or understanding mesh with and into actions of our individual and collective bodies; or, what do we do? This last question is in this historical period, alas, kidnapped by financial speculators in war, prostitution, and other drug dealers. I – we who are interested in knowing what we truly are and may be – can here-and-now only speak about knowing and only reactively about doing. As Brecht's Galileo at the end of the play, still shrewd but now less confident, maybe even panicky, not quite rightly observed: it all smells of capitulation. My (and his) excuse and small comfort in the intellectuals' Grand Hotel Abyss is – to quote Brecht from 1929 against the Brecht of 1938 – "They could not see the causes of events, because they could not get rid of the events" (*GBFA* 21: 307).

And further, a certain kind of understanding – such as understanding the preceding sentence – is also a precondition for any future action: a preparation for getting rid of the present actors. I shall articulate this further at the end.

I.2

And so, who are we, this fraction of the professional class: intellectuals? But only if standing as society's bump of consciousness and conscience. Today most of us intellectuals are mercenaries, adjunct police(wo)men keeping kids off the streets and ideas out of dangerous hands. No empirical group is exempt of class-society corruption: nobody is fit to be the angel with the flaming sword. Yet we finally need also the sword, figured in esoteric Buddhism as Fudô, the wrathful aspect of creation: not too dissimilar from Blake's sword necessary for Jerusalem in England's green and pleasant land. A first lesson: no knowledge without a fusion of experiences with imagination, that is, tropes and images; nor without allegories, that is, personifications of dismantling and rebuilding. We should cautiously and firmly wrest angels and deities away from monotheism, as Walter Benjamin did, for they might be messengers and images of our collective, always more or less cognitive, functions of demystification and critique. The path from empirical people to collective allegory is tricky and humbling. But it is the only path: and just look at the exemplary edifice Marx built upon the allegorical image of commodity as fetish!

1.3

Cognition is not split into reason and emotion, which are co-present in any proposition – I cannot argue this here, and can only refer to my essay "On Cognitive" (now also to "Emotion"). The only useful distinction is between cognition relevant for our purposes and interests (pertinent) and irrelevant (non-pertinent – cf. Prieto). For example: the classical theological conundrums about the existence of God are irrelevant to me; not so the understanding of people's position under the stars and other powers – the impulse toward salvation of communities and individuals. Thus, relevance is to be understood as pertaining to the present historical epoch and people's salvation in it, not as this day's profit. What is relevant meshes with our *salus* (health/salvation), what is irrelevant does not – and vice versa. Since our systems should be open (see Wedge 2), we cannot finally know what may at some point become relevant, but only pragmatically know what is – here and now, for such-and-such interests – not relevant. Therefore, in case of doubt relevance should be both carefully and sympathetically tested. Novelties are welcome but only if they improve well-being for one and many. Yet ill-making, damnation, must be guarded against. Example for this: to market products of pharmaceutical chemistry, and even more so of molecular genetics, as "atomic" units, without careful testing of their "thick" impacts in space and time. What profit it you to gain billions if your wives bear thalidomide babies?

1.4

Any acceptable horizon after the industrial revolution is – for better or worse, but necessarily – dynamic, a movable feast or engine. The Copernican revolution of Marx's paradigm means "[t]here is no knowledge [...] aside from critical knowledge" (Lefebvre, *Production* 323). However,

> [t]he methods get used up, the attraction does not work any longer. New problems come about and need new means. Reality is changing; to present it, the way of presentation must change. Nothing comes out of nothing, the new comes from the old, but is nonetheless new. (Brecht, *GBFA* 22.1: 410)

When the ground inevitably shifts from under our feet, what may remain constant is our orientation; our bearings or stances (called usually but less felicitously, slighting the body in favour of eyes only, standpoint or view) assume central importance. Any bearing inserts the body personal into the body politic, according to the interests which direct the mutual induction of reasons and emotions (see Suvin "Haltung").

This leads to the always final question about understanding: *What for?* All categories in which we are inescapably thought and think, acted and act, are products of a glorious but also radically tainted class history; yet some are better tools than others. Every method is shaped by experiences that history imprints upon the flesh of social classes. But both *cui bono* and "Why bother?" are such huge questions that before attempting to move them a working kit of ropes and pulleys must be assembled.

Wedge 2/ Closed Conceptual Systems Are Bankrupt; Radical Critique and Form

> We step and we do not step into the same rivers. We are and we are not.
> — HERACLITUS

2.1

Though the Christian godhead is supposed to be infinite, the closed feudal system with nostalgias of a Holy Roman world empire produced a theology which eventually, say after Aquinas, pretended to have a closed spherical system – a Ptolemaic cycle of epicycles – that explains everything. Several social formations later, it is clear to us that the explanations ultimately worked either by tautology or by derivation from a not further knowable God, to be believed on pain of loss of soul (political suppression) or indeed body (physical suppression). To update Marx with help of Brecht and Benjamin, the shape of the ideas of a ruling class is the ruling shape of the ideas in the world that class rules.

Physician heal thyself! What can we carry forward from this our hard-won understanding (Bruno still flames with a bit in his mouth!)? What does this imply for the dominant system of Objectivist science in our no less horribly polluted times? This ideology is no less absolute than medieval theology, both in its claims and its hold on the masses – though the absolutism of science is dynamic and more complex, therefore also more difficult to understand. And what, finally, does this imply for the stance or bearing from which we criticize both Objectivism and its Deconstructionist inverted mirror?

2.2   Learned Excursus on "System"

> [The "system" of all philosophers] springs from an imperishable desire of the human
> mind – the desire to overcome all contradiction.
>   — ENGELS, *Ludwig Feuerbach and the End of Classical German Philosophy*

"System" really means any articulation of propositions that can claim an architectonic unity. It was imported into English from Greek (and probably French) at the beginning of the seventeenth century to signify "the whole scheme of created things, the universe" (*OED* s.v. "system," from which are all data here). This bolstered the theological tradition through the authority of both ancient Hellenic philosophy and modern up-and-coming sciences.

In these sciences system came to mean either a set of objects and/or (a fundamental confusion!) "a set of principles, etc.: a scheme, method" which shapes and informs a department of knowledge or belief that deals with such a correlative set of objects as an organized whole. This was immediately, by the mid-century, applied to a comprehensive exposition of or treatise about some subject, that is, to a written work claiming to be for that particular "branch" of knowledge as total and authoritative as the Book or books of any among the by now rival theologies claimed to be for the universe as a whole; moreover, this horizon carried overtones of a harmonious whole that Plato had called *mousikè* (clearly grounded in politics) and which had had a *systema* to organize it. The ideological vanguard department of both knowledge and scientific belief was first, at the end of the seventeenth century, Galileian physics including astronomy, which delineated the solar system and various mechanical systems of using force and gaining power from manipulations of gravity, wind, optical knowledge, and similar.

In and after the eighteenth century the notion of "system" began to expand but also to harden. It extended first to biology where system came to mean a set of organs or parts of the same structure or function, as rendered visible by the meshing of new ideological and technological ways of looking, for example the nervous or the sanguine system apprehended by dissection and the microscope. Eventually any department of knowledge (geology, geometry, architecture ...) could have one or more systems in the sense of an organized, structurally and/or functionally connected set of objects – again, both really "out there" and validated by a science that had these objects for its object. But simultaneously, the meaning of system jelled into schemes of formal classification, perhaps most famously the Linnaean system for living beings, to be joined later by the Mendeleyev system of chemical elements and other triumphs of taxonomic organization that became the basis for whole sciences and their sweeping advances.

The ideological dominance of system meant also the setting in place of a deep and long duration topological structure – a qualitative geometry permeating all imaginable relationships – in the hegemonic collective unconscious. It then begat two important semantic derivations. First, what was anyway a dead metaphor derived semantically from the Greek for "standing up together" (*istanai* plus *syn*) and structurally from an Idealist

version of the Athenian *polis*, came to be used metaphorically for any sufficiently encompassing set of principles, scheme or method. Increasingly, this
returned to politics as a synonym for the strongly hierarchical organization
of an industrialized society composed of discrete and fixed units, which
incorporated humans as systemic parts (see Marcus and Segal 140 and
passim). And second, a reaction by the oppressed identified "the System,"
in caps, as what oppresses them: the dominant political, economic, and
social order. This reaction was first recorded in gibes at system builders
(in *Tristram Shandy* and in Diderot) or indeed system mongers by the
humanist *intelligentsia*, but came to a head in the socialist agitation of the
English working class of the mid-nineteenth century, whence it continued to (one hopes) our days. Today this reaction is, for our little historical
moment, backgrounded in favour of systems obviously constructed by
people yet nevertheless largely outside of our control: computer operating systems, systems analysis or similar technocratic management systems
of late, warmongering capitalism (see Gray 142–43, 149–65, Marcus and
Segal 129 and 243ff.), geared to totalizing efficiency in maximizing profit
inextricably wedded with killing. Nor is there much hope we can get soon
out of such anti-democratic programmings that progress smoothly from
designing weapons systems, with humans inserted into their computerized net as "information processing systems," to designing the future of the
present social system (see Lefebvre, *Cybernanthrope* 65–79, Levidow and
Robbins eds 28ff., 56ff., 152ff., and Ross 174 and passim); or that we can in
any foreseeable future get out of systems analyses.

Thus, "system" is a powerful but also very ambiguous concept. In
orthodox scientism it is used as an unverifiable tautology that poses (or,
worse, tacitly presupposes) a delimited whole apprehended as an organized or articulated unity of distinguishable parts which are not simply in
a fortuitous juxtaposition but obey a scheme or order, a "lawful" principle,
a *rule* – so that they can be called a set, a complex unity, an organization.
Even clearly manipulated technological or directly political sub-systems
claim the prestige and sanction of "nature," including human nature, and
of hidden teleologies – for example, of The Technology or The Market.
The authority of "natural laws" ("as if there were something authoritarian
and dominating in nature" – Anders 463 [see also 411–13]) obscured how

– by whom, through whom, for whom – they came about and functioned: as operative hypotheses carried out and constantly updated in the interest of precise social classes. The system's closure means the disciplining and arrest of historical flow. When astronomy or cosmology subjects anything from the Earth+Moon system up to the ensemble of red-shift galaxies to a universal law of movement, such a discipline exemplarily explicates the presupposition present, in "softer" ways, in any talk about a closed system of relationships. That the Big Bang theory of cosmology came to be dominant after Hiroshima is a wonderful case of *post hoc ergo propter hoc* (causal dependency on history): ask not where the explosion came from! Worship it in awe and wonder! (One might suspect the downfall of this theory will not come about before the "big bang" of capitalist profit expansion collapses.)

An influential minority concluded therefore from Nietzsche on that the notion of "system" ought to be abandoned as tautological, indeed immoral (*Twilight* 9). On the other hand, all intellectual activity as well as human intervention into an increasingly complicated and contradictory world would grind to a halt unless articulated wholes can be delimited and as it were cut out of it, as trees out of rhizomes, for purposes of both immediate and long-duration understanding (I have argued this in "Two Cheers"). All such purposes are historical and wedded to interests of given social groups. If that is foregrounded, then the horizons of human freedom and the incalculable contingencies of history can be constantly factored in and reconciled with a "soft" systematicity. Lenin praised the ancient Greeks for having "modes of framing questions, as it were tentative systems [...]" (367). A great pioneer of such open, in the sense of both *polycentric* and *changeable*, systematicity, Gramsci, argued that it should not be an imposed structure that goes from thought to thought but a grappling with problems presented by the process of history (see II: 1216). Another great pioneer, Ernst Bloch, openly called for an "open system" (*Gesamtausgabe* 8: 472). Such systems are then more than a closed organization of concepts incapable of feedback and change. As Lenin put it, "Practice is higher than (theoretical) knowledge, for it has not only the dignity of universality, but also of immediate actuality" (213). Containing an inalienable compo-nent of induction and analogy, such systems or provisional totalities are

constructs which nonetheless allow for grasping segments and aspects of
historical reality.

2.3

All systems assuming an unchanging nature and a fixed attribution of what is
"natural" are hidden theologies. Marx clearly refused systems (see *Grundrisse*
471: "natural or *divine* presuppositions"), and Engels even more explicitly,
e.g., in *Ludwig Feuerbach*. Any child-raiser (mother, teacher) knows "nature"
is extremely changeable and malleable. And yet, orthodox Marxism in the
positivistic Second and Third Internationals adapted to its new bearers'
– not the proletariat's – need for another scientist orthodoxy or quasi-
theological system. Insofar as theology formalizes a collective desire (for
all of us) as well as a distributive desire (for each of us) for salvation, I have
suggested above that it springs out of an unalienable necessity for a human
life not simply as we know it but also as we can imagine it. But *the formalization (shaping) into a closed system*, that is characteristic of the Euro-American
monotheistic long duration of the last 2,000 years, was always constrict-
ing and much too often hugely pernicious. It is supposedly validated by
the closure of nature as seen by a potentially all-knowing observer (God,
Science, History) but it is in fact magically analogous to this closed nature.
The working classes' revolt against the constrictive and oppressive System of
(in)human relationships fell prey to this danger of excessive systematicity,
their enemies' hierarchy of fixed classes. The reason for this is not simply
historical inertia, the millennial socialization of several continents into
comforting closures, but also the hijacking of the workers' movement by
new social groupings (the least imperfect designations for which are up to
now "despotic bureaucracy" and "labour aristocracy") whose interest was
involved in closure. This began in the nineteenth-century socialist parties
– ironically, when both poetry (Heine, Baudelaire, Rimbaud) and serious
philosophy (Marx, Kierkegaard) had abandoned rigid systems, kept alive
by third-raters like Comte or Spengler – but came to a head in Stalinism
(and in parallel though distinct ways, directly geared to the capitalist technoscientific militarization, in Fascism), again in opposition to liberatory

revolutions in politics and Einsteinian physics. Dealing with this multiple closure is indispensable in order to draw lessons from our ancestral, Fordist period (ca. 1890–1973) and the ensuing even more murderous Post-Fordism, for which central Marxian insights are still needed.

2.4

To reject the notion of an articulated whole organized according to an overarching method – which would be a provisional historical totality – would mean we could have no formalizable body of knowledge. However, a watershed between useless and useful wholes (that is, closed and open systems) can be found in the relation of a system towards *contradiction*. Already in Hegel one can find the distinction between horizons of meaning which obtain at the revolutionary beginning of a historic epoch, when the new dispensation "behaves with fanatic enmity toward the systematization of the preceding principle," and at its fulfillment when its central "principle" matures into a full subsumption of all elements from past and present (see *Wissenschaft* 15, but also his other writings, and the comments in Bodei 358–67). It follows that the earlier, "fermentation," phase is dominated by contradiction and the later, systematizing one by a consolidating affirmation. This important pointer, however, still allots maturity to the overcoming of contradiction and is to that extent to my mind too colonised by a centrally theological closure. At the latest since the Industrial Revolution contradictions can never be fully backgrounded in favour of a "positive," synthesizing principle. Only dynamically equilibrated systems, with a deniable and thus changeable rather than closed history (peddled today for example by the ideologists of the global US domination), can at these – our – times be defended.

Brecht and Benjamin – different but largely compatible formulators – have for me an exemplary status because they understood two meshing, necessary and sufficient, matters. First, like Fordist technocrats and other great Modernists (Kafka, Joyce, Lenin, Einstein), they saw how shapes, forms or frameworks determine behaviour. Second, as opposed to the Post-Fordist capitalists and their PoMo epicycle, they saw that such forms participate of contradictory historical experience which is yet open as it can be presented and intervened into. There is a huge difference between a complex emptiness or fruitful inexhaustibility, and ignorance which means possession by prejudice: between the illusion you really know vs. the Socratic knowledge you really do not know (*scio ut nesciam*). Nietzsche exiled Socrates: let us defy Lyotard and call Socrates back from the exile.

2.5

Forms are – inalienably and simultaneously – *both concepts and tropes* (metaphors). As different from concepts organized into closed systems, the metaphoric aspect is a self-criticism of ossified bureaucratized conceptual reason: full, "living" metaphors are also metamorphic, they change shapes to accommodate changing experiences (see for this the opus of Guattari and Deleuze, for example Deleuze 61, also Suvin, "On Metaphoricity"). As different from a superficial rhetorics of tropes, the conceptual backbone of such shapes is a reaffirmation of clear if corrigible steering toward a constantly moving horizon; perhaps even more clearly than concepts, metaphors presuppose a difference between the literal and the figural, the extra- and the intra-textual. (To coin a phrase: *il n'y a pas de texte sans hors-texte*; there is no text without the outside-the-text.) Micro-shapes: images, metaphors (Benjamin's "eidos, a vivid image of life" – *Correspondence* 308). Meso-shapes: metaphoric themes, sets, and types of argumentative propositions, narrations – for example, genres of writing and of other semiotic and dialogic communication (performances, paintings ...). Mega-shapes: representative (equally personal and collective) stances, bearing, horizons, behaviours, theories. Finally: mass behavioural movements. All these forms change in time (history); indeed, morphogenesis (à la Thom) constitutes history.

Eisenstein's, Heartfield's, Picasso's, Ernst's, and Brecht's "montage" as well as Benjamin's "constellations" may be attempts to negotiate all three of the above levels. To the univocal closed system, all of them oppose a kind of previously unthought-of but now *incipiently meaningful* juxtaposition, a bricolage partaking of a topological practice as much as of a conceptual presupposition. For this dynamically unstable cognitive nexus, the more powerful a system, the more it needs to be shot through and indeed counteracted (*unterwandert*) by one or preferably more metaphoric ensembles, which by definition are not quite systematic systems. Examples (which I have analyzed elsewhere): Marx's *Manifesto*, Brecht's *Life of Galileo*.

In our little epicycle, this also means there are serious limitations to the academic article or book, aping systematicity and therefore as a rule constricted, Laocoon-like, by the twin serpents of Scientificity approximating absolute Truth and fashionable Originality-for-a-Day.

Wedge 3/ Into Riemannian Interstellar Seas: Science, Truth, Open Forms

> There is only one knowledge, the knowledge of our world in its becoming; and this becoming includes the very knowledge.
> — MERLEAU-PONTY, *Adventures of the Dialectic*

3.1

The dynamics of developing sciences seem opposed to the sudden static revelation of religion. So they are, but as poles of the same globe of transcending the messy imperfection of everyday praxis.[2] There is a real difference between them, of a piece with the difference between precapitalist social formations based on agricultural space and capitalism based on industrial time and then financial spacetime. Yet the dogmatic pretension of science to get – in however deferred and lengthy ways – to a final Truth

2 Characteristically, both religion and science stake out claims to a deeper truth, visible for religion in the approximations of ideas, ecstasies, and art, and for science in mathematically laced ideas and via the new instruments of vision from microscope and telescope, cloud chamber, or photos beyond the range of the human eye. Goodman and Elgin compare and contrast the deviations from empirical visibility in medieval paintings, where the Madonna and Child are bigger than others in proportion to significance, with those in X-ray or cloud-chamber photographs (113, and see Gombrich 245–46).

about the universe (marked by a capital T) participates of the same long-durational, class-society delusion that history, with all its human interests and evaluations, can be brought to a stop. Science yoked to capitalism is still dominated by a Platonic-Christian ideology, refusing the body and femininity (Noble); it has not taken off for the open cosmic spaces or the glowing magma center.

There are by now few respectable thinkers who would not concede that of the two main kinds of scientific knowledge, "facts" and "theories," the theories – say of chemical valency – are self-evidently useful fictions (conventions), and the facts or observations an unholy amalgam of sensual evidence and semantics with theory (that is, fiction), "theory-laden to a degree that makes their contents inseparable from the theory" (Laudan 142; this still leaves enough room for criteria to adjudicate competing theories, he rightly notes). Let me take Harré's example for a factual sentence, "A blue precipitate appeared at 28°C." (80), and note its referent would be rendered quite differently in cultures which see blue as not different from green (there are many such cultures), which would instead of degrees Celsius use a qualitative scale (say, "it blushed"), and which would instead of "precipitate appears" say "Mercury has been revealed" (the alchemists would). Is the sentence "Mercury is revealed when water blushes green" really translatable into Harré's lab language without remnants? If a sentence (as any linguist would know) includes presuppositions as well as positions, it is not. Is the untranslatable part simply magical mumbo-jumbo that can be suppressed? This would depend on what additional cognition it might contain: for example, "Mercury" may well be more specific (as to its look or curative powers) than "precipitate" and thus contain more bytes of information. And what about great cultures which instead of the subject-object syntax use mainly contiguity and richer if less univocal relationships, and say something like "East Dragon – green – sudden event – blush – liquid," as I fantasize the Chinese would? How come they invented gunpowder, printing, and the South-pointing compass needle?

In sum, as Harré notes, "Many, indeed infinitely many, different sets of hypotheses can be found from which statements describing the known facts can be deduced [...]" (87; see Haraway 24–39 and passim). All attempts "to show that the methods of science guarantee it is true, probable, progressive or highly confirmed knowledge [...] have generally failed," concedes a recent prominent defender of the efficiency of science as cognition (Laudan 2). His proposed way out, that science solves important problems, passes under silence – as pragmatism usually does – what problems were picked out from brute facticity (ibid. 16) and constituted as worthy of solution at expense of other ones, as well as whom do the solutions benefit. As a whole current of philosophers has maintained since Gassendi (in 1658), theories are not true or false but good or bad instruments for research. Laudan maintains with much historical evidence that "in determining if a theory solves a problem, *it is irrelevant whether the theory is true or false, well or poorly confirmed*; what counts as a solution to a problem at one time will not necessarily be regarded as such at all times" (22–23).

Formally speaking, "atom" is the name of an agent in a story about "chemistry," just as "Mr Pickwick" is the name of an agent in a story about "the Pickwick Club" (see Harré 89), notwithstanding some different rules of storytelling in the two cases, consubstantial with the much greater historical impact of the atom-type of story upon masses of people than the Pickwick-type story. "[Theoretical f]ictions must have some degree of plausibility, which they gain by being constructed in the likeness of real things," concludes a middle-of-the-road theoretician of science (Harré 98). In other words, literary and scientific "realism" are consubstantial products of the same attitude, the quantifying immanency of bourgeois society. Yet institutionally sanctified science persists in claiming it is the pursuit of the whole truth in the form of certainty, while the apparently "weaker" and certainly more modest Dickens did not. The philosophic and other systems of belief arising out of (and constituting) science remain stuck on this two-dimensional surface. As a planet's map is regulated and shaped by the grid of cartographic projection, so is any such system based on a principle, for example the Aristotelian excluded middle or the Hegelian necessarily resolved dialectical contradiction. And this principle is also a kind of (obviously circular) meta-reflection about, or methodic key of, the system that is in turn founded on and more or less necessarily deduced from it, and that exfoliates in the form of a finite series of propositions culminating in a rounded-off certainty.

This form is finally not too different from the nineteenth century "well-made," illusionistic stage play; no wonder, for they both flow out of the Positivist orientation. The Lady with the Camelias and the Laws of Thermodynamics are sisters under the skin: both show a beautifully nec-essary death. Such a necrophilic stance is only possible in a society whose ruling class is committed to "mastery" over nature and other people. The hegemonic science "has projected and promoted a universe in which the domination of nature has remained linked to the domination of man" (Marcuse, *One-Dimensional* 166). In this section I focus on epistemology as a first step, but any stance implies a social subject, it is impelled and limited by its political interests. There are fatal limits to all cognition shaped by a clash of interests between masters and slaves, by "male identity" (Noble xiv, and see Haraway 29), and by murderous ethnocentrism, usually implying a fake "race" theory. As Foucault – among others – noted, our "Truth" is a discourse of "a few great political and economic apparatuses (university, army, writing, media)" (132), that is, it is geared to capitalist production and bourgeois power. Finally, conclusions have to be drawn from this.

3.2

What could then be the form and horizon of a possible and needful ascen-sion from the Flatland planimetry into the curved space of trigonometry or indeed the imaginary nth dimensions of higher mathematics, in which Euclid's axioms do not suffice and hold? It would be an *open form*. Its presupposition is that openness does not at all imply formlessness. There is no understanding without articulation. Combating division into social classes and domination of the upper classes is the prerequisite for a humanly sustainable ensemble of values, openly articulated according to preferen-tial interests on the agenda of humanity: not *an-archeia* but a dynamic hierarchy.

The non-Euclidian form would be open at the end. This could be a tautology ("open" implies also "open at the end") were it not necessary to firmly distinguish "language" from meta-language. Namely, in order for a form to be a form – a provisional, pragmatic cosmos with preferential orientations and not a chaos – it has to have *a provisional closure of the Signifier*: this is a condition of perceptibility for any piece of writing, mathematics, imaging or topology, or any other imaginable semiotic system – "language" in a loosely metaphoric sense. (Friedrich Schlegel remarked that we cannot live either with or without a system: updating this, we cannot do without either provisional systems or system-destroying metaphors!) But it has simultaneously, then, to beware of a magical, short-circuiting, *final closure of the Signified* – of the intended horizons toward which the piece is oriented. The orientation is not an anchor in the wild ride on the oceanic swells and currents but our firm though flexible guideline for the helm. It is determined both by the huge urgency of escaping from where we are now (our locus of capitalist terror) and an idea – however initial and vague – of the horizons which are to be refused, thus also of the horizons which call for investigation.

3.3

Nietzsche's call *auf die Schiffe!* (to the ships), leaving the comfortingly familiar but by now barren and indeed death-dealing shores, implies today several superimposed but distinguishable ways to follow or methods. First, with Bloch, it implies venturing into the open invitation of not only the optimistically Not Yet Known (as in traditional bourgeois science) but also the riskier Not Yet Existing. What rough beast may be ambling toward Bethlehem – surely not only the PoMo delight in the polymorphically perverse horrors of supercapitalism? But even further, and crucially, it then implies openness toward the Not Now Foreseeable; and indeed, toward the Not Ever Cognitively Exhaustible. Not ever exhaustible cognitively, because not ever exhaustible experientially, historically, agentially. History has no end (but untold catastrophes and triumphs). Much like a haiku echoing forth in the reader (see Suvin *Lessons*, Chapter 2); or the series of encounters along Don Quixote and Sancho Panza's road; or the ideal Brechtian pedagogy of playing; or the ideal Benjaminian arrested image, for example the Angel of History being propelled backward to an unseen future, looking at the film of ruins presenting themselves in front of him.

Shooting the fishes of facts in a closed barrel of experiences is only possible if history is viscous, arrested, finally contained. This does not seem on the agenda of any liveable future for humanity.

But then the openly signifying form would be open at any sufficiently neuralgic point of articulation, for example the cusp of a Prigoginian "catastrophe" figure. This is easily proven: a beginning and a middle exist only in function of an end. If the cessation of a semiotic piece is not its end – neither its politic *telos* nor its final reverberation in the constitutive dialog with the piece's user (say the reader) – then the piece's articulation or organization only *seems* to have an Aristotelian beginning and middle: given that the loci and even the horizon of the Signified are dynamic, the beginning could have been elsewhere, the middle can be anywhere, and any distinguishable segment or *articulum* has its own ending – up to a point open. Like a Brechtian play or a Cervantesian novel or a Marxian or Nietzschean or Benjaminian prose project, the piece demands to be rewritten for every new user-type – that is, new constellation of human relationships. Any version (and there are only versions, no "originals") must be syntagmatically closed but also paradigmatically open, always shimmering at the edges: its open signifying structure means that it can go on indefinitely, like a tapeworm, parasitic on the intestine in and from which it is nourished. This foregrounds the rewriting that any user's mind will anyway inevitably effect, but attempts to steer it according to a constant value orientation.

3.4

Therefore, what may Hegel's definition of philosophy as "the age grasped in thought" (Foreword to *Sketch of the Philosophy of Law, Werke* 7: 26) today mean? The age (historical monad) is provisional, split along class, gender, ethnic, and many other fault-lines: there are as many ages as stable and acting groups with critical and creative interests and evaluations. There are also correspondingly many "thoughts" or ways what to grasp such an age as (the correspondence is, I think, quite strict). Alas, of Aristotle's two "dianoetic virtues," philosophy and the arts, the former has paled on our historical horizon and may only be rescued by new politics. But the orientation, the acknowledgement that all is steeped in overwhelming yet open history, may remain. History is our fertile delight and cursed limitation. But history is only grasped as a *montage*, in all its senses. A montage provides the chance at critical distances and step-by-step verification by practice.

Wedge 4/ Economics of Working Bodies, Salvational Politics

> We are like somebody wha hears
> A wonderfu' language and mak's up his mind
> To write poetry in it – but ah!
> It's impossible to learn it, we find,
> Tho' we'll never ha'e ony use again
> For ither languages o' ony kind.
>   Hugh MacDiarmid, "Ode to All Rebels"

4.1

Cognition is in our times threatened by the complementary perils of solidified dogmatism and shoreless Disneyfication – both catexes of sympathy away from autonomous personalities. These twin reproducers of class hegemony are mass sects of infantilized salvation through some numinous image that invites empathizing stories: a saviour (Jesus, Stalin, Hitler) or an allegory of commodification (Mickey Mouse, the Lion King). Both entail kidnapping and fakery of the salvational impulse: the initially metamorphic and liberating Mickey Mouse, lauded by Benjamin as kin to anti-mythic folktales and to Fourier, can easily turn (has turned) into the Big Bad Wolf, and Lenin into Stalin. The religious or political personalized saviours, who mask the *apparati* they head; the institutionalized science as part of fixed capital and ideology of technocratic cadres; and, obversely, the ceaseless mania for consumption – all are arrests of imagination, corruptions of the potentially best into the worst. This may be avoided only by a permanent revolution, the constant interaction of knowing with not-knowing, of the already significantly understood and the now for the first time to be significantly understood. Cognition is generated at and from the moving

periphery of the understood, like matter and anti-matter from the seem-
ing vacuum of interstellar spaces. Wisdom arises out of the knowledge of
nescience (both in Nietzsche and his hated Socrates): "And only on this
by now solid and granite basis of nescience may science have arisen, the
will for knowing on the basis of a much more powerful will, the will for
unknowing, for the uncertain, the untrue! Not as its opposite, but – as its
improvement!" (*Jenseits* 24) Careful: this "untrue" is the opposite of the
illusionistic, for example of progress, angels, gods, UFOs or Mickey Mice
(as well as of atoms equated to Solar systems) taken for empirical existents
leading to fanatical belief; it is that which demolishes The Monolithic Truth
while preserving verifiability for any given situation.

The Knower is a deep-sea diver: "Without this kind of nescience life
itself would be impossible, it is the condition for maintaining and furthering
life: a huge and solid bell of nescience must be standing around you" (*Wille*
609). The sea of wisdom "delineates the limit even of [scientific, DS] cognition" (*Götzendämmerung* 5). Today we might think of this as the ABC of
quantum mechanics, which shatters Laplace's dream of gaining complete
information as concerns the state of a system. Even Einstein dreamed of a
Unified Theory: all our physicists are professionally monotheists, in spite
of Chaitin's Theorem which says that mathematics – which has long ago
imperialistically gobbled up logic – has a finite limit in forming significant
propositions about the complexity of any object (see Chaitin, and Rucker
287). Mathematics, Norbert Wiener noted, is finally "the most colossal
metaphor imaginable" (95).

4.2

Nonbeing is not empty but potentially pregnant: for example, the omnipotent empty space of Lao Tse, an undeveloped photographic image, Bloch's
latency, cosmic "vacuum" generating positrons, Gendlin's syntax of wordless
but not shapeless psychic conceptions awaiting semantics ... It follows that
nescience is the boundary of what we know, the permanent and permanently
moving interface with lived collective and personal history: nothing can be
fully known in advance. Lineaments of alternative possibilities may in the

best case be drawn. Aristotle thought we cannot know whether there will be a sea-battle tomorrow, but we do know that there *either* will *or* won't be one. As argued earlier, this is only pertinent for exceptional cusps and culminations of battle-readiness, of inevitability, and – most important – of salience or pertinence. But at such points new Possible Worlds may wink into being.

Will the fertility result in pregnancy? It depends on the choice of season, the plot of earth (or of other mother matter), the modes (qualities) of seeding. But first and not least, not all potentialities are worth actualizing. Even if we could know that Great King Dareiush will or will not call for his fourth concubine in Persepolis tonight, say by the watch-fire system shown at the beginning of *Agamemnon*, why should we find time and energy to know it (organize the watchers and fires, look for them, etc.)? In Aeschylus, the time was found because the signal (fall of Troy) was of supreme pertinence for the whole Hellenic world. So: if you want to know something, you must begin by caring about it, devoting labour to it: *truth is a matter of economics of working bodies* – even before capitalist political economy when financing is foregrounded as its enabling factor (see Brecht's *Dialog of Exiles*; or the history of science and technology in the age of world wars). Any formalization of embodied knowledge is a choice from among competing horizons and paths. We can check this by seeing the choice according to interests of capitalism in the atomized surface "facts" of any TV newscast.

Obversely, Laplace's hypothesis (if one knew the kinds and paths of all the atoms in the universe, one could predict with certainty everything to happen) is abstract scientism run mad. Imagine living in the world in which everything, including everybody's birth and death, was running on absolutely certain iron tracks: it should have been enough to cast doubt on the whole enterprise of atomistic and extrapolative scientism! A degenerate but equally obfuscating approximation to Laplace, a fake certainty and disneyfied constellation, are today precisely the TV news: the certainty all is as we already know and only details will vary. Within the eternal return of the same, these details are then the news: the bad guy at the global OK Corral is Iran or Iraq (or Serbia, or tomorrow China) instead of the USSR, poverty comes from heavens while the IMF is good. *Plus ça change, plus c'est la même chose*. Diametrically opposed to this is the encounter with Nonbeing: history can radically change.

4.3

A further key rearrangement of categories is implied here, diametrically opposed to the disciplinary organization of knowledge by which the bourgeoisie organizes the old maxim of "divide and conquer," suppressing the indispensable union of operative truth and life-furthering value. It is, in today's insufficient terms, a melding of science, politics, religion, and economics into a humanizing philosophical history (the only science that Marx recognized; see also Daly and Cobb 123–31). For, the way science has been practiced since Galileo is not only a cultural revolution (Jameson) but also a latent or patent political upheaval. The bourgeois civilization's main way, *via magistra*, of coping with the unknown is aberrant because it "transmut[es] nature into concepts with the aim of mastering nature" (Nietzsche, *Wille* 610): that is, it turns nature *only* into concepts and furthermore makes a more or less closed system out of concepts. It is not that the means get out of hand but that the mastery – the wrong end – *requires* consubstantially wrong means. If you want to be Master of your Company, you got to treat profit-making concepts as raw material on the same footing as profit-making labourers and iron ore. The problem lies not in the Sorcerer's Apprentice but in the Master Wizard. The scientific is the political.

A major political difference between religion and science is that entry into churches is free, while entry into the labs of technoscience is not. Religion was created for the poor classes, in order to make them bear their lot; whatever science was created for (it was to be more practical than religion in bettering everybody's lot), it is today indifferent to the sufferings it arises out of and often much intensifies. The ready subservience of science to capitalist destruction of life – theoretically speaking, the crude but still very powerful scientific Positivism and philosophical Objectivism – must be decisively abandoned if we are to preserve the human species and most organic life. Despite its terrible record, almost nullifying both its cosmic and its political utopian impulse, a new look at the other main traditional means of coping with the unknown, religion – an activity projecting upon the unknown anthropomorphic forces which may be propitiated but also a "table of contents of humanity's theoretical struggles" (Marx, *Werke* 1: 383) – is obviously on the agenda. While in present straits humanity is not fit to inquire into larger (for example cosmic) mysteries, it must be recognized that religions were often the privileged – or simply the only tolerated – site of the Utterly Different (Bloch), of the philosophical wonder and awe at the tremendous and fascinating mystery sparked by nescience. Not, I hasten to add with as much stress as I can muster, that I find any use for monotheism or for the usually quite pernicious clerical *apparati* (churches as institutions). Yet: if both the scientific and religious fixed Truth is a dangerous illusion or fakery; if understanding or wisdom is (at least since the industrial revolution) ineluctably a dynamic permeation and interfusion of the known with the unknown; and if the unknown will never be finally known since history will not freeze; then no *salvational impulse* (traditionally monopolized but also deflected first by religions and theologies, and then by technology and science) can be heedlessly tossed aside in an age of multiple catastrophes on all levels, in this polluted Unknown into which we are lurching. Profit as the Transcendental Signifier (Great Satan) means unprecedented, system-immanent quantitative and qualitative destruction of human bodies through wars, drugs, and other poisonings of air, water, food – all of them being normalized and naturalized through objectivism and hypocritical empathy.

4.4

Thus, looking at this from the scientific side, we need a salvational science, wresting the impulse away from religion. "God is not dead, he has been included into human destiny" (Benjamin). Looking at it from the side of belief, science needs to be refashioned to cope with qualities (overridingly, the quality of people's lives) and not only quantities. But I shall here follow Brecht and Benjamin and look at our historical constellation as a new animal proceeding toward the horizons of a psychophysically viable community or *polis*: as *politics* in the classical sense, materializing salvation.

True, although politics is the only way for people to collectively help themselves, it is only too rarely such. Nonetheless, classical salvational, revolutionary politics fuses the daily, "vulgar" concerns with psychophysical survival of people and the ability to cope with Paradise as well as – alas especially – with Hell (as Benjamin reiterates in his materials on the Paris Arcades, for example *Gesammelte Schriften* V: 676, 1011, 1023, and *Correspondence* 549). An earmark of Hell: its "time doesn't want to know death" (Benjamin, *Gesammelte Schriften* V: 115). An earmark of Paradise and any prefiguration of it, such as the questing Soviet of Brecht's *He Who Says No*: it can give meaning to death (see Suvin *Lessons*, Chapter 5).

The only politics working for salvation is one of democratic communities. To get at them, "the most trite Communist platitude possesses more *hierarchies of meaning* than does contemporary bourgeois profundity, which has only one meaning, that of an apologetic" (Benjamin, *Correspondence* 372–73). This may, retrospectively, be too optimistic, unless "Communist" is the ideal which worthwhile Marxists and worthwhile anarchists hold in common, rather than the ambiguous and finally corrupted Bolshevik tradition. Without the horizon of salvation for each as well as for all, communism or socialism is scientistic dogma; without politico-economic practice, "theology falls into magic" (Buck-Morss 249). Despite its terrible record, almost nullifying the utopian impulse of communism, it remains the most energetic, hopeful, and mass attempt at thisworldly salvation of modern times, and a new look at this dispossession of capitalism – beginning with a look at the grievous errors of "real communism" – ineluctably remains on any agenda to avert disaster.

Wedge 5/ Pragmatics as Method: Multiple Pertinences, Not Only But Also; Art as Emblem

> Whoever today sticks his head into sand, will grind his teeth tomorrow.
> — Graffito in Germany, 1980s

The ideal of an absolute Truth leads necessarily to Nietzsche's "illusion" – that is, faking. This Truth may be arrived at in complex ways, but it is finally supposed to be a point of rest for the weary: "simple, transparent, not contradicting itself, permanent, enduring as identical, with no crease, hidden sleight, curtain, form: a man conceives thus the world of Being as 'God' in his own image" (*Wille* 543). Such Truth (this ideal of truthfulness) is thus a lie, and whenever erected into a closed system – as in religion and in Galileian science – it compels lying, always unconscious and frequently also conscious. Any cognition developed against this fixed horizon partakes of a huge, finally deadly illusion.

Strange as this may sound, cognition is usefully to be understood not only as open-ended but also as codetermined by the social subject and societal interests looking for it: the horizons are both movable and multiple. Not only is this legitimate, it is unavoidable and all-pervasive. Quite materialistically, the object of any praxis can only be "seen as" that particular kind of object (Wittgenstein) from a subject-driven – but also subject-modifying – standpoint and bearing. Now today no society wishing to survive can afford to face the sea of dangerous unknowns seeping into the cracks of our endangered life-world without a number of competing bearings, ways of negotiating the swirls and swells of bitter matter. The absence of such competition (and of its material basis) was what doomed the USSR. Obversely, the richer societies of the global North can afford the necessary luxury of multiple class fractions within the ruling class, with their differing interpretations of common class and societal interests, presenting alternative projects for societal essence or orientation. If such societies, principally the US one, decide on closure, they too will doom themselves (and possibly all of us).

Theoreticians like Kuhn or Foucault then fold back this multi-perspective view of the Einsteinian age into historical succession. It is more interesting to note that multi-perspective view and multi-linear causality was first rehearsed at length in two semiotic clusters. One was Modernist art: in poetry since Blake and Baudelaire, in painting since Cézanne and Picasso, in prose culminating with Joyce, Kafka or Faulkner, and in theatre with Meyerhold and Brecht, while film and TV were wholly produced within this horizon (so that their massive failures can be directly attributed to capitalist alienations of their immanent possibilities, as Benjamin argued). The other was heretical cognition best represented by most Marx and some Nietzsche, but also, to my mind, by the post-Einstein revolutions in natural sciences. The strengths of people like Brecht, Benjamin, and Eisenstein lay in cross-fertilization of these two major traditions of the real novum.

5.2

This multiple as well as open-ended way of cognizing refigures the *relation of exception to rule*.

Any exception implies a very dialectical contradiction: a) there is a rule or law; yet simultaneously, b) this rule has limits – of operation and reliability, most importantly of *pertinence*. Any sufficiently sustained and important exception judges and finally demolishes the rule; but then, such exception/s stimulate and induce new horizons, norms, rules. In dynamic, even though closed or one-track systems – such as classical (Galileian) science – this (old) rule must be exchanged for a new and more encompassing one which accommodates the exception. The dynamism can here still be subordinated to the arrow of progress: higher, faster, quicker – a permanent Olympic Games of the spirit, where the Nobel Prize medals strike gold. But in equally dynamic yet open and multi-track totalities (see Suvin, "Two Cheers"), the contradiction of rule and exception is not permanently deferred in order to break out anew as a falsification of the wider paradigm. These truly open quasi-systems – always provisional and protean – incorporate the startling, anti-Newtonian realization that probably all rules are only statistical and pragmatic, for all will always have exceptions arriving from the inexhaustible life-world of history traversing and constituting our bodies (Blake was right about "Newton's sleep").

This does not mean that in any given, delimited situation there are no rules: on the contrary, we could not delimit and deal with any situation at all without proposing rules valid for them. But it indicates how to use rules (as well as situations). First, *the extreme* becomes the exemplary form of the exception, indicating the neuralgic and dialectical watershed of pertinence for the rule: we begin to realize that any dynamic and complex state of affairs can only be discussed by a feedback between its phenomena and a *pro analysi* model formed by "pure," that is in some ways extreme, elements. Indeed, it can be argued that "concept comes from the extreme" (Benjamin *Gesammelte Schriften* I.1: 215; see Lefebvre, *Production* 219).

Second, the interesting exception indicates the limits of pertinence of a rule: the rule is not invalidated, it is assigned a domain of validity *beside which* (not above or below which in any progressive sense) *other domains with other limits of pertinence may and most probably must exist.* This entails not only a division of turfs – analogous to that between atomic physics, chemistry, physics, and biology, constituted roughly by the size of its elementary unit, from quark to cell – but also, and at that in the most fruitful cases, *crossings of rule-domains* (as in Freud's "overdetermination" of dream elements; and see Gendlin). The closed "upward arrow" systems of cognition use a rigid rule with explained-away exceptions. Nietzsche calls in *Wahrheit und Lüge* some inkling of this denial an emblem of terrible powers that oppose to scientific truths quite different truths. To the contrary, Lenin noted with approval Hegel's arguments that "Law is the enduring [...] in the appearances [...], the quiescent reflection of appearances" – and therefore, he concluded, "every law is narrow, incomplete, approximate" (151). The meta-principle of open cognition, opposed to the fake *excelsior*, could be called: *not only but also* (or both/and). The best known example is perhaps the wave-corpuscle duality in modern physics, but what Jameson speaks of as the coexistence of humanizing utopia and alienating ideology in almost any human endeavour today (certainly in all artworks and philosophies) may be an even better one.

But then such a multiple cognition cannot rely on the "Olympic Games'" or "progress" model of the exception-rule spiral, nor be a prettification of existing bodies and images: "we are not talking about face lifts and liposuction" (Bolongaro) but about a change of behaviour and living. It is not a night in which all cats are grey: it is a dawn in which a societal "we" needs different cats for different purposes: say, some for petting and some for catching mice (as Deng Xiao-ping failed to realize, so that his mousers have by now turned into "capitalist roaders").

"Rule" agents and "exception" agents constitute an anthropology. Benjamin's agents, operating within the closed system of commodity capitalism, are all "exception" or marginal people, the metropolitan "Mohicans" from the jungle of cities (after Balzac, Baudelaire, Brecht, Kafka): prostitute, gambler, flâneur, collector, rag-picker, detective, last not least the *poète maudit* (behind all of whom hides the author himself). But socially marginal may be semiotically or cognitively central because extreme: his typical figures show up the System *en creux* (prostitute as the living commodity). Marx's agents are the "rule" and ruling agents: the hidden Powers-That-Be of alienating perdition, allegories of the System ("M. le Capital et Mme la Terre"), and the new redeeming Power-To-Be: "proletarians of all countries". Not much is to be found in Marx about the "system" the new Powers might set up, but if it were something like Fourier's, it would be highly complex but also open-ended and dynamically meshing. Brecht effects a sly grafting: his plebeians are alienated at much too high a price into terrible but also temporary and failing Powers – Galy Gay, Shen Te, Mother Courage, Azdak. Brecht's margins judge the center and exceptions pronounce judgment upon the rule. Nietzsche does not come off well here: the prophet on high, above the madding crowd; prefigurations of a new upper class.

5.3

The strange dialectics of both/and are thus neither closed dogmatics nor unguided, disoriented eclecticism. A new, anti-Aristotelian Golden Middle may be found here in dynamic oscillation between Not Only and But Also, a bipolarity that may render the rule/ exception dilemma obsolete. In Marx's *Capital* the searcher is confronted by *two different ways of cognizing* reality. A crucially ambiguous case is one of outer appearance vs. inner laws of movement. The unfortunate paleotechnic vocabulary of rigid laws inherited from Newton, thus finally from Christian predetermination, and issuing forth with metallic ("iron," or in the original German in fact "brazen") rigidity, can be found in Marx's quick abbreviations, most notoriously in the Preface to *Capital*. But obversely, the more dialectical relation between veiling or mystifying and unveiling or manifesting, omnipresent in Marx from *The Communist Manifesto* on, usually does not rely on laws but on critical work grounded in tendencies and constituting both these poles in an unceasing weaving back and forth between them (see for extended discussion Suvin and Angenot, and Suvin "Two Cheers"). We could derive from Marx's terminology a new illuminating vocabulary: "Beneath the apparently solid surface, they [the 1848 revolutions] betrayed oceans of liquid matter, only needing expansion to rend into fragments continents of hard rock" ("Speech at the Anniversary of the *People's Paper*," Tucker ed. 427; see on this remarkable passage Berman 90 and passim). A *rock-solid model* is opposed to an ocean-fluid or *metamorphically fluid* one here: on the one hand an uncritical linkage of notions (*Vorstellungen*) which follow a "common sense" that is usually only conceptual and out of touch with sensual dynamics, and on the other hand a critical reasoning steeped in subversive norms of desire and value that reconstructs the given in its becoming, having become, and functioning into a dialectically contradic-tory – articulated yet fluid – "concrete." This is in fact the Marxian whole or totality, prefigured already in his doctoral dissertation as the opposition of Democritus and Euclid vs. Epicure and Lucretius.

From this vantage point the necessary distinction about the uses, abuses, and limits of Nietzsche could also be undertaken. What is to be retained from him (and his best pupils in the twentieth century, such as Deleuze and Guattari) is an operative view of the universe, and our lives, as a dynamic winking in and out of a loose system of interacting forces. In that metamorphic and rhizomatic multiplicity we can – and at any pragmatic moment must, and thus always do! – freeze or cut out sufficiently stable "trees" of argumentation. This is quite compatible with the Marxian and Brechtian use of "production" or creation as form-giving fire, a magma or old mole from the depths rending all encrusted certainties.

5.4

Beside the powerful but sensually "thin" scientific method, it is *art*, the rendering of "thick" Possible Worlds, that has been the long-duration competitor of religion for wresting the unknown into the known by means of figure and narration, and for doing this in order to make present living easier. This parable-like, cognitively projective and allusive yet sensually present, function of insisting on the lateral possibilities of historical life, which might feed into a different future, remains for art in the foreseeable future. But it remains pertinent (it will be cognitive) on condition that the parable does not simply *illustrate* but *induces* the doctrine that it refers to and presupposes, that it become a critical rather than simply confirmational allegory: as Benjamin formulated in regard to Kafka and Brecht (perhaps best in Benjamin, *Correspondence* 564–65 and *Gesammelte Schriften* VI: 11–13; see Suvin, "Preliminary"). "The highest art is the art of living," noted Brecht: if this cannot today be (alas) an art of training statesmen for a State withering away, as he thought in 1930, it cannot be either an art of profit-making yuppie debauchery. Perhaps it is now the art of training critical dissenters who care for *how* as the indispensable obverse of *why*. Today, the formal is the substantial. Nonetheless, the final horizon should never be wholly forgotten: Burckhardt's State as a Work of Art – not in the murderous Renaissance but in a possibly utopian future. For if this does not happen – if we dissidents don't make it come about – utopia may, we have learned, also be dystopia: "Socialism or Barbarism" (Luxemburg 269). Radical participatory democracy from below at all levels; or profit-crazed neo-feudal oligarchy destroying us all.

Poetry (artistic production) is thus potentially a privileged form for conveying and constituting cognition, for humanizing it by means of figures and events recalling but also modifying the life-world, and for understanding what cognition is and may be. As discussed a propos the openly signifying form in Wedge 3, art foregrounds the user's interpretation but attempts to steer it according to a constant orientation. Thus, following Benjamin, worlds of art may (in the best cases) present us with radically different and/or radically better *experiences*, whose shapings are then guides to salvation. It is not without right that poetry since Baudelaire openly claimed to be the highest cognition, as did the novel since Balzac (Marx and Engels agreed with that claim). For, as Nietzsche had surmised, we have to "look at science in the light of art, but at art in the light of life" (*Birth* 19).

Part 2. What Must We Know For Blights

Increscunt animi, virescit volnere virtus.
[Wounded, the excellence grows adult and spirits stronger]
— NIETZSCHE'S motto, 1872

What remains clear is that all the problems that socialism tried and failed to solve remain even less soluble today, and insoluble within our present structures.
— HEINER MÜLLER, 1981

But may the will to truth mean this to you: that everything be transformed into the humanly conceivable [...], the humanly palpable! You have to think to the end your own senses.
— NIETZSCHE, *Thus Spoke Zarathustra*, 1880s

Wedge 6/ What for

Outside of poetry there is no Zen, outside of Zen there is no poetry.
TEN'IN RYÛTAKU, fifteenth century (paraphrasing Yen Yü, twelfth century–thirteenth century)

Let's say first of all what is not happiness, since we know that.
— LEFEBVRE, 1967

6.1

Yet further, always radically further, to the farthest horizon: It seems incontrovertible that all grasping and understanding reality is phylogenetically (for the human species) and ontogenetically (for each child) both metaphorical and literal, that the lever, microscope, movies or computer, formed in order to have a definite type of effect, change the neural pathways of humans and make them stand under a differing reality. The mediated traffic with nature determines in each historical case the human sensorium as a hermeneutic apparatus. Any (literal and metaphorical) tool defines its object-types and its subject-wielders both *as* something and *to* (*for*) something. The embodied sense-functions shape our access to the world of signifying and significant potential actions. In that sense, Marx's famous final *Thesis on Feuerbach*, enjoining understanding to change the world, would almost be superfluous. It should perhaps be read as much as a confirmation as an exhortation: this is what "the point" or the purpose of "philosophers' interpretation" has always been. No interpretation without consequences for change – but also, no change without interpretation. Any understanding intervenes into life to a certain, sometimes minimal, degree – if only by refusing to intervene. And attempts to make sense of the forces shaping our lives will run into sand unless understanding connects to practical changing of the pernicious constellations stunting our lives.

It is imperative that we realize – as the feminists have – epistemology does not function without asking the political question "what for?" or *cui bono*. It is not simply that there is no useful politics without clear perception: much more intimately, interests and values decisively shape all perception. The barrier between supposedly "cultural" discussions and politics-cum-economics is sterile categorization and blindness.

6.2

Thus, the final and overriding question for now is: where are we to look for liberating currents in this needy, paltry, poor age (*dürftige Zeit*) of ours? For if we do not at least guess at them, approximate them, try to forecast them, pave the way for them, help to make them possible, how are we to use Marx's great insight that no theory or method can be divorced from or indeed understood without the practice of social groups to which it corresponds? How are we to delineate the new sensorium humanity needs for survival?

Again, I may today only begin answering this by contraries: What are the major blights most efficiently destroying human existence, dignity, and sense in the twentieth century? I can name three: mass murders, mass prostitution, mass drugging – a consubstantial unholy trinity.

Wedge 7 / Against War

> Counter-revolution by the center against the periphery
> Blood on stone   blood and stones
> Thou shalt not get out from under world banks
>   fish mouth silently
> This is Moses and the prophets.
>   "Le Ceneri di Tito"

There have never been so many killings in the entire world history as in this one century: hundreds of millions of people slaughtered by bomb and knife, and probably billions by hunger and maladies of poverty – the class war of the few ever more rich against the many ever more poor. Tuberculosis is back in force, and even the plague has returned in India. The excuse that – proportionately to the number of people alive – the twentieth century is no worse than any other may or may not be statistically correct, but it is irrelevant. If we have the cognitive wherewithal to ensure the survival of more people beyond their twelfth month, then we surely must use it to ensure their survival to their (our) natural end. Each person is a body in hope and pain, in theological terms in direct one-to-one relation to divinity. No proportions apply.

Worse: the present Post-Fordist social system does not *need* even approximately as many producers as the Welfare State Fordism did. Consumers are still needed, but the poorer ones (non-"Whites," most women, the very old and very young) do not count for much. One average North American citizen – such as me or you – consumes thirteen times more energy than one Chinese and 1,300 times more than a Bangladeshi: in direct proportion, the US armed forces and media count carefully their own body-bags but not the dead of its bombing and starving out. In the vein of Swift's *Modest Proposal*, I can propose that for the rulers of our globe, the corporative-military complex, major demographic bloodletting is most welcome (more than a touch of racism may be found here). At the very least, unless profit lurks in the wings, there is no reason to spend money on preventing it – either wars (Ruanda, Bosnia, and further to come), epidemics, terminal drugging or endemic famines: about hunger alone, cautious international sources speak of some 40 million people dying from it each year, while "about 500 million are chronically malnourished," that is on the way to dying soon, and a further 800+ million in "absolute poverty," that is, bordering on famine and dying a bit more slowly (Drèze-Sen 35, *Human ... 1996* 20, idem, *1998*).

Continuous warfare has *never* ceased under capitalism, whose heartbeat is antagonistic competition regardless of human lives (there were more dead and maimed per year in US car crashes than US casualties at the height of the Vietnam War). However, there was an illusory truce between the Euro-American metropolitan states as of ca. 1870. But even if we date the beginning of the permanent chain of war carnages in the "North" from 1911 – the first carving up of a precapitalist European empire, the Ottoman one, and the first major world revolution, the Mexican one – then we are already within the most terrible (almost) Hundred Years War in human history. Is this an accident? No. Capitalism cannot climb out of economic depressions without huge military spending, a "war mega-dividend." As Benjamin intuited and Paul Sweezy buttressed, it is a permanent "martial law": the Welfare State was also a Warfare State. In that respect, even the fully degenerate "State socialism" of the USSR was better: it did not need war, it was bankrupted by the armaments race forced on it.

We need to zero in relentlessly on this fact: from the inception of the modern State and market, wars have always been "the greatest and the most profitable of investments" (Lefebvre, *Production* 275). No capitalism without wars: and today wars destroy the world.

This is of a piece with the maintenance of a sustainable vertebrate biosphere (cockroaches may survive). No sane ecology without going against the profit principle and unlimited growth: beginning with wars and armament industries.[3]

Wedge 8/ Against Prostitution

> Prostitution is only a *particular* expression of the *general* prostitution of the labourer, and since prostitution is a relationship which includes not only the prostituted but also the prostitutor – whose vileness is even greater – so also the capitalist etc. fall in this category.
>
> — KARL MARX, *Economic and Philosophic Manuscripts of 1844*

8.1

About prostitution, I own to a deep prejudgement: my stomach upheaves at it. I see it as a purulent rhizomatic system in which it is difficult to decide what is worse: the obvious surface, the hidden depths; the signifier or the signified; the brute fact or the allegoric imagination valorizing it and driving it on. The surface is bad enough: the mass expansion of the sexual traffic in women (and, more rarely, men) is directly caused by the low or no earnings within capitalist immiseration (Chessler-Goodman 5), as clearly shown in the flood of first African (in the 1980s) and then East European prostitutes (for "since the end of communism, women have experienced a disproportionate share of economic hardship" – "In" 39) to more affluent European countries. The average of around thirty clients per week is of a piece with the mass-production or conveyor-belt drill (in the chorus lines of Busby Berkeley movies or in brothels). Though there are no proper statistics, a 1985 estimate put the spending on US prostitution at 15 billion (Pateman 190) and a 2000 estimate in Europe ("In") at 9 billion – yes! – dollars. At any given point in time, hundreds of thousands of prostituted sexual bodies lose the oldest and perhaps most specifically

3   *Note Jan. 2008*: See now much more in the Mesnard and the two Suvin entries in the bibliography of Wedge 7.

humanizing *promesse de bonheur*, the wondrous joy of two human wholes donating each to the other, the aura of mysterious – because creative and thus never fully foreseeable – use-value.

Marx could rightly say that "the whole of human servitude is involved in the relation of worker to production, and all relations of servitude are only modifications and consequences of the worker's relation to production" ("Economic" 299); but one could with Benjamin perhaps as rightly say this for the relation of the prostitute to prostitution, in the widest sense. To vary Marx's even more famous definition of capital, which was "not a thing but a social relationship among people mediated by things" (*Kapital* I: 731), prostitution is not a whore's activity but a social relationship among people rooted in the sale of the embodied female sexuality. For, if we define a prostitute as any person for whom sexual relationships become work in view of financial gain (see Parent-Duchatelet, Goldmann, Pateman), then to begin with – as classical socialists and feminists from Mary Wollstonecraft on said – what I would call the patriarchal (not all) bourgeois marriages are largely a mono-prostitution. But even further, the sale of sexual use of a woman's bodily services as consumable commodity (which fortunately for the seller, often an exploitative middleman, miraculously regrows – up to a point of no return) means that everything can become a commodity.

Sexual prostitution is then, as the epigraph from Marx well notes, a two-sided relationship of unequal power enforced primarily by dire poverty and secondarily by bourgeois law enforcement and mores. Without falling into the noxious sentimentality of the "whores with a heart of gold," it is clear they are at least as much sinned against as sinning: and insofar as they work, unionizing and strikes must be allowed. There are claims by Post-Modern practitioners that along much disgust they sometimes enjoy prostituted sex (cf. *Sex Work* passim and Bell chapters 5 and 6). I sympathize: why should the oppressed not get pleasure where they can? Yet drug users claim this too: it remains a poisoned and poisoning relation. True, criminalizing prostitution (or drug intake) fails to check it and helps only the middlemen: laws against exploiting the workforce, coercion, violence, and child abuse suffice, and the police has no business in the bedrooms of nations. No noncoercive sexual relationship or community of adults is to be medically or legally privileged or discriminated (Rubin, McLeod 20–25; if there were to be laws, they should apply to all involved in the prostitution relationship).

8.2

But the alternative of "Starve or sell yourself," never more shamelessly enforced than at the end of this great century of democratic commodities, is an Original Sin inherent in capitalist urbanization and industrialization that ramifies into almost all the blights of its (our) period. Physical labour-power is already a quite strange commodity, vested as it is most intimately in a personal body: how can you tell the labourer from the labour? In the modern age, two super-commodities have been added to it, making sale-able objects out of what would seem at the furthest remove from com-modification: the sexual body, and the creative brain. As Daniel Defoe showed, the first was from Moll Flanders on as a rule female and lower class (with a small stratum of high-class courtesans); as Balzac showed, the second was from Lucien de Rubempré on (in *Lost Illusions*) as a rule male and "middle" class: in our age of progress both are increasingly becoming unisex. Capitalism splits (in the North) into a two-track system: patriar-chy for the poor and marginals of gender and ethnicity-race, contract for the hegemonic and affordable. Thus, sexual prostitution is also a common denominator for and bridge to all other forms of prostitution under capi-talism, as well as to subservience to the war of each against each and to drugging (Millett ed. 112–14). I have argued (Suvin, "Two Holy" 44ff.) that both erotics and writing have as their optimal horizon a utopian and cognitive practice: fullness of meaning, necessary and sufficient articula-tion without power-hierarchies, denial that what exists here-and-now is the sole possibility, uniqueness of its microworld, its passional depth and vitality. But this, their *raison d'être*, is systematically commodified into dys-topia – lives of quiet desperation or loud cynicism. The cognitive metaphor of intellectuals (and particularly media people from the rise of mass press on) as prostitutes selling their brain-power to alienating ends is a recurring and just one. Today more than ever.

Sexual prostitution itself is as a rule male possession of the living super-commodity of a performing female body, where the pleasure is not simply in the afferent genital nerves but at least equally in the masculine imagination. It is the perverted but – one must assume – intense pleasure of using a person humiliatingly reduced to obedient object, the final subsumption of highest quality under quantification (money, price), of Eros under Death – as in Baudelaire's poetry, ambiguously freezing this alienation through classical form. His attentive reader Benjamin saw how in the reified female body, which can yet give (and pretend to receive) pleasure, allegory unites with commodities. In his language, the prostituted body, the mass commodity that "celebrates its becoming human in the prostitute" (*Gesammelte Schriften* I.2: 671), is the central "phantasmagoria" of commodified capitalism. The central capitalist sacrament, so to speak, the ritual of this weird religion whose Holy Scriptures are the daily stock-market quotations, is to reduce any use-value of bodies to a fixed financial "equivalent" rather than to meet them as equipollent (and evanescently changing and inexhaustible) subjects.

The horizon of a minimally just society is the abolition of the economic and psychic pressure on women to sell and on men to buy sexual services. Both are here "participants in an exercise in human misery" (McLeod 90), in denials of humanity (see Millett ed. 47, 62–67, 85, and 131–32).

Wedge 9/ Against Drugs

> [T]he junk merchant does not sell his product to the consumer, he sells the consumer to his product [...]. He degrades and simplifies the client.
> — WILLIAM S. BURROUGHS, *Naked Lunch*

9.1

However, the latest full colonization of human inner space (but the colonization of the genome has begun) is the colonization of the brain, *brainwashing* – that quintessential term of the US 1950s, as American as apple pie, dynamite, P.T. Barnum, hype, and ads.

Insofar as prostitution is an addiction, involved with power hustling, it also belongs here (so do some springs of war and violence in general, see now Suvin "Terms"). But we need more data about it, as well as about the real effect of the mind-bending *drugs*. I shall provisionally define these as substances acting upon the human brain so as to inflect its judgment away from fundamental interests of bodily and social salvation. They are by now as a rule industrially produced for mass consumption, and include alcohol, tobacco, and marijuana, the old narcotics and opiates and the new hallucinogens and pharmacy pills. The first problem is definition and inclusion: how to differentiate the "natural" uses of mild stimulants in small concentrations (for example, wine) for euphoria or disease treatment from drugging as defined above, which is usually addictive. It is an illusory palliative, its production and consumption sprung from physical or psychic misery and in turn impeding its eradication through liberatory politics, and last not least it is big capitalist business. Mass drunkenness began with industrialization, as testified to by Hogarth's Gin Lane, and spread with it. One should not forget the second half of Marx's famous quip about religion, "opiate of the people, heart of the heartless world": all brainwashing is accepted for momentary dulling of pain in the user, be he the poorest peasant or the most competitive speculator and CEO (the upper-class drugs are therefore not really prosecuted: alcohol and pills are officially exempt, old-type cocaine unofficially). But the long-range costs are exorbitant: drugs stupefy people, often a whole people.

Data on the illegal drugs are especially secret and controversial. Around 1990 the WHO estimated the users at 50 million (all numbers should for today be augmented between 50 and 200 percent). The number of users is small in comparison to tobacco and alcohol: in the US in 1988 there were 106 million users of alcohol, 57 million of tobacco, 12 million of marijuana, 2.8 million of cocaine and ca. 0.7 million of heroin; 98 percent of deaths from use seem due to the legal drugs (Methodist 6, 10–12). But the profits in the illegal trade, bolstered by prohibition, are huge: the narcodollar income of perhaps 500 billion US$ per year, when whitewashed by banks and invested, gave by 1990 a profit of between 1,000 and 2,000 billion US$ per year (Delbrel ed. 5–6, 116). The producers get very little of this: from $100 of cocaine bought in New York, an Andean coca peasant gets maybe $2, the middlemen (Colombian mafia – or opium and hashish smugglers from Indochina and Afghanistan) maybe $4–5, the rest is profit in the USA (ibid. 117 and 214). Both this trade and the legal prescription drugs pushed by oligopolic pharmaceutical industry are predicated on unregulated research and massive international distribution. By the end of the 1990s, drug-related activities constituted ca. 2–6 percent of the world Gross Product and well over 10 percent of world trade, and were (with arms) the most profitable world commodity (George 166–67).

There is a special bond between drugs and war (also professional sports). Not to discuss the Opium Wars against China, stimulants were massively given to soldiers from World War II to the drugged US armies today, while narcodollars finance the lords of war, from the CIA organization of the Indochina heroin trade in the 1970s and Afghanistan to the UCK guerrillas in Kosovo.

9.2

All beliefs and evaluations modify the mind, with appropriate biochemical reactions inside it. There is little reason not to call drugging such relational proceedings (and not only discrete substances) as inflect people's judgment away from fundamental interests of bodily and social salvation. These proceedings also fall under William Burroughs's addictive "junk," the ideal commodity because the "junk merchant" begins by moulding the consumer: "He degrades and simplifies the client" (xxxix). I shall here mention only the brainwashing by means of *Disneyfication*: in developed capitalism, all roads lead to the Rome of bending the mind, and a proper part can stand for the whole.

I argue at length in Chapter 9, and will here only briefly repeat and bring to a point, that Disneyfication is a drug that does not function by introduction of chemical substances into the brain but by channelling adult imagination into infantilism. It works by emotional empathy into comic-book figures that propagate cheeriness, affluence, consumerism, and technoscientific progress – a simplified ideology pretending to be suburban or exotic utopia while occulting labour, hunger, lack of shelter, disease, sex or death. It is a degenerate utopia, where the succession of thrilling fake novums pre-empts radical novelty. It is abetted and massively involved in TV and other media, where the viewer is cut off from the producing of (or in) them and positioned within a mass of atomized fellow-viewers, so that an incessant desire to consume is the only participation in the social process. The abiding alienation of labour and political disempowerment is channelled into a rage for addictive consuming. There is a deep subterranean bond between the starving bellies and bacterial epidemics among the masses of the global South, and the starving minds and drugging epidemics moulding us in the North. Disneyland is a pioneering *pars pro toto* of the capitalist and especially US admass brainwash. Its central spring is what I have called *reproductive empathy*, where "the commercial glance into the heart of things [...] demolishes the space for the free play of viewing" by abolishing any critical distance (Benjamin, *Gesammelte Schriften* IV.1: 131–32). This empathy is consubstantial to transfer ideologizing, "naturalizing" and shutting out historical time as the space of alternative choices, while the foreign/ers and the natural world become the primitive, the savage, and the monstrous; and to substitution commodifying, producing a transmogrified reality by hallucinatory channelling of desire. The pervasive upshot of Disneyland is that the pursuit of happiness becomes a lifetime of shopping.

Disneyfication is a shaping of affective investment into commodifying which reduces the mind to infantilism as an illusory escape from death.

Wedge 10/ Against Apocalypse

> What is here dealt with can scarcely be presented as doctrinal opinion, certainly not as system. It seems rather a precipitate of an inalienable experience that permeates all considerations. It means that methodic stringency is worth its name only when it includes into its horizon not only experiments within the segregated lab space but also those within the free space of history.
>
> — WALTER BENJAMIN

10.1

The "cannon fodder" or mortified meat in wars, prostitution, and drugging, the mass casualties, are as a rule the oppressed of "White" patriarchal
capitalism: all the poor, most "coloureds," most women. (The exceptions,
such as the British ruling class sacrificing much of its own youth in World
War I or Stalinist despotic bureaucracy murdering off the Old Bolsheviks,
are rare, for they lead to that class's loss of mastery.) "Lower" class, race,
as well as gender expendability – paired with nauseatingly sentimental
hypocrisy, beginning (say) with Man Friday – reign: and especially when
these "non-independent" categories overlap in, say, Black members of US
armed forces or prostitutes displaced into big cities (see Davis) or indeed
prostitutes and other hangers-on servicing soldiers in poorer countries
(the "comfort women" for the Japanese Imperial Army, and today the mass
prostitution around US and UN forces abroad, from the Philippines to
Bosnia). "Colored, sexed, and laboring persons" are denied epistemological visibility and thus political agency (Haraway 32, and see 26–30), they
have traditionally not been Cartesian and Lockean "individuals" (who
were, before the onset of counterrevolutionary hypocrisy in the nineteenth
century, forthrightly defined as those who have possessions). They bear
the full weight of the enforcement of super-profits, the degradation, and
the legal persecution that with the advent of imperialism shift from the
dangerously organized male White industrial workers and intellectuals
(who advance to privileged bearers of social-democratic reformism) to the
unemployed, the "criminal," and the female people – as well as the colonial
and semi-colonial vanquished in the wars (see Marcuse 134 and passim,
Haug 190 and passim). For one relatively small example, there are at least
27 million slaves – people held by violence for economic exploitation – in
the world (Bales 23 and 280), not counting prostitutes. Both the social-
democratic and the communist movements catastrophically undervalued
the significance of this change in exploitation targeting a non-factory proletariat (though the Bolsheviks were, at their revolutionary beginning, the
first to indicate it).

10.2

War – drugs – brainwashing: these are the present dispensation's Three Riders of the Apocalypse. War is the first rider: the determining spring of life under capitalism is a continuation of war by other means. Foucault penetratingly asked: "isn't power simply a form of warlike domination [...] a sort of generalized war which assumes at particular moments the forms of peace and State?" (123). Technoscience is perhaps not simply war, as Latour sometimes implies, yet at least it is intimately shaped by use for war, literal and metaphorical. But this unnatural state of affairs generates so much misery that drugs and brainwashing have to be resorted to, in the finally vain endeavour to find a breathing space, to shut out Death. Capitalist civilization reposes on insoluble contradiction between a boundless increase of productive forces and boundless economic and psychic immiseration of people: its main product is the production of destructive novums, "undermining of the springs of all wealth: the earth and the worker" (Marx, *Kapital. Werke* 23: 530). Capital practices "systematic robbery of the preconditions for life [...], of space, air, light [...]" (ibid. 449–50), and today we could add water, silence, health in general, etc. – in fact, life and the pursuit of happiness. Post-Fordist condemnation of two thirds of adult population globally (and one third in the "rich" countries) to unemployment or piecework is a further robbery of vitality during people's youth, to be paid for in their middle and late years by defencelessness against disease and early dying. Thus behind the three riders, as always, the fourth and main one advances, *Death* as this civilization's final horizon. As Benjamin exemplarily argued on the traces of Baudelaire and Balzac, Death is the only end of gambling, excitement, novelty – of the commodity customer's experience and time horizon (for example, *Gesammelte Schriften* I.2: 668). It is clearly also the end-horizon of raping the planet by economic exploitation and ecocide. This is not the easeful death each of us has a right to: it is the collective death of humanity.

Whence such myopic folly, differing from any past dying empire only in its speed-of-light propagation? Probably it is intrinsic to the thirst for power. When Freud speculated during World War I that "the impulse of cruelty arises from the instinct of mastery" (59), we might reject obfuscating terms such as instinct but see that he put his finger on a centrally sore point. (He also rightly saw as the counter-pole an "instinct for knowledge or research" – 60.) While this is as old as class society and patriarchy, it was never so powerful, unnecessary, and necrophilic as in capitalism, driven by the unending "fix" of profits. And in particular amid the perfectly sinful Post-Fordist wars, prostitution, and druggings.

10.3

What are we, who should still call ourselves the Left, and whose conscious core should perhaps think again about assuming communism as its poetry and prose, then to do? To begin with: strive to understand and minimize the ruling-class apocalypse; look for ways to counteract the blights in articulated and organized ways. Since all blights are semiotically and materially interwoven, the only possible response to any of them is one that does not hinder a response to any other among them. Beside pragmatic reasons of achieving oppositional critical mass, Gramsci's "historical bloc" (which would itself be enough), this is what makes it necessary to shun sectarian politics like the plague, even by such potentially large groups like super-exploited women. Separatisms – the defunct *ouvrierisme* (reliance on industrial workers only, today noticeably diminished by automatization) and countryside "Maoism"; macho, feminist, and generation separatism; etc. – are the worst internal enemy of radical politics. Rainbow politics could be a good name if it is understood that while the colours are separate, so that organizing around issues limited to a given "identity" may be locally useful as a first step, the rainbow is one.

Finally (the snake bites its tail): the political equivalent of this whole endeavour of mine is the fact that the "professional-managerial" class is today – as Bloch argued in 1938 for the intelligentsia in the industrialized states (343) – the one indispensable ally in any historical bloc, say with the working classes and women, which would have a chance to get off the ground. An ally is NOT a servant: it is somebody with whom one can disagree but has strategic interests in common, a community of destiny against the terrorism of capital (see Lefebvre, *Cybernanthrope* 56–57) which may supply criteria for resolving the disagreement. And the criteria have to be built up with contributions by each. We "professionals" are professionally trained to formulate such criteria – if we can shake off capitalist corruption and listen to political experiences from below. For, "any erroneous understanding of truth is simultaneously an erroneous understanding of freedom" (Marcuse 147).

This is what the present writing, however awkwardly, attempts to clear the ground for.[4]

Works Cited

The titles are listed by the first "Wedge" in which they occur. Suggestions from Benjamin, Bloch, Brecht, Marx, and Nietzsche (where not noted in the bibliography, he is cited from *Werke*, Leipzig: Naumann, 1900–13) are too frequent to be recorded. The bibliography has been updated in 2008.

Wedge 1

Brecht, Bertolt. *Werke. Grosse kommentierte Berliner und Frankfurter Ausgabe.* 33 vols. Berlin: Aufbau, and Frankfurt: Suhrkamp, 1988–98. [cited as *GBFA*]
Deleuze, Gilles. "Intellectuals and Power." *Language, Counter-memory, Practice: Selected Essays and Interviews.* Ed. and trans. Donald F. Bouchard and Sherry Simon. Ithaca, New York: Cornell University Press, 1977.
Hegel, Georg F.W. *Werke.* 20 vols. Frankfurt: Suhrkamp, 1969–71.

---

4   My thanks go to Babette Babich, Matt Beaumont, Eugenio Bolongaro, Heather Keenleyside, and especially to Alcena Rogan. They may not share some or all of my horizon.

Lefebvre, Henri. *The Production of Space*. Trans. Donald Nicholson-Smith. Oxford: Blackwell, 1997.

Nietzsche, Friedrich. *Also sprach Zarathustra. Ein Buch für alle und keinen*. München: Goldmann, 1992.

Prieto, Luis. *Pertinence et pratique*. Paris: Minuit, 1975.

Suvin, Darko. "On Cognitive Emotions and Topological Imagination." *Versus* 68–69 (1994): 165–201.

——. "Emotion, Brecht, Empathy vs. Sympathy." *Brecht Yearbook* 33 (2008): 53–67.

——. "*Haltung* (Bearing) and Emotions: Brecht's Refunctioning of Conservative Metaphors for Agency." *Zweifel – Fragen – Vorschläge: Bertolt Brecht anlässlich des Einhundertsten*. Ed. T. Jung. Frankfurt: Peter Lang, 1999, 43–58.

Wedge 2

Anders, Günter. *Die Antiquiertheit des Menschen*. 2 vols. München: Beck, 1994–95.

[Benjamin, Walter.] *The Correspondence of Walter Benjamin 1910–1940*. Ed. Gershom Scholem and Theodor W. Adorno. Trans. Manfred R. and Evelyn M. Jacobson. Chicago: University of Chicago Press, 1994.

Bloch, Ernst. *Gesamtausgabe*, 16 vols. Frankfurt: Suhrkamp, 1959ff.

Bodei, Remo. *Dekompositionen*. Stuttgart-Bad Cannstatt: Frommann-Holzboog, 1996.

Deleuze, Gilles. *Proust et les signes*, 4th edn. Paris: PUF, 1976.

Gramsci, Antonio. *Quaderni del carcere*. 5 vols. Ed. Valentino Gerratana. Turin: Einaudi, 1975.

Gray, Chris Hables. *Postmodern War*. New York: Guilford, 1997.

Hegel, Georg F.W. *Wissenschaft der Logik*. 2 vols. Ed. Georg Lasson. Leipzig: Meiner, 1948.

Lefebvre, Henri. *Vers le Cybernanthrope*. Paris: Denoël-Gonthier, 1971.

Lenin, Vladimir I. *Philosophical Notebooks. Collected Works*. Vol. 38. Moscow: Progress, 1981.

Levidow, Les, and Kevin Robbins (eds). *Cyborg Worlds: The Military Information Society*. London: Free Association Books, 1989.

Marcus, Alan I., and Howard P. Segal. *Technology in America*. San Diego: HBJ, 1989.

Marx, Karl. *Grundrisse*. Trans. Martin Nicolaus. New York: Vintage, 1973.

Nietzsche, Friedrich. *Twilight of the Idols*. Trans. Richard Polt. Indianapolis: Hackett, 1997.

[OED] The Compact Oxford English Dictionary. Oxford: Clarendon Press, 1991.

Ross, Andrew. *Strange Weather*. London: Verso, 1991.

Suvin, Darko. "On Metaphoricity and Narrativity in Fiction." *SubStance* 48 (1986): 51–67.

——. "Two Cheers for Essentialism and Totality: Marx's Oscillation and its Limits." *Rethinking Marxism* 10: 1 (1998): 62–78.

Wedge 3

Foucault, Michel. *Power/ Knowledge*. Ed. Colin Gordon. New York: Pantheon Books, 1980.

Gombrich, Ernst. "Standards of Truth." *The Image and the Eye*. Oxford: Phaidon, 1982. 244–77.

Goodman, Nelson, and Catherine Z. Elgin. *Reconceptions in Philosophy and Other Arts and Sciences*. Indianapolis and Cambridge: Hackett, 1988.

Haraway, Donna J. *Modest_Witness@Second_Millennium*. New York: Routledge, 1997.

Harré, R[om]. *The Philosophies of Science*. London: Oxford University Press, 1972.

Laudan, Larry. *Progress and Its Problems: Towards a Theory of Scientific Growth*. Berkeley: University of California Press, 1978.

Marcuse, Herbert. *One-Dimensional Man*. Boston: Beacon, 1964.

Noble, David. *A World Without Women: The Christian Clerical Culture of Western Science*. New York: Oxford University Press, 1992.

Suvin, Darko. *Lessons of Japan*. Montreal: CIADEST, 1996.

Wedge 4

Benjamin, Walter. *Gesammelte Schriften.* Frankfurt: Suhrkamp, 1982–.
Buck-Morss, Susan. *The Dialectics of Seeing.* Cambridge, MA: MIT Press, 1995.
Chaitin, Gregory. *Information Randomness and Incompleteness.* New York: World Scientific, 1987.
Daly, Herman E., and John B. Cobb, Jr. *For the Common Good.* Boston: Beacon, 1989.
Gendlin, Eugene T. "Thinking Beyond Patterns." *The Presence of Feeling in Thought.* Ed. Bernard denOuden and Marcia Moen. New York: Peter Lang, 1991. 27–189.
Jameson, Fredric. *Postmodernism, or, The Cultural Logic of Late Capitalism.* Durham: Duke University Press, 1992.
Marx, Karl, and Friedrich Engels. *Werke (MEW).* Berlin: Dietz, 1962–.
Nietzsche, Friedrich. *Philosophy and Truth: Selections from Nietzsche's Notebooks of the Early 1870s.* Ed. and trans. Daniel Breazeale. Atlantic Highlands: Humanities, 1979.
Rucker, Rudy. *Mind Tools.* Boston: Houghton Mifflin, 1987.
Wiener, Norbert. *The Human Use of Human Beings.* Garden City: Doubleday, 1954.

Wedge 5

Berman, Marshall. *All That Is Solid Melts Into Air.* New York: Simon and Schuster, 1982.
Bolongaro, Eugenio. E-mail response to D. Suvin. 17 December 1997.
Rosa Luxemburg Speaks. Ed. Mary-Alice Waters. New York: Pathfinder, 1970.
Marx, Karl. *Das Kapital. Erster Band. MEW.* Vol. 23. Berlin: Dietz, 1993.
[——.]. *The Marx–Engels Reader.* Ed. Robert C. Tucker. New York: Norton.

Nietzsche, Friedrich. *Birth of Tragedy*. Trans. Walter Kaufmann. New York: Vintage, 1967.

Suvin, Darko. "Preliminary Theses on Allegory." *Umjetnost riječi* 1–3 (1977): 197–99.

——, and Marc Angenot. "L'aggirarsi degli spettri. Metafore e demifisticazioni, ovvero l'implicito del manifesto." *Le soglie del fantastico*. Ed. Marina Galletti. Roma: Lithos, 1997. 129–66.

Wedge 7

Drèze, Jean, and Amartya Sen. *Hunger and Public Action*. Oxford: Clarendon Press, 1989.

Human Development Report 1996. Ed. UN Development Programme. New York and London: Oxford University Press, 1996.

Human Development Report 1998. Ed. UN Development Programme. New York and London: Oxford University Press, 1998.

Mesnard y Mendez, Pierre. "Capitalism Means / Needs War." *Socialism and Democracy* 16.2 (2002): 65–92.

Suvin, Darko. "De la guerre 2001: triomphe du capitalisme sauvage." *La Chute du Mur de Berlin dans les idéologies*. Ed. Marc Angenot and Régine Robin. Montréal: *Discours social 6*, n.s. no. 6, 2002. 161–74.

——. "Sulle 'nuove guerre' identitario-territoriali." *Giano* 55 (2007): 45–53.

Wedge 8

Bell, Shannon. *Reading, Writing, and Rewriting the Prostitute Body*. Bloomington: Indiana University Press, 1994.

Chessler, Phyllis, and Emily Jane Goodman. *Women, Money and Power*. New York: Morrow, 1976.

Delacoste, Frédérique, and Priscilla Alexander (eds). *Sex Work: Writings by Women in the Sex Industry*. Pittsburgh: Cleis, 1987.

Goldmann, Emma. *The Traffic in Women and Other Essays on Feminism.* Ojai: Times Change, 1990.

"In the Shadows." *The Economist* 26 August 2000: 38–39.

Marx, Karl. "Economic and Philosophic Manuscripts (1844)." *The Writings of the Young Marx on Philosophy and Society.* Ed. and trans. Loyd D. Easton and Kurt H. Guddat. Garden City: Doubleday, 1967. 283–337.

McLeod, Eileen. *Women Working: Prostitution Now.* London and Canberra: Croom Helm, 1982.

Millett, Kate (ed.). *The Prostitution Papers.* New York: Ballantine, 1976.

Parent-Duchatelet, Alexandre J.B. *De la prostitution dans la ville de Paris.* 2 vols. Paris: Baillière, 1836.

Pateman, Carole. *The Sexual Contract.* Cambridge: Polity, 1988.

Rubin, Gayle. "Thinking Sex." *Pleasure and Danger: Exploring Female Sexuality.* Ed. Carole S. Vance. Boston: Routledge, 1984. 279–308.

Suvin, Darko. "Two Holy Commodities: The Practices of Fictional Discourse and Erotic Discourse." *Sociocriticism* 2 (1985): 31–47.

Wedge 9

For books about Disney and Disneyfication see Chapter 9 in this book.

Burroughs, William. *Naked Lunch.* New York: Grove, 1966.

Delbrel, Guy (ed.). *Géopolitique de la drogue.* Paris: La Découverte, 1991.

George, Susan. *The Lugano Report.* London: Pluto, 1999.

Suvin, Darko. "Terms of Power, Today: An Essay in Political Epistemology." *Critical Quarterly* 48.3 (2006): 38–62.

United Methodist Church. *Drugs and the Economic Crisis: Intricate Web.* Cincinnati: Task Force on the Economic Crisis, 1990.

Wedge 10

Bales, Kevin. *Disposable People*. Berkeley: University of California Press, 1999.

Bloch, Ernst. "Der Intellektuelle und die Politik." *Vom Hasard zur Katastrophe*. Frankfurt: Suhrkamp, 1972. 336–43.

Davis, Angela Y. *Women, Race and Class*. New York: Random House, 1981.

Freud, Sigmund. *Three Essays on the Theory of Sexuality*. Ed. and trans. James Strachey. New York: Basic Books, 1975.

Haug, Wolfgang Fritz. *Politisch richtig oder richtig politisch*. Hamburg: Argument, 1999.

Latour, Bruno. *Science in Action*. Cambridge, MA: Harvard University Press, 1987.

Marcuse, Herbert. *Feindesanalysen*. Lüneburg: zu Klampen, 1998.

CHAPTER 11

What Remains of Zamyatin's *We* After the Change of Leviathans? Or, Must Collectivism Be Against People? (1999–2000)[1]

To Saša Flaker and Mike Holquist, as they were in the 1950s–1960s, friends from whom I learned much

The Revolution – that is: I – not alone, but we.

— A.A. BLOK, diary note

1   I am responsible for non-attributed translation. Except for direct quotes and the book title, arguments about the philosophical "We" and "I" in and out of Zamyatin are always put into quotes with initial caps. The characters D-503 and I-330 are named (or "numbered") in full the first time they occur in any paragraph, and after that only as D- and I-. A few more words may be useful about the "braided" structure I experimentally adopted in this essay, which focuses in sections 1, 3, and 5 on the text of the novel *We*, interweaving this in sections 2, 4, and 6 with the changed state of Russia today and how this changes our eyes, that is, our view of the 1921 novel. This spiral shuttling back and forth is held together by the central concern of Zamyatin's, which has not ceased to be of interest even though its terms have more or less shifted, the discussion of the State Leviathan "We" vs. the individualist "I". This was an attempt to escape what I have increasingly felt as the ghetto of Idealist literary studies and esthetics, which take history into account only if it is the history of other books and writings. This seems to me the bad, alas also increasingly weighty, aspect of our professionalism and specialization, rashly aping natural sciences (who are anyway running into serious problems themselves). While I cannot claim for this article more than presenting one attempt at coping, it seemed much preferable to not trying anything, or (obversely) emigrating from literary studies.

I see in the near future a crisis approaching that unnerves me and makes
me tremble for my country [...]. Corporations have been enthroned and
an era of high corruption will follow [...].

     — A. LINCOLN, letter to Col. W.F. Elkins

The case against saying we seems overwhelming [...]. The epistemological and political need to say we remains, however. Neither a theory nor
a politics of irreducible singularity seems very promising.

     — N. SCHEMAN, "The Body Politic"

0. Premise

First premise (epistemological): the rereading of a text which, within radically altered circumstances of a reader, suddenly begins to look significantly
different – prompting perhaps a reconsideration of the ethical, political or
other values earlier allotted to it by the same reader – poses a puzzle about
the nature of textual meaning. It foregrounds an axiom of semiotics which
seems counter-intuitive only because our "intuition" has been shaped by

---

Note 2003: I have resisted the temptation to change this essay for two reasons,
pertaining to the twin focus and organization of the essay, evident in the opposition
between the odd and even sections. First, the writings on Zamyatin seem to have
more or less dried out, now that he is not at the forefront of Kremlinology; at any
rate I'm not aware of significant additions to the arguments I cite (say about I-330).
Second, the statistics on Russia would of course change in four years, but its economical polarization, which brings immiseration to many, probably most people, is going
on (see now Stiglitz, chapter 5), aggravated by the senseless and counterproductive
war in Chechnya.

Note 2006: Material for this essay was assembled around 1999, at what was probably the economic nadir of Russia. Today, the life expectance for males has risen, back
from fifty-five to fifty-nine years ... And there are many more millionaires, gangsters,
and prostitutes than in 1999.

positivistic prejudice: there is no object-"text" out there, independent of the collective or allegorical subject-eyes beholding it. (This does not mean there is nothing out there!) I will be speaking here of a novel, but text may be taken in the semiotic sense of any articulated signic entity able to stand still for the purpose of analysis. No fixed and unmoving central text, analogous to Ptolemy's Earth or to an unsplittable atom or personality, can be opposed to an environing "context" (or even the more recent and modish "intertext"); unless one is to say that the context permeates the text by existing beneath and between each sign-unit and determining their shapes and meanings. Such is the case of the context of any specific sociolect within natural language: Russian or English or indeed the Spanish of Pierre Ménard's word by word reconstruction of Cervantes's *Don Quijote* which nonetheless gives the nineteenth-century reader, as Borges rightly argues, a quite different novel from the reader of Cervantes's age. A text, in brief, exists in the interaction of signifiers visible on its surface with the individual or collective beholder, who allots signification and meaning to the ensemble and articulation of the signifiers. All text studies – and thus also, perhaps more clearly than other genres, SF studies – are historico-semiotic studies, or if you wish cultural studies.

Second premise (political): we have gone through – the globe is still going through – a change of Leviathans that rule and subsume us, which might be dated with 1991 in Russia as the final stage of a world-historical change datable (maybe) with 1973. I extrapolate "Leviathan" from Hobbes's meaning to that of any collective, politico-economic as well as ideological, hegemony, the World Whale inside which all of us are condemned to live. The transfer into the entrails of a new – but just as pernicious and probably more murderous – whale is surely of the utmost significance for understanding the position of all of us under the missing stars.[2] In a dialec-

---

2   After the first draft of this article I read Michael R. Krätke's excellent analysis of the limits of globalization (esp. 40–55), which proves that the multinational corporations have fully globalized only the currency and capital markets. The ca. 600 big corporations and "institutional investors" are owned and managed, and further they produce, research, and invest, overwhelmingly in one zone of the "triad" (North America, Europe, Japan and East Asia), indeed 80 out of the 100 biggest ones mainly

tical furthermore, this orientation can be of use as a defence against being totally digested by the devouring global whale, the capitalist socioeconomic formation in its new Post-Fordist shape, and indeed as modestly emboldening us to work toward preparing its downfall, from an assumed point of view based upon lineaments of some different, better, today necessarily utopian collective. Wallerstein argues that the prevailing loss of ideological ascendancy and even legitimacy by the State is a prelude to the downfall of the capitalist world-system, since the latter has never been able to exist only through the Invisible Hand of the Market without crucial State support to weaken the claims of the workers, transfer citizens' taxes to the capitalists, and defend them against stronger "foreign" competitors (32, 46–47, and passim). Whether this view may be too optimistic or not, it is at any rate crucial to understand the metamorphosis of Leviathan. And what better way to this than by feedback from a classic view of him?

It follows that our very ambiguously new Post-Fordist age – a return of the stalest meat spiced with the sharpest sauces – unambiguously forces an awake critic into new ways of envisaging and talking about text/context. The new ways have unfortunately not been fully worked out by anybody that I can see. The best I can do is to adopt a "braided" structure, which should not be too surprising for readers of Le Guin's *The Dispossessed*, Piercy's *He, She and It*, the Strugatskys' *Snail on the Slope* (see Chapter 18 and Suvin, *Positions* Chapter 11) or the even more complex shuttling in Russ's *Female Man* – as well as for readers of verse, say with the a-b-a-b rhyme. Indeed

---

in one country; exceptions can be found in the food and drink, computer, and some other consumer goods firms (McDonald's!). Based on such data, the splendid book by Kagarlitsky rightly argues that "the [...] argument about 'the impotence of the state'" both hides its abuse by financial capital and hobbles struggles for a countervailing, democratic nation-state (vi and passim; see also Went 48–50). I dissent only from his analysis of the Bosnian civil war and a few other, minor matters. Amongst them is his term of "New Big Brother" rather than New Leviathan: true, it is more immediately comprehensible but also, as I argue in Section 4, much too personalized for the capillary politics of globalization.

perhaps the compositional principle of all fictional utopias (including dystopias) is necessarily the braiding of showing and telling, lecture and action. And if you believe, as I have often argued, that all SF is not only historically a niece of utopia but is also ineluctably written between the poles of utopia and dystopia, then to the degree this is correct, it further follows that such braiding or more generally patching is also the compositional principle of SF.

All of this finally means that the pretence at a "final" explanation of anything has been well lost. But my project is even more modest: I think it may be too early to achieve a full new overview of *We* (for one thing, most regrettably, many writings by Zamyatin still remain inaccessible or indeed unpublished), and I wish this contribution to be simply a first shot across the bows by a devil's advocate – whom my subject himself would salute as necessary.[3]

---

3   A smattering of letters to and about Zamyatin was published in Russia and abroad beginning with the *glasnost* years. Yet there is still a great deal of unpublished writings by him in the archives at Columbia University, in Paris – including a ten-page film synopsis of *We* called *D-503* from 1932 – and in Russia.

It might also be useful to immerse Zamyatin more decisively into his precise locus. First of all, *We* and some of his most significant essays were written in and as a response to the period of War Communism ca. 1917–21, the time of fierce military struggle, direct State dictatorship, and the crudest collectivist hyperboles (for example by the "proletarian" poets and the enthusiasts for Taylorism); Stalin's post-1928 or post-1934 reign of terror is a rather different period – for one thing, open opposition à la Zamyatin was not tolerated any more. There are indications that a number of Zamyatin's later and not yet fully accessible works (as the unfinished novel about Attila) again turned to a critique of the West. Second, he would profit from much more comparison to his contemporary Futurist poets or Constructivist painters (see Heller); and within SF and utopia/dystopia, only some first parallels have been drawn to two other major Russian SF works of the 1920s with world-historical horizons, deeply preoccupied with, respectful of, yet not necessarily starry-eyed about the price of revolutionary politics – Alexey Tolstoy's *Aelita* and Ilya Ehrenburg's *Trust D.E.* (see Striedter). All three were written by intellectuals who had been living not only in Russia but also in western Europe, of which they were rather critical. All three oscillated in their attitude toward the Bolshevik authorities, Zamyatin being the most resolutely and stridently critical of them.

For Zamyatin himself was and constantly remained both a convinced heretic and a convinced utopian socialist.[4]

So then: just how different is today, after the sea-change of whales inside which we Lucians, Sindbads, Pantagruels or Nemos live, the text of Zamyatin's novel *We*? For one question, which is a technical way of putting it within the debates of Utopian Studies: is it still a living "anti-utopian" novel when nobody can even pretend that the utopia it was "anti" to is still a major, observable actuality?

I

It is well known (and rehearsed from Gregg to Beauchamp) that *We* takes its central agential constellation as well as some of the most important value horizons from a heretical reworking of the orthodox Christian myth of Eden, which echoes powerfully in Milton and Dostoevsky.[5] In mildly

4   A remarkable unpublished article draft from 1921 propounds: "Only those who do not believe or insufficiently believe in socialism want an orthodox socialist literature and fear unorthodox literature. I believe. I know: socialism is inevitable. It has already ceased to be a utopia, and precisely because of this it is the business of true literature to build new utopias. [...] [T]he future has become the present, it has acquired flesh, earth, steel, it has become heavy, current – and that is why it no longer [...] carries the pathos of utopia and imagination – so that it is necessary to build for man a new utopia of tomorrow and the day after tomorrow" (Russian original in Malm'stad and Fleishman 107–08).

5   So far as I am aware, having followed criticism on Zamyatin in the main European languages, most critics – many of whom are listed in the bibliography of *Metamorphoses* – who speak about his relation to Dostoevsky mention only aspects from *The Brothers Karamazov*, *The Possessed*, and *Notes from the Underground* (but see the pioneering Shane). Yet Zamyatin knew his Dostoevsky very well indeed, and I think a thorough confrontation of *We* with Dostoevsky's whole opus is a desideratum that one hopes the Slavists could put high up on their agenda, just after the publication of Zamyatin's collected works, even though grants might have dried up. It would be a shame if we had to find out that most Slavists had in reality been more interested in Cold War Kremlinology than in literary cognition when they extolled Zamyatin.

semiotic or narratological terms, and confining myself solely to paradigmatic aspects, one could characterize it as a conflict between a Protagonist (God) – who is both the supreme power and the supreme value – and an Antagonist (Satan as the Serpent tempter) over the Pentateuch's and the Bible's overriding Value – the obedience of Man (Adam) to God. I find it useful for further discussion to present this as a little graph:

Table 1: Agential Constellation behind *We*

SCHEME OF CONFLICT

Protagonist, force ⟵⟶ Antagonist, anti-force

Value, stake

BIBLE–MILTON

God ⟵⟶ Satan

Adam   Eve

Salvation of mankind

Already in *Paradise Lost* Satan had ambiguously acquired some traits of a political heretic not too dissimilar from examples in the English Revolution of Milton's age; focussing on those traits, Blake could then read Milton as being of the Devil's party without knowing it, and Mary Shelley could rework the Miltonic template into Dr Frankenstein as a bungling and culpable Creator vs. his Creature as a righteous antagonist more sinned against than sinning. This may suffice here as a shorthand to indicate how, between Milton and Zamyatin, the huge earthquakes of the second, overtly political series of revolutions, centered on 1789 and its results, had changed the landscape. The great lesson from the failure of the radical *citoyen* project, from the bourgeois compromise with the old rulers, was for the Romantics that the heaven's god(s) turned tyrants. Some of the best Blake or Percy Shelley belongs here, while Byron's and then Baudelaire's pseudo-Satanism, echoing throughout European culture, is the strategic hinge to all later *poètes maudits*. Russian poetry (from Pushkin and Lermontov to Zamyatin's elder contemporaries) and the equally great prose of "Romantic realism" after Gogol (see Fanger) were powerfully swimming in the same current, in ways exasperated by a country which had not managed even an initial bourgeois revolution. Theirs was a bitter protest, sometimes revolutionary but in the *fin-de-siècle* Symbolists more and more just privately (for example, erotically) blasphemous – even though its principal names, Bryusov and Blok, came to sympathize more or less actively with the October Revolution. As a rule, the world "out there" was felt as offensive and the real values as residing in the poetic persona's "inner" creativity – Shelley's ambivalent "caverns of the mind" (in Frye 211), or in the Symbolist poet as hypnotic visionary.

Zamyatin became – as did his colleagues Belyi and Bulgakov – a "terminal point" (to adapt the argument for *1984* in Frye 204) of this Romantic subversion. Substituting life in the Unique State, a futuristic glass city walled-in against the outside "Green World" (supposedly because of devastation in century-long wars), to life in the Garden of Eden, he followed the Romantics by resolutely disjoining power and goodness in the new agent that took the place of God as both ruler and addressee of people's absolute worship – the totally planned State, and its head and symbol, the dictator Benefactor, "the new Jehovah, coming down to us from heaven" (140).

Even further, if we take the proper narratological approach that the Protagonist is that agential force which initiates most of the narrated action, the new Protagonist is laicized from God to Man: as in *Frankenstein*, he is a male scientist-creator, the mathematician D-503, chief constructor of the first spacecraft whose possession is supposed (rather vaguely) to ensure victory to the possessing side. As in Blake, Percy Shelley or Byron, he is faced with tyrannical paternal authority; but he will also, as in the more conservative Mary Shelley, get faced with his own inadequacies. The Powers-That-Be still rule, but their basis in Man's obedience is in the story both shown as increasingly shaken and shown up as simply repressive: their dogmatic pretence to divine infallibility, transferred from Christianity to science, has turned them into the negative Antagonist, taking the place of Satan from the Judeo-Christian myth. The new Adam is not only an exemplary (that is, primarily allegorical) Protagonist, but also his own supreme Value. This constellation, prefigured in Frankenstein's Creature, is here derived from the Man-God Jesus opposed to the Church as Power in Dostoevsky's Grand Inquisitor legend (see Gregg 66–67), but Zamyatin's atheist individualism reduces salvation to what narratology calls narcissism. It is articulated as obedience to the protagonist D-503's own (that is, humanity's) sensual or "shaggy" nature, which is therefore easily swayed by the supposedly Satanic (but in Zamyatin liberatory) figures from the Miltonic model. The ideal goal or *salus*, the Grail of this quest, is not sinless life in a renewed Paradise but the dismantling of the fake paradise of all-pervasive, Leviathanic politics in favour of either passionate life and/or a freer or more "natural" political life. The salvation of the allegorical Protagonist lies no longer in listening to a collective, institutionally codified and enforced story but in fashioning a new story for himself through sexual passion which is magically analogous to ideological heresy and political subversion; erotics takes the place of theology and largely of politics also:

Table 2: Agential Constellation in *We*

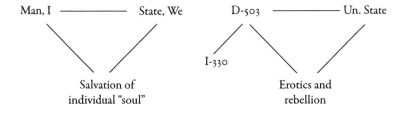

This is not only a most ingenious refashioning of the best-known narrative constellation or "master narrative" of European culture from Palestine to the industrial and bourgeois revolutions. It is also articulated in a masterly, almost Cubist texture of splinters (see Parrinder 137 and my brief discussion in *Metamorphoses*), which has aged as well as the best wine. Further, it also reuses, through the sole narrator's (tardy) education by events, possibly the second most powerful European narrative. It is the story which spelled the religious one in bourgeois individualism from Bunyan and Fielding on, was best codified probably in Goethe's *Wilhelm Meister*, and meandered through innumerable variants down to Heinlein and today – the hero's voyage to a true understanding of himself, the "educational novel" (*Bildungsroman*) of what might be called individualistic religion. The hero is simultaneously – and not wholly convincingly – "humanly" representative and yet atomically individual, an investment of the authors' core personal values and yet an example for all the readers insofar as they are all supposed to be individuals, only individuals, and nothing but individuals. In the best Modernist and dystopian fashion, the educational voyage is at the unhappy end aborted, but its values should have inoculated the reader. We approach here possibly the central contradiction or *aporia* of individualism, clearly shared by Zamyatin: In the end, we are all unsplittable atoms (say of hydrogen), but every atom is possessed of a different, unique, and most precious soul. And yet the soul needs exterior validation – God, or more prosaically, social life (see Marx's *Holy Family* 148 and passim).

Finally, Zamyatin throws into this rich mix the pairing of the Protagonist with an erotic seductress. I shall return to this in section 5.

2

However, if my argument at the beginning, that the "contextual" side shapes all parts and aspects of the text, has any merit, the long duration model of the preceding Section is always renewed by major synchronic constraints produced in a new historical period. In order to attend to this overriding determination, I propose to you my (not at all original, I am happy to say) first sketch of the change of Leviathans. It will not have the elegance of Zamyatin's construction but it may have the persuasiveness of recognizability. I will begin the closest I can to the new dispensation of global Post-Fordist rule, and my initial argument is taken from an internet article by Michel Chossudovsky. He is not alone in arguing that we are in the midst of a possible worldwide crisis whose scale already makes it "more devastating than the Great Depression of the 1930s. It has far-reaching geopolitical implications; economic dislocation has been accompanied by the outbreak of regional conflicts, [...] and in some cases the destruction of entire countries. This is by far the most serious economic crisis in modern history."[6]

It is not simply that, in what I see as an omen, 2,300 billion dollars of "paper profits" could in a few weeks after mid-July 1998 evaporate from the US stock market: a plague on its house (except that we all live in this house). More to the point right here, since we are speaking about Russia, from 1992 to 1998 "some 500 billion dollars worth of Russian assets – including plants of the military-industrial complex, infrastructure and natural resources – have been confiscated (through the privatization programmes and forced bankruptcies)" (2). They have been plundered by new domestic as well as the Western speculative capitalists, not interested in long-term investment and production but only in immediate profit: the percentage of investments into durable production is half of the US one, so that productive fixed capital is being reduced by 5–10 percent of Russian GDP per year. The industrial production, the GDP, and the real wages have since the collapse of the USSR plummeted by at least half, and continue to fall. The Russian median income in 2000 was ca. 50 US$ a month and also falling: incomplete estimates put the majority of population in present-day Russia, that is more than 80 million people, under the poverty threshold,

6   Chossudovsky, "Financial," "electronic p." 1; further cited by the number of "virtual page." Chossudovsky is professor of economics in Ottawa; see also for Russia his *Globalisation*, chapter 11. My thanks to him for generously permitting extensive quotation.

and probably 30 percent more at a very bare subsistence level; "50–80 percent of school-age children are classified as having a physical or mental defect" (Cohen 23). The life expectancy for males has fallen from 65 to 55 years, the level of the famine countries of mid-Africa, compared to the life expectancy of seventy-four years in Cuba (see Cabanne and Tchistiakova, updated by Stuckler). The World Health Organization reported in 1997 an unmonitored rise in diseases for 75 percent of Russians who in the new "free" Leviathan live in poverty without social services, including a 3,000 percent rise of syphilis (Redford, see McMurtry 270), while Holmstrom and Smith report (6) a doubling of suicides and tripling of deaths from alcohol abuse: the population in Russia is falling by about one million people per year (but no humanitarian outcries have been heard from the NATO governments and media)! To the contrary, 2 percent of Russian population have possessed themselves of 57 percent of the total national economic wealth. This super-rich gangster-capitalist oligarchy in banking and export-import has, in collusion with the global corporate raiders dealing almost exclusively in asset-stripping and speculation, illegally transferred out of its country at least 250 billion dollars, and possibly the double of that amount (Clairmont 18, see Flaherty, Holmstrom-Smith, Menshikov and Skuratov). Russia is a country in moral and material ruins.

In cases of refractory States that refuse embedding into world capitalist finances, mercenary armies may still be used, as in Nicaragua, Iraq or Serbia. But Russia is the prime object-lesson that, as a rule, the takeovers by our new Leviathan of private corporate capital substitute for invading armies complex speculative instruments for "control over productive assets, labour, natural resources and institutions" (Chossudovsky 2). Its new paradigm is "concentration of control combined with decentralization of production" (Kagarlitsky 4). The often obnoxious State centralized planning by bureaucracy has been replaced by the no less huge and more powerful global planning by hundreds of millions of "globalization" bureaucrats, from corporations and stockmarkets to international bodies, whose cost is by now 20 percent of the produced commodities (McMurtry 287). Banks, not tanks; computer terminals or cell phones instead of artillery or bombers: the devastation for the lives of millions of powerless people outside the relatively very small ruling class is identical. After Mexico and Eastern

Europe, this "financial warfare" has in a few months of 1997 "transferred over 100 billion dollars of East Asian hard currency reserves into private financial hands. At the same time, real earnings and employment plummeted virtually overnight, leading to mass poverty in countries which had in the postwar period registered significant economic and social progress." (Chossudovsky 3)

The crises of the 1990s mark "the demise of central [national] banking, meaning national economic sovereignty," that controlled money creation on behalf of what was at least susceptible of being an overt will of that society. The demise is by no means confined to the "inferior races" of Africans, Asians or Slavs. It is by now threatening both the Nazis' and the World Bank's favourite "honorary Whites," Japan, as "a handful of Western investment banks [...] are buying up Japan's bad bank loans at less than one tenth of their face value." It is also hitting countries such as Canada, "where the monetary authorities have been incapable of stemming the slide of their national currencies. In Canada, billions of dollars were borrowed from private financiers to prop up central bank reserves in the wake of speculative assaults" (Chossudovsky 3–4).

Who funds the IMF bailouts, asks Chossudovsky? Where did the money come from, to finance these multi-billion dollar operations from Mexico to Indonesia or Japan? Overwhelmingly – from the public treasuries of the G7 countries, constituted by working citizens' taxes (businesses as a rule pay no taxes), and leading to significant hikes in the levels of public debt. Yet in the USA, say, "the issuing of US public debt to finance the bail-outs is underwritten and guaranteed by the same group of Wall Street merchant banks involved in the speculative assaults." These same banks will

ultimately appropriate the loot (e.g., as creditors of Korea or Thailand) – i.e., they are the ultimate recipients of the bailout money (which essentially constitutes a "safety net" for the institutional speculator) [...]. [As a result], a handful of commercial banks and brokerage houses have enriched themselves beyond bounds; they have also increased their stranglehold over governments and politicians around the world. (Chossudovsky 5)

The new Leviathan is at least equally powerful as the old one was and even less accountable to democratic control from below. It ruthlessly subordinates the whole of civil society and democratic self-determination to the objectives of financial capital (see McMurtry, Clarke 356 and passim, Kagarlitsky 29–31). It needs and uses States for public brainwashing and coercion to destroy the Keynesian and ensure the globalized Leviathan (see Kagarlitsky 14–19): internally as backup apparatuses for plundering the taxpayers and keeping them quiet by electoral charades and police, and externally as pressure and finally war machines against recalcitrants.

3

If my preceding section seems a detour, this is due to the rigid, strongly ideologized boundaries of our disciplinary division of labour, which fortunately does not prevail in utopian studies. For, the change of Leviathans – of the hegemonic collectives or "We"s inside which we all live – is at the root of my revisiting *We*, and revisioning it with this new insight. From the 1950s on, many of us defended Zamyatin against those who did not recognize his pregnancy – not only against Stalin but against all religious and crypto-religious dogmatisms. If we ever get nearer to a *Handmaid's Tale*-type society, no doubt we will have to return to some form of such defence. But today, we have to delimit within Zamyatin by holding fast to what is still relevant in his vision but also by recognizing that there are at least as relevant limits to it. His novel's title is an ellipse, unfolded in the text as a sarcastic unveiling into which he positions the reader: it should fully be "the false We vs. the True or Inner I" (see Parrinder 135). My thesis is that the central emotional and notional axis indicated by this device, the opposition of positive individuality to the negative collectivity of State centralization, does not seem relevant any more: both of its poles are by now untenable. Here is one small set of examples, composed of a number of significant, more or less overt uses of this opposition in the novel.

It begins in Entry 1: "I, D-503, Builder of the Integral, [...] shall merely attempt to record what I see and think, or, to be more exact, what we think (precisely so – we, and let this We be the title of my record)."[7] And continues in a number of places where D-503 is still or again a loyal "number"-cog in the mechanism of the State, for example in Entry 20 when he compares "I" to a gram and "We" to a ton: "[...] on one side 'I,' on the other 'We,' the [Unique] State [...]. And the natural path from nonentity to greatness is to forget that you are a gram and feel yourself instead a millionth of a ton."

While there is a lot of semi-overt reference to collectivism in the presentations of Taylorism (the Table of Hours, the machine-like work rhythms on the construction site – Entries 7 and 15), a clear indication of D-'s disarray comes about in Entry 18, a Gogolian grotesque of dismemberment:

> imagine a human finger cut off from the whole, from the hand – a separate human finger, running, stooped and bobbing, up and down, along the glass pavement. I was that finger. And the strangest, the most unnatural thing of all was that the finger had no desire whatever to be on the hand, to be with others.[8]

This opposition is conceived exclusively in terms of a power struggle and irreconcilable conflict: either "We" will eat up (dominate, enslave) "I," or "I" will eat up (subvert, destroy) "We." Either "'We' is from God, and 'I' from the devil" (Entry 22), or the obverse: no dialectics may obtain. The former case prevails at the beginning of the novel, as indicated by the first two quotes. The latter case develops slowly and bursts into the open before

7   Given the several translations in print and used pell-mell in criticism so far, I shall be citing by "Entry" (as the chapters in *We* are called) and not by page of the Ginsburg translation I used. I have checked them all against the original Russian (*My*, New York: Inter-Language Literary Associates, 1967).

8   This image comes from an old tradition, formulated for example by Plato in the *Politeia* (4: 462d) and Aristotle in *Metaphysics* Z 10: 1035b, where the natural and essential priority of the community to the individual is exemplified precisely as that of the body to the finger. It thence ran through the Stoics and Catholic Schoolmen to Spinoza and the conservative Romantics. It is recalled in 1837 by Emerson in protest against a state of society "in which the members have suffered amputation from the trunk, and strut about so many walking monsters" (54).

the middle of the novel (Entry 16) when D-503 develops the malady of "soulfulness" and an increasing anxiety which can only be allayed – and his isolation rendered tolerable and indeed emotionally validated – by what one might call the privatized mini-collective of the erotic couple: D-503's desire for I-330. A further "We" is less than clearly and somewhat inconsistently sketched out when D- and Zamyatin proceed to interpret the opposed, "natural" and "shaggy," Mephi in terms of a unanimous collective where "everybody breathes together" (Entry 27), so that D- "cease[s] to understand who 'They' are, who are 'We'" (Entry 28).⁹

This absolutistically individualist horizon was indeed Zamyatin's enthusiastic creed, identified as the supreme value of the Russian intelligentsia. In an essay that echoes the language of *We* he spelled it out both in national terms – "the stormy, reckless Russian soul" (no less) – and in class terms: "This love, which demands all or nothing, this absurd, incurable, beautiful sickness is [...] our Russian sickness, *morbus rossica*. It is the sickness that afflicts the better part of our intelligentsia – and, happily, will always afflict it" (*A Soviet* 223). In a number of other pronouncements, he speaks of such an idealist "romanticism" as the true artistic attitude toward the world (see for example Shane 52 and 53).

On the contrary, the combinatory of what I shall simply call Value vs. Social Horizons is much richer than the Manichean opposition between "We" and "I" (and other ideological binaries such as public vs. private, reason vs. emotion, *et j'en passe* – so that a strong suspicion arises all such binaries are finally untenable). I cannot imagine any self-aware collective movement (political, religious, and even professional) without a communitarian "We" epistemology that it necessarily implies and invokes. This does not mean that some such "Us" orientations can not be pernicious

---

9   Huntington's subtle analysis notes a number of such positive "We"s in the novel, issuing in the Entry 37 query "Who are we? Who am I?" This jibes with his argument that the confusion in the novel is a deliberate strategy, but seems too strong a reading to me. It is tempting to posit an "unconscious" Zamyatin-the-artist working against the ideologist, but it may be too easy. Nonetheless, as Huntington's analyses of "thou" also suggest (all 132–34), we have only scratched the surface of this rich artefact: it may surprise us yet.

– examples abound throughout history down to today, the latest being the super-corporate collectivity of the international financial market to which I shall return. However, the "Me" epistemologies and orientations may not only be as pernicious, they are also self-contradictory in a way that the "We" ones are not: for, as Aristotle observed, people who can live outside of community are either beasts or gods. This does not mean that any easy black-and-white way out obtains; indeed I believe that both the strictly collectivist and the strictly individualist ideologies situate themselves in the same double bind, from which we must step out.

In other words, even if we agree to the dubious dichotomy of "We" and "I," the combinatory allows for at least four cases of pairing the collective and the individual:

Table 3a: Combinatorics of Social Life (Overview)

Social Horizons

Collective	Individual	
+	+	Good
		Value
–	–	Bad

The Upper Left plus Upper Right case or (+ +), a good collective interacting with good individuals, is the best imaginable one, Paradise or Utopia. The Lower Left and Lower Right or (– –) one, the corrupt collective interacting with corrupt individuals, is the worst case, Hell or total dystopia. I would argue that the World Bank/ IMF/ WTO system is today fast approaching this condition, while hypocritically pretending that it is if not the best imaginable at least the best of all realistically possible worlds (we are in *Candide* country here). Zamyatin however considers only the diagonal cases, LL+UR (−\+, bad collectivism stifling good individualism) that masquerades to boot as UL+LR (+/−, a good collectivism voiding bad individualism). This is what his strong but reluctantly admiring critic Voronsky, in certainly the best Soviet response *We* received, called the usual bourgeois equation of Communism with a super-barracks (171 and ff.). For, Zamyatin is here dealing with a nightmarishly distorted version of Leninist War Communism equated with medieval Catholicism (a type of configuration which Stalin did his best to bring about ten years later). Yet this assiduous reader of Dostoevsky ought to have taken into account that Christianity moved between the poles of the Grand Inquisitor, from whom his Benefactor is derived by way of metallurgic metamorphosis, and Jesus, whose method has been fairly called a "Communism of Love" (Bloch) – much different from the privatized frenzy of the D-I couple.

Table 3b: Combinatorics of Social Life (Listing)

Possible pairings:

(++) Upper ←———→ = Earthly Paradise

(−−) Lower ←———→ = Earthly Hell

(+/−) Diagonal U.L. to L.R. = pretense of Unique State

(−/+) Diagonal L.L. to U.R. = reality of Unique State

4

For, what is the Leviathan – briefly glimpsed in section 2 above – that we are facing today? No doubt, it is again a negative collectivism, but in a different form from the still existing one of the brute militarized State gang that returned from colonial ventures to rule Europe in the industrialized and Taylorized World War I, which echoes strongly in this novel by a naval engineer: "The soldiers on the front lines recognized that the [First World

W]ar was like work in an abominable factory" (Gray 121). The high cost of Nazism and high-tech destruction has taught our ruling classes that empowerment by direct physical violence, including mass torture and murder, is to be used only when some of the forcibly impoverished countries, regions, and cities today threaten to revolt. While when necessary we in the richer North can remain in comfortable cahoots with the Francos, Pinochets, and Suhartos of the world, we are today overwhelmingly ruled by the psychophysical alienation of corporate capitalist collectivism. It is, politically speaking, a variant disguising the leaden weight of gang power – but morally indistinguishable from it – by a "velvet glove" in the archipelago of upper-class and (shrinking) middle-class enclaves, while retaining open militarized suppression outside those enclaves. Directly relevant to our immediate concerns here is that this hegemony also functions by fostering the ideological illusions of "individual expression" in the middle classes, while remaining in fact other-steered at least to the same degree as in the Catholic Middle Ages or under Stalinism.

This Post-Fordist collectivism means unemployment, totalizing alienation of labour and dispossession in the working place – including bit by bit but quite clearly the working places of intellectuals such as universities or research groups. It means increasing political impotence of not only the working classes proper but also the "professional-managerial" classes (with the exception of some important groups of mercenaries among the CEOs or the media, sports and scientific stars, equivalent to the military generals). Its insidious alienation constitutes what I would tentatively call *emptying* negative collectivism as opposed to the *brutal* negative collectivism of mass paleotechnic uniformity dreaded and rebelled against in *We*. While the ruled are encouraged to indulge in faddish (and deep-down also uniform) surface garishnesses of dress or music consumption, the rulers are a faceless, diffuse congeries of interlocking directorates: one cannot imagine Mr Greenspan (of the US Federal Reserve) or M. Camdessus (of the IMF) as the Benefactor – the capitalists have learned that Hitler was too dangerous a tool. To what Čapek in his *War with the Newts* called the "male horde" of overt brutal collectivism, there gets substituted in the North a genderless rule by grey suits and attaché cases, which can co-opt women like Mrs Thatcher or Ms MacKinnon. It is "the impersonal Nothing represented by the manager" (Kracauer 160), and articulated for us in Kafka and Beckett or the best cyberpunk and Piercy. As opposed to the despotic configuration Dostoevsky and Zamyatin attributed to medieval Catholicism, exasperated in overt Fascism and Stalinism, it suppresses individuality by brainwashing the disoriented majority into Disneyfied consumer contentment or at least stupefaction, and driving a minority of us into unhappy isolation. Instead of Medieval choral music or Zamyatin's State odes and music-making machines instilling the sense of the rulers, the emptying terrorism uses senseless *muzak*. Instead of universal ideologies hiding race, nation, and gender by rejecting it Outside, as in the city-State of *We*, racism, sexism, and ethnic exclusivism get now foregrounded in the rule over the motley crowds of our megalopolises and their identity politics. Instead of the Sexual Hours we have commodified pornography and S/M (see Kern 20). Instead of the Unique State's Institute of State Poets and Writers, today in the USA – and thus almost in the world – twenty interlocking media monopolies (in TV, films, publishing) and their bankers "constitute a new Private Ministry of Information and Culture" (Bagdikian xxviii). Everybody is democratically free to be physically and psychically hungry while chewing abundant junk food. The Catholic God acquires in this perspective a certain grim nobility, not to mention the truly noble *Nirvāna* of Gautama the Enlightened (Buddha).

Nonetheless, to the old plus new Leviathans of negative collectivism we ought in reason and with passion to oppose the possibility of (++), the utopia of a radically better communal arrangement, "an association in which the free development of each is the condition for the free development of all" (Marx, *The Manifesto of the Communist Party* 238). As Rabbi Hillel put it almost two thousand years ago: "If I am not for me – who is for me?", but also "If I am only for me – who am I?" Or, as Blok noted while writing his great poem *The Twelve*, testifying to the ubiquity of Zamyatin's theme in that historical moment but also to the availability of a diametrically opposed poetic vision on it, "The Revolution – that is: I – not alone, but we" (Dement'ev ed. 420).[10] Today, it has grown clear that collectivism is in our overcrowded – massified and urbanized, electric and electronic – mode of life absolutely unavoidable. The only choice we have is between the bad collectivities, suppressing freedom from as well as freedom for, and the good collectivities which, whatever form they may take, would be in feedback and mutual induction with non-narcissistic personalities: it is either "We" against "I" or "We" in feedback with "I"; either Zamyatin or Blok. In such a feedback, as Le Guin put it in *The Dispossessed* (see Chapter 18), "to be whole is to be part."

On top of classical heresies and liberal revolutions, from Gautama and Spartacus to J.S. Mill, we have in this century a number of quite good, if alas too brief, examples of "temporary liberated zones" (the Temporary Autonomous Zones of Hakim Bey) from which to draw lineaments of such a positive collectivism. Eschewing even the best blueprint sketches, such as Lenin's *State and Revolution*, and the imaginative articulations which are to be found in the SF of Mayakovsky, Platonov, Russ, Le Guin, Charnas or Piercy, let me stress here only the experiences of actual liberation movements. These comprise all non-corrupted unions, cooperatives or similar people-power struggles, and culminate in the popular revolutions whose promising beginnings and sad suffocations from without and within mark the twentieth century, from the Russian and Mexican series to Yugoslavia, China, and Vietnam (Cuba may still be largely an exception). A positive collectivism is also posed in religious terms, where all believers are members of a higher body: "Members of a Church congregation enter upon a

---

10   Many similar statements, not all by second-rate poets, could be found at the time; full titular coincidences are, for example, the great movie director Dziga Vertov's *We: A Variant of the Manifesto* of 1922 and Mayakovsky's poem "We" already in 1914.

       It must be acknowledged that all bad variants of collectivism, prominently including Stalinism, stress the individual's subsumption under a Leviathan: the tell-tale semantic sign here is the insipid and covertly religious hypostasis of the collective into a singular unit, either named Leader or allegorical Party, e.g., in Becher's *Kantate 1950*: "Du grosses Wir, Du unser aller Willen:/ [...] / Dir alle Macht, der Sieg ist Dein, Partei!" ("Thou great We, Thou will of all of us:/ [...] All power to Thee, victory is Thine, O Party!"). Brecht's dialectics of "we are it" is here spurned.

'We' which signifies the commonality of creatures that both sublates and founds all the distinctions and unifications which cleave to the proper name" (Kracauer 167). Zamyatin was certainly cognizant of this powerful and ancient tradition, reacting as he was against both the decayed Tsarism with Orthodox Christianity and the lineaments of a new modernized Leviathan – both of them unbearably autocratic. His Unique State is what Sartre would call a serial collectivity, one in which each member is alien to others and himself, as opposed to the very unclear possibility of Sartre's "fused group" (306–19, 384–96) among the Mephis.

Of the "fused" or inclusive traditions I shall choose here only the nearest to us in spacetime, the quarter-revolution of Western feminism, and use for that purpose the representative texts by Mellor, Rich, and Gearhart. I shall begin with Mellor's book for "a Feminist Green Socialism" which contrasts, in the wake of Carol Gilligan, a "male-experience [...] ME-world" to "[a decentralised and safe] WE-world." The "We"-world was prefigured by Fourier and Marx, "but subsequently sidelined by later Marxists and socialists" and reactualized in "the interests and experience of women" (250). I would object to the traces I find here of an undialectical tendency to lump all women together as positive – though I imagine feminists might want to except Thatcher, Schlafly, and I much hope also the Fortune fifty female CEOs or the corporate astronauts (certainly Rich does so, 15–16) – and, more cutting, to lump all men as more or less lost causes. Still, I would accept Gilligan's opposition of personality-types whose relationships are centered on responsibility and care vs. those who are centered on "integrity" as separation, self-actualization, and (in my terms) conflict, and who ultimately depend on "direct exploitation of [not only, DS] women's time and labour" (Mellor 270–71).

My critique is much advanced by Rich's truly rich and dialectical keynote speech at the Utrecht 1984 conference. Her engagement with the pronouns "I" and "We" begins with a twin axiom: "there is no liberation that only knows how to say 'I,'" and "[t]here is no collective movement that speaks for each of us all the way through"; and issues in the conclusion: "We – who are not the same. We who are many and do not want to be the same" (16–17). One can find in Rich also a wonderful meditation, based on her visit to the Sandinista Nicaragua, on what she identifies as "the deepfreeze of history." Her description exemplarily encompasses both the bad approach to collectivism and a new "We" resisting it, and is thus most cognate to my discussion of *We*:

> Any US citizen alive today has been saturated with Cold War rhetoric, the horrors of communism, the betrayals of socialism, the warning that any collective restructuring of society spells the end of personal freedom. And yes, there have been horrors and betrayals, deserving open discussion. But we are not invited to consider the butcheries of Stalinism alongside the butcheries of [W]hite supremacism and Manifest Destiny. [...]. Discourse itself is frozen at this level. [...]. Words which should possess a depth and breadth of allusions, words like socialism, communism, democracy, collectivism – are stripped of their historical roots. [...]. Living in the climate of an *enormous either/or*, we absorb some of it, unless we actively take heed. (14, emphasis added)

In a more restricted genre discussion, Gearhart points out that the practice of most feminist utopian fiction is characterized by a tendency both toward "collective values as opposed to the individual values [of] male writers [...]," and toward a group protagonist, somewhere between participatory democracy and "out-and-out anarchism" (for example in Charnas, Gearhart, Russ, Wittig). She recognizes there are also different tendencies, as in Le Guin, but argues that even there (in my words) a full focus on the empathetic, "I am Madame Bovary" protagonist never obtains (42–43). Gearhart attributes all such changes in figuration to a "we feeling" that identifies women as vehicles of humanity for collective co-operation "[...] with the earth, with animals, and with each other" (41). I shall not go into ways by which her little essay could be supplemented and even respectfully criticized (beyond the remnants of a "We-I" dichotomy, I think it is by now fatally self-defeating to confine our hopes to women only and in particular to posit lesbian feminists as the vanguard of this struggle) but only note that I would accept the points cited as a part of any good collectivism.

Finally, this "good We" is also a commonplace of communist and other revolutionary movements, as is within SF evident in all works with a however modified eutopian horizon, say Stapledon's *Last and First Men* (see on him now Suvin, "Science Fiction Parables"), Le Guin's *The Dispossessed* or Piercy's *He She and It*. In "warm Marxist" terms, Brecht's poem "Ballad of the Waterwheel" articulates a utopian plebeian "We" of suffering and rebellious solidarity:

> Ach wir hatten viele Herren
> Hatten Tiger und Hyänen
> Hatten Adler, hatten Schweine
> Doch wir nährten den und jenen [...]. (Brecht 14: 207)[11]

Many other works of his, say the radio-play *Ocean Flight* or other poems, delve at more length into the "We" vs. "I," indeed "We" vs. "It" syndrome. As Jakobson commented about another Brecht poem, "'we' is here an unalienable part of 'I' as well as of 'thou.' But [...] [this is] the inclusive 'we,' which includes the addressee" (668–69).

Philosophically,

> the indisputable and exacting consciousness of "human rights" always risks masking by its legitimacy the other legitimacy that has been and remains indispensable: that we ought to be able to say "we" [...], at the point where neither God nor master says it for us [...]. For, not to be able to say "we" throws each "I" – individual or collective – into the madness of not being able to say "I" either. (Nancy 62)

5

In this light, and facing the Leviathans of today and not yesterday, it seems to me decisive that Zamyatin lived at a historical moment when non-individualist utopianism, in a wide spread from theocracy to warm Marxism (from Solovyov through Lenin to Bogdanov) had been debated and when its possibility, however precarious, was on the agenda of the post-1917 revolutionary openings. In numerous articles, he situated himself within

11   Non-poetic translation: "Oh we had so many bosses / They were tigers or hyenas / They were eagles, also swine, / But we fed this one and that one [...]".

this debate and pleaded for a radical utopia, one of tomorrow and not – as the Bolshevik one – of today; and I do not wish to retract my argument from *Metamorphoses* that *We* judges its nightmare from the vantage of such a utopian-socialist tomorrow. Yet he was unable to imagine a workable utopian variant (the "soft primitivism" of the country Mephi is obviously not such, which is acknowledged in the novel by the attempt to take over the city). This is both the strength and the weakness of *We*. The strength resides in his fierce concentration on the creator-diarist D-503, the weakness in the consubstantial absence of views and norms alternative to the Romantic individualism Zamyatin and this creature of his come to share. The hiatus or indeed contradiction between his overt doctrine of permanent heresy or revolution and his covert untranscendable doctrine of individualism grows into what Marx called "the Robinson Crusoe fiction," not only born of alienated relationships typical of capitalism but also acquiescing in the dichotomies that constitute the alienation. E.J. Brown may be one-sided when he focuses on the "belated Rousseauism" of the fact that "[t]here is no adequate attempt in [Zamyatin, Orwell or Huxley] to examine the concrete social or economic factors that would lead to the debasement of human values: they offer only an abstract argument in favor of the simple and primitive as against the complex and cultivated" (222); but he is also right.

I have argued in Section 1 that Zamyatin is a terminal point of such Romantic individualism. My examples were drawn mainly from English Romanticism but, except for Byron, Zamyatin was more familiar with the German tradition, in Goethe's *Faust* (from whose denying figure his Mephi took their name) and in the late Nietzsche's distinction of elite vs. herd which exactly matches the relationship both of D-503 to the grey masses of the Unique State and of I-330 to the colourful subversives she leads (though D- oscillates guiltily while I- is sardonically uninhibited). The novel's Romanticism has been rightly found in the contrast between innocence and experience, in the pathetic fallacy equating nature with D-'s moods, in the "noble savage" notion present both in the Mephi primitivism and in D-'s shagginess (Edwards 44 and 62, see Hoyles 108), and in the lineage of Zamyatin's heroes which comes from the solitary and brooding, rebellious or even salvational, Byronic types in Russian culture, such as the male outcast – often the sensitive artist – right down to Gorky (see Scheffler 91, Barratt 355). This was blended with Zamyatin's overwhelming inspiration from Dostoevsky.

Paradoxically, however, in comparison to that theocratic populism Zamyatin's atheist stance is both less clear and more elitist. Who is in *We* the equivalent of the heretic Christ confronting the *apparatchik* Great Inquisitor? D- is too weak for this role, and the true heretic I- and her Mephi Green World are not only finally defeated but also to my mind an ambiguous brew of incommensurable, if potent, erotic and political traits. In this Section I shall focus on I-, an object of much libidinal investment inside and outside the text, who has disturbed a number of critics as functionally a self-interested political Snake yet axiologically part of the book's core values, sex (and brains) as heretic rebellion: the point is that she is, richly but confusingly, both.[12]

---

12   Critics' opinions about the role of Zamyatin's splendid I-330 have been diametrically opposed. A brief sample of a few more recent ones yield some extreme pro and con opinions.

    Pro: In Ulph, one of the most stimulating critics, I find references to "dialectic duality – siren and revolutionary [...] Superwoman [...] Belle Dame Sans Merci [...] one of the most sadistic, frenetic and comical seductions of the faltering male by the determined vamp in Western [?!] literature [...]" (82–85 passim). In Hoisington, whose entire article is praise of I-330 as the real heroine of this novel "[...] both in the sense of the mover and the character who best exemplifies the novel's governing values," I- "is the stimulating, fertilizing force"; "a rebel [...] who chooses to remain true to her beliefs, to suffer and to die rather than recant" (82–85).

    Con: For Mikesell/Suggs I- is failed trickster, "the love she demands [of D- has] destructive effects," "the world desired by I-330 and her Mephi [...] harbors [...] violence and deceit," and "finally she is not a facilitator but, like the Benefactor himself, a tyrant" (94 and 98). For Barratt, I- is "a Mata Hari figure, who has been using her sexual attractiveness as a means [...]"; her ultimate aim is freedom but paradoxically "her initial act [...] was to enslave [D-] by luring him against his will into compromising his allegiance to the One State" (346 and 355). For Petrochenkov "I-330's most ominous feature [are] [...] the vaginal teeth that castrate [...]. Her mouth is associated with a knife and dripping blood [...]" (246–47).

    It should be noted, first, that the critics' opinion does not follow their gender; and second, that most "pro" critics note I-'s ambiguous (both-and) characteristics,

Zamyatin spoke of pathos and irony as the cathode and anode between which the literary current is created (*A Soviet* 130); but if the irony suddenly loses relevance, pathos is the only (inert) pole that remains. As some of his novel's other central devices, the *femme fatale* I-330 (see Praz, chapter 4) is taken from the overheated, reach-me-down quasi-Romanticism of the European *fin-de-siècle*, and in particular from the Russian Symbolists' mysterious and supremely alluring Beautiful Lady (*prekrasnaia dama* – see *A Soviet* 32), also descended from the Byronic semi-demonic female (Lamia), and characterized by stock Decadent props such as the sharp liqueur (probably out of Huysmans's *A rebours*, 1884; English as *Against Nature*). This figure-type is, of course, a figment of the (male) imagination reacting after the mid-nineteenth century against the threat of transgressive female independence. However, I- is overdetermined in complex ways, so that it is imperative to distinguish, in the tradition begun by Propp, her narratological plot position and her characterological role.

I-330 is narratologically placed in the position of Eve from the Biblical-Miltonic model. In his essay "On Synthetism," Zamyatin claimed this literary movement of his was sublating in a Hegelian fashion – assuming and transcending – the tragically unattainable "Eve as Death" from Vrubel and Blok; so that instead of Schopenhauer they were following the ecstatic Nietzsche. But whatever the theory, the transcendence is not noticeable in *We*.[13] Rather, it hesitates between Symbolism (mystery) and Cubism (new understanding). Furthermore, the plot of *We* is quite consciously taken (see Entry 18) and refunctioned from popular penny-dreadfuls: it is a political

---

while the "con" critics concentrate on the negative ones. The problem seems to me to be which of the undoubtedly present two aspects of I- predominates within the plot and the ethico-political concerns of Zamyatin – and then, our concerns today.

13   See Zamyatin, *A Soviet* (82); see also Scheffler (29, 92, and passim), and Rooney. To my mind Zamyatin's handling of Hegelian historiosophy as well as of Nietzsche's Superman vs. herd is rather simplified. He was a *bricoleur* in the philosophy of history and of politics. While this may be quite enough for writing one novel, it will not do to extrapolate his pronouncements as indubitable cognitions about the State Leviathan in general and the Soviet State in particular; as a theorist he catches fire only when he can integrate his overriding Modernist avant-garde allegory of entropy vs. energy with other symbolism.

spy-thriller with a vamp who comes to a bad end, as popularized at the time by the sensational Mata Hari case. (By the way, this became, mainly through Orwell, the template of much subsequent SF in the "new maps of hell," most often losing the redeeming qualities of *We* and just keeping the stereotype of individual – anguished protagonist – plus female sidekick vs. State machine.) The seductive Satanic force from *Genesis*, Milton, and the Romantics has been fully laicized and displaced from the position of antagonist (now reserved for the rulers), though echoes of its former status richly if somewhat confusingly persist. In *We* the most alluring sexual and political seductress I-, aided by the eponymous S-for-Satan-4711, turns out to be politically and ideologically positive. Thus I- oscillates between two narratological positions. Traditionally, she would have been an aide or satellite to D-: Juliet to his Romeo, or better Eve to his Adam. But in *We*, consonant with her characterological upgrading as pillar of heretic strength, she is Snake rather than Eve (besides its role in Eden, the Snake was also a nineteenth century theatre role of faithless *femme fatale*); that is, I- becomes an *al pari* co-protagonist, who in fact initiates all the political and most of the erotical actions in the plot (though she is not a co-narrator).

Characterologically, I-330 is much stronger than the sensitive and inde-cisive D- who is, in a subversion of the usual gender roles, "feminized" by her bee-sting of pollination, her vampirical pointed teeth, her sexual initiative fulfilling him, and her politico-ideological leadership and guru or commis-sar status (see Hoisington 83). Yet she is also, against the grimly Puritanical Unique State, the emancipated flapper in a world of Symbolist decadence, materialized in the Ancient House – a commonplace of the SF-cum-utopian tradition from William Morris through Wells's *Time Machine* – and whose forbidden and intoxicating qualities are emblematized by the sharp green liqueur (absinthe?). A further way of characterizing her is to oppose her, in a series of very effective love-and-jealousy triangles – taken from the theatrical conventions of vaudeville, melodrama, and boulevard comedy near and dear to Zamyatin the playwright – to O-90 (and subsidiarily to U-). This furthermore employs Dostoevsky's usual contrast between two strong female types: the gentle, mild, and humble woman vs. the predatory woman with demonic traits, corresponding to epileptic hyper-sensitivity of her male prey. It is O- who is the Eve to D-'s Adam (Entry 19) where I- is

Lilith. O- is round and rosy where I- is straight line and associated with extreme colours, O-'s love and sex are comfortable where I-'s are "bitterly demonic and untamed" (Edwards 65, from Billington 502), O- is transparent where I- is opaque, O- is maternal where I- is non-procreative though intellectually and erotically "pollinating" D- (see Hoyles 104–05). In Entry 19, however, O- begins to take on some traits of I-: she is energized and subverted through her love for D- and the child she bears, the maternal becoming the political (somewhat like Gorky's *Mother*). Finally (Entries 29 and 34), I- saves O- and her child among the Mephi.

The unresolved ambiguities about I-330 may be understood as the confusion of two forms of Zamyatin's overriding positive principle of energy: political subversion and erotic passion. In Zamyatin's novel, these two forms and goals, co-present only in the pivotal I-, are equated. But they can coincide only if, as Orwell realized, a love affair is also a political subversion of the State. Empirically, this is nonsense in any mass State; in this respect, Huxley's *Brave New World*, where sex is a drug in the hands of rulers, has proven much nearer to our unromantic concerns today than Zamyatin or his imitation in Orwell. The novel can only work if D-503 is taken as the axiologically representative subject of the Unique State, that is, not a "realistic" character but an allegorical protagonist. As constructor of the politically crucial spaceship, he is much too important to be simply Everyman: rather, he is the allegorical Intellectual, without whose support no revolution can win. Both as creator of spaceship and as creator of the diary entries, D- is the archetypal creative individual: an enthusiastic scientist and a reluctant artist. Written at the same time as Joyce, Zamyatin's novel might be called, among other things, a "portrait of the artist as (sexually) awakening dystopian." After seducing D- sexually, I- therefore sets about persuading or educating him politically – with mixed success. But the sexual carnality remains entirely non-allegorical, it is a (no doubt very appealing and brilliantly executed) carry-over of Dostoevskian possession, a matter of depth psychology and possibly theology but not of politics. Within the political strand of the plot, the carnal affair with D- must necessarily be backgrounded, so that he comes to function as a patsy, used for the advantages he can bring the Revolution by delivering the spaceship to its side. The Benefactor tells him so, though D- does not really want to hear it.

However, Zamyatin uses the political strand of the plot much as I- uses D-: as means to a higher end – the sexual growth into a "soul." His aim is to show a sincere believer turned inside out by *what is missing* in the Unique State: the pleasure of the senses, a feedback loop between the brain and sexual *jouissance*, the colours, tastes, smells, and hormonal delights experienced by his body, an eversion that would translate as a sub-version. Very realistically, D- really wants only such "soulful" erotics, and he is dragged into politics reluctantly and with relapses. That he would be dragged into subversion at all belongs to the penny-dreadful, melodramatic hinge between politics and sex. But sexuality in *We* is not heretical in the utopian "constructivist" or "synthetist" sense announced by Zamyatin's essays. Rather, it is strung between proclamations of freedom and experiences of death: D- associates it with caveman violence, fever, and death (not only the "little death" of epileptic and orgasmic fits).[14] At the end, the exemplary sexual pair D-I is sorted out into death as liquidation (I-) vs. indifferent looking-on (D-). Erotics and individualism seem defeated, while the political struggle remains undecided.

Besides the emblematic I-330, the Mephi outside the Wall are supposed to be another incarnation of the union between great sex and liberatory politics. But apart from her preaching, in a philosophically to my mind unimpeachable but politically rather vague way, the necessity of permanent revolution, what alternative program are we given in the Mephi world, even in glimpses? Back to the land? For a mass industrialized society? Even to pose such questions shows that *We* is concerned with politics only in the sense of individual protest against its course, but not really in the high philosophical or cognitive sense claimed by Zamyatin. A critic in

---

14   It would be interesting to compare this with Walter Benjamin's views on the woman's body in Baudelaire's civilization as "death-body, fragmented-body, petrified body" and "a metaphor for extremes," issuing in the Baudelairean abyss (or, I would add, Zamyatin's vertigo); the quotes are from the approach to this aspect of Benjamin in Buci-Glucksmann 226 and 228. A crucial question for *We*, so far as I remember not yet posed, would here be: "Who is D-'s diary really addressed to?"

the mid-1990s could therefore rightly observe that Zamyatin and similar dystopians had "lost almost [all] of their interest and relevance" shortly after their publication in the Russia of the late 1980s: "it is as if 'we' had won the battle against the 'One State,' but what we find beyond the Green Wall is increasingly not what we expected ..." (Lahusen 678, ellipsis in the original). This is what I attempted to discuss earlier by way of the "We" vs. "I" dichotomy.

6

Zamyatin commented in 1932 that *We* "is a warning against the twofold danger which threatens humanity: the hypertrophic power of the machines and the hypertrophic power of the State" (Lefèvre 1). The comment may say more about how the author's stresses had shifted in the intervening dozen years – and pursuing his ideological shifts after the mid-1920s, apparently to the Left, might prove very revealing – than about the much more ambiguous treatment of technoscience in the novel.[15] This fascination with and yet mistrust of technoscience can be taken beyond State sponsorship of massive drives such as the Soviet Five-Year Plans and the US Manhattan Project or Marshall Plan, so that it remains applicable to our concerns today: the Post-Fordist capitalist corporations' full symbiosis with computers, automation, and gene manipulation; and of course to the ever more horrifying ways of mass military murders in "small" (but tomorrow perhaps

---

15   As a number of critics from Lewis and Weber on have remarked, insofar as the ideology of "mechanized collectivism" is the target, *We* is a polemic with the school of Proletkult poets propagating the extension of Taylorism (see for those themes also Scheffler 186–91) – the pet focus of Zamyatin's sarcasm from his English 1916 stories on – into all areas of life. It is not a polemic with super-technological ways of life in Russia, quite non-existent there until recently, but was in fact meant by Zamyatin equally, if not more, for the capitalist "West" (see Myers 75–77).

again global) wars.[16] Yet should we not focus on who (what social group) deals with the machines of technoscience how, what for, in whose interest and to whose detriment?

Finally, amid all the mathematics, architecture, and construction technology, it may be still cognitively useful, and thus acceptable, that *We* is inhabited by faceless crowds marching four abreast. Perhaps one can even accept as realistic for 1920 that these crowds then resolve into women in various variants of sexual desire – named stereotypically by "soft" I, O, and U vowels – or of janitoring, and into men as doctors, poets or secret-service "Guardians" – named by "hard" consonants D, R, and S. After all, *We* is a novel, grotesque, Cubist kind of allegory (though again, Zamyatin had some doubts about Picasso and especially abhorred Le Corbusier's architecture of cubes – *A Soviet* 134–35). But it is built around a central absence: except for some brief and not very enlightening scenes in the shipyard, there are within the horizons of Zamyatin's novel no economics, nor productive labour, nor working people – no accounting for the distribution and maintenance of the food, housing, "aeros," telephones, electric whips, walls for fencing in, and streets for marching. The anonymous (unnumbered?) masses are there only as a backdrop for D- and I-. The "I vs. We" translates as private vs. public. Most perniciously perhaps, reason is insistently identified with "We," and emotion (or imagination) with "I." This aspect in Zamyatin is late, impoverished, ideological individualism.

However, I would not like to end merely on a negative note about a dialectically contradictory masterpiece I still in many ways admire. If the

---

16   As in all nations which had quickly to recapitulate "western" modernization, and thus serve to show its underlying structure, modern science was in Russia too first introduced for military purposes as part of a centralized State; the first use of the term *nauka* (science) was in a 1647 military manual in the sense of "military skill" (Billington 113). It is most eye-opening that the one thing the two Leviathans, Zamyatin's Fordist one and our Post-Fordist one, have obviously in common (remember the imperialist interplanetary rocket D- is building!) is the massive war technology and nationalist propaganda playing it up, both of which they're not only engaged in but in fact deeply dependent on; this is the visible tip of the iceberg of continuing murderous class-rule.

humanization of the overwhelmingly center-stage protagonist has been defeated and the temptress firing his imagination and organizing rebellion has been cruelly suppressed in the best Jehovaite tradition, at least two important aspects remain relevant and fertile today. The first and perhaps most important one may be signalled by the inferences hidden in its technology of writing: for all meaning resides in the form, and form cannot be disjoined from meaning. As Voronsky was one of the first to have pointed out, Zamyatin was a master of the word, the sharp observer of incisive details. His Cubist texture and some other aspects (for example the astounding believability of the rather improbable D-503 and I-330) have only rarely been matched since in any SF – utopian or dystopian or anti-utopian. A post-realistic or properly Modernistic texture, say, can be found in a very few items after the 1960s: much William Burroughs, one text by Golding (see Parrinder 139), some Bester or Le Guin (for example "New Atlantis"), Harlan Ellison, and Kathy Acker. Thus, like his revered Wells, Zamyatin has rightly entered world literature. Furthermore, I have in this essay dealt more or less solely with the paradigmatic aspect of this allegorical narration, its central conflict. I have scarcely touched upon its very rich syntagmatic unfolding, from the tripartition of each Entry to the full agential constellation and the intermingling of the action with dreams, comments, and so on, and to its metaphoric scaffolding. A salient point is that while the story of D- and I- ends in total defeat, the novel's ending remains ambiguous, not quite closed: the battle rages on, and O-90 has left the State to bear D-'s child. Most important: as I argued in *Metamorphoses*, the defeat IN the novel is not the defeat OF the novel – that is, of its potentially liberatory effect on the reader.

The warnings against capitalist industrialization with its military drill incorporated in the paleotechnic machines, and the Soviet enthusiasm for it, are incorporated strangely and richly into the precision and economic clarity of *We*, where even the "irrational number" enters into a system of lucidly functional oppositions and mathematics turn into ambiguous metaphor if not allegory.[17] The novel's organization, texture, and "style" (see Heller 235–37) evince a Cubist or Constructivist confidence which is not only utopian but also deeply complicitous with, indeed unthinkable without, the very urbanization and industrialization whose one, malevolent variant they so doggedly stigmatize. They bear the imprint of Zamyatin the engineer and shipbuilder, the extoller of the persecuted theoretician of science Robert Mayer, and constitute the hidden positive, utopian socialist, values in the name of which the repressive aberrations are envisaged and judged. I doubt this would provide any comfort to the present-day savage corporate capitalism subjugating national states, the new Leviathan.

And second, more narrowly but perhaps more acutely, the old State apparatus is neither fully nor definitely off the agenda of present history. The Global Corporate vs. State Leviathans do not spell each other as participants in a relay race or train connections. Rather, they relate at least as intimately as do geological strata, where a new formation can for long stretches be interrupted by remains or even re-emergences of the old formation upheaving and sticking up as whole mountain ranges.[18] Though the "transnational" corporations are still mainly "national companies with

17   The shock or even horror at such numbers as square roots or similar, well conveyed by the mistranslation of "irrational" (from *alogon*, see Russo 56), arises from their enforcing abandonment of the ancient Pythagorean conception that a line is constituted by an enumerable succession of points. In other words, one cannot explain basic relationships in the real world by means of whole numbers only.

18   Perhaps the succession of not only modes of production but also of their main stages might best be understood as imbricated articulation rather than simple abolition, see Jameson 67. – As to my little geological metaphor: any metaphor or model has limits of applicability. But if we were to proceed to a meta-level of theorizing, it should be noted that Marx's key notion of "social formation" refunctions the geological "formation" of his admired Lyell, which wittily fuses a historically specific process and its result. In geology, terms like primary and secondary formation suggest simultaneously the nature/structure and the evolutionary collocation of rock strata (see Godelier 343); if not metaphors they are at least puns. In that sense the historical figures of the two capitalist Leviathans of centralized Fordist State and globalized Post-Fordist speculative finances are both distinct ideal types and inextricably commingled within the latter's contradictory domination over the former.

a transnational reach" (Wood 7, and see Krätke), the partnership and collusion between the capitalist global corporations and the nation-States seems to me finally dominated by the former. Yet, as we have seen in the mendacious and cruel war against Serbia, the old State Leviathan can be summoned into operation at the touch of a cellular phone call or of a computer button whenever the new Leviathan needs it: they are, after all, still instruments of class rule, brothers under the skin. State apparatuses have largely become local enforcing committees of the big oligopolies conveniently designed as the IMF/WTO/World Bank triad; it may in fact turn out that the new Leviathan is a true dialectical sublation of the old one, both denying and preserving it in selected aspects. Dialectically, the old Leviathan is also, at given propitious places and times, available for useful work, bundling and accelerating a large national consensus in order to improve life, for example, to institute medicare or social insurance. That was especially the case in some approximations to popular sovereignty in poorer states brutally attacked by the subversive forces of international capital. This was prefigured by the Mexican and Kemalite revolutions, this is what Lenin's State decayed into at its best moments of defence of the USSR, and this is what continued into the postwar experiences of the "non-aligned" peoples from Tito through Nkrumah and Nehru to Castro. But where are the snows of yesteryear?

Even so, Zamyatin's generous indictment of life in a "super-barracks" society is of a much diminished importance for getting our bearings in a super-Disneyland society. *We*'s bad collectivism recycles what are by now "paleotechnic" (Mumford) or Fordist elements and attitudes predating speculative finance capitalism. The insipid food in *We*, made from petroleum and distributed by the State, does not collate to our problems with the overspiced and cancerogenously hormonized "macdonaldified" burgers pushed by brainwashing us in the "free" market. Even less does it speak to the hungry and freezing unpaid millions of "freed" Russia.[19]

---

19   My thanks go to colleagues connected with the Society for Utopian Studies November
      1998 meeting where a briefer version was first presented: Naomi Jacobs; Carol Franko
      whose writing led me to Adrienne Rich's article, which she kindly sent me; and

Works Cited

Bagdikian, Ben. *The Media Monopoly* 4th edn. Boston: Beacon, 1992.

Barratt, Andrew. "Revolution as Collusion: The Heretic and the Slave in Zamyatin's *My*." *Slavonic and East European Review* 62.3 (1984): 344–61.

Beauchamp, Gorman. "Of Man's Last Disobedience." *Comparative Literature Studies* 10 (1973): 285–301.

Becher, Johannes R. "Kantate 1950." *Neues Deutschland*. 27 May 1950.

Billington, James H. *The Icon and the Axe*. New York: Vintage, 1970.

Brecht, Bertolt. *Werke. Grosse kommentierte Berliner und Frankfurter Ausgabe*. 33 vols. Berlin: Aufbau, 1988–98.

Brown, Edward J. "*Brave New World, 1984* and *We*: An Essay on Anti-utopia." *Zamyatin's We*. Ed. Gary Kern. Ann Arbor: Ardis, 1988. 209–27.

Buci-Glucksmann, Christine. "Catastrophic Utopia: The Feminine as Allegory of the Modern." *Representations* 14 (1986): 222–29.

Cabanne, Claude, and Elena Tchistiakova. *La Russie*. Paris: Colin, 2002.

Chossudovsky, Michel. "Financial Warfare": 22 September 1998 <http://www.southside.org.sg/souths/twn/title/trig-cn.htm>.

——. *The Globalisation of Poverty*. London: Zed Books, 1997.

Clairmont, Frédéric F. "La Russie au bord de l'abîme." *Le Monde Diplomatique* 18 March 1999: 18–19.

Clarke, Simon. *Keynesianism, Monetarism and the Crisis of the State*. Aldershot: Elgar, 1989.

Savas Barkçin, my co-panelist, whose paper on Kemalism reminded me of what became my next-to-last paragraph. They also go to Patrick Flaherty for sending me some unpublished papers of his on Russia today, from which I learned much, and to Dubravka Juraga's critiques. I did not note in my first overview of *We*, the less than 2,000 words in the chapter on Russian SF from *MOSF*, and should now, that the direct stimulus to deal with it was for me, within the general Titoist reappraisal of the Soviet experience, my (then) friend's Saša Flaker's rediscovery of Zamyatin in his book *Heretici i sanjari* (*Heretics and Dreamers*, Zagreb 1958).

Cohen, Stephen F. "American Journalism and Russia's Tragedy." *The Nation* 2 October 2000: 23–30.

Dement'ev A.G et al. (ed.). *Istoriia russkoi sovetskoi literatury.* Vol. 1. Moscow: Nauka, 1967.

Edwards, T.R.N. *Three Russian Writers and the Irrational.* Cambridge: Cambridge University Press, 1982.

Emerson, Ralph Waldo. "The American Scholar." *Essays and Poems.* Ed. Joel Porte. New York: American Library, 1983. 53–71.

Fanger, Donald. *Dostoevsky and Romantic Realism.* Cambridge, MA: Harvard University Press, 1965.

Flaherty, Patrick. "Putin, Praetorianism and Revolution." Unpublished paper.

Frye, Northrop. "The Drunken Boat." *The Stubborn Structure.* Ithaca: Cornell University Press, 1970. 200–17.

Gearhart, Sally. "Female Futures in Science Fiction." *Proceedings of the Conference Future, Technology and Women.* San Diego: Women's Studies Department, San Diego State University, 1981. 41–45.

Ginsburg, Mirra (ed. and trans.). *A Soviet Heretic: Essays by Yevgeny Zamyatin.* Chicago: University of Chicago Press, 1970.

Godelier, Maurice. "Formazione economico-sociale." *Enciclopedia Einaudi.* Vol. 6. Turin: Einaudi, 1979. 342–73.

Gray, Chris Hables. *Postmodern War.* New York: Guilford Press, 1997.

Gregg, Richard A. "Two Adams and Eve in the Crystal Palace: Dostoevsky, the Bible, and *We.*" *Zamyatin's We.* Ed. Gary Kern. Ann Arbor: Ardis, 1988. 61–9.

Heller, Leonid. "La prose de E. Zamjatin et l'avant-garde russe." *Cahiers du monde russe et soviétique* 24.3 (1983): 217–39.

Hoisington, Sona Stephan (ed.). "The Mismeasure of I-330." *A Plot of Her Own: The Female Protagonist in Russian Literature.* Evanston: Northwestern University Press, 1995. 81–88.

Holmstrom, Nancy, and Richard Smith. "The Necessity of Gangster Capitalism: Primitive Accumulation in Russia and China." *Monthly Review* 9 (1999): 1–15.

Hoyles, John. *The Literary Underground.* New York: St Martin's Press, 1991.

Huntington, John. "Utopian and Anti-Utopian Logic: H.G. Wells and His Successors." *Science Fiction Studies* 9.2 (1982): 122–46.

Jakobson, Roman. "Der grammatische Bau des Gedichts von B. Brecht 'Wir sind sie.'" *Selected Writings*. Vol. 3. Ed. Stephen Rudy. The Hague: Mouton, 1981. 660–71.

Jameson, Fredric. *The Cultural Turn*. London: Verso, 1999.

Kagarlitsky, Boris. *The Twilight of Globalization*. London: Pluto, 2000.

Kern, Gary (ed.). "Introduction". *Zamyatin's We*. Ann Arbor: Ardis, 1988. 9–21.

Kracauer, Siegfried. *Das Ornament der Masse*. Frankfurt: Suhrkamp, 1977.

Krätke, Michael R. "Kapital global?" *Turbo-Kapitalismus. Gesellschaft im Übergang zum 21. Jahrhundert*. Ed. Elmar Altvater et al. Hamburg: VSA, 1997. 18–59.

Lahusen, Thomas. "Russian Literary Resistance Reconsidered." *Slavic and East European Journal* 38.4 (1994): 677–82.

Lefèvre, Frédéric. "Une heure avec Zamiatine." *Les nouvelles littéraires* 497 (23 April 1932): 1, 8.

Lewis, Kathleen, and Harry Weber. "Zamyatin's *We*, the Proletarian Poets, and Bogdanov's *Red Star*." *Zamyatin's We*. Ed. Gary Kern. Ann Arbor: Ardis, 1988. 186–208.

Mal'mstad, Dzhon, and Lazar' Fleishman. "Iz biografii Zamiatina." *Stanford Slavic Studies*. Vol. 1. Stanford: Stanford University Press, 1987. 103–51.

Marx, Karl. *Selected Writings*. Ed. David McLellan. Oxford: Oxford University Press, 1977.

McMurtry, John. *The Cancer Stage of Capitalism*. London: Pluto, 1999.

Mellor, Mary. *Breaking the Boundaries*. London: Virago, 1992.

Menshikov, Stanislav. "Russian Capitalism Today." *Monthly Review* 3 (1999): 81–99.

Mikesell, Margaret Lael, and Jon Christian Suggs. "Zamyatin's *We* and the Idea of the Dystopic." *Studies in Twentieth Century Literature* 7.1 (1982): 89–102.

Mumford, Lewis. *Technics and Civilization*. New York: Harcourt, 1963.

Myers, Alan. "Zamyatin in Newcastle." *Foundation* 59 (1993): 70–78.

Nancy, Jean-Luc. *Être singulier pluriel.* Paris: Galilée, 1996.

Parrinder, Patrick. "Imagining the Future: Wells and Zamyatin." *H.G. Wells and Modern Science Fiction.* Ed. Darko Suvin. Lewisburg: Bucknell University Press, 1977. 126–43.

Petrochenkov, Margaret Wise. "Castration Anxiety and the Other in Zamyatin's *We.*" *Critical Studies: The Fantastic Other.* Ed. Brett Cooke et al. Amsterdam: Rodopi, 1998. 243–55.

Praz, Mario. *The Romantic Agony.* New York: Oxford University Press, 1970.

Redford, Tim. "Europe faces disease invasion from East." *Guardian Weekly* 13 April 1997: 7.

Rich, Adrienne. "Notes toward a Politics of Location." *Women, Feminist Identity and Society in the 1980's.* Ed. Myriam Díaz-Diocaretz and Iris M. Zavala. Amsterdam and Philadelphia: Benjamins, 1985. 7–22.

Rooney, Victoria. "Nietzschean Elements in Zamyatin's Ideology." *Modern Language Review* 81.3 (1986): 675–86.

Russo, Lucio. *La rivoluzione dimenticata.* Milano: Feltrinelli, 2003.

Sartre, Jean-Paul. *Critique de la raison dialectique.* Paris: Gallimard, 1960.

Scheffler, Leonore. *Evgenij Zamjatin: Sein Weltbild und seine literarische Thematik.* Bausteine zur Geschichte der Literatur bei den Slaven. Vol 20. Tübingen: Böhlau, 1984.

Shane, Alex M. *The Life and Works of Evgenij Zamjatin.* Berkeley: University of California Press, 1968.

Skuratov, Iurii. *Variant drakona.* Moscow: DP, 2000.

Stiglitz, Joseph. *Globalization and its Discontents.* London: Allen Lane, 2002.

Striedter, Jurij. "Three Postrevolutionary Russian Utopian Novels." *The Russian Novel from Pushkin to Pasternak.* Ed. John Garrard. New Haven: Yale University Press, 1983. 177–201.

Suvin, Darko. *Metamorphoses of Science Fiction.* New Haven: Yale University Press, 1979.

——. *Positions and Presuppositions in Science Fiction.* London: Macmillan, 1988.

———. "Science Fiction Parables of Mutation and Cloning as/and Cognition." *Biotechnological and Medical Themes in Science Fiction.* Ed. Domna Pastourmatzi. Thessaloniki: University Studio, 2002. 131–51.

Ulph, Owen. "I-330: Reconsiderations on the Sex of Satan." *Zamyatin's We.* Ed. Gary Kern. Ann Arbor: Ardis, 1988. 80–91.

Voronsky, Aleksandr K. "Evgeny Zamyatin." Trans. P. Mitchell. *Russian Literature Triquarterly* 3 (1972): 157–75.

Wallerstein, Immanuel. *Utopistics.* New York: The New Press, 1998.

Went, Robert. *Globalization.* Trans. T. Smith. London: Pluto, 2000.

Wood, Ellen Meiksins. "Labor, Class, and State in Global Capitalism." *Labor in the Age of "Global" Capitalism.* Ed. Ellen M. Wood et al. New York: Monthly Review, 1998, 3–16.

Zamyatin, Yevgeny. *We.* Trans. Mirra Ginsburg. New York: Avon Books, 1983.

CHAPTER 12

What May the Twentieth Century Amount To: Initial Theses (1999–2000)

To Marc Angenot: we learned from each other for the three last decades of that century (and I took the epigraphs to Part 5 from his *"Religions de l'humanité" et "Science de l'histoire"*)

Quid sum miser tunc facturus?
Quem patronem rogaturus?
[Poor me, what am I to do?
Which master do I plead to?]
— THOMAS OF CELANO, *Dies irae*

Gott hätte seine Hand bei allem im Spiel, nur bei unsern Irrthümern nicht?
[God's hand should be everywhere present, except in our errors?]
— G.E. LESSING, *The Education of the Human Race*

Wer sagt, er könne beweisen
wer sagt, er hätte kapiert
und tut nichts/ und tut nichts/ und tut nichts
der kann nichts beweisen
und hat nichts kapiert.
[Whoever says he can prove it, /Whoever says she's got it, /And does nothing, [tris] /He can prove nothing /And she's got nothing.]
— BARBARA STROMBERG, "Wer sagt," in her CD *Gerade jetzt*, Meltemi music – ORF 1993.

Stupidity is a cosmic force.
— MIROSLAV KRLEŽA, *Na rubu pameti* [*At the Limits of Reason*]

Part 1. The Question, and How Not to Answer It

> So viele Hoffnungen, so viele Entwürfe, so viel Vergeblichkeit, und bei alledem: so
> viel gültige Leistung ... Jetzt wirken sie für mich zusammen: das Gedächtnis und
> die Geschichte.
> [So many hopes, so many projects, so much futility, and nonetheless: so much valid
> accomplishment ... Memory and history: now they converge for me.]
> — HANS MAYER, "Gedächtnis und Geschichte"

1

Overwhelmingly, this twentieth century is a time of betrayals. Great expectations, enormous efforts, at a few supremely important points (1917, 1945) wondrous, breathtaking breakthroughs authorizing the most sweeping hopes (Bloch) – and yet at the end of it, looking backward at it, a huge disappointment. The hope was a historical wager, and the wager did not pay off. The enemies outside and inside ourselves were too many, too tough.

2

In this collapse of good collectives and utter malignancy of the bad collectives ruling us, we must fall back on identifying ourselves and others. Who betrayed what? I speak as one who would like to be a "writing revolutionary from the bourgeois class" (Benjamin III: 225). I wish to retain the stance of a radical socialism – maybe we can today mark its indispensable refurbishing by getting back to Marx's term "communism." I try to puzzle out what this stance may be today. But it is at least clear that a dispossessing social justice is now *the only*, if at the moment feeble, hope for the survival of this *kalpa* of humanity.

But before we get to "who" and "what", we still have to ask "how come"? The present flows into the future by way of the past: or it flows very badly.

3

Why? The best people, the greatest achievements, lead to the worst horrors. Einstein and the physicists, the DNA discovery and the geneticists, Wiener and the cyberneticists, result in the genosuicidal madness of nuclear bombs and the (still threatening) balance of unimaginable ABC terror. The yearning energies for well-being and justice of hundreds of millions of downtrodden people from Pugachev and Pushkin through the Narodniks to Trotsky and Lenin lead to the grotesque deep-sea monster of Muscovite despotism. Fascism draws its energies from perverting, with the enthusiastic support of banks and armament industries, the same millennial Joachimite urgency. The open spaces of Populist friendliness, breaking through the stock-market ice-crust in the New Deal when Mr Deeds went to town, recongeal into the antiutopia of numb Disneyfication below, orgies of shamelessness among the soon to be ruined cracked speculators above, and dozens of small or medium wars outside, on city streets and the peripheries of empire: triple drug-systems mocking and gunning down the pursuit of happiness.

4

Why is this then?
   One answer: the attempts at practical utopianism were so flawed that they were doomed from the start. "You should not have tried it." Or: "The conditions were not ripe." This Social-Democratic (Menshevik, the Compromiser of Mayakovsky's *Mystery Bouffe*) standpoint is to be rejected. In some ways conditions are never and yet always ripe (the old half-full vs. half-empty glass), and nothing ever comes about unless radicals and revolutionaries try. Just look at the alternative: the billion-slaughtering World Wars, hungers, psyche-devouring humiliations! Lenin was right to insist on seizing the day, truly "shot through with a chip of messianic time" (Benjamin). This does not mean he was then right about everything else: but he was right about the provisionally essential matter in 1917. Consider the ant, thou sluggard: try, try again! Above all: learn how to try, perhaps

differently! Learn the proper stance to take up (Brecht), how to tread the
Way (= the method).

5

One exception from utter betrayals, perhaps the hugest Stonehenge of fragments and warmest comfort to be shored against our interplanetary cold
ruins: the best of art (in the widest sense). The best surviving articulation
of lived non-official experience is in Joyce, Kafka, Meyerhold, Mayakovsky,
Chaplin, Brecht, Krleža, Andrić, Picasso, Tatlin, Larionov, Magritte, Ernst,
Eisenstein, Benjamin, Lorca, Neruda, Bartok, Shostakovich ... Even when
they were at some times forced to compromise, the compromises (*Life of
Galileo, Ivan the Terrible, The Leningrad Symphony, The Dove of Peace*)
are usually honourable, engaged, and advance our understanding. This
too carries a lesson, a glimpse of how to evaluate the betrayals by concrete
contraries. If only we could develop this glimpse – Bartók's *Piano Concerto
no. 2*, the *Inspector General* direction, *The Ballads of Petrica Kerempuh,
Battleship Potemkin*, "Josephine the Songstress," *Modern Times, St Joan of
the Stockyards, The Buckow Elegies, The Private Tutor* direction – into an
articulated plank, a reliable guide to action!

6

Most of the purely conceptual instruments have fared badly in the vertigi-
nously rapid mutations of this century. Have we really had, in any non-fictional writing or indeed other sign-systems of this time, an equivalent to the
long-range validity, to the power of anti-hegemonic generalization, allowing
specification, of Marx and – to a lesser extent – of Nietzsche? Maybe in
the mathematically laced writings (for example, Einstein)? But how much
pertinent cognition to help us overcome the New World Disorder will
remain from the best people? Perhaps only methodological hints, and at that
overwhelmingly the *pars destruens* (in Lenin, Gramsci, Wittgenstein ...)?

If so, how can we fail to note Marx and Nietzsche most intimately intertwine conceptual logic with metaphors and figures?

Part 2. What To See History As; What To See History For

> We know only one science: the science of history.
> — KARL MARX and FRIEDRICH ENGELS, *The German Ideology*

> Car ce n'est une légère entreprise [...] de bien connaître un état qui n'existe plus, qui n'a peut-être point existé, qui probablement n'existera jamais, et dont il est pourtant nécessaire d'avoir des notion justes, pour bien juger de notre état présent.
> [It is no easy enterprise to know well a state which exists no more, which has perhaps never existed, which will probably never exist, and which it is yet necessary to understand correctly in order to judge well our present state.]
> — J.-J. ROUSSEAU, *Discours sur l'origine et les fondements de l'inégalité parmi les hommes*

7

Why is, for example, Fredric Jameson (himself caught up in viscous history, of which we are all viscidly constituted) so much more cognitively useful than Ernest Mandel – within ostensibly compatible and perhaps even, in "thin" conceptual terms, identical historiosophic horizons? It is in part a matter of breadth: Mandel remains encased within an even generous, politically informed economics; this is of interest to a commonality outside of professionally closed ghettoes, or to a public sphere, only as semi-finished product for a thinker like Jameson or as a hint for overriding analogies that shatter disciplinary boundaries (untranscended example: Marx's great theory of commodity fetishism). Lacking either, the "professionally" inflected urge (such as chasing the "long cycle of crises" hypothesis) becomes formalized, loses the radical antithesis, and peters out in sterility, the *caput mortuum* of concepts chasing each other's tail in a circle.

A persuasive complement, where both the "cultural" and the "political" have the same exemplary, allegorical breadth and depth, is the convergence from these two starting points between Raymond Williams and Antonio Gramsci. Or – probably the most fertile stance articulated in our century – the interplay between Brecht's poetic persona and the self-assembled (*bricolé*), intervening Gramscian Marxism of his. But then, both Williams and Brecht knew at first hand the tools of metaphoric and narrative (that is not only conceptual) articulation.

8

The most urgent reconsideration on the agenda of the Left as I see it is of Lenin himself as a companion of names from section 5 (and antitypes such as Henry Ford). His masterpieces – October 1917, or in written form *The Philosophical Notebooks* and *The State and the Revolution*; his compromises – the NEP; his mistakes – absolutizing an "objective" materialism and the then and there probably correct but contingent Russian theory of the revolutionary Party: all of them have to be faced and evaluated in the same spirit of a "thick" pragmatic critique, in order to possibly "reacquire Lenin out of Leninism" (Haug). Nothing is gained and overmuch is lost by erasing and tabooing this experience of the century's most important liberation and betrayal. An excellent beginning: Luxemburg's critique and yet support.

Not so irrelevantly, any decision about Leninism (i.e., organized revolution by working classes, including intellectuals) is largely also a decision about Modernism. This does not at all mean that Modernism is Leninism, and even less vice versa: rather they have the same origin as answers to the crisis of capitalism and the bourgeoisie, run sometimes parallel and sometimes diverge or confront each other inimically, as competing vanguards. But it does pose the question of teleology: What is their activity for? As Lenin insisted: *cui bono*?

9

Theories – including this attempt at hypothesis – have always been toolkits. A toolkit can only be validated and finally adjusted in practice:

> Like trees with many branches but few roots
> Are those whose wisdom exceeds their deeds.
> The winds come and easily uproot them.
> (*Pirke Avot – Wisdom of Our Fathers*)

But only tools with a chance at working well – opening doors, pulling the brake, switching on the current, reaching the Internet, solving the equation, finding rhyme and reason – should be tested. Even solidly rooted trees can only prosper if they have enough leafy branches: their photosynthesis is indispensable for the roots to become and remain solid.

10

In this century, a major mutation in existence and experience has pivoted on the Faustian *bourgeois* moulting into globally violent capitalist. Faust's *citoyen* soul was given up, and simultaneously, in the dominant "democratic" variant centered in the USA, also hypocritically retained as fake fraternity. Understanding the huge and growing existential inequality of layered human classes means coping with, discounting and seeing through a formal, legal equality of individuals. The old images as well as concepts do not correspond to this existence and experience in the age of world wars. What we see life's events and existents as (culture; or theory, as its possible critique) is no longer like unto a tree with roots and leafy branches. Rather it may be like a banyan-tree, whose rhizome-roots descend from the branches: *tout se tient*.

Even more extremely, this apparently topsy-turvy mutation may have to take cognitive precedence in teaching us how to see the stymied century, in so many ways more similar to a new Gothic or Hellenistic Age than to the crown of progress. Such is our filial wisdom.

11

This is not a plea for "cultural materialism," unless culture is to mean equally what we have impoverished into the categorical compartments of politics, economics, religion, psychology, anthropology, etc. It is a plea for Marx's (and Vico's) history as the only knowledge, for historical materialism centered on many struggles of many classes, where "final instances" depend on the investigating subject as well as the investigated object, as the only epistemic and political chance of our intelligence to minimize the catastrophe, to fruitfully "organize pessimism" (Naville and Benjamin).

12

If so, self-enclosed art is not enough. The twenty-first century desperately, imperatively needs liberatory political movements by groups and classes responding to the fierce class struggle from above by an at least equally determined, persistent, and witty struggle from below. And the struggle of working people against the stifling hegemony must largely begin as the struggle of intellectuals – for we too are workers and share the same destiny – against universal brainwashing; and anybody is a potential intellectual insofar as she or he attempts to make sense of the forces shaping our lives (Gramsci, Brecht). Attempts to make sense of the forces shaping our lives will run into sand unless understanding connects to practical changing of the pernicious constellations stunting our lives. "The highest art is the art of living" (Brecht).

This is the horizon against which all our toolkits have to be judged. No toolkit is viable unless fusing the lessons of political and artistic practice. No politician should be trusted unless he has learned literary understanding (wit). No cultural critic should be trusted unless she is engaging in empirical politics. (Therefore, I am not to be trusted either, unless we optimistically think that past engagement can confer some wisdom upon one's present stance and glance when in search of present engagement.) "Politics" and "art" meet first in practice: they come out of and return to our everyday lives. But then, they cognitively meet on epistemological ground: how, what, and why do people take their circumstantial relationships *as* and *for*.

Part 3. A Little Philosophy of History

> We might have been otherwise, and might yet be.
> — DONNA HARAWAY, *Modest_Witness@Second_Millennium*

13

The macro-periodization of human history proposed by the *Manifesto of the Communist Party* is a powerful tool. This lens worked through two analogies or allegories. The first was an extrapolation, by the two Rhinelander authors, of the French Revolution of 1789 into the shortly coming proletarian revolution of all countries (but starting in France and Germany). The second was an extrapolation of the *Gemeinschaft* (commonality) of tribal societies into the classless society. This results in the Hegelian triad of tribal → class → classless societies.

14

Experiences of the last 150 years have thoroughly shaken the first allegory. It may well be (though we do not know enough) that the bourgeoisie of 1789 – and earlier English or Dutch forerunners – is the only class to come to durable power by sudden insurrection after slow and thorough economic incubation. Also, in a system of communicating vessels, it is the first ruling class consciously foregrounding perpetual growth-dynamics of production (alienated labour). The proletarian productivity of immediate producers requires dis-alienated labour, so that it cannot properly incubate before the revolutionary phase itself (Luxemburg) – except in some prefigurations, including much art. Thus the analogy between bourgeois and proletarian revolution seems not to hold. A further argument is the radically changed technoscientific environment which has added the survival of the Homo sapiens and other vertebrate species – that is, global dynamic equilibrium of people with their "environment" – to the revolutionary goal. A third is the economico-sexual oppression and stultification out of which the feminists speak: in USA, the most productive country of the world, the median earning of a woman is well below half of a man's, and about three quarters of women could not alone support a child. Other reasons for the failure of this analogy may be found.

There are some arguments that the metamorphoses of labour in computerized production may – at least in the North – create a working class whose productivity will be potentially more disalienated: both based on collective creativity and hindered by the profit motive. Even in that case, it will have to be examined whether the participation in the extraprofits of global capitalism allows this class to become as revolutionary as the *tiers état*.

15

The second, long-duration analogy is one between primitive or tribal communism, where low productivity enforced absence of classes in the modern sense, and a society without class antagonisms – though never without contradictions and clashes of interests – based on high productivity. Even if this forgets the huge drawbacks of tribal life (what was the average length of life?), the argument remains unshaken and more indispensable than ever. But that reformulates the theory of history into a tetrad: tribal → precapitalist (tributary) → capitalist → classless societies. In other words (as can be, for example, read out of Morus's *Utopia* or Chinese history): capitalism was not providentially necessary, a Happy Fall ensuring final redemption; nor will it be providentially overcome.

More mileage is here latently present: for one thing, we may have to reformulate the price for any further failure as not simply "socialism or barbarism" but a more horrifying spectre of some variant of decennial or centennial fascism, fusing aspects from all the worst capitalist, feudal, despotic, and slave-owning societies in the interest of the new rulers. Which lay godhead may guarantee this is not possible?

16

How can we not remember Hitler, the huge shadow out of this century cast upon our future? Born and reborn of despairs and rages inseparable from capitalism, Hitler is for us immortal just like socialism. Next time, the Iron Heel would be using drugs and genetics for its supermen.

But obversely and always, "all poets are Yids" (Tsvetaeva): the critical and irritating marginals, enunciating annunciations. So are all other millions or billions of people who understand very well that they are rejected, humiliated, and exploited by this shameless capitalism without a human face: they are all Mitteleuropean Jews railroaded into extinction by Himmler's and the IMF's progress. But in their wit, all these millions understand just as well as – or better than – intellectuals the utopian chink of "les choses pourraient être autrement" (Ruyer: things could have been otherwise). Brecht's confrontation of the monster Hitler with the plebeian joker (*Witzereisser*) Schweyk at the end of his eponymous play must be a focus for all our catastrophic defeats and victories to come in the extremely dangerous twenty-first century.

17

What then remains of Marx? Many things. Centrally: the realization that the figure of Destiny is in capitalism Political Economy. Tykhe is swallowed into the Stockmarket, Anangke rides on the profit-bringing and profit-enforcing bombers. Hell is the sweatshops of China and Montreal, the cubicles of solitary rooms.

Part 4. The Question of How; "Science"

Salus rei publicae suprema lex.
[The health/ salvation of the commonwealth is the overriding law.]
                                                    — Ancient Roman rule

Man kann nicht sagen, dass etwas ist, ohne zu sagen, was es ist.
[We cannot say that something is without saying what it is.]
                                    — F. SCHLEGEL, *Athenäumsfragment*

18

If the "why" of Part 1 is here and now too difficult to answer directly, the crucial detour through "how" seems required. How are we to go about answering the question of the century, correctly posed at its outset as "What Is to Be Done"? What kind of optics has a chance at looking around the corner or at the gathering galaxies?

19

Beside and beyond the bourgeois "commonsense," the ruling theoretical answer of the last quarter millennium, displacing theology, was – by means of, under the flag of science. It is a powerful answer, seductive precisely for the intellectuals we need, yet on the whole a misleading one. Transmuted into technoscience, it intervenes with exponential force and speed into everybody's daily life: soon the filthy rich shall have chimaeras and sphinxes as pets.

So: What does science do? How does it do what it does? Is the power of intervention gained by this method worth the price we are paying for it (genocide, ecocide)?

20

With Descartes, Galileo, and Newton, "science" separated itself out of wisdom – what Kant still called *wissenschaftliche Lebensweisheit* or "cognitive wisdom of living," whose backbone is care for health and salvation – on the basis of quantifying (mathematics). The underlying "laws" of the universe were those that could be mathematically described and repeated in calculatable practice. This displaced the wrong qualities of theological knowledge, for example Aristotelian "qualitative physics." But it also displaced, in the interest of the bourgeoisie, the supreme law of the commonwealth's *salus*. It dispensed with any quality, except the quality of being quantified. It thus divorced scientific fact from value. The relationship of science to nature became consubstantial with the relationship of scientists to ignorant others (workers, women).

The price seemed right for 300 years. It became too high around 1848, and has grown exorbitantly ever since. It proved impossible to substitute for the exploitation of one class by another an exploitation of Nature by Man (Saint-Simon). In the age of world wars this has resulted in the full dominance of "barbarian experts" (C.P. Snow), blind servants of the Iron Heel. Alas, scientists, especially those wedded to capitalist profit and ideology (in my optimistic days I think they are only 97 percent), are of no use in our first tasks, stopping the destruction of the planet by war and ecocide.

21

We are forced to conclude: the project of human survival is consubstantial with a return of "specialized" sciences – most urgently the most powerful ones – into their matrix of cognitive wisdom. Truly democratic science – by and for (the) people – has to espouse being publicly taken to account as to each and every of its uses and consequences: which would be no more dictatorial than the strict control relentlessly exercised over it today by and for profit, debasing all that is not instantly marketable as quantified bytes of "information."

Modern natural science itself has given us hints how to do this spirally, by not abolishing Newton but subsuming him under Einstein as a specialized case. Human affairs are certainly messier than the Lorentz algebraic transformations which can quantify that particular subsumption. We shall have to declare that big chunks or aspects equivalent to Newton (Bacon, Descartes ...) are counterproductive and not usable after a given point of people's relationships with each other and with the environment, such as 1848 in the rich North. Use-value qualities are by now an intrinsic and inalienable part of facts. As a fact for us air is only air if breathable and water only water if drinkable. Chunks or aspects of science compatible with this may be – must be – subsumed. But the weight of proving that it is compatible must lie on the patent-appliers and must be incorporated into every scientific result.

Not against science but for a science saturated with consciously chosen values. Not back to Aristotle but forward from Marx and Nietzsche.

Part 5. Poetic Justice vs. Murderings

De quel nom te nommer, heure obscure où nous sommes?
[By which name to name you, hour of obscurity wherein we are?]
    — VICTOR HUGO "Prélude" in his *Chants du crépuscule* (1835)

Eh! Où en êtes-vous dans la route du bien quand la mendicité, l'agiotage, la banqueroute, la mauvaise foi règnent plus que jamais dans votre dégoûtante Civilisation?
[Well! Where are you on the road to goodness when beggary, speculation, bankruptcy, bad faith reign more than ever in your disgusting Civilisation?]
    — CHARLES FOURIER, *Égarements de la raison montré par les ridicules de la science incertaine* (1847)

22

How may we generalize the lesson from the ingent exception of art (see 5)? One way is that poetry is a form of wit, bringing out the unexpected from the encrusted. Another way is that the artistic spacetime, the "thickly" different world, "fixes" the unexpected as a latent picture is fixed by the chemical bath into the photographic negative. It is coproduced by the user's imagination: by whomever and however created, art presupposes a user, an ideal "we." What is fixed is also articulated; it can be understood, contradicted, sifted. The overriding law of the bourgeois world is Franklin's "time is money," the highway of exchange-value destroying the fertile wetlands. In traffic with art, "time is a form of wealth to be spent at leisure and with detachment" (Calvino), the worlds are manipulable and possibly different. "It ain't necessarily so" (the Gershwin brothers): use-values do not have to be given up. In poetry's (art's) utopian glimmer, probe, and epitome, alternatives for humanity can be – cheaply! – rehearsed. It is at its best, in its horizons, a perennial playful childhood of human kind. But also – for the triumphant side may today not be disjoined from the militant side – the wrathful aspect of creation identifying and fettering the poisoners.

23

Poetry (artistic production) is then potentially a privileged form for conveying and constituting cognition, for humanizing it by means of figures and events recalling but also modifying the life-world, and for understanding what cognition is and may be. Art foregrounds the user's interpretation but attempts to steer it according to a constant orientation. Art is not simply imagistic evasion from the chained world of stale concepts (Lukács) but a new interpenetration of concept with an always oriented (topological) imagery. Neither weavers of wreaths hiding bourgeois chains nor hunters bringing fresh meat to the lords, artists must sit as equals at the symposium of understanding. The worlds of art may – in the best cases – present us with radically different experiences, whose shapings are then guides to salvation. Hegel's judgment at the beginning of the nineteenth century that art is no longer our supreme mental necessity but has to be spelled by more systematic forms of cognition, such as philosophy, has to be turned upside-down at the beginning of the twenty-first century. The triumphalist statics of his esthetics forgets his splendid dialectics. It leads to his surely strange sentence that the thought of a killer is more significant than the most beautiful spectacle of nature. Well, maybe – and if so, so much the worse for significance – but it is certainly no more useful to us, his incorporate fellow-humans.

It is understandable that ruling classes intuitively distrust and hinder humanized cognition and salvation. But the unbelievable obtuseness of all shades of Marxist politics so far toward art, of a piece with their refusal to renew their thinking by bathing in ongoing history, raises serious doubts about their liberatory interests (as opposed to change of ruling class-blocs). As Nietzsche had surmised, we have to "look at science in the light of art, but at art in the light of life."

24

But, of course: the potentiality of this poetically just privilege can only be realized "when it will be understood that every literature that refuses to walk hand in hand with science and philosophy is a homicidal and suicidal literature" (Baudelaire). And today we have to add to these tacit assistants of murderers all artistic experience that refuses to at least expose itself to, face and understand, the deepest emancipatory currents of its age; that does not refuse the programmatic destruction of life's qualities, the aggressive destruction of nurturing or care.

Doctrine: More Departures from Heine #14

Drummer, drum on & have no fear
And kiss the bare–breast Liberty!
This is the whole of science and art
The sum of all philosophy.

Drum & inveigle the drowsy people
Send the snake's hiss and roar of lions,
One step in front, ready to die,
This is the sum of art and science.

This is old Karl's dialectics
Of all philosophy it is the Summa.
I've understood it by steadily looking,
& seeing the Revolution one Summer.

25

What then may be workable, embodied answers to the peculiar, stunted rationality of wars, of the exchange-value rule of bureaucracy and army? We have to find this out in action. As Vico argued, whatever we cannot intervene into, we cannot understand (say, the cosmos). But, clearly: only use-values can stand up to capitalist unequal exchange. This holds in spades for the last three-quarters of a century, predominantly operating on "brain labour," so that the capitalist instauration of the hegemony of economics instead of politics and theology must be sublated under the hegemony of culture (in the widest sense). Ancient designations for these use-values were compassion, indignation, and love: that is, today, communism and poetry. We need to realize that there is no poetry without communism, and no communism without poetry. All poets know this, often in fantastic metamorphoses; few communists have allowed their suspicion to flower. When sundered, what we get are caricatures which compromise the potential horizon of either.

26

Thus, the overriding question is now: where are we to look for liberatory currents in this penurious, indigent, shabby, needy, mean, paltry, poor time of ours? For if we do not at least guess at them, approximate them, try to forecast them, pave the way for them, help – however feebly – to make them possible or maybe bring them about, how are we to use Marx's great insight that no theory or method can be divorced from or indeed understood without the practice of social groups to which it corresponds? How are we to delineate the new sensorium humanity needs for survival?

27

This may today be only answered by contraries: What are the major blights most efficiently destroying human flesh, dignity, and sense? I have named three in Chapter 10: mass murders, mass prostitution, mass drugging. They are simultaneously literal and metaphoric – so poetry is needed to plumb them fully. They intertwine.

Murders are done to bodies by bullet, bomb or knife, and to psyches by pressures of misery enforced by State or group terror. Prostitution of sex has been foisted mainly upon females, of intellect mainly upon males. Drugging is not only crack, alcohol, and industrially produced pill but also Disneyfication (the rage for commodity consumption), scientism, and all variants of tribal religion, whether the tribe number two thousand or two billion members.

Ours is an age of violence multiplied by the unprecedented powers of capitalist technoscience, inflicted upon pain-ridden people in their hundreds of millions, and whoever does not write, create, work because, in spite of, and against this violence, is co-responsible for it. The violence corresponds to obfuscating language and imagery – either facelessly generalized or individually demonizing (the enemy is either The Moslems or Milošević). This is where we can, and therefore must, *begin* to intervene.

We can only do this at length, and collectively. It may be painful, but not doing it will be immensely more painful.

28

What are we, who should still call ourselves the Left, and whose conscious core should perhaps think again about assuming communism as its poetry and prose, then to do? I attempt to identify some preconditions in chapter 10, section 10.3, to which I refer the patient reader.

P.S. (2002)

Theses must be brief. I have resisted the temptation, three years later, to update this to "terrorism," which I do elsewhere. I hope it is clear this look backward was, like Bellamy's, searching for a basis to look forward. If it works, it may be readily applied to today.

Works Cited

Longer arguments and large bibliographies may be found in some other works of mine (shamelessly stealing from dozens of wiser people and the practice of millions), including Chapters 8–10 of this book, and further in:

Suvin, Darko. "De la guerre 2001: triomphe du capitalisme sauvage." *La Chute du Mur de Berlin dans les idéologies*. Vol. 6. Ed. Marc Angenot and Régine Robin. Montréal: Discours social, 2002. 161–74; see Pierre Mesnard y Mendez. "Capitalism Means/ Needs War." *Socialism and Democracy* 16.2 (2002): 65–92, also <www.sdonline.org>.
——. "Haltung (Bearing) and Emotions: Brecht's Refunctioning of Conservative Metaphors for Agency." *Zweifel – Fragen – Vorschläge: Bertolt Brecht anlässlich des Einhundertsten*. Ed. Thomas Jung. Frankfurt: Peter Lang, 1999. 43–58.
——. "Two Cheers for Essentialism and Totality: On Marx's Oscillation and its Limits (as well as on the Taboos of Post-Modernism)." *Rethinking Marxism* 10.1 (1998): 66–82.

CHAPTER 13

A Tractate on Dystopia 2001

To Gianni Maniscalco Basile, friend and fellow dystopian

"Usà puyew usu wapiw"
["Backward going forward looking,"]
Swampy Cree tribe phrase and image taken from a porcupine backing
into a rock crevice – lifted from U.K. Le Guin

Premises

1

All of us on the planet Earth live in highly endangered times. Perhaps the richer among us, up to 10 percent globally but disproportionately concentrated in the trilateral USA–Western Europe–Japan and its appendages, have been cushioned from realizing it by the power of money and the self-serving ideology it erects. But even those complain loudly of the "criminality" and in general "moral decay" of the desperately vicious invading their increasingly fortress-like neighbourhoods. We live morally in an almost complete dystopia – dystopia because anti-utopia – and materially (economically) on the razor's edge of collapse, distributive and collective.

2

Utopianism is an orientation toward a horizon of radically better forms of relationships among people. It establishes vectors of people's desire, need, and imaginative understanding toward radically better horizons. This was being discussed at length in the 1960s and 1970s. But in the endangered today this is, while still supremely necessary, not enough. Utopian reflections, in and out of fiction, have now to undertake openings that lead toward agency: action.

3

We therefore have to talk first about epistemology (imagination, semiotics, semantics, art) and then about ontology (application of imagination to really existing power relationships, politics). "Reality is not at all the same as the empirical being – reality is not a being, it is a becoming [...] the moment in which the new is born. Reality is admittedly the criterion of accurate thinking. But it does not just exist, it becomes – not without participation of the thinking." (Lukács).

A. Epistemology and Utopia

Introduction

The discourse around utopia/nism is not far from the Tower of Babel. Its ideological cause (capitalist maligning of non-capitalist alternatives) is difficult to affect. But it behoves us to try and affect secondary semantic muddiness. A toolkit needed to talk intelligibly has to be proposed, subsuming my own earlier attempts and selected illuminations from criticism in English, German, Italian, French, and so on.

4

UTOPIA will be defined as: the construction of a particular community where sociopolitical institutions, norms, and relationships between people are organized according to a *radically different principle* than in the author's community; this construction is based on estrangement arising out of an alternative historical hypothesis; it is created by discontented social classes interested in otherness and change. All utopias involve people who radically suffer of the existing system and desire to radically change it.

Gloss 4a: This definition backgrounds the tradition arising out of Morus's island and title, in which the relationships between people are organized according to a radically more perfect principle than in the author's community. I believe we have to abandon the meaning and horizon of utopianism as automatically entailing radically better relationships. More perfect relationships have to be proved (or disproved) for each particular case or type of texts. Confusing *radical otherness* and *radically greater perfection* leads to muddle: incommunicability or wilful obscurantism.

Gloss 4b: Estrangement (Shklovsky's formal *ostranenie* issuing into Brecht's political epistemic of *Verfremdung*) is a cognitive strategy of perception-cum-evaluation based on radical critical desire. It comports multiple possibilities of anamorphosis and eversion of salient aspects in the author's world, which has as its purpose the recognition that the reader truly lives in a world of topsy-turvy values.

5

In case the imaginatively constructed community is not based principally on sociopolitical but on other, say biological or geological, radically different principles, we are dealing with Science Fiction (SF). The understanding that sociopolitics cannot change without all other aspects of life also changing has led to SF becoming the privileged locus of utopian fiction in the twentieth century.

Gloss 5: This means that utopian fiction is, today and retrospectively, both an independent aunt and a dependent daughter of SF. The lines of

consanguinity begin to intertwine in H.G. Wells's sociobiological SF, where
biology is mainly a metaphor for social class.

6

Utopia may be divided into the polar opposites of: EUTOPIA, defined
as in 4 but having the sociopolitical institutions, norms, and relationships
between people organized according to a *radically more perfect* principle
than in the author's community; and DYSTOPIA (cacotopia), organized according to a *radically less perfect* principle. The radical difference
in perfection is in both cases judged from the point of view and within
the value-system of a discontented social class or congeries of classes, as
refracted through the writer.

   Gloss 6a: As in all other entities in these theses, we are dealing with
ideal types. Example of proximity to eutopia: Morus's *Utopia*; to dystopia:
Zamyatin's *My (We)*.

   Gloss 6b: If utopia is a sociopolitical beast, it is also imaginary. It is
not simply that all sociopolitical notions are such, as Anderson famously
concluded of "nation," and that this is more evident in counterfactual
speculations. Further, utopia provides ways of understanding both how
to refuse the sociopolitics and *Lebenswelt* of here-and-now and how to go
about constructing countermodels. Models are not reality (there are no
isobars on the surfaces of continents): they are speculative possibilities and
guidelines. Utopia is an epistemological beast: a method and not a state.
This disbars it from being translated in any straightforward way into the
ontological sphere. Nonetheless its reason for existing is such a translation
and anamorphosis. In eutopia, it is Moses on Mount Horeb: the Promised
Land will be expugnated by Joshua. Dystopia operates by contraries.

7

Dystopia in its turn divides into anti-utopia and what I shall call "simple" dystopia. As Jameson notes, the anti-utopia is a structural inversion of eutopia, "formally quite different from the dystopian narrative."

ANTI-UTOPIA is a significantly different locus which is explicitly designed to refute a currently proposed eutopia. It is a pretended eutopia – a community whose hegemonic principles pretend to its being more perfectly organized than any thinkable alternative, while our representative "camera eye" and value-monger finds out it is significantly less perfect, a polemic nightmare. Thus, it finally also turns out to be a dystopia.

"SIMPLE" DYSTOPIA (so called to avoid inventing yet another prefix to "topia") is a straightforward dystopia, that is, one which is not also an anti-utopia.

Gloss 7a: The intertext of anti-utopia is, historically, the strongest "currently proposed" eutopia. Ca. 1915–75 the intertext was therefore anti-socialism, but both earlier (from Souvestre to Kafka's *Penal Colony*) and later other intertexts, say of militarist or market violence, may prevail.

The intertext of "simple" dystopia has been and remains more or less radical anti-capitalism. Zamyatin, individualist but avantgarde critic of mass society, straddles both.

Gloss 7b: Examples of proximity to anti-utopia: all the weaker followers of Zamyatin, from Ayn Rand and Orwell on; of proximity to "simple" dystopia: Pohl–Kornbluth's *Space Merchants* (and in general the US "new maps of hell") or the movies *Soylent Green* and *Blade Runner*.

8

More clearly than for other genres of writing, all the delimitations above function only if understood within the *historical spacetime*, i.e., within the unrepeatable social formation and horizon, of a text's inception. For a post-industrial reader the statics of Plato's *Politeia* (*Commonwealth*) or Campanella's *Civitas Solis* (*City of the Sun*) translate the historically intended eutopian horizon into a dystopian one.

However, while eutopia and anti-utopia are more akin to satire and pamphlet (Frye's "anatomy") and "simple" dystopia to the standard individualist novel, to the extent they employ narrative agents and chronotopes, all of these remain (pace Jameson) fictional strategies jelling into narrative genres.

Gloss 8a: A reader of Plato in, say, the twentieth century is reading against a different horizon of experiences and values, which colours all, so that the shadow of the *SS* falls on the Guardians' politics and erotics; we might call this the "Pierre Ménard" syndrome or law.

Gloss 8b: This is not a defect but a strength of utopian horizons and artefacts: born in history, acting upon history, they laicize eternity and demand to be judged in and by history.

9

For this reason alone, it is mandatory to insert the overtly estranging *satire* into the utopian tradition, at the latest since Cyrano's *États et Empires de la Lune* (*States and Empires of the Moon*). It took the second major step in that tradition: to import into utopia's other spatial (later: temporal) locus a radically worse sociopolitical organization, and to do this by developing the perceptive and evaluative strategy of estrangement into an array of deeply critical micro-devices. Historically and psychologically, dystopia is unthinkable without, and as a rule mingled with, satire.

Gloss 9: Untranscended example: Swift's *Gulliver's Travels*; but the twentieth-century SF texts from Lem to Sheckley, Dick, and Banks run a close second.

10

To use Swiftian terms: in utopia a Thing Which Is Not is posited as being (in eutopia as being supremely valuable), while in satire a Thing Which Is is posited as being despicable; one condemns what is by indirection and the other by direction. If utopia is to be seen as a formal inversion of salient sociopolitical aspects of the writer's world which has as its purpose the recognition that the reader truly lives in an axiologically inverted world, then satire wittily foregrounds the inherent absurdity, and thus counteracts utopia's necessary but often solemn doctrinal categorization. It adds the Ass to the Saviour's crib and entry into Jerusalem.

11

We have here, as already in 4, come up against the necessity of another set of analytic tools. From Plato's term *topos ouranios* (heavenly place) on, it is clear that utopia's location, while a very important signifier, is only seemingly spatial: it abounds in maps but it is not photographable. In the best cases it is less significant than the orientation toward a place somewhere in front of the oriented; and furthermore, even the place to be reached is not fixed and completed: it moves on. It is thus situated in an imaginary space which is a measure of and measured as value (quality) rather than distance (quantity).

The necessary elements for utopian movement – of which stasis is a zero-form – are an agent that moves, and an imaginary space (or time – but all the metaphors for time are spatial) in which it moves. The agential aspects, to be approached at the end, open up the properly political problematic of who is the bearer of utopia/nism. The pertinent aspects of space are: a/ the place of the agent who is moving, his *locus*; b/ the *horizon* toward which that agent is moving; and c/ the *orientation*, a vector that conjoins locus and horizon.

Gloss 11: It is characteristic of horizon that it moves with the location of the moving agent, as demonstrated by Giordano Bruno. But it is, obversely, characteristic of orientation that it can through all the changes of locus remain a constant vector of desire and cognition.

12

A combinatorics of locus/horizon gives the following possibilities:

1. H > L: *open-ended or dynamic utopia;*
2. L = H or L > H: *closed or static utopia;*
3. L (H = 0): *heterotopia;*
4. H (L = 0): *abstract or non-narrative utopia(nism).*

There seems to be no obstacle to applying these terms (as well as a further set of agential terms) as analytic tools to the whole range of utopian studies – fictions, projects, and colonies.

Gloss 12: #1 is the *dominance of Horizon over Locus*: Locus does not coincide with but interacts with Horizon: this makes for a dynamic, open utopia (e.g., Platonov's *Chevengur*, Le Guin's *The Dispossessed*). #2 is a Locus that coincides with or swallows Horizon: this makes for a dogmatic, static, closed utopia (e.g., Campanella's *Civitas Solis*, Cabet's *Voyage en Icarie*). #3 is *Locus alone*, without a utopian Horizon: this makes for heterotopia (e.g., Foucault, in fiction his disciple Delany). #4 has *Horizon alone*, without a utopian Locus; this is where non-localized "utopian thought" belongs, such as all the abstract blueprints, utopian programs, etc.

I have difficulty in seeing how could, in any strict sense, either a horizon without concrete locus – without Bakhtin's chronotope (#4) – or a locus with no horizon (#3) be a good or bad utopia (though they can be the utopia's contradiction).

13

Finally: what is not usefully discussed as utopia but as some other beast? Among other things, any construction, I would say, that does not significantly deal with a radically changed community but with dreams of individual felicity within the social status quo (Don Juan) or outside of society (Robinson Crusoe). No doubt, these too are multiply connected with utopianism, by contraries or eversion, but arraying all dreams of betterment under the illicit metaphor of utopia – as in the most meritorious Ernst Bloch – leads to a loss of all explicative clarity. While supremely important today, utopia is not the same as Being, or even as Supreme Good.

Gloss 13: Much of the otherwise highly interesting SF, from Dick through Delany to cyberpunk, backgrounds, fragments or indeed represses all kinds of utopianism so strongly that, although inescapably written between the eutopian and dystopian horizons, it would need too complicated analogical mediations to be usefully discussed here.

B. Politics and Dystopia

If in Part A a critic can be formal and impersonal, calling attention to the rules of method (suggesting what delimitations may be required), this is scarcely the case for the following Parts B and C. Even where I do not expressly introduce the first person singular, it is implied, so that the following theses are largely stimuli for what may be further debated.

B1 Post-Fordism

14

If history is a creatively constitutive factor of utopian writings and horizons, then we also have to recognize the epistemic shift beginning in the 1930s and crystallizing in the 1970s: *capitalism co-opts all it can from utopia* (not the name it abhors) and invents its own, new, dynamic locus. It pretends this is a finally realized eutopia (end of qualitative history) but since it is in fact for about 90 percent of humanity clearly, and for 8–9 percent in subterranean ways, a lived dystopia, it demands to be called anti-utopia. We live in an ever faster circulation of a whirligig of fads that do not better human relationships but allow heightened oppression and exploitation, especially of women, children, and the poor, in "a remarkably dynamic society that goes nowhere" (Noble). The economists and sociologists I trust call it *Post-Fordism* and global commodity market – unregulated for higher profit of capital, very regulated for higher exploitation of workers.

15

The unprecedented Post-Fordist mobilization and colonization of all non-capitalized spaces, from the genome to people's desires, was faced with the insufficient efficacy of orthodox religions (including scientism and liberalism). After "belief became polluted, like the air or the water" (de Certeau), *culture* began supplying authoritative horizons for agency and meaning. It does so either *as information* **or** *as esthetics*: information-intensive production in working time (for example biotechnology, whose output is information inscribed in and read off living matter) and "esthetic" consumption in leisure time, the last refuge of desire. The new orthodoxy of belief proceeds thus "camouflaged as facts, data and events" (de Certeau) or as "culture industry" images.

16

Early on within Post-Fordism, Raymond Williams sniffed the winds of change and drew attention to a new dominant in pragmatic as well as cultural history in which radical change (communist revolutions) has failed, largely because capitalism has managed to co-opt change. This went beyond the superficial yearly fashions, consubstantial to consumerist capitalism (Benjamin), to a different mode of doing business, soon to be known as globalization and Post-Modernism. Change is now permanently on the agenda but "primarily under the direction and in the terms [I would add: and on terms] of the dominant social order itself" (Williams). It led to the battle-cry "death to systems," meaning in practice not what the working classes earlier meant when opposing the System but an end to all-inclusive alternative projects.

Those taking up the cry with Lyotard, Colletti, and co. did not mean that they themselves should not form a system of institutional and other power ties and that their writings should not become the institutionalized academic form of criticism known as Deconstruction, but that all talk of wholeness and totality be henceforth terrorized into extinction. The dogmas of Soviet-type pseudo-socialism were fiercely ripped apart, the dogmas of "free market" (meaning demolition of public control over huge capitalist conglomerates) – which, I would argue, are at least as pernicious and murderous – were not questioned. This transfers into utopianism, Williams noted taking up terms by Miguel Abensour, as *heuristics* vs. systematics, and he went on to discuss even–handedly their strengths and weaknesses.

Gloss 16a: I can here identify three exemplary Post-Fordist constructions, all "esthetic." One is dystopian and anti-utopian: Disneyland (points 18–20), and two are reworkings of old stances and genres, Fallible Utopia and Fallible Dystopia (points 21–24). This already points to the fact that hegemonic bourgeois ideology (say in TV and newspapers) has kept resolutely systematic, albeit in updated guises such as Disneyfication. Obversely, what may perhaps be called the "new" Left has in and after the 1960s found new ways to proceed in heuristic guise.

Gloss 16b: Of course, the overarching dystopian construct is the "informational" one of Post-Fordism and global capitalism itself, the killer whale inside which we have to live, but obeying my point 13, I shall not discuss it directly here.

17

However, heuristic means "serving to find out" and it is not incompatible with systematic, which originally meant both pertaining to "the whole scheme of created things, the universe" and to "a set of principles, etc.: a scheme, method" (*OED*): you can very well find out a universal scheme. Systematisation became rigid in the nineteenth century, when Engels ironically noted that "the 'system' of all philosophers [...] springs from an imperishable desire of the human mind – the desire to overcome all contradiction." Rather, the heuristic should be contrasted to what philosophers call the "ostensive" mode: concentrating on the right formulation of a question vs. handing down received wisdom. The heuristic method induces the questioner to collaborate in finding the answer, which is indispensable in times of fast change, in learner or world. No wonder that in computer programming it has come to mean cognizing by continual trial-and-error stages.

But any teacher – or other practitioner, say practical theologian (Bastian) – would know that you cannot reach anybody without using both methods: only on the basis of existing understanding can new knowledge be gotten. When vanguard knowledge began to proceed heuristically – as of 1905, when Einstein did not call his paper on relativity a theory but considerations from a "heuristic viewpoint," or indeed as of Marx, who called his considerations not a theory but "a critique" – it was disputing improperly absolutized, closed systematisation.

Gloss 17: This can be clearly seen in the static eutopias that infested the Positivist age (Mercier, Cabet, Bellamy), which swallowed horizon in locus. They were fiercely combated by the Right because of their system (in anti-utopias such as Souvestre's) and by the Left because of their method (in metamorphic eutopias such as Restif's or Morris's).

B2 Disneyfication as Dystopia

18

An exemplary (bad) case of a dystopian misuse of eutopian images are the edulcorated fables and fairy-tales of Disneyland. I shall use it as a privileged *pars pro toto* of the capitalist and especially US admass brainwash. Its spatial rupture with everyday life masks its intensification of commodity dominance. Its central spring is what I shall (adapting Louis Marin) call *reproductive empathy*. As Benjamin remarked, "the commercial glance into the heart of things demolishes the space for the free play of viewing" by abolishing any critical distance. This empathy functions, perverting Freud's dream-work, by *transfer ideologizing* and *substitution commodifying*.

Gloss 18a: Transfer ideologizing is the continually reinforced empathizing immersion, the "thick," topologically and figurally concrete, and seamless false consciousness, that injects the hegemonic bourgeois version of US normality into people's neurons by "naturalizing" and neutralizing three imaginative fields: historical time as the space of alternative choices; the foreign/ers; and the natural world. Historical time is turned into the myth of technological progress, while the foreign and nature become the primitive, the savage, and the monstrous.

Gloss 18b: In substitution commodifying, the Golden Calf is capillarized in the psychic bloodstream as *commodity*. The upshot of Disneyland, life as "a permanent exchange and perpetual consuming," commodifies desire, and in particular the desire for happiness as signification or meaningfulness. The dynamic and sanitized empathizing into the pursuit of commodity is allegorized as anthropomorphic animals who stand for various affects that make up this pursuit. The affects and stances are strictly confined to the petty-bourgeois "positive" range where, roughly, Mickey Mouse introduces good cheer, the Lion King courage and persistence, etc.

19

Psychologically, the Disneyfication strategy is one of *infantilization* of adults. Its images function as a "security blanket," producing constantly repeated demand to match the constantly recycled offer. The infantilization entails a double rejection. First, it rejects any intervention into the real world that would make the pursuit of happiness collectively attainable: it is a debilitating daydream which appeals to the same mechanism as empathizing performances and publicity in our "society of spectacle." Second and obverse, it rejects any reality constriction of one's desire, however shallow or destructive. Wedded to consumer dynamics of an ever expanding market, Disneyland remains deeply inimical to knowledge, which crucially includes an understanding of limits for any endeavour – and in particular of the final personal limit of death. Snow White must always be magically resuscitated, to circulate again.

Gloss 19: "Main Street, USA," the central thoroughfare of Disneyland, was constructed as an exact replica of the main street of Walt Disney's boyhood town, except that it was, "down to every brick and shingle and gas lamp," five-eighths of the normal size, and that it created a sense of depth, both shortening and stretching the perception, by having each exterior level be larger than the one above it: "the intended effect was to recall the main street of every adult's distanced youth [...] with the remembered perspective

of a child's eye." Disney passed most days inside his apartment above Main
Street, "where he would stand by the window with tears streaming down
his face as people walked along the boulevard of his dreams" (M. Eliot).

20

In sum: Disneyland's trap for desire, this fake Other, is a violence exercised
upon the imaginary by its banalized images. Disneyfication is a shaping of
affective investment into commodifying which reduces the mind to infantilism
as an illusory escape from death: a mythology. It can serve as a metonymy of
what Jameson has discussed as the Post-Modern "consumption of the very
process of consumption," say in TV. It pre-empts any alternative imagination, any fertile possibility of a radical otherness or indeed simply of shuttling in and out of a story.

B3   Fallible Eu/Dystopia

21

From Moylan's pioneering delimitation and the wealth of his analyses
of fictional and critical texts in *Demand*, I draw the following scheme
for what I prefer to call the *Fallible Eutopia*, a new sub-genre of the US
1960s–1970s:

1. the society of textual action is eutopian, in open or subtle contra-
    diction to the human relations and power structures in the writer's
    reality;
2. this new Possible World is revealed as beset by dangers – centering
    on inner contradictions, but often including also outer, hegemonic
    counter-revolutionary violence – that threaten to reinstate class
    stratification, violence, and injustice;
3. our hero/ine, often a multifocal collective, combats this threat with
    some chance of success.

This form supplements the usual utopian critique of the writer's (dystopian) reality with a second front against the involution and downfall of the eutopian society.

Gloss 21a: Examples: Robert Nichols's wonderful tetralogy *Daily Lives in Nghsi–Altai*; Naomi Mitchison's *Solution Three*; Sally M. Gearhart's *Wanderground*; Suzy M. Charnas's *Motherlines* dilogy (now trilogy); the culmination of the first wave of this form, Ursula K. Le Guin's *The Dispossessed*, explicating in its two loci, braided chapter structure, and the subtitle of "An Ambiguous Utopia" the two fronts; and K. Stanley Robinson's work culminating so far in the Mars *Trilogy* and *Years of Rice and Salt*, the masterpieces of its second, dialectically post-feminist wave.

Gloss 21b: These works are based in the counter-hegemonic US and European movements of the times, from anarchist ascendancies through the centrally situated feminist ones to other counter-cultural ones (gay, ecological, "rainbow"). This is clear in the "plague on both your houses" thrust typical of the anti-Stalinist "New Left." It is confirmed by the abrupt cessation of its first wave with the advent of Reagan and its reappearance when the shock of Post-Fordism had been digested.

22

From Moylan's pioneering delimitation and the wealth of his analyses of fictional and critical texts in *Scraps*, I draw the following scheme for what I prefer to call the *Fallible Dystopia*, a new sub-genre arising out of both the shock of Post-Fordism and its imaginative mastering:

1. the society of textual action is dystopian, in open extrapolation from or subtle analogy to human relations and power structures in the writer's reality;
2. this new Possible World is revealed as resistible and changeable, by our hero/ine, often with great difficulty.

This form proposes that no dystopian reality is nightmarishly perfect, and that its seams may be picked apart.

Gloss 22a: In the best cases, such as K. Stanley Robinson and Marge Piercy, this form begins to visit the "periphery" of capitalism, usually the Arab world. Obversely, the escape to a eutopian enclave as illusion of bliss, finally to the stars, inherited from earlier dystopian SF (for example *The Space Merchants*), is an individualist temptation persisting in SF from John Brunner (if not A.E. Van Vogt) to Octavia Butler.

Gloss 22b: Examples: Pamela Sargent's *The Shore of Women*, an exceptionally explicit self-criticism of separatist feminism; Robinson's *Gold Coast*; Piercy's *He, She and It*; Butler's *Parable of the Sower*; and Ken MacLeod's *Star Fraction*. The great ancestor is London's *Iron Heel*, while Huxley's *Island* already prefigured the fall from Fallible Eutopia into Fallible Dystopia. Pat Cadigan's *Synners* melds the Fallible Dystopia and cyberpunk. A ludic variant at its margin is the "Culture" series by Iain M. Banks beginning with *Consider Phlebas* (1987). The reader should draw her own conclusion from the preponderance of female names, within an incipient regrouping of opposition to unbridled speculative capitalism.

23

The epistemic and political impulse of those two sub-genres or forms seems very similar, since they reflect upon the causes and implications of fatal politics "as systemic" (Moylan), in a flexible or "soft" totalizing interrogation (Jameson, Suvin "Two Cheers") carried by the epic and heuristic narrative. Both oppose monolithism and foster dialogues. Both redound back on the reader's reality, potentially investing its bleakness with indignant affect. Their differences stem mainly from the different structure of cognitive feeling in their historical moments (this can be well seen in Robinson's switch from the mainly dystopian *Gold Coast* [1988] to the mainly eutopian *Pacific Edge* [1990]). Rooted in a Gramscian "pessimism of the intellect, optimism of the will," interweaving glimpses of far-off horizons with the closure inside the belly of the beast, these are hybrid and often polyphonic writings. In the pragmatic absence and indeed breakdown of collective agencies, such as centralized parties, the writings focus on the *choices* by one or more focal agents, themselves endangered and fallible, who undergo a heuristic awakening to be followed by the reader – not least toward new collective agencies from the bottom up. Sometimes this is formalized as different time-horizons or histories flowing out of some crucial choice (Russ, Le Guin, Piercy).

Fallible Eutopia had to devise more innovative textual strategies to counteract the dogmatic systematisation of its tradition and make room for the presence of the old hegemony inside and outside the eutopians. It is therefore as a rule heuristic and open, fit for epic action and articulation of change as process and not blueprint. Fallible Dystopia, with a shorter tradition, has no such rigid format to break, either formally or ideologically (nobody ever set out to realize a dystopia): it can simply follow the river-bed of societal history. Since this kind of Dystopia can incorporate rather than – as Eutopia – counteract the ancestral proceedings, its strategies seem more similar to dystopian SF from Wells and Čapek through the post-1945 "new maps of hell" to Dick and Disch.

Gloss 23: The Fallible Eutopia and the Fallible Dystopia are ideal types which allow for a spectrum of intermediate, often ambiguous possibilities. Fallible Eutopia recognizes the threatening twofold dystopia; Fallible Dystopia shows at least a glimpse of eutopia as the locus of oppositional values. A balance of eutopian and dystopian horizons makes of Joanna Russ's *Female Man* and Marge Piercy's *Dance the Eagle To Sleep*, which deal partly or wholly with a flawed eutopian struggle within a fierce repression, ancestors of both these genres. Samuel Delany's *Triton* rejects both horizons in favour of showing up the micropolitics of his anti-hero, and seems to me not to belong in either sub-genre. (Generic categorization shows relevance to a given discussion, not necessarily quality.)

24

In sum, the strategies of what we may call a refurbished utopianism for sadder and possibly wiser times add to the panoply of deeply critical devices for creating inverted worlds whose salient aspects show up the author's pragmatic world as one of upside-down, death-dealing values and rules. This enriched horizon clarifies and activates liberating desire by means of textually embodied – not only ideological – alternative images and actions. To the illusory mythology of Disneyfication (as example of hegemonic strategies for "commodity esthetics"), a Lotus-land for the weary, they oppose epic struggle. To addictive consumption they oppose cognitive and practical creation. Through narrative choices, they affirm the possibility of a radical otherness, indeed its absolute necessity for the survival of human values and lives.

Table 1: Shifts of Utopian Features

	CORPUS	Different Exemplary LOCUS	RUPTURE	Utopian QUALITY (E or D)	Axiological RELATION TO HEGEMONY
1	Morus	space – far[i]	static – cut off[ii]	better socio-political organization: E	*opposed*
2	*Gulliver* Books III–IV	as above	as above	worse socio-political organization: D+/–	*opposed*
3	Bellamy – Morris	time – future	static – vision	better socio-political organization: E	*opposed*
4	Nineteenth- to Twentieth-century Anti-utopias	as above	as above	worse socio-political organization: D–	*opposed to opposing*: back to hegemony
5	Wells I: *The Time Machine* and *The First Men in the Moon*	time as socio-biological space	dynamic – machine	inverted socio-biological organization: D+	*opposed*
6	Wells II: other[iii]	Possible Worlds[iv] with one different variable each	invasion of different reality[v]	mixture of all five above: E	*opposed*
7	Disneyland (Disneyfication)	space – contiguous	intercalary dynamic (money, rollercoaster)	identification with desire for commodities: D-	*intensified*: back to hegemony in spades

| 8 | Fallible Eutopia | Possible World of flawed/ endangered E | Possible World both different from hegemony and internally split | struggle for E as process | *opposed – but also to static E* |
| 9 | Fallible Dystopia | Possible World of resistible D | Possible World intensifies hegemony, internally split | struggle against D | *opposed* |

E = eutopia/n
D = dystopia/n (D- = dystopia which is anti-utopia, D+ = "simple" dystopia)

i   Borrowed from Antiquity, medieval religiosity, and folktales (Plato – Dante – Cockayne). Each name stands for a paradigm – in row 1, for example, for the "alternate islands" of Bacon, Campanella, etc.

ii   Paradigm: King Utopus cuts the isthmus connecting Utopia to a continent.

iii   Wells I = *The Time Machine* and *First Men in the Moon*; all ruptures after this are dynamic. Wells II = for example *Days of the Comet, Food of the Gods, Modern Utopia, Men Like Gods*; while *War of the Worlds* contaminates Wells I and Wells II.

iv   Possible Worlds can be any variant of spacetime, including esthetic and virtual reality (semiotic spacetime).

v   Borrowed from horror stories.

C. *Ausklang* on Agents: Who Are We? Where Are We Going To? (Free after Gauguin)

25

At the end of Piercy's *He, She and It*, an anti-capitalist alliance is in the making between the dissident high-technology intellectuals and politicized urban gangs of youngsters and labourers, under the aegis of a fighting eutopian emissary ...

While it is not useful to blur the ontological differences between fact and fiction, both partake of, act upon, and are shaped by the same human imagination. It seems to me mandatory to end these much too long theses (testimony to the confusing times which we live through and which live through us) by talking about agency, in a brief attempt to identify who might be here talking to whom, in this endangered moment under the stars. My answer is (maybe alas): various stripes or fractions of *intellectuals*.

What can, and therefore must, an intellectual do today within, under, and against dystopia? If I may define this type as one who responds, who is responsive and responsible, a possible answer is: not too much; yet perhaps, with much effort and much luck, this might prove just enough.

Gloss 25: The above Bakhtinian dialogical definition excludes of course the great majority of those whom sociologists call "the professionals," people who work mainly with images and/or concepts and, among other functions, "produce, distribute and preserve distinct forms of consciousness" (Mills): the engineers of material and human resources, the admen and "design" professionals, the new bishops and cardinals of the media clerisy, most lawyers, as well as the teeming swarms of supervisors (we teachers are increasingly adjunct policemen keeping the kids off the streets). The funds for this whole congeries of "cadre" classes "have been drawn from the global surplus" (Wallerstein): none of us has clean hands. I myself seem to be paid through pension funds deriving in part from loans to the Québec government by German banks, or ultimately by the exploitation of people like my ex-compatriots in Eastern Europe.

26

This our intermediate class-congeries in the world has since 1945 in the capitalist core-countries been materially better off than our earlier counterparts: but the price has been very high. Within the new collectivism, we are "a dominated fraction of the dominant class" (Bourdieu). We live a contradiction: while essential to the *encadrement* and policing of workers, we are ourselves workers who may sit down. Excogitating ever new ways to sell our expertise as "services" in producing and enforcing marketing images of happiness, we decisively further the decline of people's self-determination and non-professionalized expertise. We are essential to the production of new knowledge and ideology, but we are totally kept out of establishing the framework into which, and mostly kept from directing the uses to which, the production and the producers are put. Our professionalization secured for some of us sufficient income to turn high wage into minuscule capital. We cannot function without a good deal of self-government in our classes or artefacts, but we do not control the strategic decisions about universities or dissemination of artefacts.

27

And what of the swiftly descending future? The hope for an eventual bridging of the poverty gap both worldwide and inside single countries is now over. It is very improbable the Keynesian class compromise can be dismantled without burying under its fallout capitalism as a whole. Will this happen explosively, for example in a quite possible Third World War, or by a slow crumbling away which generates massive breakdowns of civil and civilized relations, on the model of the present "cold civil war" smouldering in the USA and indeed globally, which are (as Disch's forgotten masterpiece *334* rightly saw) only comparable to daily life in the late Roman Empire? And what kind of successor formation will then be coming about? Worst fears and maddest hopes are allowable. The age of individualism and free market is over, the present is already highly collectivized, and demographics as well as insecurity will make the future even more so: the alternative lies between the models of the oligarchic (that is, centrally Fascist) war-camp and an open plebeian-democratic commune.

28

In this realistically grim perspective, facing a dangerous series of cascading bifurcations, our liberatory class interests as intellectuals are twofold and interlocking. *First*, they consist in securing a high degree of self-management, to begin with in the workplace. But capitalism without a human face is obviously engaged in large scale "structural declassing" of intellectual work, of our "cultural capital" (Bourdieu, and see Guillory). There is nothing more humiliating, short of physical injury and hunger, than the experience of being pushed to the periphery of social values (and thus of financing) which all of us have undergone in the last quarter century. Our younger colleagues are by now predominantly denied Keynesian employment, condemned to part-time piecework without security. Capitalism has adjoined to the permanent reserve army of industrial labour that of intellectual labour.

Thus our interests also consist, *second*, in working for such strategic alliances with other fractions and classes as would consent us to fight the current toward militarized browbeating. This may be most visible in "Confucian capitalism" from Japan to Malaya, for example in the concentration-camp fate of the locked-in young women of its factories, but it is well represented in all our "democratic" sweatshops and fortress neighbourhoods as well as fortress nation-blocs, prominently in USA (see Harvey). It can only be counteracted by ceaseless insisting on meaningful democratic participation in the control not only of production but also of distribution of our own work, as well as of our neighbourhoods. Here the boundary between our as it were dissident interests within the intellectual field of production and the overall liberation of labour as their only guarantee becomes permeable.

29

The Modernist oases for exiles (the Left Bank, Bloomsbury, lower Manhattan, major US campuses) are gone the way of a Tahiti polluted by nuclear fallout and venereal pandemic: some affluent or starving writers à la Pynchon or Joyce may still be possible, but not as a statistically significant option for us. Adapting Tsvetaeva's great line "In this most Christian of all worlds/ All poets are Yids" (V ètom khristianneishem iz vsekh mir/ Vse poèty zhidy), we can say that fortunately all intellectuals are partly exiles from the Disneyland and/or starvation dystopia, but we are an "inner emigration" for whom resistance was always possible and is now growing mandatory. The first step toward resistance to Disneyfied brainwashing is "the invention of the desire called utopia in the first place, along with

new rules for the fantasizing or daydreaming of such a thing – a set of narrative protocols with no precedent in our previous literary institutions"
(Jameson). This is a collective production of meanings, whose efficacy is
measured by how many consumers it is able to turn, to begin with, into
critical and not empathetic thinkers, and finally into producers.

30

All variants of dystopias and/or eutopias sketched above pivot not only on
individual self-determination but centrally on collective self-management
enabling and guaranteeing personal freedom. Whoever is not interested
in this horizon will not be interested in them: and viceversa.

Lucca, September 2001

A Post Scriptum (2006)

0

I wrote the "Tractate on Dystopia" in Summer 2001 and sent it to some
friends a few days before September 11. They included Raffaella Baccolini
and Tom Moylan, so that in our protracted e-mail discussions (which can be
followed in our common contribution to *Nuovissime*) the new atmosphere
became a major intertext. Much could be added after five years of this new
intertext imposed on the world by the dogmatic competition of radical
monotheisms under capitalism: the contribution of capitalist globalization
has been that today, Voltaire would have to put his slogan "Écrasez l'infâme"
into the plural. I have in fact made some minor changes and additions in
half a dozen sections, and tightened up the phrasing in a number of places,

but this is far from beginning to render the baleful perspectives deepening every day of those five years and going on (seemingly) without end in sight. However, it is not at all clear to me that additional understanding of such perspectives would best be made under the rubric of Dystopia/nism: I have tried to reach them under the rubrics War, Terrorism, *The Communist Manifesto*, Exile, Power/Violence ... Inversely, if I attempted to accommodate even significant echoes of such new rubrics into the form and horizons of my *Tractate*, it would become another animal. For better or worse, it has now jelled into its own form.

Thus I am now adding only some general thoughts which are both a Post Scriptum to the 2001 tractate and might buttress it in 2006. They are in two parts, on the intertext leading to a discourse about dystopia, and on my coupling of literary fiction and Disneyland in that discourse.

I

Why talk about dystopia today, here?

Because we have to talk about our lives, here, today. We have to both testify and delve into, try to illuminate, what is happening to us all, in and around each of us.

What is that? This modest P.S. cannot pretend to say it with any precision, but perhaps it can suggest some neuralgic knots and calcifications of our body politic.

It is a devolution of the post-1917 Welfare-and-Warfare State, which has lost its welfare wing and is being rapidly devolved to Warfare-and-Bamboozlery State. Warfare is exported outside the – relatively, for a smaller and smaller minority – rich State-system of the metropolitan (capitalist, patriarchal) North, well represented by the Trilateral group of North America, west-central Europe and Japan plus a smattering of their outcrops (the "little tigers" of East Asia, the "White dominions" of ex-British Empire). But combined with the dismantling of the minimum solidarity and justice that brought about and sustained the Welfare State in both its Leninist and (reactively) Keynesian wings, violence as war abroad means also increasing violence as repression within, needed to quell the rising despair over, and eventually protests against, the devolution of public health, education, housing, and all other services and of all controls over savage capitalism without a human face, most prominently the shameless exploitation of immigrant workers without civic rights. It means the spectre haunting us today of the police State, returning from the US-organized dictatorships around the world to roost in the native soil, first hypocritically and now openly with the dominion of the Bush Jr. administration. That this is practically invisible in all of our embedded mass media constitutes the bamboozlery wing of what, modifying President Eisenhower, we now have to call corporate-military-media complex ruling us. Each reader at all interested in dystopia can fill in the list of moral and political reasons for our indignation at such a huge impoverishment and militarization of our lives.

But why talk about it under the guise of dystopia rather than in essays or pamphlets within the disciplines of political or economic science ("science"?), or even of philosophy? Because – as was said about ascending Mount Everest – it is there, and because it has some cognitive privileges. Dystopia as a literary and media form is alive and well everywhere the public sphere and public reflection has still the chance to function beyond a fight for immediate survival. Such a psychophysical fight leaves no money and time for writing and reading fiction: indeed I believe the "precarization" of intellectuals and of the youth is a political conspiracy to prevent them from thinking. Yet however precarious, some oases in the simooms of desertification still exist. To change my image, this speech from the belly of the new Leviathan is both dystopia's strength and, no doubt, its limitation.

Some results of our academically fragmented disciplines in the social sciences or *Geisteswissenschaften* may be admirable and indispensable, especially those which militate against this fragmentation. However, even at best we critics lack the means to convey the feel of "thick" life and its experiences inside, with, and against Leviathan. There is something within storytelling, the imagination of alternative actions by agents in an alternative Possible World, which hearkens back to the rich primitive syncretism of singing dances around the campfire from which all our arts have evolved, as can be felt in the clearest of such throwbacks, music. For all such alternatives, however roundabout and disguised, are alternatives for different paths that could be taken by humankind and its key social groups. *Mutato nomine de te dystopia narratur*: as all other imaginative fiction but perhaps more clearly so, the estrangements of eutopia and dystopia are warnings, proposals, and weighing of costs for each of us – here, today.

Why not then write about utopia, or (as we have increasingly come to more properly call it) eutopia, the depiction of radically better Possible Worlds, rather than dystopia, the depiction of radically worse Possible Worlds? Again, first of all because eutopian writings are not there any more, in close parallel to the loss of belief in actually proposed eutopian models of a more or less radically socialist kind. True, fictional eutopias had a very interesting last (so far) flurry within the feminist movement, mainly in the English-speaking countries, for a dozen years from the late 1960s on, in the work of Charnas, Piercy, Wittig, Gearhart, and others, culminating to my mind in the rich "ambiguous utopia" of Le Guin's *The Dispossessed*. But already, these were often rather ambiguous texts, incorporating doubts not so much what eutopia was against but what it was for, or better, how it went about getting out of what it was against; and eutopias have since become rare and even more hybrid. To the contrary, dystopia has increasingly come to the fore since Wells's reactualization of the ancestral tradition from Cyrano and Swift onwards, and it has become characteristic of our days after the "mainstream" triad of Zamyatin's *We*, Huxley's *Brave New World*, and Orwell's *1984* (the quality of which to my mind descends as we go on, in direct opposition to their fame). These pioneering texts and their followers dealt principally with the State Leviathan. However, I have argued in my essay on Zamyatin that the Leviathan has mutated from State to (mainly) corporative dictatorship. Where we are at today is perhaps better prefigured in the cluster of US dark forebodings within science fiction, following upon Jack London's *Iron Heel* and identified in a pioneering survey by Kingsley Amis as the "New Maps of Hell" from Vonnegut to Walter Miller Jr.

To what Amis discussed we'd have to add today also dystopia's strong presence in the early Soviet writings of Mayakovsky and Platonov, the feminist prefigurations of Burdekin and Boye, the follow-up in some works by Lem in Poland and the brothers Strugatsky in Russia, the later feminist dystopias mentioned above, and the great flowering of US and UK "awful warning" SF in the 1960s and early 1970s. Much of it was sparked by fears of a nuclear holocaust and its aftermath, but some of it identified also more mundane economico-political processes as leading to devolution and breakdown, say in some works of Dick, Burgess, Vance, Spinrad, Brunner, Disch, Ballard, Russ, and Le Guin. This has not abated after the sea-change of the mid-1970s, in the dystopian tenor of the best "cyberpunk" SF by Gibson, Cadigan or Spinrad, the anti-war SF from Joe Haldeman to Joan Slonczewski, Dick's splendid late *A Scanner Darkly*, and the emergence of new voices from the 1990s on. The most powerful of them seems to me K.S. Robinson who went on, after the closely observed US "autopia" (life dominated by cars and drugs) of *Gold Coast*, to reinstate the clash of dystopia and eutopia into ongoing history with his *Mars* trilogy and *Days of Rice and Salt*. Alongside the continuation of the feminist impulse in the completion of Gearhart's trilogy, Suzette Haden Elgin's recently completed trilogy *Native Tongue*, and Atwood's *The Handmaid's Tale*, the most prominent voices of dystopian writing from the last two decades include a disproportionate number of women writers, such as Marge Piercy's remarkable *He, She and It*, some novels by Slonczewski, or Octavia Butler's *Parable of the Sower*. However, I do not claim to have exhausted the richness or complexity of the dystopian vein, say in the latest Ballard or in Ken MacLeod (to mention only two UK names) but merely to have indicated that it is very much "here".

Last not least, why call our theme and focus "dystopia", a neologism invented by J.S. Mill in 1868? Again, one of the reasons is that it was widely picked up by criticism from the 1950s on. As I discuss at length above, there is by now wide scholarly consensus that the term of "anti-utopia" should be reserved for a specific subsection of dystopias written to warn against an existing utopia, not (as in most dystopias) against the existing status quo. But why did "dystopia" rightly win out against Bentham's earlier proposed term of "cacotopia" (the Google frequency count of references is more than 4000:1)? Notionally, possibly because the Greek root "dys", meaning bad, unlucky or generally negative, is not only richer than "kakos", meaning evil or ugly, but it is also widely used in medicine and science (dyslexia, dysentery, dysfunction, dyspepsia, dyspnoea). But I suspect more poetic reasons are prominent here. Dystopia is not only shorter but it also amalgamates despair and utopia: it keeps the utopian (eutopian) impulse but subjects it to the test of desperate, desolate, desertifying peril. As in Derrida's *pharmakon*, it simultaneously identifies a poison in and offers an antitoxin to the body politic.

2

The term "Utopia" (with capital "U") started out as a work of imagination in literary fiction, which playfully pretended to an obviously unbelievable and not to be believed geopolitical factuality. To enhance its particular type of pretence, the term pretended further to identify and describe in all strategic details a country on a par with England but as far from it as Muscovy, India, or the new Americas, and yet its anamorphical image (round instead of triangular and so on). But the pretence was at the same time cognitively constitutive of utopia as such. This led to readings which forgot Morus's horizon and intention, the complex contraries and eversions in which this cognition dwells, and which I would call *cognitive fictionality*.

This new tool for thinking soon begat the general stance or horizon of "utopianism," of orientation toward utopia, meaning originally (as Morus's Latin title had it) a discourse about "the best state of the polity," or at least – as more dynamic ages added – about a radically better state of such a commonwealth (country, State). But I would claim that, however literal-minded the readings, no discursive derivation of this orientation (say "utopian thought") managed to free itself from the inalienably imaginary, and furthermore fictional, character of that felicitous naming as No-place – in Swiftian terms The Place That Was Not. The cognition which the utopian *organon* both carries and necessitates is complex and roundabout, not to be literally realized: as I argued a third of a century ago, utopia can only be heuristically applied, not physically realized. True, "dystopia" (and "cacotopia") originated in the conceptual discourse of political philosophy amid the nineteenth-century rise of the industrial bourgeoisie and capitalism. But just like the blatantly parasitic term of "anti-utopia," they were always already derivative of a fictional state of affairs and country, depending on and from the Morean paradigm of "utopia" (with lower-case "u").

How is it in this light to be defended that in this *Tractate* I treat upon the same footing phenomena of literary fiction and phenomena of imaginative and playful (though deeply corrupt) involvement in an ideology such as Disneyfication, objectivized in the various mini-loci or allegorically compressed mini-countries of Disneyland or Disney World? What makes Disneyland more akin to a eutopia and/or dystopia than to England, France or indeed the USA of which it is part (and as I argue, a *pars pro toto*)?

A first answer is that there is a central existential difference between a life-world one is necessarily inside of and a secondary creation one may be outside of. In any really existing country people willy-nilly live and work, must die and may get children: their bodily, psychophysical life is fully engaged in and committed to their location. To the contrary, a piece of utopian literature, a Fourierist blueprint or Disney World does not fully enclose any person: one may visit it, but not live in it, one may dwell on but not in it, one is finally outside not inside. (Utopian colonies attempting to span this abyss therefore regularly cracked up.) The Book of Nature is not really a book, in whatever hieroglyphs it may be written; the Stage of Life (or of Society) is not really a stage, whatever games may on it come and go. The metaphoric (topic) relationships and traffic between these entities – I shall call them Possible World Zero and Possible Worlds One-to-N (PW_0, PW_{1-n}) – are multiple and complex, and constitute indeed much of the critic's daily bread, but for the most important purposes the entities themselves remain as distinct as any two entries in a semiotic encyclopaedia may be. Traffic piles up unless it goes between two distinct places.

It remains then, in this brief defence of my methodology or epistemology, to ask whether these two species of my genus dystopia, the literary dystopia and Disneyland, exhaust the PW_{1-n} group. Of course they do not: other examples for species could surely be added. But while craft is long, life is short, and anyone paddling on such a vast and tempest-tossed ocean can count oneself lucky to have lashed together a catamaran of two flimsy hulls.

Note

My thanks go to comments by Rich Erlich and Tom Moylan. Errors and opinions remain mine.

Works Cited in Tractate

Full references with pagination may be found in my earlier publications, adduced at end by chronology – especially in the earlier chapters of this book, here summarized, added to, and brought to a point. My pervasive debt to Raymond Williams's and Fredric Jameson's work is not well indicated by the one reference for each. Much work of Lyman Tower Sargent and other colleagues from the Society for Utopian Studies and elsewhere is also implied. The section listing my works at the end is a ploy to prevent this being called "A Huge Tractate."

Bastian, Hans-Dieter. *Verfremdung und Verkündigung*. München: Kaiser, 1965.
Benjamin, Walter. *Gesammelte Schriften*. Ed. Rolf Tiedermann and Hermann Schweppenhäuser, 7 vols. Frankfurt: Suhrkamp, 1980–87.
Bloch, Ernst. *Das Prinzip Hoffnung*. 2 vols. Frankfurt: Suhrkamp, 1959.
Bourdieu, Pierre. *In Other Words: Essays Towards a Reflexive Sociology*. Trans. Matthew Adamson. Stanford: Stanford University Press, 1990.
de Certeau, Michel. "The Jabbering of Social Life." *On Signs*. Ed. Marshall. Blonsky. Baltimore: Johns Hopkins University Press, 1985. 146–54.
Eliot, Marc. *Walt Disney: Hollywood's Dark Prince*. New York: Carol, 1993.
Engels, Friedrich. *Ludwig Feuerbach and the End of Classical German Philosophy*. Karl Marx and Friedrich Engels. *Selected Works in One Volume*. London: Lawrence and Wishart, 1968. 594–632.

Guillory, John. "Literary Critics as Intellectuals: Class Analysis and the Crisis of the Humanities." *Rethinking Class*. Ed. Wai Chee Dimock and Myron T. Gilmore. New York: Columbia University Press, 1994. 107–49.

Harvey, David. *Justice, Nature and the Geography of Difference*. Oxford: Blackwell, 1996.

Jameson, Fredric. *The Seeds of Time*. New York: Columbia University Press, 1994.

Lukács, Georg. *Geschichte und Klassenbewusstsein*. Berlin and Neuwied: Luchterhand, 1968.

Marin, Louis. *Utopiques: jeux d'espaces*. Paris: Minuit, 1973.

Mills, C. Wright. *White Collar*. New York: Oxford University Press, 1953.

Moylan, Tom. *Demand the Impossible*. New York: Methuen, 1986.

———. *Scraps of the Untainted Sky*. Boulder: Westview, 2000.

Noble, David F. *America by Design*. New York: Knopf, 1977.

Wallerstein, Immanuel. *Historical Capitalism with Capitalist Civilization*. London: Verso, 1996.

Williams, Raymond. *Problems in Materialism and Culture*. London: Verso/NLB, 1980.

***

Suvin, Darko. *Metamorphoses of Science Fiction: On the Poetics and History of a Literary Genre*. New Haven and London: Yale University Press, 1979.

———. *Positions and Presuppositions in Science Fiction*. London: Macmillan, 1988.

———. "Locus, Horizon, and Orientation: The Concept of Possible Worlds as a Key to Utopian Studies" (Chapter 3 in this book).

———. "Where Are We? How Did We Get Here? Is There Any Way Out?: Or, News From the Novum" (Chapter 8 in this book).

———. "Two Cheers for Essentialism and Totality." *Rethinking Marxism* 10.1 (1998): 66–82.

——. "Utopianism from Orientation to Agency: What Are We Intellectuals under Post-Fordism To Do?" (Chapter 9 in this book).

——. "Horizon (Utopian)" and "System." Entries for "Lexicon: 20th Century A.D." *Public*, Toronto 19 (2000): 72–75 and 20 (2000): 81–84.

——. "Reflections on What Remains of Zamyatin's *We* after the Change of Leviathans: Must Collectivism Be against People?" (Chapter 11 in this book).

Works Cited in Post Scriptum

Most references for this piece may be found in the items under my name of the *Tractate* above. I add one more item of mine, for the context within which both were written.

Jameson, Fredric. *Archaeologies of the Future*. London and New York: Verso, 2005 [surely the most important work on utopia/nism since Bloch].

Maniscalco Basile, Giovanni, and Darko Suvin (eds). *Nuovissime mappe dell'inferno: Distopia oggi*. Roma: Monolite, 2004.

Suvin, Darko. "Circumstances and Stances." *Publications of the Modern Language Association* 11.3 (2004): 535–38.

Seven Poems from the Utopian Hollow: Diary Notes of 2000–2005

I'm Into Your World

Mi pesano gli anni venturi
[The coming years lie heavily upon me]
Ungaretti

I'm into your world but not entirely of it
Not into the coil of writhing serpentine lies
Hissing with laid-on charm from TV & PC monitors
Eternal Truths of claudicant metaphors
Murdering en masse with the invisible hand of smart bombs.

I know the acrid sweat of the on & off Filipino labourer
& more intimately the smouldering rage of the scribe
Impotent to stop the lies dictated into his mind:
By your empire moulded, its stamp burning
In their brain convolutions & their muscle flesh.

What may i do? With eyes wide open
Steer my paraplegic wheels
      while the nightingale
Goes on singing as if all were right
Into the thrilling strata of the planet's air

& i await the dove
Of a differing Flood.

6400

(We Shall Behold)

We shall behold our love lie down
Like an evening
In the streets singing with the firefly's shine

& when bells suddenly ring
It shall be
A different morning.

But why do i sleep badly?

6400

Ex: Fudō 2000

To Predrag M.

Headnote: Fudô = esoteric Buddhist godhead of wrath, irate aspect of Enlightenment: blue-black face appearing amid flames, sword in one hand and rope in other hand to cut off and bind evil passions. – Please observe the deviant stresses on the <i>s in ll. 2 and 7.

What poems, mind of mine, may you now sing
When corrupt desire rules the ex-communìsts
When massy murder brainwash & whoring enlists –
Few are saved – their lust for easeful things?

What hopes may now be found to grow new wings?
We in our youth, emerged from bloody mists,
Saw Fudō's sword in hands of antìfascìsts
& the people's rule a real thing,

Wrathful & kind.
      Now i let my country go,
Murderously after false gods a-whore.
When surgical verse cuts deep it is to know,
To find at understanding's furthest shore
Why poison invades the brain's every pore.
Yet every poem encodes: I loved you so!

                          30500

Three Doctrines from Heine

3.
Red-eyed bloody business weather!
One-eyed profit-ordered town!
How i wonder when – not whether –
Earthquakes rise to break you down.

11.
When we lie together in post-coital bliss
Don't ask me about Yugoslavia, how grand it
Was, how come it got pushed so bloodily amiss:
There are good reasons – i cannot stand it.

I beg you, leave Yugoslavia in peace
Don't mention world banks – NATO – elites – bandits
Don't call up traitors or errors, just give me a kiss:
There are good reasons – i cannot stand it.

One i loved in those bygone, far-off, beautiful days
Now calls it "Serbo-bolshévik", our youth's season,
& sighs for more civilized (European) ways:
I cannot stand it – there are good reasons.

5.
For on this rock we shall erect
The Church that works from downside up
The Third Age church of Holy Bodies
Both personal & congregational:

See: hunger, killings are not needful
The pie in TV skies deceives
Give us today our daily sweets
Give us down here the sacred hearts & sense.

Return to body its merry pump
Rid of the fat that has enclogged it
The overeating brought by hunger
The ulcers caused by profit slash & burns.

Return to brain its hormonal bath
Disturbed by wolfish enmities
To people & birds & beauteous trees –
When heart & brain work well, we shall be saved.

If you, O masters, will not let us
Be saved, entirely we must
Remove you: profit is the fat
In bloodstream, profit brings the early stroke.

Your lying church will be dismantled
Our Earth at last inhabitable,
Polluted eyes may see no godheads
The cleansed may go to many-coloured stars.

When holiness meets wholeness
& the people absolute,
Washed clean of Class Division Sin
We may aspire to the cosmic Lute.

6–700

In The Ruins of Leningrad*: A Medieval Allegory

Counterproject to Elder Olson's "In the Ruins of Macchu Picchu"

What Hope had built, cruel Greed has spilled
– Witness the city of Ilyich & Peter –
But what Greed's unbuilt, Hope can rebuild.

Where are the mountains of starving & killed?
The dead of Yudenich, Yagoda & Hitler?
What Hope had built, cruel Greed has spilled.

The hunger for Justice walks forth unstilled
The hunger for bread makes Her still sweeter
Greed's power unbuilds, Hope can rebuild.

Between Greed & Justice, what grain will be milled?
The outcome's uncertain, balances teeter:
What Hope had built, cruel Greed has spilled.

When Winter has stricken flesh to the hilt
Struck flesh will strive to unseat her
Greed cruelly kills but Hope can rebuild.

A counterpower can also be willed
To Death Love beats a countermeter
What Hope had built, cruel Greed has spilled.
A sterile mule is Greed: Hope can rebuild.

* Or Beograd, or Sarajevo, or …

311200

Reading the Secret Treasury [Hizôhôyaku]

The deranged in command of armies do not know they're mad
Blind people leading the nations do not see their blindness
Reproduced by deep class interests, they're in the dark all their lives
Dying time & time again, they take revenge in killing others
At the end of their deaths they've forgotten there was light.

8402

Aequinox

The victories & the defeat in the lowlands are behind us
The defeats & the victory in the highlands are before us
What we need today is embodied reason, & a caress.

13305

Living Labour and the Labour of Living: A Tractate for Looking Forward in the Twenty-first Century (2004)

To Colin MacCabe, sympathetic editor in scanty times: he asked for more

Vain is the word of a philosopher which heals no human suffering.

— EPICURE

0. Introduction[1]

0.1

I wish to articulate an initial approach within which: a/ the insight of Karl Marx is indispensable to any looking forward that attempts to avoid catastrophe for humanity; b/ this insight is best understood as being constituted by a fusion of three domains and horizons (*cognition*, *liberty*, and *pleasure*), with a set of regulative principles (*dialectic*, *measure*, *absolute swerve*), and a focus applying them to the determining factor of capitalist and any post-capitalist life: work, or better *living labour*.[2]

---

1   My argument, especially in Part 1, was triggered by Preve's wondrous *Il filo di Arianna*, from which it departs. My thanks for comments leading to improvements go to Sam Noumoff and Joan Roelofs.
2   Other ways of understanding the place and significance of Marx may be, of course, legitimate for other purposes. For example, Lenin's definition of "The Three Sources

It will be seen that the mortification of living labour, effected by trading creativity for alienation, leads with accelerating speed to personal and collective death. This is the reason for a radical refusal.

0.2

Faced with global capitalism and its colonization of the habitats, hearts, and minds of people, we need allies to understand its devastations well. The best one I can find is the teacher for life, history, in its precapitalist achievements. It may supply an estranging mirror.

The richest and most articulated counter-cultures would be the ones of the Chinese cultural circle (China and Japan) and of the Indian tradition. Alas, each needs one lifetime of study. A third possibility would be the European medieval tradition, but it is coded in theological terms which would need too much decoding for a brief approach. The classical Greco-Roman tradition, and then the classical communist tradition culminating in the nineteenth and twentieth centuries, are therefore, in the position we find ourselves, the best detours in hope of a springboard: *reculer pour mieux sauter.*

---

and Three Component Parts of Marxism" as being the best of "German philosophy, English political economy, and French socialism" (23) is obviously correct, given his horizons; I shall have something to say about each of them. Yet I would claim that today, in direr straits than in Lenin's time, we have to go back to the ultimate roots.

1. Three Interlocking Domains: Cognition, Liberty, Pleasure

1.1 Cognition

Cognition or understanding (*sapientia*) is in Marx on the one hand science but on the other hand integral human practice. I have argued in three earlier essays ("Transubstantiation," "Utopian," and "What") how *Wissenschaft* or knowledge was in German subsumed by Kant to mean a systematic body of cognition with a proper correlation of principles and consequences. Now, on pain of having no transmittable knowledge, scientific or other, we cannot do without systems in the sense of articulated wholes or provisional totalities organized according to an overarching method; yet only dynamically equilibrated systems, with a deniable and thus changeable rather than closed history can today be defended. Therefore, we may still wish (I would) to retain the methods and name of science for strictly articulated and formalized cognition, as opposed to what Aristotle called "opinion" (*doxa*). But this can be rescued from its present dominant use as a death-dealing variant of absolutist belief, enslaved to capitalist profit, only if it gets into continual feedback with values and interests from human practice.

Science is nothing without humanity: as Gramsci remarked, whether the universe would exist in the absence of humanity is for us (today) an empty question. It is not outside history: "One basis for life and *another* for *science* is in itself a lie" (Marx, "Private" 311). Yet this is what happens under capitalism, where living labour is incorporated into variable capital while technoscience is opposed to it as alien fixed capital. But we would need for science an analysis as rigorous as Marx's of labour and production as use-value vs. exchange-value. For, simultaneously, science as use-value is that form of human practice from whose ideal horizon all partial interests (of a class, gender or other limited group) have been expunged: "its dialectic consists in the fact that science is simultaneously a rigorously non-anthropomorphic vision of the world and in exclusive service of human happiness and serenity" (Preve 26). It has its first and noblest systematic form in Hippocratic medicine, which differentiates people only by the environment that pervades them.

1.2 Liberty

Liberty or freedom is the power of each person, but then also of each human class by which the person's possibilities are as a rule determined and constricted, to choose a stance and most actions. The problem consists in how to reconcile two usually clashing realities: history is real (there is a sufficiently stable Being out there determining us) and yet human choice is also real (there is a possibility for people to intervene into Being determining it); as Marx put it, people make history but constricted by conditions not of their choosing. Marx found in Epicure, whose stance he prefers to determinism in his doctoral dissertation, a strictly materialist explanation of freedom through unforeseen, casual but unavoidable, swerves of atoms from the straight path because of their inherent weight; but he adopted it for deep reasons of his time where the personal coincided with the political: the bright hope of the French Revolution, and the fact that even a well-off middle-class youngster and rising star such as himself could choose to become its devotee. The weight is the atom's participation in the material world, and following the deviation's effect in the world made of Epicure, in Hegel's opinion, the inventor of empirical natural science (cf. Asmis and Serres). The *parenklisis* or swerve (*clinamen* in Lucrece's Latin) was invented from an analogous necessity to imagine the possibility of a Hellenic intellectual refusing the social relationships of his time without resorting to gods or other heavenly sanctions (see Thomson), and the same held for his interpreter Lucrece and his best readers through centuries: Machiavelli, Erasmus, Montaigne, Bruno – who found in him an infinity of worlds – or Savinien Cyrano, Gassendi's pupil in seventeenth-century Paris. It is an *avoidance* of the fated straight line by the swerving atoms, of pain by the body, and of the declining world as a whole by the blessed gods in the intermundia and (as far as possible) by the adepts in the Epicurean communities or Gardens.

Why does this straight line, asks Derrida, fall from above to below; what does the provenience of case (*casus*, in German *Fall*), chance, and accident from the root for falling, *cadere*, entail (22)? It is because they come from the above, a place of power not subject to human will, of whimsical Gods or blind Nature, and may fall or break in upon any of us, like meteorites – or their symmetrical obverse, the freewheeling and imprevisible idea (*Einfall*). In fact, Epicure properly scoffs at the anthropomorphic idea that in the infinite there is an up and down. The fixed destination of Destiny may be perturbed and deviated by some action (Derrida 24). For Lucrece, the swerve breaks the chains of Fate, and sanctions "the free will of people living in the world / [...] By which we move wherever pleasure leads each of us."[3] It opens a free space for choice, where causal strings dilate and possible Being may be born from Non-Being (as sub-atomic particles from interstellar vacuum). This rescues accident and unforeseeability from its marginal status in the pioneering discussion of Aristotle (*Metaphysics* V–VI), and transfers it from the casual to the causal realm. It may thus serve as basis for, and it is of a piece with, an analogous rescue of pleasure, Lucrece's High Venus, from Aristotle's somewhat lukewarm treatment in *Nicomachean Ethics*. Marx rightly sees this alienation (*Entäusserung*) and contradictoriness as the heart-piece of Epicure's philosophy, its strengths and its limit: the atom is defined equally by the possibility of movement and of deviation (*Texte* 154, 150, and passim). There is no necessity to live under necessity: finally, life itself can be avoided or withdrawn from. Such an avoidance simultaneously denies the norm and yet observes it as its presupposition (ibid. 100–02, 142, 150–52, and 158).

Of course, in modern class society possibly no concept has been more abused than liberty. As Hegel noted: "When freedom is mentioned, one must always be careful to see whether it is not really private interests that are being spoken of" (Lenin enthusiastically approved, see *Philosophical* 311).

---

3 Lucretius II: 254–8. Historians of science as a rule sneer about Epicure's swerve, but it seems to be less extravagant than many a contemporary scientific tenet (see Andrade IX and passim, Georgescu-Roegen 168). The pioneer of a proper revaluation was Marx's dissertation and its preparatory notes, see *Texte* 59ff., 99–103, 142, and 148–58. By the way, *clinamen*, the de-clination or deviation, is akin to Haraway identification of language as "made of tropes, constituted of bumps that make us swerve from literal-mindedness" (11): this should make believers in linguistics as the hegemonic epistemology like Epicure. In fact, about his system as expounded by Lucrece, Serres concludes that post-Einsteinian science is fully compatible with it: their hands meet across the centuries of Newtonian quantification.

Beside Epicurean hedonism, the other great classical idea of freedom
was the Stoic freedom as the recognition of necessity, a universal concatena-
tion of causal nets. It proved indispensable for the revolutionary and communist movements both then and after Marx, as it taught steadfastness in
face of adversity and sacrifice, and it was together with Epicureanism the
first to affirm world brotherhood in the expanding world of Mediterranean
empires. However, predestination is fine while you seem to be the winning
wave of the future, but after epochal defeat it easily becomes a confirmation
of and justification for a necessary, destined unfreedom. This happened to
Stoicism too: the so-called Middle Stoa became in the Alexandrian age the
doctrine teaching Roman oligarchy how to use philosophy in conjunction
with State-enforced religion for purposes of rule. Marx's Epicureanism is
a better ally for and mainspring of a movement toward freedom, though
I would differ from Preve in stressing the inescapable necessity for revolutionary movements to practice a dialectical interaction between a final
horizon of hedonism and the immediate crutch of stoicism while hobbling
toward it. This dialectics can also be thought of in medieval clerical terms
as one between the triumphant and militant horizons of the movement.
Thence Lenin's love of Chernyshevsky's *narodnik* asceticism: but the crutch
should not be taken for the horizon.

For stoicism is a philosophy of permanent losers, often complemented
by a vague messianism. As such, it has no answer to the two central questions
of praxis and practical philosophy: the limit of life in a relatively early *death*,
and the duration of life (very often, much too often) as *unhappiness*.

1.3 Pleasure

Epicure's breakthrough was to conjoin being wise, honourable, and friendly
(that is, more than simply just) with felicity or pleasure (maxim 5), and furthermore, using a healthy individualism, to found all the rest on pleasure,
insisting primarily on the evacuation of pain. Sensual experience is the basis
for understanding, but it is steered by wise decision. Natural science (*fysi-
ologia*) is needed to know how to cope with pleasure and pain (*maxim* 11),
and wisdom to distinguish natural, necessary, and vain pleasures (maxim

29), to illuminate their proper measure. The passion for wealth is at best sordid (maxim 30), but friendship (*filia*) a cosmic principle of blessedness (maxim 35) in human affairs. State and right were founded on a utilitarian agreement between people (maxims 33, 36–38). A life in concord without war, and indeed (as the early Christian Eusebius realized – see Farrington, *Faith* 78) a commonwealth without class strife, was prefigured in the Epicurean "Gardens" which admitted the unlearned, women, and even slaves. Centrally, this intellectual intuition or penetration (*epibole tes dianoias*) issues in freedom – in Lucrece's poetic words:

> [...] with pitiless judgment
> Evaluate, and if things seem true to you,
> Give yourself up to them, but if something is wrong, take up arms
> Against it. For the spirit seeks reasons
> [...] as far as thought desires to look
> And the thrust of the spirit freely flies across.
> (II: 1041–47)

The fusion of the domains I indicate as central to Marx is contained here in a first approximation.

Epicure's original answer (and it may have been better than we know, as it has come to us mutilated by unceasing persecution) adapted the unitary materialism of Greek philosophy by providing weight to the primordial atoms and thus a capacity for self-originated motion and deviation. This was a decisive step, and Marx remembered it much after his dissertation. Perhaps self-critically, a note on "points not to be forgotten" at the end of his "Introduction" on the foundations and critique of political economy reads: "*This whole conception* [i.e., of his outline of capitalism] *appears as a necessary development*. But legitimation of chance [...]. Of freedom also [...]" (*Grundrisse* 109). I shall argue in Part 4 why it is doubtful that capitalism was unavoidable (its failure to arise in medieval China weighs heavily against this necessity) and that the laudation in the *Communist Manifesto* would have to be balanced with an even longer list of the blights the bourgeoisie is responsible for. Parallel to this cosmic self-management, Epicure posited as principle of human existence pleasure instead of necessity. His pleasure is not immaterial but rooted in the belly (*gaster*), the seat of desires for food, drink, and sex.

True, Epicure intended his hedonism for small communities of sages, effacing pain by opting out of class society and its politics. Here the limits of avoidance or refusal understood as simple abandonment of what is general by the "abstractly single" (Marx, *Texte* 152), in order to achieve a sage suppression of troubling passions (*ataraxia*), become apparent. Yet such a secession is unavoidable at the beginning of any potentially revolutionary sect, from Epicureanism and Christianity to Feminism (though finally this does not suffice, and especially in the invasive world of technoscientific and worldwide capitalism). As Spinoza expanded it, already halfway to Fourier, the yearning to exist (*conatus existendi*) encompasses both avoiding pain and searching for pleasure, and furthermore it is not simply an instinct of self-preservation (*conatus sese conservandi*) but also and primarily a yearning to understand (*conatus intelligendi*) carried by bodily passions and ideas (*Ethics* III, prop. VI and LIII): people are defined by desire, which is "appetite together with consciousness of appetite" (*Ethics* III, prop. XCVI).[4]

Thus, full Epicurean hedonism not only faces the two questions of death and unhappiness but also provides an approach that can be built upon. It starts from the place of our bodies in the scheme of things. It collapses death into the question about life: "the art of living well and of dying well is the same" (*Letter to Menecaeus* – see Fallot, and Farrington, *Science*). Epicure and Lucrece remark rightly that no-one can be hurt when one is not – though perhaps this is not quite sufficient today, for one will know that her/his dear ones will be hurt and that one's infelicity may greatly increase by not having time to accomplish certain sense-making actions. At any rate, all hinges on the sensuous quality of living (even if in Epicure's particular situation wisdom meant for him contenting oneself with the indispensable minimum). The socialist and communist movements also started from and for this, with Fourier and Marx, but then largely neglected it in pursuit of quantitative competition with capitalist life-style: a philo-

---

4   For the filiation Spinoza-Marx see De Vries 50 and passim, Rubel, and Negri.

sophically (cognitively) and politically (pragmatically) equally disastrous failure of nerve and backslide.

1.4 Plebeians and Philosopher-Poets

The third pertinent current in ancient Greece, arising not out of intellectuals but out the dispossessed and exploited plebeians, was Orphism. Its mystical worship of Dionysus was co-opted by Pisistratus in the City Dionysia and thus gave rise to Athenian tragedy. Though encoded in mythologemes, which we can partly read off Hesiod and Empedocles, these were significant: Justice (*Dike*) sits beside the throne of Zeus looking at the dispossessors, ending the reign of force as physical coercion (*bia*); and Love, yearning for the reunion of what was dispersed and recovery of what was lost, is a revered creative power: "To the nobility Love was a dangerous thing, because it implied desire, ambition, discontent [...]. [To the Orphics] the world is best when Love overcomes Strife."[5]

The failure of classical hedonism to effect an alliance with the plebeians, to engage in sweeping collective movements, is repeated, as in a mirror image, in the failure of official Marxism to articulate the horizon of happiness through radical existential choice, left to mainly individualist schools, say from Kierkegaard to Sartre, when not to burgeoning sects. Against Marx, the most advanced philosophy (and poetry!) was again disjoined from radical mass politics. The suicides of Mayakovsky and Tsvetaeva dramatically point out the closure of an epoch that opened with Blake, Hölderlin, Shelley, Hugo, and Heine.

5   Thomson 238. It might be tempting to substitute Love for Pleasure in this sketch, as Cicero did (*hedone* certainly embraces also Joy). Alas, the former term has been sullied first by Plato and the Christian churches, and then by Rousseau and Hollywood, to the point of near uselessness.

1.5 In Sum

These three domains cannot be fruitfully disjoined, even for analysis. Each qualifies, delimits, and throws into relief elements of the other two; most importantly, each solidifies the other two. Of Jefferson's triad, liberty is the precondition for a life worth living and for the pursuit of happiness or pleasure. However, liberty without cognition is blind narcissism and without pleasure it is dutiful subservience. In Epicureanism, "the three criteria for cognition (feeling, affection, and expectation) are at the same time criteria for pleasure" (Fallot 8). Cognition without either liberty or pleasure is self-defeating elitist self-indulgence: this is masterfully articulated in Brecht's *Life of Galileo*. Pleasure without liberty is Sadean corruption, without cognition it is empty.

In sum, life, liberty, and the pursuit of happiness and understanding are nothing without and outside humanity. Humans are certainly not cosmically free to choose one's birth, often not to choose one's death, and our control of life in between is still shaky, because we are ruled by the blind gods of capital. For most of life below the upper mammals and all of inorganic nature, the question of liberty is senseless. For humanity, it is a question of to be or not to be.

2. Regulative Principles: Dialectic, Measure (Justice), the Swerve

2.1 The Dialectic

The dialectic is, as mentioned in section 1.1, an inalienable part of valid cognition today. It is also its method. It starts by saying no to empirical reality, and goes on, as Heraclitus put it, by fusing disbelief with belief: most things (in the ways our societies and languages apprehend them, I would add) simultaneously are and are not; a thing at variance with itself agrees with itself, we step and do not step into the same river:

The universe, which is the same for all, has not been made by any god or man; it has always been, is now, and shall always be ever-living fire, kindled by measure, quenched by measure. (fr. 22B30, translation modified)[6]

The universe is, much as in Daoism, timeless and self-regulating through fluctuating changes based on such unstable unities of opposites. The "fire" is an image and universal equivalent for ceaselessly metamorphic matter: "All things are an exchange for fire and fire for all things, as goods for gold and gold for goods" (fr. 22B90); fire is "want and satiety, fire shall come and judge all things" (fr. 22B65). We are in a world of far-flung trade embracing two and a half continents, where "war is what all things have in common and justice is strife" (fr. 22B80), soon to be frozen and destroyed by the full penetration of slave work, and reborn only in modern industrial capitalism that spanned the globe. This is not only why the dialectic is now our daily bread but also why its zealous detractors (willy-nilly) prevent us from understanding what is to be done.

Already the Orphics managed dialectics: Ares is invoked to bring peace, Pan to free them from panic terror, Death to ensure longevity (Cassola 297). And Aristotle's careful discussion of potentiality identified it as something which both may be and may not be actualized. This openness, the "potentiality of contraries" (*dynamis ton henantion, Metaphysics* IX, 2, 1046b5) in all creative activities, is what founds the onto-epistemological status of this liberating category. Epicure improved on such Hellenic attempts at dialectics, from Heraclitus on, by his central insight how chance and necessity (or determination and liberty) interpenetrate, applied to the relationship between humans and nature and to the zigzags of human history. Finally, Hegel's dialectic, based on the strategic centrality of contradiction within a reason that thinks totalities, is omnipresent in social reality. Yet Lenin was right to call for a "society of materialist friends of Hegel": for we cannot do without Hegel's sweeping rediscovery of the dialectic for the epoch of

---

6   Except perhaps in ancient China and India, which I am too ignorant to judge fully, I do not know of a better encapsulation of valid cosmology than this fragment of Heraclitus. Lenin would agree (see Lefebvre, ch. 3D): his *Philosophical Notebooks* show the greatest interest, after Hegel, in Heraclitus and then Epicure.

swiftly changing capitalism, where each determination is also a manifold negation, but – dialectically – we cannot use it without rejecting all traces of his arrogant Christian theory of history either (and of his esthetics).

Marx usually did this. His dialectic begins with the Hegelian liquefaction of rigid entities into relationships between social beings (such as the capital), where all movements arise and flow from fiery and fluid magmatic depths, as in Lucrece. However, he does not use the pain of the antithesis – the blood, sweat, and tears of "the wrong side of history" – as a rhetorical ploy on the order of a double negation necessarily ending in the victory of the good synthesis: that is, for what Hegel called a theodicy (justification of Providence). Induced from the ways people cohabit and relate in the epoch of capitalist economics, it is not an illustration of pre-existing speculative schemes but an open-ended process, and Marx stresses the unforeseen ruses of history. If history is necessarily a dialectic of free vs. unfree self-creation through struggles of societal classes and fractions, which is since the rise of capital centered on the existential tug-of-war of living labour versus commodification and fetishism, then it has no end (but untold catastrophes and triumphs: Rosa Luxemburg's "socialism or barbarism"). Marx's dialectics, so far as I can see yet untranscended, turns Hegel's frequent teleology into open-ended history. The key concepts are posited as historically contingent, referred to material and fleshly reality of the living labour. Given A and B in the concrete totality C (see Suvin, "Two Cheers"), D necessarily follows, but A and/or B could have been otherwise, is the unspoken presupposition. This kind of dialectic, "development as a unity of opposites [...] furnishes the key to the >self-movement< of everything existing; [...] to the >leaps,< to the >break in the continuity,< to the >transformation into the opposite,< to the destruction of the old and the emergence of the new" (Lenin, *Philosophical* 358). It is the only tool for understanding movement.

Just as science, the dialectic is nothing without humanity: it is not an exclusive property either of the scientific mind or of the universe itself, but of their interaction. The interaction is here more complex than in the case of (human) life, liberty, and pursuit of happiness, clearly sociopolitical animals. To my mind, it is legitimate to find in physical nature instances of the dialectic, if and when one can; but since all our facts to conclude from are constituted by human social history (Marcuse), there is no dialectic of nature (the universe).

Both philosophy and science begin by transforming practice into mythical personifications and then micro-metaphors, and end in one vast macro-metaphor (as, for example, Wiener's definition of mathematics goes). They cannot reflect upon themselves unless they recognize how deeply consubstantial they are to poetry: Eros turns into Newton's attraction, geometry into gravitational fields, the wayfarers' horizon into Einstein's relativities. When most at strife with itself, the subject-object opposition agrees with itself.

2.2 Measure, Justice

Thomson has magisterially shown how the passage from tribal to class society led from the matriarchal ancestresses and avenging deities to Dike, first as habitual punishment through revenge, and then, passing through judgment, to the abstraction of Justice (goddess and notion of right or equity). The praise of justice as the highest virtue, because it does not concern only oneself but primarily the other citizens, was best synthesized in Aristotle (*Nicomachean Ethics* Book V, especially 1129b and 1130a). There is no Freedom without Justice, and viceversa. Most interestingly, Dike is in Hesiod associated with proper order, civic peace, and labour, while it punishes transgression against the due measure (*metra, metron*): in Solon's words, against "snatch[ing] and steal[ing] from one another without sparing sacred or public property" – that is, against undue enrichment and violence. "Metron" is in the pseudo-Hesiodic *Certamen* the measure of oneself as an independent worker-owner, and in Solon the measure proper to a city-state which avoids the perpetual violence of covert polarization between the rich and the debt slaves or of overt civil war. It can be generally formulated as "the convenience or fitness (*convenance*) of one being to another or to itself" (Nancy 205). Its violation is, from Solon through Aeschylus to Sophocles, *violent excess (hybris)*.

Yet the reasonable efforts of mediators, recalling that we all sit in the same boat and sink with it, came up squarely against the new introduction of coinage, of riches not as land but as money and commercial capital. While the landed space is finite, money can be accumulated in time, so that "Riches have no limit" (both quotes from Solon in Thomson 232 and 233); this will be repeated by Aristotle: "There is no limit to the aim of money-making" (*Politics* 1.9.13), and for our epoch by Marx: "The circulation of capital has therefore no limits" (*Capital* I: 159 Kerr 1993 edn).

To summarily suggest another filiation, the Latin one: *modus* seems to be a close analogue to *metron*, a measure which is not quantitative but "presupposes reflection and choice, thus also decision." It is "not [...] a mensuration, but a moderation, [...] a measure of limitation or of constraint," and he who is provided with such a measure is *modestus*. In bodily balances, personal or political, the alternative root in med- gives *medeor*, to heal, and *medicus*, the healer (Benveniste 2: 123ff.).

Philosophically speaking, as best defined in Hegel, measure is "a qualitative quantity": "All things have their measure: i.e., the quantitative terms of their existence, their being so or so great, does not matter within certain limits; but when these limits are exceeded by an additional more or less, the things cease to be what they were." (Part One of the *Encyclopedia of Philosophical Sciences*: "The Logic," First Subdivision, VII. 85). Thus, the stakes here are very high – it is a matter of naturalness vs. denaturing: Hegel concludes the preceding quote by emphatically affirming that measure is the way to arrive from a discussion of Being to that of Essence, and follows it up with a long discussion in sections 107ff. where measure is needed to complete the characterization of Being, and is indeed compared to God who is the measure of all things. There is a danger here, I would add, that – just as in the Hellenic tradition – measure (and qualitative nature) can become fixed and static, but this does not apply to properly historicized and dynamic measure or indeed Essence (see Suvin, "Two").

For Aristotle it was still obvious that economy was the art of living well, consubstantial to use-values whose measure is emphatically limited by the uses a human body can put them to. The communal ship or trireme, Athens as freedom on the seas (Thucydides), withstood the Persian aggressors but could not withstand the hurricanes of private possessiveness. Individualism needs slavery and empire. One generation later, looking at the havoc-ridden downfall of the seemingly boundless empire erected by Aristotle's pupil

Alexander, Epicure needed only (only!) to refuse the existing political order to get to his pleasure principle as just measure, opposed to unlimited desires.

In modern capitalism, we have progressed indeed: the boat being sunk by this boundless movement is not only a particular political unit (Athens) or group of units (Greece) but also the environmental eco-system, vertebrate life globally. The "techno" part of technoscience indicates well the presence of competence in a quite limited domain together with the absence of asking why, that is, the absence of a measure – a qualitative, thoughtfully applied *modus* or *metron*, moderate and modest – what is the technique for and what are its human costs (see Anders, esp. vol. 2). As Pythagora reportedly defined it, the lack of measure (*ametria*) includes illness in the body, ignorance in the psyche, sedition in the community, and discord in the house (Iamblichus, in Pitagora 2: 340). Or, as Hegel remarked, when the measure is exceeded, the quality of the quantity changes radically (*Encyclopädie* paras 107–09 and *Wissenschaft* I.1.3).

2.3 The Absolute Swerve: Fourier I

Marx's argument is today still overlaid by his intermittent nineteenth-century urge toward Newtonian scientificity; yet in Marx cognition is in no way bound by those "positive" parameters, but inextricably fused with the visionary or poetic elements (which are not irrational but supply what conceptual reason has yet no instruments for). In order to understand him properly, the strengths of his greatest precursor and complement, Charles Fourier, have to be factored in.

Fourier's major strength is to have responded to the system of bourgeois "industry" (which for him means artisanal work and commerce) by an "absolute swerve" (*écart absolu*) based on the pleasure principle, both personally sensual and socially combinatory, as a totalizing horizon; and his major weakness is that he did not understand revolutions, industrial or political (just as Epicureans never understood labour). But he caught supremely well their consequences.[7]

Fourier judged "civilization" (class society, in particular bourgeois commercialism) to be, in a popular image, a "world upside down" (*Nouveau* 14). In it, the lawyer has to wish for "good lawsuits," the physician for a "good fever," the officer for "good wars, that killed half of his colleagues," the priest for the "good dead, that is, funerals at one thousand francs apiece," the monopolist for a "good famine, which doubled or tripled the price of bread," the wine merchant for "good frosts," and the builders for "a good conflagration to consume a hundred houses and further their trade" (*Théorie* I: xxxvi); family means adultery, riches mean bankruptcy, work is constraint, property ruins the proprietor, abundance leads to unemployment, and the machine to hunger. There is no reforming this ridiculous and pernicious set-up except by a new set-up, the harmonious association based on passionate attractions among people.

Extrapolating from the cognitive tradition formulated in Lucretius, all change and meaning arise out of interaction between a linear continuation of tradition and a deviant modification (*tropos*), between pious stability and heretic mutation. But now, faced with the radical nonsense that dynamically constitutes the everyday world of the bourgeoisie, the Epicurean fortuitous swerve must become a radical refusal.

2.4 Passionate Attraction: Fourier II

People are by ineradicable nature bundles of passions for Fourier, and these can only be steered and organized. Passions stand in Fourier for all the central human faculties: sensations, feelings, stances, bearings – much as in the young Marx's focus on human senses, pleasure (*Genuss*), and needs, which could be fully developed only after abolishing private property ("Private Property and Communism," in *Writings* 305–09). The central problem of

---

7   I have taken over some formulations from my *Metamorphoses*, where eleven titles of
     secondary literature up to 1975 may be found.

bourgeois individualism was how to shape a community which would, as Rousseau put it, protect the person and goods of each without making him obey anybody but herself. Fourier's politics are a radical quest for sensual happiness for one and all: from him stems the socialist slogan that the degree of female emancipation is the measure of a society's freedom. He starts from enlightened egotism and aims for a society where the individual can only find his/her benefit through operations profitable to the whole community; he calls this new regime of free association the Phalanstery. As in the Orphics and eighteenth-century sensual materialism, appetite or passionate attraction is a universal principle, and Fourier extends it from Newton's matter to the other three worlds of plant, animal, and social life. People and their passions are not equal but varied yet complementary. Therefore, their appetites, primarily sexual and gustatory, are in Phalanstery developed and harmonized by composing them into series where classes of people (by sex and age) are, by an intricate and even maniacal system of idiosyncratic analogies (see Jameson), composed into a "calculus of Destinies."

This extends to the future and the universe: from the eighteen different creations on Earth, ours is the first and worst, having to go through five horrible stages from Savagery down to Civilization, before ascending through Guarantism (the economico-sexual welfare state of the federated *phalanstères*) to Harmony. At that point there will be no more sexual or economic repression, hunger, war, States, nations, illnesses or struggle for existence. Most important for Marx, there will also be no split between intellectual and manual labour, or labour and "leisure" (see *Critique of the Gotha Programme*, and Debout). The blessed life of Harmony, innocent of private property and salaried work, of nuclear family and the split between city and country, will right the proceedings of class Power: courts and priests will be Courts of love and priesthoods of sex, wars will turn into competitions of (e.g.) pastry-making, armies will clean, plant, and reconstruct, work will become attractive as play and art, and swerving abnormality the norm of society.

Fourier's shattering interplay of maniacal poetry and ironical dialectic, rooted in the deep longings and genuine folk imagination of ancient working classes just being crushed by commerce and industry, was the first to take into account the necessities of huge demographic agglomerations. It will reappear in garden cities and kibbutzim, in Marx (see *Grundrisse* 712) and the hippies. What it lacked was a reckoning with industrial labour and capital, and with the deep-seated, internalized and normalized, violence its reign and its leaping technoscience bring.

2.5 *In Sum*

Dialectic is the way the swiftly and harshly transforming world works. Justice is the minimal – and Epicure's friendliness the optimal – measure to be observed in those workings if the society is not to tear itself apart. Even the most extreme speculations by Fourier are an attempt to apply measure to the passions of possession or self-affirmation, which is what was traditionally called wisdom. The absolute deviation or swerve is the wise measure within the dialectics of the present epoch: the urgent necessity to turn upside down the murderously transformed world in order to make it livable.

3. Marx I: Production, Creation – Living Labour

3.0

Two presuppositions are quite central to Marx's analysis of the "material mode of production" constituting capital and capitalism. The first one is living labour (*lebendige Arbeit*), "the living source of value" (*Grundrisse* 296–97); Preve perspicaciously notes that this "absolute starting point [...] functions for him as a true Being" (144)[8] and Dussel that it is "the category which generates all other categories by Marx; fetishism being

---

8   Marx, *Grundrisse*; a long list of secondary literature to Marx and the *Grundrisse* was given in Suvin "Transubstantiation" and Suvin-Angenot, to which today at least

the lack of reference to it" (39). Marx's definition of men is one of beings who "produce [...] their material life" (*German* 37). As against the Idealist definition of human being as *animal rationale*, it might be one of *animal laborans*, or the animal with labour power (*Arbeitskraft*) (Arendt 86 and 88). The second presupposition, to be initially approached in Part 4, is the measuring of living labour as time.[9]

3.1 Alienation of Value-Creation

Creative power is appropriated by capital:

> The worker [...] sells labour only in so far [...] as its equivalent is already measured, given; capital buys it as living labour, as the general productive force of wealth [...]. [I]n exchange for his labour capacity as a fixed, available magnitude, [the worker] surrenders its *creative power*, like Esau his birthright for a mess of pottage [...]. The creative power of his labour establishes itself as the power of capital, as an *alien power* confronting him. He divests himself of [externalizes, alienates – *entäussert sich*] labour as the force productive of wealth; capital appropriates it, as such. (*Grundrisse* 307)

Antonio Negri's *Marx beyond Marx* (Brooklyn, NY, and London: Autonomedia and Pluto, 1991) should be added.

9   I am aware that I here rush into an area that is hotly debated through hundreds of pages by commentators of Marx, of which I have read only a part. Even more important, Marx has in works posterior to the *Grundrisse*, especially the later parts of *Capital* and the *Theories of Surplus Value*, had more to say on Smithian production, with at least partly new ways of envisaging it (that include a distinction between the two approaches to "production," e.g., *Theorien* I: 125 or 356). I hope to return to this in a following article to deal with time and quality; in the meantime I trust that, in this most knotty field, following Marx's own development and dilemmas is not the worst way to proceed.
    I need to add that much after publishing this essay I finally laid my hands on some works that Enrique Dussel has been publishing since 1985 and which I had sought in vain in major European libraries. I was happy to see we came to the same view of living labour, though he does it at more length and with a stress on the labourer's corporeality, poverty, and denudation which I have now no space for. The single quote from him does not adequately represent my appreciation.

Labour not as object, but as activity; not as itself *value*, but as the *living source* of value. (*Grundrisse* 296)

The productivity of labour becomes the productive force of capital [... C]apital itself is essentially *this displacement, this transposition [of the productive force* of labour], and [...] *this transubstantiation*; the necessary process of positing its own powers as alien to the worker. (*Grundrisse* 308)

The worker is impoverished by the process of production, during which s/he must enter into and be transformed by an "absolute separation between property and labour, between living labour capacity and the conditions of its realization, between objectified and living labour, between value and value-creating activity." His/her "value-creating possibility" is transformed into

capital, as master over living labour capacity, as value endowed with its own might and will, confronting him in his [...] poverty. He has produced not only the alien wealth and his own poverty, but also the relation of this wealth as independent, self-sufficient wealth, relative to himself as the poverty which this wealth consumes, and from which wealth thereby draws new vital spirits into itself, and realizes itself anew [...]. The product of labour appears as [...] a mode of existence confronting living labour as independent [...]; the product of labour, objectified labour, has been endowed by living labour with a soul of its own, and establishes itself opposite living labour as an *alien power*. [...]. As a consequence of the production process, the possibilities resting in living labour's own womb exist outside it [...] as *realities alien* to it [...]. (*Grundrisse* 452–54)

In brief, as Marx concluded, living labour is transformed into production of commodity plus surplus-value, both "incorporated" into capital in unequal exchange (*Theorien* I: 353 and passim).

3.2 *Fantastic Metamorphoses and Anamorphoses*

The product of a subject (labour) is unnaturally born out of it as not simply an objectified reality (like a baby or an artefact) but as a malevolent usurper, taking from the subject its "vital spirits," vitality or indeed soul. This is not too bad an approximation to a Gothic tale, in two variants, with a male and female protagonist: the first, in which the unclean capitalist Power seeds the womb of labour (here a *succuba*) with a demon birth; the second, in which the unsuspecting hero is beset by a power he unwittingly let loose out of his soul-substance or vitality, and which turns upon him to suck the rest of such "vital spirits" – from the Sorcerer's Apprentice tale (already used in *The Communist Manifesto*) to the popular image (though not the more sophisticated original novel) of Dr Frankenstein and his monster.

Or, "[t]he accumulation of knowledge and of skill, of the general productive forces of the social brain is thus absorbed into capital [...]" (*Grundrisse* 694). As in horror-fantasy, brain-forces are absorbed into the villain, the "*animated monster*" of capital (*Grundrisse* 470). In older language, he practices soul-extraction, soul-transferral or soul-eating. For when value becomes capital, living labour confronts it "as a mere means to realize objectified, dead labour, to penetrate it with an animating soul while losing its own soul to it" (*Grundrisse* 461). The underlying image of vampirism and vampiric reincarnation, the evil incarnation process, is reproduced in Marx's very syntax:

> Capital posits the permanence of value (to a certain degree) by incarnating itself in fleeting commodities and taking on their form, but at the same time changing them just as constantly; alternates between its eternal form in money and its passing form in commodities; permanence is posited as the only thing it can be, a passing passage-process-life. But capital obtains this ability only by constantly sucking in living labour as its soul, vampire-like. (*Grundrisse* 646)

3.3 Two Meanings of Production

The radical alienation of all relationships under the hegemony of capital (living labour vs. alienated labour, use value vs. exchange value, and so on and on) can perhaps most clearly be seen in the two diametrically opposite meanings for which Marx – in a shorthand – uses the term "production" in the *Grundrisse*:

Marx was perfectly clear about the distinction between "production in general" and "capitalist production." Indeed it was the claim of the latter, through its political economy, to the universality of its own specific and historical conditions, that he especially attacked. But the history had happened, in the language as in so much else. What is then profoundly difficult is that Marx analysed "capitalist production" in and through its own terms, and at the same time, whether looking to the past or the future, was in effect compelled to use many of the same terms for more general or historically different processes. (Williams 90)

I shall use P1 for economic *"production founded on capital"* (*Grundrisse* 415) and defined from the capitalist point of view, that is, as producing surplus value while producing use-value only insofar that is "the bearer of exchange-value" (see Marx, *Theorien* I: 53, 121, 116, and 267). Here Marx reuses the classical bourgeois meanings from Smith on; the briefest definition I found is *"Productive work* is thus that which – within the system of capitalist production – produces *surplus value* for its employer [...], that is work that produces its own product as capital" (*Theorien* I: 359). Obversely, I shall use P2 for meta-economic or better *meta-capitalist production* of use-values in the sense of *creative force* (*schöpferische Kraft*, *Grundrisse* 307):

> What is *productive labour* and what is not, a point very much disputed back and forth since Adam Smith made this distinction [Adam Smith, *Wealth of Nations* II, 355–85], has to emerge from the dissection of the various aspects of capital itself. *Productive* [P1] *labour* is only that which produces *capital*. Is it not crazy, asks e.g., (or at least something similar) Mr. Senior, that the piano maker is a *productive worker*, but not the *piano player*, although obviously the piano would be absurd without the piano player? [Senior, *Principes fondamentaux* 197–206].But this is exactly the case. The piano maker reproduces *capital*; the pianist only exchanges his labour for revenue. But does not the pianist produce [P2] music and satisfy our musical ear, does he not even to a certain extent produce [P2] the latter? He does indeed: his labour produces [P2] something; but that does not make it *productive labour* in the *economic sense* [P1]; no more than the labour of the madman who produces [P2] delusions is productive [P1] [...]. (*Grundrisse* 306; and see *Grundrisse* 273)

"The poet, the madman, the lover" (to use a phrase from Marx's favourite writer) are to the bourgeois economist the very exemplars of unproductivity. Their production is purely qualitative creation.

The two meanings of production arise from the fact that Marx must *simultaneously explain and criticize* Smith's and Malthus's political economy. As he lucidly put it in the letter to Lassalle of 22 February 1858: "The present work [...] is at the same time presentation of the system of bourgeois economy and its critique by means of the presentation" (*Werke* 29: 550). Thus, he must meticulously account for the epoch-making innovation of capitalist production [P1] and sweepingly condemn it by indicating the anthropological limitation which renders it unable to subsume human production outside of the realm of necessity, i.e., the "species-specific" production [P2], that would not reproduce capital.[10]

Smith also opposes actors producing [P2] a play to those being productive [P1] by increasing their employer's wealth (*Grundrisse* 328–29). It is not accidental that Smith, Senior, and Marx all use examples from spiritual or esthetic production, which is clearly both potentially creative from Marx's anthropological standpoint (as opposed to the alienation of labour power) and yet unproductive from the standpoint of bourgeois political economy. This production [P2] has in bourgeois society only been preserved in non-capitalized enclaves, of which the most valuable may be artistic production and love. This is why the development of labour as use-value "corresponds generally [...] [to a] half-artistic relation to labour" (*Grundrisse* 587), and obversely why one of the best Marxists of the twentieth century, Brecht, returns to the concept of love as production [P2].[11]

While production had been confiscated by the rulers in all class societies, Marx's wrath implies that it is now for the first time both unnecessary (in view of the giant development of the forces of production, see, e.g., *Grundrisse* 705–06) and covered up by a giant ideological mystification of the new ruling class that pretends to freedom and integral humanism but

10 "For Marx, assumption of bourgeois perspective and voice, through what might be termed a heuristically useful travesty, was thus a frequent counter-ideological procedure" (Terdiman 23).

11 On Brecht, see Suvin "Haltung" and "Emotion." About Marx on art and production see the lucid distinctions – mostly on the material of the *Theories of Surplus Value* – by Sánchez Vázquez, 181ff.

whose only horizon is P1, which Marx will after the *Grundrisse* define as production of surplus-value appropriated by and constituting capital.

3.4 *Labour as Living Fire*

The most incisive formulation may be:

> Labour is the living, form-giving fire; it is the transitoriness of things, their tempo-rality, as their formation by living time. In the simple production process [...] the transitoriness of the forms of things is used to posit their usefulness. When cotton becomes yarn, yarn becomes fabric, fabric becomes printed etc. or dyed etc. fabric, and this becomes, say, a garment, then (1) the substance of cotton has preserved itself in all these forms [...]; (2) in each of these subsequent processes, the material has obtained a more useful form, a form making it more appropriate to consumption; until it has obtained at the end the form in which it [...] satisfies a human need, and its transformation is the same as its use. (*Grundrisse* 361)

"Living labour" is thus not a reified abstraction but the human bodily energy and skill, where body includes mind, the force of the living subject being invested in and basic to production. Labour power is a *vis viva*, the human incarnation of the "natural property of matter [being] movement [...] as *impulse, vital spirits, tension*", a tradition going from Aristotle's *entelekhia* and final cause to what Bloch will call latency-cum-tendency (*Prinzip* 1625ff.).[12] Perhaps it is by now not startling that "the advance of popula-tion [...] too belongs with production" [P2] (*Grundrisse* 486). From Marx's very beginnings, such a formulation, in which the goal of and reason for labour is the production [P2] of life (see Arendt 88), where the "mode of

---

12   Marx–Engels, *The Holy Family* 152. The term *vis viva* is derived from Marx's read-ings in – and then Engels's full impregnation by – Leibniz (see Marx's "Auszüge"), in particular Leibniz's *Specimen dynamicum* [...] *circa corporum vires*, a polemic against Descartes's reduction of motion to purely quantitative, pleading for a self-developing finality from inside any monadic form. This knot is discussed at length in Bellinazzi (73, 116–17, 136–37, 257–59, and passim). Marx's monad is here sensual human activity, as found in labour (see the *Grundrisse*; also *The Marx–Engels Dictionary* s.v. "Force" by J. Russell).

production [...] is [...] a definite *mode of life*" (Marx–Engels,*German* 37), was permanently present in him. It is confirmed by Engels's famous preface to *The Origin of the Family*: "the production and reproduction of immediate life [...] is of a twofold character. On the one hand, the production of the means of subsistence [...]; on the other, the production [P2] of human beings themselves" (455).

As opposed to production of exchange-values for profit [P1], the production of use-values for consumption [P2] is a beneficent metamorphosis of life into more life, human quality into another human quality: "*living labour makes instrument and material in the production process* into the body of its soul and thereby resurrects them from the dead [...]*" (*Grundrisse* 364). The classless society or realm of freedom necessitated by the qualitative logic of human vitality, which sublates the quantitative logic of political economy, is one which has turned the vampiric dispossession of labour and its vitality into a Heraclitean but even more a Promethean "form-giving fire," into a means of renewed life. Humanized production or creativity replaces death with life: the essential Marxian argument is as "simple" as this.

3.5 In Sum

Thus the *Grundrisse*, and then *Capital*, are the high point and crown of a whole millennia-old (if not millenary) plebeian tradition of metamorphic imagery, omnipresent already in Lucretian poetics. In it the immortal labouring people constitute the world's body in metamorphic feedback with the world's goods, refashioned by, in, and as their bodies – a tradition best set forth in Bakhtin's *Rabelais and His World*. This tradition runs on the affirmative side from early metamorphic myths – such as the central one here, Prometheus as both fire-bringer and shape-giver (*pyrphoros* and *plasticator*) – and from folktales, through what Bakhtin calls "prandial libertinism" such as the Cockayne stories and Rabelais – positing a magically unimpeded direct appropriation of nature without war, scarcity or work – to Fourier's future of passionate attractions. On the negative side, Carnival is accompanied by Lent: all that falls short of such full contentment is treated as a demonically unnatural state of affairs, a misappropriation of the people's living forces or vital spirits by vampiric villains. To mention only Marx's most likely sources, such a filiation runs again from the horrific elements in myths and folktales, culminating in those of the Grimm brothers, through classical antiquity (Homer's Circe and Lucretius rather than Ovid's codification of metamorphoses), to the Romantic elaborations on these motifs (e.g., from Goethe's *Faust*, see also *Grundrisse* 704). The subversive plebeian genres (or the twin genre) of horror fantasy cum utopian alternative, radically alienated from the seemingly solid and unchangeable status quo and therefore committed to seemingly fantastic processual and metamorphic imagery, supplied Marx in the *Grundrisse* with the popular, spontaneously materialist imaginative tradition formulating the lot of exploited people as a struggle between living renewal of their forces and a zombie-like death-in-life.

Marx changed and fulfilled this tradition by fusing it with the materialist and dialectical intellectual traditions which stem from similar roots but developed somewhat independently from Heraclitus and Epicure to Hegel and Feuerbach, briefly fusing with the plebeian tradition also at such earlier high points as Lucretius, Rabelais, and Cyrano. Marx's main innovation was to alter *the people's body* into *labour's living body*, which makes out of the cosmic presupposition of ever-living fire a concrete, everyday matter of *living labour's formative fire*. This radically transcended the dominant Greek vision of activity split between the *praxis* of free and wealthy citizens and the *poiesis* of the plebeian "mechanics," slaves, and women: "there is no effective liberty which would not also be a material transformation, [...] but also no work which is not a transformation of one's self [...]."[13] Marx's Copernican revolution substituted for the *polis* dichotomy, already rejected by Vico and Kant, the deeper binary relationship of living labour and vampiric capital. The Epicurean swerve, exasperated into a total refusal in Fourier, found its source in living labour.

---

13   Balibar 40–41. But such a doctrine of "ongoing transformation" (*Fortbildungslehre*) has been a ground bass of Ernst Bloch; see his final formulation in *Experimentum* 132.

Where labour was before the development of productive forces under capitalism traditionally an outgrowth and warding off of poverty (which is evident in the semantic kinship between the two terms, *ponos* and *penia* in Greek, *Arbeit* and *Armut* in German), Locke noted that it is the source of all property, Adam Smith that it is the source of all wealth: yet both believed it needed money for fructification. Though already Fichte objected, taking his cue from the radicals in the French revolution, that "as soon as anybody cannot live from his labour, [...] the [social] contract [on which the right to property is based] is in respect to him fully abrogated" (cited in Lukács 71), it was only in Hegel that labour was taken as the realization of human essence, as a formative or materially shaping force (see ibid. 378). Noting this, Marx however not only raised to central position the view that labour was the sole source of all creativity (see Arendt 101), possessing its own undying fire, he also changed Hegel's recognition of "the positive side of labour" by stressing that it was the realization of man "within alienation, or as alienated person" (*Writings* 322, translation modified). Marx thus added to the plebeian defence of the consuming and hedonist body, culminating in Fourier, as well as to Spinoza's understanding by means of bodily passions and idea, the crucially new cognition and trope of *the producing body*, which both incorporated and criticized (that is, dialectically sublated) bourgeois political economy.[14] A marginal but programmatic note of his in *The German Ideology* posits: "The human body. Needs and labour" (44). That is why his understanding will last as long as the economy of alienated labour and the need to imagine a radical alternative to it.

14 For arguments how well Marx knew Fourier, see Bowles, Lansac 119–34, Larizza, and Zil'berfarb.

4. Marx II: Capitalism as a New Thing under the Sun

4.1 Time as Quantity

The second mainspring of Marx's analysis of capital and capitalism is denaturing living labour by *measuring it in time* as an exchangeable quantity.
It takes up and hugely enriches the classical argument that the only way
to avoid the daily and unceasing violence of creeping or leaping civil war
or, in Orphic or medieval terms, to practice the supreme civic virtue of
justice, is the observation of due measure: "The circulation of capital has
no limits" (*Capital* 129).

All production happens in time, but only capitalist productivity is
measured per time unit. Piano playing is most precisely time-bound (each
note has a time-duration), but – unless a music impresario exploits a player's
labour – only piano-making produces wages and capital. In all uses of living
labour there occurs a transmigration and metamorphosis of labour's soul
and vitality. This creativity becomes demonic when reproducing capital,
which is effected by measuring labour in the linear time of potentially
limitless capital accumulation: "*Labour time as the measure of value* posits
wealth itself as founded on poverty [...]" (*Grundrisse* 708). The distinction
between the two senses of production is also one between maintaining
the *qualitative* nature of human living labour, which reposes on a finite
measure (like the Hellenic *metron*), or losing it for mere *quantity* in order
to enable it as exchange-value:

> Use value is not concerned with human activity as the source of the product, [...] but
> with its being for mankind. In so far as the product has a measure for itself, it is its
> natural measure as natural object, mass, weight, length, volume etc. Measure of utility
> etc. But as effect, or as static presence of the force which created it, it is measured only
> by the measure of this force itself. The measure of labour is time. (*Grundrisse* 613)

> As a *specific, one-sided, qualitative* use value, e.g., grain, its quantity itself is irrel-
> evant only up to a certain level; it is required only in a specific quantity; i.e., in a
> certain *measure* [...]. Use value in itself does not have the boundlessness of value as
> such. Given objects can be consumed as objects of needs only up to a certain level.
> (*Grundrisse* 405)

An incipient dialectic of time as duration, horizon, and value is at work in Marx, which it would behove us to learn from and develop.

4.2 From Community to Loneness

Marx's *Grundrisse* starts thus from the "first presupposition [...] that capital stands on one side and labour on the other, both [...] alien to one another" (*Grundrisse* 266), so that labour time must be exchanged for money. This is not at all a natural state of affairs. Historically, "[a]nother presupposition is the separation of [...] [labour] from the means of labour and the material for labour [...] the dissolution of small, free landed property as well as of communal landownership [...]" (*Grundrisse* 471). Before capitalism, the "labouring individual" existed as a member of a community (tribe, Asian or medieval village, etc.) whose "communal landed property [was] at the same time *individual possession*" (*Grundrisse* 492); he had "an *objective mode of existence* in his ownership [i.e., stewardship] of the land, an existence *presupposed* to his activity [...]" (*Grundrisse* 485). Capital presupposes the full annihilation of "the various forms in which the worker is a proprietor, or in which the proprietor works." This means above all: 1) dissolution of the worker's relation to land and soil, "the workshop of his forces, and the domain of his will"; 2) "dissolution of the relations in which he appears as the proprietor of the instrument"; 3) dispossessing the worker of "the means of consumption [...] during production, *before* its completion" (all 497). Capitalism having done away with the worker's "self-sustenance, his own reproduction as a member of the community" (*Grundrisse* 476), he has now been forcibly separated from materials and tools for labour, so that, as Marx ironically notes, "[i]n bourgeois society, [...] the thing which *stands opposite* [the worker] has now become the true commonality [*Gemeinwesen*], which he tries to make a meal of, and which makes a meal of him" (*Grundrisse* 496).

With the historical sketch of "Precapitalist Production Forms" (*Grundrisse* 471–514) it becomes clear "that the capitalist mode of production depends on social connection assuming the 'ideological' form of individual dis-connection" (Hall 24). Robinson Crusoe on his desert island is a totally mystified myth of origin for political economics. But he is a powerful emblem for the "disconnected" status of the manual and mental worker. "[T]he same process which divorced a mass of individuals from their previous [affirmative] relations to the *objective conditions of labour*, [...] freed [...] land and soil, raw materials, necessaries of life, instruments of labour, money or all of these from their *previous state of attachment* to the individuals now separated from them. They are still there on hand, but [...] as a free fund, in which all political etc. relations are obliterated." (*Grundrisse* 503). This means that the disconnection and integral bodily repression went very deep. Marx's vampiric, cannibalic, and demonic imagery indicates this well; and it also modulates into the language of dispossession, the result of which is the individual's objective *loneness* (isolation, *Vereinzelung*): "the individual worker [...] exists as an animated individual punctuation mark, as [the capital's] living isolated accessory" (*Grundrisse* 470).

This is a historically unique reshaping of living labour and use-value "into a form adequate to capital. The accumulation of knowledge and of skill, of the general productive forces of the social brain is thus absorbed into capital [...]" (*Grundrisse* 694). It amounts to a major cultural revolution, and has also been remarked upon by culture critics from the Right as a somewhat unclear "dissociation of sensibility" (T.S. Eliot). On the Left, it was best articulated by Lukács and Bakhtin as the descending curve of the novel from the collective values of Cervantes and Rabelais to the unhappy individualism of Gogol and Flaubert. This is both a consequence and an emblem of the disintegration of precapitalist communities and commonalities under the onslaught of the capillary rise to power of exchange-value, use-value turned into money and reproducing capital.

The disintegration of precapitalist communities, however subordinated and exploited they were as a whole, led to the ferocity of individualist aloneness. For, capitalism destroyed not only common land and co-operative work, but the further impalpable but quite real use-values of pride in work, skill, common values and beliefs, and overt numinosity. This leads to sweeping disenchantment (Weber), where most people come to lead lives of noisy or quiet despair (Thoreau). It is testified to by mass social

movements such as alcoholism, Luddism, and emigration but may be seen
most clearly in the Realism of Stendhal's and Balzac's age.

4.3 Reshaping the Time-Horizons of History

Capitalism thus means the steady, at times explosive but always relentless,
disintegration of most prior forms of people's relationships to each other
and to the universe of society and nature. It means a consubstantial change
in both overt value horizons and the depths of the human *sensorium*.

I shall pursue this in another place. Here I wish to note that, if this
is correct, then the historical overview proposed by the *Manifesto of the
Communist Party* and other works of Marx, Engels, and the whole tradition flowing out of them needs a central correction. I have in an earlier chapter (Part 3 of Chapter 13) doubted the Hegelian triad necessarily
evolving through tribal, class, and higher classless societies. First, I do not
see a preordained necessity of such – possibly of any – evolution; that it
happened is no proof that it had to happen. Second, neither are elements
lacking which speak against taking class society (the Asiatic, slave-owning,
feudal, and capitalist social formations) as a fully meaningful unit. Marx's
own investigations in "Precapitalist Production Forms" give substance to my
doubt. Political economy is a bourgeois beast, and it is not to be extrapolated
backwards, he implies (see *Grundrisse* 497). Before the rise of capital, the
aim of acquiring wealth was at least counterbalanced by other aims, such as
stabilizing society – for example, by creating good citizens (in "Antiquity",
Grundrisse 487). Wealth was certainly important, and decisive in some
pursuits, such as long-range commerce, but landed communities could
survive without it at times of political collapse. In its "bourgeois form,"
wealth is on the contrary "a complete emptying-out [...] [and] sacrifice of
the human end-in-itself to an entirely external end" (*Grundrisse* 488). The
separation of "living and active humanity" from "their metabolic exchange
with nature [...] is completely posited only in the relation of wage labour
and capital. In the relations of slavery and serfdom this separation does not
take place" (*Grundrisse* 489). "For capital, the worker is not a condition
of production [as the slave and serf were], only work is," remarks Marx

presciently: "If it can make machines do it, or even water, air, so much the better." (*Grundrisse* 498) All of this does not mean that slavery or serfdom were better, only quite different: in them, "use value predominates, production for direct consumption [and payments in kind] [...]" (*Grundrisse* 502). Finally, only in capitalism the rise of monetary wealth leads to the industrial revolution; and only in capitalism is there conquest of production in time rather than of the products in space (see *Grundrisse* 506 and 512). In fact, Marx concludes that slavery and serfdom – and a fortiori the Asiatic mode of production – were more akin to the clan system, whose forms they modify (*Grundrisse* 493)!

This conclusion (and the whole astounding argument in *Grundrisse* 493–95) goes even further than I would advocate, for it might lead us to posit a new triad of modes of production: precapitalist, capitalist, postcapitalist. I shall content myself with being non-Hegelian and proposing instead the tetrad: tribal → precapitalist → capitalist → classless societies.[15] Beyond the depth processes in economics mentioned above, capitalism adds to precapitalist or tributary class societies at least five further, key factors: first, the huge development of productive forces; second, the complete supersession of direct relationships between oppressor and oppressed, exploiter and exploited (as opposed to the situation of slaves, tributaries or serfs); third, the rise of nation-states; fourth, the replacement of religion as undoubted *doxa* by political economy and its ideologies of productivity (which draws surplus value out of labour) and of technoscience (frozen labour that does not strike) as well as – alas to a lesser degree – by the public opinion of civil society; and fifth, the convergence of profit urge and technological means in increasing globalization, culminating in our days. This means then that capitalism was not providentially necessary, a

---

15   When I put up my hypothesis of quadripartition of historical mega-periods or social
      formations in Chapter 12, sparked by hints in Marx both in the *Grundrisse* and in
      his further rethinking when studying Russia in 1873–74, it was mainly derived from
      Thomas More and Chinese history, and secondarily from Karl Polanyi and E.P.
      Thompson. But I now find, culpably late (but life short, craft vast), that this point
      has been argued by Dobb in 1947, Bookchin in chapter 6 of his *Ecology*, first version
      1982, and by Wood throughout the 1990s, as can be seen in her *Origin*.

Happy Fall ensuring final redemption – more likely, it might have been "a break in the cultural history" (Amin 53, and see 59–61)! This can be also read out of Utopia, and few people are for me more authoritative than Thomas More about the rise of capitalism; and it can be found in Marx's repeated disclaimers in his correspondence with Russians in 1877–81 against the use of his depiction of "how capitalism arose in western Europe" for erecting "a theory of the general development prescribed by destiny to all peoples" (Marx–Engels, *Geschichte* 192–93, and see 191–213)! More mileage for the twenty-first century is here latently present: for this also means that capitalism will not be providentially overcome. I concluded that we may have to reformulate the price for further failure as not simply a "return to barbarism" but a more horrifying spectre of a decennial or centennial fascism, fusing aspects from all the worst capitalist, feudal, despotic, and slave-owning societies in the interest of the new rulers.

4.4 Consecrating Creation

Not the least interesting argument in the "Precapitalist Production Forms" is the one about the deification of the community's (tribe's etc.) appropriation of land in labour. The "comprehensive unity" that stands above and sanctions the real communities' hereditary possession appears "as a *particular* entity above the many real particular communities [...] and [the] surplus labour takes the form of [...] common labour for the exaltation of the unity." Marx rightly identifies this person, the condensate of the everyday sacrality inherent in the creative relation between labour and land, as partly the despot, the patriarchal "father of many communities," and partly "the imagined clan-being, the god" (*Grundrisse* 473); but to my mind the numinous force or god is the original personification of the imaginary substance of the community, a vision (and increasingly an illusion) of its life of unitary sense, while the emperor is only "the Son of Heaven" or living deity on earth.

Here too, capitalism is at the alienating antipodes. Its unceasing alienation of creative power does not affirm and guarantee it but *withdraws* it from the subject and object of labour. Its "value-creating possibility"

(*Grundrisse* 452) results in an emptying out of value for the worker – in the widest sense (that is, everybody excluding the capitalists and their henchmen, who revel in the value of domination). The impoverishment of the labourer, discussed in my Part 3, is not simply economical, it seamlessly extends to matters of life and death: political disempowerment over relations to other people and "religious" disempowerment over relations to the universe. Where the transitoriness of the worked-on objects led to usefulness and use-values and was renewable as cyclical life, the arrow of time brings now subjection to monstrous powers which are faceless, as it were dissolved into the world of commodified relations and only dimly apprehended as deadly consequences. Weber's disenchantment can and should finally be identified with the loss of a structure of feeling of unitary sense in people's works and days.

We can today see that intolerable disenchantment further leads, in a classical return of the repressed, to even worse – because unacknowledged – re-enchantment (Balibar 59ff.). It is not only that from the oceanic depths of the capitalist mode of production there monstrously appear new religions and sects. It is not even that all varieties of revolutionary politics and socialism seem to be necessarily a mixture, in diverse modes and proportions, of disenchantment and re-enchantment. It is primarily that the everyday life gets split into work and leisure, and that both of them impact upon the sensorial system, people's consciousness, and their sense of values in totally new ways.

To reach for an understanding of these ways it is indispensable to take Marx's fetishism hypothesis seriously, which means also literally, and redo it for the age of world wars and TV sensationalism. This would begin with taking in and valorizing all the main passages in which Marx dealt with fetishism and depth mystification inherent in the capitalist production process and mode of life, and not merely the famous chapter in Book One of *Capital*. Not that his views had centrally changed after 1857–58, when he wrote the *Grundrisse* (which I used here as the first and probably the richest formulation of this subject-matter). But in Book 3 of *Capital*, as already in *Theories of Surplus Value* (written in 1861–63), he advanced from what he confined himself to in *Capital* 1 to a first consideration of interest-bearing capital, which he called its "most fetishized form", and then followed up "the enchanted and topsy-turvy world of capital" from production into the circulation process, determined not only by labour time but also by circulation time, and clearly implied this was even more "mystical" (*Werke* 25: 404 and 835–36 *Theorien* 3: 451–65).

If, as all creation, love as well as child-bearing and child-rearing belong to production in the non-bourgeois and anti-capitalist sense, then Marx takes this sense [P2] for his implicit yardstick with which to measure the wrong character of capitalist production [P1]; but it is right to say that he, and the whole Marxist tradition, does not focus on this production as creation. Though many women and children worked in Marx's time on turning labour into reproduction of capital, this was eventually found less profitable than using them for the hidden costs of reproducing the labour force, and industrial labourers became as a rule male. There was much reason in his focussing on the problem as it concerned these male labourers, on labour as abstractly genderless, but that does not excuse the neglect after him. Epicure deposed his will in the temple of Demeter, the Great Earth Mother which grows trees, grain, and people, the goddess of natural needs and their fulfillment; and practically consubstantial to it was the great Epicurean Aphrodite-Venus, Lucretius's "human and divine pleasure" (Fallot 34–35, and see Cassola 327, 332, and 436–37). We have to recover this lost legacy where women and their living labour are the indispensable second pole for human freedom, cognition, and pleasure – and as the more oppressed sex/ gender, a measure for all of them.

A crucial and vital updating of Marx's insights for the twenty-first century must use at least two new currents of cognition. First, the insights of critics of bourgeois presuppositions to economics, from Polanyi to present-day ecological debates, beginning with the absolutely necessary dethroning of the Gross National Product (GNP) as yardstick for well-being. Second, the insights of materialist feminism. Beside adding new foci, such as the intertwining of the producing and the gendered body, they add new methods. There should be no deep obstacles for such an alliance (though many contingent ones, arising mainly out of opposed interests of male and female elites competing at the capitalist poker table). To the Marxian demonic birth, Feminist and Brechtian holy birth – all creation that consecrates life – has to be added.

4.5 An Economy of Death

I cannot enter here into the properly economic discussions flowing out from Marx's two mainsprings. But as Preve remarks, all political economy "is an attempt to measure what is by nature measureless, and only the dialectic allows us to measure the measureless": he could have added that mathematicians had for the same reasons to invent the differential and integral account. He caps this fulgurant argument by noting that the problem of determining bounds to the boundless means in philosophical language a determination of totality, and that "the idea there could be a critique of political economics without the dialectic seems like the joke of a bad comic: one laughs, but only out of courtesy" (Preve 54–55). The bourgeois practice and theory of political economy are thus erected on quicksand: their basic move is to pretend the measureless can be arithmetically measured with sufficient precision to go immeasurably on. They have no inkling of life's being a small island of negentropy within an ocean of entropy that tends toward absolute zero, so that each manifestation of life is cosmically rare and must be cherished. They use for all their fatal decisions such obviously nonsensical instruments as the GNP, where crime and war officially contribute to riches, while the costs of air, water, health assistance, and all other life-enhancing activities yielding no profit on capital are kept out of its figures. This is logical: capitalist political economy is an ally of entropy; it is an economy of death rather than life [see Appendix].

Therefore, as Benjamin and Gramsci came to realize, whenever unions or revolutionary movements adopted the perspective of a merely quantified time, where the present is perpetually sacrificed for a shining future, they also swallowed the capitalist view of production as profit and sacrificed the union of intellectual freedom with material and poetic creation: the revolution turns into a shortcut to subaltern reform.

Necrophilia cannot be reformed, only done away with. Any life-affirming conservatism, muzzling the boundless and boundlessly destructive "aim of money-making," leads thus today not to the middle way of Aristotle but to a Marxian, revolutionary absolute swerve.

5. Prospect

Another great forebear of ours, Spinoza, says in *Ethics* that "[the] knowledge [of a free man] is a meditation on life, not on death" (584). Paradoxically, however, only in view of death, knowing how to meet it fearlessly in integral Epicureanism – which means getting away from life as duration in favour of life as the freedom of cognitive pleasure – is such a proper life and pursuit of happiness possible. Engels somewhere says that the human hand, with its opposable thumb, is the key to the hand of the ape. In exactly that sense, living labour and its liberation is the key to our present labour of living, to the horizons – the prospects as well as the just and unjust limits – of life.

Appendix on Political Economy and Entropy[16]

0

I have been asked to expand on the compressed remarks about political economy with special attention to possible alternatives today. Now I am no economist, and dozens of weighty tomes have been written about the hugely destructive effects of our final phase of capitalism. Thus I can here only summarize a few most salient arguments. In Polanyi's pioneering terms, when labour, nature, and even money are turned into commodities, then people are alienated and humiliated, the planet's resources recklessly

---

16   My thanks for bibliographic indications in this brave new continent for me go to Matko Meštrović and Richard Wolff. Today (*2008*) the uselessness of GNP is well established in professional discourse, and there is a plethora of further instruments, surveyed in Talberth. The estimate of the Iraq invasion costs by Stiglitz is at least 3,000 billion dollars and the Daly–Cobb index of well-being ISEW would definitely be back at the level of the 1930s.

squandered, and money subsumed under financial speculation. Both natural
resources and human life have become extremely cheap: probably around
1,500 million people live today in the most abject poverty, which means
more or less slowly dying of hunger and attendant diseases, facing the few
thousand billionaires – so that the hundred million dead and several hundred million other casualties of capitalist warfare in the twentieth century
seem puny in comparison (though their terror and suffering is not). The
purpose of economy is found to be compatible with mass dying and unhappiness, at best with social stability in the upper two thirds of the Northern
metropolis of global capitalism, while it clearly ought to be the survival
of the human species and other species ecologically linked to us (which
means practically all). Our run-away sciences, which could have finally
made (as Brecht put it after 1945) this planet habitable, have been turned
into providers of enormous quantities of commodities without regard to
quality of life. Economic growth benefits "only the richest people alive
now, at the expense of nearly everybody else, especially the poor and the
powerless in this and future generations [...]. Life on planet Earth itself is
now at risk." (Ayres 2) The "higher growth" of (as I shall argue) all our fake
economical statistics is largely synonymous with more pollution, resource
plunder, environmental destruction.

I shall attempt to deal in this Appendix with some discussions about
the relation of official income to actual well-being and conclude with an
indication of the entropy calculus as a basis for any future program of
human survival.

I

It is indispensable to start at "the accounting assumptions at the very heart
of industrial capitalism, the statistic known as the Gross National Product"
(Greider 452), further GNP. It measures the yearly monetary transactions
involved in the production of goods and services, the flow of money paid
out by producers for all their costs: wages, rents, interests, and profits, also
depreciation and excise taxes. It is founded on defining "capital" as the
manmade assets producing goods and services, and leaves out the natural

assets depleted by production (not to speak of surplus extraction of value from workers). It further ignores services and goods transacted without payment, the entropic costs (to which I shall return), and it throws into the same bag useful and murderous goods and services. For example, any known monetary transactions in arms, drugs, prostitution, and crime, any repairs after natural or manmade devastations, unnecessary lawsuits or medical interventions, all count as increase of richness. Ridiculous paradoxes ensue: if prices fall, richness is officially reduced; if family help to the sick is monetarized by hiring a nurse, or if a family member's death is followed by payment of insurance, richness grows. Finally, GNP does not at all deal with "non-monetarizable" exchanges of services and goods – not only the illegal "black market" of smuggling and immigrant work but also housework, leisure and volunteer activities, etc. – which some accounts estimate at almost two thirds of total work in industrialized countries (Möller cols 67–68). Therefore, the GNP's elaborate rows of numbers purporting to prove rising richness, and trumpeted ceaselessly by all governments and world capitalist bodies, conceal falling well-being and destruction of nature. The GNP may have been a useful instrument to measure capitalist production at the beginning of the industrial age, in what Mumford called paleo-technics, but beyond a certain level long ago achieved by industrialized countries, it becomes simply an instrument of ideological brainwashing, a Disneyland for the economists.

Pioneering demurrals against the GNP were entered in the first half of twentieth century by Irving Fisher, John Hicks, and Kenneth E. Boulding, but the critique picked up steam from the 1960s on in Baran, Sametz, Nordhaus-Tobin, Economic Council of Japan, Zolotas, and culminated in various more encompassing proposals at the end of the 1980s (see for this history Leipert 55, 62–63, 68–72, and 331ff.). Most of them concluded that the GNP is not "even a reasonable approximation [of economic wellbeing]" (Nordhaus and Tobin, cited in Ayres 5), and proposed to modify it more or less drastically to achieve such an approximation.

2

The most systematic, encompassing, and reasonable proposal for modifying the GNP by subtracting the real if hidden, and therefore difficult to estimate precisely, costs of capitalist life – production and consumption – was Daly and Cobb's magnum opus *For the Common Good* (1989, rev. edn with slightly less pessimistic calculations 1994). They proposed to effect not only a better measurement of real income but also to relate that income to what I am calling well-being (welfare being by now associated with doling out).[17] Accepting the framework of capitalism, proposals such as theirs were naively meant as a sanitizing of its savage aspect. But insofar as they dealt with people's real well-being rather than their monetarized richness, they were – intentionally or not – radical.

Daly and Cobb identify the GNP as mainly oriented toward measuring market activity but with modest adjustments in the direction of well-being, which it also claims to judge. Instruments like GNP are thus impure, a result of ideologico-political negotiation. They are a multi-purpose compromise: an example is the non-market accounting for capital depreciation (which raises the GNP: a total depreciation, the loss of all value to capital assets, would theoretically give a maximum rise to the GNP!). And since some GNP entries relate to well-being positively, some negatively, and some neutrally, Daly and Cobb concluded they can be extended to cover, say, depreciation of natural assets. By a series of such manoeuvres – subtracting thirteen categories such as environmental damage and depletion or foreign debt, and adding 4 categories that estimate household labour and some services (such as public expenditure on health and education) – they arrive first at so-called Hicksian income, that is, what can be consumed without impoverishment in the future, and then at their estimate of well-

---

17   A good formulation of human welfare in the sense of well-being is in Ruskin's *Unto This Last*: "There is no wealth but life. Life, including all its powers of love, of joy and of admiration. That country is the richest which nourishes the greatest number of noble and happy human beings; that man [sic] is richest who, having perfected the functions of his own life to the utmost, has also the widest helpful influence ... over the lives of others."

being called Index of Sustainable Economic Welfare (ISEW). In order to measure consumption (well-being) rather than production (riches), they underline the per capita amount arrived at (Table A1, 418–19). Here is their staggering difference with the GNP (all figures as US$ per capita):

	Official GNP	*Daly–Cobb's ISEW*
1950:	3,512 dollars	2,488 dollars
1973:	5,919 dollars	3,787 dollars
1986:	7,226 dollars	3,403 dollars

This means that the US per capita income, recalculated to measure well-being better (but still not fully oriented to use-value) passed since 1961 through two phases: 1961–73 it did not rise (as per GNP) 44 percent but did rise 26 percent, still a considerable achievement; 1974–86 it did not rise (as per GNP) 24 percent but *fell 9 percent*! Thence, the average US well-being was in 1986 back to where it was in the mid-1960s. (One shudders to think what that might be in 2003, when the pumping of hundreds of billions of dollars in military expenditures into the US economy would also be subtracted to arrive at an index of well-being – back at 1950? inching into the 1930s?) Quite beyond Daly–Cobb's horizon, subtracting from GNP the income of the upper (say) 2 percent would disastrously lower the per capita for the 98 percent that remain.

In sum: capitalist growth since 1973 – the onset of Post-Fordism – impoverishes the great majority of US people in terms of human well-being. This would hold *a fortiori* for most other countries of the North, except a few with remnants of the welfare State, while for the South, that is three quarters of mankind, the abyss of poverty for the majority grows daily larger.

This figuring in of the "social costs" of a profit economy, defined by Kapp (Chapters 4–9 and 13) as those costs caused by capitalist producers but not paid by them, signals that above a certain medium level of industrialized affluence, in a society based largely on "brain labour," the ability to buy more regardless of all other factors influencing life – the GNP – is by itself a poor measure of well-being. Beyond that level the official economic growth proves nothing: it "reflects increasingly frantic activity, especially trade, but little or no progress of human welfare in 'real' terms (health, diet, housing, education, etc.)" (Ayres 2, and see 2–5 passim). It is dubious also whether increase of competitiveness – the ideology of capitalist globalization – significantly contributes to well-being. The much-touted "sustainable economic growth" is an oxymoron: growth raises the GNP but probably damages at least as much as it improves well-being.

3

Of course, there can and must be sustainable development in the sense of a "qualitative improvement without quantitative growth beyond the point where the ecosystem can regenerate" (Greider 455). For now we pass beyond tinkering with exploitative and destructive economics to consideration of *ecology and survival*, where the aim changes from maximum to optimum production. The ideologized commitment of the world's major powers – governments and corporations – to infinite growth on a finite globe, collides with the elementary fact that "[a]ny physical system of a finite and nongrowing Earth must itself also eventually become nongrowing" (Daly–Cobb 72). It follows that the major focus must be to optimize production by raising the productivity of its scarcest element – today, the natural resources. This is possible to achieve, but only if the real social costs of using air, water, soil, and labour are figured in and unproductive consumption (most marketing and PR, useless innovations, artificial obsolescence, unceasing turnover of fashion trends, and other similar activities extraneous to use-values) is rigorously taxed. This means that both population growth in the poorer countries (the South) and per capita consumption in the richer countries and classes (the North) must be strongly, if reasonably, curbed. (The only fair and efficient way to curb population growth is, of course, making the poor richer – that is, meeting poverty head on rather than furthering it as the capitalist globalization does.) Their common denominator is the total consumption of energy. However, I shall vault over the, to my mind, intermediate discussion of energy (see Georgescu-Roegen 138–40 – or even Einsteinian matter-energy, however eye-opening its consequences would already be – to focus on what seems to me the furthest reach of today's discussions: the management of *entropy*.

Entropy, the central term of thermodynamics, is usually explained as the inverse measure of the energy available to do work, but it is trickier than that. As Georgescu-Roegen's pioneering text, written in the 1960s (which I gloss in this Section), applies it to economic philosophy, the Second Law of Thermodynamics means that the entropy of any isolated structure increases not only constantly, but also irreversibly (6). Since life is tied to activity, any life-bearing entity survives (maintains homeostasis) by sucking low entropy from the environment, and thereby accelerating the transformation of the environment into one of higher entropy. The Entropy Law founds a different physics: it leads away from motion, which is in principle reversible, and opens onto irreversible qualitative change. It has no time quantification – how fast will it happen – and no particularization or specification – exactly what will happen at any particular point (10–12 and 169). Thus, beyond being a branch of physics dealing with heat energy, thermodynamics underlies any biophysics of life and activity (including thinking).

Life is characterized by a struggle against entropic degradation of matter, but its activities always *pay a clear price*: the price of life is the degradation of the neighbouring universe or total system – for example Earth. "*[A] given amount of low entropy can be used by us only once*" (278), so that "the basic nature of the economic process is entropic" (283). Since any collectively significant activity must be paid in the coin of less chance for future activity, the importance of purpose, what is something done for, becomes overwhelming. Aristotle's final cause and the old Roman tag *cui bono?* (in whose interest?) are rehabilitated as against scientism's narrow concentration on the efficient cause, how to manipulate matter (194–95). If, as the Second Law of Thermodynamics recites, the entropy of the universe at all times tends toward a maximum, then we are in the domain of "a physics of economic value" (276). For, "low entropy is a necessary condition for a thing to be useful" (278): for example, copper in a bar has much lower entropy than copper diffused in molecules, or coal than ashes. The economic process is, regardless of local fluctuations, entropically unidirectional. This means it will always be generating irrevocable waste or pollution, and foreclosing some future options (use of oil after it has been burned). Since, however, it also generates not only life but also all possibilities for "enjoyment of life" (281–82), we must become careful stewards, on the constant lookout for minimizing entropy.

For example, it is from the point of view of minimizing entropy that we must switch from the present huge raising of entropy inherent in using terrestrial energy (oil, gas, and coal) to solar energy, which we get from outside the Earth system. The proportions in the mid-1980s were oil, gas, and coal 82 percent, nuclear 2 percent (its use depends on both safety and the entropic cost of waste disposal, probably too high), renewables 16 percent, and today it is probably worse. This has already brought upon us the climate change only hired guns in science pretend not to notice, with economic damages on the order of untold billions of dollars which will be rising geometrically (but the partial combating of which uses up even more energy, raising the entropy – and the GNP!). And since solar energy is huge – all terrestrial stocks of energy (low entropy) are equivalent to four days of sunlight – and practically free except for the initial cost of R&D plus installations, yet limited in its yearly rate of arrival to Earth, the preparations for the increase of its proportion in our energy consumption, which is the only alternative to a civilizational crash, should begin as soon as possible. Photosynthesis is our best bet, and if gasoline need be for limited purposes, it should be gotten from corn instead of feeding it to cattle (see 304). Our wars for oil are a testimony not only to gigantic cruelty but also to gigantic imbecility and a lemming-like suicidal urge among our ruling classes and their brainwashed followers.

4

So what is to be done? Again I can only mention a few general orientations towards maximizing life.

An idea by Georgescu-Roegen could be developed into a pleasing calculus of preconditions for felicity. He pleads for a "maximum of life quantity," defined as the sum of all the years lived by all humans, present and future, and stresses it "requires the minimum rate of resource depletion"

(20–21). We could refine this, possibly by adding past humans too, certainly by specifying minimum conditions of dignified life, etc. Clearly the goal is *a maximum stock of life quality*, but quality presupposes a minimum quantity. Since this is an anti-entropic (negentropic) enterprise par excellence, a minimum program toward it would have to include a shift to an economics of stewardship not ownership (see Brown), such as seems to have obtained before class society. The biosphere is indispensable to human physical and psychic survival, even beyond the need for photosynthesis. The flourishing of humanity is predicated on a substantial decrease of the human ecological niche as well as of the human boosting of entropy (see Daly–Cobb 378). This ties into the diminution and eventual elimination of dire poverty, since desperation cannot be expected to spare the environment (for example, locate farming where it does the least ecological damage). Such orientation toward a maximum of use-values compatible with a low rise of entropy must override all globalization based not only on financial speculation but also on the sole goal of profit.

Various sets of measures will be necessary for this, and have been for years now debated in the "new global" movements. Greider proposes reasserting political governance – where possible international, where need be national – over capital; an old-fashioned and entirely legal way of doing this is by taxing the worst corporate entropy-mongers more and restoring purchasing power to the middle and lower classes by taxing them less. A first, very simple and minimal step towards this was the 1980s proposal of the "Tobin Tax", a small exit-and-entry toll at major foreign-exchange centres, which would greatly reduce the unproductive daily speculation in money values and yield hundreds of billions of dollars for good purposes (257). Abandoning the GNP and reformulating the meaning of growth in all our public statistics is another necessary prerequisite, for something like Daly–Cobb's instrument would both educate the public as to the more realistic costs of what we do and open the door for recognition and tax support of what Frigga Haug calls "activity by and for a collective" and a "community-oriented economy" (Möller cols 71–2): the unpaid work in the family or elsewhere discussed earlier and taking up more time than the paid work (especially among women).

"[...] in the meantime" (Greider wisely continues) "defend work and wages and social protection against the assaults by [capitalist corporations]" (472). The working time per week, growing by leaps and bounds in the last 30 years as the reality underlying the GNP, is a good rule-of-thumb measure of exploitation, and the 35-hour week of the French Socialist Party was the right idea (which they did not have the will to really defend). This holds for the North and has to be accompanied *pari passu* with the alleviation of poverty in the South by introducing work for a living wage and social protection there – for without such an alliance in the long term both will come to nothing. The huge and hugely growing inequalities between North and South would remain the breeding ground of terrorism responding to Northern State terrorism.

The ecological imperative to focus on use-values instead of exchange-values brings us, finally, back to Marx's living labour. For if his horizon is valid, then such a focus cannot be accomplished without a radical change of social formation. It is by now obvious that the speculative globalization in capitalism is causally crucial for the planetary ecological disaster.

Two major difficulties would immediately arise. Capitalism functions by distancing the privileged Northern consumer from the true costs of production. Let me take the clearest case of energy prices in the North. As Kapp and others have argued, the Northern consumer buys not only that commodity but also the hidden content of ecological quality destroyed by the production of energy. The ecological replacement cost has to be added to the energy price, or entropy will spiral away and the sporadic crashes of our energy supply will grow systematic. Figuring such costs in was in the 1980s calculated as adding up to two thirds of the present prices for densely populated industrialized countries (Leipert 32–33 and 39–40, and see Greider 446 and passim). Persuading a family to pay 165 dollars or pounds instead of 100 in order to save our planet would be a major task of political education, probably impossible without access to power and thus to the mass media. The case of energy can be extended, perhaps less starkly, to other instances of what William Morris called the unnecessary offers of the market.

Second, as Wallerstein has pithily remarked, "the implementation of significant ecological measures [...] could well serve as the coup de grâce to the viability of the capitalist economy" (81). When people like Samir Amin speak of a "transition beyond capitalism" as the only alternative to hugely destructive warfare on all social levels (85), when they say the present crisis of misery and ecocide cannot be overcome within capitalism and yet must be overcome if we are not to fall back into barbarism (114) – or perhaps a genetic caste society – I believe they are right. But the question then arises: how is that to be organized and brought about? We have seen military destruction brought upon Serbia, Iraq or Afghanistan by the US government when much smaller and further-off threats were perceived. I have remarked upon the political naivety of proposals such as Daly–Cobb's: this was tolerable at the time of Carter perhaps, but is not at the time of Bush Jr.

Works Cited in Main Chapter

Amin, Samir. *Spectres of Capitalism*. Trans. Shane H. Mage. New York: Monthly Review, 1998.

Anders, Günter. *Die Antiquiertheit des Menschen*. 2 vols. München: Beck, 1994–95.

Andrade, E.N. da C. "The Scientific Significance of Lucretius." Introduction to *Lucreti De rerum Natura*. Ed. and trans. H.A.J. Munro. London: Bell, 1928.

Arendt, Hannah. *The Human Condition*. Chicago: University of Chicago Press, 1958.

Aristotle. *Etica Nicomachea*. – *Ethika Nikomakheia* [bilingual]. Ed. and trans. Carlo Natali. Roma and Bari: Laterza, 1999.

——. *Politics*. Trans. C.D.C. Reeve. Indianapolis: Hackett, 1998.

Asmis, Elizabeth. *Epicurus' Scientific Method*. Ithaca: Cornell University Press, 1984.

Balibar, Etienne. *La philosophie de Marx*. Paris: La Découverte, 1993.

Bellinazzi, Paolo. *Forza e materia nel pensiero di Marx ed Engels*. Milano: Angeli, 1984.

Benveniste, Émile. *Le vocabulaire des institutions indo-européennes*. Vol. 2. Paris: Minuit, 1969.

Bloch, Ernst. *Das Prinzip Hoffnung*. 2 vols. Frankfurt: Suhrkamp, 1959.

——. *Experimentum mundi*. Frankfurt: Suhrkamp, 1976.

Bookchin, Murray. *The Ecology of Freedom*. Oakland and Edinburgh: AK, 2005.

Bowles, R. "The Marxian Adaptation of the Ideology of Fourier." *South Atlantic Quarterly*. 2 (1955): 185–93.

Cassola, Filippo. (ed.). *Inni omerici*. Milano: Mondadori, 1997.

Debout, Simone. *L'Utopie de Charles Fourier*. Paris: Payot, 1978.

Derrida, Jacques. "Mes chances: Au rendez-vous de quelques stéréophonies épicuriennes." *Confrontation* (printemps 1988): 19–45.

De Vries, Theun. *Baruch de Spinoza*. Hamburg: Rowohlt, 1970.

Dobb, Maurice. *Studies in the Development of Capitalism*. New York: International, 1963.

Dussel, Enrique. *Un Marx sconosciuto*. Ed. A. Infranca. Roma: manifestolibri, 1999.

Engels, Frederick. "The Origin of the Family, Private Property and the State." *Selected Works in One Volume*. Karl Marx and Friedrich Engels. London: Lawrence and Wishart, 1968. 455–593.

Fallot, Jean. *Il piacere e la morte nella filosofia di Epicuro*. Torino: Einaudi, 1977.

Farrington, Benjamin. *The Faith of Epicurus*. London: Weidenfeld and Nicolson, 1967.

——. *Science and Politics in the Ancient World*. London: Allen and Unwin, 1946.

Fourier, Charles. *Le Nouveau Monde industriel et sociétaire. Oeuvres complètes de Charles Fourier*. Vol. VI. Paris: Librairie sociétaire, 1841–1848.

——. *Théorie de l'unité universelle. Oeuvres complètes de Charles Fourier*. Vol. II–V. Paris: Librairie sociétaire, 1841–48.

Georgescu-Roegen, Nicholas. *The Entropy Law and the Economic Process*. Cambridge, MA: Harvard University Press, 1971. Rpt. New York: to Excel, 1999.

Hall, Stuart. "Marx's Notes on Method: A 'Reading' of the '1857 Introduction' [to the *Grundrisse*]." *Working Papers in Cultural Studies* 6 (1974): 132–69.

Haraway, Donna. *Modest_Witness@Second_Millennium*. New York: Routledge, 1977.

Hegel, G.W.F. *Encyclopädie der philosophischen Wissenschaften*. Ed. Johannes Hoffmeister. Leipzig: Meiner, 1949.

——. *Wissenschaft der Logik*. Ed. Georg Lasson. Leipzig: Meiner, 1948.

"Heraclitus." *A Presocratics Reader*. Ed. Patricia Curd. Trans. Richard D. McKirnahan Jr. Indianapolis: Hackett, 1997.

[Hesiod. Erga kai hemerai.] Esiodo. Le opere e i giorni [bilingual]. Milano: Rizzoli, 1998.

Jameson, Fredric. "Fourier, or, Ontology and Utopia." *Archeologies of the Future*. London and New York: Verso, 2005. 237–53.

Lansac, Maurice. *Les conceptions méthodologiques et sociales de Charles Fourier*. Paris: Vrin, 1926.

Larizza, Mirella. "L'interpretazione marx-engelsiana della dottrina di Fourier." *Nuova rivista storica* 52.3–4 (1968): 249–90.

Lefebvre, Henri. *La Pensée de Lenine*. Paris: Bordas, 1957.

Lenin, Vladimir I. *Philosophical Notebooks. Collected Works*. Vol. 38. Moscow: Progress, 1981.

——. "The Three Sources and Three Component Parts of Marxism." *Selected Works in One Volume*. Karl Marx and Friedrich Engels. London: Lawrence and Wishart, 1968. 23–7.

[Lucretius Carus, Titus. *De rerum natura*.] – Lucrezio. *La natura delle cose* [bilingual]. Ed. Guido Milanese. Milan: Mondadori, 2000.

Lukács, Georg. *Der junge Hegel*. Berlin: Aufbau, 1954.

Marcuse, Herbert. *Reason and Revolution*. Boston: Beacon, 1966 (esp. ch. II.1.7 "The Marxian Dialectic").

Marx, Karl. "Auszüge zu Leibniz." *MEGA*. Frankfurt, Berlin and Moskau 1927–1935. Abt. 4, 1: 186–208.

——. *Capital*. Vol. 1. London: Lawrence and Wishart, 1946.

——. "Critique of the Gotha Programme." *The Marx–Engels Reader*. Ed. Robert C. Tucker. New York: Norton, 1972. 383–89.

———. *Doktordissertation [und Vorarbeiten]. Texte zu Methode und Praxis.*
Vol I. Reinbek: Rowohlt, 1969. 54–189 (the dissertation itself is also
in Marx–Engels. *Collected Works*, Vol. 1. New York: International,
1975).

———. *Grundrisse.* Trans. Martin Nicolaus. New York: Vintage, 1973.

———. *Texte zu Methode und Praxis.* Vol. I. Hamburg: Rowohlt, 1969.

———. *Theorien über den Mehrwert.* 3 vols. Berlin: Dietz, 1956–62.

———. *Writings of the Young Marx on Philosophy and Society.* Ed. and trans.
Loyd D. Easton and Kurt H. Guddat. Garden City: Doubleday,
1967.

———, and Friedrich Engels. *German Ideology.* Moscow: Progress, 1976.

———. *Geschichte und Politik.* Vol. 1. *Studienausgabe III.* Frankfurt: Fischer,
1971.

———. *The Holy Family. Selected Writings.* Ed. David McLellan. Oxford:
Oxford University Press, 1977. 131–55.

———. *Werke [MEW].* Berlin: Dietz, 1962–.

The Marx–Engels Dictionary. Brighton: Harvester, 1981.

Nancy, Jean-Luc. *Être singulier pluriel.* Paris: Galilée, 1996.

Negri, Antonio. *The Savage Anomaly.* Trans. Michael Hardt. Minneapolis:
University of Minnesota Press, 1991.

Pitagora. Le opere e le testimonianze. 2 vols. [bilingual]. Ed. Maurizio
Giangiulio. Milano: Mondadori, 2000.

Preve, Costanzo. *Il filo di Arianna.* Milano: Vangelista, 1990.

Rubel, Maximilien. "Marx à la rencontre de Spinoza." *Études de marxologie*
19–20 (1978): 239–65.

Sánchez Vázquez, Adolfo. *Art and Society.* New York and London: Monthly
Review, 1973.

Serres, Michel, *La Naissance de la physique dans le texte de Lucrèce.* Paris:
Minuit, 1977.

Spinoza, Baruch. *Ethics. The Collected Works of Spinoza.* Vol. 1. Ed. and
trans. Edwin Curley. Princeton: Princeton University Press, 1985.

Suvin, Darko. "Emotion, Brecht, Empathy vs. Sympathy." *Brecht Yearbook*
33 (2008): 53–67.

——. "For Lack of Knowledge: On the Epistemology of Politics as Salvation." *Working Papers Series in Cultural Studies, Ethnicity, and Race Relations.* Pullman: Washington State University [No. 27], 2001. 1–32.

——. "*Haltung* (Bearing) and Emotions: Brecht's Refunctioning of Conservative Metaphors for Agency." *Zweifel – Fragen – Vorschläge: Bertolt Brecht anlässlich des Einhundertsten.* Ed. Thomas Jung. Frankfurt: Peter Lang, 1999. 43–58.

——. *Metamorphoses of Science Fiction.* New Haven and London: Yale University Press, 1979.

——. "Transubstantiation of Production and Creation." *the minnesota review* 18 (1982): 102–15.

——. "Two Cheers for Essentialism and Totality." *Rethinking Marxism* 10.1 (1998): 66–82.

——. "'Utopian' and 'Scientific': Two Attributes for Socialism from Engels." *the minnesota review* 6 (1976): 59–70.

——. "What May the Twentieth Century Amount To: Initial Theses." *Critical Quarterly* 44.2 (2002): 84–104 (now Chapter 12 in this book).

——, and Marc Angenot. "L'aggirarsi degli spettri. Metafore e demifisti-cazioni, ovvero l'implicito del manifesto." *Le soglie del fantastico.* Ed. Marina Galletti. Roma: Lithos, 1997. 129–66.

Terdiman, Richard. "Counter-humorists." *Diacritics* 9.3 (1979): 18–32.

Thomson, George. *Studies in Ancient Greek Society.* Vol. 2. *The First Philosophers.* London: Lawrence and Wishart, 1977. [orig. 1955].

Williams, Raymond. *Marxism and Literature.* Oxford: Oxford University Press, 1977.

Wood, Ellen Meiksins. *The Origin of Capitalism.* London: Verso, 2002.

Zil'berfarb, Ioganson I. *Sotsial'naia filosofiia Sharlia Fur'e i ee mesto v sotsialisticheskoi mysli pervoi poloviny XIX veka.* Moscow: Nauka, 1964.

Works Used for Appendix

The works specifically cited are those by Ayres, Brown, Daly and Daly–Cobb, Georgescu-Roegen, Greider, Kapp, Leipert, Möller, Polanyi, and Wallerstein.

Ayres, R[obert] U. *Limits to the Growth Paradigm*. Centre for the Management of Environmental Resources, Working Paper 96/18/EPS. Amsterdam: Elsevier Science, 1996.

Baran, Paul E. *The Political Economy of Growth*. New York: Monthly Review, 1957.

Brown, Peter G. "Why We Need an Economics of Stewardship." *University Affairs*, Ottawa, November 2000, 37 and 42.

Daly, Herman E. *Steady-State Economics*. San Francisco: Freeman, 1977.

——. *Steady-State Economics*. 2nd edn. Washington, DC, and Covelo, CA: Island, 1991.

——, and John B. Cobb, Jr. *For the Common Good*. Boston: Beacon, 1989 (rev. edn, 1994).

Delphy, Christine. *Close to Home*. Trans. Diana Leonard. Amherst: University of Massachusetts Press, 1984.

[Economic Council of Japan.] *Measuring Net National Welfare of Japan: Report of the NNW Measuring Committee*. [Tokyo]: Economic Council of Japan, 1974.

Ekins, Paul (ed.). *The Living Economy*. London: Routledge and Kegan Paul, 1986.

Georgescu-Roegen, Nicholas. *The Entropy Law and the Economic Process*. Cambridge, MA: Harvard University Press, 1971. Rpt. New York: to Excel, 1999.

Greider, William. *One World, Ready or Not: The Manic Logic of Global Capitalism*. New York: Simon and Schuster, 1997.

Haug, Frigga. "Arbeit." *Historisch-kritisches Wörterbuch des Marxismus*. Vol. 1. Ed. Wolfgang F. Haug. Hamburg: Argument, 1994. Cols 401–22.

Kapp, Karl W. *Soziale Kosten der Marktwirtschaft*. Frankfurt: Fischer, 1979.

Lee, Keekok. *Social Philosophy and Ecological Scarcity*. London: Routledge, 1989.

Leipert, Christian. *Die heimlichen Kosten des Fortschritts*. Frankfurt: Fischer, 1989.

Mies, Maria, and Vandana Shiva. *Ecofeminism*. London: Zed Books, 1993.

Möller, Carole. "Eigenarbeit." *Historisch-kritisches Wörterbuch des Marxismus*. Vol. 4. Ed. Wolfgang F. Haug. Hamburg: Argument, 2000. Cols 66–73.

Nordhaus, William D., and James Tobin. *Is Growth Obsolete?* Ann Arbor and London: University Microfilms, 1981.

Polanyi, Karl. *The Great Transformation*. Boston: Beacon, 1957.

Sametz, Arnold W. "Production of Goods and Services: The Measurement of Economic Growth." *Indicators of Social Change*. Ed. Eleanor B. Sheldon and Wilbert E. Moore. New York: Russell Sage, 1968. 77–96.

Talberth, John. "A New Bottom Line for Progress." *The State of the World 2008*. Chapter 3. Washington, DC: Worldwatch Institute, 2008.

Wallerstein, Immanuel. *The End of the World as We Know It*. Minneapolis: University of Minnesota Press, 2001.

Zolotas, Xenophon E. *Economic Growth and Declining Social Welfare*. New York: New York University Press, 1981.

CHAPTER 16

Inside the Whale, or *etsi communismus non daretur*: Reflections on How to Live When Communism Is a Necessity but Nowhere on the Horizon (2006–2007)

For Tom Moylan, who denounced and announced

It will then become apparent that it is not a matter of drawing a huge dividing line between past and future, but of fulfilling the thoughts of the past.
(Es wird sich dann zeigen, dass es sich nicht um einen grossen Gedankenstrich zwischen Vergangenheit und Zukunft handelt, sondern um die Vollziehung der Gedanken der Vergangenheit.)
— MARX, Letter to Ruge of 1843

A world of female sorrow is waiting for salvation.
(Eine Welt weiblichen Jammers wartet auf Erlösung.)
— ROSA LUXEMBURG, *Gesammelte Werke*

The true conception of historical time reposes entirely on the image of salvation.
([D]ie echte Konzeption der historischen Zeit beruht ganz und gar auf dem Bild der Erlösung.)
— BENJAMIN, *Gesammelte Schriften*

I thank thee, Jew, for teaching me that word.
— SHAKESPEARE, *The Merchant of Venice*

Truth appears in Light, Falsehood rules in Power,
To see these things to be, is cause of grief each hour. [...]
Where knowledge does increase, there sorrows multiply,
To see the great deceit which in the World doth lie [...].
— WINSTANLEY, *Law of Freedom*

1. Where Are We: Amid Deep Defeat, How Is Our Stance To Be Reshaped?

1.0

The following essay is an attempt to articulate a deep unease, that I have seen paralyse many former communists, Marxists, and/or other radicals about the stance (*Haltung*), tools, and horizons indispensable for the present historical moment, which we can date roughly with the fall of the "Soviet" system and implosion of almost all communist parties and cognate movements. But the paralysis is much more widespread. Thus, I hope the essay could be, in some central positions, here offered for discussion, also pertinent for anybody with a consistently anti-capitalist stance. Labels such as "communist," though I would be in favour of giving it fresh meaning, are significant but finally not central. Even an orientation toward this or that cosmological belief or creed matters little here: if anybody truly follows the insight that the strategic source of all our social ills is capitalism, I would hope that s/he could join, or at least debate seriously, my twin central points here: the need for Salvation, and the refusal of The One Full and Final Truth.

Such a clarification is, to my mind, an indispensable part of laying the fundaments for clear theoretical horizons. If so, it is a *precondition for consistent anti-capitalist action* that coheres in space (globally) and in time (through years and decades), and therefore has a chance for success. A century ago Lenin wrote "Without revolutionary theory there is no revolutionary party"; refusing taboos on either, we need today to discuss anew in the light of experiences what he meant by Party, and what we should today envisage as Revolution. With these provisos, I hold he was correct.

In philosophical language, this means that we the subjects are constitutively co-involved in any understanding of the reality that is the case. Therefore, it is self-defeating not to reflect on our deepest presuppositions, while holding to our final horizons. If this will lead to some revisions and indeed paradoxes, they ought to be judged on their merits, in light of those horizons.

Even further, while agreeing with Marx that any concrete step of the movements for liberation is most important, I would maintain that the present chaos in such movements as to both the horizons and the ways to advance toward them makes theoretical self-reflection the indispensable next step.

1.1

In this essay I wish to debate the pertinence for our reflexions and practices of insights and partial cognitions from what have traditionally been religious formulations. I find two clusters supremely pertinent: positively, that of Salvation; negatively, that of One Full Truth. How do they speak to our presently ongoing history?

From 1848 to perhaps 1989, it was legitimate for communists to believe they might see their political victory in flesh, so to speak. This is in some deep ways parallel, or analogous, to the expectation of the early Jewish Christian communities (who lived in economic primitive communism, see Acts 2:43–46 and 4:32–35) that they would see in flesh the Second Coming of Jehoshuah the Messiah. The atmosphere is encapsulated by Otto as: "Jesus announces [...] the Kingdom has approached. It is quite near. So near, that one is tempted to translate this as: it is here. At least one feels already, in a mysterious *dynamis*, the pressure of that which wants to break in."[1] A deep crisis came about when this began to be felt as unbelievable, solved then by Paul with a deep and thoroughgoing *perestroika* (incomparably more successful than Gorbachev's) from Jews to Gentiles. Today, however, what Otto calls the atmospheric pressure (*Luftdruck*) of approaching communism is no longer here: no overall or even major victory is believable for all those among us who are of a certain age (at least

---

1   Otto 42. The parallel between early Christianity and nineteenth-century communists/ socialists is formulated clearly already by Engels in "Zur Urgeschichte."

over fifty, but maybe forty or even lower), only an uphill struggle against worse *imbarbarimenti* (barbarizations).

On the other hand, victorious capitalism daily sharpens insoluble structural contradictions that lead (perhaps swiftly) to a deep crisis. The boomerang effect of immiserated billions has already spilled over into all metropolitan cities, ecocide poisons people and all budgets, the world oil economy is ending (nobody knows how abruptly), and the breakneck Eternal Holy Wars will add size and speed to the boomerang. Among other matters, this asks us to deal with the fake holiness of mass murder by State and group terrorists. Finally, the crisis posits a hidden horizon: what if societal unravelling begins to proceed catastrophically, creating radical opposition so virulent that we would have to go back to the two World Wars for its precedents? Can anything be done in our thinking, its tools and its findings, which could turn significant segments of this opposition from fascist to liberatory?

We must therefore face again the urgent question "What is to be done?": how could we get to some initial orientations for a thoroughgoing restructuring indispensable for communists (but not only for us) today? And first, what might its guiding principles be?

1.2

I shall pose as my two axioms, first, that the age-old dream of communism is fully worldly, fleshly and material; it is therefore a radical and consistent variant of the yearning for a simultaneously personal and collective salvation from misery, in all senses. It involves "a build-up of super-individual structures and higher organisational forms that would confer meaning upon and sanctify individual living" (Landauer 10).[2] *Communism is a*

---

2   True, Landauer would have said this at best of a kind of anarchocommunism, but
     we should not forget this martyr of ours either, not only because he was a sometimes
     very wise and sometimes very naive poet, but also because in the blue distances of
     his *longue durée* of "topias" and utopias the enemy brothers anarchism and com-
     munism, both guilty of bad mistakes and in particular in relation to each other, are

salvational belief, or it is nothing. It is a temporal and universalized variant of Israel's Exodus from the oppression and shrinking fleshpots of Egypt to a future country of abundant justice. Without the horizon of a fleshly salvation, of less difficult – more tolerable, more just, and more beautiful – living, communism has no purchase upon history.

Second, communism, meaning for me the way out of institutionalized oppression and humiliation as the central articulation of society, has been decisively inflected by two consubstantial cognitive insights of Karl Marx (and then his companions and continuators), which might be thought of as a double helix. The first or salvationist one, which radicalized the bourgeois (and Jewish) insight that material history is the privileged framework of human destiny, is the insight about capitalism, the labour source of value, the class conflict, and similar doctrinal tenets, which in brief reveals that societal injustices are based on exploitation of *other people's living labour.* The second, quite anti-religious insight is that the proper way to talk about the capitalist exploitation which determines all our lives is not in the *a priori* form of dogma, a closed system, but in the *a posteriori* form of *critique.* The latter means that legitimate cognition is strategically developed by arguing for a radically deviant stance against a dominant in a given historical situation (see one of the first and best such discussions in Marcuse).

Yet decisively does not at all mean finally. The rapid mutations of capitalism and imperialism after Marx's death, its descent into most violent barbarism with organized dumbing down of people into media-dominated masses, have produced at least two overlapping waves of refurbishing for Marxism and communism. The first one is marked by the First World War, revolutions, Fordism, and Leninism with all its strengths and limitations; the second one is marked by rolled-back revolutions and revolts, uninterrupted peripheral warfare, hugely increased capitalist control over people's time, bodies, and minds, Post-Fordism, and a hugely dominant lack

---

finally reconciled. It should be stressed that originally Salvationism was oriented to clearly plebeian and thisworldly interests and that salvational religions, though often formulated by small groups of "intellectuals," were responses to mass sufferings (Weber, *Economy* VI, esp. 399–401 and 481–529, also *Soziologie* 404–11).

of theoretical understanding. Therefore, whatever else our anti-capitalist
movements may lack, we have today to face the limitations from which the
project of updating Marx (and then Lenin and others) suffers.

In the straits in which we are, we are entitled to turn for help wherever
we can find it. Since ours is an attempt to materialize salvation as earthly
and political, we cannot exclude humanity's millenary experiences with
seeking salvation. I do not claim they could or should be our only crutch,
but I do propose that we use these experiences, often theologically theorized (see Weber, *Soziologie* 336), for our purposes. We should proceed to
a good part in the wake of Benjamin, and while we can approach his saying
"god is not dead, he has been included into human destiny" with caution
and cavils, we should use it. Indeed I would claim that classical radical and
revolutionary politics was always also salvational, fusing the daily "vulgar"
concerns for psychophysical survival of people with the ability to manage
Paradise as well as with – alas especially – Hell.[3]

Without politico-economic practice, theology dissolves into pseudo-
magic or tautology; without the horizon of salvation for each as well as for
all, communism ossifies into scientistic dogma and despotism.

1.3

All precapitalist societies have been characterized by a more or less religious
cosmology justifying human life in both its avoidable and unavoidable
sufferings, and by a "ritual penetration" consubstantial with sense-making
as well as with power networks. Marx penned into the *Grundrisse* a brief
but to my mind extremely important sketch of "the imagined clan-being,"
despot or god, who incarnates the "comprehensive unity" that stands above
and sanctions the real communities' hereditary possession of land and their
work on it (473). The numinous force or godhead is the personification of

---

3   See Benjamin's materials on the Paris Arcades – for example *Gesammelte Schriften*
      V: 676, 1011, 1023, and *Correspondence* 549; also Shelley's "Hell is a city much like
      London" (*Peter Bell the Third*).

the imaginary substance of the community, a vision, and increasingly an illusion, of its life of unitary sense. There is relatively little mysticism, though very much straightforward hierarchical dispossession, in this condensation of the everyday sacrality, inherent in the creative relation between labour and land, into an active, anthropomorphic guarantor who then becomes also the creator.

This creative or productive relationship in social formations where people relate to human and non-human nature only as community members is not divided into our categories of religion, politics, and economics. Godelier even argues that in such societies, from tribes to the Inca State, politics and religion are "two forms of the same process, two elements of the same content which exists simultaneously at different levels" (XIV): in the Pygmies' forest cult, the idea that the forest donates their food, health, social harmony, etc., is articulated in a way that *reworks* – as Freud's dream-work does – some strategic junctures of their natural ecosystem and their social organization. Just so, precapitalist peasant communities, in Marx's analysis, reworked their (limited but for certain purposes efficient) cognition of organization for survival into the tribal/ communal godhead/s.

1.4

Still, all organized religion, dialectically, soon grows into a fetter for freedom and creativity, because it downgrades all thisworldly horizons and collective autonomy from below. All Churches begin as more or less communist communities but then buy into hierarchical and exploitative power, as a rule violently. When a power group (a priestly religion, as Kant sneeringly remarked) has wedded the pretense to possessing the One Full Truth – of which more later – to the claim of sacrality, it loses all restraints against mortifying people's flesh (see Suvin, "Keywords"). In Marxist terms, religions too are prominent sites of class confrontation about the horizons of life.

As against religious faith, capitalist rationalization has by means of demystification within a pugnacious thisworldliness solved many problems eluding other historical forms. It has achieved a productivity that for the first time since tribal societies makes this planet habitable for all. But, in Merleau-Ponty's good formulation, "Demystification is also depoeticization and disenchantment. One should keep from capitalism its refusal of the exterior sacred [or: of the sacred as exterior, *du sacré extérieur*] but revive the need for absolute which it has abolished." He also recalls Max Weber's pregnant remark that capitalism is like the shell secreted by the dead religious animal, and that "Nobody knows yet who shall in the future inhabit this shell [...]. Will there be a new renaissance of all thoughts and ideals or, on the contrary, a petrification [*Versteinerung*] by mechanism, masked by a kind of anxious importance" (36–37). Two facets arise from capitalist rationalization.

First, Weber's disenchantment should finally be identified with the loss of a structure of feeling of unitary sense in people's works and days. We can today see that intolerable disenchantment, the alienation under the lay godheads of Money and Commodity, can easily lead, in a classical return of the repressed, to open re-enchantment (see Chapter 15 in this book). From the oceanic depths of the capitalist mode of production there monstrously appear new religions and sects, from Lutheranism and post-Tridentine Catholicism to Methodism and the newly aggressive Churches of today, as well as a not uninteresting Neo-Paganism. As Weber puts it, "The old plural gods, disenchanted and therefore in the form of impersonal forces, rise from their graves and seek power over our lives [...]" (*Soziologie* 330).

Second, even where the religious animal is apparently dead, its ghost haunts our societal shell. This is clearest in the capitalist religion of the Invisible Hand of the Market, a Hidden God of Profit inherited from Calvinist strands. It should be developed, much further than I can do here, using Marx's concept of commodity fetishism, where the ensemble of objectified commodities is – like the West African deity represented by a palpable, humanly made wooden statue – also an impalpable, material yet transcendental, thing (*sinnlich unsinnlich* – *Kapital* 85), which rules human relationships.[4] The laicized religiosity of profit has proved "[equal]

---

4   See also the pioneering and very illuminating Dussel on the pervasive theological metaphorics of Marx (more than 250 citations from the Bible, 212–13). They are

in effectiveness [...] to the most violent outbursts of religious fervour in history" (Polanyi 31) – and equally bloodthirsty. As Derrida notes: "In these times, language and nation form the historical body of all religious passion"; and "Wars or military interventions, led by the Judeo-Christian West [...], are they not also, from a certain side, wars of religion?" (*Faith* 44 and 63).

Symmetrically obverse, the devolution of capitalist rationality and official science into a tool of oppressions undermines its original hugely liberatory elements. Today the only way to defend reason is to redeploy it against capitalism and its daily mass destructions.

Conclusion 1

We are in a period of bitter disenchantment and desperation: the whole of humanity is faced with a triumphant reduction of all valuation to the cash nexus. From this dogmatic blindness to use-values there flow untold destructions of people and planet, as well as (since human nature abhors vacuum of values) the rise of false gods justifying this: the pseudo-religions of the Market and nationalism, neo-religious political dogmatism (usually called fundamentalism), even sadistic joy of destruction. The place all other social formations had for qualitative values is now empty. It was earlier mainly filled by religion. *We have to find and staunchly propagate a new value system*, centered in liberation of labour and creativity, which is *in that respect* functionally analogous to religion (as lungs are to gills), but also has a fundamentally different orientation: a thisworldly vertical of creativity by means of people's empowerment from below upwards. Last not least, a value can only exist together with a clear goal, or at least horizon.

---

clustered in his investigation of capital, and enrich commodity fetishism with a lai-cized figure of the Jewish idolatry and the Christian satanic force. The young Marx's "alienation" seems to have come to Hegel from Luther's translation of Christ's *ekenose* as "entäussert sich" in Paul's Phil. 2:6–7 (19).

2. To Keep Salvation in Sight While Living On:
How To Use Benjamin via Bonhoeffer (with Cavils)

2.1

In pre-monotheistic beliefs there is a central rich ambiguity in a semantic cluster that includes the Latin *salus* (also its Hellenic and Hebrew equivalents), meaning both fleshly health and axiological salvation, as well as *damnare*, meaning to "fetter" somebody by causing him/her both material ills and axiological evil, or its opposite *redimere*, meaning to unbind from both material fetters and ill fortune. This is in organized religions today subordinated to, if not suppressed in favour of, saving and redeeming an entirely phantomatic "soul" against a brute "body." However, even in a monotheistic religion like Christianity some strong currents speak of the "present futurity of God" and of a "salvation that is unconditionally a present and simultaneously wholly the future" (Schmitthals 119–20), although churches generally, in proportion to their political conservativeness, then stress the divinely preordained and largely transcendental future.

The major difference between transcendental religion and communism as beliefs is, then, that Christians – and other monotheists at least – expect their salvation in the other world, our glory (and perhaps limit) is not to do so. For, even if Paradise were proved to us, it could never cancel the sufferings and despair of all the bombed and tortured billions of class history. All official religions dispense entirely too much opium to their followers, and we have to remember with Marx that though opiate may be of use to momentarily deaden the pain of the fleshly creature, it has never healed anybody. We communists should however stick to such uses as *Salus rei publicae suprema lex*: the salvation (freeing, unfettering) of the political body or commonwealth is one of our supreme aims and norms; to which must today be added the salvation of particular people serially (in particular, defending them against unjust communities). All other cosmological mysteries have a chance to be approached with understanding only after having put our Gaia house in order. In the meantime, nobody can be saved alone, and even Candide's solution to cultivate his own garden is unreachable for most and endangered for all.

2.2 Negations

I do not speak in favour of anybody's turning religious or philosophical Idealist in any variant. I am firmly committed to materialism and immanence, though I also think some present-day religions were originally fully (Daoism) or mostly (Buddhism) such. I also recognize the dangerous historical precedent of defeated revolutionary movements turning into religious communities, as happened e.g., to Buddhism and Quakers, and do not at all wish to contribute to such a sliding path. I agree with what I think Gramsci was getting at when he defined Marxism as "A historicist understanding of reality which is free from any residue of transcendence and theology" (II: 1226). What I would like to see is, with all needed differences, an updating of the somewhat too triumphal but still valuable Ernst Bloch (see especially "Originalgeschichte"): a co-optation of energies inherent in myth and religious faith, and sometimes in radical theology, for our still fully immanent belief, "a firm faithfulness of reason to its own atheology" (Nancy 41). Belief means enjoying a system of clear and strong values within an all-embracing stance which also makes sense of social reality and of actions to affect it (see Goldmann 98–99 and passim, and Weber, *Economy* 450–51), and is not at all to be equated with religion, which is its mystified form. Belief can and should be based in reasoned argument; religious faith is based in indisputable command (Nancy 79): *ipse dixit*. There is no collective or indeed individual action without a framework of belief. As to "communism," the term itself comes from *munus* = obligation, indicating a belief into reciprocity "in common" (see Derrida, *Passions* 79).

Here it is mandatory to mention the overwhelmingly corrupt and cruel pseudo-communism of the Stalinist stripe, with its worship of a refurbished State hierarchy. Inside any radical movement for liberation today, the old conundrum of means and ends, or of the Goal and the Way to it, has to be abandoned for a better toolkit. Lenin cited with approval Hegel's argument that means are more honourable than ends (189–90).

Yet anarchists have remembered better than communists that how we walk the way will codetermine the shape of any (always provisional) goal we may arrive to.

2.3

Thus, we have to begin asking ourselves in intelligent, articulated, and collective ways *how* is it today *possible to live* – in all the meanings of these three underlined terms. What are the possible ways and modes for meaningful living for each of us personally and then all of us serially and collectively? The question was, in the sense worried at here, asked first by some writers and artists plus some heterodox Marxists from Luxemburg, Brecht, Marcuse, and Benjamin on, then some heterodox Protestants from Bonhoeffer and Metz on and heterodox Catholics from Küng to Liberation Theology, and I would imagine many other people I do not know of. While nobody has a full answer, we should begin by identifying the ground we stand on – when we can stand (as a witty title of W.F. Haug's rehearses it). This space in which we live and take up our stance (*Haltung*) is also "the present in which the personality [of the historical materialist] writes history" (Benjamin I: 702). I believe we are here and now, in this epoch, facing three complex imperatives:

1. To live (with the inevitable pragmatic compromises) satisfactorily and fruitfully in this fleshly and societal world.
2. To live without hope that we personally shall see any approximation to victory.
3. Yet in spite of all, to go on living, first, without losing the hope for some future possibility of the classless society, or whatever an integral societal justice will then be called, and second, consubstantially and crucially, without losing the values that flow from this belief for our present.

Such a not entirely easy reorientation would mean recapturing the motives, energy, and persistence that kept so many communists, anarchists, and other radicals going throughout an entire life, *usque ad mortem*, even under the gravest hardships and persecutions; however, this would be fused with the quasi-religious understanding that, in this historical epoch, the victory is not for us in the flesh. It would mean melding the stances enunciated, more or less at the same time, by Kafka: "Es gibt unendlich viel Hoffnung, nur nicht für uns" ("There is infinitely much hope, only not for us"), and by Gramsci following Sorel: "Pessimism of reason, optimism of will."

2.4

In other words, what we need (along much else) if we wish to hold to a set of salvational values is what Benjamin would call a new philosophy of history. Or, not to be immodest, we need at least some strong pointers towards the horizons of such a new philosophy. To start with the *pars destruens* of Benjamin's parting little tractate which has been wrongly called *Theses on the Philosophy of History*: his denial of automatic progress in social relationships is today our obvious ABC. But the alphabet goes on from D to Z and maybe even to new letters, and we have to attempt, with a Benjaminian bold subtlety, erecting a *pars construens* – which he also held to firmly under the name of Messianism, though even he did not know how to articulate it. Just as in the case of Saul of Tarsus, at some point the question of a new addressee as bearer of such horizons, the new Gentiles, shall have to be faced. As soon as possible, perhaps, but (beside saying it must be some alliance of the downtrodden from the rich and the poor parts of the world) I am not at all sure this would be possible right now, before clearing up in little circles as much as we can for a set of values and orientations that can be proposed to such a new "universal class" as basis for a program.

What I am arguing is that when we do not yet understand, in however approximate ways, "scientifically" (by lay cognition) the deep currents in thisworldly reality, we can use – circumspectly! – the phantasmatics (Godelier) of religiously coded partial cognitions, intimations, and suggestions to get at some salient aspects of what to do, how to behave. The ideal would be, of course, to subsume them – as Marx did for fetishism – into a lay explication. Failing this optimal ideal, we have to follow Brecht's principle of "Not Only But Also." On the one hand, to repeat, a minimum due prudence is to refuse in principle not only actually existing Churches and monotheism, but all dogmatic theism as an explanation of reality. But on the other hand we can (and therefore must) learn from any sources which do not go in for "weak thought" – as Italian admirers call the Post-Modernism vulgate of Lyotard, Baudrillard, and co. – but for pertinent thought.

I shall here speak only about some salvationist philosophical, indeed quasi-theological sources. This would include, first, some heterodox tendencies in modern Christian theology which have abandoned the Father for the Son (nobody, except writers like Octavia Butler, has yet gone on to the Daughter or back to the Jewish female Shekinah), that is, abandoned the triumphal "theocratic theology" of all Popes, ayatollahs, and head rabbis, just as we have had to abandon the triumphal beliefs into predestined victories through Party, State, and similar. Second, it would pick up and modify some pointers of the later Derrida, centering in the opposition between the monotheistic mirage of a perfect and omnipotent One God (*theos*) and the diffuse, protean and multiform Sacral or Numinous (*theion*), whose forms and effects would be by definition imperfect and variously potent.

Of the first horizon, I wish to touch here, no doubt only initially, upon a few reflections by Dietrich Bonhoeffer, to whom we should listen seriously in part because he was hanged by the Nazis for his participation in the July 1944 plot to remove Hitler: his theory was very laudably accompanied by clear political options. His central thesis is for me that it is necessary to learn how to live in a godless world *etsi deus non daretur*. This means literally "even if God were not [a] given," but then, paradoxically, also in spite of that: keeping God in reserve so to speak. He then focused on Christ as the impotent and suffering god: both as being (in an orthodox vein) the symbol of the world's salvation, and as being (more interestingly for us) a model for ethico-political behaviour, for what Brecht would call the *Haltung* or stance of the believer. This imitation of Christ would lead the Bonhoefferian believer to a "being present for others" (*Für-Andere-Dasein*): "Vor und mit Gott leben wir ohne Gott" ("Standing before god and with god, we live without god", Bonhoeffer 241). Since this for Bonhoeffer entails not only actively sharing and practicing solidarity with other people's pain and suffering, but even a worldly and political commitment to alleviate them and if possible eliminate their causes, it is a stance which I propose we should ponder and in large measure godlessly cannibalize.[5] For example, unlike the great majority of present-day religious and lay theoreticians, faced with Nazism Bonhoeffer does not renounce violence: tyranny justifies tyrannicide. Today, and even more tomorrow, there is no easy, abstract answer to the violence conundrum, for it is true that violence engenders counter-violence but also that non-violence aids and abets violence; and sometimes, as in the antifascist struggle of World War II, violence can stop even worse violence. This knot cannot be solved by any a priori yes or no but only by a discussion of values and of situations (I pointed to this in "Keywords"). Even the sayings attributed to Jehoshua of Nazareth contain opposites, as his movement politically vacillated: "My reign is not of this world" (John 18:36), but also "I have not come to bring peace but a sword" (Matthew 10:34) and "if you have no sword, sell your cloak and buy one" (Luke 22:36).

How does one godlessly ingest and digest a theology, however heterodox it might be towards its religious tradition? To quote Benjamin's *Löschblatt* (blotter) parable: "My thought is entirely imbued with theology, as a blotter is with ink. But if the blotter had its way, no writing should remain." ("Mein Denken verhält sich zur Theologie wie das Löschblatt zur Tinte. Es ist ganz von ihr vollgesogen. Ginge es aber nach dem Löschblatt, so würde nichts was geschrieben ist, übrig bleiben" – V: 588.) The death of God should not mean the death of humanity. If God and Socialism are dead, it is not the case that everything is permitted (Dostoevsky updated by Post-Modernist cynicism): it is rather the case that everything has to be rethought, and the rethinking has then to be tried out in practice.

---

5   Michael Löwy has rightly reminded me of a position similar yet prior to Bonhoeffer's, that of Pascal and the "bet" in his fragment 233, as interpreted by Goldmann's splendid pages on this tragic horizon of the Hidden God (315 ff.) – which Goldmann elsewhere connects to twentieth-century Marxism.

Conclusion 2

We have to invert Benjamin's image of the wizened dwarf inside the chess-playing automaton being Theology and the chess-playing puppet Turk being Marxism (we can easily call the two also Religion vs. Communism). Today, the wizened and ugly creature that must hide out of public sight is Communism and the recognized upfront agent is Religion. What I propose is the dwarf is using the puppet, not viceversa. If we are to *use some carefully chosen cognitive aspects of religion* (themselves as a rule flowing out of communist fraternity, however limited), *it must be strictly inside a thisworldly and liberatory historical horizon*; that is, taking over the salvational aspect of religion but atheistically denying (or at least agnostically bracketing for our whole historical period) its otherworldly aspect: and most of all its dogmatic horizons. I now come to this.

3. Against Monoalethism: Self-Reflexive vs. Dogmatic Belief, the Repressive One Full Truth and the Protean Numinous; with a Proposal for Skeptical Belief

3.0

Is using quasi-theological philosophy not dangerous, if we need to be strictly opposed to the present irrationalist seepage of weirdest religious mish-mashes as well as to the obscurantist assumption that you miraculously know the Truth once and for all, with the cannibalic consequences we have witnessed? Yes it is – like using fire or water. But I believe the dangers can be neutralized by two moves.

The first is the blotter paradox, quoted earlier. In other words, we should appropriate the strengths of salvationism by Hegelian *Aufhebung* (sublation). As noted above, today our situation is reverse from Benjamin's: Marxism seems ugly and dwarfed, hiding out of shame. Yet nonetheless: if it openly assumes the strengths of salvationism, nobody can, as Benjamin remarked, win against it. True, truth by itself wins no battles, only people in proper groupings do. Benjamin wrote his optimistic saw at a time when what seemed to be liberatory Marxist and communist organizations were strong. We would have, parallel to what I write about here, to undertake forging equally strong but wiser organizational mediations.

The second is a stress on the old theological insight that the corruption of the best engenders the worst, the shining Lucifer becoming the Devil when fallen (*corruptio optimi pessima*). As Shakespeare put it, lilies that fester smell far worse than weeds. In other words, just as the precondition and safeguard for reassuming the term and tradition of communism is that we fiercely scrutinize and reject its corruption in all variants of State worship, culminating in Stalinist terrorism against its own people, from the USSR to Kampuchea: so the precondition and safeguard for practicing a proximity to the religious theories and practices of salvationism is that we identify and strenuously denounce its main aberration. In both cases, the aberration is consubstantial with the dogmatic faith which I shall call MONOALETHISM.

3.1

Monoalethism is the belief in *One Full (and therefore Final) Truth* which has been revealed to us by a set of holy, non-amendable books and holy, unquestionable prophets. The believers in its God are set apart and saved.

Such an ontotheology, that not only defines the truth of religion as absolute knowledge but also posits that God is One and in all ways supremely perfect, is a West Asian invention from the age of the large empires (see Weber, *Economy* 448–50 and passim). When not bloodily busy as Lord of Hosts, God is here an oriental potentate shaping a world to dispel his boredom and increase the glory and adoration rendered unto him (also his priests' possessions). But he has become transcendental: as opposed to all previous pantheons and *numina*, the Divinity is, first, no longer together in the world with men, as two species distinguished by powers and mortality but not radically Other (Homer's gods may be wounded). Second, the monoalethic God's Universal Uniqueness converts Him (goddesses are disallowed) from a superhuman person – the micro-ethnic Yahwe – to a principle, source, and/or Law, the *logos* of late Hellenic Platonism, in whom all possible truths and qualities reside (see Nancy 28–30, 35–39, and passim). The alterity then functions as a magnet ordering the believer in all important moments and soliciting him to lose herself in Him. (Not so incidentally, this radically alters the idea of Death, which grows into a haunting obsession.) This runs in the Euro-Mediterranean tradition from post-Babylonian Judaism through the Christian churches and Islam's warrior religion to Rousseau's "civic religion" and Hegel (see Derrida, *Faith* 53–54), and thence to nationalism and all other absolutist faiths, theist or atheist. Historically, it marks the necessity of a totality at the point where the world is politically growing into empires but has societally lost the value of creative work and productive labour.

This motif of "oneness" – Unity, Unicity, and Universality of Power and Truth – is fraught with both significance and paradox. In order to think about anything, and especially about matters of human destiny, it is necessary to delimit a field of inquiry, with a – however provisional and historically changeable – strategic essence (see Suvin, "Two Cheers"). A flexible, momentary, situated totality is implicit in our languages, where A is not B but the one and only A=A. But even more (or earlier), it is to my mind implicit in our sensorium, for example in the visual and motoric metaphor of *horizon* as orientation from the locus where one stands (see Chapter 5 in this book): yet for all that, such unity is never excusive or hierarchic (in the pre-Socratics, the One is not the Only but the womb of everything, Thales's "the world is full of gods"). The undialectical and unhistorical approach of centralized power represses the fact that a unity can only come about from a more or less democratic plurality. The monotheistic Unity (all religions run to the capital beginning letters of Power) acts downward from an Emperor of Heavens: "All the errors of polytheism were then destroyed," recounts Eusebius of Caesarea. "Polyarchies, tyrants, or democracies existed no more, ... but One God only was preached to all: one single Empire (*basileia*), the Roman one, flowered for ever [...]" (Meslin-Palanque 213; see for the Chinese "Sovereign on high" Onians 526). Since this imperial Unity is also supreme, that is, untranscendable, any denial of a part or aspect threatens the whole. Thence follows what has been well dubbed the monotheist *odium theologicum*, casting out sinner together with sin and resulting in untold slaughters and auto-da-fés. William Blake's poetic Jehovah put this monomania perhaps best:

> Let each choose one habitation,
> [...]
> One command, one joy, one desire,
> One curse, one weight, one measure,
> One King, one God, one Law.
> (*The Book of Urizen*, ll. 79, 81–83)

The process of taming tribal democracy begins with the rise of the State (see Clastres 179–85) but is rendered impermeable by the centralized States of capitalism, enforcing their own Full Unity which is intrinsically, overtly or covertly, monotheistic. There is the (non-human) One and below Him Eusebius's All: the humans who could not be saved by their own efforts (the latter claim by the tribally raised Pelagius was condemned by the imperial bishops – see Joxe 402). Finally, colours tend to disappear and shapes not to really matter within the black-and-white thinking (evident also in the ex-Orthodox seminarist Djugashvili) where the only criterion is the participation in a homogeneous, in-different Truth (see Nancy 61–62, 112–14). What a difference from Lenin, who glossed Hegel's "truth is infinite" with "its finiteness is its denial" (93)!

3.2

Let me dwell a bit more on monotheism, since we are again faced with the huge ravages in the world at large of dogmatically revealed religion. Nancy has characterized it as ranging from disavowal of reason to an ignoble exploitation of misery and suffering (20). The underlying incoherence of monotheism is that the concept of One and Only Omnipotent God, Blake's Nobodaddy, immediately suffers shipwreck on a reef that can be understood in two ways, axiological and ontological. First, axiologically, any radical dissenter is not merely wrong but satanic, and his uprooting by all means conceivable is not only a regrettable necessity but a holy service to the Lord. Going far beyond the necessary self-defence practiced by every society, this is morally and politically quite unacceptable. Second, ontologically and indeed logically, *cur malum*? or *unde mala*? (whence evil/s, Boethius). If God is also a benevolent father, how to explain the overwhelming, permanent, not only hugely murderous but deeply oppressive and humiliating injustices and evils of this world: "what god made [...] shark" (*Moby-Dick* chapter 66)? Monotheism has in fact always oscillated between a repressive unity and an equally tormented and inconclusive Manichean dualism of God vs. Satan (see Martelli 59–69). The internal logic of such a Uniqueness generates other Uniquenesses, in holy warfare with each other (see Nancy 62) ...

The *aporia* of this Universality is that it is Unilateral, that is, exclusive. For example, Rousseau emphatically equates the intolerance of his civil religion with theological intolerance: "It is impossible to live in peace with people we take to be damned. To love them would mean to hate God who punishes them: we must necessarily convert or persecute them."[6] Now we know where Bush and Bin Laden come from: an unholy alliance of theocratic and lay religiousness (see Ali)! True, not all monotheism has been fundamentalism, which can be defined as the attempt to subordinate the State to one religious ideology. Nonetheless, we can today see that fundamentalism is the permanent horizon of monotheism and often, such as at our historical moment, its dominant.

Finally, we cannot simply shrug this off as religious blindness: the same deep springs that have fed the three monotheist religions continued to operate in the workers' movement, even when its overt (for example Weitlingian) religiosity was expunged by a so-called Marxism. The insistence on the One Undoubted Truth and the One Ultimate Cause by most of its theoreticians and leaders from Kautsky to Stalin has often amounted to a true *furor theologicus* (see Gramsci 1445). Instead of finding out what

---

6   *Contrat social*, Book IV, chapter IX. I owe this reference and much stimulation about theology vs. fundamentalism to Martelli.

humanity would mean – the lighting of a Promethean, anti-theistic fire – the goal was often (as the title of a feeble utopia by H.G. Wells rehearses it, aping the Edenic Snake) Men Like Gods. One notes with interest that the leaders of successful revolutions, Lenin, Tito, Mao or Ho, were much less dogmatic.

This is not at all meant to deny the great demystificatory advances already achieved by some monotheism. I think here of the fierce Jewish insistence on self-determination, indeed of belief's dissidence against dominant values, and on salvation within – and as – a history changeable by people, even to radical transgression (as symbolized in Jacob's fight against the Angel), and in some prophets such as Amos of the insistence on social justice; however, this is restricted to one people and paid for by aggressiveness, "the harsh expression of male will, and the often cruel negation of Nature" (Bookchin 174). I think of Jehoshua's religion of the Son and of compassion. I think further of the ecumenicism of the Pauline tradition, translating insights from Greek philosophy and West Asian salvationism into a mass practice, and of the primitive communism of early Christian communities, a spectre which was to recur persistently through Joachim of Fiore to later sects. No doubt, other religions could also be investigated for such elements. The positive and even the negative aspects of religion can be used for Benjamin's "*lay illumination*" (*profane Erleuchtung*, emphasis by Benjamin), a materialist, anthropological inspiration "to which [...] religion can be a *Vorschule* [preparatory course, elementary introduction]" ("Der Sürrealismus," II/1: 295–310) – though he added there can be many other such prefigurations, notably love.

Nonetheless, we must finally affirm that all culture as we know it, including scientific knowledge, "is by definition secular. It requires a broad-mindedness of which no religion will ever be capable" (Arendt 299). It is in Europe a heritage of both the tribal traditions and the plebeian access to democracy symbolized by Athens and the Renaissance, which burst through the mythical and religious straitjacket.

3.3

I shall proceed here using Derrida's latter phase. Though signalled by his in many ways splendid *Spectres of Marx*, it is of unequal value both in itself and for our purposes, so that I shall focus only on some aspects of his *Foi et savoir*.[7] I shall use three tools from his toolbox groping toward a skeptical faith: the self-reflexive faith or belief, the *theion* or protean numinous, and finally the post-Benjaminian messianic.

Faith and Knowledge at one point discusses Kant's first "Parergon," added (in the second edition) at the end of the appropriate section of his *Religion within the Limits of Reason Alone*, where Kant sets up the opposition between two types of belief, *reflektierendes* and *dogmatisches Glauben*. The dogmatic belief ignores the difference between faith and knowledge since they are presupposed to be inextricably fused in divine revelation. Dogmatism or fundamentalism refuses hermeneutics and historicity: it pretends that some admittedly fallible people have been endowed with the power to not only hear but also so fully understand the Word of God that scriptural interpretations are univalent (which is obviously absurd, since each religion has spawned a huge host of contending commentators throughout history), and that historical situation plays no part in the understanding of the sacred texts. To the contrary, Derrida paraphrases Kant's simple definition of *self-reflexive belief* as a process: "one must act as though God did not exist or no longer concerned himself with our salvation" (50). This is for Derrida a temporary suspension for certain purposes of the existence of "God [...], the soul, the union of virtue and happiness"; thus a good Christian "must endure in this world, in phenomenal history, the death of God, well beyond the figures of the Passion [...]" (51). Bonhoeffer's meditations on *etsi deus non daretur* are thus an activist Protestant reworking of self-reflexive belief. Most important is that "faith has not always been

---

7   One of Derrida's weakest texts is to my mind, unfortunately, his meditation on Benjamin's "Zur Kritik der Gewalt", called *Force de loi*, so that I shall focus only on some aspects of his *Foi et savoir*. I use it here in possibly uncouth ways: a) only pp. 43–57 of *Faith*, a quarter of its sixty pages; b) cutting, adding, splicing, that is, deforming him for *our* purposes – as he too often did for his purposes.

and will not always be identifiable with religion [...]. All sacredness and all holiness are not necessarily [...] religious" (48).

Second, I shall attempt to apply Derrida's distinction (53ff.) between theology and *theiology*, the latter being a discussion of *to theion*, the numinous, holy or sacred quality – within which I am here interested only in the salvational rather than the saved aspect. "Theiology" is a term Derrida only hints at, and he warns against its Heideggerian connotations. However, I find potentially useful its foregrounding of a numinosity or salvificalness which might be illustrated by a little mental experiment. Let us set up a topological (and probably historical) series which would retraverse backwards a supposed "development" of religious horizons. Beyond monotheism we would find polytheism, including the paramount god of the politically sovereign space (e.g., the polis), as an exclusive cultic community. The pantheon was not fixed, new gods (such as Dionysus) could be added to it. They were not disembodied but possessed a different kind of body – unaging and capable of entering different avatars. Further back, a kind of animism is found in which each important space (river, mountain) or even type of action could have its own godlet or daimon, a personification of its mundane importance for the community, or indeed be a godhead (as Agni, the Fire). We find there also other imaginary beings, say "gods without any personal name, [...] designated only by the name of the process they control" (Weber, *Economy* 402; see Vico 6). Indeed, gods could even be openly fabricated by an imperial court, as was the case with Serapis under Ptolemy I (Fraser 1: 246–59). Dead leaders could also be *numina*: in the original Shintoism, if one invented, say, a new carpentering stroke which would permit better cutting and shaping of wood, then one could become the *kami* (High One, Lord) of that stroke and be invoked by the carpenters' guild at the beginning of each important segment of such work.[8]

Suppose we continued backwards even from this stage, we might find a diffuse, not at all anthropomorphic sacrality of wonder and awe, which

---

8   Outside the works of Japanese and Chinese origin, some of which I discuss in Suvin, *Lessons*, this has been best brought home to me by Selver's growth into the godhead of anti-colonialist warfare in Le Guin's *Word*.

has no room for the distinction between natural and supernatural (see
Spivak's dream of "animist liberation theologies [...] [for] an ecologically
just world," 339). In it, all the entities a tribe recognizes have both being
and subjectivity or spirit, and hierarchy finds little room in a world of
diverse but qualitatively incommensurable subjects. This sacrality underlies Benjamin's attempts at describing the aura, and I find it well characterized by Tacitus speaking of the German tribes' non-antropomorphic
"veneration of a mysterious reality (such as woods and forests) to which
they give the name of gods and which they understand by devotion only"
(14, section 9). Dumézil reads the evidence from Saxo and Caesar about
German customs of land ownership as strictly analogous to the projections they made into the numinous sphere, so that the rise of worshipping
single gods, as against the earlier heroic "unanimism," signals the overthrow
of yearly communist (he calls it "totalitarian" – so much for scientific
objectivity) land redistribution (130–32).This unanimous numinosity
had no need for a special name because it was potentially everywhere.[9]
Derrida hints at this when he asks whether revealability (*Offenbarkeit*),
which I would interpret as a diffuse and omnipresent potentiality, is more
primordial than any frozen revelation (*Offenbarung*), and hence independent of all religion. If so, he further hints this might be where Kant's
reflektierendes Glauben at least originates, if not being such a belief itself
(54–55). To the contrary, the abstract concept of gods eternally identical
to themselves and only revealed in this or that place or time can only be
sustained by cultic associations tending toward esoteric priesthood (see
Weber, *Economy* 407ff.).

This proceeding of dissolving god/s back into the numinous effects a
de-alienation of the salvific quality, that human relationships surely need,
away from all "personality cult" and tending to the sublimity of the Chinese
Dao (Way): an impersonal quality and force prior to and more fundamental

---

9   The term *to theion* became in Greek only possible after neuter adjectives could,
    from the fifth century BCE, be substantivized to express an abstract notion. It is thus
    anachronistically applied to anything prior. Also, in the early Presocratics such as
    Anaximander, it seems to have been a way to Unicity.

than any godhead (see Derrida 48 and passim). But much beyond that, its importance lies in an applicability to all major monoalethic categories, to all "god words" (Science, History, Nation, and so on), stand-ins for the Unique Truth as a necessity of the Unique State in Evgeniy Zamyatin's prescient novel *We*. To take one such present term, The Democracy: there would be no further use to discuss what it is and to certify its presence or absence as a digital 1 or 0, but only to discuss the presence and analog strength of the democratic *element or impulse* (which I fantasize might be called *to demokratikon*), of plebeian democratization, in any particular State or proceeding.

3.4

Finally, how useful is Derrida's post-Benjaminian *messianic*, "the opening to [...] the coming of the other as the advent of justice" (56)? I differ from Derrida by believing we cannot dispense either with a (mildly skeptical) horizon of expectation or with classical prophetic prefiguration – which always, from Cassandra and Yeremiyahu on, implied "if you don't listen to this, then ...". The expectation and the threat should be tied to Rosa Luxemburg's alternative of socialism or barbarism, so obviously being played out today before our very eyes. But within such a horizon, Derrida rightly stresses that "death – and radical evil – can come as a surprise at any moment," just as well as the advent of justice: in the US maxim, the only certainties we have are death and taxes. Skepticism has always been a kind of truncated dialectics, whose role is for Hegel to demonstrate "contradiction or antinomy in every concept" (Lenin underlines this with approval, 116). Nonetheless, the more moderate skeptics held also that there are reasonable criteria (the *eulogon*) for justifying our actions without dogmatic certainty. Skepticism is not incompatible with an *als ob*, a hypothetical belief: "An invincible desire for justice is linked to this expectation [...] [belonging] to the experience of faith, of believing, of a credit"; "this faith without dogma [...] makes its way through the risks of absolute night [...]." This justice "alone allows the hope [...] of a universalisable culture of singularities" (56–57). For once, Derrida allows that this abstraction, "without denying faith, liberates a universal rationality and the political democracy that cannot be dissociated from it." (57) And communism is for me the precondition for a radical justice.

Thus it might be best to retain from the murky discussions of messianism not so much the term as its horizon of expectation, however allied with skepticism; its prophetic strain, as clarified by Luxemburg; and its reasonable but firm commitment to the desire for justice amid the risks of "absolute night." An alternative lay terminology is at hand: the desire, form, and horizon called utopia (see Bloch *Prinzip*, Jameson, Moylan, and Chapters 1, 2, and 9 in this book).

3.5 *The Hypothetical Imperative*

These considerations, proceeding from our experiences as illuminated by Benjamin aided by Bonhoeffer and by the latter Derrida, suggest an epistemological and therefore also ethical regulating principle. I would call it the *hypothetical imperative*. A hypothetical imperative would state: in this historical macro-situation, which we explain, as best we know, as being this-plus-that; and if we accept, for given reasons, such-and-such premises; then X necessarily follows. A set or open system of such Xs is a doctrine to enunciate and propagate as guide for action. It is in that particular spacetime as absolute as any religious belief or Kant's categorical imperative. In particular, for class society as a whole, Marx's radical call is still non-negotiable: "the categorical imperative to overthrow all conditions in which man is a degraded, enslaved, forsaken, contemptible being" ("Toward" 257–58, *MEW* 1: 385).

However, the premises or even the whole situation might rapidly change, or indeed practice might show that our reasoning was at some point deficient. In that case Y would follow: Brecht, still a vanguard beacon for us, rehearsed this in a brilliant pair of small *Lehrstücke*, the "plays for learning" *Der Jasager* and *Der Neinsager* (*He Who Says Yes* and *He Who Says No*).[10]

Conclusion 3 For a Skeptical Salvational Belief

Thus, I believe we imperatively need (among other things) a salvational doctrine for one and all. Without it, any liberatory movement shall fail: no revolution without revelation. However, our doctrine's limits of interpretation as well as (more rarely) of revision have to be constantly movable, like the posts in Alice's mad croquet game. We ought to bestow upon it in some patches a long-duration and in other patches a provisional assent, both being open to correction. Nonetheless, in certain situations we must also be prepared to suffer or die for it. My initial question as to a proper way of living is inseparable from a readiness to face death, an *ars moriendi*.

This is what I mean by skeptical belief. It is correlative to dialectics (see Chapter 15 in this book) and indispensable for "the unsated requirement which has been called 'communism'" ("l'exigence inassouvie qui fut nommée 'communisme,'" Nancy 30).[11]

10   See my lengthy discussion in *Lessons*, chapter 5: "The Use-Value of Dying: Magical vs. Cognitive Utopian Desire in the 'Learning Plays' of Pseudo-Zenchiku, Waley, and Brecht." Also, on open system, the section "Wedge 2" in Chapter 10 of this book.

11   My thanks go to opinions about and critiques of earlier versions by Rich Erlich (who even did a heroic colour-code comment on the whole), Gene Gendlin, Christina Kaindl, Sylvia Kelso, Marcelline Krafchick, U.K. Le Guin, Michael Löwy, Edoarda Masi, Tom Moylan, Richard Ohmann, Jan Rehmann, Ulrich Schödlbauer, and Victor Wallis, and the encouragement of W.F. Haug. Also to Loren Kruger and Christoph Türcke for counsel about critical literature, including the latter's own stimulating works. While the text has been much improved by their sometimes strong objections, the responsibility remains mine, including that for all translations of non-English passages. Two matters of great importance that would have to be discussed if one were to go beyond a brief article would be a new look at love, Saul's *agape*, based on Brecht and feminism (I approach it in "Emotion"), and a new look at Marx's notion of fetish/ism.

Works Cited

Ali, Tariq. *The Clash of Fundamentalisms*. London: Verso, 2002.

Arendt, Hannah. *The Jewish Writings*. New York: Schocken, 2007.

Benjamin, Walter. *Gesammelte Schriften*. Frankfurt: Suhrkamp, 1980–87.

Bloch, Ernst. "Originalgeschichte des Dritten Reichs." *Vom Hasard zur Katastrophe*. Frankfurt: Suhrkamp, 1972. 291–318.

——. *Das Prinzip Hoffnung*, 2 vols. Frankfurt: Suhrkamp, 1959.

Bonhoeffer, Dietrich. *Widerstand und Ergebung: Briefe und Aufzeichnungen aus der Haft*. Ed. Eberhard Bethge. München: Kaiser, 1970.

Bookchin, Murray. *The Ecology of Freedom*. Oakland and Edinburgh: AK, 2005.

Clastres, Pierre. *La Société contre l'État*. Paris: Minuit, 1974.

Derrida, Jacques. "Faith and Knowledge: The Two Sources of Religion at the Limits of Reason Alone." *Acts of Religion*. Ed. Gil Anidjar. Trans. Samuel Weber. New York and London: Routledge, 2002. 42–101 [orig. "Foi et savoir: Les deux sources de la 'religion' aux limites de la simple raison." *La religion*. Ed. Jacques Derrida and Gianni Vattimo. Paris: Seuil, 1996, 9–86].

——. *Passions*. Paris: Galilée, 1993.

Dumézil, Georges. *Mitra-Varuna: An Essay on Two Indo-European Representations of Sovereignty*. Trans. Derek Coltman. New York: Zone Books, 1988.

Dussel, Enrique. *Las metáforas teológicas de Marx*. Estella, Navarra: Verbo Divino, 1993.

Engels, Friedrich. "Zur Urgeschichte des Christentums." Karl Marx and Friedrich Engels. *Werke (MEW)* 22. Berlin: Dietz, 1992. 447–73.

Fraser, Peter M. *Ptolemaic Alexandria*. 3 vols. Oxford: Clarendon Press, 1998.

Godelier, Maurice. *Horizon, trajets marxistes en anthropologie*. Paris: Maspéro, 1973.

Goldmann, Lucien. *Le Dieu caché*. Paris: NRF-Gallimard, 1955.

Gramsci, Antonio. *Quaderni del carcere*. 4 vols. Torino: Einaudi, 1975.

Jameson, Fredric. *Archeologies of the Future*. London and New York: Verso, 2005.

Joxe, Alain. *Voyage aux sources de la guerre*. Paris: PUF, 1991.

Landauer, Gustav. *Die Revolution*. Frankfurt: Rütten and Loening, 1907.

Le Guin, Ursula K. *The Word for World Is Forest*. New York: Berkeley, 1976.

Lenin, Vladimir I. *Philosophical Notebooks. Collected Works*, Vol. 38. Moscow: Progress, 1981.

Marcuse, Herbert. *Reason and Revolution*. Boston: Beacon, 1960.

Martelli, Michele. *Teologia del terrore*. Roma: Manifestolibri, 2005.

Marx, Karl. *Grundrisse*. Trans. Martin Nicolaus. New York: Vintage, 1973.

——. *Das Kapital: Erster Band. MEW*, Vol. 23. Karl Marx and Friedrich Engels. Berlin: Dietz, 1993.

——. "Toward the Critique of Hegel's Philosophy of Law: Introduction." *Writings of the Young Marx on Philosophy and Society*. Ed. and trans. Loyd D. Easton and Kurt H. Guddat. Garden City: Doubleday, 1967, 249–64 ("Zur Kritik der Hegelschen Rechtsphilosophie (Einleitung)," *MEW* 1. Berlin: Dietz, 1976, 378–91, or www.mlwerke.de/me/me01/me01_378.htm).

Merleau-Ponty, Maurice. *Les Aventures de la dialectique*, Paris: Gallimard 2000.

Meslin, Michel, and Jean-Rémy Palanque (eds). *Le Christianisme antique*. Paris: Colin, 1967.

Moylan, Tom. *Scraps of the Untainted Sky*. Boulder: Westview, 2000.

Nancy, Jean-Luc. *La Déclosion*. Paris: Galilée, 2005.

Onians, Richard B. *The Origins of European Thought: About the Body, the Mind, the Soul, the World, Time and Fate*. Cambridge: Cambridge University Press, 2000.

Otto, Rudolf. *Reich Gottes und Menschensohn*. Munich: Beck, 1940.

Pocket Interlinear New Testament. Ed. Jay P. Green Sr. Grand Rapids: Baker, 1983.

Schmitthals, Walter. *Die Apokalyptik*. Göttingen: Vanderhoek and Ruprecht, 1973.

Spivak, Gayatri Chakravorty. "Cultural Talks in the Hot Peace."
Cosmopolitics. Ed. Pheng Cheah and Bruce Robbins. Minneapolis
and London: University of Minnesota Press, 1998. 329–48.
Suvin, Darko."Emotion, Brecht, Empathy vs. Sympathy." *Brecht Yearbook*
33 (2008): 53–67.
——. "Keywords of Power, Today: An Essay in Political Epistemology."
Critical Quarterly 48.3 (2006): 38–62.
——. *Lessons of Japan*. Montreal: CIADEST, 1996.
——. "Two Cheers for Essentialism and Totality." *Rethinking Marxism*
10.1 (1998): 66–82.
Tacitus, Cornelius P. *De origine et situ Germanorum*. Milano: A. Mondadori,
2001.
Vico, Giambattista. *Principi di scienza nuova*. Ed. Marco Veneziani. Firenze:
Olschki, 1994.
Weber, Max. *Economy and Society*. 2 vols. Ed. Günther Roth and Claus
Wittich. Berkeley: University of California Press, 1978.
——. *Soziologie. Weltgeschichtliche Analysen. Politik*. Ed. Johannes
Winckelmann. Stuttgart: Kröner, 1964.

Five Farewell Fantasies of 2006–2008

For Ursula K. Le Guin

A Martial Epigram on Martians

Qui legis Oedipoden caligantemque Thyesten
Martial X.4

Why are you staring so raptly into Orcs & Elves
Why gulping down Conan, Potter & th'insufferable Lewis
What are to you rebelling robots, or what help
To your wasting lives the circenses of media clerics
Brainwashing the new imperial plebeians?
                                                    Imbibe
What life shall recognize & call out "This is mine!"
Even if Aliens or Dragons, such story shall taste of us humans,
The ways we oppress & love each other, in what cave
Are we ourselves & how may we get out into the light
Of the blue Sun.
                    But no, mr. Jones, you don't want to
See yourself, cognize your killing cruelties: so at least
Read your Tolkien! You may shut the book & think
Why he loved cleansing wars.
                                                    26706

Cold Comfort (Intrumo)

In a dream a dragon came to me, looked at me,
Splendour of shimmering copper scales
& scarlet thorns, scythe-taloned. I looked
Back, at the amber mist around his huge eyes, above

The fuming nostrils. The red-black smoke from her mouth
Hissed: "Don't despair, short-lived Earthling. Soon
You shall die, soon will expire your kind's cosmic contract.
This muddied globe your Mother is unforgiving as our winds.

But in the new creation the Mother shall whelp, a few shards
May be dug up & deciphered by successor populations,
Hexapods perhaps, stabler far, winged like ourselves:

A few testimonials, like the ones you found of Gilgamesh
& Anarres, shall show yours was a redeemable kind.
>What a pity!< the unsentimental hexapods will chirrup,

Winging on to their inscrutable business of conviviality."
                                                          26806

Pillaging the Gnostics

Et in hora mortis nostrae

See, i talk so that i may leave
I tell you what i heard & saw
In the leaves of grass in the drawn sweaty faces,
I teach you as i slowly learned it
I talk that i may leave this world
Where i never had enuf time
        In peace.

I lived on Earth a short time, i didn't have time.
A short span of time. Pay attention
So you can hear me. If i came, who
May i be, may i have been, may
I have become? I drank the water of life
The water of pleasure. Now i advance toward
      The water of forgetfulness.

Greetings to you, my sister & my brother!
Do not be so deathly afraid of sweet-gifting Venus,
Mother & lover, not yet known! I lived on Earth
A short time, i praised it, i suffered it.
I learned a little, i taught a little, a multitude
Of sisters, of companions, only
      A few knew me,

I knew only a few, only little. I tell you
Disintoxicate yourself! Renounce your deadly path,
Walk on the Way which leads you to be free.
No Yahweh no kings to dominate, no masters
Except the Masters who know, so far as they know.
You are self-condemned, self-enchained. Renounce
      The chains you forged.

You made for yourself a heavenly Lord & leader.
He turned around & enslaved you, shut
Your eyes & ears, raised up an inbred caste
Inimical to Justice & Knowledge, to Venus Of All People.
You turned to derision this house given unto you
As a heredity & a promise, it will be
      Pulled quite down.

Only knowledge can unfold liberty, an
Undying desire. Let this tree grow, so you may grasp
The fruits of freedom. All of us possess
A chip of knowledge, a teardrop of liberty
Within ourselves. Do not let this pearl
Drop into the viscous flow of arrested
       Time. Wake up

From the drugged dream of reason. Who
Are you? Whose brother & sister are you?
Where are you going? Do you judge all matters
In order to be judged? O the anxiety of not reaching,
Of reaching & not grasping! Do you see
High Venus, star moving across resplendent skies?
       I tell you truly:

This is the hour of our death
This is the cosmic hour of persecution
This the hidden hour of our ignoble oblivion.
You can live toward a good death or a bad death.
Life is when two sexes are in each other as light
Liberty, as amity. Thus we become citizens of
       Fair Earth, Heaven.

                           5–7307

Haecceitas (This Here & Now)

Things are there   a this   a shape
Necessary for this here & now
Exposed   unchanged in the light that they bathe
The space that they are.

& i? Am i a thing or a looker-on?
Both – &? & you too
With this red hair & those green eyes
That nose mouth breasts moist lap?
Enter: here too are gods.

Bitter truth: we know we shall not be.
Animals, more & less than.
Things, more & less than. Forms that feel.

Warmth is a dissipative structure
Your smooth skin a miracle of negentropy
The small adorable crow's-feet at your eyes
Forerunners of tectonic crevasses   drought
The lap will bear children & desiccate
It will not be. Yet things are there.

What is done has been done
What is undone has been undone
When they are redone it will not be this.
Things are reversible but not for us.

Seize the shining day   seize the fertile night
Deep deep down   the dark shore
There-things & not-there non-things   unreal
Amid non-persons here there & everywhere
I too am here   now   with you
Athirst for justice   unreconciled

My green essence:
Psyche, Chloe.

                                        11–211007

Sonnet for Reinventing Tomorrow (Reading Patraquim)

A slow step   à la derive
the way lost   how does one make maps
Athirst for a face to drink in
another map of coloured stone   stony

The prospect for a simple gesture of elegance
inaugurating us   the seventh day
From dictionary the entries justice   incarnate
& you on the tornado shore

Yet the corrupt gods   shaping us   woe is me
as we invented them   overhead a roof
The wrong solitude   so common
as gills in the sea   apnoeic
The hands that drove the rivers crazy
unused   useless   today

2–4908

CHAPTER 18

Cognition, Freedom, *The Dispossessed* as a Classic (2007)

To Don Theall, who hired me to teach SF within our common humanist horizon

Part 1.   On Le Guin's *The Dispossessed* and its Liberating Librations: A Commentary[1]

1.1   A Pointer to Fictional Articulation, Poetry, Freedom

I have argued elsewhere at length three points about narrative in general.

First, that fictional narrative (as any thinking) can be understood as based on *thought experiments and models* (see Suvin, "Can People"). Re-presentation in fiction takes model images of people and spacetimes from non-fictional ways of understanding and reconstructing social reality into a process that (in good or significant cases) develops roughly as follows: the new schemes of how people live together glimpsed by the writer go about subverting the heretofore received fictional norms of agential and chronotope structuring; but as this is happening, the schemes themselves are in turn modified in and by some autonomous principles of fictional articulation. All of this together enables the resulting views of relationships among people, elaborated by the restructured piece of fiction, to return into

---

1   I adopt the abbreviations: *TD* = *The Dispossessed*, Sh = Shevek, A = Anarres, U = Urras. The citations are keyed to the Avon 1975 paperback edition of *TD*. Unacknowledged translations are all mine.

our understanding represented and reformulated *with a cognitive increment* (that can range from zero through very partial to very large). This better understanding permits what Brecht called intervenient, effective or engaged thinking (in the technical sense of meshing or being engaged in gear). It allows the reader to pleasurably verify old and dream up new, alternative relationships: to *re-articulate*, in both senses of the word, human relationships to the world of people and things. As Aristotle argued in *Politics* (I.2), humans necessarily live in political communities. Thus, all central human relations are, in this widest sense, communal or communitarian, what we humans have or are in common: significant fictional re-presentation of relations among people presents the reader with the possibility of rearticulating our political relationships.

Second, that any text unfolds a *thematic-cum-attitudinal field*, and that fiction does so by necessarily presenting relationships between fictional agents in a spacetime. According to the way these are presented, a fictional text is either simply metaphorical (as some non-narrative poems) or narrative. My contention is that all texts are based on a certain kind of metaphoricity, but that the narrative texts add to metaphorical ones a concrete presentation in terms of space and time, the chronotope. I cannot argue it here but only indicate my text "Metaphoricity and Narrativity," which has at least the virtue of discussing a large bibliography. I end up with the definition of narrative as a finite and coherent sequence of actions, located in the spacetime of *a possible world* (*PW*), proceeding from an initial to a final state of affairs, and *signifying possible human relationships* (the agential signifiers or vehicles can, of course, be gods, Martians, Virtues, talking animals or Bauhaus machines, and the chronotopic ones any spacetime allowing for coherent events). All fictional (and non-fictional) texts are in this view "analogical mappings" (Gentner 109) of one semantic domain upon another. Among the great virtues of Le Guin's *The Dispossessed* (further *TD*) is the fact that such a mapping is discreetly foregrounded in it by means of Odo's Analogies.

Third but not least, my essay "The Science-fiction Novel as Epic Narration" (where I briefly touched upon *TD*), argued that there is a central distinction to be made between what I called *the epic and mythological horizons* and their ways to articulate fiction. In principle, the epic events are presented as contingent and not fully foreseeable (and thus historical and as a rule reversible), while the mythological events are cyclical and predetermined, foreseeable descents from the timeless into the temporal realm. The verse or prose epic therefore foregrounds the plot, which was a foregone conclusion in mythology. Thus, an epic text will be meaningful only if each significant event is the result of a value *choice*, as opposed to a pre-established or automatic sequence reposing on unquestionable fixed values of the mythological text. That choice constitutes the poetry of post-mythological prose, opposed to the myth's incantatory repetitions of always already given names and patterns. Choice shapes the agential relationships within the narration in unforeseeable and therefore potentially new and better ways. It is the narrative equivalent and rendering of freedom.

I could easily document how much of the above is consonant with Le Guin's views about fiction. But I think it is better if I do so on the material of *TD*, and restrict myself here only to one essay, her thoughts on narrative ("Some"). She focuses, in Odo's "ethical mode," on the fact that all actions imply choices and entail consequences: "[Narrative] asserts, affirms, participates in directional time, time experienced, time as meaningful" (39). In the syntactic or epistemological mode (if I may add one), she cheers George Steiner's suggestion "that statements about what does not exist and may never exist are central to the use of language," which often means a "refusal to accept the world as it is" – though she rightly notes that celebrating some choice aspects of a world is often as significant (43–44). The "scientific" focus on statements of fact is ably swatted as a noxious fly:

> Surely the primary, survival-effective uses of language involve stating alternatives and hypotheses. We don't, we never did, go about making statements of fact to other people, or in our internal discourse with ourselves. We talk about what may be, or what we'd like to do, or what you ought to do, or what might have happened: warnings, suppositions, propositions, invitations, ambiguities, analogies, hints, lists, anxieties, hearsay, old wives' tales, leaps and crosslinks and spiderwebs. (44)

Le Guin's conclusion speaks to what I also want to come to as a main horizon of *TD* – a kind of freedom:

> The historian manipulates, arranges, and connects, and the storyteller does all that as well as intervening and inventing. Fiction connects possibilities, using the aesthetic sense of time's directionality defined by Aristotle as plot; and by doing so it is useful to us. If we cannot see our acts and being under the aspect of fiction, as "making sense," we cannot act as if we were free.
>
> Only the imagination can get us out of the bind of the eternal present, inventing or hypothesizing or pretending or discovering a way that reason can then follow into the infinity of options, a clue through the labyrinths of choice, a golden string, the story, leading us to the freedom that is properly human, the freedom open to those whose minds can accept unreality. (45)

1.2 A Hypothesis on The Dispossessed

I am attempting in the rest of Section 1 a commentary on Le Guin's *TD*, following the stance of "commentaries" on Bertolt Brecht by Walter Benjamin, who noted this genre presupposes the classical status of the text to which it refers. *The Dispossessed* will be here treated as the qualitative culmination of the great SF age or wave of 1961–75, which indeed crested and broke with it. A classic.

I wish to focus first on the most striking feature of *TD*: its organization into two parallel narrative "strands," the Anarres (A) and Urras (U) one, which body forth the central and all-pervasive concern with a unity-through-dualism. I shall proceed as inductively as possible.

The two plot strands, the Urras story and the Anarres pre-story of Shevek (further in the Tables Sh), proceed each sequentially in linear time. Table 1 provides a first orientation:

Table 1

Chapter 1: (A→)U1, pp. 1–20. Sh, age 38, travels in Urrasti ship from A to U and lands there.

Chapter 2: A1, pp. 21–50. Sh's growth and education from baby to age ca. 19.

Chapter 3: U2, pp. 51–73. Sh surveys the "possessed" U.

Chapter 4: A2, pp. 74–101. Sh, age 19–20, comes to A capital, he and we learn about Anarresti society and a worm in the apple.

Chapter 5: U3, pp. 102–24. Sh begins to learn about the inner workings of U society.

Chapter 6: A3, pp. 125–54. Sh, age 21–24, learns in Abbenay further about walls inside Anarresti minds but also about friendship (Bedap) and partnership (Takver).

Chapter 7: U4, pp. 155–87. Sh finds out how wrappings work in U (Vea).

Chapter 8: A4, pp. 188–217. Sh, age 29–30, writes a book and has a daughter but faces drought.

Chapter 9: U5, pp. 218–46. Sh breaks through in his work and in meeting the U rebels. Revolt on U is put down bloodily, Sh hides.

Chapter 10: A5, pp. 247–69. Sh, age ca. 33, reunites with Takver after four dry years, realizes what is possession, and decides to found a printing "syndicate."

Chapter 11: U6, pp. 270–82. Sh in Terran Embassy on U. He has understood time and politics. The ansible equations will be broadcast to everybody.

Chapter 12: A6, pp. 283–305. Sh, age ca. 38, decides to go to U.

Chapter 13: U→A, pp. 306–11. Sh returns in Hainish ship with prospect of unbuilding the wall around A.*

---

*   I have read an interview by Le Guin, but I cannot find it again, in which she credits me for pointing out there should be a separate thirteenth chapter. I remember well reading the MS. of *TD* and two small textual changes I gingerly proposed (she accepted one and firmly rejected the other) but I do not remember at all this proposal. I do not doubt I committed it, and I shall gladly take whatever small credit thus accrues to me, though I much doubt Le Guin's highly colourful dramatization of our dialogue, which makes me out as much bolder with her than I would ever dare. As to Chapter 1, it technically begins on A and thus might in a very formalized notation be rendered as A + (A→U₁). But I think this would be superfluous: it deals after all with going away from A.

However, my hypothesis is that the two strands are woven together not only as history and prehistory of the protagonist but at least as much as adjoining two-by-two pairs in analogic space. A unified thematic-cum-attitudinal common denominator and trope obtains in Chapters 1–2, and then a different one each in Chapters 3–4, 5–6, 7–8, 9–10, and 11–12. There is also a final inversion between the "spaceship" Chapters 13 and 1 – the humiliation, disorientation, and boxing in of the outbound voyage vs. the spacious hope of the inbound return – which brings it all together. The analogic space exemplifies what the thematic development is all about, it is the how of its what. Thus, the following pairs will be presented at a somewhat higher level of generalization. For one thing, I shall here disregard focalization and the frequent use of "free, indirect discourse," the interplay between the authorial explanatory voice and Shevek's experiences, which is increasingly slanted toward the latter and to my mind works admirably (though I shall have a not unimportant cavil at the end). The parallels between U and A chapters are expressly pointed out in the first pair of Table 2 but they continue until they are mentioned again as diverging in the fifth pair (see right).

As a quondam drama critic, let me note that this plot uses in its own way, with temporal and thematic overlaps proper to a novel, the classical scheme of presentation – collision – crisis – (ambiguous) resolution. Taking into account also its intimate moulding by time's quirks, we might say it is Aristotle twisted through Shevek's Temporal Theory.

1.3 Some Buttressing

Having set out this hypothesis, I better substantiate it inductively. Alas, it is impossible to capture the richness of a true novel (rather than an extended long-story, which many SF long prose fictions marketed as novels have been) into a critic's mesh, so this commentary can only suggest it by probes. I begin with the chronological beginning, Chapter 2 (Chapter 1 is a kind of fortissimo overture to the book, an alluring taste for the reader to find out more). It is divided into eight situations, instantaneous snaphots from the flow of time in and around Shevek.

Table 2

First pair (*Chapters 1–2*), 50 pages: presentation of being walled-in, walls as imprisonment, and the reaction to it, direct and through the education of Sh: in Urras, beginning with the confinement in the Urrasti ship, and in Anarres, as baby and youngster.

Second pair (*Chapters 3–4*), 51 pages: overview, anthropological look from a height, mainly through Sh's interactions with the community of people and of physics.

Third pair (*Chapters 5–6*), 54 pages: experience of living and working inside the society, getting deeper into it or behind the scenes, glimpsing the central problems such as power; Sh's first important contacts with people.

Fourth pair (*Chapters 7–8*), 63 pages: attempts at breakout and frustration at obstacles: Vea, Sabul; first fruits but also drought.

Fifth pair (*Chapters 9–10*), 52 pages: crisis, direct battering at walls – divergent possibilities in A (unbuilding difficult but feasible) and U (violent suppression); building the edifice of time.

Sixth pair (*Chapters 11–12*), 36 pages: the walls are getting breached, the time theory and Sh get out of confinement.

Singleton round-off (*Chapter 13* – contrasting with Chapter 1), 6 pages: walking through the wall; "true voyage is return": open but hopeful ending.

(The first five pairs are roughly of the same size, while the last three chapters rush towards an end.)

Situation 1, pp. 21–22: It begins – parallel to the famous opening sentence of chapter 1 and the book, "There was a wall" – with the paragraph: "In a square window in a white wall is the clear, bare sky. In the center of the sky is the sun." Shevek's father and the nursery matron discuss his permanent stay after the separation of parents. (Separation is a running theme and image of the book; it applies analogously to people, planets, and instants of time.) Infant Shevek sits in the square of sunlight and has a fit of rage at being crowded out of it. It is a very rich situation, a rule in this book of richly observed or "thick" relationships shot through with sense-making. It gives us the first glimpse of Anarresti ethics: "Nothing is yours. It is to use. It is to share.": possessiveness is childish. It establishes the recurrent imagist equation of Shevek and the light, while his refusal to share it prefigures both his problems as highly gifted individual in conformist societies of different kinds and the symmetrical refusal of profiteers in both A and U to let him share the gift: "The baby [...] hid his face in the darkness of the lost sun."

Situation 2, pp. 23–25: Shevek, age eight, tells a children's Speaking-and-Listening circle his vision of Zeno's Paradox (if time is divisible, the arrow can never get to its target), is scolded by the adult pedagogue for not sharing understandable, two-way speech, and excluded for this "egoizing" (to share is another running, specifically Anarresti, theme). He finds comfort in thinking of the harmonies between the "cool and solid" numbers, which are always just, always in a balanced pattern.

Situation 3, pp. 25–27 (it could perhaps be called 2b, a continuation of 2 above; the intervals in my closely printed edition are not always clear): two months later, Shevek, who had had to learn how to wait or endure time, gets from his father the logarithmic tables, and finds transcendence in mathematics; he dreams of a huge fearful wall barring his homecoming through a desert and destroyed by the number 1, "that was both unity and plurality," but can neither recover that piercing joy nor forget it.

Situation 4, pp. 27–32: Shevek, age 12, plays a game of "prison" with his friends Tirin, Bedap, and others. The prisoner is locked into an improvised dark space for a night, he beshits himself; Shevek vomits (as in 7: 186 in Urras, explained in 9: 219).

Situation 5, pp. 33–37: Shevek, age ca. 16, and three friends look at their moon, Urras, and argue about it; Tirin begins doubting how valid are today the Odonian movies of 150 years ago and why the PDC (Production and Distribution Coordination, the central institution on A) will not let anybody go there. With its rare focus on Tirin the artist – who had imagined the prison of situation 4, and who will be later psychically destroyed in an asylum for deviance – this could be called "another part of the prison."

Situation 6, pp. 37–43: at age 18, Shevek works in an afforestation group in the desert (a forest in a previous geological age). He is already set apart by his interests and personality. He glimpses in this project the Odonian principle of Causative Reversibility, "ignored by the Sequence school of physics currently respectable on Anarres." Sex rears its bewildering head, and he finds in one such experience another transcendence of self and time.

A brief coda is constituted by a discussion with a travelling partner about sex, women, and possessing/possession.

Situation 7, pp. 43–47: Shevek, age 19, is back "home" at the North-setting Regional Institute of the Noble and Material Sciences (scene of the first five situations, his upbringing). Authorial glimpse forward to his final Temporal Theory which asserts that "home," the return so important to Shevek, is not a point but a process melding transience and eternity. He finds his male friends mostly callow and women friends wary. An answer to his first paper on physics by Sabul, physicist at Abbenay, is waiting. His teacher pleads it is Shevek's duty to go to the center, but warns him that power is there; he doesn't (yet) understand.

Situation 8, pp. 47–50: the night before leaving, at a climactic party for Shevek, the group of friends discusses time and life. Shevek orates on unavoidable suffering, on sharing it in solidarity but also attempting to go beyond it and forget the self – a high point of this chapter. Only Bedap and a girl with short hair fully agree. We later learn (6: 146) she was Takver and the speech was decisive for her life.

In this chapter, we are not merely following the hero's education in youth, and getting intense glimpses of his friends and A. It is also, richly, a sequence of metaphors (in a wide sense, i.e., tropes) and analogies. I would approximately identify them as, in order of appearance (but then they go on through the novel, additively): a) the difficulty of the seeker after light (situation 1); b) his loneliness, both necessary and due to societal narrowness, and a way of resolving it through mathematical physics (situations 2–3); c) showing and debating the prison, the darkness (situations 4–5); d) the political is the epistemological, social or political activity is how we humans understand the world (here, causative reversibility); true journey is not only an arrow but also a circle bending back to its origin, an origin that one then finds changed; so it is a kind of spiral, as in his later Time Theory (situations 6–7); e) a highly suggestive, though inconclusive, debate on the sense of life, on how to justify this world of too much pain (situation 8).

I note a repetition in this micro-example of the narrative macro-syntax of chapters, each of which is separate yet most are also twinned. Exceptions are the beginning and ending, which must be sensitive to other plotting needs. This might be a general narratological device of *TD*, but to establish this more probes would be necessary. At any rate, I think there would be a major difference at the macro-level. The value insights in this Anarresti chapter are mostly *additive* (e.g., Chapter 4 shows a concrete prison and Chapter 5 then generalizes or "abstracts" this by debate, a technique recommended by G.B. Shaw). To the contrary, I think the common denominator of each pair of chapters in Table 2 is mostly developed as Anarresti cognitive freedom-as-solidarity vs. Urrasti possessiveness, with the important proviso that possessiveness is infiltrating the freedom in unforeseen ways: the value insights are *contrastive* rather than additive.

All together, the chapter might perhaps be called "an introduction to Shevek's world and views": world as view and view of the world. This is then foregrounded at the beginning of the twinned Chapters 3 and 4, as the view from a height - from an imaginary dirigible (3: 52) and a literal one (4: 74), A being as always the open materialization of U but with contrasting value-horizons (Sh takes his looking down from dirigible on A as wonder and clarity, on U as confusion and lack of involvement). Musically speaking, chapter 1 has five movements, with a brief but very important tone-setting beginning (*Auftakt*) and a widening or crescendo with a clear culmination, after which the wave of sense subsides in a pause and we begin anew in Chapter 3 (as well as 4) - understanding the "possessed" and the dispossessed society, always as Shevek's field of consideration and action. The sequence of thematico-analogic movements goes from the personal through the communal to the politico-epistemological, and finally to the metaphysical. I am not sure how representative is this chapter for the whole novel, and therefore whether the sequence indicates the growing importance of these four stages. I tend to doubt this as too "sequential," but at any rate note with relief that the metaphysical discussion is self-confessedly inconclusive. I believe polluted class humanity is not ready for serious, i.e. cosmological metaphysics: if Urras (a phonetically distended echo for Earth) ever finds its way to Anarres, after some centuries we might begin to grow ready.

1.4 Simulsequentiality, or Preaching by Example

The reconstructable causal temporality of events in the narration vs. its actual sequence as it unfolds for the reader, what the Russian Formalists called story (*sjuzhet*) and plot (*fabula*), are here foregrounded as systematically disjoined. The story may be reconstructed in linear time as: U1 to U6→A1 to A6→return; or, in the chapter numerations, 2–4–6–8–10–12→1–3–5–7–9–11–13. Yet two analogical, circular and/or timeless, movements contrast and complement the linearity, on what I shall call the meso (middlesized) and macro (overall) levels.

The meso level are the analogic pairs as shown in Table 2, where the great contrasts between U and A – Sh as growing and (mainly) adding wider understanding on A vs. Shevek as grown and (mainly) facing inimical manoeuvres on U – are infiltrated by the common metaphoric tenor of each pair. This does not result in six or seven stories, for the common denominators or metaphors are themselves fitted into the double (A and U) linear developments: the linear and circular movements are both two and one, they are a duality and unity, varying in a quite different shape the balancing of the yang-yin symbol. In a critical X-ray, the paired chapters would stand skeletally out as introductions of the metaphoric themes of walls (pair 1), cognitive overview (2), thick inside cognition (3), obstacles (4), assault on walls (5), and their breaching (6+7). The template for this sequence and for the overall liberating feel and horizon of *TD* might be section c) of Chapter 2: realizing there is a prison, often very concrete but always centrally consisting of what Blake called "mind-forged manacles," and acting against it, attempting to get out. In propertarian hypocrisy the prison might be a rich campus and colourful wrappings (and when this fails helicopter gunships as murderous enforcers), in Urrasti bleakness it might be concrete walls, in both cases they are so to speak consubstantial with false categorization and dogmatic prejudice. In fact, Anarres is, as Shevek comes to understand at the end, the truth of Urras: it is what the Formalists would call "the baring of the device" (of the ploy, proceeding, category) of power and repression so carefully hidden out of sight in wrapped-up Urras. Its bareness is also a poetic and cognitive metaphor, a cutting to the bone and showing of the joints, an X-ray. Metaphors are so indispensable and useful because they invoke sensually based evidence, validated by central human needs and desires, against the current ossified, often wilfully faked, categories. They explode literal semantic and referential pertinence and propose a new, imaginative pertinence by rearranging categories that shape our experience. Metaphor sketches in, thus, lineaments of "another world that corresponds to other possibilities of existence, to possibilities that would be most deeply our own [...]" (Ricoeur, *Rule* 229).

One of Shevek's formulations of his time theory, perhaps the pithiest because put into a debate on U, runs:

> There is the arrow, the running river, without which there is no change, no progress, or direction or creation. And there is the circle or the cycle, without which there is chaos, meaningless succession of instants, a world without clocks or seasons or promises. (7: 180)

To unpack this a bit, adding some of his other terms: The arrow is dynamic becoming, which yet has no sense unless it feeds a recognizable – changeable but sufficiently firm – being: in the case of humans, a person and/or a society with needs in the present based on memories of the past and desires for the future. Both together constitute a unity-in-duality (or vice versa). One-sided change, such as the overheated bourgeois "progress" over, say, the last 150 years, is meaningless and thus destructive. Le Guin has been permanently fascinated by what Lévi-Strauss called the "cool," tribal societies (and she will come to rate them higher in her later works such as *Always Coming Home*, having despaired of progress altogether). However, their one-sided permanence is, as Shevek remarks, boring. Once we have eaten of the apple of knowledge, I would say, there is no way back to the "primitive communism" of tribe, animal or plant, repressed by physical necessities. We have the choice between growing class repression or libertarian communism on a higher rung of the spiral, such as the one Le Guin is attempting to get at in *TD*.

The macro-circle is constituted by the novel's whole, Chapter 13 circling back on a higher level of understanding and achievement to chapter 1 in the novel, the A→U voyage coming back home to A. While a good way to think of the overall structure – which Le Guin might prefer – is as librations in a dynamic balance, the union of arrow and circle results

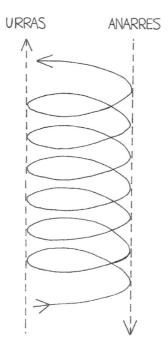

also in Time's simulsequential spiral (here open-ended, ongoing in historical time). The circlings (the six pairs of chapters) open up to a spiral which we might optimistically think as going upward. The upward arrow of progress is not seen but implied; however, as I have argued, it could be represented by the dotted lines touching the left (A) and right-hand (U) side of the circles as drawn below. The arrow of historical time begins with the original choice by the Odonians to accept exile on A (to which I shall return in my cavil) somewhere below the beginning of the spiral, points at the end to the future choices flowing out of Shevek's return with a representative of the Hainish, and includes everything in between. The spiral is an image out of dialectics, but I advance it with some hesitation, for the clean perfection of geometric curves much oversimplifies messy human relationships, and I don't know how to draw a fuzzy spiral. Most important, it shows the finished product without the process creating it: the spiral metaphor leaves out the element of choice, the catastrophe-theory bifurcations lurking at many turns. It is useful only if Hegel's own religious connotations of an automatic, predestined course are refused. In perhaps the only useful instrument Po-Mo has left us, it is indispensable that the spiral be there as a model but it is also indispensable that it be "under erasure" – as it is in Marx, who simultaneously expects collapse of capitalism and works for revolution.

At any rate, the too neat spiral is in the novel balanced both by the complex, on the whole advancing but also often see-sawing meso-structures, and even more by the subtle yin-and-yang of the micro-level, well exemplified by the superb sentence I cited from the end of situation 1, "The baby [...] hid his face in the darkness of the lost sun." To cognition by contraries – or (dare I say) by dialectic contradictions between and within people and chronotopes.

But what is the or at least one focus around which *TD* turns or librates? It might be found in one of its richest semantic clusters, that of *possession*, melding as it does the meanings of ownership and of something stronger than obsession: a subjection to demoniacal powers (in some ways a counterweight to Dostoevsky's anti-nihilist *Besy*, literally *The Demons*, translated into English as *The Possessed*). The possessors possess both things (on U) and power over others (on U and, more rarely but crucially, in the power center of A). Yet the coin has another side: things (that is, reified human relationships) are in the saddle and ride mankind – or manunkind, as e.e. cummings would phrase it:

> You the possessors are possessed. You are all in jail. Each alone, solitary, with a heap of what he owns. You live in prison, die in prison. It is all I can see in your eyes – the wall, the wall. (7: 184)

The terminological family of "possessed" is a set of brilliant portmanteau words, but it has a not unimportant drawback. The U possession as capitalist alienation of and from central characteristics of humanity calls forth on A a dispossession that is simultaneously a/ lack of property ownership, b/ lack of demonic possession (class power), and c/ lack of things. The last term of the triad, my c/, is on the whole negative – as testified by the permanent siege mentality on A enforced by the drought and culminating in the near-famine of Chapter 8. Politico-economically speaking, the last term of the triad muddles up the positive meanings of dispossession.[2] Le Guin's equally wondrous neologism "propertarian" (noun and adjective) has an analogous drawback: it is a mixture of legal and ethical language, without political economy, so that it might be mistaken for ascetic refusal of worldliness. I am not sure the word capitalism is ever used in *TD*: only its consumer effects are shown in Shevek's astonishment at money, the shopping mall, etc.

The question that follows is, in theological language, why do the wicked prosper? It is not a minor question, for no monotheism has so far been able to answer it – from Job through the Parable of the Tares to the Dr Faust(us) legend – without inventing Satan. In anthropological terms, the questions in *TD* would be: is there a necessary or only an accidental connection, first, between anarchist bareness as well as the immediate readability of direct human relationships on A and its meager, largely desert ecology (see Jameson's pioneering meditation on *TD*, *Archaeologies* 155–59, and many passages in *TD*, perhaps most explicitly in the Shevek–Bedap discussion of Chapter 6: 131–39); second, between the lush fertility and the manifold propertarian (capitalist) wraps and traps of U; and third, between the two planetary situations, encompassed in the image of twins circling about each other?[3] Surely William Morris was right when he called for a radical diminution of unnecessary (usually kitsch) things accompanied by useless toil ("Useful"); yet, must capitalism be always (as here) associated with abundance, however unjustly gotten and distributed,

---

2   There are at least two further semantic variations to be mentioned here: a) a further positive meaning of possession, arising in and from shamanic possession of or by the goal (Radin 132); but it would scarcely fit Shevek to say he was possessed by the Time Theory; b) the ironic danger, materializing on A, of its becoming again possessed by propertarianism and domination.

3   It would be instructive to compare *TD* with the first (the only readable) *Dune* novel by Frank Herbert. I heard a talk by him in Berkeley 1965 where he claimed the desert grew from his newspaper writing about the Oregon deserts, not too far from Le Guin. He blew them up, of course, into a super-Arabia that mixes T.E. Lawrence, Aramco, and his own Baroque galactic twists at the borders of Fascist sword-and-sorcery. *TD* is in almost all ways an anti-*Dune*.

and communism with scarcity, however puritanically useful as stimulus in adversity and heroically battled against by a united collective? Here we get into the domain of competing social systems and ways of life, a properly historico-political critique, which I shall face at the end of this essay. To be able to do so, I need a long detour.

Part 2. Some Propositions about Cognition in Science and Fiction[4]

2.0

Le Guin's *TD* is that actually rather rare thing, a real *science fiction* novel: a work of fiction seriously exploring science or systematic cognition – both as a human way of knowing and as human social activity. To understand this better, I proceed here with a discussion of cognition. I wish to deal with two varieties of science: one, the positive older sister (below called "S1"); the other, the troublesome younger brother, let's say for now, problematic ("S2"). But I need to introduce this by first considering science as a way of asking how to understand the universe, that is, science in terms of epistemology. I shall then come to fiction as cognition.

2.1 Central Orientation Points for Epistemology

I am not aware of a systematic basis for epistemology we could today use, but I postulate that our interpretations of what is knowledge or not, and how can we know that we know, are largely shaped by the "framework of

---

4   Sections 2.1–2.3 are a much abridged summary of a long discussion in my "On the Horizons."

commitments" we bring to them. Catherine Z. Elgin usefully formulated in 1982 a strategic "soft" skepticism that still allows such commitments:

> Philosophy once aspired to set all knowledge on a firm foundation. Genuine knowledge claims were to be derived from indubitable truths by means of infallible rules. The terms that make up such truths were held to denote the individuals and kinds that constitute reality, and the rules for combining them ... were thought to reflect the real order of things. – This philosophical enterprise has foundered. Indubitable truths and infallible rules are not to be had.

Instead, thinking always begins with working approximations based on "our best presystematic judgments on the matter at hand" (Elgin 183). As we advance toward understanding, we often discover these approximations are untenable or insufficient – but there is no other ensemble to be had.

Scientists of a positivist inclination will discourse on evidence, in the sense of proof. Evidence is important, but it is always "theory-laden," determined by "our conception of the domain and [...] our goals in systematizing it [...]" (Elgin 184–85). The *New York Times* claims it brings "All the news that's fit to print," but who determines what is fit of the news? Alternatively, a tradition from the more radical Skeptics through the Post-Modernists and extreme constructionists has questioned whether there is a reality to be known and whether, if it is there, we could know it or talk about it. Neither tradition is satisfactory. The horizon I am sketching is characterized by Elgin and Nelson Goodman in 1988 as "reject[ing] both absolutism and nihilism, both unique truth and the indistinguishability of truth from falsity" (3). A univocal world – *the* fixed reality out there – has been well lost, together with the Unique Final Truth (divine or asymptotically scientific) and other Onenesses of the monotheist family. A sense of panic at the loss of this clear world, at the loss of theological certitude, not only permeates dogmatists of all religious and lay kinds, but has also engendered its symmetrical obverse in an absolutist relativism. How is a third way possible beyond this bind?

It can begin by recognizing that right and wrong persist, but that rightness can no longer be identified with correspondence to a ready-made, monotheistic Creation, but must be created by us, with skill and responsibility. Goodman and Elgin think that the term "truth" as usually conceived is too solidly embedded in faiths and certitudes of monotheistic allegiance to be safe and useful; categories and argument forms that are products of continual human cognition, on the other hand, are better instruments for practical use, testable for situational rightness. Truth is strictly subordinate to rightness in this approach, and this rightness is dependent on our various symbol systems (see Aronowitz vii–xi and passim). One consequence is that science loses its epistemic primacy: like art and everyday perception, "[it] does not passively inform upon but actively informs a world" (Elgin 52–53). The arts and sciences overtly repose on intuitions, which are for science buried in their axioms as indubitable certainties. Whether you prefer Marx's or Balzac's description of nineteenth-century France will depend on your general or even momentary interests, but they're in no way either incompatible or subsumed under one another: and both are cognitive.

Sketching an operative epistemological way can further proceed by recognizing that there are still some logical ways if not of defining truth then at least of defining untruth (Goodman and Elgin 136). As Orwell might have put it, all opinions are constructed and relatively wrong or limited, but some are more wrong than others. This holds pre-eminently for those I would call *monoalethist* (from *alethe*, truth): all those – from monotheists to lay dogmatists (Fascists, Stalinists, and believers in the Invisible Hand of the Market) – who hold they have the Absolute Truth, including the belief that relativism is absolute (see more in essay 16). Only belief in the absolute right – Haraway's "God-trick" ("Situated" 589) – is absolutely wrong.

2.2 Cognition Is Constituted by and as History: Multiple Sources and Methods

In a remarkable passage right at the beginning of *Works and Days*, Hesiod invents the myth (or allegory) of the two Erises, the benign and the malign one (I: 11–26). The bad Strife favours wars and civil discords. But the first-born is the good Strife, whom Zeus has placed at the roots of the earth, for she generates emulation: one vase-maker or poem-singer envies the other, the lazy and poor peasant imitates the industrious and richer one.

This *polar splitting of concepts* seems to me a central procedure of critical reason, dissatisfied with the present categorizations and trying to insinuate opposed meanings under the same term. I shall adopt this Hesiodean procedure for knowledge and then science.

The principal ancestors to this endeavour may be found in Marx and to a minor, but still significant degree in Nietzsche. I take from Nietzsche that belief in the correspondence of intellect to thing/s – an Aristotelian correspondence of knowledge to reality – is an ideal impossible to fulfil and leads to faking and skepticism. This Truth is a lie, and whenever erected into a system, as in religion and in Galileian science, compels lying. Any cognition developed against this fixed horizon partakes for Nietzsche of a huge, finally deadly "illusion" (*Zur Genealogie* 128). The constructivist account, on the other hand, is a creative transference of carrying across, in Greek *meta-phorein*, whence his famous hyperbolic statements that knowing is "Nothing but working with the favourite metaphors" (*Philosophy* xxxiii). For Nietzsche wisdom arises out of the knowledge of nescience: "And only on this by now solid and granite basis of nescience may science have arisen, the will for knowing on the basis of a much more powerful will, the will for *unknowing*, for the uncertain, the untrue! Not as its opposite, but – as its improvement!" (*Jenseits* 24). Nietzsche is not necessarily a source for Le Guin, she rightly prefers the Dao, but nescience and non-being are important ideas for her. Yet take care: in terms of Le Guin's worlds and ours, these horizons are the opposite of the illusionistic one, they rule out angels, UFOs, Mickey Mice, and the Invisible Hand of the Market. Nescience demolishes The Monolithic Truth while preserving verifiability for any given situation, and denies the illusions that so often lead to fanatical belief.

More useful still is Marx, whose relevant views I discuss at length elsewhere (Chapter 15 in this book and "On the Horizons"; see also Aronowitz, especially chapters 2 and 3). Suffice it here to say that Marx had a dual view: on the one hand he rejected positivistic approaches, pouring his scorn on the falsities of bourgeois political economy, but simultaneously he chastised all attempts to subject science or cognition to "a point of view from the outside, stemming from interests outside science" (*MEW* 26.2: 112). *Capital* itself is presented as a project of "free scientific research," which assumes the task to clarify the inner relationships of the phenomena it deals with without imposition from the outside, and in particular against "the Furies of private interest" (*MEW* 23:16). His two major, consubstantial cognitive insights are first, that societal injustices are based on exploitation of other people's living labour; but second, the insight that the proper way to talk about the capitalist exploitation which rules our lives is not in the *a priori* form of dogma, a closed system, but in the *a posteriori* form of critique. Legitimate cognition is epistemically grounded in the process it describes, and strategically developed by developing and articulating a radically deviant stance against a dominant in a given historical situation (see Marcuse). After Marx, it should be clear that "All modes of knowing presuppose a point of view [...]. Therefore, the appropriate response to [this is] [...] the responsible acknowledgement of our own viewpoints and the use of that knowledge to look critically at our own and each others' opinions." (Levins 182) The rightness of a theoretical assertion depends on evidence as interpreted by the assertor's always socio-historical needs, interests, and values.

Approaching science from this epistemological basis, I suggest the Hesiodean procedure of splitting the institutionalized horizons of science-as-is fully off from those of a potentially humanized science-as-wisdom, which would count its casualties as precisely as the US armed forces do for their own (but not for those they bomb). I wish I could call the latter "science" and the former something else, perhaps technoscience, but I do not want to give up either on science or on technology. I shall provisionally call the firstborn, good science "Science 1" (S1), and the present one, whose results are mixed but seem to be increasingly steeped in the blood and misery of millions of people, "Science 2" (S2). S1 is always situational and situated, S2 pretends to be timelessly valid. The medieval theologians would have called them *sapientia* vs. *scientia*, though in those early days they optimistically believed *scientia* could be tamed by the former, by knowledge which was the highest intellectual virtue. This splitting can be philosophically justified by Hegel's observation that truth as such is essentially a cognitive process, so that life (social practice) has to be figured in (469).

These are ideal types only, intermixed in any actual effort in most varied proportions: also, the beginnings of S2 are in S1, and amid its corruption it retains certain of its liberatory birthmarks to the present day. Nonetheless, the fixation on *domination* and the consubstantial *occultation of the knowing subject* in S2 "is a particular moment in the division of labor." The avoidance of capricious errors "does [not] protect the scientific enterprise as a whole from the shared biases of its practitioners." In sum, "The pattern of knowledge in science is [...] structured by interest and belief [...]. Theories, supported by megalibraries of data, often are systematically and dogmatically obfuscating." It is not by chance that "major technical efforts based on science have [led] to disastrous outcomes: pesticides increase pests; hospitals are foci of infection; antibiotics give rise to new pathogens; flood control increases flood damage; and economic development increases poverty" (Levins 180, 183, and 181).

Bourgeois civilization's main way of coping with the unknown is aberrant, said Nietzsche, because it transmutes nature into concepts with the aim of mastering it as a more or less closed system of concepts. It is not that the means get out of hand but that the mastery – the wrong end – *requires* wrong means of aggressive manipulation. S2 is not only a cultural revolution but also a latent or patent *political* upheaval. The scientific, finally, is the political.

There are strong analogies and probably causal relations between a determinist "search for truth, proclaimed as the cornerstone of progress" and "the maintenance of a hierarchical, unequal social structure," within which capitalist rationalization has created the large stratum of "administrators, technicians, scientists, educators" it needed (Wallerstein, *Historical* 82–83). In particular, it created the whole new class of *managers*. As Braverman's *Labor and Monopoly Capital* pointed out, "to manage" originally meant to train a horse in his paces, in the manège (67). F.W. Taylor did exactly this – he broke "the men," calling in his *Shop Management* for "a planning department to do the thinking for the men" (Braverman 128). Later, since "machinery faces workers as *capitalized* domination over work, and the same happens for science" (Marx, *Theorien* 355), control was built into the new technologies. During the nineteenth century, "science, as a generalized social property" (S1) was replaced by "science as a capitalist property at the very center of production." This is "the scientifico-technical revolution" (Braverman 156), while technoscientific ideology becomes, as Jameson notes, "a blind behind which the more embarrassing logic of the commodity form and the market can operate" (*Singular* 154). Already by the early 1960s, three quarters of scientific R&D in the USA was corporate, financed directly or through tax write-offs by the Federal government, that is, by money taken from tax-payers, while profits went to corporations (164–66). It is almost a century by now that scientific research is mainly determined by expected profits to the detriment of S1 (see Kapp 208ff.), where it is not neglected for purely financial speculation. It has become "commodity scientism" (see the discussion in Chapter 8, section 4.1).

The supposition that science does not deal in values, which began to be widely doubted only after the Second World War, had as "its actual function to protect two systems of values: the professional values of the scientists, and the predominant [status quo] values of society as they existed at that moment [...]." (Graham 9, and see 28–29). The stances of "objectivity" and erasure of the subject actively fostered a treatment of people (workers, women, patients, consumers) as objects to be manipulated as a part of nature. As a hierarchical institution devoted to manipulation, S2 was easily applicable to "human resources": the Nazi doctors' experiments were only an extremely overt and acute form of such *Herrschaftswissen*, knowledge used for domination.

We must ruefully accept, with due updating, Gandhi's harsh verdict about science: "Your laboratories are diabolic unless you put them at the service of the rural poor" (Gandhigram). S2 is Power (over people); S1 is Creativity (within people). In this view science is a usable and misusable ensemble of cognitions, not an absolute truth we can approach asymptotically. It is principally a "by whom" and "for what" – an "impure" productive relationship between (for example) workers, scientists, financiers, and other power-holders, as well as an institutional network with different effects upon all such different societal groups, which can and must become less death-oriented. S1 must be based on holistic understanding, which would englobe and steer analytical knowledge (Goodman and Elgin 161–64). This would not at all diminish its impressive status as institution; on the contrary, S1 would finally be as truly liberating, both for its creators and its users, as its best announcers have, from Bacon to Wiener and Gould, claimed it should be. It could at last embark not only on the highly important damage control but also on a full incorporation of aims for acting that would justify Nietzsche's rhapsodic expectation: "An experimenting would then become proper that would find place for every kind of heroism, a centuries-long experimenting, which could put to shame all the great works and sacrifices of past history" (*Fröhliche* 39) – truly, a joyous science. It would have to ask: what questions have not been asked in the last 400 years, and for whose profit have we ignored them?

2.3 Whither Science Now?

In 1932, sensing the worse to come (which has not ceased coming), Brecht asked:

> Faced with all these machines and technical arts, with which humanity could be at the beginning of a long, rich day, shouldn't it feel the rosy dawn and the fresh wind which signify the beginning of blessed centuries? Why is it so grey all around, and why blows first that uncanny dusk wind at the coming of which, as they say, the dying ones die? (*GBFA* 21: 588)

He went on for the rest of his life to worry at this image of false dawn through the example of Galileo. His final judgment was that Galileo (reason, science, the intellectuals) failed, and helped the night along, by not allying himself with a political dawn-bringer. But then, we might ask today, where was he to find a revolutionary class who wanted such an ally, and where indeed was Brecht to find it after 1932?

So, what would an updated, sophisticated S1 mean – how can we really get a science for (the) people, science wedded to easing human life and to a humane quality of life? This is a question dealt with by fictional cognition in *TD*. For our world, I shall suggest (consistently with Le Guin) that our first necessity is radical social justice, so that rethinking would get a chance.

Second, we must truly learn the lesson that our technical competence, based on an irresponsible S2 yoked to the profit and militarism that finance it, vastly exceeds our understanding of its huge dangers for hundreds of millions of people and indeed for the survival of vertebrate ecosphere (cockroaches and tube worms might survive). To survive, we imperatively have to establish and enforce a graduated system of *risk assessment* (Beck) *and damage control* based on the negentropic welfare of the human community and the eco-system in which we are embedded. This means retaining, and indeed following consistently through, Merton's famous four basic norms of science – universalism, scepticism, public communism, and personal disinterestedness (see also Collingridge 77–85 and 99ff.) – as well as strict scientific accountability, adding to the sense of not falsifying findings the sense of being responsible for their consequences. This means practicing science from the word go, its teaching, as most intimately co-shaped by the overriding concerns of what and who such an activity is for: "A stronger, more adequate notion of objectivity would require methods for systematically examining all the social values shaping a particular research process [...]" (Haraway, *Modest* 36, building on Harding; see also Wallerstein, *End* 164–67, 238–41, and 264–65).

Major scientific projects should not be allowed to become "in house" *faits accomplis* without a public debate that follows the juridical norm of hearing more than one side: "Every decision involves the selection among an agenda of alternative images of the future, a selection that is guided by some system of values" (Boulding 423). Hence, all individuals, including corporate "fictive individuals," involved in screening, testing, and monitoring should provide the "bias statement" demanded already a third of a century ago by the American Academy of Sciences: a list of all previous major research funding, occupations, investments – and even public stands on political issues (cited in Collingridge 186, with disfavour).

These suggestions are just the beginning of a first pass at a solution. Among the huge gaps in my quick survey is lack of discussion on who should establish and administer such reviews and controls, and how to prevent an unnecessarily cumbersome bureaucracy to take root. These are however not beyond human ingenuity, if transparency and democratic accountability are achieved.

2.4 Narrations in Science and Fiction

Kant had a major difficulty in the *Critique of Judgment:* judgments deal with particulars, which is the only logical category to be actual. But how is one to account for any particular, notoriously contingent and as it were anarchic, for which the general concept has still to be found? He sometimes finessed this by using examples, which hide a generalized allegory: the particular Achilles is the example of Courage in general. This welcome subterfuge pointed already to the untenability of claims for science as the best (or only) knowledge, since an example partakes both of image and of an implied story, as Achilles before Troy. It reintroduced history as a story, enabling us to understand why the *Iliad* was an unsurpassed cognitive fount for the Hellenes. It follows that science and other ways of cognition (say art) do not relate as "objective" vs. "subjective" (or strong male vs. weak female), but as human constructions guided by different constraints for coherence and different conventions of anchoring or "entrenchment." As Bruner argues, the arts are differently entrenched from sciences: they implicitly cultivate hypotheses, each set of which requires a Possible World but not the widest possible extension for applying that set in our World Zero, that is, testability in the scientists' sense; rather, they must be recognizable as "true to conceivable experience" or verisimilar (52 and passim). However, I would argue that arts quite compensate for this by showing in "thick" detail what may be a lived truth of a conceivable experience, or how to both contextually arrive at cognition and how to live with it further.

For one thing, sciences may have a "long duration" additiveness, until the paradigm and the powerful institution supporting it changes. Science deals with univocal and stereotypic contrivances or arrangements – that is, those in theory repeatable with identical effects (though every engineer knows practice is different). Yet this horizon is not unknown in art: think of Athenian or Renaissance performance, supported (like science) by institutions geared to foreseeable results. This is also the ideal horizon of the more decentralized institutionalization of the publishing of poetry or the novel in periodicals and books, operating with statistical projections. Institutionalization then turns out to be largely necessary for both, but not necessarily from top down: from bottom up is the tradition of S1 and most art. When one gets down to the non-institutionalized creator or artefact, the univocity wavers: in the case of people, projects and stereotypes (for example, genre conventions, from the epic poem to SF) are enmeshed with the creator's complex past and present histories, with not quite foreseeable choices. The novel has since its birth, and poetry has since the Romantics, played off constant cognitive innovation against the generic enablement, the New against the recognizable. A computer is foreseeable, a human brain is not. Science is what can be fully repeated, art what can not.

What are then a few of the relevant differences and similarities between the cognitive horizon and route of science (S1) and of creative writing, poetry in the wider sense? The horizon, source, and finally the aim (the Supreme Good) of both is to my mind the same: making life, that precious and rare cosmic accident, richer and more pleasurable; fighting against entropy by making sense, in different ways, of different segments of nature, very much including human relationships. In brief, both are cognitive tools and pursuits. But more particularly, both participate in the definition of *poiesis* which Plato seems to have been the first to propose: "action causing something to emerge from non-being to being" (*Symposium* 205b). Against his upper-class snobbery, Aristotle pointed out this entails that any *tekhne*, "art and craft", is deeply akin to ethico-political praxis in that its field is "that which might also be otherwise," a *hexis poietike* (*Nicomachean Ethics* I.i and VI.4: 1140a), a creative stance or bearing of potential novelty, of open possibility. This *tekhne*, an artful third way beyond the determinism-chance split, relates to technique as S1 does to S2 (see Castoriadis 231–35).

Therefore, both S1 and poetry deal with *situations* against a horizon of human interest and evaluation. The formalizations of S2 try to taboo this horizon and to erect the very specialized, fenced-in lab as the exemplary situation-matrix extrapolatable to reality (which then fails immediately and obviously in all social and biological studies, say primate research). The chronotope of an S2 experiment is manipulated so as to be mathematically explainable, the human agents must be kept out. Yet both the situations of fiction and today's science are constructed or taken up for (different but converging) purposes co-defined by the interests of the subject constructors. Each has necessarily a formal closure – involving among other matters a beginning, middle, and end, as Aristotle phrased it for plays – but they are often open-ended, and their multiplicity is always such. Further, a longer work (a theory or a novel) is articulated like a chain or a tapeworm, in a series of delimited events which stand together (this is a literal translation of Aristotle's *systasis pragmaton*) as segments to result in as final unity. When, in several branches of quantum mechanics, and similarly in catastrophe theory, a whole battery of models is regularly used, and "no one thinks that one of these is the whole truth, and they may be mutually inconsistent" (Hacking 37), the differences to Balzac's *Comédie humaine* series or the set (the macrotext) constituted by the poetry of – say – Byron, Shelley, and Keats remain obvious, but the overall formal similarities as cognitive pursuits do not deserve to be slighted either.

I shall conclude with a pertinent excerpt from a longer discussion in Chapter 10: Formally speaking, "atom" is the name of an agent in a story about "chemistry," just as "Mr Pickwick" is the name of an agent in a story about "the Pickwick Club" (Harré 89), though there are different rules of storytelling in the two cases. "[Theoretical f]ictions must have some degree of plausibility, which they gain by being constructed in the likeness of real things," concludes the middle-of-the-road historian of science Harré (98). If we take the example of literary and scientific "realism," we find they are consubstantial products of the same attitude or bearing, the quantifying thisworldliness of bourgeois society. This is a contradictory stance, with great strengths (obvious from Cervantes and Fielding on) based on looking steadily at this world as a whole, and increasingly great dangers based on possessive reification of bourgeois atomized individualism. The dangers surface when institutionally sanctified science stakes out a claim to being the pursuit of *the whole truth* in the form of *certainty*, while the apparently weaker and certainly more modest Dickens escapes them. S2 science likes to think of itself as deductive. However, as a planet's map is regulated and shaped by the grid of cartographic projection, so is any system based on a deductive principle, for example the Aristotelian excluded middle or the Hegelian necessarily resolved dialectical contradiction. And this principle is also a kind of meta-reflection about, or key to the method of, the system that is in its (obviously circular) turn founded on and deduced from it. When a philosophical or scientific system develops in the form of a finite series of propositions culminating in a rounded-off certainty, its form is finally not too different from the nineteenth-century "well-made," illusion-istic stage play; no wonder, for they both flow out of the Positivist orienta-tion, where decay of value leads to despair. The Lady with the Camellias and the Laws of Thermodynamics are sisters under the skin: both show a beautifully necessary death.

2.5 The Poet's Politics: Thinking as Experience

Poetry or fiction always implies a reader standing for a collective audience, ideally his/her whole community (this is foregrounded in plays). It was the accepted norm not only for ancient Greece but also for Leibniz or Kant that such creations in words reach some transmittable understand-ing of human relationships, so that Baumgarten called his foundational *Aesthetica* of 1750 the "science of sensual cognition." In proportion to its coherence, richness, and novelty a work of art gives shape and voice to a previously uncognized, mute and non-articulated, category of being – that is, of human relationships to other people and the universe. For many poets it then became logical and ethical to think of translating such cognition into politics as concrete human relationships of power.

How may artistic creators *professionally* participate in politics? This was no problem in the era of Homer, Alcman, or Solon but became complicated when political units grew larger as well as more acutely based on divergent class interests and the attendant oppression of a major part of the body politic. Ever since the advent of class society, tales, romances, ballads, love songs, have been principally a plebeian delight, often transmitted orally. Plato clearly felt poets as worrisome competitors to his philosopher-king and advocated banning all those who did not fit his norms. After many painful experiences, including the splendid but today not often applicable attempts of the Romantics to either participate directly as bards of revolt or turn away totally from politics (which means leaving it to the status quo), we may today follow the lead by Rancière (but see on poetry as cognition also Spivak 115ff.) and posit something like the following:

The poet-creator can (in fact, cannot but) participate in politics but only paradoxically. This means, literally, that she is one who doubts the reigning commonplace opinions, one who swerves from it by infringing old usages and meanings and, implicitly or explicitly (this is a matter of situation and personal temperament), creating new ones. Epicure's ruling principle of the atoms *swerving* from the automatically straight path may stand as the great ancestor of all creative methods and possibilities (see Chapter 15 in this book); from Epicure's interpreter Lucretius it passed on – via Cyrano – to Swift, Wells, and thence lay into the foundations of SF.

Yet an operative, efficient or creative paradox is inherent in language (and this is foregrounded in poetry). Sensually perceived reality contains only particulars. However, this cannot be fixed and formulated in language without an indispensable anchoring in the general. Both are wonderful and necessary tools of cognition *sine quibus non*; yet dialectically, when isolated, both the particular concrete and the general abstraction are alienated from the plenitude of reality which is in feedback with human understanding. Therefore, as a place of useful thinking (not sundered from feeling), verse and prose poetry – and SF – have often been a different but converging mode of cognition (*alter non alius*), that filled in the voids left by institutionalized science and institutionalized philosophy, and of course by most institutionalized politics. The latter use generalization, irremediably wedded to concepts, which cannot fully account for the relationship between people and nature, the finite and the infinite. Symmetrically obverse, sensual representation focuses on the particular as immediately apparent and needs generalizing tools (both concepts and figures such as allegory) that go beyond the here and now. Poetic creation sutures conceptual thought to justification from recalled immediate sensual, bodily experience which is (thus far) much more difficult to falsify or disbelieve.

This creative stance, however, immediately leads to an intimately personal paradox of living in politics as an anti-politics. All that is commonly taken for politics – for us, say, since the effects of the antifascist wars, such as peace and the Welfare State, have been largely or fully expunged – is alien and inimical, where not actively threatening and deadly. Where personality is valued for and as consumption and carefully shaped phrases pertain increasingly to mendacious advertising, art has to upset. Our immediate major poetic ancestor, Rimbaud (in a filiation beginning with many Romantics and Baudelaire), was led to exasperation at having to reconcile

his deep hatred of the bourgeoisie and existing society with the irrefragable
fact of having to breathe and experience within it:

> [...] industrialists, rulers, senates:
> Die quick! Power, justice, history: down with you!
> This is owed to us. Blood! Blood! Golden flame!
> All to war, to vengeance, to terror [...]. Enough!

> [...] I'm there, I'm still there.
>   ("Qu'est-ce pour nous [...]," 113)

The obverse of this (the *assez* vs. *j'y suis toujours*) aporia is Thomas
More's great coinage of utopia: the radically different good place which is
in our sensual experience not here, but must be cognized – today, on pain
of extinction. What is not here, Bloch's Yet Unknown, is almost always
first adumbrated in fiction, most economically in verse poetry. From many
constituents of the good place, I shall here focus, as does Rancière (92–93),
on freedom – Wordsworth's "Dear Liberty" (*Prelude* l. 3) which translates
the French revolutionary term of *liberté chérie* – that then enables security,
order, creativity, and so on. It is of freedom that Rimbaud's *Boat* is drunken:
the method or *epistemic principle* of great modern poetry from him on (and
prose too, in somewhat differing ways), is *freedom as possibility of things being
otherwise*. This is to be understood by interaction between what is being said
and how it is being said, in a consubstantiality of theme and stance. Poetic
freedom is a historically situated, political experience of the sensual, which
is necessarily also polemical swerve from and against the *doxa*, in favour of
fresh cognition. The common, brainwashed understanding includes much
what has in the past truly been liberating politics but has retained only a
few impoverished slogans from its heroic ages (the liberal, communist, and
antifascist ones) when it directly flowed out of human senses. Therefore,
"creators have to retrace the line of passage that unites words and things"
(Rancière). And in prose, I would add, the line that unites human figures
and spacetimes. As we see in *TD* and the desire, personified in Shevek, for
"a landscape inhabitable by human beings" (*TD* 10: 268).

Part 3. *The Dispossessed* Seen as Fictional Cognition – Laudation with a Cavil

3.0

I have long been proposing that we treat SF as loose modern parables or *exempla*. If this is the privileged way for understanding SF texts, is Shevek the parable's vehicle, on the order of Jesus' Mustard Seed? And what is then the tenor, the worldly and therefore imperfect (ambiguous) Kingdom of Heaven? What is Shevek more precisely an example of or exemplary for? I shall first focus on him as the central signifying figure of *TD* and then on what his course signifies.

3.1 Shevek's Situations and the Binary Librations

Critics of *TD* have often accounted for its plot by following the education and struggle for freedom of Shevek. But as always in Le Guin, and in all proper anthropology, he is "A person seen [...] in a landscape" ("Science Fiction" 87). He is obviously *en situation*, an instance of what Haraway was to recommend as "situated knowledge." Shevek is centrally an interactor with and interpreter of his twin worlds. He is that in relation to what we (but not *TD*) wrongly separate into the categories of freedom and cognition; discussing Enlightenment, Kant quite unambiguously defines political freedom as "to make public use of one's reason at every point" (4). Perhaps the central duality or binary of this novel is: how does the individual person's urge for these Siamese twins, that is, for unbuilding walls, fare on both worlds, the anarchist and the capitalist one; how is it both modifying and being modified by them?

I shall therefore neglect here, with one brief exception, the interesting characteristics balancing Shevek's exemplariness, making him humanly fallible and believable even while he is outgrowing them, such as a self-reliance bordering on egocentrism even while it is done in the service of the Cause (physics as freedom), a puritanic narrowness making for loneliness in the first two chapters on A, and so on. The exception is the Shevek-Takver binary, of which I shall mainly consider its wondrous lyrical inception (6: 145–54). There would be much to infer from it about *TD* as focused not only on clarity and knowledge but also, consubstantially, on passion and dark suffering. However, I shall approach Takver through her two Tinguelyan mobiles – airy sculptures of wire suspended from the ceiling, the "Occupations of Uninhabited Space," contrasting Shevek's pre-Takver void, and later the "Inhabitations of Time," complementary to his theoretical inhabitation of it. They show how the binary couple's unity is one of separate and complementary equals, Takver the biologist bringing in the immediate life-oriented presentness as the convex of Shevek's concave long-range abstractions in physics. She is Shevek's other illumination beside cosmology: the whole final third of chapter 6 is suffused by an unearthly radiance, rising in the dark as the silvery Moon (Urras) does and piercing it, like the joy between them, to propagate as well as celebrate clarity. This relationship comes to a head in the pillow-talk coda on being in the middle of life vs. looking at it "from the vantage point of death" (154). True, a separatist sectarian might note that the two characterizations are based on a variant of the hegemonic ascription of male and female qualities, say female concreteness vs. male abstraction. But first, the basis is not the whole beautiful edifice, there is much more in the text to contradict any banal polarization. And second, hegemony also means "a lived system of meanings and values" (Williams 110), in tension between ideology and utopia. The Takver–Shevek pair is a mini-utopia, an ethical harmony quite analogous to the final Simulsequentiality Theory. No ambiguities in either.[5]

---

5   My original plan for a commentary to *TD* included a section demolishing Samuel R. Delany's "To Read *The Dispossessed*." I believe he has not only failed to read most of what is there, but that the few elements he focuses on and blames, such as heterosexuality and ongoing identities, are those which diverged from his own writerly practice and ideology, so that it is (to put it mildly) very ungenerous to imply everybody should write like himself. Lack of space prevented me from doing a detailed anti-commentary. I am not totally displeased at this, for two reasons. I hope my analysis shows the untenability of his pseudo-destructions. I would also not enjoy

I now regretfully pass over the thickly populated world of A to focus on Shevek. Centrally, he is of the family of Sun Heroes, bringers of the light and slayers of pestilential dragons. Light is of course the opposite of blindness (as in Oedipus and Lear), it is knowledge of oneself as part and parcel of the world as society and as universe. I mentioned that the very first situation of the book, the baby in the sun ray, begins to establish the strong imagery of light as the (physical and cognitive) clarity and "difficult to arrive at simplicity"[6] which recurs often – sometimes as light reflected in Shevek's face or eyes (see 2: 45 and 11: 280) or ideas that crave light (3: 58) or his transparent moral personality (6: 146). Yet suns and light are not quite the same after Relativity Theory: light dare not forget (nor does Shevek) it is the left hand of darkness, as life is of death, about which I shall have more to say at the end of this sub-section. And heroes are not the same after socialism and feminism (cf. Le Guin's pendulum swing away, "Carrier Bag" 167–69): they are no more given by mythological decree but have to struggle through epic choices, they are Light *Seekers*, a two-legged permanent revolution incompatible with a macho killer role (I agree with Milner's observation that *TD* is "unambiguously feminist" [209]).

Nonetheless, Shevek is also a founding hero, renewer of Odo's correct but corrupted message (see 4: 88), inaugurator of communist freedom in physical theory and (perhaps) in social practice. Like many heroes, he has to pass through a desert exile, first on A (the physical desert in Chapter 8 and the moral desert of corrupt power in Chapter 10) then amid the lush city jungle and fleshpots as well as the underground hideouts of U. We leave him – a wise cut-off – before he enters the Promised Land (openly named in 1: 7), returning from afar with a new physical Law which does not mean power for one chosen people, caste or gender but breaking down the walls between people in the whole universe, no less (the ansible). A dissident

---

pointing out the glaring sectarianisms of a writer I have read with enjoyment and respect, though to respect creative truth it probably should be done.

6   This is one of Brecht's definitions of communism in the poem "Praise of Communism" (11: 234). I hope and trust he would in the 1970s not have withheld the appellative from the equally anti-authoritarian *TD*.

and unbuilding builder, the opposite of the channel-digging King Utopus; Remus more than Romulus.

Shevek is presented as having a strong self. But that is to be understood in terms of *TD*'s all-pervasive librations. It is perhaps best shown a propos the first piece of Shevek's world we see: "There was a wall." Yet immediately after that proposition we are led to see (first swing of the pendulum of meaning) it is also not a wall, for it does not bar the road. It is "an idea of boundary." Yet again "the idea was real," it is a wall – second swing of the pendulum. Wall 1, the physical one, was not important; Wall 2, the notional one, is the most important thing/ notion on A. The method here is not a hesitation from Yes through No to Yes, it is rather a movement that returns by way of depth analysis from notion 1 (mere physical wall) to a changed notion 2 (wall as all-important idea of boundary that bars passage), where both notions use the same term yet destabilize and dynamicize it. Analogously, Shevek's Self is continually shifting, encountering inner and outer walls and working to unbuild them, infiltrating and being infiltrated by the two worlds of A and U, by the possessed situations, characters, spaces, relationships of U and by the dispossessed – but sometimes repossessed – ones on A. Very roughly, this shift may be thought as spirally progressing from the isolated individual, through dispossession from egotism by select interaction with his community, to creator. Shevek's rich libration is the incarnation of Odo's tombstone inscription: "To be whole is to be part; true voyage is return" (3: 68); this is signalled in his encounter with her a dozen pages later.

Of a piece with this is Shevek's delving into or affinity with pain (e.g., his speech on 2: 48–50) and death. The very method of librating between Being 1→Unbeing→Being 2 is a sequence of little deaths and joyful rebirths, as his first step onto Urras shows: "[H]e stumbled and nearly fell. He thought of death, in that gap between the beginning of a step and its completion, and at the end of the step he stood on a new earth" (1: 16). Surely this is a conscious subverting of the PR trumpets and cymbals anent the US colonel's landing on our Moon, just a few years before *TD*. The small step for Shevek is not necessarily a giant leap for anything; it is certainly not a step on the upward arrow of progress towards the excelsior of bigger and better military technology (like, say, the giant match-cut leap at the beginning of *2001*) ... I cannot make here a thorough survey, but only give two more small instances. First is the little death of sexual orgasm, that letting go of the self (2: 41, and then both death and renewal with Takver, from 6: 148 on). Second is the violent death, such as that of the Urrasti demonstrator (9: 243–46), which is horridly different because unnecessary, but possibly part of the same cycle. However, this indispensable theme is pervasive: parting is (as in the French proverb) also a little death, and travel is in Le Guin usually accompanied by loss of consciousness and a (more or less useful and successful) rebirth into a new one, as in Shevek's spaceship experience of chapter 1.

3.2 *The Exemplary Reach for Integrality, and a Limit*

Thus, what does Shevek's parable ideally stand for? I think for a double unity-in-duality. The first or thematic one is that of *physics and politics*, in our poor terms: of natural vs. human/social science. Shevek stands for their integrality in the sense of the Presocratics' *physis* or of our ambiguous "physical," usable for Einstein and Olivia Newton-John. Unbuilding propertarian possession of human nature cannot be divided from the same effort about the world and vice versa, as we realize today in the capitalist destruction of climate and other eco-systems. We cannot fully imagine any of this, since history has both insufficiently and often wrongly developed our sense(s) – so that Jameson is right to insist throughout *Archaeologies* that utopia/nism relates to the present and not to the future. But perhaps what all of us intellectuals have the greatest difficulty to imagine even feebly is the unbuilding of the division of labour between mental and bodily work, which *TD* exceptionally attempts to envisage. Now Shevek, as all major poetry, also stands for the second, attitudinal or methodological integrality of *the thematic What* with *the relational How*. The metaphors and analogies of the How, steeped in relationships between people and their products, unbuild obsolete categories, as in Rimbaud: "Blood! Blood! Golden flame!/ All to war, to vengeance, to terror [...]. Enough!/ [...]./ [...] I'm there, I'm still there." The plot arrow may then, in the best of cases, begin to show, to make visible and understandable, the coming into being of better categories. Only together can the two result in the fully disalienating melding of sense as meaning with the sensual evidence of poetry fitting words to the world.

TD brings this off superbly up to Shevek's encounter with the U revolt. But measured by the very high level that far, at that point I grow uneasy. I shall approach this by factoring in Jameson's characterization of Le Guin's SF as world reduction or ontological excision.

The most salient example Jameson gives is the reduction of human sexuality to the periods of "heat" (*kemmer*) in *The Left Hand of Darkness*, though others such as the lack of animals there and even more so on Anarres could be added. He notes that the method is one of "'thought experiment' in the tradition of great physicists," citing Le Guin's pointers to Einstein and Schrödinger in "Is Gender" – it is "the experimental production of an imaginary situation by excision of the real [...]" (274). Returning to *TD*, he characterizes the Anarresti utopia as a place "in which [humanity] is released from the multiple determinisms (economic, political, social) of history itself [...], precisely in order to be free to do whatever it wants with its interpersonal relationships ..." (275). As with *The Left Hand*, it is thus "[an] attempt to rethink Western history without capitalism" (277). This rich, anthropological vein – validated by the excision of unlimited sex or animals – attains a persuasiveness much higher than exclusive Morean or Bellamyan focusing on sociopolitics would.

Let me try to rephrase this as an ambiguous polarity, inherent in the A landscape or nature, between *bareness* as facilitator of understanding by poetic analogy (A as truth, discussed in 1.4 above) and *barrenness* as Cold War stigmatizing of all revolutionary politics by identifying it with inescapable stagnation in poverty (and attendant rise of a new privileged class). In the A chapters the stark poetry clearly prevails. The lushness itself of U in Chapters 3, 5, and 7 is a corrupt denial of bareness when observed by Shevek's sarcastic utopian eye. But in the middle of chapter 9 the stance shifts. Where Shevek encounters the protesters and repression, he is merely our camera eye justifying scattered glimpses about a major social movement of which we know little. His usual overview, coupled with the authorial generalizations, is lacking. We do not know the context in any way even faintly similar to the richness of details about A and the propertarian wraps in U; we are restricted to Shevek's fugitive glances. There is a generic kinship to the city revolutions of *News from Nowhere* or *The Iron Heel*, but the U revolt resembles perhaps more something out of *The Sleeper Wakes* (in terms of Le Guin's opus, maybe out of Orsinia) than any later depiction. Yet compared to Morris or London, we do not know much about the Urrasti oppositional movement. It is an alliance of non-violent syndicalists /?/ and centralizing communists (9: 239), and seems largely followed by the lower classes, but was it really insurrectionary in intent? It seems to have been suppressed, but it is not clear how permanently. However, the political revolt finds no further place in the novel; I'm not sure it's even mentioned during the return to A.

Correction: there is one movement, nearest to the author, which *TD* melds with the pre-WW1 template: the mainly non-violent (except on the government side) anti-Vietnam protests, violently put down in Chicago 1968 and in the shootings at Kent State and Jackson State Universities in 1970. In the *TD* demonstration, the Vietnam War helicopters shoot people at home. It is after all sparked by a war abroad, in Benbili – the Third World of U. Le Guin's view of it shares the 1960s protesters' generosity of spirit, radical swerve, and political limitation.

My sense of something lacking here, of a major failure of interest, is rendered more acute by contrast to the splendid beginning of Chapter 9, Shevek's breakthrough to his time theory, which is a culmination of this novel, in particular of the wall vs. light imagery:

> The wall was down. The vision was both clear and whole. What he saw was simple [...]: and contained in it all complexity, all promise. It was revelation. It was the way clear, the way home, the light.
> The spirit in him was like a child running out into the sunlight. There was no end, no end [...]. (9: 225)

These are also among the best pages of speculation on the creative, here specifically scientific, process of discovery that I know. If SF is to be examined in its relationship to science and creativity, it will stand out as a beacon with a very few matching examples (say Lem's more systematic tour de force on the history of Solaristics).

It is not fair to demand that the incandescent intensity of such passages be sustained everywhere. But in the whole account of the U revolt, only Shevek's speech at the demonstration comes near to it. (Even there, I either do not understand or disagree with the final dichotomy: "You cannot make the Revolution. You can only be the Revolution.") The rest is seen in an accelerated blur. Workable enough, but predicated on exclusive focus through and on Shevek. Chapter 9 culminates in the Time Theory, and the rest is anti-climactic. The wall is down for the time theoretician but not for the Urrasti insurgents. The splendid analogy between physics and politics seems confined to A. It resurrects forcefully in Shevek's speech to the Terran ambassador (11: 280–81), but restricted to the general philosophy of time. It is not clear whether much hope is left for U: this is not left in the balance, it is dropped. (Of course, historians may argue Le Guin has been prophetic in this too. When has a revolution ever succeeded at the centre of an empire unless the empire was already in bad disarray?)

Yet since utopia is about the present, and ours is in 2007 different from the present of the early 1970s, we have to judge this writing in our world. In it, the heaviest artillery of capitalism, the persuasiveness of which eventually brought down State pseudo-communism, was that capitalism delivers the goods while communism does not. Capitalism claimed and claims what is in *TD* the lush and teeming beauty of U with its ecologically full or overcrowded niches of plant, animal, and city life. Le Guin probably tried to weaken such a claim with the contrast between Urras and ruined Terra in Keng's speech. While an effective bit of eco-criticism on its own, this does not erase the impact of the union, indeed consubstantiality, between communism (however morally admirable) and poverty as shown on A.

We thus get to an imbalance between the morally admirable and the corporeally easy or even feasible, dispossession as lack of ownership with its demons and as lack of things – back to an opposition between purity and (as final horizon denied by poverty) survival. It is politically of a piece with the Odonians' accepting exodus from their society instead of revolution inside it, and Shevek's following this pattern by forgetting his Urrasti brothers. He had, after all, identified the basement where he and other defeated insurgents on U had to hide as Hell (9: 244); but even this hero was not up to a Harrowing of Hell.[7] By this I do not, of course, mean to indicate psychological or moral stains in a fictional character, and even less to "blame" the poet-author who had discovered for us more than anybody else: it is a matter of the novel as a whole arriving at its own boundary or wall. The properly economico-political critique – that capitalism proceeds by finally ruining the forces of production (people, earth, air, water) at least as thoroughly as it had developed them at its beginnings, that it increasingly delivers destruction – is missing in the U story. It is a void as significant as the absence of industrial production at the heart of *News from Nowhere*, the concave that defines its convexities. I do not at all believe this nullifies the great insights and delights of *TD*. But while the ambiguity between authoritarian and libertarian utopia is a very fertile one, the ambiguity between capitalism and fertility (however corrupt) is simply misleading.

Still, the overriding story in much the greater part of *TD* is one of rare imaginative sympathy by a writer in full command of rich narrative shaping against an explicitly cognitive horizon. I hope I have suggested in this

---

7   In sum, "The Odonians on Anarres have created a good society, but even they might have done better to have stayed home on Urras and ensured the Revolution on Urras" (Erlich chapter 8). Odo's plans were based on "the generous ground of Urras," not on "arid Anarres" (4: 77), quite parallel to Marx's expectation of revolution starting in the most developed countries of France and perhaps England. The aridity of A is analogous to the Odonians opting for separation rather than permeation, for a revolution only for a vanguard and then exile group instead of for all the Urrasti people. Interestingly, it seems Marx blamed Cabet's plan of communists forming utopian colonies in the USA instead of working for the revolution in France. But then, he himself had to become a mainly (but not fully) theorizing exile ... Another analogy is the separation of the "Soviet experiment" from the rest of the world, first imposed from the outside by a capitalist *cordon sanitaire*, then assumed by Stalin, as well as the sectarianism of the parties and people oriented mainly to the defence of the USSR rather than change in their own spaces. Certainly the corruption of the revolution by a rising bureaucracy comes from there, as well as from subsidiary separatisms such as the one to and in Zionist kibbutzes in Palestine. But in the background of everything Le Guin does is her rootedness in the USA, so the fact *TD* was written a few years before the US 200th anniversary (roughly as long as the existence of A) and that many on the Left hold the promise of American Revolution was betrayed is another factor.

article some of the main admirable facets of *TD*, very rare in and beyond SF (or utopian fiction if you wish). But in a final abstraction, beyond the great and not to be underrated delights of its micro- and meso-levels, what might be identified as its so to speak transportable insight and horizon for us readers today? What I was getting to at the beginning of this sub-section is – put in an allegorical way – that Shevek brings about the marriage of Freedom and Knowledge (Cognition, including S1 and poetry). It is the vision of *freedom as critical cognition* – which in our epoch means two things: first, solidarity with others of the same horizon, a defence of civil society; second, a radical orientation by contraries to the hegemony stifling us. With warts and all, *TD* establishes a horizon of thisworldly justice centered on people and their knowledge. This is where my cavil at the separation of freedom and knowledge in his final relationship with the Urrasti people comes from: it is a fall back into our "pure," S2 science. Nonetheless, the overall vision of *TD* is one where freedom and poetico-scientific cognition embrace, sustained by our interest and belief in Shevek's trajectory. What Augustine of Hippo put as, "When truths are reached, they renew us," holds both for the hero and us readers insofar we sympathize with him and his understanding.

I do not believe this can get obsolete as long as injustice obtains – and it has been steadily deepening. Truth shall make ye free (if you organize).[8]

---

8   My thanks for help with materials go to Johan Anglemark and the Carolina Library in Uppsala, and to Rich Erlich for comments and editing assistance much beyond normal collegiality. I wish to stress that James Bittner was the first to broach thoroughly and interestingly in his 1979 University of Wisconsin dissertation many central problems of *TD*, and I think with pleasure of our discussions at that time, from which much must have continued to work in me subconsciously.

Works Cited

Aronowitz, Stanley. *Science as Power.* Minneapolis: University of Minnesota Press, 1988.

Beck, Ulrich. *Risk Society.* Trans. Mark Ritter. London: Sage, 1992.

Boulding, Kenneth E. "Truth or Power." *Science* 190 (1975): 423.

Braverman, Harry. *Labor and Monopoly Capital: The Degradation of Work in the Twentieth Century.* New York and London: Monthly Review, 1974.

Brecht, Bertolt. *Werke. Grosse kommentierte Berliner und Frankfurter Ausgabe.* 33 vols. Berlin: Aufbau, 1988–98.

Bruner, Jerome. *Actual Minds, Possible Worlds.* Cambridge MA: Harvard University Press, 1986.

Castoriadis, Cornelius. *Crossroads in the Labyrinth.* Trans. Kate Soper and Martin H. Ryle. Brighton: Harvester, 1984.

Collingridge, David. *Social Control of Technology.* New York: St Martin's, 1980.

Elgin, Catherine Z. *With Reference to Reference.* Indianapolis: Hackett, 1982.

Erlich, Richard D. *Coyote's Song: The Teaching Stories of Ursula K. Le Guin.* A Science Fiction Research Association Digital Book: <http://www.sfra.org/Coyote/CoyoteHome.htm>. 5 September 2007.

Gandhigram Rural University: <http://www.gandhigram.org>. 5 September 2007.

Gentner, Dedre. "Are Scientific Analogies Metaphors?" *Metaphor: Problems and Perspectives.* Ed. David S. Miall. Brighton: Harvester Press, 1982, 106–32.

Goodman, Nelson, and Catherine Z. Elgin. *Reconceptions in Philosophy and Other Arts and Sciences.* Indianapolis: Hackett, 1988.

Graham, Loren R. *Between Science and Values.* New York: Columbia University Press, 1981.

Hacking, Ian. *Representing and Intervening.* Cambridge: Cambridge University Press, 1983.

Haraway, Donna. *Modest_Witness@Second_Millennium*. New York and
    London: Routledge, 1997.
——. "Situated Knowledge." *Feminist Studies* 14.3 (1988): 575–99.
Harding, Sandra. *Whose Science? Whose Knowledge?* Ithaca: Cornell
    University Press, 1991.
Harré, R[om]. *The Philosophies of Science*. London: Oxford University
    Press, 1972.
Hegel, Georg W.F. *Wissenschaft der Logik*. Vol. 2. Frankfurt: Suhrkamp,
    2003.
Jameson, Fredric. *Archaeologies of the Future*. London and New York: Verso,
    2005.
——. *A Singular Modernity*. London and New York: Verso, 2002.
Kant, Immanuel. *On History*. Ed. Lewis W. Beck. Trans. Lewis W. Beck et
    al. Indianapolis: Bobbs-Merrill, 1963.
Kapp, K. William. *The Social Costs of Private Enterprise*. Cambridge MA:
    Harvard University Press, 1950.
Le Guin, Ursula K. *The Dispossessed: An Ambiguous Utopia*. New York:
    Avon, 1975.
——. "Is Gender Necessary? Redux." *Dancing at the Edge of the World*.
    New York: Grove, 2002. 7–16.
——. "Science Fiction and Mrs Brown." *The Language of the Night*. New
    York: Berkley, 1978–94.
——. "Some Thoughts on Narrative." *Dancing at the Edge of the World*.
    New York: Grove, 2002. 37–45.
Levins, Richard. "Ten Propositions on Science and Antiscience." *Science
    Wars*. Ed. Andrew Ross. London and Durham: Duke University Press,
    1996. 180–91.
Marcuse, Herbert. *Reason and Revolution*. Boston: Beacon , 1960.
Marx, Karl. *Theorien über den Mehrwert*. Vol.1 Berlin: Dietz, 1956.
——, and Friedrich Engels. *Werke* (*MEW*). Berlin: Dietz, 1962–.
Milner, Andrew. "Utopia and SF in Raymond Williams." *Science Fiction
    Studies* 30.2 (2003): 199–216.
[Morris, William.] "Useful Work versus Useless Toil." *William Morris*.
    Centenary edn. London: Nonesuch, 1948. 603–23.

Nietzsche, Friedrich. *Die fröhliche Wissenschaft.* Munich: Goldmann, 1959.

———. *Philosophy and Truth: Selections from Nietzsche's Notebooks of the Early 1870s.* Ed. and trans. Daniel Breazeale. Atlantic Highlands, NJ: Humanities, 1979.

———. *Werke.* Leipzig: Naumann, 1900–13.

———. *Zur Genealogie der Moral.* Ed. W.D. Williams. Oxford: Blackwell, 1972.

Radin, Paul. *Primitive Religion.* London: Hamilton, 1938.

Rancière, Jacques (ed.). "Transports de la liberté." *La politique des poètes.* Paris: Michel, 1992. 87–130.

Ricoeur, Paul. *The Rule of Metaphor.* Toronto: University of Toronto Press, 1978.

Rimbaud, Arthur. *Oeuvres complètes.* Ed. Louis Forestier. Paris: Laffont, 1992.

Spivak, Gayatri Chakravorty. *In Other Worlds.* New York and London: Routledge, 1988.

Suvin, Darko. "Can People Be (Re)Presented in Fiction?" *Marxism and the Interpretation of Culture.* Ed. Cary Nelson and Lawrence Grossberg. Urbana: University of Illinois Press, 1988. 663–96.

———. "On the Horizons of Epistemology and Science." (forthcoming in *Critical Quarterly* 52.1).

———. "On Metaphoricity and Narrativity in Fiction." *SubStance* 48 (1986): 51–67.

———. "The Science-fiction Novel as Epic Narration." *Positions and Presuppositions in Science Fiction.* London: Macmillan, and Kent: Kent State University Press, 1988. 74–85.

Wallerstein, Immanuel. *The End of the World as We Know It.* Minneapolis: University of Minnesota Press, 1999.

———. *Historical Capitalism with Capitalist Civilization.* London: Verso, 1996.

Williams, Raymond. *Marxism and Literature.* New York: Oxford University Press, 1981.

Index of Names and Works

Ralahine Utopian Studies

Ralahine Utopian Studies is the publishing project of the Ralahine Centre for Utopian Studies, University of Limerick, and the Department of Intercultural Studies in Translation, Languages and Culture, University of Bologna at Forlì.

The series editors aim to publish scholarship that addresses the theory and practice of utopianism (including Anglophone, continental European, and indigenous and postcolonial traditions, and contemporary and historical periods). Publications (in English and other European languages) will include original monographs and essay collections (including theoretical, textual, and ethnographic/institutional research), English language translations of utopian scholarship in other national languages, reprints of classic scholarly works that are out of print, and annotated editions of original utopian literary and other texts (including translations).

While the editors seek work that engages with the current scholarship and debates in the field of utopian studies, they will not privilege any particular critical or theoretical orientation. They welcome submissions by established or emerging scholars working within or outside the academy. Given the multi-lingual and inter-disciplinary remit of the University of Limerick and the University of Bologna at Forlì, they especially welcome comparative studies in any disciplinary or trans-disciplinary framework.

Those interested in contributing to the series are invited to submit a detailed project outline to Professor Raffaella Baccolini at Department of Intercultural Studies in Translation, Languages and Culture, University of Bologna at Forlì, Forlì, Italy or to Professor Tom Moylan or Dr Joachim Fischer at the Department of Languages and Cultural Studies, University of Limerick, Republic of Ireland.

E-mail queries can be sent to oxford@peterlang.com.

Series editors:
Raffaella Baccolini (University of Bologna, at Forlì)
Joachim Fischer (University of Limerick)
Tom Moylan (University of Limerick)
Managing editor:
Michael J. Griffin (University of Limerick)

Ralahine Centre for Utopian Studies, University of Limerick
http://www.ul.ie/ralahinecentre/

Volume 2   Michael J. Griffin and Tom Moylan (eds):
            Exploring the Utopian Impulse. Essays on Utopian Thought
            and Practice.
            434 pages. 2007. ISBN 978-3-03910-913-5

Volume 3   Ruth Levitas:
            The Concept of Utopia. (Ralahine Classic)
            280 pages. 2010. ISBN 978-3-03911-366-8

Volume 4   Vincent Geoghegan:
            Utopianism and Marxism. (Ralahine Classic)
            189 pages. 2008. ISBN 978-3-03910-137-5

Volume 5   Barbara Goodwin and Keith Taylor:
            The Politics of Utopia. A Study in Theory and Practice.
            (Ralahine Classic)
            341 pages. 2009. ISBN 978-3-03911-080-3

Volume 6   Darko Suvin:
            Defined by a Hollow. Essays on Utopia, Science Fiction and Political
            Epistemology. (Ralahine Reader)
            616 pages. 2010. ISBN 978-3-03911-403-0

Volume 7   Andrew Milner (ed.):
            Tenses of Imagination: Raymond Williams on Science Fiction, Utopia
            and Dystopia. (Ralahine Reader)
            253 pages. 2010. ISBN 978-3-03911-826-7

Vol. 13, No. 1   2002
UTOPIAN STUDIES

A PUBLICATION OF THE SOCIETY FOR UTOPIAN STUDIES

Utopian Studies

Nicole Pohl, editor

Utopian Studies is a peer-reviewed publication of the Society for Utopian Studies, publishing scholarly articles on a wide range of subjects related to utopias, utopianism, utopian literature, utopian theory, and intentional communities. Contributing authors come from a diverse range of fields, including American studies, architecture, the arts, classics, cultural studies, economics, engineering, environmental studies, gender studies, history, languages and literatures, philosophy, political science, psychology, sociology and urban planning. Each issue also includes dozens of reviews of recent books.

Founded in 1975, the Society for Utopian Studies is an international, interdisciplinary association devoted to the study of utopianism in all its forms. For information on becoming a member of the society, please contact Alex MacDonald. Membership of the Society includes a year's subscription of the journal and a newsletter, *Utopus Discovered*, and details on publications in the field.

"Utopian Studies . . . is a scholarly production whose particular interest lies in its interdisciplinary approach to social and political issues. . . . [It] offers scholarly commentary on utopias old and new, and a forum for all those who are fascinated by alternative futures."

-Barbara Goodwin, *TLS Review*

Alex MacDonald
Secretary/Treasurer
Society for Utopian Studies
c/o Campion College, University of Regina
3737 Wascana Parkway
Regina, SK S4S 0A2
Canada
alex.macdonald@uregina.ca

Institutions should contact the Johns Hopkins University Press for Print Subscription information.
Phone: 1-800-548-1784
Outside USA and Canada: 410-516-6987
Email: jrnlcirc@press.jhu.edu

ISSN: 1045-911X | Semi Annual Publication

penn state press

820 N. University Drive, USB 1, Suite C | University Park, PA 16802 | info@psupress.org
WWW.PSUPRESS.ORG | 1-800-326-9180